GRAMMAR
FOR THE WELL-TRAINED MIND
YELLOW WORKBOOK

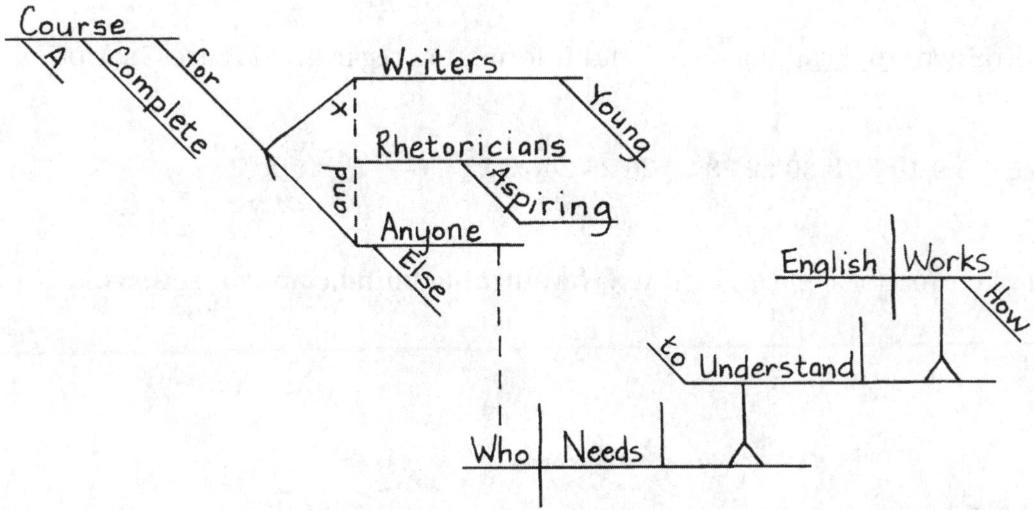

By Susan Wise Bauer
with Jessica Otto and Audrey Anderson,
Diagrams by Patty Rebne

Layout and Design by Shannon Zadrozny

Visit welltrainedmind.com for additional information regarding Figures in Motion.

1 2 3 4 5 6 7 8 9 10 B&B 30 29 28 27 26 25 24 23 22

GYS-1022

For a list of corrections, please visit **www.welltrainedmind.com/corrections**.

Table of Contents

FOREWORD

Welcome to *Grammar for the Well-Trained Mind*!

This innovative grammar program will take you from basic definitions ("A noun is the name of a person, place, thing, or idea") all the way through detailed analysis of complex sentence structure. Once you complete it, you'll have all the skills needed for the study of advanced rhetoric—persuasive speech and sophisticated writing.

WHAT MAKES UP THE FULL PROGRAM

Each year of study in *Grammar for the Well-Trained Mind* requires three books.

The nonconsumable *Core Instructor Text* is used for each year of study. It contains scripted dialogue for the instructor, all rules and examples, and teaching notes that thoroughly explain ambiguities and difficulties.

There are four *Student Workbooks* with accompanying *Keys*. Each consumable workbook provides a full course of exercises and assignments. Each corresponding key gives complete, thoroughly explained answers. Your goal is to complete all four *Workbooks* before the student finishes high school. (See *How the Program Works*, below.)

Two optional reference books are also available. All rules and definitions, with accompanying examples, have been assembled into a handy reference book, *The Grammar Guidebook*. This handbook will serve the student for all four years of study—and will continue to be useful as the student moves through advanced high school writing, into college composition, and beyond. In addition, all diagramming rules covered in the course are summarized in *The Diagramming Dictionary: A Complete Reference Tool for Young Writers, Aspiring Rhetoricians, and Anyone Else Who Needs to Understand How to Diagram English Sentences*.

HOW THE PROGRAM WORKS

Language learning has three elements.

First: You have to understand and memorize *rules*. We call this "prescriptive learning"—grasping the explicit principles that govern the English language and committing them to memory. *Grammar for the Well-Trained Mind* presents, explains, and drills all of the essential rules of the English language. Each year, the student reviews and repeats these rules.

Second: You need *examples* of every rule and principle ("descriptive learning"). Without examples, rules remain abstract. When you memorize the rule "Subjunctive verbs express situations that are unreal, wished for, or uncertain," you also need to memorize the example "I would not say such things if I were you!" Each year, the student reviews and repeats the same examples to illustrate each rule.

Third: You need *practice.* Although the four workbooks repeat the same rules and examples, each contains a completely new set of exercises and writing assignments, along with a *Key* providing complete answers.

The combination of *repetition* (the same rules and examples each year) and *innovation* (brand-new practice materials in every workbook) will lead you to complete mastery of the English language.

HOW TO USE GRAMMAR FOR THE WELL-TRAINED MIND

When you first use the program, begin with the *Core Instructor Text* and any one of the *Workbooks* with its accompanying *Key* (*Purple, Red, Blue,* or *Yellow*). Keep *The Grammar Guidebook* and *The Diagramming Dictionary* on hand for reference.

During this first year, you won't necessarily grasp every principle thoroughly. Simply go through the dialogue with your instructor, complete the exercises, check the answers, and discuss any mistakes.

You may need more than one year to complete your first *Workbook*; the exercises increase in complexity and difficulty from Week 20 on. That's absolutely fine. Feel free to take as much time as necessary to finish this workbook.

When your first *Workbook* is completed, you and your instructor will go back to the beginning of the *Core Instructor Text* and start over, this time using a *Workbook/Key* combination of a different color. You'll go over the same dialogue, the same rules, and the same examples—with an entirely fresh set of exercises. This combination of repeated information along with new and challenging exercises will truly begin to build your competence in the English language.

Follow this same procedure for the third and fourth years of study, using workbooks of the remaining two colors, along with their matching keys.

Regular reviews are built into the program. Every three weeks, take some extra time to do the exercises reviewing what was covered in the three weeks before. After Week 27, the reviews double in scope: twelve exercises review the material all the way back to the beginning of the course. These reviews, beginning with Review 9, become one week's work each. During review weeks, try to do three exercises per day, and then go back and review the rules and principles of any exercise in which you miss two or more sentences/examples.

WHICH WORKBOOK?

Because each workbook makes use of the same rules and examples, you may use any one of the four workbooks during your first year in the program. It is highly recommended, however, that you then go back and finish the earlier workbooks as well. The program is designed to take *at least* four years, no matter where you begin.

IMPORTANT PRINCIPLES OF LEARNING

As you study, keep the following in mind.

- Language is a rich, complicated tapestry. It is occasionally logical, and sometimes irrational. Mastering its complexities takes time and patience. Don't expect to master—or even completely understand—every principle the first time through. Repetition and practice will eventually bring clarity. Be diligent—don't abandon the curriculum because of frustration! But accept occasional confusion as a natural part of learning. If you don't understand subjunctives the first time through, for example, accept it, move on, and then repeat the following year. Eventually, the concepts will come into focus.
- Always ask for help if you need it. This isn't a test. It's a learning process.
- From Week 19 (halfway through the course) on, you are encouraged to read sentences out loud. Reading out loud is an important part of evaluating your own writing. Follow the directions—don't ignore them and read silently.
- Take as long as you need to finish each lesson. As noted above, it's perfectly acceptable to take more than one year to finish a workbook (particularly the first time through). The earlier lessons are shorter and simpler; they increase in both complexity and length as the book goes on. But especially in the later lessons, don't worry if you need to divide a lesson over two days, or take more than one week to complete a week's worth of lessons. In subsequent years, you'll go much more quickly through the earlier lessons, giving you time to stop and concentrate on areas of challenge later on.

ABOUT DIAGRAMMING

Grammar for the Well-Trained Mind uses diagramming exercises throughout.

Diagramming is a learning process. Think of the diagrams as experimental projects, not tests. Attempt the diagram, look at the answer, and then try to figure out why any differences exist. Expect these assignments—particularly in the second half of the book—to be challenging. Ask for help when you need it. Always diagram with a pencil (or on a whiteboard or blackboard), and expect to erase and redo constantly.

Also remember that diagramming is not an exact science! If you can explain clearly why you've made a particular choice, the diagram might be correct even if the key differs. To quote a 1914 grammar text: "Many constructions are peculiar, idiomatic, and do not lend themselves readily to any arrangement of lines" (Alma Blount and Clark S. Northup, *An English Grammar for Use in High and Normal Schools and in Colleges*).

WEEK 1

Introduction to Nouns and Adjectives

— LESSON 1 —

Introduction to Nouns
Concrete and Abstract Nouns

A noun names a person, place, thing, or idea.
Concrete nouns can be observed with our senses. Abstract nouns cannot.

Exercise 1A: Abstract and Concrete Nouns

Decide whether the underlined nouns are abstract or concrete. Above each noun, write *A* for abstract or *C* for concrete. If you have difficulty, ask yourself: Can this noun be touched, seen, or experienced with another one of the senses? If so, it is a concrete noun. If not, it is abstract.

A loose tooth will not rest until it's pulled out. (African proverb)

Two wrongs don't make a right. (English)

Make haste with leisure. (German)

Draw not your bow 'til your arrow is fixed. (Russian)

He who digs too deep for a fish may come out with a snake. (African)

Shared joy is a double joy; shared sorrow is half a sorrow. (Swedish)

It's better to light a candle than curse the darkness. (Chinese)

Evil enters like a needle and spreads like an oak tree. (Ethiopian)

Turn your face to the sun and the shadows will fall behind you. (New Zealander)

Exercise 1B: Using Concrete and Abstract Nouns

Identify each noun as concrete or abstract. Write a sentence that includes the given noun and at least one noun of the opposite type (so, if the given noun is a concrete noun, you must use it and also include an abstract noun of your choice).

Underline the additional noun in your sentence and label it as *C* for concrete or *A* for abstract. (It's fine to use more than one extra noun, but you only need to label one.)

The first is done for you.

	C or *A*?	Your Sentence
happiness	A	She laughed with happiness during the movie. (C: movie)
mug		
boots		
delight		
exhaustion		
oats		

— LESSON 2 —

Introduction to Adjectives
Descriptive Adjectives, Abstract Nouns
Formation of Abstract Nouns from Descriptive Adjectives

An adjective modifies a noun or pronoun.
Adjectives tell what kind, which one, how many, and whose.
Descriptive adjectives tell what kind.
A descriptive adjective becomes an abstract noun when you add *-ness* to it.

cheerful cheerfulness
grumpy grumpiness

Exercise 2A: Descriptive Adjectives, Concrete Nouns, and Abstract Nouns

Decide whether the underlined words are concrete nouns, abstract nouns, or descriptive adjectives. Above each, write *DA* for descriptive adjective, *CN* for concrete noun, or *AN* for abstract noun.

The sentences below were taken from *The Boxcar Children*, by Gertrude Chandler Warner. Some have been slightly adapted.

Not a soul passed them on the country road. All the houses they saw were dark and still.

Benny tumbled into the bed with a great sigh of satisfaction.

Each of them quickly scraped together a fragrant pile for a pillow, and once more lay down to sleep with hardly a thought of fear.

Jess saw an old freight or box car. Her first thought was one of fear; her second, hope of shelter.

It stood on rusty broken nails which were nearly covered with dead leaves. Then the thunder cracked overhead.

It seemed to the children that the sky would split, so sharp were the cracks of thunder.

But not a drop of rain reached them in their roomy retreat.

Exercise 2B: Descriptive Adjectives and Abstract Nouns

For each sentence, identify the underlined word as *DA* for descriptive adjective or *AN* for abstract noun. Then change the underlined word to the other form (adjective to noun or noun to adjective) and rewrite the sentence with the new form. You may rearrange, add, or subtract words as necessary to make a sensible sentence. Your new sentence doesn't have to match the original exactly in meaning, but it should be close.

The first is done for you.

AN
The house had a charm that appealed to me.

The charming house appealed to me.

Bertie's favorite book is one filled with silly stories.

___

The puppy was easy to train because of her intelligence.

___

The loudness of the drums drowned out the singers' voices.

____

Chloé wrote a story filled with danger and excitement!

____

Alex is a graceful performer on the stage.

____

Exercise 2C: Color Names

Underline all the color words in the following sentences. Then write *A* for adjective or *N* for noun above each underlined color word.

These sentences are taken from Ruth Plumly Thompson's *Grampa in Oz*. Some have been slightly adapted.

King Fumbo of Ragbad shook in his carpet slippers. He had removed his red shoes, so he could not very well shake in them.

He turned a sickly green and began to tremble violently.

Then, muttering apologies, the old soldier seized a curtain cord and tied Fumbo to a red pillar.

The country of the west, which was settled by the Munchkins, was marked in blue; the northern Gilliken country in purple.

But soon these villages became farther and farther apart, and the country more wild and unsettled, and just as the sun slipped down behind the treetops they came to the edge of a deep blue forest.

Beneath slithered the road and not until the last length of yellow had flashed by did Dorothy and Percy Vere let go.

Urtha, wearied by her strange adventures, had fallen fast asleep in the middle of counting the stars, and lay in a fragrant heap, her lovely violet eyes closed tight.

As he straightened up, the long, green bottle of patent medicine caught his eye.

And the loyal little Winkies have built him a splendid tin castle in the center of their pleasant yellow country.

— LESSON 3 —

Common and Proper Nouns
Capitalization and Punctuation of Proper Nouns

A common noun is a name common to many persons, places, things, or ideas.
A proper noun is the special, particular name for a person, place, thing, or idea.
Proper nouns always begin with capital letters.

Capitalization Rules

1. Capitalize the proper names of persons, places, things, and animals.

boy	Peter
store	Baskin-Robbins
book	*Little Women*
horse	Black Beauty
sea	Sea of Galilee
port	Port of Los Angeles
island	Isle of Skye

2. Capitalize the names of holidays.

Memorial Day
Christmas
Independence Day
Day of the Dead

3. Capitalize the names of deities.

Minerva (ancient Rome)
Hwanin (ancient Korea)
God (Christianity and Judaism)
Allah (Islam)
Gitche Manitou or Great Spirit (Native American—Algonquin)

4. Capitalize the days of the week and the months of the year, but not the seasons.

Monday	January	winter
Tuesday	April	spring
Friday	August	summer
Sunday	October	fall

5. Capitalize the first, last, and other important words in titles of books, magazines, newspapers, movies, television series, stories, poems, and songs.

book	*Alice's Adventures in Wonderland*
magazine	*National Geographic*
newspaper	*The Chicago Tribune*
movie	*A River Runs Through It*
television series	*The Waltons*
television show	"The Chicken Thief"
story	"The Visit of the Magi"
poem	"The Night Before Christmas"
song	"Joy to the World"
chapter in a book	"The End of the Story"

6. Capitalize and italicize the names of ships, trains, and planes.

ship	*Titanic*
train	*The Orient Express*
plane	*The Spirit of St. Louis*

Exercise 3A: Capitalizing Proper Nouns

Write a proper noun for each of the following common nouns. Don't forget to capitalize all of the important words of the proper noun. If the proper noun requires quotation marks, include them.

You may either write your answers below or use a computer. If you are handwriting your answers, underline any proper noun that should be italicized.

Common Noun	**Proper Noun**
book	______________________________
song	______________________________
movie	______________________________
store	______________________________
state	______________________________
team	______________________________

Exercise 3B: Proper Names and Titles

On your own paper, rewrite the following sentences properly. Capitalize and punctuate all names and titles correctly.

sesame street is the longest-running television show of all time.

the orient express is a train made famous by the author agatha christie.

in 1893, two sisters, patty and mildred hill, wrote the song happy birthday to you.

shel silverstein created many humorous poems, including where the sidewalk ends.

lucy maude montgomery was the author of the popular novel entitled anne of green gables.

Exercise 3C: Proofreading for Proper Nouns

In the following sentences, indicate which proper nouns should be capitalized by underlining the first letter of the noun three times. This is the proper proofreader's mark for "capitalize." The first word in the first sentence is done for you.

harriet tubman was born in maryland between 1820 and 1825.

her original name was araminta harriet ross, but she later changed it to harriet.

she was born a slave, but she escaped in 1849 through the secret network called the underground railroad.

during her lifetime, tubman used the underground railroad to lead more than 300 slaves to freedom.

she was given the nickname "moses" because of her brave actions which led many to safety.

— LESSON 4 —

Proper Adjectives
Compound Adjectives (Adjective-Noun Combinations)

1. Capitalize the proper names of persons, places, things, and animals.
2. Capitalize the names of holidays.
3. Capitalize the names of deities.
4. Capitalize the days of the week and the months of the year, but not the seasons.
5. Capitalize the first, last, and other important words in titles of books, magazines, newspapers, movies, television series, stories, poems, and songs.
6. Capitalize and italicize the names of ships, trains, and planes.

A proper adjective is formed from a proper name. Proper adjectives are capitalized.

	Proper Noun	Proper Adjective
Person	Aristotle	the Aristotelian philosophy
Place	Spain	a Spanish city
Holiday	Valentine's Day	some Valentine candy
Month	March	March madness

Shakespeare wrote a number of sonnets.
I was reading some Shakespearean sonnets yesterday.

Mars is the fourth planet from the sun.
The Martian atmosphere is mostly carbon dioxide.

On Monday, I felt a little down.
I had the Monday blues.

The English enjoy a good cup of tea and a muffin.
Gerald enjoys a good English muffin.

The German-speaking tourists were lost in Central Park.
The archaeologist unearthed some pre-Columbian remains.

Words that are not usually capitalized remain lowercase even when they are attached to a proper adjective.

A compound adjective combines two words into a single adjective with a single meaning.

When the mine collapsed, it sent a plume of dust sky high.
I just had a thirty-minute study session.

N ADJ
sky high

ADJ N
thirty minute

N ADJ
user friendly

ADJ N
high speed

The sky-high plume of dust could be seen for miles.
My study session was thirty minutes.

Those directions are not user friendly!
I prefer user-friendly directions.

The connection was high speed.
He needed a high-speed connection.

Exercise 4A: Forming Proper Adjectives from Proper Nouns

Form adjectives from the following proper nouns. (Some will change form and others will not.) Write each adjective into the correct blank below. If you are not familiar with the proper nouns, you may look them up online on Encyclopaedia Britannica, Wikipedia, or some other source (this will help you complete the sentences as well). This exercise might challenge your general knowledge! (But you can always ask your instructor for help.)

Italy	Iraq	Buddha	Alaska	Mars
Hippocrates	Japan	Greece	Antarctica	Maccabeus

The National Cherry Blossom Festival is an annual event in Washington, D.C., showcasing the gift of ________________ cherry trees to our country and celebrating the friendship between our nations.

One of my favorite dishes is avgolemono soup, a traditional ________________ food.

Hanukkah celebrates the second-century victory of Jewish people over their enemies during the ________________ Revolt.

The Safafeer market in Baghdad is a famous place to buy beautiful copper pieces made by ________________ artisans.

Taking an ________________ cruise is a popular way to see glaciers and amazing wildlife such as humpback whales, sea otters, and bald eagles.

James took a class to learn true ________________ cooking, such as pasta e fagioli.

Tibet has hundreds of monasteries dedicated to the study of the ____________ religion.

Scientists must determine how humans can survive the ________________ climate in order for astronauts to attempt life on that planet.

Because of the continent's location, the ________________ summer begins in October.

Doctors must take the ________________ oath and promise to protect their patients.

Exercise 4B: Capitalization of Proper Adjectives

In the following sentences, correct each lowercase letter that should be capitalized by underlining it three times.

Then, underline each proper adjective. Finally, circle each proper adjective that has not changed its form from the proper noun.

the seven wonders of the world include the brazilian statue known as christ the redeemer.

in 2017, alex honnold became the first person to reach the el capitan summit without the use of any ropes or safety equipment. his incredible feat was filmed and turned into a documentary, which later won an oscar award.

hungarian designer erno rubik invented the rubik's cube in 1975. more than 300 million of the toys have now been sold. the fastest solving time was set by chinese speedcuber yusheng du, who finished the puzzle in 3.47 seconds.

jane goodall is a british scientist who has dedicated her life to the study of chimpanzees. she is most famous for her studies of chimp behavior in a tanzanian game reserve, which is now known as gombe stream national park. in 2002, she was given a united nations award for her contributions to science.

the world record for high diving was set by dana kunze in 1983, when he dove from a height of 173 feet. Later, swiss diver oliver favre attempted to break the record but injured his back in the process.

Exercise 4C: Hyphenating Attributive Compound Adjectives

Hyphens prevent misunderstanding! Explain to your instructor the differences between each pair of phrases. The first is done for you. If you're confused, ask your instructor for help.

friendly-looking puppy
friendly looking puppy
(both a dog who looks friendly and a friendly dog whose purpose is to look around)

sweet-smelling flower
sweet smelling flower

cold-blooded animal
cold blooded animal

off-campus housing
off campus housing

green-eyed monster
green eyed monster

WEEK 2

Introduction to Personal Pronouns and Verbs

— LESSON 5 —

Noun Gender
Introduction to Personal Pronouns

Exercise 5A: Introduction to Noun Gender

How well do you know your animals? Fill in the blanks with the correct name (and don't worry too much if you don't know the answers . . . this is mostly for fun).

Animal	Male	Female	Baby	Group of Animals
duck	______	______	duckling	flock
ant	______	queen	______	______
hawk	______	______	eyas	______
pig	______	______	piglet	______
zebra	______	mare	______	dazzle OR zeal of zebras
tiger	______	tigress	______	______
whale	bull	______	calf	______
goose	gander	______	______	______

Nouns have gender.
Nouns can be masculine, feminine, or neuter.
We use *neuter* for nouns that have no gender and for nouns whose gender is unknown.

Subha Datta set off for the forest, intending to come back the same evening. He began to cut down a tree, but he suddenly had a feeling that he was no longer alone. As it crashed to the ground, he looked up and saw a beautiful girl dancing around and around in a little clearing nearby. Subha Datta was astonished, and let the axe fall. The noise startled the dancer, and she stood still.

Subha Datta thought he was dreaming.

Although she did not yet know it, the fairy had not convinced Subha Datta.

A pronoun takes the place of a noun.
The antecedent is the noun that is replaced by the pronoun.
Personal pronouns replace specific nouns.

I	we
you	you (plural)
he, she, it	they

Exercise 5B: Nouns and Pronouns

Write the correct pronoun above the underlined word(s). The first is done for you.

Marie Curie was awarded the Nobel Prize for important discoveries in the field of
She
radiation. Curie discovered the radioactive elements plutonium and radium.

French scientist Louis Pasteur created pasteurization, a process which prevents bacteria from growing in liquids such as milk and wine and allows them to last longer before spoiling. Pasteur also developed a vaccine for the deadly disease of rabies.

Bacteriologist Alexander Fleming discovered that mold, growing on a slide in his laboratory, kept bacteria from reproducing. Alexander Fleming studied the effects of mold on bacteria, and Alexander Fleming used the results of his work to invent penicillin, a life-saving medicine.

In 2019, the first known images of a black hole were taken. The algorithms used to capture the image of the black hole were developed by researcher Katie Bouman and her team. The image Katie Bouman helped to obtain will allow scientists to learn more about the mysterious black hole and the function of the black hole in space. In an interview after the image was revealed, Katie remarked, "The one Katie and her team showed a picture of is 55 million light years away!"

In 1895, Wilhelm Roentgen was working in his lab and observed crystals growing on a table near a cathode ray tube. Roentgen discovered that the rays could not pass through bone, but the rays could go through tissue. Roentgen began to study the rays, which led to the invention of the modern-day X-ray.

Exercise 5C: Substituting Pronouns

The following passage is from E. Nesbit's *The Enchanted Castle.* This version sounds very awkward because the pronouns *I, you, he, she, it, we,* and *they* have all been replaced by nouns.

Choose the nouns that can be replaced by pronouns, cross them (and any accompanying words such as *the*) out, and write the appropriate pronouns above them.

You may also need to cross out and replace some verbs or helping verbs if necessary to maintain agreement.

The incident of the invisible Princess had surprised, and the sudden decision to be a detective had brought its own anxieties... Only now a new feeling had come to Gerald as Gerald walked through the gardens; by day those gardens were like dreams, by night like visions. Gerald could not see his feet as Gerald walked, but Gerald saw the movement of the dewy grass-blades that his feet dispersed. And Gerald had that extraordinary feeling so difficult to describe, and yet so real and so unforgettable: the feeling that Gerald was in another world, that had covered up and hidden the old world as a carpet covers the floor. The floor was there all right, underneath, but what Gerald walked on was the carpet that covered the floor, and the carpet was drenched in magic, as the turf was drenched in dew.

The feeling was very wonderful; perhaps the reader will feel the feeling someday. There are still some places in the world where the feeling can be felt, but the places grow fewer every year...

Something enormously long and darkly grey came crawling towards Gerald slowly, heavily... As the thing writhed past Gerald, Gerald reached out his hand and touched the side of its gigantic tail. The thing was of stone.

Exercise 5D: Pronouns and Antecedents

Circle the personal pronouns in the following sentences, and draw an arrow from each pronoun to its antecedent. If the noun and pronoun are masculine, write *m* in the margin. If they are feminine, write *f*; if neuter, write *n*. If the gender of the noun and pronoun are unknown, write *u* in the margin. Look carefully. Some sentences may have more than one personal pronoun, and some personal pronouns may share an antecedent! In addition, some antecedents may not actually appear in the sentences provided.

These sentences are from *The Story of Doctor Dolittle*, by Hugh Lofting. Some have been slightly adapted.

But soon the animals began to get worried. And one evening when the Doctor was asleep before the kitchen-fire, they began talking in whispers.

So it was agreed that the monkey, Chee-Chee, was to do the cooking and mending; the dog was to sweep the floors; the duck was to dust and make the beds; the owl, Too-Too, was to keep the accounts, and the pig was to do the gardening. They made Polynesia, the parrot, housekeeper and laundress, because she was the oldest.

Then the animals made a vegetable and flower stall outside the garden-gate and sold radishes and roses to the people that passed by along the road. But still they didn't seem to make enough money to pay all the bills—and still the Doctor wouldn't worry.

Then the crocodile and the monkey and the parrot were very glad and began to sing, because they were going back to Africa, their real home.

And one day when an old lady with rheumatism came to see the Doctor, she sat on the hedgehog who was sleeping on the sofa and never came to see him anymore, but drove every Saturday all the way to Oxenthorpe, another town ten miles off, to see a different doctor.

So, as time went on, the Doctor got more and more animals; and the people who came to see him got less and less. Till at last he had no one left.

"I can never be quite sure of my age," said Polynesia. "It is either a hundred and eighty-three or a hundred and eighty-two."

— LESSON 6 —

Review Definitions
Introduction to Verbs
Action Verbs, State-of-Being Verbs
Parts of Speech

A noun names a person, place, thing, or idea.
A common noun is a name common to many persons, places, things, or ideas.
Concrete nouns can be observed with our senses. Abstract nouns cannot.
An adjective modifies a noun or pronoun.
Adjectives tell what kind, which one, how many, and whose.
Descriptive adjectives tell what kind.
A descriptive adjective becomes an abstract noun when you add *-ness* to it.

A verb shows an action, shows a state of being, links two words together, or helps another verb.

Part of speech is a term that explains what a word does.

State-of-Being Verbs
am were
is be
are being
was been

Exercise 6A: Identifying Action Verbs

Underline the verbs in the following passage. Mark them as *A* for action verbs or *B* for being verbs. This passage has been slightly adapted from *The Wonders of the Jungle: Book One*, by Prince Sarath Gosh.

Here come all the animals! The buffaloes, the blue deer, the red deer, the wild pigs, the hyenas, the wolves, the red dogs, and many others. Watch and see how each kind of animal comes. The moon shines clear above the trees, and we see a long way up the stream.

See the buffaloes! They come a little above the elephants. But they do not come one behind another in a line, like the elephants. They come three or four together.

The buffaloes drink three or four at a time because they are like a body of soldiers, one row behind another. Sometimes twenty or thirty rows make up a herd. We see only the first row drinking now, but soon we see the others behind.

And why do the buffaloes come like a body of soldiers? Because they fear their enemy—the tiger! Once upon a time the buffaloes scattered about, and the tiger ate many of them, one at a time. Then those that escaped from the tiger joined together like a body of soldiers, so that they could beat off the tiger. But now watch the first row drinking. They are all bull buffaloes, the Papas of the herd; you can tell that by their huge horns, a yard long on each side of the head. You see how the buffaloes stand side by side, so that their horns almost touch one another. That is the way the buffaloes march to the stream from their feeding place—horn to horn. Why? Because no prowling tiger passes those horns.

Watch the first row as it finishes; the whole row wheels around to the side like soldiers. Then those march to the back of the herd, and stand there in a row.

Meanwhile the second row in the front steps to the water. These also are bull buffaloes. When they finish, they also wheel, march to the back of the herd, and there stand behind the first row. In this way four or five rows of bulls drink, one after the other, and go to the back of the herd.

Next come about a dozen rows of cow buffaloes and their calves, or children. You see again, like the elephants, the Mammas and children among the buffaloes are also in the middle, safe from all harm.

Then at the end there are four or five rows of bull buffaloes again. They guard the Mammas and the children from enemies in the back.

Exercise 6B: Choosing Verbs

Provide both an appropriate action and state-of-being verb for each of the following nouns or pronouns. The first is done for you.

	State-of-Being	Action
The computer	is (or was)	crashed
Some students		
We		
He		
The clouds		
An insect		
Cells		
The door		
Tomato plants		
Owls		

Exercise 6C: Strong Action Verbs

Good writers use descriptive and vivid verbs!

In the following sentences, replace the underlined state-of-being and action verbs, which are bland and general, with more vigorous and colorful action verbs. The first is done for you.

You may use a thesaurus if necessary.

Camille Flammarion, the author of *Astronomy for Amateurs*, from which these sentences were taken, used much more interesting verbs! Your instructor will show you her original sentences when you're finished.

The crimson disk of the Sun has gone beneath the ocean.
The crimson disk of the Sun has plunged beneath the ocean.

These exquisite double stars go in gracious and splendid couples around one another, as in some majestic valse, marrying their multi-colored fires in the midst of the starry firmament.

Everywhere we find the Sun; everywhere we see his work, extending from the infinitely great to the infinitely little.

We embark upon a ray of light, and move rapidly to the portals of our Universe.

The fable of the dragon eating the Sun or Moon during the eclipses is universal.

Our Sun, that _is_ so calm and majestic, is in reality the seat of fierce conflagrations.

The molecules _light_ and burn like true stars with a brilliancy that is often magnificent.

There is an immense variety in the brilliancy of the shooting stars, from the weak telescopic sparks that _go_ like a flash of lightning, to the incandescent *bolides* or *fire-balls* that _glow_ in the atmosphere.

The globe of fire _changes_, and splits up into luminous fragments, scattered in all directions.

Here, we constantly _get_ a pure and dazzling white light from our burning luminary.

Its ray, indeed, _has_ the potentiality of every conceivable color, but picture the fantastic illumination of the worlds that _are_ round these multiple and colored suns as they shed floods of blue and roseate, red, or orange light around them!

The glacial zones are where the Sun _is_ constantly above or below the horizon for several days.

— LESSON 7 —

Helping Verbs

Part of speech is a term that explains what a word does.

Exercise 7A: Action and Helping Verbs

Underline the action verbs in both columns of sentences once. The sentences in the second column each contain at least one helping verb. Underline these helping verbs twice. These sentences are adapted from "Our Dog Rolf," by Frau Paula Moekel in *Muenchner Nachrichten*.

COLUMN 1	COLUMN 2
Rolf recognized letters and numerals.	He was wagging his tail with delight!
Rolf understood me.	Rolf can recognize any money.
He reads his own name easily.	He would rap "yes" or "no."

COLUMN 1	COLUMN 2
He remembers names and numbers over quite a period of time.	The numbers were written down.
Rolf used the same paw for decimals and units.	At the close of his tests, Rolf was rewarded with a cake.
One public appearance brought him praise from a large circle of acquaintances.	Rolf has made frequent public appearances.

Helping Verbs

am, is, are, was, were
be, being, been
have, has, had
do, does, did
shall, will, should, would, may, might, must
can, could

Exercise 7B: Providing Missing Helping Verbs

Fill in each blank with a helping verb. Sometimes, more than one helping verb might be appropriate.

This excerpt is adapted from *The House on the Borderland*, by William Hope Hodgson.

Right away in the west of Ireland lies a tiny hamlet called Kraighten. It ________________ situated, alone, at the base of a low hill. Far around there spreads a waste of bleak and totally inhospitable country; where, here and there at great intervals, one ________________ come upon the ruins of some long desolate cottage—unthatched and stark. The whole land is bare and unpeopled, the very earth scarcely covering the rock that lies beneath it, and with which the country abounds, in places rising out of the soil in wave-shaped ridges.

Yet, in spite of its desolation, my friend Tonnison and I __________ elected to spend our vacation there. He __________ stumbled on the place by mere chance the year previously, during the course of a long walking tour, and discovered the possibilities for the angler in a small and unnamed river that runs past the outskirts of the little village.

It was early one warm evening when my friend and I arrived in Kraighten. We ______ reached Ardrahan the previous night, sleeping there in rooms hired at the village post office, and leaving in good time on the following morning, clinging insecurely to one of the typical jaunting cars.

It ______________ taken us all day to accomplish our journey over some of the roughest tracks imaginable, with the result that we were thoroughly tired and somewhat bad tempered. However, the tent had to be erected and our goods stowed away before we ______________ think of food or rest. And so we set to work, with the aid of our driver, and soon had the tent up upon a small patch of ground just outside the little village, and quite near to the river.

Then, having stored all our belongings, we dismissed the driver, as he had to make his way back as speedily as possible, and told him to come across to us at the end of a fortnight. We ______________ brought sufficient provisions to last us for that space of time, and water we ______________ get from the stream. Fuel we ______________ not need, as we ______________ included a small oil-stove among our outfit, and the weather was fine and warm.

Tonnison ______________ got the stove lit now and was busy cutting slices of bacon into the frying pan; so I took the kettle and walked down to the river for water. On the way, I had to pass close to a little group of the village people, who eyed me curiously, but not in any unfriendly manner, though none of them ventured a word.

— LESSON 8 —

Personal Pronouns

First, Second, and Third Person
Capitalizing the Pronoun *I*

Personal Pronouns

	Singular	**Plural**
First person	I	we
Second person	you	you
Third person	he, she, it	they

Although they are not very hungry, I certainly am.

ich i I

As the German-built plane rose into the air, I experienced a strange loneliness.

Exercise 8A: Capitalization and Punctuation Practice

Correct the following sentences. Mark through any incorrect small letters and write the correct capitals above them. Insert quotation marks if needed. Use underlining to indicate any italics.

In september of 1622, the ship named nuestra señora de atocha set sail from havana, cuba, as a part of a large fleet of ships headed to spain. the atocha bore so much gold, silver, copper, and jewels that workers had labored for two months simply to load all of the wealth. the cargo included valuables from peru, mexico, colombia, venezuela, and panama, and the ship was heavily armed with more than 18 bronze cannons. it was manned by a crew of more than 200 sailors and slaves. it was only a short distance into the journey when a hurricane overcame the fleet, sinking seven vessels and scattering the wreckage across the ocean floor, just off the coast of the islands now known as the florida keys.

king philip iv sent another group of ships to recover the lost treasure, but after many years, only half of the contents of one vessel, the santa margarita, were brought to the surface, and all efforts to rescue the items were eventually abandoned.

the atocha lay undisturbed on the ocean floor until 1969, when treasure hunter mel fisher began his quest for the missing ship. he and his crew searched the depths, only locating tiny pieces of the massive treasure over a span of several years. then, one day in 1985, fisher's son sent his father a message, declaring, "We have found the main pile!"

fisher's discovery included emeralds, gold, silver, coins, cannons, and jewelry estimated at a value of $400 million. some items from both the atocha and the santa margarita are now housed at the mel fisher maritime museum in key west, florida, where the public can view them.

Exercise 8B: Person, Number, and Gender

Label each personal pronoun in the following selection with its person (*1*, *2*, or *3*) and number (*S* or *PL*). For third-person singular pronouns only, indicate gender (*M*, *F*, or *N*). The first is done for you.

The selection below is adapted from Agatha Christie's *Poirot Investigates*.

As usual, Poirot was right. After a short interval, the American film star was ushered in, and we (1PL) rose to our feet.

Mary Marvell was undoubtedly one of the most popular actresses on the screen. She had only lately arrived in England in company with her husband, Gregory B. Rolf, also a film actor. Their marriage had taken place about a year ago in the States and this was their first visit to England. They had been given a great reception. Every one was prepared to go mad over Mary Marvell... All these details passed rapidly through my mind as I joined with Poirot in greeting our fair client.

Miss Marvell was small and slender, very fair and girlish-looking, with the wide innocent blue eyes of a child.

Poirot drew forward a chair for her, and she commenced talking at once.

"You will probably think me very foolish, Monsieur Poirot, but Lord Cronshaw was telling me last night how wonderfully you cleared up the mystery of his nephew's death, and I felt that I just must have your advice. I dare say it's only a silly hoax—Gregory says so—but it's just worrying me to death."

She paused for breath. Poirot beamed encouragement.

"Proceed, Madame. You comprehend, I am still in the dark."

"It's these letters." Miss Marvell unclasped her handbag, and drew out three envelopes which she handed to Poirot.

WEEK 3

Introduction to the Sentence

— LESSON 9 —

The Sentence

Parts of Speech and Parts of Sentences

Subjects and Predicates

A sentence is a group of words that contains a subject and predicate.

part of speech — noun verb

The cat sits on the mat.

part of the sentence — subject predicate

The subject of the sentence is the main word or term that the sentence is about.
Part of speech is a term that explains what a word does.
Part of the sentence is a term that explains how a word functions in a sentence.
The predicate of the sentence tells something about the subject.

part of speech ________ ________

The *Tyrannosaurus rex* crashes through the trees.

part of the sentence ________ ________

Exercise 9A: Parts of Speech vs. Parts of the Sentence

Label each underlined word with the correct part of speech AND the correct part of the sentence.

part of speech ________ ________

The water is cold.

part of the sentence ________ ________

part of speech ________ ________

We roasted marshmallows.

part of the sentence ________ ________

part of speech ________ ________

The goat munched our reservation.

part of the sentence ________ ________

part of speech ________ ________

He laughed at us.

part of the sentence ________ ________

Exercise 9B: Parts of Speech: Nouns, Adjectives, Pronouns, and Verbs

Label each underlined word with the correct part of speech. Use *N* for noun, *A* for adjective, *P* for pronoun, and *V* for verb.

These sentences are from *The Mysterious Stranger*, by Mark Twain.

We passed out through the parlor, and there was Marget at the spinnet teaching Marie Lueger. So one of the deserting pupils was back; and an influential one, too; the others would follow. Marget jumped up and ran and thanked us again, with tears in her eyes—this was the third time—for saving her and her uncle from being turned into the street, and we told her again we hadn't done it; but that was her way, she never could be grateful enough for anything a person did for her; so we let her have her say. And as we passed through the garden, there was Wilhelm Meidling sitting there waiting, for it was getting toward the edge of the evening, and he would be asking Marget to take a walk along the river with him when she was done with the lesson. He was a young lawyer, and succeeding fairly well and working his way along, little by little. He was very fond of Marget, and she of him. He had not deserted along with the others, but had stood his ground all through. His faithfulness was not lost on Marget and her uncle. He hadn't so very much talent, but he was handsome and good.

Exercise 9C: Parts of the Sentence: Subjects and Predicates

In each of the following sentences, underline the subject once and the predicate twice. Find the subject by asking, "Who or what is this sentence about?" Find the predicate by saying, "Subject what?"

Orcas are large dolphins.

They hunt in groups.

These giant animals are carnivores.

Sometimes, they are called "killer whales."

Orcas are extremely intelligent and social animals.

Each pod uses its own language of sounds for communication.

These mammals can be found in all oceans of the world.

— LESSON 10 —

Subjects and Predicates

Diagramming Subjects and Predicates
Sentence Capitalization and Punctuation
Sentence Fragments

A sentence is a group of words that contains a subject and predicate.
The subject of the sentence is the main word or term that the sentence is about.
The predicate of the sentence tells something about the subject.

He does.
They can.
It is.

Hurricanes form over warm tropical waters.

Hurricanes | form

A sentence is a group of words that contains a subject and a predicate.
A sentence begins with a capital letter and ends with a punctuation mark.

No running in the kitchen.

> Can we measure intelligence without understanding it? Possibly so; physicists measured gravity and magnetism long before they understood them theoretically. Maybe psychologists can do the same with intelligence.
>
> **Or maybe not.**
>
> —James W. Kalat, *Introduction to Psychology* (Cengage Learning, 2007)

Because he couldn't go.
Since I thought so.

A sentence is a group of words that usually contains a subject and a predicate.
A sentence begins with a capital letter and ends with a punctuation mark.
A sentence contains a complete thought.

Exercise 10A: Sentences and Fragments

If a group of words expresses a complete thought, write *S* for sentence in the blank. If not, write *F* for fragment.

since the beach is crowded __________

let's go get ice cream __________

it is fine to leave our bicycles here __________

she likes mint chocolate chip ice cream best __________

that snow cone looks refreshing __________

the empty sunscreen bottle __________

if we need more __________

Exercise 10B: Proofreading for Capitalization and Punctuation

Add the correct capitalization and punctuation to the following sentences. In this exercise you will use proofreader's marks. Indicate letters which should be capitalized by underlining three times. Indicate ending punctuation by using the proofreader's mark for inserting a period: ⊙ Indicate words which should be italicized by underlining them and writing *ital* in the margin.

on august 25, 1916, president woodrow wilson signed a law creating national parks in the united states

the first park to open was yellowstone national park

today, there are 58 national parks in america

alaska and california have the most parks of any state

the most popular park is the great smoky mountain area, which stretches across parts of north carolina and tennessee

arizona is home to one of the most famous parks, the grand canyon

yellowstone contains one of the most popular tourist sites in any park, a geyser known as old faithful

grand teton national park in wyoming is home to diverse and fascinating wildlife, such as black bears, grizzly bears, elk, moose, and bald eagles

photographer ansel adams brought attention to the beauty of the parks with his stunning images

his book, parmelian prints of the high sierras, brought attention to the need to preserve these incredible areas of land

Exercise 10C: Diagramming

Find the subjects and predicates in the following sentences. Diagram each subject and predicate on your own paper. You should capitalize on the diagram any words that are capitalized in the sentence, but do not put punctuation marks on the diagram. If a proper name is the subject, all parts of the proper name go onto the subject line of the diagram.

The first one is done for you.

A light rain fell in the morning.

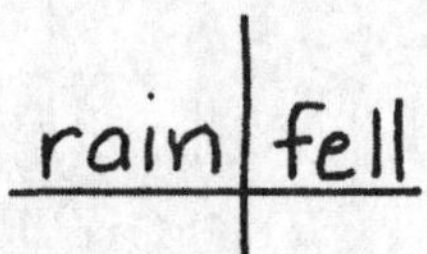

Frogs croaked loudly in the lake.

Yellow flowers bloomed on the path.

Baby birds ate worms in their nest.

Horses grazed happily.

Maram picked vegetables from the garden.

I mowed the grass.

Mom drank coffee on the porch.

— LESSON 11 —

Types of Sentences

A sentence is a group of words that usually contains a subject and a predicate.
A sentence begins with a capital letter and ends with a punctuation mark.
A sentence contains a complete thought.

A purple penguin is playing ping-pong.

A statement gives information. A statement always ends with a period.
Statements are declarative sentences.

An exclamation shows sudden or strong feeling.
An exclamation always ends with an exclamation point.
Exclamations are exclamatory sentences.

A command gives an order or makes a request.
A command ends with either a period or an exclamation point.
Commands are imperative sentences.

Sit!
Stand!
Learn!

The subject of a command is understood to be *you*.

(you) | Sit

A question asks something.
A question always ends with a question mark.
Questions are known as interrogative sentences.

He is late.
Is he late?

He | is   he | Is

Exercise 11A: Types of Sentences: Statements, Exclamations, Commands, and Questions

Identify the following sentences as *S* for statement, *E* for exclamation, *C* for command, or *Q* for question. Add the appropriate punctuation to the end of each sentence.

	Sentence Type
Do you know how to play an instrument	_________
I learned a new piece on the piano	_________
Practice piano every day	_________
Please learn this new song by next week	_________
What a lovely sound this piano makes	_________
Could I practice in the morning	_________
I can't wait for my recital	_________
My brother plays the violin	_________
Are my grandparents coming to the recital	_________
Cover the piano to protect it from dust	_________

Exercise 11B: Proofreading for Capitalization and Punctuation

Proofread the following sentences. If a lowercase letter should be capitalized, draw three lines underneath it. Add any missing punctuation by writing it into the sentence.

what a perfect day for a hike

please refill the water bottles

have you seen my backpack

pack some extra snacks

what trail should we take

don't forget the bug spray

the hike to the waterfall is amazing

Exercise 11C: Diagramming Subjects and Predicates

On your own paper, diagram the subjects and predicates of the following sentences. Remember that the understood subject of a command is *you*, and that the predicate may come before the subject in a question.

Are you tired?

Read this book before Friday.

Close the oven.

Maureen walked here.

The dog loved his new toy.

Thunder boomed loudly!

Did the movie begin?

The water is cold!

— LESSON 12 —

Subjects and Predicates
Helping Verbs
Simple and Complete Subjects and Predicates

The subject of the sentence is the main word or term that the sentence is about.

The simple subject of the sentence is *just* the main word or term that the sentence is about.

Mary	had a little lamb.
Its fleece	was white as snow.
...the lamb	was sure to go.

The complete subject of the sentence is the simple subject and all the words that belong to it.

The predicate of the sentence tells something about the subject.
The simple predicate of the sentence is the main verb along with any helping verbs.
The complete predicate of the sentence is the simple predicate and all the words that belong to it.

Complete Subject	**Complete Predicate**
Lambs born in the spring	must remain with their mothers until July.
Plentiful turnips	should be provided for them.

Exercise 12A: Complete Subjects and Complete Predicates

Match the complete subjects and complete predicates by drawing lines between them.

In the forest, a lion	captured the mouse with his paw.
A tiny mouse	was in pain and roared loudly.
The surprised and angry lion	ran to the lion and ate through the rope, freeing him.
The frightened mouse	accidentally ran across the lion's nose.
Intrigued by the mouse's offer, the lion	became caught in a hunter's trap tied with rope.
Several days later, the lion	lay sleeping under a tree.
Stuck in the trap, the lion	heard the lion's cry.
From across the forest, the mouse	let the mouse go.
Quickly, the mouse	begged for her freedom and promised to help the lion in return.

Exercise 12B: Simple and Complete Subjects and Predicates

In the following sentences, underline the simple subject once and the simple predicate twice. Then, draw a vertical line between the complete subject and the complete predicate.

The first is done for you.

These sentences are adapted from J. M. Barrie's *Peter and Wendy.*

Hook | stood shuddering, one foot in the air.

The astounded brothers were dragged away to hack and hew and carry.

The little house looked so cosy and safe in the darkness.

Peter was a superb swordsman and parried with dazzling rapidity.

"In two minutes, the ship will be blown to pieces!"

A million golden arrows were pointing it out to the children.

Of all delectable islands, Neverland is the smallest and most compact.

Neverland is always more or less an island, with astonishing splashes of color here and there.

Exercise 12C: Diagramming Simple Subjects and Simple Predicates

On your own paper, diagram the simple subjects and simple predicates from Exercise 12B.

— REVIEW 1 —

Weeks 1-3

Topics:
Concrete/Abstract Nouns
Descriptive Adjectives
Common/Proper Nouns
Capitalization of Proper Nouns and First Words in Sentences
Noun Gender
Pronouns and Antecedents
Action Verbs/State-of-Being Verbs
Helping Verbs
Subjects and Predicates
Complete Sentences
Types of Sentences

Review 1A: Types of Nouns

Fill in the blanks with the correct description of each noun. The first is done for you.

	Concrete / Abstract	Common / Proper	Gender (M, F, N)
Maya Angelou	C	P	F
cookie	______	______	______
Puerto Rico	______	______	______
calendar	______	______	______
queen	______	______	______
excitement	______	______	______
nephew	______	______	______
bell	______	______	______
Smithsonian Magazine	______	______	______
surprise	______	______	______
Andes Mountains	______	______	______

Review 1B: Types of Verbs

Underline the complete verbs in the following sentences. Identify any helping verbs as *HV*. Identify the main verb as *AV* for action verb or *BV* for state-of-being verb.

The northern lights occur in the skies near the earth's poles.

They can appear as bright green, red, violet, or blue lights.

The lights dance in the sky.

They may shine as rippling bands or a steady light.

In some countries, such as Greenland, people can see the lights almost every night.

The southern lights transform skies in Antarctica and New Zealand.

The lights form from gases such as oxygen and nitrogen.

These gases collide with electrically-charged protons and electrons.

That collision causes the lights.

Review 1C: Subjects and Predicates

Draw one line under the simple subject and two lines under the simple predicate in the following sentences. Remember that the predicate may be a verb phrase with more than one verb in it. If the subject is an understood *you* in a command, write "(you)" in the left margin and underline it once to indicate that it is the simple subject.

Bridges permit travel over waterways and canyons.

The first bridges were built in Greece for chariots.

Early bridges in China were made from stone.

Roman architects used cement for very strong bridges.

Suspension or hanging bridges were constructed in South America.

Today's bridges are formed from steel and concrete.

Arches make a bridge stronger.

The arches distribute the weight more evenly.

You can create your own bridge from a log or beam.

Make it a strong and sturdy bridge!

Review 1D: Parts of Speech

Identify the underlined words as *N* for noun, *P* for pronoun, *A* for adjective, *AV* for action verb, *HV* for helping verb, or *BV* for state-of-being verb.

The following passage is from Louisa May Alcott's *Jo's Boys*.

"If anyone had told me what wonderful changes were to take place here in ten years, I wouldn't have believed it," said Mrs Jo to Mrs Meg, as they sat on the piazza at Plumfield one summer day, looking about them with faces full of pride and pleasure...

Jo put her hand on her sister's, and both sat silent for a little while, surveying the pleasant scene before them with mingled sad and happy thoughts.

It certainly did look as if magic had been at work, for quiet Plumfield was transformed into a busy little world. The house seemed more hospitable than ever, refreshed now with new paint, added wings, well-kept lawn and garden, and a prosperous air it had not worn when riotous boys swarmed everywhere and it was rather difficult for the Bhaers to make both ends meet. On the hill, where kites used to be flown, stood the fine college which Mr Laurence's munificent legacy had built. Busy students were going to and fro along the paths once trodden by childish feet, and many young men and women were enjoying all the advantages that wealth, wisdom, and benevolence could give them.

Just inside the gates of Plumfield a pretty brown cottage, very like the Dovecote, nestled among the trees, and on the green slope westward Laurie's white-pillared mansion glittered in the sunshine; for when the rapid growth of the city shut in the old house, spoilt Meg's nest, and dared to put a soap-factory under Mr Laurence's indignant nose, our friends emigrated to Plumfield, and the great changes began.

Review 1E: Capitalization and Punctuation

Use proofreading marks to indicate correct capitalization and punctuation in the following sentences. Be careful: Some of these may have more than one sentence, so ending punctuation will need to be inserted to split sentences correctly!

small letter that should be capitalized: ≡ beneath the letter.

italics: single underline | insert period: ⊙ | insert exclamation point: ↑
insert question mark: ? | insert quotation marks: " | insert comma: ,

charles lindbergh completed the first solo flight across the atlantic ocean in his plane, the spirit of st. louis

robert louis stevenson wrote many children's poems, including bed in summer, which describes how hard it is to sleep when it is still light outside

the u.s.s. arizona was sunk at pearl harbor on december 7 1941

did you know that mario is the most famous nintendo character of all time

gifted violinist itzhak perlman became famous at age 13, when he appeared on the ed sullivan show

kitagawa utamaro was a master of the japanese art of woodblock printing

in 2019 at a meet held in monaco, sifan hassan ran a mile in 4 minutes and 12.33 seconds, setting a new world record for women

the national anthem of great britain is entitled god save the queen the queen herself does not sing it when it is played in her presence

the book goodnight moon appeared on reader's digest's list of the greatest children's books of all time

Review 1F: Types of Sentences

Identify the following sentences as *S* for statement, *C* for command, *E* for exclamation, or *Q* for question. If the sentence is incomplete, write *I*.

These sentences are adapted from "The Fir Tree," by Hans Christian Andersen.

	Sentence Type
The sun shone, and the soft air fluttered its leaves.	________
Fell to the earth with a crash.	________
Look what is sticking to the ugly old fir tree.	________
"Do you know where those trees were taken?"	________
The young fir tree wished very much to know.	________
What would become of them?	________
This is beautiful!	________
Rejoice in your youth.	________
How do I know this is so?	________
"Will the trees of the forest come to see me?"	________
Who came and peeped among the branches.	________
Christmas time drew near.	________
Many trees were cut down.	________

WEEK 4

Verb Tenses

— LESSON 13 —

Nouns, Pronouns, and Verbs

Sentences

Simple Present, Simple Past, and Simple Future Tenses

A noun names a person, place, thing, or idea.
A pronoun takes the place of a noun.
A verb shows an action, shows a state of being, links two words together, or helps another verb.

State-of-Being Verbs

am	were
is	be
are	being
was	been

Helping Verbs
am, is, are, was, were
be, being, been
have, has, had
do, does, did
shall, will, should, would, may, might, must
can, could

A sentence is a group of words that usually contains a subject and a predicate. A sentence begins with a capital letter and ends with a punctuation mark. A sentence contains a complete thought.

A verb in the present tense tells about something that happens in the present.
A verb in the past tense tells about something that happened in the past.
A verb in the future tense tells about something that will happen in the future.

Exercise 13A: Simple Tenses

	Simple Past	Simple Present	Simple Future
I			will shop
You	laughed		
She		calls	
We	liked		
They		skip	

Form the simple future by adding the helping verb *will* in front of the simple present.
A suffix is one or more letters added to the end of a word to change its meaning.

Forming the Simple Past
To form the past tense, add *-ed* to the basic verb.

sharpen–sharpened
utter–uttered

If the basic verb ends in *-e* already, only add *-d*.

rumble–rumbled
shade–shaded

If the verb ends in a short vowel sound and a consonant, double the consonant and add *-ed*.

scam–scammed
thud–thudded

If the verb ends in *-y* following a consonant, change the *y* to *i* and add *-ed*.

cry–cried
try–tried

Exercise 13B: Using Consistent Tense

When you write, you should use consistent tense—if you begin a sentence in one tense, you should continue to use that same tense for any other verbs in the same sentence. The following sentences use two verb tenses. Cross out the second verb and rewrite it so that the tense of the second verb matches the tense of the first one.

The first sentence is done for you.

For a bit of fun, see if you can guess which movie each of these sentences is referring to!

contained
Hagrid delivered a letter to Harry that ~~contains~~ his invitation to Hogwarts.
(Harry Potter and the Sorcerer's Stone)

Luke discovers that Darth Vader was his father.

Buzz Lightyear and Woody became good friends, but they begin as enemies.

Carl will ride his hot-air balloon to Paradise Falls, and his explorer pal Russell helped him along the adventurous route.

Charlie won the golden ticket and chooses his grandfather as his guest for the fantastical tour.

Dorothy will find her way home, and she was reunited with Aunt Em and Uncle Henry.

Nemo becomes lost at sea, and his father, Marlin, needed Dory's help to find his son.

Exercise 13C: Forming the Simple Past Tense

Using the rules for forming the simple past, put each one of the verbs in parentheses into the simple past. Write the simple past form in the blank. Be sure to spell the past forms of regular verbs correctly, and to use the correct forms of irregular verbs.

These sentences are taken from "Shippeitaro," translated by Valfrid Hedman.

Long, long ago, in the good old days when there ____________ (are) still fairies and giants, trolls and dragons, valiant knights and distressed maidens, a brave young warrior ____________ (goes) into the world in search of adventure.

For a while, he ____________ (pauses) without encountering anything more special, but finally one evening, he ____________ (finds) himself next to a deserted and lonely mountain. No village, no cottage visible, not even a charcoal burner's hut, although they are so often ____________ (find) on the outskirts of the forest. He ____________ (follows) a weak and well-grassed path, but at last he also ____________ (loses) sight of it. Twilight ____________ (approaches) and in vain he ____________ (struggles) to find the lost path. With each attempt, he ____________ (seems) more and more hopelessly clinging to thorn bushes and long grass that grew densely everywhere. Weak and tired, he ____________ (fumbles) forward in the ever-increasing darkness until he suddenly ____________ (arrives) at a small deserted and half-ruined temple. However, it still ____________ (contains) a sanctuary. There ____________ (is), of course, shelter from cold dew, and so he ____________ (decides) to spend his night in the temple. He ____________ (has) no food;

tangled in his cloak and placing his excellent sword beside him, he ___________ (falls) to rest and soon ___________ (falls) into a deep sleep.

At midnight, he ___________ (wakes) up to a horrible noise. At first he ___________ (thinks) he ___________ (dreams), but the noise ___________ (continues), and the whole building ___________ (echoes) with the most horrible cries and howls. The young warrior ___________ (lifts) gently and ___________ (looks) out of the hole in the dilapidated wall. He ___________ (sees) a strange and creepy vision. A group of disgusting cats ___________ (spin) a wild and horrible dance, and their screams ___________ (echo) into a quiet night. From their horrible cries, the young warrior ___________ (distinguish) the following words:

"Tell it not to Shippeitaro!
Listen for his bark!
Tell it not to Shippeitaro!
Keep it close and dark!"

A beautiful full moon ___________ (illuminates) this horrible play with its rays, which the young warrior ___________ (watches) in amazement and horror. When midnight ___________ (is) over, the ghost cats ___________ (disappear) and everything ___________ (is) quiet again.

— LESSON 14 —

Simple Present, Simple Past, and Simple Future Tenses
Progressive Present, Progressive Past, and Progressive Future Tenses

A verb in the present tense tells about something that happens in the present.
A verb in the future tense tells about something that will happen in the future.
A verb in the past tense tells about something that happened in the past.

study will study studied

Forming the Simple Past:
To form the past tense, add *-ed* to the basic verb.
If the basic verb ends in *e* already, only add *-d.*
If the verb ends in a short vowel sound and a consonant, double the consonant and add *-ed.*
If the verb ends in *-y* following a consonant, change the *y* to *i* and add *-ed.*

Exercise 14A: Forming the Simple Past and Simple Future Tenses

Form the simple past and simple future of the following regular verbs.

Past	Present	Future
	bake	
	close	
	beg	
	challenge	
	brush	
	add	
	fix	
	end	
	cry	

Yesterday, I cried. I was crying for a long time.
Today, I learn. I am learning my grammar.
Tomorrow, I will celebrate. I will be celebrating all afternoon.

A progressive verb describes an ongoing or continuous action.

Exercise 14B: Progressive Tenses

Circle the ending of each verb. Underline the helping verbs.

is singing

am riding

are sewing

have been hiking

will be walking

am thinking

were studying

had been kayaking

The progressive past tense uses the helping verbs *was* and *were*.
The progressive present tense uses the helping verbs *am, is,* and *are*.
The progressive future tense uses the helping verb *will be*.

Spelling Rules for Adding *-ing*
If the verb ends in a short vowel sound and a consonant, double the consonant and add *-ing*.
skip–skipping
drum–drumming

If the verb ends in a long vowel sound plus a consonant and an *-e*, drop the *e* and add *-ing*.
smile–smiling
trade–trading

Exercise 14C: Forming the Progressive Past, Present, and Future Tenses

Complete the following chart. Be sure to use the spelling rules above.

	Progressive Past	Progressive Present	Progressive Future
I sweep	I was sweeping	I am sweeping	I will be sweeping
I cook			
I take			
I swim			
You count	You were counting	You are counting	You will be counting
You type			
You flip			

	Progressive Past	Progressive Present	Progressive Future
You plant			
We wish	We were wishing	We are wishing	We will be wishing
We live			
We hug			
We care			

Exercise 14D: Simple and Progressive Tenses

Fill in the blanks with the correct form of the verb in parentheses.

In 1890, George Washington Carver ________________ (progressive past of *study*) art at college when a professor noticed how well Carver ________________ (simple past of *sketch*) plants and ________________ (simple past of *encourage*) him to pursue a degree in botany.

Carver was an excellent student and ________________ (simple past of *graduate*) as the first African American to receive a Bachelor of Science degree. His reputation as a skilled botanist led him to Tuskegee University, where he ______________ (simple past of *work*) and researched.

While Carver ________________ (progressive past of *examine*) soil chemistry, he discovered that farmers who ________________ (progressive past of *grow*) the same crop for many years ________________ (progressive past of *deplete*) the soil.

Carver ________________ (simple past of *observe*) that nitrogen was added back to the soil when the farmers ________________ (progressive past of *plant*) other crops such as peanuts, sweet potatoes, and soybeans.

However, since many farmers ________________ (progressive past of *harvest*) these plants, there was now a surplus of them, and the growers ________________ (progressive past of *become*) frustrated with what to do with the abundance of crops they could not sell.

Carver ________________ (simple past of *decide*) to learn what other products could be made from peanuts and sweet potatoes.

After much research, Carver ________________ (simple past of *learn*) that these plants could be used in over 300 items which ________________ (simple past of *range*) from foods to cleaning products to office supplies.

Today, when you ________________ (progressive present of *enjoy*) a baked sweet potato, or perhaps you ________________ (progressive present of *bake*) it into a pie, you can thank Dr. Carver for helping to make this humble vegetable so popular!

— LESSON 15 —

Simple Present, Simple Past, and Simple Future Tenses
Progressive Present, Progressive Past, and Progressive Future Tenses
Perfect Present, Perfect Past, and Perfect Future Tenses

A progressive verb describes an ongoing or continuous action.

Yesterday, I was studying tenses.
Today, I am studying tenses.
Tomorrow, I will be studying something else!

NEWS BULLETIN!
A diamond theft occurred at the National Museum yesterday. The thief had already fled the scene when a security guard discovered that the diamond was missing.

A perfect verb describes an action which has been completed before another action takes place.

I practiced my piano.
I was practicing my piano all day yesterday.
I had practiced my piano before I went to bed.

Perfect Past	Perfect Present	Perfect Future
I had practiced yesterday.	I have practiced.	I will have practiced tomorrow.
I had eaten before bed.	I have eaten already.	I will have eaten by bedtime tomorrow.
I had seen the movie a week ago.	I have seen the movie once.	I will have seen the movie before it leaves the theater.

Perfect past verbs describe an action that was finished in the past before another action began.

Helping verb: *had*

Perfect present verbs describe an action that was completed before the present moment.

Helping verbs: *have, has*

Perfect future verbs describe an action that will be finished in the future before another action begins.

Helping verb: *will have*

Exercise 15A: Perfect Tenses

Fill in the blanks with the missing forms.

Simple Past	Perfect Past	Perfect Present	Perfect Future
I wondered	I had wondered	I have wondered	I will have wondered
I skipped			
I lied			
I climbed			
We inspected	We had inspected	We have inspected	We will have inspected
We opened			

Simple Past	Perfect Past	Perfect Present	Perfect Future
We clapped			
We debated			
He carved	He had carved	He has carved	He will have carved
He tripped			
He illustrated			
He dined			

Exercise 15B: Identifying Perfect Tenses

Identify the underlined verbs as *perfect past*, *perfect present*, or *perfect future*. The first one is done for you.

perfect present
I have decided to learn karate.

I had studied martial arts before, and I had enjoyed my classes.

I have started lessons this week, and my sensei has given me exercises to practice at home, too.

By next month, I will have learned enough skills to earn my yellow belt.

My sensei has taught karate for many years, and she had earned her black belt when she was a teenager.

Some students from my karate studio have competed and have won trophies in competitions around the area.

At the end of the year, I will have practiced enough to compete as well.

Exercise 15C: Perfect, Progressive, and Simple Tenses

Each underlined verb phrase has been labeled as past, present, or future. Add the label *perfect*, *progressive*, or *simple* to each one. The first one has been done for you.

simple
PAST PAST PAST
Khadija finished her breakfast. She had eaten, but she was almost too excited to taste

PAST PRESENT PRESENT FUTURE
the food, because she thought, "I know what is happening today: My family will be going

to the state fair!"

FUTURE PAST PRESENT
Khadija's mother declared, "We will need tickets," so Khadija announced, "I volunteer to

PAST PAST
wait in the line!" While she waited, Khadija was enjoying the sounds of music and

PAST
was savoring the smells of delicious fried treats she would enjoy. Suddenly, the breakfast

PAST PAST
she had eaten seemed so long ago! After several hours had passed, Khadija and her family

PAST PAST
began the long walk back to the van. They were laughing about all the fun they

PAST
had experienced that day.

FUTURE PAST PAST
"We will be doing this again next year!" Khadija exclaimed; and the whole family agreed.

— LESSON 16 —

Simple Present, Simple Past, and Simple Future Tenses
Progressive Present, Progressive Past, and Progressive Future Tenses
Perfect Present, Perfect Past, and Perfect Future Tenses
Irregular Verbs

go	run	are	know	make
go-ed	run-ned	ar-ed	know-ed	mak-ed
went	ran	were	knew	made

Exercise 16A: Irregular Verb Forms: Simple Present, Simple Past, and Simple Future

Fill in the chart with the missing verb forms.

	Simple Past	Simple Present	Simple Future
I			will begin
You			will go
She	shrank		
We		choose	
They		hold	
I	made		
You		shine	
He			will pay
We		ride	
They		teach	
I			will take

	Simple Past	Simple Present	Simple Future
You	swept		
It		stinks	
We	bore		
They			will wake
I		win	
You	became		
We		break	
They		weep	

	Simple Past	Simple Present	Simple Future	Progressive Past	Progressive Present	Progressive Future	Perfect Past	Perfect Present	Perfect Future
go	went	go	will go	was going	am going	will be going	had gone	have gone	will have gone
eat	ate	eat	will eat	was eating	am eating	will be eating	had eaten	have eaten	will have eaten

Exercise 16B: Irregular Verbs: Progressive and Perfect Tenses

Fill in the remaining blanks. The first row is done for you.

Simple Present	Progressive Past	Progressive Present	Progressive Future	Perfect Past	Perfect Present	Perfect Future
begin	was beginning	am beginning	will be beginning	had begun	have begun	will have begun
eat						

Simple Present	Progressive Past	Progressive Present	Progressive Future	Perfect Past	Perfect Present	Perfect Future
blow						
choose						
lend						
make						
flow						
tear						
spend						
wake						
hold						
fly						
see						
bring						

Simple Present	Progressive Past	Progressive Present	Progressive Future	Perfect Past	Perfect Present	Perfect Future
send						
sell						
forget						
dig						
get						

WEEK 5

More About Verbs

— LESSON 17 —

Simple, Progressive, and Perfect Tenses
Subjects and Predicates
Parts of Speech and Parts of Sentences
Verb Phrases

I yawn today. Yesterday, I yawned. Tomorrow, I will yawn.
I am yawning today. Yesterday, I was yawning. Tomorrow, I will be yawning.

A progressive verb describes an ongoing or continuous action.

I have yawned today already.
Yesterday, I had yawned before I had my dinner.
Tomorrow, I will have yawned by the time the sun goes down.

A perfect verb describes an action which has been completed before another action takes place.

Exercise 17A: Simple, Progressive, and Perfect Tenses

All the bolded verbs are in the past tense. Label each bolded verb as simple (*S*), progressive (*PROG*), or perfect (*PERF*). These sentences are adapted from *The Radio Boys' First Wireless*, by Allen Chapman.

"I **was going** to hear what the doctor has to say. I **got** a letter the other day from a cousin of mine out in Michigan, and he **told** me all about a set that he made and **put** up himself and **said** he was just crazy about it. He wanted me to go into it so that he and I might talk together. Of course, though, I guess he **was kidding** me about that. Michigan is a long way off, and it takes more than a day to get there on a train."

"My dad **was reading** in the papers the other night about a man in New Jersey who **was talking** to a friend nearby and told him that he **was going** to play a phonograph record for him. A man over in Scotland, over three thousand miles away, **had heard** every word he **had said** and the phonograph too. A ship two thousand miles out on the Atlantic heard the same record, and so did another ship in a harbor in Central America."

There **was** a loud guffaw behind the lads, accompanied by snickers, and the friends turned around to see three boys who were following them.

"What's the joke, Buck?" asked Bob coldly, as he **looked** from one to the other.

"You're the joke," **answered** Buck insolently; "that is, if you believe all that stuff I heard you pulling off just now."

"I **wasn't talking** to you," replied Bob, restraining himself with some difficulty.

"Telephoning without wires! You might as well talk of walking without legs." This argument **seemed** to him so overpowering that he **swelled** out his chest and looked triumphantly at his two companions, whose faces instantly **took** on the same expression.

"But say, fellows, forget about Buck and listen to this," said Herb. " It's a good one that I **had heard** yesterday. Why is—"

He was interrupted by a shout from Bob.

"Look," he cried, "look at that auto! It's running wild!"

---

had rejoiced.
will have rejoiced.

A phrase is a group of words serving a single grammatical function.

have greatly rejoiced
They will have all rejoiced

The subject of the sentence is the main word or term that the sentence is about.
The simple subject of the sentence is *just* the main word or term that the sentence is about.

The predicate of the sentence tells something about the subject.
The simple predicate of the sentence is the main verb along with any helping verbs.

Part of speech is a term that explains what a word does.

A noun names a person, place, thing, or idea.

A pronoun takes the place of a noun.

Part of the sentence is a term that explains how a word functions in a sentence.

A verb shows an action, shows a state of being, links two words together, or helps another verb.

Exercise 17B: Identifying and Diagramming Subjects and Predicates, Identifying Verb Tenses

Underline the subject once and the predicate twice in each sentence. Be sure to include both the main verb and any helping verbs when you underline the predicate. Identify the tense of each verb or verb phrase (*simple past*, *present*, or *future*; *progressive past*, *present*, or *future*; *perfect past*, *present*, or *future*) on the line. Then diagram each subject and predicate on your own paper.

These sentences are adapted from Mabel Powers's *Stories the Iroquois Tell Their Children*.

Summer is the time for work. ______________________

Bees store their honey. ______________________

Squirrels will gather their nuts. ______________________

It was at the time of the Harvest Moon. ______________________

A line of fires was burning around the camp. ______________________

The wind had thrown them off the trail. ______________________

The Peacemaker listened to the grievance of the one and then the other. ______________________

The two will depart in peace—no longer enemies, but friends. ______________________

"On my great wings, I will bear him far away from the hunters." ______________________

A rabbit was running swiftly down the trail. ______________________

Who will fly the Great Sky Trail? ______________________

We have given them soft hearts and kind minds. ______________________

"A deep sleep will fall on him." ____________________

— LESSON 18 —

Verb Phrases

Person of the Verb

Conjugations

	Progressive Past	Progressive Present	Progressive Future
I run	I was running	I am running	I will be running
You call	You were calling	You are calling	You will be calling
He jogs	He was jogging	He is jogging	He will be jogging
We fix	We were fixing	We are fixing	We will be fixing
They call	They were calling	They are calling	They will be calling

PERSONS OF THE VERB

	Singular	**Plural**
First person	I	we
Second person	you	you
Third person	he, she, it	they

Simple Tenses

REGULAR VERB, SIMPLE PRESENT

	Singular	**Plural**
First person	I pretend	we pretend
Second person	you pretend	you pretend
Third person	he, she, it pretends	they pretend
First person	I wander	we wander
Second person	you wander	you wander
Third person	he, she, it wanders	they wander

REGULAR VERB, SIMPLE PAST

	Singular	**Plural**
First person	I wandered	we wandered
Second person	you wandered	you wandered
Third person	he, she, it wandered	they wandered

REGULAR VERB, SIMPLE FUTURE

	Singular	Plural
First person	I will wander	we will wander
Second person	you will wander	you will wander
Third person	he, she, it will wander	they will wander

Perfect Tenses

REGULAR VERB, PERFECT PRESENT

	Singular	Plural
First person	I have wandered	we have wandered
Second person	you have wandered	you have wandered
Third person	he, she, it has wandered	they have wandered

REGULAR VERB, PERFECT PAST

	Singular	Plural
First person	I had wandered	we had wandered
Second person	you had wandered	you had wandered
Third person	he, she, it had wandered	they had wandered

REGULAR VERB, PERFECT FUTURE

	Singular	Plural
First person	I will have wandered	we will have wandered
Second person	you will have wandered	you will have wandered
Third person	he, she, it will have wandered	they will have wandered

Exercise 18A: Third-Person-Singular Verbs

In the simple present conjugation, the third-person-singular verb changes by adding an *-s*. Read the following rules and examples for adding *-s* to verbs in order to form the third-person singular. Then, rewrite the first-person verbs as third-person-singular verbs. The first of each set is done for you.

Usually, add *-s* to form the third-person singular verb.

First-Person Verb	Third-Person Singular Verb	
I like	he	likes
I speak	she	____________
I work	it	____________

Add *-es* to verbs ending in *-s*, *-sh*, *-ch*, *-x*, or *-z*.

First-Person Verb	Third-Person Singular Verb	
we watch	it	watches
we fix	he	________
we fish	she	________

If a verb ends in *-y* after a consonant, change the *y* to *i* and add *-es*.

First-Person Verb	Third-Person Singular Verb	
I cry	he	cries
I fly	she	________
I worry	it	________

If a verb ends in *-y* after a vowel, just add *-s*.

First-Person Verb	Third-Person Singular Verb	
we say	she	says
we destroy	he	________
we journey	it	________

If a verb ends in *-o* after a consonant, form the third-person singular by adding *-es*.

First-Person Verb	Third-Person Singular Verb	
I overdo	she	overdoes
I forgo	it	________
I go	he	________

Exercise 18B: Simple Present Tenses

Choose the correct form of the simple present verb in parentheses, based on the person. Cross out the incorrect form.

Rishi and Anju (decide/decides) to build a computer.

Rishi (research/researches) what parts to buy, while Anju (make/makes) a list of them.

They (go/goes) online to order the parts.

Rishi (ride/rides) his bike to the post office when the siblings (hear/hears) that their order is ready.

"We should (count/counts) all the parts to make sure they are all here," (say/says) Anju.

"While you (check/checks), I will set up a work table," Rishi (reply/replies).

Rishi and Anju (spend/spends) all day on their computer, only stopping when their dad (tell/tells) them it is time to eat.

At the dinner table, they (talk/talks) about their project. They (look/looks) forward to a fun summer working together!

Exercise 18C: Perfect Present Tenses

Write the correct form of the perfect present verb in the blank. These sentences are slightly adapted from Mark Twain's *A Connecticut Yankee in King Arthur's Court.*

How I ______________ [long] for you!

Then I ______________ [sleep] well, sure enough.

I couldn't keep from thinking about it, and contemplating it, just as one does who ______________ [strike] oil.

Chains cease to be needed after the spirit ______________ [go] out of a prisoner.

You ______________ [see] that kind of people who will never let on that they don't know the meaning of a new big word.

The handsome and popular Sir Charolais of Gaul, who ______________ [win] every heart by his polished manners and elegant conversation, will pull out to-day for home.

— LESSON 19 —

Person of the Verb
Conjugations
State-of-Being Verbs

English	Latin		
conjugate	*conjugare*	*con*	+ *jugare*
to join a verb to each person in turn	to join together	with	+ to yoke

REGULAR VERB, SIMPLE PRESENT

	Singular	Plural
First person	I conjugate	we conjugate
Second person	you conjugate	you conjugate
Third person	he, she, it conjugates	they conjugate

REGULAR VERB, SIMPLE PAST

conjugated

REGULAR VERB, SIMPLE FUTURE

will conjugate

REGULAR VERB, PERFECT PRESENT

	Singular	Plural
First person	I have conjugated	we have conjugated
Second person	you have conjugated	you have conjugated
Third person	he, she, it has conjugated	they have conjugated

REGULAR VERB, PERFECT PAST

had conjugated

REGULAR VERB, PERFECT FUTURE

will have conjugated

REGULAR VERB, PROGRESSIVE PRESENT

am conjugating

STATE-OF-BEING VERB, SIMPLE PRESENT

	Singular	Plural
First person	I am	we are
Second person	you are	you are
Third person	he, she, it is	they are

Exercise 19A: Forming Progressive Present Tenses

Fill in the blanks with the correct helping verbs.

Regular Verb, Progressive Present

	Singular	Plural
First person	I ______________ finishing	we ______________ finishing
Second person	you ______________ finishing	you ______________ finishing
Third person	he, she, it ______________ finishing	they ______________ finishing

STATE-OF-BEING VERB, SIMPLE PRESENT

	Singular	Plural
First person	I am	we are
Second person	you are	you are
Third person	he, she, it is	they are

STATE-OF-BEING VERB, SIMPLE PAST

	Singular	Plural
First person	I was	we were
Second person	you were	you were
Third person	he, she, it was	they were

STATE-OF-BEING VERB, SIMPLE FUTURE

	Singular	Plural
First person	I will be	we will be
Second person	you will be	you will be
Third person	he, she, it will be	they will be

STATE-OF-BEING VERB, PERFECT PRESENT

	Singular	Plural
First person	I have been	we have been
Second person	you have been	you have been
Third person	he, she, it has been	they have been

STATE-OF-BEING VERB, PERFECT PAST

	Singular	Plural
First person	I had been	we had been
Second person	you had been	you had been
Third person	he, she, it had been	they had been

STATE-OF-BEING VERB, PERFECT FUTURE

	Singular	Plural
First person	I will have been	we will have been
Second person	you will have been	you will have been
Third person	he, she, it will have been	they will have been

STATE-OF-BEING VERB, PROGRESSIVE PRESENT

	Singular	Plural
First person	I am being	we are being
Second person	you are being	you are being
Third person	he, she, it is being	they are being

STATE-OF-BEING VERB, PROGRESSIVE PAST

	Singular	Plural
First person	I was being	we were being
Second person	you were being	you were being
Third person	he, she, it was being	they were being

STATE-OF-BEING VERB, PROGRESSIVE FUTURE

	Singular	Plural
First person	I will be being	we will be being
Second person	you will be being	you will be being
Third person	he, she, it will be being	they will be being

Exercise 19B: Forming Progressive Past and Future Tenses

Fill in the blanks with the correct helping verbs.

Regular Verb, Progressive Present

	Singular	Plural
First person	I ____________ jumping	we ____________ jumping
Second person	you ____________ jumping	you ____________ jumping
Third person	he, she, it ________ jumping	they ____________ jumping

Regular Verb, Progressive Past

	Singular	Plural
First person	I ____________ jumping	we ____________ jumping
Second person	you ____________ jumping	you ____________ jumping
Third person	he, she, it ________ jumping	they ____________ jumping

Regular Verb, Progressive Future

	Singular	Plural
First person	I ____________ jumping	we ____________ jumping
Second person	you ____________ jumping	you ____________ jumping
Third person	he, she, it ____________ jumping	they ____________ jumping

— LESSON 20 —

Irregular State-of-Being Verbs

Helping Verbs

Forms of the State-of-Being Verb *Am*

SIMPLE PRESENT

	Singular	Plural
First person	I am	we are
Second person	you are	you are
Third person	He, she, it is	they are

SIMPLE PAST

	Singular	Plural
First person	I was	we were
Second person	you were	you were
Third person	he, she, it was	they were

SIMPLE FUTURE

	Singular	Plural
First person	I will be	we will be
Second person	you will be	you will be
Third person	he, she, it will be	they will be

PERFECT PRESENT

	Singular	Plural
First person	I have been	we have been
Second person	you have been	you have been
Third person	he, she, it has been	they have been

PERFECT PAST

	Singular	Plural
First person	I had been	we had been
Second person	you had been	you had been
Third person	he, she, it had been	they had been

PERFECT FUTURE

	Singular	Plural
First person	I will have been	we will have been
Second person	you will have been	you will have been
Third person	he, she, it will have been	they will have been

PROGRESSIVE PRESENT

	Singular	Plural
First person	I am being	we are being
Second person	you are being	you are being
Third person	he, she, it is being	they are being

PROGRESSIVE PAST

	Singular	Plural
First person	I was being	we were being
Second person	You were being	you were being
Third person	he, she, it was being	they were being

PROGRESSIVE FUTURE

	Singular	Plural
First person	I will be being	we will be being
Second person	you will be being	you will be being
Third person	he, she, it will be being	they will be being

Exercise 20A: Simple Tenses of the Verb *Have*

Try to fill in the missing blanks in the chart below, using your own sense of what sounds correct as well as the hints you may have picked up from the conjugations already covered. Be sure to use pencil so that any incorrect answers can be erased and corrected!

Simple Present

	Singular	Plural
First person	I have	we ______
Second person	you ______	you ______
Third person	he, she, it ______	they ______

Simple Past

	Singular	Plural
First person	I ________	we ________
Second person	you ________	you ________
Third person	he, she, it ________	they ________

Simple Future

	Singular	Plural
First person	I will ________	we ________
Second person	you ________	you ________
Third person	he, she, it ________	they ________

Exercise 20B: Simple Tenses of the Verb *Do*

Try to fill in the missing blanks in the chart below, using your own sense of what sounds correct as well as the hints you may have picked up from the conjugations already covered. Be sure to use pencil so that any incorrect answers can be erased and corrected!

Simple Present

	Singular	Plural
First person	I ___do___	we ________
Second person	you ________	you ________
Third person	he, she, it ________	they ________

Simple Past

	Singular	Plural
First person	I ________	we ________
Second person	you ________	you ________
Third person	he, she, it ________	they ________

Simple Future

	Singular	Plural
First person	I will ________	we ________
Second person	you ________	you ________
Third person	he, she, it ________	they ________

I will be
You will run
He, she, it will sing
We will eat
You will shout
They will cavort

I shall be
You will run
He, she, it will sing
We shall eat
You will shout
They will cavort

I shall be!
You shall run!
He, she, it shall sing!
We shall eat!
You shall shout!
They shall cavort!

I **will** go to bed early.
When I was young, I **would** always go to bed early.

I **would** like to go to bed early.
I **should** probably go to bed now.

I **would** eat the chocolate caramel truffle.
I **should** eat the chocolate caramel truffle.
I **may** eat the chocolate caramel truffle.
I **might** eat the chocolate caramel truffle.
I **must** eat the chocolate caramel truffle.
I **can** eat the chocolate caramel truffle.
I **could** eat the chocolate caramel truffle.

Am, is, are, was, were, be, being, and *been* are forms of the verb *am.*
Have, has, and *had* are forms of the verb *has.*
Do, does, and *did* are forms of the verb *do.*
Shall and *will* are different forms of the same verb.
Should, would, may, might, must, can, and *could* express hypothetical situations.

WEEK 6

Nouns and Verbs in Sentences

— LESSON 21 —

Person of the Verb
Conjugations
Noun-Verb/Subject-Predicate Agreement

SIMPLE PRESENT

	Singular	**Plural**
First person	I enjoy	we enjoy
Second person	you enjoy	you enjoy
Third person	he, she, it enjoys	they enjoy

PERFECT PAST

	Singular	**Plural**
First person	I had been	we had been
Second person	you had been	you had been
Third person	he, she, it had been	they had been

PROGRESSIVE FUTURE

	Singular	**Plural**
First person	I will be running	we will be running
Second person	you will be running	you will be running
Third person	he, she, it will be running	they will be running

Complete Conjugation of a Regular Verb

SIMPLE PRESENT

	Singular	**Plural**
First person	I grab	we grab
Second person	you grab	you grab
Third person	he, she, it grabs	they grab

SIMPLE PAST

I grabbed, etc.

SIMPLE FUTURE

I will grab, etc.

PERFECT PRESENT

	Singular	Plural
First person	I have grabbed	we have grabbed
Second person	you have grabbed	you have grabbed
Third person	he, she, it has grabbed	they have grabbed

PERFECT PAST

I had grabbed, etc.

PERFECT FUTURE

I will have grabbed, etc.

PROGRESSIVE PRESENT

	Singular	Plural
First person	I am grabbing	we are grabbing
Second person	you are grabbing	you are grabbing
Third person	he, she, it is grabbing	they are grabbing

PROGRESSIVE PAST

	Singular	Plural
First person	I was grabbing	we were grabbing
Second person	you were grabbing	you were grabbing
Third person	he, she, it was grabbing	they were grabbing

PROGRESSIVE FUTURE

I will be grabbing, etc.

Exercise 21A: Person and Number of Pronouns

Identify the person and number of the underlined pronouns. Cross out the incorrect verb(s) in parentheses. The first one is done for you.

These sentences are adapted from Madeline Yale Wynne's "The Little Room."

	Person	Singular/Plural
She (is / ~~are~~) an echo, that's all.	third	singular
"It (is / are) a pretty story, Pepita."		
"The house is just as it was built; there have never been any changes, so far as we (knows / know)."		
"They (makes / make) me think of the Maine woman who wanted her epitaph to be: 'She was a hard-working woman.'"		
I (wonder / wonders) if the other people in the car can hear us?		
"Don't, Roger. You have no idea how loud you (speaks / speak)."		
You (does / do) well to remember him.		
Margaret looked at her husband. He kissed her, "I (does / do) not like to hear you speak of your mother in connection with it."		

SIMPLE PRESENT

	Singular	**Plural**
Third person	He, she, it grabs	They grab
	The man grabs	The men grab
	The woman grabs	The women grab
	The eagle grabs	The eagles grab

PERFECT PRESENT

	Singular	**Plural**
Third person	He, she, it has grabbed	They have grabbed
	The boy has grabbed	The boys have grabbed
	The girl has grabbed	The girls have grabbed
	The bear has grabbed	The bears have grabbed

PROGRESSIVE PRESENT

	Singular	**Plural**
Third person	He, she, it is grabbing	They are grabbing
	The father is grabbing	The fathers are grabbing
	The mother is grabbing	The mothers are grabbing
	The baby is grabbing	The babies are grabbing

PROGRESSIVE PAST

	Singular	**Plural**
Third person	He, she, it was grabbing	They were grabbing
	The king was grabbing	The kings were grabbing
	The queen was grabbing	The queens were grabbing
	The dragon was grabbing	The dragons were grabbing

Exercise 21B: Identifying Subjects and Predicates

Draw two lines underneath each simple predicate and one line underneath each simple subject in the following sentences. If a phrase comes between the subject and the predicate, put parentheses around it to show that it does not affect the subject-predicate agreement.

Sloths often reside in Central and South America.

Trees in tropical rainforests create the perfect home for these mammals.

Algae on the sloths' fur provides excellent camouflage.

Three-toed sloths usually perch on the branches.

The diet of a sloth consists of vegetation like flowers and leaves.

Once a week, sloths slowly descend from their trees.

The meal in a sloth's stomach will digest over the course of an entire week.

Exercise 21C: Subject-Verb Agreement

Cross out the incorrect verb in parentheses so that subject and predicate agree in number and person. Be careful of any confusing phrases between the subject and predicate.

The teacher of the science classes (choose/chooses) Jasmine and Gabriel to work on the project.

Jasmine and Gabriel (decide/decides) to demonstrate how oil spills harm animals.

Jasmine, using library books, (research/researches) the effect of oil spills on birds.

She and Gabriel (gather / gathers) supplies so that they can (conduct / conducts) an experiment.

Gabriel gently drops a bird feather into a pan of water and the students in the class (watch / watches) the feather repel the moisture.

Next, Jasmine, with a dropper, (place / places) oil in the water, and Gabriel, using brushes, (coat / coats) the feather in the oil and water mixture.

The students around the table (observe / observes) that the oil (cause / causes) the feather to lose its natural waterproofing, which is what (happen / happens) to birds in an oil spill.

— LESSON 22 —

Formation of Plural Nouns
Collective Nouns

A collective noun names a group of people, animals, or things.

Exercise 22A: Collective Nouns

Write the collective noun for each description. Then fill in an appropriate singular verb for each sentence. (Use the simple present tense!) The first one is done for you.

Description		Collective Noun	Verb	
a group of bees	The	swarm	enters	the hive.
group of fish	The	__________	__________	to the surface.
people who determine a verdict	The	__________	__________	a decision.
many ants	The	__________	__________	our picnic.
several newborn kittens	The	__________	__________	in the basket.
group of dancers	The	__________	__________	the ballet.
many pearls put together in a row	This	__________	__________	around her neck.

Exercise 22B: Plural Noun Forms

Read each rule and the example out loud. Then rewrite the singular nouns as plural nouns in the spaces provided.

Usually, add *-s* to a noun to form the plural.

Singular Noun	Plural Noun
cat	cats
trail	____________
paper	____________
ring	____________

Add *-es* to nouns ending in *-s*, *-sh*, *-ch*, *-x*, or *-z*.

Singular Noun	Plural Noun
bus	buses
flash	____________
lunch	____________
tax	____________
waltz	____________

If a noun ends in *-y* after a consonant, change the *y* to *i* and add *-es*.

Singular Noun	Plural Noun
sky	skies
curry	____________
strawberry	____________
theory	____________

If a noun ends in *-y* after a vowel, just add *-s*.

Singular Noun	Plural Noun
kidney	kidneys
chimney	____________
decoy	____________
highway	____________

Some words that end in *-f or -fe* form their plurals differently. You must change the *f* or *fe* to *v* and add *-es*.

Singular Noun	Plural Noun
leaf	leaves
afterlife	____________
half	____________
midwife	____________

Words that end in *-ff* form their plurals by simply adding *-s*.

Singular Noun	Plural Noun
spinoff	spinoffs
whiff	________________
tariff	________________

Some words that end in a single *-f* can form their plurals either way.

Singular Noun	Plural Noun
turf	turfs/turves
scarf	________________

If a noun ends in *-o* after a vowel, just add *-s*.

Singular Noun	Plural Noun
bamboo	bamboos
duo	________________
ratio	________________
stereo	________________

If a noun ends in *-o* after a consonant, form the plural by adding *-es*.

Singular Noun	Plural Noun
potato	potatoes
mosquito	________________
domino	________________
buffalo	________________

To form the plural of foreign words ending in *-o*, just add *-s*.

Singular Noun	Plural Noun
avocado	avocados
grotto	________________
staccato	________________
tempo	________________
palazzo	________________

Irregular plurals don't follow any of these rules!

Singular Noun	Irregular Plural Noun
tooth	teeth
louse	lice
trout	trout

axis	_______________
baggage	baggage
dozen	dozen/dozens
swine	_______________
ellipsis	ellipses

Exercise 22C: Plural Nouns

Complete the following excerpt by filling in the plural form of each noun in parentheses. The following passage is slightly adapted from *The Fatal Eggs*, by Mikhail Bulgakov.

"Undernourishment!"

The scientist was perfectly right. Vlas should have been fed with flour and the (toad) _______________ with flour (weevil) _______________, but the disappearance of the former determined that of the latter likewise, and Persikov tried to shift the twenty surviving (specimen) _______________ of tree-(frog) _______________ onto a diet of (cockroach) _______________ ... Consequently, these last remaining specimens also had to be thrown into the rubbish (pit) _______________ in the Institute yard. (Thing) _______________ went from bad to worse. When Vlas died the Institute (window) _______________ froze so hard that there were icy (scroll) _______________ on the inside of the (pane) _______________. The (rabbit) _______________, (fox) _______________, (wolf) _______________, and (fish) _______________ died, as well as every single grass-snake. Persikov brooded silently for days on end, then caught pneumonia, but did not die. When he recovered, he started coming to the Institute twice a week and in the round hall, where for some reason it was always five (degree) _______________ below freezing point irrespective of the temperature outside, he delivered a cycle of (lecture) _______________ on "The (Reptile) _______________ of the Torrid Zone" in galoshes, a fur cap with ear-(flap) _______________ and a scarf, breathing out white steam, to an audience of eight. The rest of the time he lay under a rug on the divan in Prechistenka, in a room with (book) _______________ piled up to the ceiling, coughing, gazing into the (jaw) _______________ of the fiery stove which Maria Stepanovna stoked with gilt (chair) _______________, and remembering the Surinam toad. But all (thing) _______________ come to an end. So it was with 'twenty and 'twenty-one, and in 'twenty-two a kind of reverse process began. Firstly, in place of the dear departed Vlas there appeared Pankrat, a young, but most promising zoological caretaker, and the Institute began to be heated again a little. Then in the summer with Pankrat's help Persikov caught fourteen common (toad) ____________. The (terrarium) ________________ came to life again... In 'twenty-three Persikov gave eight lectures a week, three at the Institute and five at the University, in 'twenty-four thirteen a week, not including the (one) ________________ at workers' (school) ______________, and in the spring of 'twenty-five distinguished himself by failing no less than seventy-six (student) ________________, all on (amphibian) ________________. "What, you don't know the difference between amphibians and reptilia?" Persikov asked. "That's quite ridiculous, young man. Amphibia have no (kidney) ________________. None at all. So there. You should be ashamed of yourself."

"Well, kindly retake the exam in the autumn," Persikov said politely and shouted cheerfully to Pankrat: "Send in the next one!" Just as amphibians come to life after a long drought, with the first heavy shower of rain, so Professor Persikov revived in 1926 when a joint Americano-Russian company built fifteen-story apartment (block) ________________ in the centre of Moscow, beginning at the corner of Gazetny Lane and Tverskaya, and 300 workers' (cottage) ________________ on the (outskirt) ________________, each with eight (apartment) ________________, thereby putting an end once and for all to the terrible and ridiculous accommodation shortage which made life such a misery for Muscovites from 1919 to 1925.

You would not have recognised the Institute either. They painted it cream, equipped the amphibian room with a special water supply system, replaced all the plate glass with (mirror) ________________ and donated five new (microscope) ________________, glass laboratory tables, some 2,000-amp arc lights, reflectors and museum (case) ____________.

— LESSON 23 —

Plural Nouns
Descriptive Adjectives
Possessive Adjectives
Contractions

An apostrophe is a punctuation mark that shows possession. It turns a noun into an adjective that tells whose.

Possessive adjectives tell whose.

An adjective modifies a noun or pronoun.
Adjectives tell what kind, which one, how many, and whose.
Descriptive adjectives tell what kind.
A descriptive adjective becomes an abstract noun when you add *-ness* to it.

Form the possessive of a singular noun by adding an apostrophe and the letter *-s*.

Exercise 23A: Introduction to Possessive Adjectives

Read the following nouns. Choose a person that you know to possess each of the items. Write that person's name, an apostrophe, and an *s* to form a possessive adjective.

Example: Pablo ______ Pablo's ______ bicycle

______ dog

______ phone

______ soccer ball

______ bedroom

______ bowl

Form the possessive of a plural noun ending in *-s* by adding an apostrophe only.

Form the possessive of a plural noun that does not end in *-s* as if it were a singular noun.

Exercise 23B: Singular and Plural Possessive Adjective Forms

Fill in the chart with the correct forms. The first is done for you. Both regular and irregular nouns are included.

Noun	Singular Possessive	Plural	Plural Possessive
backpack	backpack's	backpacks	backpacks'
glass			
city			
man			
tomato			
ray			
ocean			
gas			
wife			

mouse ________ ________ ________
roof ________ ________ ________

	SINGULAR		PLURAL	
	Pronoun(s)	**Possessive Adjective**	**Pronoun**	**Possessive Adjective**
First person	I	my	we	our
Second person	you	your	you	your
Third person	he, she, it	his, her, its	they	their

INCORRECT	CORRECT
I's book	my book
you's candy	your candy
he's hat	his hat
she's necklace	her necklace
it's nest	its nest
we's lesson	our lesson
they's problem	their problem

Contraction	**Meaning**
he's	he is
she's	she is
it's	it is
you're	you are
they're	they are

A contraction is a combination of two words with some of the letters dropped out.

Exercise 23C: Common Contractions

Drop the letters in grey print and write the contraction in the blank. The first one is done for you.

Full Form	Common Contraction	Full Form	Common Contraction
I am	I'm	they have	
who would		who has	
you had		it would	
we are		must not	
could have		when is	
it will		how is	
had not		why will	
I would		might not	

— LESSON 24 —

Possessive Adjectives
Contractions
Compound Nouns

A contraction is a combination of two words with some of the letters dropped out.

Contraction	Meaning	Not the Same as
he's	he is	his
she's	she is	her
it's	it is	its
you're	you are	your
they're	they are	their

It's hard for a hippopotamus to see its feet.
It is *hard for a hippopotamus to see its feet.*
It's hard for a hippopotamus to see ***it is*** *feet.*

You're fond of your giraffe.
You are *fond of your giraffe.*
You're fond of ***you are*** *giraffe.*

They're searching for their zebra.
They are *searching for their zebra.*
They're searching for ***they are*** *zebra.*

Exercise 24A: Using Possessive Adjectives Correctly

Cross out the incorrect word in parentheses.

(Your / You're) missing (your / you're) keys.

(Their / They're) new house is the one (their / they're) building down the street.

(Yours / your's) is the blue cup next to (hers / she's).

(Its / It's) the cafe around the corner. You will see (its / it's) red awning.

My seat is next to (yours / your's) and in front of (his / he's).

(Its / It's) time for the dog to get (his / he's) vaccinations.

We wanted to watch (their / they're) show, but (their / they're) sold out of tickets.

If (your / you're) sleepy, I think that (your / you're) sleeping bag is next to (theirs / theres).

(Hers / She's) will be the last car to arrive. (Hers / She's) running late.

(Its / It's) a mystery which has never been solved. (Its / It's) resolution will be a relief!

A compound noun is a single noun composed of two or more words.

One word	shipwreck, haircut, chalkboard
Hyphenated word	self-confidence, check-in, pinch-hitter
Two or more words	air conditioning, North Dakota, *The Prince and the Pauper*

Exercise 24B: Compound Nouns

Underline each simple subject once and each simple predicate (verb) twice. Circle each compound noun.

Many people perished because of the lack of lifeboats on the *Titanic*.

My sister-in-law was a taxi driver for twelve years.

Before our trip, we ate breakfast at sunrise.

Can you find the train station?

I put my workbook on the bookshelf.

We ate our takeout dinner in the dining room.

It was the three-year-old's birthday!

The trial of the famous safecracker began today at the courthouse downtown.

If a compound noun is made up of one noun along with another word or words, pluralize the noun.

passerby passersby passerbys

If a compound noun ends in *-ful*, pluralize by putting an *-s* at the end of the entire word.

truckful trucksful truckfuls

If neither element of the compound noun is a noun, pluralize the entire word.

grown-up growns-up grown-ups

If the compound noun includes more than one noun, choose the most important to pluralize.

attorney at law attorneys at law attorney at laws

Exercise 24C: Plurals of Compound Nouns

Write the plural of each singular compound noun in parentheses in the blanks to complete the sentences.

Every year during our camping trip, all the (grown-up) ______________________ and kids in our family pick (blackberry) ______________________.

The recipe called for two (handful) ______________________ of chocolate chips.

All of my (hairbrush) ______________________ are missing!

My community's pool has three (diving board) ______________________ and two (concession stand) ______________________.

The group of (passerby) ______________________ kindly helped with our flat tire.

All of the (five-year-old) ________________ were scooping up (bucketful) __________ of sand on the beach.

Both (father-in-law) ______________________ lit the (candlestick) ________________ that were on the wedding tables.

The awards were given to the winner and both (runner-up) ______________________.

— REVIEW 2 —

Weeks 4-6

Topics
Simple, Progressive, and Perfect Tenses
Conjugations
Irregular Verbs
Subject/Verb Agreement
Possessives
Compound Nouns
Contractions

Review 2A: Verb Tenses

Write the tense of each underlined verb phrase on the line in the right-hand margin: *simple past, present,* or *future*; *progressive past, present,* or *future*; or *perfect past, present,* or *future*. Watch out for words that interrupt verb phrases but are not helping verbs (such as *not*).

These sentences are adapted from Frances Hodgson Burnett's *A Little Princess*.

Verb Tense

"Oh, I never had such a dream before." She scarcely dared to stir; but at last she pushed the bedclothes aside, and put her feet on the floor with a rapturous smile. ____________ ____________

"I am dreaming—I am getting out of bed," she heard her own voice say; ____________ ____________

"I don't know who it is," she said; "but somebody cares for me a little. I have a friend." ____________ ____________

"You must introduce me and I will introduce you," said Sara. "But I knew her the minute I saw her—so perhaps she knew me, too." ____________ ____________

"Yes, little Sara, it is. We have reached it at last." And though she was only seven years old, she knew that he felt sad when he said it. ____________ ____________

The fact was, however, that she was dreaming and thinking odd things… about grown-up people and the world they belonged to. ________________ ________________

"She says it has nothing to do with what you look like, or what you have. It has only to do with what you THINK of, and what you DO." ________________ ________________

"The streets are shining, and there are fields and fields of lilies, and everybody gathers them." ________________ ________________

He had made wonderful preparations for her birthday. Among other things, he had ordered a new doll in Paris. ________________ ________________

"Miss Minchin knows she will have worked for nothing. It was rather nasty of you, Lavvy, to tell about her having fun in the garret." ________________ ________________

"You will go to a nice house where there will be a lot of little girls, and you will play together, and I will send you plenty of books…." ________________ ________________

"She has locked herself in, and she is not making the least particle of noise." ________________ ________________

And the streets are shining. And people are never tired, however far they walk. They can float anywhere they like. ________________ ________________

She only said the kind of thing little girls always say to each other by way of beginning an acquaintance, but there was something friendly about Sara, and people always felt it. ________________ ________________ ________________

Review 2B: Verb Formations

Fill in the charts with the correct conjugations of the missing verbs. Identify the person of each group of verbs.

PERSON: ___________

	Past	Present	Future
SIMPLE	she worried	she	she
PROGRESSIVE	she	she is worrying	she
PERFECT	she	she	she

PERSON: ___________

	Past	Present	Future
SIMPLE	I	I	I will whistle
PROGRESSIVE	I	I	I
PERFECT	I had whistled	I	I

PERSON: ___________

	Past	Present	Future
SIMPLE	you	you	you
PROGRESSIVE	you were wondering	you	you
PERFECT	you	you	you will have wondered

PERSON: ___________

	Past	Present	Future
SIMPLE	they	they guess	they
PROGRESSIVE	they	they	they will be guessing
PERFECT	they	they	they

Review 2C: Person and Subject/Verb Agreement

Cross out the incorrect verb in parentheses.

Do I not (destroys/destroy) my enemies when I (makes/make) them my friends?
—Abraham Lincoln

Remember always that you not only (has/have) the right to be an individual, you (has/have) the obligation to be one.
—Eleanor Roosevelt

Whoever (is / are) happy will make others happy, too.
—Anne Frank

She (walks / walk) in beauty like the night / Of cloudless climes and starry skies.
—Lord Byron

I (likes / like) these plants that you (calls / call) weeds. —Lucy Larcom

You (has / have) brains in your head. You (has / have) feet in your shoes. You can steer yourself any direction you (chooses / choose).
—Dr. Seuss

Forgiveness (is / are) the attribute of the strong.
—Mahatma Gandhi

How glorious a greeting the sun (gives / give) the mountains!
—John Muir

The sun (looks / look) down on nothing half so good as a household laughing together over a meal.
—C. S. Lewis

We (was / were) scared, but our fear (was / were) not as great as our courage.
—Malala Yousafzai

I (believes / believe) every human has a finite number of heartbeats. I don't intend to waste any of mine.
—Neil Armstrong

Review 2D: Possessives and Compound Nouns

Complete the chart below, writing the singular possessive, plural, and plural possessive of each singular pronoun or compound noun. The first one has been done for you.

Noun	Possessive	Plural	Plural Possessive
professor	professor's	professors	professors'
chairperson			
he			
book			
you			
wolf			
deer			
I			
dragonfly			
bedroom			
it			

class	__________	__________	__________
she	__________	__________	__________
schoolbus	__________	__________	__________

Review 2E: Plurals and Possessives

In the following sentences, provide the possessive, the plural, or the plural possessive for each noun in parentheses as indicated. These sentences are from *The Swiss Family Robinson*, by Johann David Wyss.

The forest still extended about a (stone, singular, possessive) __________ throw to our right, and Fritz, who was always on the look-out for (discovery, plural) __________ observed a remarkable tree, here and there, which he approached to examine; and he soon called me to see this wonderful tree, with (wen, plural) __________ growing on the trunk.

In the (captain, singular, possessive) __________ cabin we found some (service, plural) __________ of silver, pewter (plate, plural) __________ and (dish, plural) __________, and a small chest filled with bottles of choice wines. All these we took, as well as a chest of (eatable, plural) __________, intended for the (officer, plural, possessive) __________ table.

I had looked at (Jack, singular, possessive) __________ site for the bridge, and thought my little architect very happy in his selection; but it was at a great distance from the timber. I recollected the simplicity of the harness the (Laplander, plural) __________ used for their reindeer. I tied (cord, plural) __________ to the (horn, plural) __________ of the cow.

She wanted, also, some wild (fowl, plural, possessive) __________ (egg, plural) __________ to set under her (hen, plural) __________. Francis wished for some (sugarcane, plural) __________.

Then, with the hatchet making an opening at each end, we took (wedge, plural) __________ and (mallet, plural) __________, and the wood being tolerably soft, after four (hour, plural possessive) __________ labour, we succeeded in splitting it completely.

I slept on moss and cotton in Mr. (Willis, singular, possessive) ____________________ room, with my two younger (son, plural) ____________________. Everyone was content, waiting till our (arrangement, plural) ____________________ had been completed.

However, I assured her, our new guest would need no attention, as he would provide for himself at the river-side, feeding on small (fish, plural) ____________________, (worm, plural) ____________________, and (insect, plural) ____________________.

Fritz and I then, with a chisel and small axe, made an opening about three (foot, plural) ____________________ square, below the (bee, plural possessive) ____________________ entrance.

Review 2F: Contractions

In the following sentences, form contractions from the words in parentheses. These sentences are adapted from *Violets and Other Tales,* by Alice Moore Dunbar-Nelson.

"____________________ (I am) so warm and tired," cried Mama Hart plaintively.

"____________________ (You had) better come with us, Flo. ____________________ (You are) wasting time."

Still, for all the suffering ____________________ (I have) experienced, ____________________ (I would) be willing to go through it all again just to go over those five months.

____________________ (There is) none I place above you.

I ____________________ (cannot) imagine where you get your meddlesome ways from.

"Dinner! ____________________ (Who has) got time to fool with dinner this evening?"

"Maybe ____________________ (it will) snow," he muttered.

"Then ____________________ (will not) I have fun! Ugh, but the wind blows!"

"Gracious man, ____________________ (we have) tried."

And ____________________ (he will) be the victor longer than anyone else.

"____________________ (She is) a good girl, that Lillian."

"Besides, we must. ____________________ (It is) late, and you ____________________ (could not) find your crowd."

"Why, my Louis says ____________________ (they are) putting canvas cloths on the floor."

"____________________ (They will) never miss you; ____________________ (we will) get you a rig."

"____________________ (Let us) go on!"

There were tears in her eyes, hot, blinding ones that ____________________ (would not) drop for pride.

I wonder what ____________________ (he is) up to now.

There ____________________ (is not) much warmth in a bit of a jersey coat.

There ____________________ (was not) one of us who imagined we would have only to knock ever so faintly on the portals of fame and they would fly wide for our entrance into the magic realms.

WEEK 7

Compounds and Conjunctions

— LESSON 25 —

Contractions
Compound Nouns
Diagramming Compound Nouns
Compound Adjectives
Diagramming Adjectives
Articles

A contraction is a combination of two words with some of the letters dropped out.

Exercise 25A: Contractions Review

Write the two words that form each contraction on the blanks to the right. Some contractions have more than one correct answer. The first is done for you.

Contraction	Helping Verb	Other Word
he'll	will	he
wasn't	________	________
I'll	________	________
wouldn't	________	________
you're	________	________
isn't	________	________
who're	________	________
didn't	________	________
you've	________	________

Our air conditioning is working!

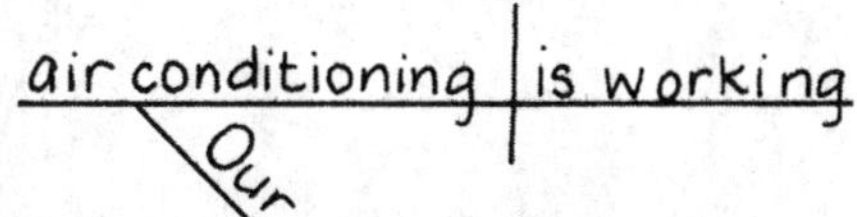

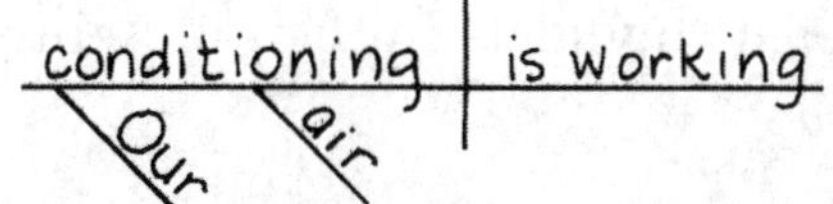

Exercise 25B: Diagramming Adjectives and Compound Nouns

On your own paper, diagram every word of the following sentences.

Sydney's fishtank bubbled.

A tiny music box played.

My dishwasher broke.

The mayor-elect spoke.

The large-headed monster had twenty-seven teeth.

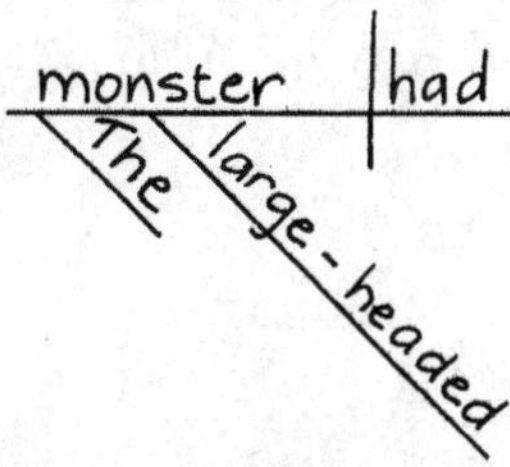

The articles are *a*, *an*, and *the*.

Exercise 25C: Compound Nouns

Using the list of words below, make as many single-word compound nouns as you can. Many words in this list can be used twice or more.

Column A	Column B	
hair	world	____________
swim	ache	____________
back	style	____________
tooth	paper	____________
wall	take	____________
under	bone	____________
out	suit	____________

Exercise 25D: Compound Adjectives

Correctly place hyphens in the following phrases.

fifty two weeks

cold blooded animal

a five year winning streak

the three page well written paper

a middle aged person

a strong willed toddler

the brightly lit soccer field

Exercise 25E: Diagramming Adjectives, Compound Nouns, and Compound Adjectives

On your own paper, diagram every word in the following sentences. These are adapted from *The Magical Land of Noom*, by Johnny Gruelle.

A pale blueish-green tint slanted.
The homemade Flying Machine disappeared.
The soft-voiced cow was eating.
A steady buzz-buzz grew.
All pretty fairy tales end.

— LESSON 26 —

Compound Subjects
The Conjunction *And*
Compound Predicates
Compound Subject-Predicate Agreement

The fireman hurries.
The policeman hurries.
The fireman and the policeman hurry.

SIMPLE PRESENT

	Singular	**Plural**
First person	I hurry	we hurry
Second person	you hurry	you hurry
Third person	he, she, it hurries	they hurry

Compound subjects joined by *and* are plural in number and take plural verbs.
A conjunction joins words or groups of words together.

The farmer plants.
The farmer harvests.
The farmer plants and harvests.

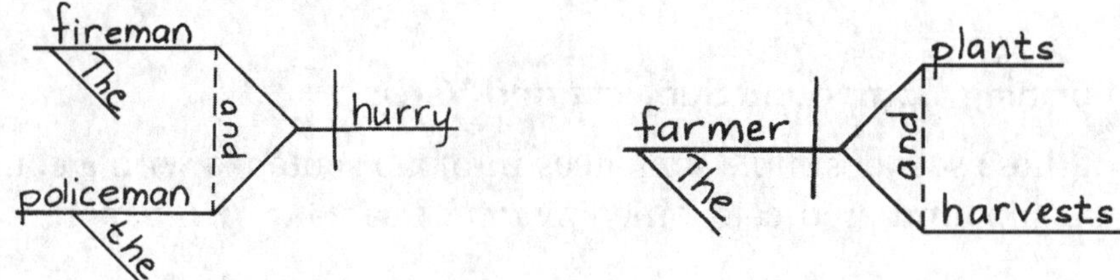

Exercise 26A: Identifying Subjects, Predicates, and Conjunctions

Underline the subjects once and the predicates twice in each sentence. Circle the conjunctions that join them. The first one is done for you.

These sentences are adapted from Solomon Northup's *Twelve Years a Slave.*

With the return of spring, Anne (and) I conceived the project of taking a farm in the neighborhood.

We reached that city before dark, and stopped at a hotel southward from the Museum.

Towards evening, on the first day of the calm, Arthur and I were in the bow of the vessel.

The roar of cannon and the tolling of bells filled the air.

I bowed my head upon my fettered hands, and wept most bitterly.

Pen, ink, and paper were furnished.

Exercise 26B: Diagramming Compound Subjects and Predicates

Draw one line under the subject[s] and two lines under the predicate[s] in the following sentences. Circle any conjunctions that connect subjects and/or predicates. When you are finished, diagram the subjects, predicates, and conjunctions ONLY of each sentence on your own paper.

These sentences are adapted from "Maese Perez, the Organist," by Gustavo Adolfo Becquer. Translated by Rollo Ogden.

The confusion and clangor lasted a few seconds.

The two women turned and disappeared.

I went to the choir and opened the door.

The Mother Superior and the nuns rushed to the organ-loft.

The organ gave a strange sound and was silent.

Light and sound were expressed by the organ's hundred voices.

Exercise 26C: Forming Compound Subjects and Verbs

Combine each of these sets of simple sentences into one sentence with a compound subject and/or a compound predicate joined by *and*. Use your own paper.

The ducks waddle in the yard.
The ducks eat insects in the yard.

The nurse takes my temperature.
The nurse gives me medicine.
The nurse checks my blood pressure.

Matteo toured the exhibit at the museum.
Lucia toured the exhibit at the museum.
Martina toured the exhibit at the museum.

During the storm, rain fell from the sky.
During the storm, hail fell from the sky.

The glass blower heated the glass.
The glass blower rolled the glass.
The glass blower shaped the glass.

Exercise 26D: Subject-Verb Agreement with Compound Subjects

Choose the correct verb in parentheses to agree with the subject. Cross out the incorrect verb.

The veterinarian and her assistant (talk/talks) calmly to the nervous puppy.

The assistant (pet/pets) the puppy while the vet carefully (give/gives) the vaccination.

While the puppy (chew/chews) on a treat, the vet and her assistant (examine/examines) him.

After the assistant (weigh/weighs) the puppy, the vet (make/makes) notes on the chart.

Before the puppy leaves, the vet and her assistant (inform/informs) the animal's owner that the puppy is healthy.

The owner and his puppy (walk/walks) out of the office and (get/gets) in the car to drive home.

— LESSON 27 —

Coordinating Conjunctions
Complications in Subject-Predicate Agreement

A conjunction joins words or groups of words together.
A coordinating conjunction joins similar or equal words or groups of words together.

and, or, nor, for, so, but, yet

Indonesia and Greater Antilles are groups of islands.
I will nap or go running.
They will not help me, nor you.
I ran after them, for I needed help.
I stubbed my toe, so now my foot hurts.
I was exhausted, but my sister was still full of energy.
He was laughing, yet he seemed sad.

Exercise 27A: Using Conjunctions

Fill the blanks in the sentences below with the appropriate conjunctions. You must use each conjunction (*and, or, nor, for, so, but, yet*) at least once. (There is more than one possible answer for many of the blanks!)

These sentences are adapted from *Among the Meadow People*, by Clara Dillingham Pierson.

I have been telling the Daisies and the Cardinals that they should grow in such a place, ____________ they wouldn't listen to me.

One may have a comfortable home, kind neighbors, and plenty to eat, ____________ if he is in the habit of thinking disagreeable thoughts, not even all these good things can make him happy.

During the days when the four beautiful green-blue eggs lay in the nest, Mrs. Robin stayed quite closely at home. She said it was a very good place, ____________ she could keep her eggs warm and still see all that was happening.

The Robin on the fence huddled down into a miserable little bunch, ____________ thought: "They don't care whether I ever have anything to eat. No, they don't!"

When you have lived as long as I have, you will know that neither Grasshoppers ______ Tree Frogs can have their way all the time.

That was much pleasanter than having to grow up all alone, as most young Frog-Hoppers do, never seeing their fathers and mothers _____________ knowing whether they ever would.

The more he thought about it the more he squirmed, until suddenly he heard a faint little sound, too faint for larger people to hear, _____________ found a tiny slit in the wall of his chrysalis.

Still it had held him for eight days already and that was as long as any of his family ever hung in the chrysalis, _____________ it was quite time for it to be torn open and left empty.

She loved her babies so that she almost disliked to see them grow up, _____________ she knew it was right for them to leave the nest.

If they heard their father _____________ their mother flying toward them, they would stretch up their necks and open their mouths.

You can just fancy what a good time the baby Spiders had. There were a hundred and seventy of them, _____________ they had no chance to grow lonely, even when their mother was away.

He thought this, _____________ he didn't say it.

Compound subjects joined by *and* are plural in number and take plural verbs.

I am friendly.
George and I are friends.

The policeman or the fireman hurries.

The dog and the cat are sleeping on the sofa.
The dog or the cat is sleeping on the sofa.
The dogs or the cat is sleeping on the sofa.

When compound subjects are joined by *or,* the verb agrees with the number of the nearest subject.

The pies were scrumptious.
The pies on the table were scrumptious.
The box of pencils is on the top shelf.

A can of red beans sits on the table.

The young man at all of the meetings was bored.

Fractions are singular if used to indicate a single thing.
Fractions are plural if used to indicate more than one thing.

Three-fourths of the pie was missing.
Three-fourths of the socks were missing.

Expressions of money, time, and quantity (weight, units, and distance) are singular when used as a whole, but plural when used as numerous single units.

Thirty dollars is too much to pay for that shirt.
Thirty dollars are spread across the table.

Seven years is a long time to wait.
The minutes tick by.

A thousand pounds is far too heavy for that truck.
Fifty gallons of water are divided among the refugees.
Four miles is too far to walk.

Collective nouns are usually singular. Collective nouns can be plural if the members of the group are acting as independent individuals.

The herd of cattle was grazing quietly.
The herd of cattle were scattered throughout the plains.

Exercise 27B: Subject-Predicate Agreement: Troublesome Subjects

Circle the correct verb in parentheses so that it agrees with the subject noun or pronoun in number.

Six miles (is / are) the distance of the race.

Three-fourths of the cake (was / were) eaten by the children.

The horses or the donkey (grazes / graze) in the field.

Jerry's cheerleading squad (has / have) won the championship!

This batch of muffins (smell / smells) delicious!

The baseball team (run / runs) laps every day before practice.

Ten pounds of produce (weigh / weighs) too much for this bag.

Five bottles of juice (is / are) divided among the students.

One cup of chocolate chips (need / needs) to go into the batter.

The jury (vote / votes) on the verdict today.

My aunt and uncle (visit / visits) us each summer, and our whole family (stay / stays) at the beach together.

One-half of the Lego pieces (was / were) dumped across the table.

The rabbit in the bushes (hide / hides) from predators.

The flock of geese (scatter / scatters) across the field.

The flock of geese (fly / flies) in a formation.

She and her friends (organize / organizes) a charity auction each year.

Exercise 27C: Fill in the Verb

Choose a verb or verb phrase that makes sense to complete each sentence. Put that verb or verb phrase in the present tense. Be sure the verb or verb phrase agrees in number with its subject!

The boat in the waves __________________ wildly during the storm.

The plot of vegetables __________________ during the summer.

Sixty dollars __________________ too much for that game.

The students' essays about the short story __________________ interesting thoughts.

The chickens in the coop __________________ all day long.

Those pickles in the jar __________________ like homemade.

A sample of cheeses __________________ the appetizer.

The plates or the platter __________________ sits on the shelf.

Two-thirds of the class __________________ the test.

— LESSON 28 —

Further Complications in Subject-Predicate Agreement

Many nouns can be plural in form but singular in use: *measles*, *mumps*, *rickets*, *politics*, *mathematics*, *economics*, *news*.

Mathematics is my favorite subject.

Singular literary works, works of art, newspapers, countries, and organizations can be plural in form but are still singular in use.

Little Women was written by Louisa May Alcott.
The United States is south of Canada.

Many nouns are plural in form and use but singular in meaning: *pants, scissors, pliers, glasses.*

Pants are too hot in the summertime.

In sentences beginning with *There is* or *There are*, the subject is found after the verb.

There is a skunk in the brush.
There are three skunks in the brush.

***Each* and *every* always indicate a singular subject.**

In Masai villages, each woman cares for her own cattle.
In Masai villages, each of the women cares for her own cattle.
In Masai villages, each cares for her own cattle.

In Masai villages, women care for their own cattle.

Every man needs friends.
Men need friends.

Compound nouns that are plural in form but singular in meaning take a singular verb.

Fish and chips is my favorite British dish.

Compound subjects joined by *and* take a singular verb when they name the same thing.

The owner and manager of the ice cream shop is also working behind the counter.

Nouns with Latin and Greek origins take the singular verb when singular in form and the plural verb when plural in form.

The data suggest otherwise.

Singular	**Plural**
medium	media
datum	data
criterion	criteria
phenomenon	phenomena
focus	foci
appendix	appendices

Exercise 28A: Subject-Verb Agreement: More Troublesome Subjects

Find the correct verb (agrees with the subject in number) in parentheses. Cross out the incorrect verb.

The Wind in the Willows (is / are) her favorite book.

Each of the paintings (hang/hangs) in a different part of the museum.

Highlights (is / are) a magazine for children.

Statistics (is / are) my favorite class.

Thirty percent of the team (practice / practices) every weekday.

The popular British dish of fish and chips (taste / tastes) delicious with malt vinegar.

There (is / are) three packages in the mailbox.

Every one of the performers (take / takes) a bow.

Checkers (is / are) an easy game to learn.

Pliers (belong / belongs) in this tool box.

Here under the bed (is / are) the missing library books.

Physics (has / have) to be taken before you graduate.

Cacti (contain / contains) water which many animals use.

The Philippines (celebrate / celebrates) Independence Day on June 12.

Ellipses (mark / marks) a missing portion of a quote.

Anne of Green Gables (take / takes) place in Prince Edward Island, Canada.

There (is / are) a new movie I want to see.

Every one of the women (own / owns) a small business.

Bangers and mash (appear / appears) on many menus in Scotland.

Each of the fonts (show / shows) up differently on the screen.

Exercise 28B: Correct Verb Tense and Number

Complete each of these sentences by writing the correct number and tense of the verb indicated in the blank. The sentences are adapted from Harriet Pyne Grove's *Greycliff Wings*.

There [simple present of *am*] _______________ her letter, Virgie. I forgot to tell you to read it.

Then she laughed. "Please forgive me, Miss West, I did not realize what I [progressive past of *say*] _______________."

"There [simple present of *am*] _______________ so many places about the campus that would make a fine setting."

A vineyard of well-trained grape-vines [simple past of *am*] _______________ on a slope and stretched for quite a distance.

"I suppose that shed or something down there [simple present of *am*] _______________ for the hydroplane."

The black letters of the name [progressive past of *show*] _______________ clearly against a pearl-grey side.

The glasses [simple past of *am*] _______________ all focused upon the little hollow before them, Hilary's face growing brighter as she watched.

Remember to keep your wits about you and feel that the game depends on how well each of you [simple present of *play*] _______________.

Early after lunch, a number of girls [simple past of *start*] _______________ off for their ride.

A procession of worn, dusty men [progressive past of *march*] _______________ away toward the camp.

Two or three of the girls [progressive present of *rush*] _______________ to help Hilary up.

Neither Lilian or I [simple present of *appear*] _______________ really small enough for fairies, but in the costumes we look smaller.

Juniors and seniors on the bank [progressive past of *hold*] _______________ their breath.

WEEK 8

Introduction to Objects

— LESSON 29 —

Action Verbs
Direct Objects

A direct object receives the action of the verb.

Cara built a bonfire.
We roasted marshmallows over the bonfire.
Tom ate the delicious cookie.
Julia, hot and thirsty, drank the fresh-squeezed lemonade.
She visited her grandfather.
He had forgotten her name.
She found peace.

We roasted marshmallows.

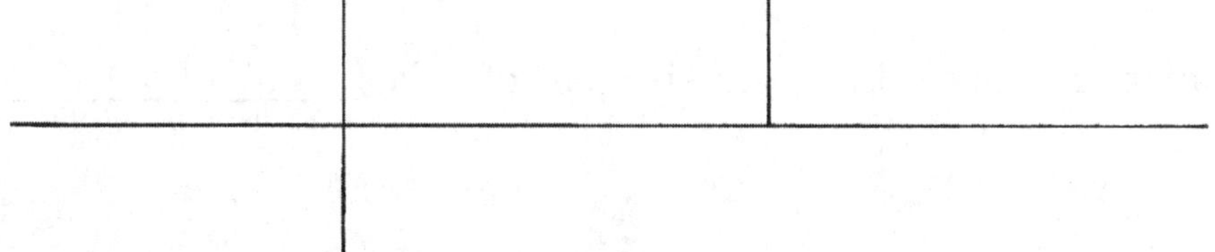

We roasted soft marshmallows and beefy hot dogs.

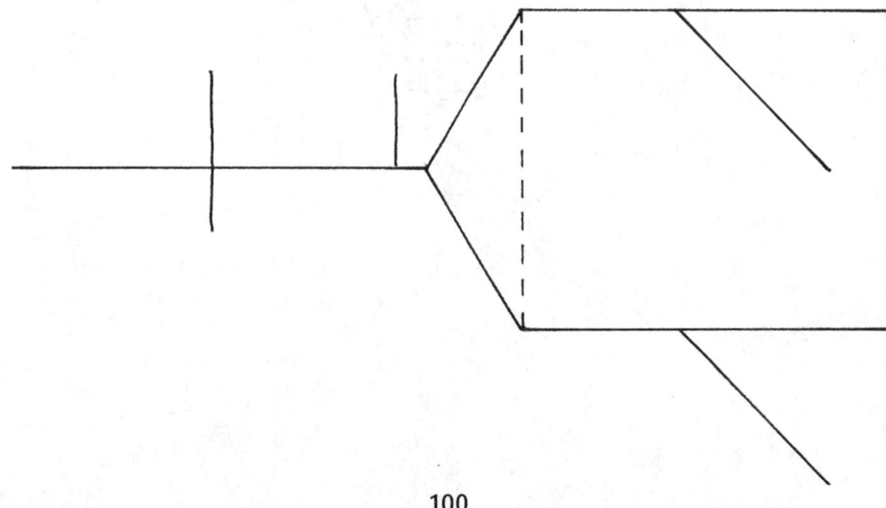

My friend and I rode roller coasters and ate popcorn and cotton candy.

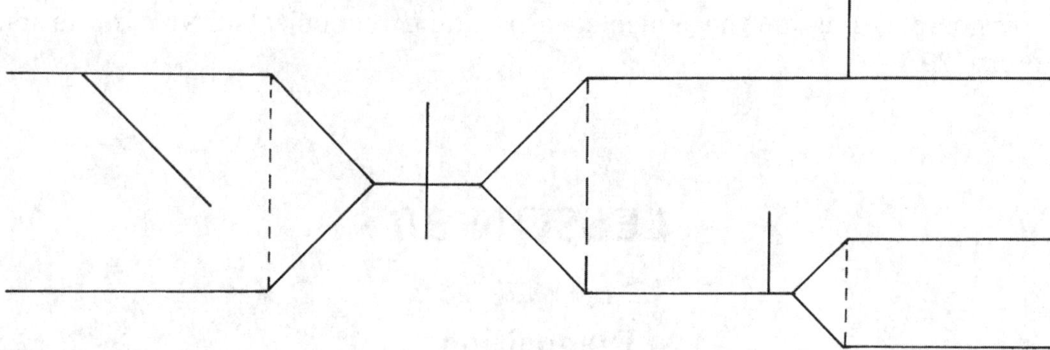

Exercise 29A: Direct Objects

In the following sentences, underline the subjects once and the predicates twice. Circle each direct object.

Ancient Egyptians were building pyramids around 2780 BC.

The workers used limestone and granite for the structures.

They carved the stone with chisels.

Laborers dragged immense, heavy stones to the building site with sleds.

After a pharaoh's death, embalmers mummified the pharaoh's body.

Often, the embalmers would mummify the pharaoh's pets, too.

Craftspeople placed furniture and treasures into the pyramid.

The pharaoh and his family would need these items in the afterlife.

Egyptian culture valued the afterlife.

Workers and priests laid the pharaoh's body inside the pyramid.

The priests sealed the tomb.

Sadly, many tomb robbers opened the pyramids.

They stole jewels, gold, and silver.

In 1923, archaeologist Howard Carter discovered King Tut's tomb and found valuable items.

He and his team recovered many important artifacts.

Exercise 29B: Diagramming Direct Objects

On your own paper, diagram the subjects, verbs, and direct objects ONLY in the sentences from Exercise 29A.

— LESSON 30 —

Direct Objects
Prepositions

I broke my breakfast plate!
The pottery plate broke into pieces.

A preposition shows the relationship of a noun or pronoun to another word in the sentence.

Prepositions
aboard, about, above, across
after, against, along, among, around, at

before, behind, below, beneath
beside, between, beyond, by

down, during, except, for, from
in, inside, into, like

near, of, off, on, over
past, since, through, throughout

to, toward, under, underneath
until, up, upon
with, within, without

Exercise 30A: Identifying Prepositions

In the following sentences (adapted from "The Monkey and the Crocodile," in *Jataka Tales*, retold by Ellen C. Babbitt), find and circle each preposition.

The monkey soon moved away from that tree. But the Crocodile found him, far down the river, living in another tree. In the middle of the river was an island covered with fruit-trees.

Half-way between the bank of the river and the island, a large rock rose from the water. The Monkey could jump to the rock, and then to the island. The Crocodile watched the Monkey crossing from the bank of the river to the rock, and then to the island.

He thought to himself, "The Monkey will stay on the island all day, and I'll catch him on his way home at night."

The Monkey had a fine feast, while the Crocodile swam, watching him during the day.

Exercise 30B: Word Relationships

The following sentences all contain action verbs. Underline each subject once and each action verb twice. If the sentence has an action verb followed by a direct object, write *DO* above the direct object.

If the sentence contains a preposition, circle the preposition and draw a line to connect the two words that the preposition shows a relationship between. The first two are done for you.

The geese near the lake honked noisily.

DO

Savannah likes popcorn with butter.

Five tiny caterpillars ate the leaves of the milkweed plants.

Jonatan bakes fresh bread every Saturday.

We visited the park under the St. Louis Arch.

The scariest scene of the movie is happening now!

After class, Jayden and Naveah taught the new choreography.

Ali was fishing from the new pier.

Is Roma coming to the class?

The lime slushy spilled on the seat.

The *Mona Lisa* hangs in the Louvre.

Did you find your phone yet?

Exercise 30C: Diagramming Direct Objects

On your own paper, diagram the subjects, predicates, and direct objects ONLY from the sentences above. If a sentence does not have a direct object, do not diagram it.

— LESSON 31 —

Definitions Review
Prepositional Phrases
Object of the Preposition

A noun names a person, place, thing, or idea.
An adjective modifies a noun or pronoun.
A pronoun takes the place of a noun.
A verb shows an action, shows a state of being, links two words together, or helps another verb.
A conjunction joins words or groups of words together.
A coordinating conjunction joins similar or equal words or groups of words together.
A phrase is a group of words serving a single grammatical function.
A preposition shows the relationship of a noun or pronoun to another word in the sentence.

Prepositions
aboard, about, above, across
after, against, along, among, around, at
before, behind, below, beneath
beside, between, beyond, by
down, during, except, for, from
in, inside, into, like
near, of, off, on, over
past, since, through, throughout
to, toward, under, underneath
until, up, upon
with, within, without

A brook sluggishly flows (through) low ground.

Dark draperies hung (upon) the walls.

The tunnel wound (into) the green hill.

A prepositional phrase begins with a preposition and ends with a noun or pronoun. That noun or pronoun is the object of the preposition.

Put your hand beneath your workbook.

Calvin ran across the floor.

I baked a pie for my mother.

Exercise 31A: Objects of Prepositional Phrases

Fill in the blanks with a noun as the object of the preposition to complete the prepositional phrases.

The cat's favorite spot is by the ______________________.

Under the ______________________, Mom found the missing book.

The whole family hiked to the ______________________.

Matt puts ketchup on his ______________________.

A large bear was spotted near the ______________________.

Will Mia sing during the ______________________?

Exercise 31B: Identifying Prepositional Phrases

Can you find all eleven of the prepositional phrases in the following excerpt, adapted from "The Four Dragons," a traditional Asian folktale?

Underline each complete prepositional phrase. Circle each preposition. Draw a box around each object of a preposition.

The four dragons went happily back. But ten days passed, and not a drop of rain came down. The people suffered more, some eating bark, some grass roots. Seeing all of this, the four dragons felt very sorry, and they knew the Jade Emperor only cared about pleasure, and never took the people to heart. They could only rely upon themselves and could relieve the people of their miseries. But how? Seeing the vast sea, the Long Dragon said that he had an idea.

"What is it? Out with it, quickly!" the other three demanded.

"Look, is there not plenty of water in the sea where we live? We should scoop it and spray it toward the sky. The water will be rain drops and will save the people and their crops," said Long Dragon.

"Good idea!" said the others as they clapped their hands with joy.

Exercise 31C: Remembering Prepositions

Can you remember all forty-six prepositions without looking back at your list? The first letter of each preposition has been given for you.

A	B	D	E	F	I	L
aboard	______	______	______	______	______	______
______	______	______		______	______	
______	______				______	
______	______					
______	______					
______	______					
______	______					
______	______					
______						
______						

N	O	P	S	T	U	W
______	______	______	______	______	______	______
	______			______	______	______
	______			______	______	______
	______			______	______	
					______	

— LESSON 32 —

Subjects, Predicates, and Direct Objects
Prepositions
Object of the Preposition
Prepositional Phrases

The subject of the sentence is the main word or term that the sentence is about. The simple subject of the sentence is *just* the main word or term that the sentence is about.

The complete subject of the sentence is the simple subject and all the words that belong to it.

The warrior saw on the opposite mountain two great globes of glowing fire.

The predicate of the sentence tells something about the subject.
The simple predicate of the sentence is the main verb along with any helping verbs.
The complete predicate of the sentence is the simple predicate and all the words that belong to it.
A direct object receives the action of the verb.
A preposition shows the relationship of a noun or pronoun to another word in the sentence.

Prepositions
aboard, about, above, across
after, against, along, among, around, at
before, behind, below, beneath
beside, between, beyond, by
down, during, except, for, from
in, inside, into, like
near, of, off, on, over
past, since, through, throughout
to, toward, under, underneath
until, up, upon
with, within, without

A prepositional phrase begins with a preposition and ends with a noun or pronoun.
That noun or pronoun is the object of the preposition.

The warrior | saw on the opposite mountain two great globes (DO) of glowing fire.

The warrior saw two great globes.

The Dragon King with his retainers accompanied the warrior to the end of the bridge, and took leave of him with many bows and good wishes.

____

____

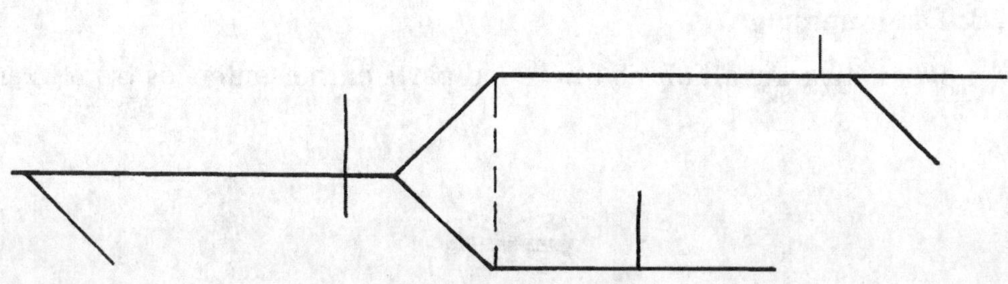

Exercise 32A: Identifying Prepositional Phrases and Parts of Sentences

In the following sentences, circle each prepositional phrase. Once you have identified the prepositional phrases, underline subjects once, underline predicates twice, and label direct objects with *DO*.

Things to watch out for:

1) Words that could be prepositions but are acting as other parts of speech instead. If it doesn't have an object, it's not a preposition!
2) In some of these sentences, subjects and predicates are inverted so that the predicate comes first. Find the verb first, then ask, "Who or what [verb]?" to find the subject. Remember that the subject will not be the object of a preposition!

These sentences are adapted from "The Story of Ali Cogia, Merchant of Bagdad," a traditional Arab folktale. The first is done for you.

DO
Ali Cogia lived (in Bagdad) and owned a shop.

He planned a journey to Mecca.

He took a large vase, placed money in the bottom, filled it with olives, and carried it to his friend for safekeeping.

After many months, the friend in Bagdad looked into the vase and saw the gold.

He took the gold and hid it.

After another month, Ali Cogia returned to Bagdad and asked for his vase.

The gold was missing from the vase.

Ali Cogia asked for the truth.

The merchant denied the charge against him.

In the end, the truth of the theft was discovered by a wise child's discerning questions.

Exercise 32B: Diagramming

On your own paper, diagram all of the uncircled parts of the sentences from Exercise 32A.

WEEK 9

Adverbs

— LESSON 33 —

Adverbs That Tell How

A sneaky squirrel stole my sock slowly.
A sneaky squirrel stole my sock sleepily.
A sneaky squirrel stole my sock cheerfully.
A sneaky squirrel stole my sock rapidly.

An adverb describes a verb, an adjective, or another adverb.

An **exceptionally** sneaky squirrel stole my sock slowly.
A sneaky squirrel stole my sock **very** rapidly.

Adverbs tell how, when, where, how often, and to what extent.

Adjective	Adverb
serious	seriously
fierce	_________
thorough	_________
crazy	crazily
scary	_________
cheery	_________

He left hurriedly.
Hurriedly, he left.
He hurriedly left.

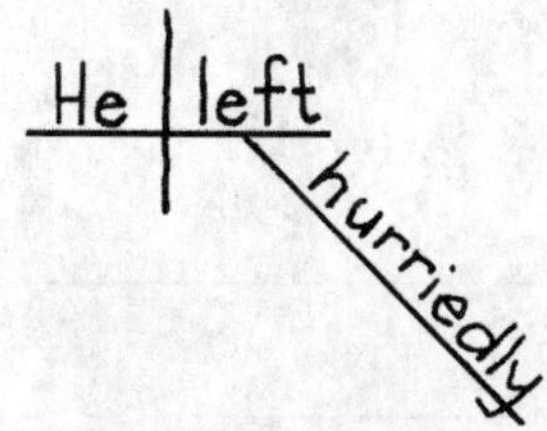

Exercise 33A: Identifying Adverbs That Tell How

Underline the adverbs telling how in the following sentences, and draw arrows to the verbs that they modify.

Amelia Earhart famously flew across the Atlantic Ocean, the first woman to do so.

She quickly became famous and began writing honestly about her experiences as a pilot.

Earhart bravely piloted from Honolulu to California in 1935, a risky journey.

She and Fred Noonan, an experienced navigator, carefully planned a new challenge: a flight around the world.

News organizations excitedly reported every step of the preparation for the trip.

Earhart had skillfully handled dangerous flying conditions on many occasions.

However, this trip would have many errors which caused the plane to drift significantly off course.

On July 2, 1937, a naval ship in the area received a radio transmission in which Earhart briefly described the plane's problems.

Besides being off course, the plane was rapidly running out of fuel.

Tragically, Earhart and Noonan disappeared that day. They were never found.

People still study how the pair mysteriously vanished. This event is considered an unsolved mystery of the modern era.

Exercise 33B: Forming Adverbs from Adjectives

Turn the following adjectives into adverbs.

Adjective	Adverb	Adjective	Adverb
rapid	____________	happy	____________
careful	____________	generous	____________

easy	_______________	merry	_______________
safe	_______________	warm	_______________
powerful	_______________		

Exercise 33C: Diagramming Adverbs

Diagram the following sentences on your own paper.

The baby goat leaps energetically.

I quickly dropped the hot pan.

The movie ended abruptly.

Did you listen intently?

Anna slowly savored the warm cookie.

The chef deftly whisked the ingredients.

— LESSON 34 —

Adverbs That Tell When, Where, and How Often

Exercise 34A: Telling When

Martin dropped his recipe cards for crêpes. Help him get organized by numbering the following sentences from 1 to 6 so he can make the crêpes.

_______ Whisk 1 1/2 cups of flour into the wet ingredients.

_______ Pour only a few tablespoons of batter into the hot pan, and spread the batter around the pan in a thin layer.

_______ Serve warm with either a sweet or savory filling.

_______ First, preheat a buttered skillet or crêpe pan.

_______ When bubbles start to form on the crêpe, flip it over and cook the other side.

_______ While the butter is melting in the pan, beat two eggs with three cups of milk in a separate bowl.

An adverb describes a verb, an adjective, or another adverb.
Adverbs tell how, when, where, how often, and to what extent.

Yesterday I washed my dog outside.

The dog ran away.

Then the dog lay down.

Now my dog is sleeping there.

My glasses are lying there.

My red book is sitting here.

There are my glasses.

Here is my red book.

Now my dog is sleeping there.

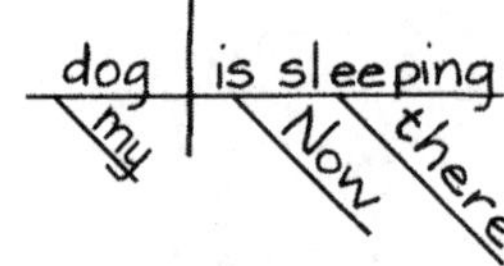

There are my glasses.

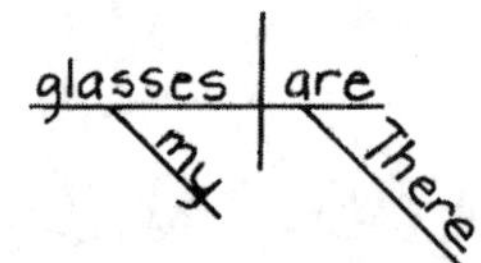

Here is my red book.

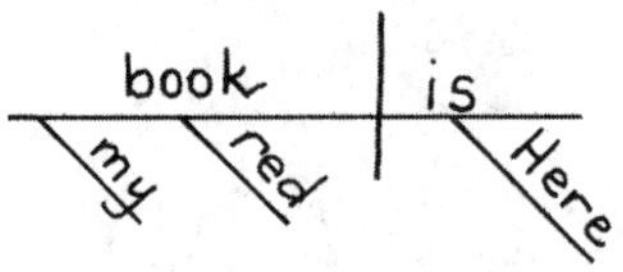

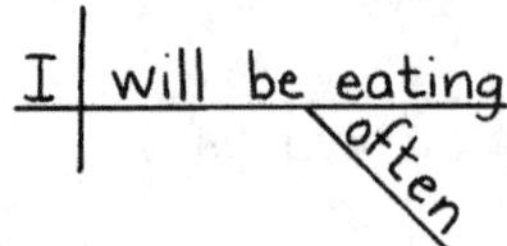

***Here* and *there* are adverbs that tell where.**

I wash my dog weekly.
Richie is always looking for adventure.
I will often be eating.

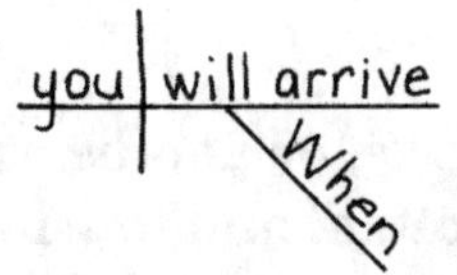

When will you arrive?

Where is my hat?

How are you doing?

you will arrive When.

my hat is Where.

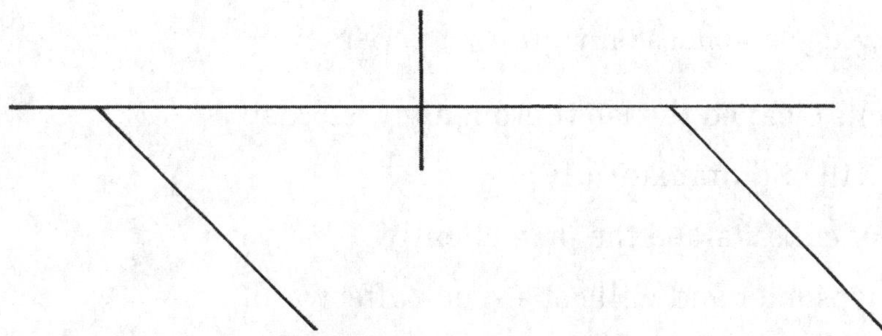

Exercise 34B: Distinguishing Among Different Types of Adverbs

Put each of the following adverbs in the correct category, according to the question each one answers.

badly	safely	seldom	second
away	wearily	usually	soon
constantly	then	far	anywhere

When	**Where**	**How**	**How Often**
______________	______________	______________	______________
______________	______________	______________	______________
______________	______________	______________	______________

Exercise 34C: Identifying Adverbs of Different Types

Underline the adverbs in the following sentences that tell *when*, *where*, or *how often*. For now, do not underline any prepositional phrases acting as adverbs.

The violinist bowed first and the concert began.

My dad makes homemade pizza weekly.

The team meets downstairs.

Emma's kitten destroyed the chair immediately.

There is a canoe by the dock.

Blizzards happen rarely in this part of the country.

Sylvia arrived early for the show.

Our vacation begins tomorrow.

Please take the trash outside.

Here are your keys.

Exercise 34D: Diagramming Different Types of Adverbs

Diagram the following sentences on your own paper.

The science students cleaned the lab thoroughly yesterday.

Tonight, the play will end dramatically.

The lioness and her cubs stalked the prey silently.

Marieke will run laps later and will eat a snack afterward.

The delighted dog's tail wagged wildly.

— LESSON 35 —

Adverbs That Tell To What Extent

An adverb describes a verb, an adjective, or another adverb.
Adverbs tell how, when, where, how often, and to what extent.

The extremely humid day was unpleasant.
Sharon runs quite quickly.
Larry shrieked especially loudly.

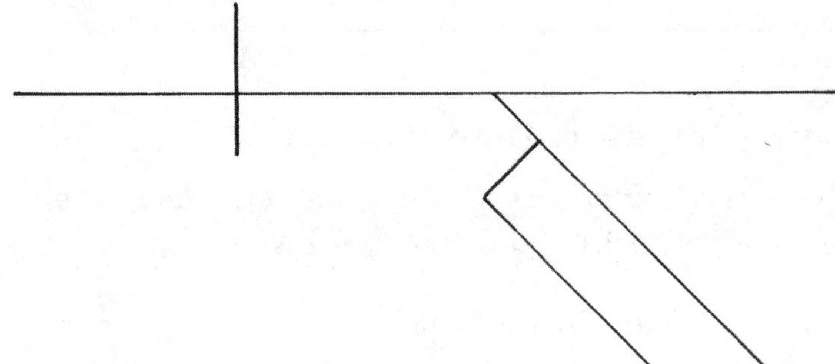

Extremely skittish Larry ran away.

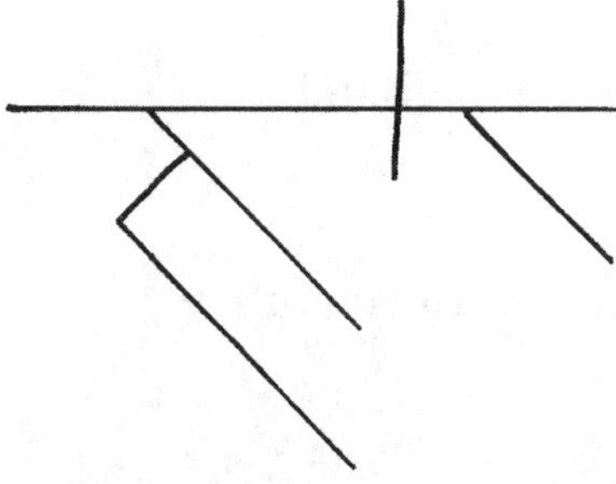

Exercise 35A: Identifying the Words Modified by Adverbs

Draw an arrow from each underlined adverb to the word it modifies. These sentences are from Jules Verne's *An Antarctic Mystery.*

Desolation Islands is the only suitable name for this group of three hundred isles or islets in the midst of the vast expanse of ocean, which is constantly disturbed by austral storms.

"Cannot we talk very well here?" I observed.

I lived there for several weeks, and I can affirm, on the evidence of my own eyes and my own experience, that the famous English explorer and navigator was happily inspired when he gave the islands that significant name.

"My ship is not intended to carry passengers. I never have taken any, and I never intend to do so."

Captain Len Guy proved himself a true seaman, James West had an eye to everything, the crew seconded them loyally, and Hunt was always foremost when there was work to be done or danger to be incurred.

Hunt stepped back a few paces, shaking his head with the air of a man who did not want so many compliments for a thing so simple, and quietly walked forward to join his shipmates, who were working vigorously under the orders of West.

We had no longer to do with completely frozen vapor, but had to deal with the phenomenon called frost-rime, which often occurs in these high latitudes.

Success seemed very nearly assured, as the captain and the mate had worked out the matter so carefully and skilfully.

In my rambles on the shore, I frequently routed a crowd of amphibians, sending them plunging into the newly released waters.

Besides, when it came to the question of cooking, it mattered very little to him whether it was here or there, so long as his stoves were set up somewhere.

Patterson's note-book says nothing, nor does it relate under what circumstances he himself was carried far away from them.

More than five hundred thousand sheep yield over four hundred thousand dollars' worth of wool yearly.

With these words Captain Len Guy walked quickly away, and the interview ended differently from what I had expected, that is to say in formal, although polite, fashion.

Exercise 35B: Diagramming Different Types of Adverbs

Diagram the following sentences on your own paper.

Read the test instructions very carefully.
You must read the lines much more confidently.
Yesterday, some incredibly fragrant roses bloomed.
Matteo plays the classical guitar quite skillfully.
Did you see the extremely elaborate tapestry?
Where are we driving today?

— LESSON 36 —

Adjectives and Adverbs
The Adverb *Not*
Diagramming Contractions
Diagramming Compound Adjectives and Compound Adverbs

An adjective modifies a noun or pronoun.
Adjectives tell what kind, which one, how many, and whose.

An adverb describes a verb, an adjective, or another adverb.
Adverbs tell how, when, where, how often, and to what extent.

It matters naught.

It does not matter.

A contraction is a combination of two words with some of the letters dropped out.

It doesn't matter.

It's not there.

Tall and wide arches weren't often built.

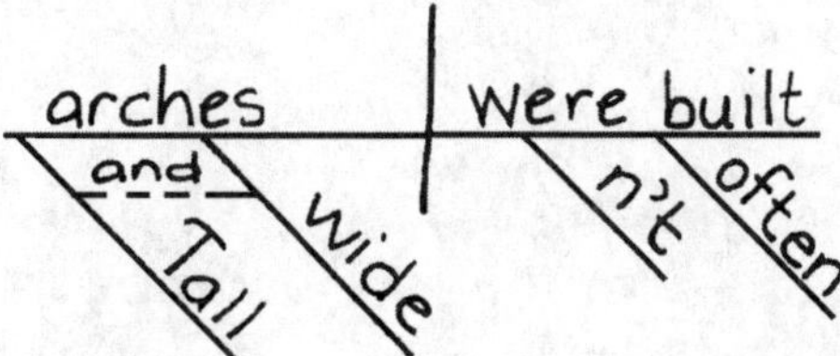

The idea was deeply and widely held.

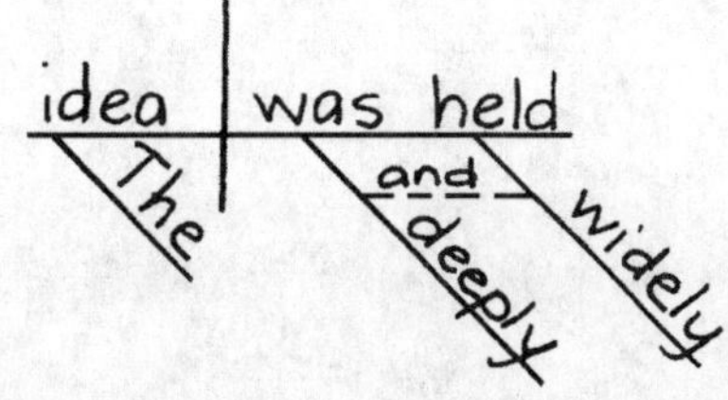

Exercise 36A: Practice in Diagramming

On your own paper, diagram every word of the following sentences. They are adapted from *Home Life in All Lands*, by Charles Morris.

The pig finds the truffles and roots them eagerly.

Pigs will swallow kitchen slops greedily.

Pigs actually prefer dry and clean sleep spaces.

A cat's claws don't touch the ground.

The cat hunts quietly and cautiously.

No mouse can pass it safely.

Various cattle breeds differ very much.

The goose can strike a strong and hard blow.

Geese can guard a farm and wake very easily.

The goose's loud noises can rouse the entire household.

— REVIEW 3 —

Weeks 7-9

Topics
Parts of Speech
Compound Parts of Sentences
Prepositions
Prepositional Phrases
Objects of Prepositions
Subjects and Predicates
Subject-Verb Agreement
Verbs and Direct Objects

Review 3A: Parts of Speech

In the passage below from Henry David Thoreau's *Walden*, identify the underlined words as *N* for noun, *ADJ* for adjective, *ADV* for adverb, *PREP* for preposition, or *CONJ* for conjunction. The first is done for you.

N

The shore is composed of a belt of smooth rounded white stones like paving stones, excepting one or two short sand beaches, and is so steep that in many places a single leap will carry you into water over your head; and were it not for its remarkable transparency, that would be the last to be seen of its bottom till it rose on the opposite side. Some think it is bottomless. It is nowhere muddy, and a casual observer would say that there were no weeds at all in it; and of noticeable plants, except in the little meadows which recently overflowed, which do not properly belong to it, a closer scrutiny does not detect a flag nor a bulrush, nor even a lily, yellow or white, but only a few small heart-leaves and potamogetons, and perhaps a water-target or two; all which however a bather might not perceive; and these plants are clean and bright like the element they grow in. The stones extend a rod or two into the water, and then the bottom is pure sand, except in the deepest parts, where there is usually a little sediment, probably from the decay of the leaves which have been wafted on to it so many successive falls, and a bright green weed is brought up on anchors even in midwinter.

Review 3B: Recognizing Prepositions

Circle the forty-six prepositions from your list in the following bank of words. Try to complete the exercise without looking back at your list of prepositions.

whose near there that until
with in her on again
before here around those across
up for except but by
item into like yet and
within very nor under of
behind was upon from going
above along of between begin
the an since past to
during aboard at this without
against what if beneath toward
among underneath below after while
either an beside about beyond
my inside good off
throughout down through over its

Review 3C: Subjects and Predicates

Draw one line under the simple subject and two lines under the simple predicate. Watch out for compound subjects or predicates! Also, remember that in poetry, sometimes the order of words is different than in normal speech—once you have found the verb, ask "who or what" before it to find the subject.

The following lines are from the poem "The Lady of Shalott," by Alfred, Lord Tennyson.

The yellow-leaved waterlily, the green-sheathed daffodilly tremble in the water chilly.

The sunbeam showers break and quiver.

Four gray walls and four gray towers overlook a space of flowers.

A charmed web she weaves always.

Over the water near, the sheepbell tinkles in her ear.

Sometimes a troop of damsels glad, an abbot on an ambling pad, a curly shepherd lad, or long-hair'd page in crimson clad goes by to tower'd Camelot.

The sun came through the leaves, and flamed upon the brazen greaves of bold Sir Lancelot.

The helmet and the helmet-feather burned like one flame together.

The mirror cracked from side to side.

She chanted loudly, chanted lowly.

She loosed the chain, and down she lay.

Review 3D: Complicated Subject-Verb Agreement

Circle the correct verb form in parentheses.

The cupcake or the cookies (is / are) available for dessert.

The squadron (cheers / cheer) for the graduating officers.

Because of the intense storm, the herd (is / are) split up across the valley.

Three-fourths of the lights (has / have) gone out.

She decided that five dollars (was / were) too much for the coffee.

Ang and Dara (hands / hand) out water to the volunteers.

Where (is / are) the scissors?

A basket full of peaches (sits / sit) on the kitchen counter.

"Hansel and Gretel" (tells / tell) the story of a brother and sister who were lost in the forest.

Two-thirds of the apple (has / have) rotted.

Boxes for the delivery truck (sits / sit) on the porch.

Review 3E: Objects and Prepositions

Identify the underlined words as *DO* for direct object or *OP* for object of preposition. For each direct object, find and underline twice the action verb that affects it. For each object of a preposition, find and circle the preposition to which it belongs.

These sentences are from *Stella by Starlight*, by Sharon Draper.

Even Dusty was quiet, folded at her feet, but he sniffed the air, watchful and alert.

None of the boys in the school, not even those taking high school classes, could beat him in a footrace.

He won two gold medals in track at the Olympics this summer.

Stella said bye to Tony and grabbed a broom without being told.

Most every plank of pine wood inside the house was covered with old newspapers.

She found three fresh eggs and hightailed it back to the warmth of the house.

Maybe it was because she lived in such a small speck of a town, and she liked how the newspaper helped her feel like she was part of something bigger.

"I'm the queen of the world!" she shouted to the sky.

Mama filled Papa's mug back up. "It's chilly out there, Jonah," she said, deliberately changing the subject.

WEEK 10

Completing the Sentence

— LESSON 37 —

Direct Objects
Indirect Objects

She gave **Odysseus** bread and sweet wine and sent him forth.

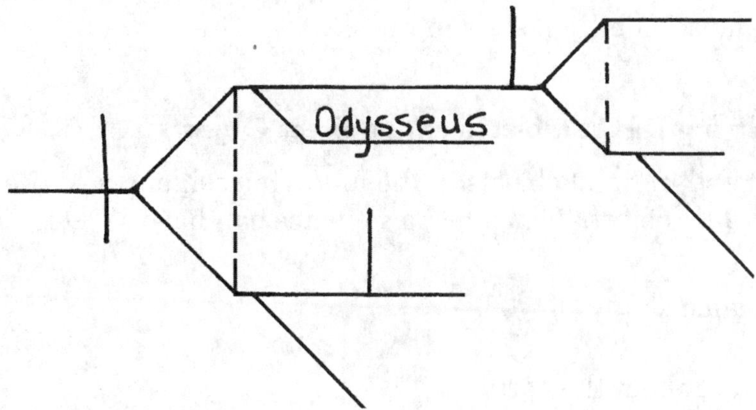

A direct object receives the action of the verb.
An indirect object is the noun or pronoun for whom or to whom an action is done.
An indirect object comes between the action verb and the direct object.

Odysseus asked the stranger a question.
Brandon sent his cousin and uncle an email.

Odysseus | asked | question
a
stranger
the

Brandon | sent | email
an
cousin
his
and
uncle

Exercise 37A: Identifying Direct Objects

Underline the action verbs and circle the direct objects in these sentences. Remember that you can always eliminate prepositional phrases first if that makes the task easier.

The sentences are adapted from R. J. Palacio's *Wonder.*

I like the sound of science.

I did not destroy a Death Star or anything.

At the beginning of every month, I will write a new precept on the chalkboard.

By the end of the year, you will have your own list of precepts.

Everyone in the world should get a standing ovation once in their lives.

Via kissed Daisy on the nose.

You would look up and see a billion stars in the sky.

Exercise 37B: Identifying Direct Objects and Indirect Objects

Underline the direct and indirect objects in the following sentences. Write *DO* for direct object and *IO* for indirect object. Remember, a sentence can have a *DO* without an *IO.*

Give your sister the game.

Rohan sent Anika a text about the party.

Mom baked us muffins for breakfast today.

Is Aidan bringing the book after class?

I sent my grandmother a card yesterday.

Please put the ice cream in the freezer.

Gabrielle read her little sister a story before bedtime.

The director showed the cast a movie after practice.

Exercise 37C: Diagramming Direct Objects and Indirect Objects

On your own paper, diagram the following sentences.

Arianna drew me a lovely picture.
Read me the description.

The professor handed us the tests and gave us instructions.
The entire crowd cheered and stomped their feet.
Kaito handed the children juice and snacks.
I asked Sara and Dylan the questions.
Will you give your parents the packages tomorrow?

— LESSON 38 —

State-of-Being Verbs
Linking Verbs
Predicate Adjectives

The tiny, jewel-colored hummingbird is strong and frantically energetic.

A verb shows an action, shows a state of being, links two words together, or helps another verb.

A linking verb connects the subject to a noun, pronoun, or adjective in the complete predicate.

A predicate adjective describes the subject and is found in the complete predicate.

The subject of the sentence is the main word or term that the sentence is about.
The simple subject of the sentence is *just* the main word or term that the sentence is about.
The complete subject of the sentence is the simple subject and all the words that belong to it.

The predicate of the sentence tells something about the subject.
The simple predicate of the sentence is the main verb along with any helping verbs.
The complete predicate of the sentence is the simple predicate and all the words that belong to it.

State-of-Being Verbs

am	were
is	be
are	being
was	been

I am.
I am hungry.

They are being.

They are being loud.

The sunset was.

The sunset was spectacular.

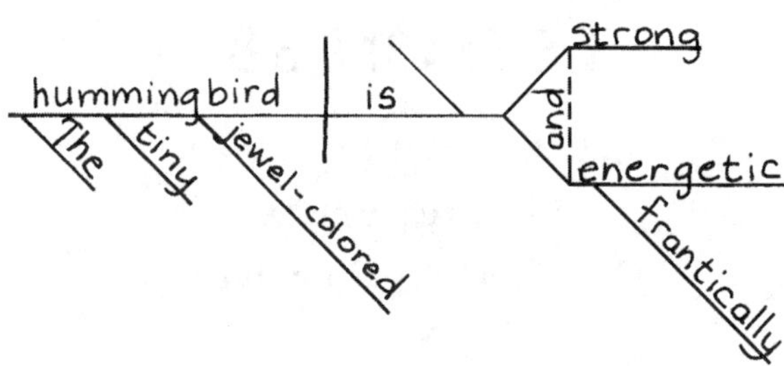

LV PA
Hummingbirds are tiny.

AV DO
Tiny hummingbirds sipped sweet nectar.

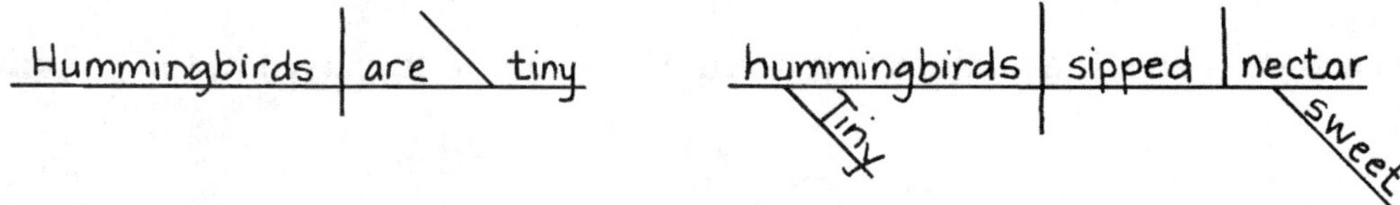

Exercise 38A: Action Verbs and Linking Verbs

In the following sentences, underline the subjects once and the predicates twice. If the predicate is a linking verb, write *LV* above it, circle the predicate adjective, and label it *PA*. If the predicate is an action verb, write *AV* above it, circle the direct object, if any, and label it *DO*. The first is done for you.

These sentences are slightly condensed from Rudyard Kipling's *Just So Stories*.

AV DO DO
The Whale ate the starfish and the garfish.

He was grey and woolly.

They could see stripy shadows and blotched shadows in the forest.

"They are too clever on the turbid Amazon for poor me!"

The cabin port-holes are dark and green.

His enemies were hiding in the bushes and would see him.

The Camel's hump is black and blue.

"The sun is very hot here."

Can the Leopard change his spots?

The tree trunks were exclusively speckled and sprottled.

Suleiman-bin-Daoud was wise and strong.

The Djinn took a bearing across the desert, and found the Camel.

His dear families went in a hurry to the banks of the great grey-green, greasy Limpopo River.

Exercise 38B: Diagramming Direct Objects and Predicate Adjectives

On your own paper, diagram ONLY the subjects, predicates, and direct objects or predicate adjectives (along with any conjunctions used to connect compounds) from the sentences in Exercise 38A.

— LESSON 39 —

Linking Verbs
Predicate Adjectives
Predicate Nominatives

I am unpopular.
I am a flower.
I am a berry.

A predicate adjective describes the subject and is found in the complete predicate.
A predicate nominative renames the subject and is found in the complete predicate.

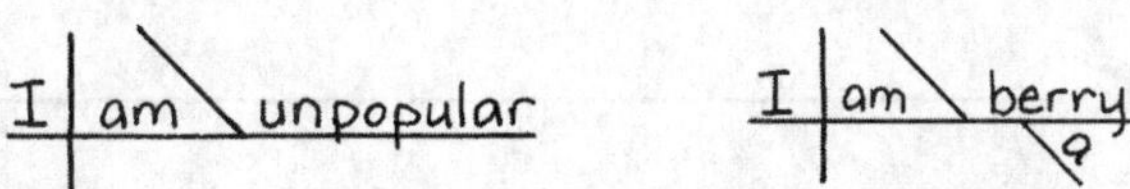

Iguanas are reptiles.
Iguanas = reptiles (predicate nominative)

Iguanas are scaly.
scaly iguanas (predicate adjective)

reptiles iguanas   not a predicate adjective
iguanas ≠ scaly   not a predicate nominative

Exercise 39A: Identifying Predicate Nominatives and Adjectives

In the following sentences, underline the subjects once and the predicates twice. Circle the predicate nominatives or adjectives and label each one *PN* for predicate nominative or *PA* for predicate adjective. Draw a line from the predicate nominative or adjective to the subject that it renames or describes. There may be more than one of each.

Crocodiles are fascinating animals.

These animals are carnivorous.

They are incredibly fast swimmers and hunters.

Australia is home to the freshwater crocodile.

Freshwater crocodiles are quite bashful.

The freshwater crocodile's diet is mostly insects and fish.

Birds, mammals, and fish are the preferred food of a saltwater crocodile.

Their jaws are powerful and dangerous.

Exercise 39B: Writing Predicate Nominatives and Adjectives

Finish each sentence in two ways: with a predicate nominative and with a predicate adjective. If you need to use more than one word in a blank to complete your sentence, circle the word that is the predicate nominative or predicate adjective.

The first is done for you.

Sewing is ______ my favorite (hobby) ______. (predicate nominative)
Sewing is ______ enjoyable ______. (predicate adjective)

The Belgian waffles were ______________________. (predicate nominative)
The Belgian waffles were ______________________. (predicate adjective)

The cure is ______________________. (predicate nominative
The cure is ______________________. (predicate adjective)

Cucumbers are ____. (predicate nominative)

Cucumbers are ____. (predicate adjective)

Many of the books on the shelf are ______________________. (predicate nominative)

Many of the books on the shelf are ______________________. (predicate adjective)

The little child's hiding place was ______________________. (predicate nominative)

The little child's hiding place was ______________________. (predicate adjective)

Exercise 39C: Diagramming Predicate Adjectives and Predicate Nominatives

On your own paper, diagram every word of the following sentences.

The cave exploration was exciting!
Tonight's sunset is bright orange and red.
Her studio was an old barn.
Caron made us bacon and eggs.
Bats are mammals.
Submit the new homework.
The class learned new dance steps.
Are you tired?
The washer and the dryer broke.

— LESSON 40 —

Predicate Adjectives and Predicate Nominatives
Pronouns as Predicate Nominatives
Object Complements

A linking verb connects the subject to a noun, pronoun, or adjective in the complete predicate.

A pronoun takes the place of a noun.
The antecedent is the noun that is replaced by the pronoun.

I	we
you	you (plural)
he, she, it	they

It is I.
The winner is you.
My best friend is she.

It = I
winner = you
friend =she

(plural noun) ______________________________ are we.

(singular noun) ______________________________ has been you.

(plural noun) ______________________________ were they.

We elected Marissa leader.
The explorers found the camp abandoned.
He painted the fence white.

An object complement follows the direct object and renames or describes it.

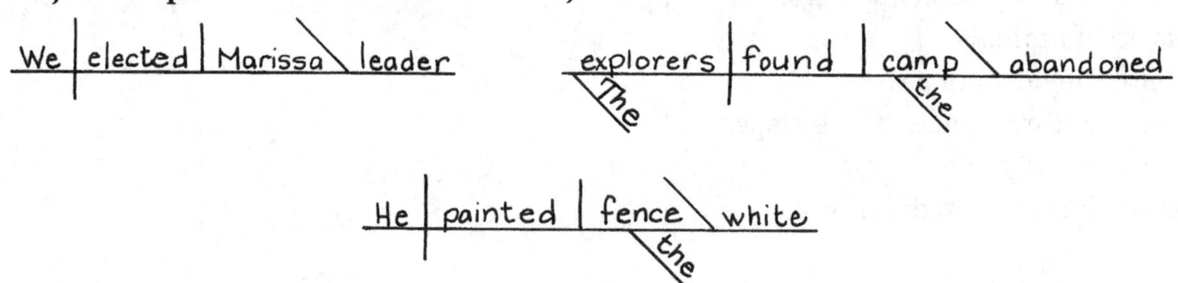

An adjective that comes right before the noun it modifies is in the *attributive position.*

They are user-friendly directions.

An adjective that follows the noun is in the *predicative position.*

Those directions are user friendly.

My friend dyed his hair purple.
My friend dyed his purple hair.
My friend dyed his purple hair orange.

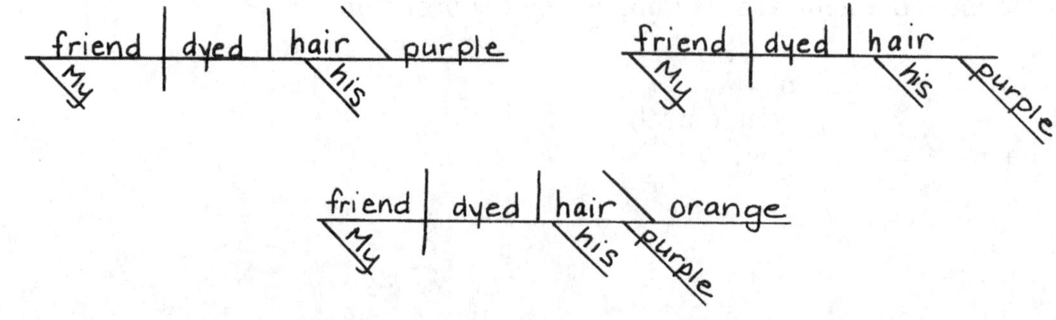

Exercise 40A: Reviewing Objects and Predicate Adjectives and Nominatives

Identify the underlined words as *DO* for direct object, *IO* for indirect object, *OP* for object of preposition, *PN* for predicate nominative, or *PA* for predicate adjective.

- For each direct object (or direct object/indirect object combination), find and underline twice the action verb that affects it.
- For each object of the preposition, find and circle the preposition to which it belongs.
- For each predicate nominative and predicate adjective, find and draw a box around the linking verb that it follows.
- When you are finished, answer the questions at the end of the selection.

The following passage is from *Esperanza Rising*, by Pam Muñoz Ryan. It has been condensed and slightly adapted.

Papa handed Esperanza the knife. This job was usually reserved for the eldest son of a wealthy rancher, but Esperanza was an only child and Papa's pride and glory. She was given the honor.

The August sun promised a dry afternoon in Aguascalientes, Mexico. Everyone who lived and worked on El Rancho de las Rosas was gathered at the edge of the field.

The grapevine clusters were heavy. Papa declared them ready. Esperanza's parents stood nearby. Mama was tall and elegant, her hair in the usual braided wreath that crowned her head, and Papa, barely taller than Mama, his graying mustache twisted up at the sides. He swept his hand toward the grapevines, signaling Esperanza. When she walked toward the arbors and glanced back at her parents, they both smiled and nodded, encouraging her forward. When she reached the vines, she separated the leaves and carefully grasped a thick stem. She put the knife to it, and with a quick swipe, the heavy cluster of grapes dropped into her waiting hand. Esperanza walked back to Papa and handed him the fruit. Papa kissed it and held it up for all to see.

1. Find the object complement in this passage. Write it in the blank below and cross out the incorrect choices. ______________________________ is an (adjective/noun) that (describes/renames) the direct object.

2. Find the compound adjective in this passage. Write it in the blank below and cross out the incorrect choice. ______________________________ is in the (attributive/ predicative) position.

Exercise 40B: Parts of the Sentence

Label the following in each sentence: *S* (subject), *LV* (linking verb), *AV* (action verb), *DO* (direct object), *OC-A* (object complement-adjective), *OC-N* (object complement-noun), *IO* (indirect object), or *PN* (predicate nominative).

The girl named her hamster Peggy.

The girl gave her hamster water.

We painted the walls blue.

We painted the walls carefully.

The hard-working volunteers gave the children a wonderful event.

The hard-working volunteers made the event a reality.

They called the painting a masterpiece.

I considered the salsa spicy.

The judges were strict.

The judges named the horse the winner.

The judges gave the horse a blue ribbon.

Exercise 40C: Diagramming

On your own paper, diagram the sentences from Exercise 40B.

WEEK 11

More About Prepositions

— LESSON 41 —

Prepositions and Prepositional Phrases
Adjective Phrases

Prepositions
aboard, about, above, across
after, against, along, among, around, at
before, behind, below, beneath
beside, between, beyond, by
down, during, except, for, from
in, inside, into, like
near, of, off, on, over
past, since, through, throughout
to, toward, under, underneath
until, up, upon
with, within, without

A preposition shows the relationship of a noun or pronoun to another word in the sentence.
A prepositional phrase begins with a preposition and ends with a noun or pronoun. That noun or pronoun is the object of the preposition.
A phrase is a group of words serving a single grammatical function.

I could have been running away.

Speed of Sound

Ring of Fire

Bridge Over Troubled Water

Time of Your Life

The Sound of Silence

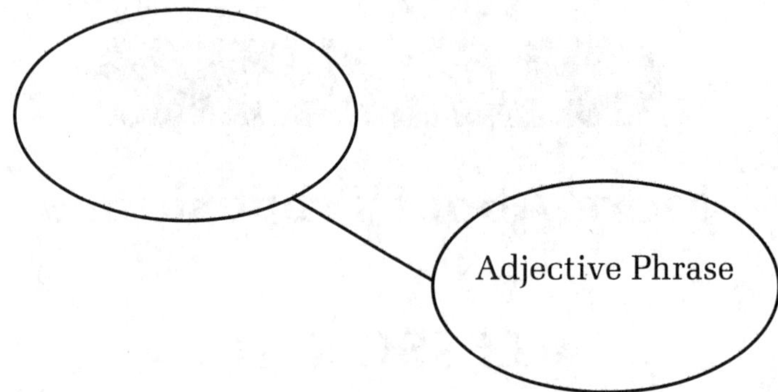

Prepositional phrases that act as adjectives are also called adjective phrases.

The boy with the freckles was whistling.
The old man on the bench hummed a tune.
Arthur borrowed a book of mine.

Adjective phrases usually come directly after the words they modify.

Caleb climbed a tree with thick branches.

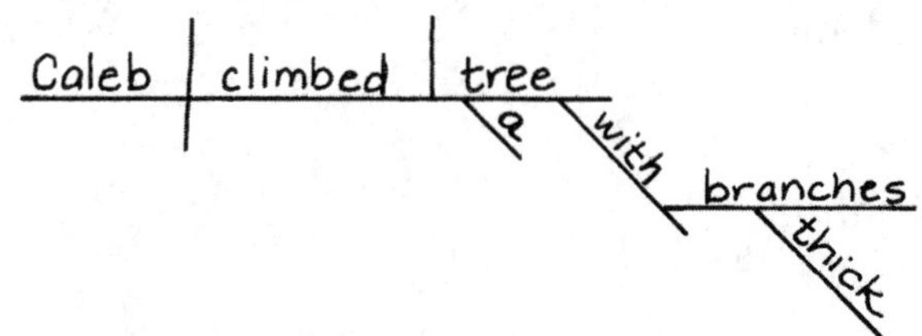

The children in the house were sleeping.

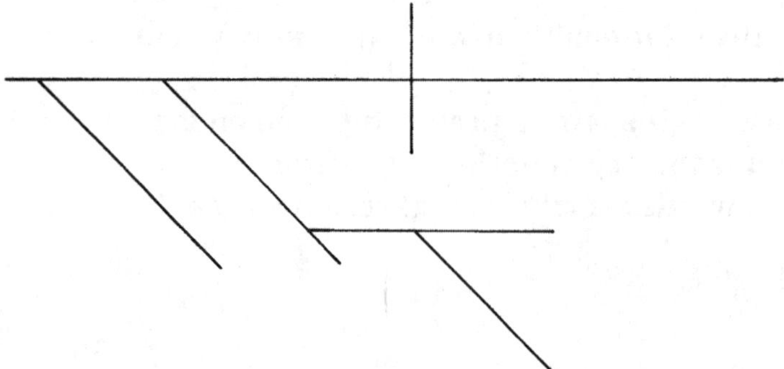

Exercise 41A: Identifying Adjective Phrases

Underline the adjective phrases in the following sentences. Draw an arrow from each phrase to the word it modifies. The first is done for you.

A fifty-mile span <u>of land</u> was the site <u>of the Panama Canal</u>.

It would shorten a ship's journey and avoid travel around Cape Horn.

Many of the workers on the Canal kept contracting malaria and yellow fever.

These illnesses caused many deaths and caused delays to the construction.

Major Ronald Ross discovered the connection between mosquitoes and these diseases.

The Canal's location on the Isthmus of Panama was an environment with hot, wet weather.

This weather caused an increase in the mosquito population.

The U.S. Army Sanitary Department began work on disease prevention.

The Sanitary Department dug drainage ditches and drained many pools around the Canal area.

The Sanitary Department also built buildings with screens.

The number of deaths decreased rapidly.

Exercise 41B: Diagramming Adjective Phrases/Review

Diagram each sentence from Exercise 41A on your own paper. Follow this procedure, and ask yourself the suggested questions if necessary.

1. Find the subject and predicate and diagram them first.
   What is the verb?
   Who or what [verb]?
2. Ask yourself: Is the verb an action verb? If so, look for a direct object.
   Who or what receives the action of the verb?

   If there is a direct object, check for an indirect object.
   To whom or for whom is the action done?

   Remember that there may be no direct object or no indirect object—but you can't have an indirect object without a direct object. If there is an indirect object, it will always come between the verb and the direct object.
3. Ask yourself: Is the verb a state-of-being verb? If so, look for a predicate nominative or predicate adjective.
   Is there a word after the verb that renames or describes the subject?
4. Find all prepositional phrases. Ask yourself: Whom or what do they describe?
5. Place all other adjectives and adverbs on the diagram. If you have trouble, ask for help.

— LESSON 42 —

Adjective Phrases
Adverb Phrases

Prepositional phrases that act as adverbs are also called adverb phrases.
An adverb describes a verb, an adjective, or another adverb.
Adverbs tell how, when, where, how often, and to what extent.

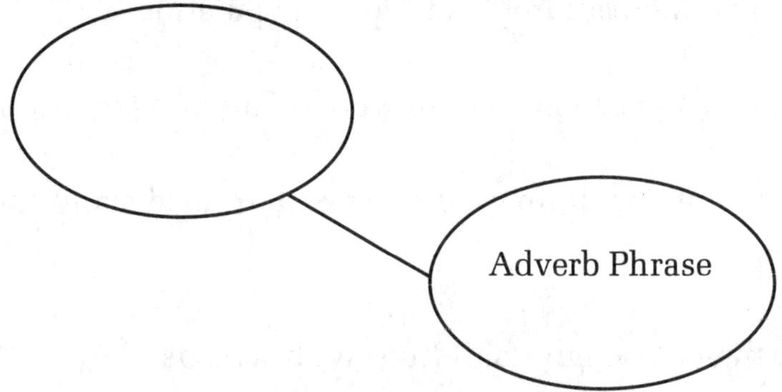

Fly Me (to) the Moon

I Fall to Pieces

Wake Me at Sunset

Sitting on the Dock of the Bay

Cameron scuba-dives in Hawaii.
At 6:00 a.m., Cameron wakes.

Adverb phrases can be anywhere in a sentence.

With great confidence, Hank Aaron swung the bat through the air.

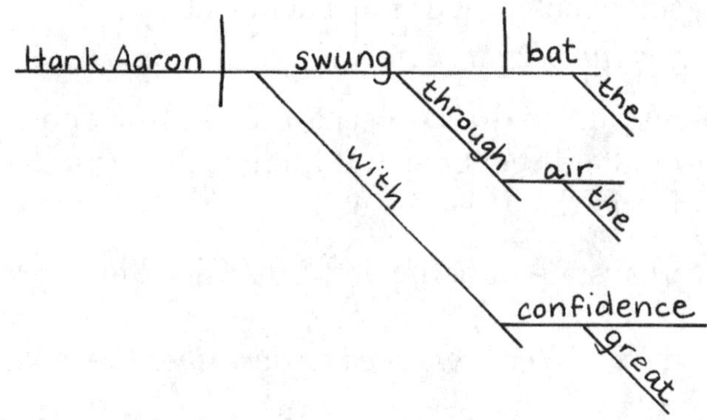

In summer, the car was hot beyond belief.

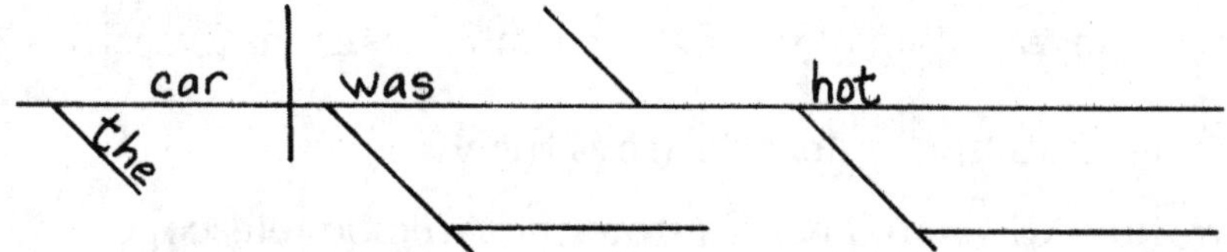

Exercise 42A: Identifying Adverb Phrases

Underline the adverb phrases in the following sentences and circle the preposition that begins each phrase. Draw an arrow from each phrase to the word it modifies. Be careful not to underline any prepositional phrases that function as adjectives! These sentences are adapted from *What If? Serious Scientific Answers to Absurd Hypothetical Questions*, by Randall Munroe.

The first is done for you.

The common cold is caused by various viruses.

After a few days, your immune system destroys the virus.

When you fight the virus, you are immune to that particular rhinovirus strain.

Earth's most powerful radio signal beams from the Arecibo telescope.

This massive dish sits in Puerto Rico and can function like a radar transmitter.

Signals bounce off Mercury and the asteroid belt.

The Curiosity rover is sitting in Gale Crater on Mars.

Liquid water does not last on Mars, because it is too cold and there's too little air.

The power delivered to the ground by sunlight outweighs the power delivered to the ground by lightning.

Perpetual nighttime thunderstorms occur in Lake Maracaibo.

The Empire State Building is frequently struck by lightning.

Exercise 42B: Diagramming Adverb Phrases

On your own paper, diagram the following five sentences from Exercise 42A.

After a few days, your immune system destroys the virus.

Earth's most powerful radio signal beams from the Arecibo telescope.

This massive dish sits in Puerto Rico and can function like a radar transmitter.

Perpetual nighttime thunderstorms occur in Lake Maracaibo.

The Empire State Building is frequently struck by lightning.

— LESSON 43 —

Definitions Review
Adjective and Adverb Phrases
Misplaced Modifiers

An adjective modifies ______________________________.

Adjectives tell ______________________________.

A preposition shows ______________________________
word in the sentence.

A prepositional phrase ______________________________
______________________ **or pronoun.**
______________________________ **object of the preposition.**

A phrase is ______________________________ **function.**

Prepositional phrases that ______________________________
adjective phrases.

Adjective phrases usually ______________________________.

An adverb describes ______________________________.

Adverbs tell ______________________________ **extent.**

______________________________ **are also**
called adverb phrases.

Prepositions

A ____________, **a** ____________, **a** ____________, **a** ____________.

A ________, **a** ________, **a** ________, **a** ________, **a** ________.

B ____________, **b** ____________, **b** ____________, **b** ____________.

B ____________, **b** ____________, **b** ____________, **b** ____________.

D __________, **d** __________, **e** __________, **f** __________, **f** __________.

I ________________, **i** ________________, **i** ________________, **l** ________________.

N __________, **o** __________, **o** __________, **o** __________, **o** __________.

P ____________, **s** ____________, **t** ____________, **t** ____________.

T ____________, **t** ____________, **u** ____________, **u** ____________.

U ____________, **u** ____________, **u** ____________.

W ____________, **w** ____________, **w** ____________.

The cat scratched Brock's sister with the striped tail.

A misplaced modifier is an adjective phrase in the wrong place.

The beautiful girl was dancing with the handsome man in the red dress.

On the pizza, Molly ate the mushrooms.

I cut my finger while I was cooking badly.

I saw that the toast was burned with a glance.

I spotted the dog chewing on the sofa leg from the stairs.

Exercise 43A: Distinguishing Between Adjective and Adverb Phrases

Underline all the prepositional phrases in the following sentences. Write *ADJ* above the adjective phrases and *ADV* above the adverb phrases. These sentences are adapted from Marguerite Henry's *Misty of Chincoteague*.

A wild, ringing neigh shrilled from the hold of the Spanish galleon.

The wind was dying with the sun.

It was not the cry of an animal in hunger.

The captain's eyes were fixed on his men, but his thoughts raced to the rich land where he was bound.

His beady eyes darted to the lookout man in the crow's nest, then to the men on deck.

The stallion neighed to the mares, who were struggling to keep afloat.

The ponies were exhausted and their coats were heavy with water, but they were free!

With wild snorts of happiness, they buried their noses in the long grass.

Then they rolled in the wiry grass and they gave great whinnies of happiness.

The sea gave them protection from their fiercest enemies.

Exercise 43B: Correcting Misplaced Modifiers

Circle the misplaced adjective and adverb phrases in the following sentences. Draw an arrow to show where the phrase should be.

For some of the sentences, the phrase may make sense where it is—but if a phrase doesn't communicate what the author wants it to, it is misplaced. Assume that each sentence contains a phrase that is misplaced (that is, a different meaning was intended), correct as instructed above, and explain to your instructor how the placement changes the meaning.

The first is done for you, with a sample explanation provided.

Under the surfboard, the surfer spotted the shark swimming.

Under the surfboard as initially placed indicates that the surfer was positioned under the board itself. In the corrected position, the phrase tells the reader where the shark was located.

The car was going too quickly down the road with blue stripes.

The musician played my favorite song in a sparkly, sequined hat.

The nurse in my shoulder gave me a shot.

With long whiskers, Gerald carried the cat.

Under the plate, he found one more cookie.

The old, haunted house finally collapsed on the beach.

From the garden, Dad fried zucchini.

In the freezer, Amelia saw the ice cream.

The class debated the verdict in the library.

The zookeeper feeds the lion in the green jacket.

The mud covered my shoes from the yard.

— LESSON 44 —

Adjective and Adverb Phrases

Prepositional Phrases Acting as Other Parts of Speech

The ship went down into the Gulf of Guinea and, with many stops on the way, approached the mouth of the Congo.

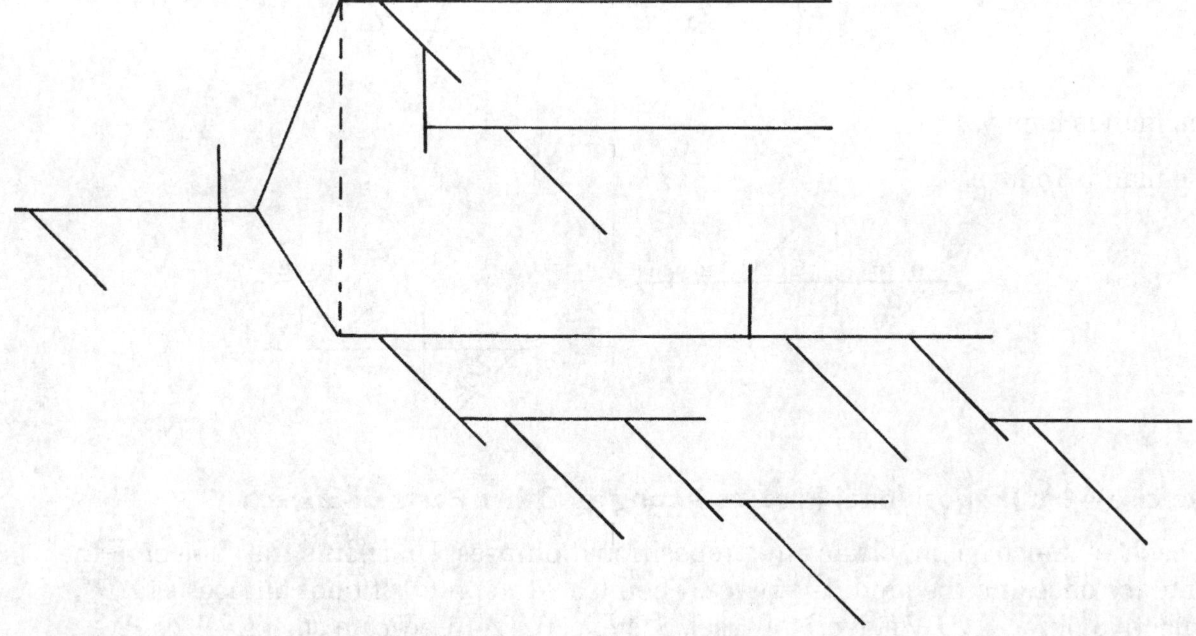

A swamp is not a safe place.

Under the bridge is not a safe place.

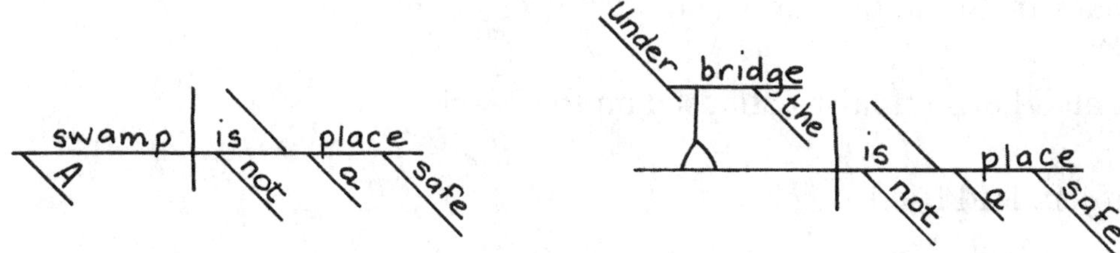

The best place for the treasure is my closet.

The best place for the treasure is under the bed.

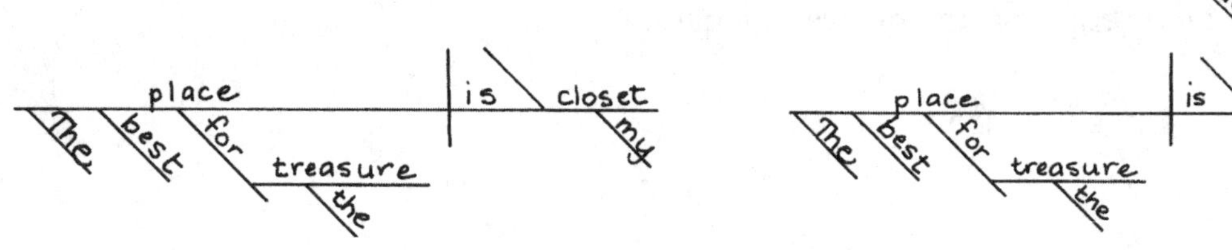

He stepped from the dark.

He stepped from behind the tree.

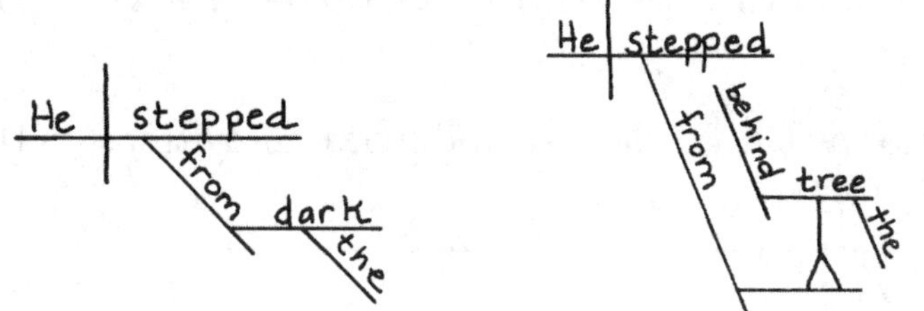

The man is happy.

The man is in love.

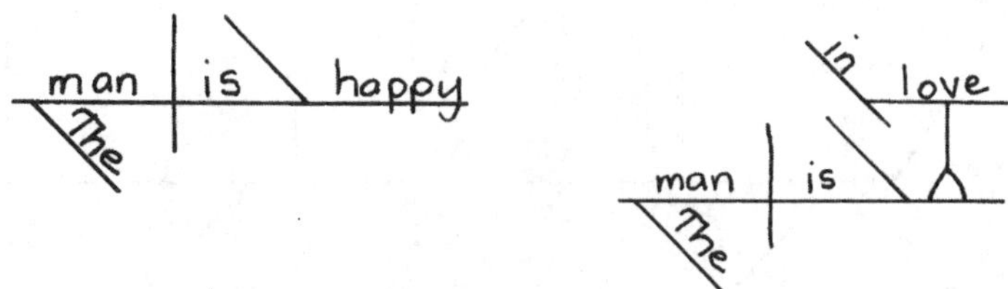

Exercise 44A: Prepositional Phrases Acting as Other Parts of Speech

In each sentence below, circle any prepositional phrases. Underline the subject of the sentence once and the predicate twice. Then label the prepositional phrases as *ADJ* (adjective phrase), *ADV* (adverb phrase), *S* (subject), *PA* (predicate adjective), or *PN* (predicate nominative).

In the wind is bitterly cold.

The hotel down the street is under construction.

Now sing with your loudest voice.

During the class is a bad time for a nap.

The Yeoman Warders are in their stately red uniforms.

The snake slithered down the porch steps, through the flower bed, and under the old house.

My favorite place is at the beach.

The bike with a flat tire swerved off the road.

You are in a bad mood!

The train in the station was ready for passengers.

Exercise 44B: Diagramming

On your own paper, diagram these sentences from Exercise 44A.

In the wind is bitterly cold.
The hotel down the street is under construction.
Now sing with your loudest voice.
During the class is a bad time for a nap.
The Yeoman Warders are in their stately red uniforms.
The snake slithered down the porch steps, through the flower bed, and under the house.
My favorite place is at the beach.
The bike with a flat tire swerved off the road.
You are in a bad mood!
The train in the station was ready for passengers.

WEEK 12

Advanced Verbs

— LESSON 45 —

Linking Verbs
Linking/Action Verbs

State of Being/Linking Verbs
am, is, are, was, were
be, being, been

Additional Linking Verbs
taste, feel, smell, sound, look
prove, grow
remain, appear, stay
become, seem

I tasted the candy.

The candy tasted delicious.

The fried chicken tasted crispy.

The chicken tasted the birdseed.

Thomas felt the baby chick.
Thomas felt sad.

ACTION	LINKING
He proved the theory.	He proved unreliable.
The farmer grew wheat.	The farmer grew tired.
The dog remained on the porch.	The dog remained wary.
The cloud appeared in the sky.	The cloud appeared threatening.
We stayed home.	We stayed happy with our home.

The student became confused.
The grammar seemed difficult.

Exercise 45A: Distinguishing Between Action Verbs and Linking Verbs

Underline the predicates in the following sentences. Identify each main verb as *AV* for action verb or *LV* for linking verb. If the verb is followed by a direct object (*DO*), predicate adjective (*PA*), or predicate nominative (*PN*), label it.

Remember that a verb with no direct object, predicate adjective, or predicate nominative will most likely be an action verb. Also remember that direct objects, predicate adjectives, and predicate nominatives are never found in prepositional phrases.

The corn grew quickly in the summer.

The fire grew cold.

The milk tastes spoiled.

I tasted the balsamic vinegar.

The pig seems happy.

Those actions look suspicious.

Are your shoes new?

The honeysuckle smelled sweet.

Terrance smelled the lavender bush.

Katarzyna became the lead actress.

The butterflies are migrating.

The fireflies are appearing in the sky.

The desert appeared endless.

When is the director giving notes to you?

Exercise 45B: Distinguishing Among Different Kinds of Nouns

Underline all the nouns in the following sentences. Identify them as *S* for subject, *OP* for object of a preposition, *IO* for indirect object, *DO* for direct object, or *PN* for predicate nominative.

Imani loves horses.

They are her favorite animals.

Her aunt lives on a ranch and owns two horses.

She gives Imani riding lessons.

Her aunt is a veterinarian.

Imani cleans the horses' stalls and feeds the animals apples and carrots.

Eventually, Imani will own a farm and horses.

Exercise 45C: Diagramming Action Verbs and Linking Verbs

Diagram the following sentences.

The old road feels bumpy.
Oviraptors were omnivores.
Oviraptors would eat eggs.
Can you bring me the keys?
The sky grew dark.
Stefan grew sunflowers.

— LESSON 46 —

Conjugations
Irregular Verbs
Principal Parts of Verbs

Verbs in the simple past, simple present, and simple future describe actions that simply happen.
Verbs in the progressive past, progressive present, and progressive future describe actions that go on for a while.
Verbs in the perfect past, perfect present, and perfect future describe actions which have been completed before another action takes place.

Exercise 46A: Forming Simple, Perfect, and Progressive Tenses

Fill in the missing blanks in the chart below.

Simple Present

	Singular	Plural
First person	I jump	We ______________
Second person	You ______________	You jump
Third person	He, she, it ______________	They jump

Simple Past

	Singular	Plural
First person	I ______	We ______
Second person	You ______	You ______
Third person	He, she, it ______	They jumped

Simple Future

	Singular	Plural
First person	I ______	We ______
Second person	You will jump	You ______
Third person	He, she, it ______	They ______

Perfect Present

	Singular	Plural
First person	I ______	We ______
Second person	You ______	You ______
Third person	He, she, it has jumped	They ______

Perfect Past

	Singular	Plural
First person	I ______	We ______
Second person	You ______	You had jumped
Third person	He, she, it ______	They ______

Perfect Future

	Singular	Plural
First person	I will have jumped	We ______
Second person	You ______	You ______
Third person	He, she, it ______	They ______

Progressive Present

	Singular	Plural
First person	I ______	We are jumping
Second person	You ______	You ______
Third person	He, she, it ______	They ______

Progressive Past

	Singular	Plural
First person	I ____________	We ____________
Second person	You were jumping	You ____________
Third person	He, she, it ____________	They ____________ jumping

Progressive Future

	Singular	Plural
First person	I will be jumping	We ____________
Second person	You ____________	You ____________
Third person	He, she, it ____________	They ____________

Simple Present	Simple Past	Simple Future
build	built	will build
buy	bought	will buy
choose	chose	will choose
sell	sold	will sell

Exercise 46B: Spanish and English Words

Draw lines to match each English word with its Spanish equivalent. Because English and Spanish have similar backgrounds, you should be able to complete this exercise easily, even if you've never learned any Spanish!

English	Spanish
problem	correctamente
action	entrar
anniversary	estudiante
community	acción
student	aparecer
correctly	artista
difficulty	problema
appear	comunidad
enter	dificultad
artist	aniversario

English verbs have three principal parts.

First principal part: the simple present (present)

(I) conjugate *(I)* ____________

Second principal part: the simple past (past)

(I) conjugated *(I)* ____________

Third principal part: the perfect past, minus helping verbs (past participle)

(I have) conjugated *(I have)* ____________

Exercise 46C: Principal Parts of Verbs

Fill in the chart with the missing forms.

	First Principal Part Present	Second Principal Part Past	Third Principal Part Past Participle
I	wait	waited	waited
I	file		filed
I			needed
I	cry		
I		talked	
I			invented
I	worry		
I		appeared	
I	shop		
I			swayed

Exercise 46D: Distinguishing Between First and Second Principal Parts

Identify each underlined verb as *1* for first principal part or *2* for second principal part. These sentences are from Mary Norton's *The Borrowers.*

Mrs. May lived in two rooms in Kate's parents' house in London; she was, I think, some kind of relation.

"In fact, you might almost say that he became a borrower himself..."

"You waste hours on those birds," Homily would say.

In the morning, the sun streams in on the toast and marmalade.

She gazed downwards at the upturned face and then she smiled and her eyes slid away into distance.

— LESSON 47 —

Linking Verbs
Principal Parts
Irregular Verbs

Linking Verbs
am, is, are, was, were
be, being, been
taste, feel, smell, sound, look
prove, grow
remain, appear, stay
become, seem

Present	Past	Past Participle
(I) taste	(I) tasted	(I have) tasted
(I) become	(I) became	(I have) become
(I) feel	(I) felt	(I have) felt

COMMON IRREGULAR VERBS

Present	Past	Past Participle	
SAME PRESENT, PAST & PAST PARTICIPLE:			
beat	beat	beat	(OR beat beat beaten)
burst	burst	burst	
cost	cost	cost	
cut	cut	cut	
fit	fit	fit	
let	let	let	
put	put	put	
quit	quit	quit	
hit	hit	hit	
hurt	hurt	hurt	
set	set	set	
shut	shut	shut	
SAME PAST & PAST PARTICIPLE:			
bend	bent	bent	
send	sent	sent	
lend	lent	lent	
bleed	bled	bled	
feed	fed	fed	
feel	felt	felt	
keep	kept	kept	
lead	led	led	
leave	left	left	
meet	met	met	
read	read	read	
sleep	slept	slept	
bring	brought	brought	
buy	bought	bought	
catch	caught	caught	
fight	fought	fought	
seek	sought	sought	
teach	taught	taught	
think	thought	thought	
lay	laid	laid	
pay	paid	paid	
say	said	said	
sell	sold	sold	
tell	told	told	

Present	Past	Past Participle
lose	lost	lost
shoot	shot	shot
find	found	found
wind	wound	wound
dig	dug	dug
sit	sat	sat
win	won	won
stand	stood	stood
understand	understood	understood
hear	heard	heard
make	made	made
build	built	built

DIFFERENT PAST AND PAST PARTICIPLE:

awake	awoke	awoken
bite	bit	bitten
break	broke	broken
choose	chose	chosen
forget	forgot	forgotten
freeze	froze	frozen
get	got	gotten
give	gave	given
drive	drove	driven
eat	ate	eaten
fall	fell	fallen
hide	hid	hidden
rise	rose	risen
shake	shook	shaken
speak	spoke	spoken
steal	stole	stolen
take	took	taken
write	wrote	written
ride	rode	ridden
become	became	become
begin	began	begun
come	came	come
run	ran	run

Present	Past	Past Participle
drink	drank	drunk
shrink	shrank	shrunk
ring	rang	rung
sing	sang	sung
swim	swam	swum
draw	drew	drawn
fly	flew	flown
grow	grew	grown
know	knew	known
tear	tore	torn
wear	wore	worn
do	did	done
go	went	gone
lie	lay	lain
see	saw	seen

— LESSON 48 —

Linking Verbs
Principal Parts
Irregular Verbs

Linking Verbs
am, is, are, was, were
be, being, been
taste, feel, smell, sound, look
prove, grow
remain, appear, stay
become, seem

Verbs in the simple past, simple present, and simple future describe actions that simply happen.
Verbs in the progressive past, progressive present, and progressive future describe actions that go on for a while.
Verbs in the perfect past, perfect present, and perfect future describe actions which have been completed before another action takes place.

PRINCIPAL PARTS
present, past, past participle

Exercise 48A: Principal Parts

Fill in the blanks in the following chart of verbs.

Present	Past	Past Participle
light	________	________
weave	________	________
________	began	________
________	________	burnt
________	foresaw	________
pay	________	________
________	________	thrust
swell	________	________
________	________	ground
________	flung	________
________	________	dealt
forsake	________	________
let	________	________
________	________	lost
________	________	strung
________	stank	________
________	________	slunk
cost	________	________
________	sought	________
________	rose	________
________	________	sprung
slit	________	________
shine	________	________
________	________	spun
________	rid	________
mean	________	________

Present	Past	Past Participle
______	______	laid
______	______	sped
wring	______	______
strive	______	______
______	______	cut
______	______	forecast
spend	______	______
______	met	______
______	______	driven
______	______	bid
______	lay	______
______	______	understood
throw	______	______
sell	______	______
______	kept	______
______	______	rewound

Exercise 48B: Forming Correct Past Participles

Write the correct third principal part (past participle) in each blank. The first principal part is provided for you in parentheses.

The first is done for you.

I had broken (break) the plate.

Her friends have ______ (send) her birthday cards.

Mathilde has never ______ (fly) by herself.

The fishing rod had nearly ______ (bend) in half by the time he had ______ (catch) the huge fish!

Have you ______ (choose) which cupcake you would like?

Yesterday, Ben had ______________ (drive) to the nursery and had ______________ (buy) two trees for the yard.

Petra had ______________ (find) her phone after I texted her.

Exercise 48C: Forming Correct Past Tenses

Write the correct second principal part (past) in each blank. The first principal part is provided for you in parentheses.

The first is done for you.

Liam __wrote__ (write) a paper about Aaron Burr.

We ______________ (swim) for an hour yesterday.

Charlotte ______________ (bring) cucumbers that she ______________ (grow) in her garden.

I ______________ (blow) out the candle just before I ______________ (hear) the first clap of thunder.

Oliver's ankle ______________ (feel) bruised after he ______________ (fall) down the steps.

The witness ______________ (keep) insisting that the defendant was not the person she ______________ (see).

Tyra ______________ (give) me the rope and ______________ (hold) onto the end while I climbed down.

Exercise 48D: Proofreading for Irregular Verb Usage

In the passage below, from Jean Craighead George's *My Side of the Mountain*, you will find seven errors in irregular verb usage. Cross out the incorrect forms and write the correct ones above them.

I looked up to see how much higher I had to go. Then I seed them. There sitted three fussy whitish gray birds. Their wide-open mouths gived them a startled look.

"Oh, hello," I sayed. "You are cute."

When I speaked, all three blinked at once. All three heads turned and followed my hand as I swinged it up and toward them.

Something hit my shoulder. I turned my head to see the big female. She had hitted me. She winged out, banked, and started back for another strike.

Exercise 48E: Diagramming

On your own paper, diagram the following four sentences.

Who announced Secretariat the winner of the race?
The fog over the lake seems mysterious.
Abuela cooked the chicken and warmed the rice.
Near the waterfall is the best spot for a swim.

— REVIEW 4 —

Weeks 10-12

Topics:
Direct and Indirect Objects
Linking Verbs
Predicate Adjectives
Predicate Nominatives
Articles
Adjective Phrases
Adverb Phrases
Action vs. Linking Verbs
Irregular Verbs
Principal Parts (Present, Past, Past Participle)

Review 4A: Action vs. Linking Verbs

Identify the underlined verbs as *A* for action or *L* for linking.

A young bottlenose dolphin swam happily in the warm waters of the Florida coastline.

The nets of a crab trap were invisible to her, and she became its victim as she grew tangled in the rope.

She twisted and tried to free herself, but she soon felt exhausted.

A fisherman noticed the moving trap and found the entrapped dolphin.

Rescuers arrived and freed the frightened animal.

They took her to their facility and treated her wounds so that she could become strong again.

The rescuers named her Winter and fitted her with a prosthetic tail to help her swim and play.

Winter grew famous for her incredible recovery and story.

She is an inspiration to many people who come visit her each year at Clearwater Marine Aquarium.

Review 4B: Predicate Adjectives and Predicate Nominatives

Underline the linking verb in each of the following sentences. If the sentence concludes with a predicate nominative or predicate adjective, circle each and write *PA* for predicate adjective or *PN* for predicate nominative above it.

Geodes are beautiful rocks.

The inside of a geode is hollow.

A geode's exterior looks unremarkable.

However, the interior appears sparkling and colorful.

Minerals such as quartz and pyrite are common in geodes.

The mineral is a liquid and then it crystallizes.

The crystals usually look blue or purple.

Geodes are quite popular among rock collectors.

Review 4C: Adjective and Adverb Phrases

In the following excerpt from Joseph Marshall III's *In the Footsteps of Crazy Horse*, identify each underlined prepositional phrase as *ADJ* for adjective phrase or *ADV* for adverb phrase.

Jimmy smiled as he loped across the prairie. He was riding Little Warrior, a small but sturdy buckskin quarter horse. Grandpa was riding on Dancer, a muscular bay quarter horse stallion. Grandpa Nyles had, a small herd of horses.

Their chore was checking Grandpa Nyle's twelve miles of fence. They stopped along Horse Creek, which flowed into the Smoking Earth River. Grandpa wanted to rest the horses and let them graze. Besides, it was always good to relax in the shade of some big, tall cottonwood trees. Jimmy took a long stick and poked around in the grasses before he sat down. It was a way to scare away snakes. Grandpa had taught him that.

As they sat against the trunk of a giant cottonwood tree, they listened to the creek gurgling and watched the horses munch on grass.

Review 4D: Forming Principal Parts

Complete the following excerpt by writing the correct principal part of the verb (first, second, or third) in parentheses. Sentences are adapted from Arthur Conan Doyle's *The Sign of the Four.*

It was a September evening, and not yet seven o'clock, but the day had ____________ (be, 3rd PP) a dreary one, and a dense drizzly fog ____________ (lie, 2nd PP) low upon the great city. Mud-coloured clouds drooped sadly over the muddy streets. Down the Strand the lamps ____________ (be, 2nd PP) but misty splotches of diffused light which ____________ (throw, 2nd PP) a feeble circular glimmer upon the slimy pavement. The yellow glare from the shop-windows had ___________ (stream, 3rd PP) out into the steamy, vaporous air, and ___________ (throw, 3rd PP) a murky, shifting radiance across the crowded thoroughfare. There ___________ (be, 2nd PP) something eerie and ghost-like in the endless procession of faces which flitted across these narrow bars of light,—sad faces and glad, haggard and merry. I ___________ (be, 1st PP) not subject to impressions, but the dull, heavy evening, with the strange business upon which we were engaged, combined to make me nervous and depressed. I had ___________ (see, 3rd PP) from Miss Morstan's manner that she had ___________ (suffer, 3rd PP) from the same feeling. Holmes alone ___________ (rise, 1st PP) superior to petty influences. He ________ (hold, 2nd PP) his open note-book upon his knee, and from time to time he jotted down figures and memoranda in the light of his pocket-lantern.

Review 4E: Irregular Verbs

Find and correct the SIX errors in irregular verb usage in the following excerpt from *Mr. Popper's Penguins,* by Richard and Florence Atwater. Cross out the incorrect form and write the correct form above it.

The reason Mr. Popper was so absentminded was that he was always dreaming about far-away countries. He had never goed out of Stillwater. It would have be nice, he often thinked, if he could have saw something of the world.

Whenever he heared that a Polar movie was in town, he was the first person at the ticket-window, and often he sitted through three shows.

Review 4F: Misplaced Modifiers

Circle the misplaced adjective and adverb phrases in the following sentences. Draw an arrow to the place where each phrase should be.

The ring belonged to the man of silver.

With red roses, I gave the plants to the customer.

Behind the stadium of leather, she found a wallet.

Bri showed us pictures of her vacation after dinner.

He put a piece of toast on the plate with jam.

The bat ate the fruit with leathery wings.

Gina made with noodles chicken soup for her mom.

The bird ate from the feeder with red feathers.

Review 4G: Diagramming

Diagram the following sentences.

King's Day is an annual celebration in Amsterdam.

People gather and celebrate the monarch's birthday.

Citizens wear orange in honor of the House of Orange.

Some people in the celebrations dye their hair orange.

Vendors bake the celebrants a special pastry.

Tompouce is a puff pastry with cream filling.

The baker also tops the specialty with pink frosting.

Many boaters will decorate their vessels and sail down the canals of the city.

WEEK 13

Advanced Pronouns

— LESSON 49 —

Personal Pronouns
Antecedents
Possessive Pronouns

Lindsay woke up when Lindsay heard Lindsay's mother call Lindsay. Lindsay ate Lindsay's breakfast and brushed Lindsay's teeth and got ready for Lindsay's day.

A pronoun takes the place of a noun.
The antecedent is the noun that is replaced by the pronoun.

Personal Pronouns

	Singular	**Plural**
First person	I	we
Second person	you	you (plural)
Third person	he, she, it	they

Exercise 49A: Personal Pronouns and Antecedents

Circle the personal pronouns in the following sentences, adapted from *Commodore Perry in the Land of the Shogun*, by Rhoda Blumberg. Draw an arrow from each pronoun to the antecedent. In the margin, write the gender (*f*, *m*, or *n*) and number (*S* or *PL*) of each pronoun.

People panicked, and they carried valuables and furniture in all directions in order to hide from invading barbarians!

The Emperor Komei was isolated in the royal palace at Kyoto. Although he was worshiped as a divine descendent of the sun goddess, Amaterasu, he was a powerless puppet.

Commodore Matthew Calbraith Perry was in command of the squadron. He had not come to invade. He hoped to be a peacemaker.

Perry's mission was to unlock Japan's door. It had been slammed shut against all but a few Dutch and Chinese traders, the only ones officially allowed in for over 200 years.

Personal Pronouns (Full List)
I, me, my, mine

you, your, yours

he, she, him, her, it

his, hers, its

we, us, our, ours

they, them, their, theirs

Possessive Adjectives (same as Possessive Pronouns)

my	our
your	your
his, her, its	their

Peter's sword ________ sword

The Pevensie children's wardrobe ________ wardrobe

The tree's silver leaves ________ leaves

Lucy's cordial ________ cordial

The tree's silver leaves glistened.
Its silver leaves glistened.

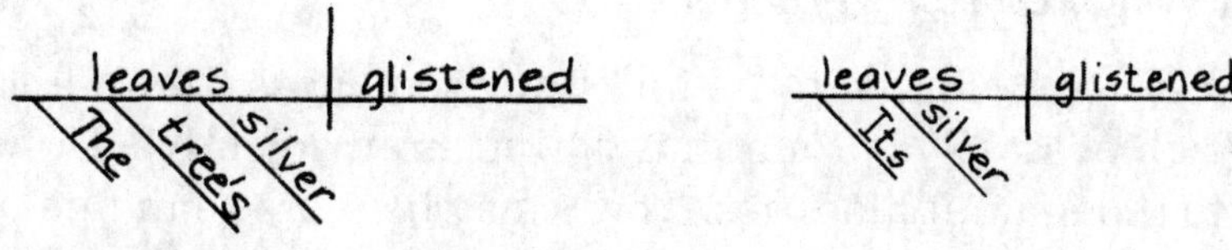

Lucy's cordial healed Edmund.

Her cordial healed Edmund.

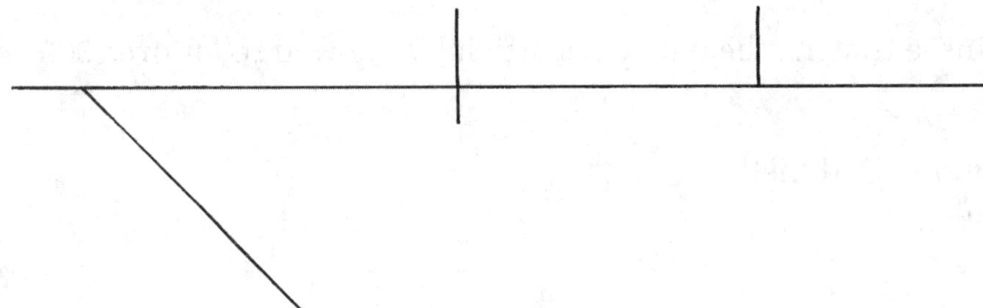

The chocolate is my candy.
The chocolate is mine candy.
The chocolate is mine!

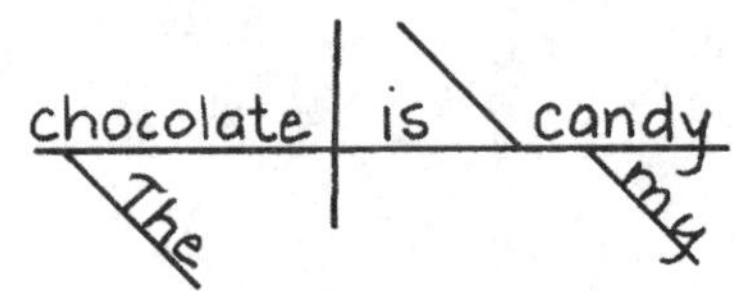

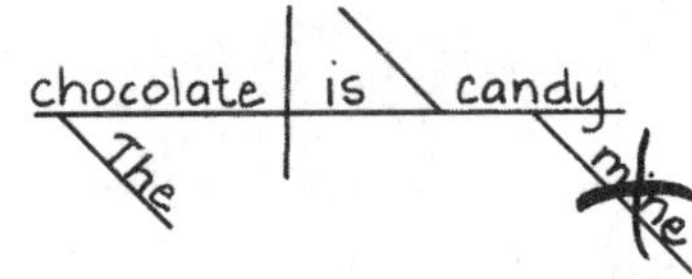

chocolate | is \ mine
The

He is your baby brother.
He is yours baby brother.
The baby brother is yours!

He | is \ brother
your baby

He | is \ brother
yours baby

brother | is \ yours
The baby

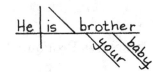

Exercise 49B: Identifying Possessive Pronouns

Underline the possessive pronouns in the following sentences from *Shiloh,* by Phyllis Reynolds Naylor. Each possessive pronoun is acting as an adjective. Draw an arrow from the pronoun to the noun it modifies. There may be more than one pronoun in each sentence.

Dara Lynn is dipping bread in her glass of cold tea, and Becky pushes her beans up over the edge of her plate in a rush to get them down.

I don't know anybody who likes him much, but folks around here like to keep to their own business.

Dara Lynn and Becky came up the lane with their packages.

The dog goes as far as the sycamore tree, lies down in the wet grass, head on his paws.

Exercise 49C: Using Possessive Pronouns

In the following sentences, write the correct possessive pronoun above the underlined noun(s).

Patrick and Catherine O'Leary lived in Chicago in the 1800s. They never imagined what legend would start because of the actions of Patrick and Catherine O'Leary's cow.

On the evening of October 8, 1871, an immense fire started in Chicago, and many people claim that it started when the O'Learys' cow kicked over a lantern in the barn, as Catherine was going about Catherine's evening chores.

The fire spread quickly, aided by Chicago's famous wind blowing down the streets and the fact that many of Chicago's buildings were made of wood.

When the fire was finally extinguished, over 300 people had lost the people's lives.

The city had also lost over 17,000 of the city's buildings.

Chicago began to rebuild and soon became known as an architectural wonder. Famous architect Frank Lloyd Wright built many of Frank Lloyd Wright's famous houses there.

For 25 years, the Sears Tower in Chicago held the record for being the tallest building in the world. People travelled from all over to get the people's pictures taken on the top floor of the tower.

Famous baseball player Babe Ruth once said of the baseball stadium, "I'd play for half Babe Ruth's salary if I could hit in Wrigley Field all the time."

American poet Carl Sandburg wrote a poem about Chicago, in which he answered critics, stating, "to those who sneer at this Carl Sandburg's city...proud to be Hog Butcher, Tool Maker, Stacker of Wheat, Player with Railroads and Freight Handler to the Nation."

Exercise 49D: Diagramming Possessive Pronouns

On your own paper, diagram every word in the following sentences, slightly adapted from *The Tale of Peter Rabbit*, by Beatrix Potter.

They lived with their Mother in a sand-bank, underneath the root of a very big fir tree.

Then old Mrs. Rabbit took a basket and her umbrella.

He got caught by the large buttons on his jacket.

— LESSON 50 —

Pronoun Case

Personal Pronouns (Full List)
I, me, my, mine
you, your, yours
he, she, him, her, it
his, hers, its
we, us, our, ours
they, them, their, theirs

My crown, I am; but still my griefs are mine.
—William Shakespeare, *Richard II*

Object pronouns are used as objects in sentences.
me, you, him, her, it, us, them

Mark each bolded pronoun as *DO*, *IO*, or *OP*.

For **me**, my lords, I love **him** not, nor fear **him.**
—William Shakespeare, *Henry VIII*

Give **us** notice of his inclination.
—William Shakespeare, *Richard III*

A virtuous and a Christian-like conclusion,/To pray for **them** that have done scathe to **us**.
—William Shakespeare, *Richard III*

Subject pronouns are used as subjects and predicate nominatives in sentences.
I, you, he, she, it, we, they

Mark each bolded pronoun as *S* or *PN*.

I am **he**.
—William Shakespeare, *Richard III*

Stand **we** in good array; for **they** no doubt,/Will issue out again and bid us battle.
—William Shakespeare, *Henry VI*

I blame her not, **she** could say little less;/**She** had the wrong. But what said Henry's queen?
—William Shakespeare, *Henry VI, Part III*

You need to learn grammar. I will teach you.

I met her at the park. She was wearing her jacket.

It is not very hard. I will learn it.

CORRECT	*INCORRECT*
I am he.	I am him.
The students are we.	The students are us.
The teachers are they.	The teachers are them.

The kitten licked Jim. The kitten licked _________.

The winners were Judy and Diane. The winners were _________.

OP OP
Give the prize to Madison and him. NOT: Give the prize to *he.*

S S
Dad and I made brownies. NOT: *Me* made brownies.

Exercise 50A: Subject and Object Pronouns

Underline all the personal pronouns in the following sentences. Identify them as *S* for subject, *O* for object, or *P* for possessive.

These sentences are from *Life on Surtsey: Iceland's Upstart Island,* by Loree Griffin Burns.

Iceland sits on the edge of the Arctic Circle, meaning it's cool. In winter, when the Arctic Circle is tilted away from the sun, Icelanders barely see it during the day. Glaciers, summer days that last twenty hours, and regular volcanic eruptions may sound extreme to you and me, but to the average Icelander, it is all pretty humdrum.

As kids, "we stayed outside all the time, when not doing our homework," said Erling Ólaffson, a resident of Iceland.

But on November 14, 1963, an epically unusual event shook the country. A volcano exploded under the sea—she gave birth to an island. When ash and cinder began to spew violently, all Iceland watched them. The materials settled back into the sea, the volcano's base grew wider, and its top grew taller.

Stories of the eruption spread. Erling read them in his local paper. Unlike most people, he could take in the drama from his house. The eruption cloud eventually stretched high enough to be clearly seen in Erling's town of Hafnarfjördur, and his family watched it from their windows.

"I could see smoke over the mountains to the southeast," Erling said. "We saw just a stable smoke column, with no movement. But there was something about it."

Exercise 50B: Using Personal Pronouns Correctly

Choose the correct word(s) in parentheses and cross out the incorrect choice(s). Be sure to choose the grammatically correct choice for writing and not the choice that sounds the best.

My mother and sister and (me/I) decided to take a trip to Prince Edward Island, Canada.

My sister researched train tickets for (us/we), and (me/I) booked a rental car for our stay on the island.

Mom gave (my sister and me/my sister and I) a bag of our favorite snacks for the trip.

During the train ride, (us/we) talked about the places on PEI that were most interesting to (us/we).

Once (us/we) left the train, Mom navigated the map for my sister while (her/she) drove the rental car all around the beautiful island.

The trip was magical and gave (us/we) wonderful memories together.

As Mom, my sister, and (me/I) journeyed back home, Mom commented that her favorite travel companions of all were (us/we).

Exercise 50C: Diagramming Personal Pronouns

On your own paper, diagram the following sentences. Personal pronouns are diagrammed exactly like the nouns or adjectives they replace.

I bought her a gift.

Do you see it?

His teammates were we.

It is she.

They showed us the quilts.

He won it!

— LESSON 51 —

Indefinite Pronouns

Gollum wanted the ring. He longed for it.
Everyone hoped that Frodo would succeed.

Indefinite pronouns are pronouns without antecedents.

Indefinite Pronouns
Singular

anybody	anyone	anything
everybody	everyone	everything
nobody	no one	nothing
somebody	someone	something
another	other	one
either	neither	each

Plural
both, few, many, several

Singular or Plural
all, any, most, none, some

All of the cake was eaten.

All of the pieces were eaten.

Most of the people . . .

None of the water . . .

All | was eaten
of
cake
the

All | were eaten
of
pieces
the

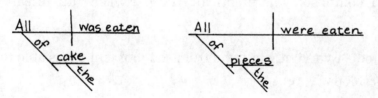

Many of the guests arrived early.

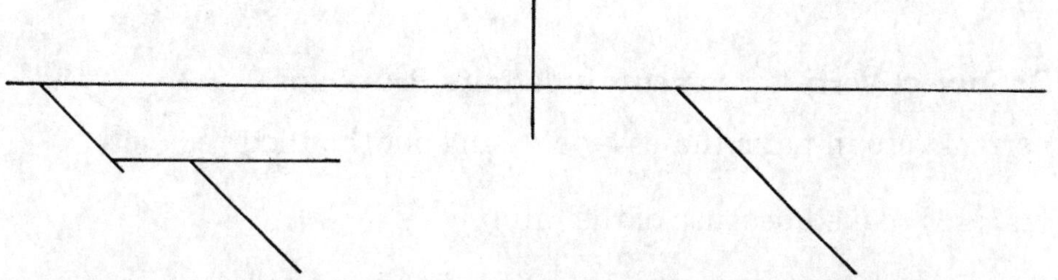

Many guests arrived early.

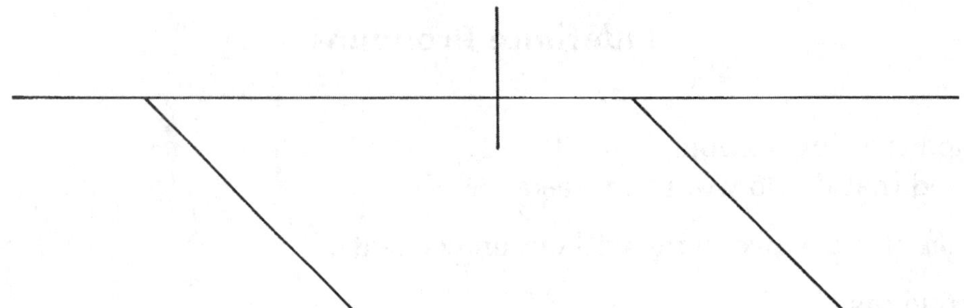

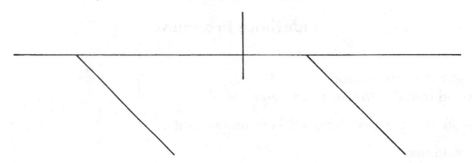

Exercise 51A: Identifying Indefinite Pronouns

Underline all of the indefinite pronouns in the following sentences. Each sentence may contain more than one pronoun.

These sentences are drawn from *Spooked!: How a Radio Broadcast and The War of the Worlds Sparked the 1938 Invasion of America*, by Gail Jarrow.

No one knew that a group of adults was plotting a different sort of mischief for October 30, 1938.

Men and some of the women would report back to their jobs, if they were lucky enough to have them.

His business in shambles, he decided he had nothing to lose.

Many had lost their houses and farms because they couldn't pay their debt.

One was organized, composed, and practical. Another was wildly creative, intense, and arrogant.

Welles later admitted, "Everybody told me from the moment I was able to hear that I was absolutely marvelous."

Someone in the family switched the radio on and twirled the dial to the evening's entertainment.

Exercise 51B: Subject-Verb Agreement: Indefinite Pronouns

Choose the correct verb in parentheses by crossing out the incorrect verb.

Everything (is/are) soaked because of the rain!

Most of the tree limbs (was/were) still intact on that giant oak.

Several of the garden plants (seems/seem) to be flattened.

Each of the cars (appears/appear) unscratched.

I saw that something (is/are) lying near the shed.

Someone from the family (needs/need) to check it.

On the roof, none of the shingles (was/were) damaged.

I checked on the chickens, and all of them (acts/act) like the storm never happened.

(Do/Does) anyone see the beautiful rainbow?

Exercise 51C: Diagramming Indefinite Pronouns

On your own paper, diagram the following sentences, which are all quotes from the works of William Shakespeare.

Nothing will come of nothing. (*King Lear*)
We shall part with neither. (*Comedy of Errors*)
All men make faults. ("Sonnet 35")
Both of you are birds of self-same feather. (*King Henry the Sixth*, Part III)
Few are angels. (*King Henry the Eighth*)

— LESSON 52 —

Personal Pronouns
Indefinite Pronouns

Personal Pronouns
I, me, my, mine
you, your, yours
he, she, him, her, it
his, hers, its
we, us, our, ours
they, them, their, theirs

Subject pronouns: ____

____

______________________ am delighted to be doing grammar.

______________________ are delighted to be doing grammar.

______________________ is delighted to be doing grammar.

Object pronouns: ____

____

The walrus splattered water all over ________________________.

The rain drenched Kim and ________________________________.

Possessive pronouns/possessive adjectives in attributive position: ____________________

____

I grabbed ___________________________________ umbrella.

The cloud began dropping _____________________ moisture.

The soaked tourists ran for ____________________ cars.

Possessive pronouns/possessive adjectives in predicate position: ______________________

____

That raincoat is ____________________________________.

Those waterproof ponchos are ________________________.

Indefinite pronouns are pronouns without antecedents.

Singular Indefinite Pronouns

anybody	anyone	anything
everybody	everyone	everything
nobody	no one	nothing
somebody	someone	something
another	other	one
either	neither	each

Everyone _________ in the kitchen.

Nobody ___________ in the dining room.

Neither of them ___________ in the garden.

Plural Indefinite Pronouns

both, few, many, several

Both _________ cooking eggplants.

A few of the crowd _________ objecting to eggplant.

Several _________ quite happy with the prospect of eggplant.

Singular or Plural Indefinite Pronouns

all, any, most, none, some

All of the fire engines _________ there.

All of the mansion _________ destroyed in the fire.

Is everyone coming to get _________ Christmas present?

____

Are they all coming to get their Christmas presents?

Exercise 52A: Subject and Object Pronouns

In the following sentences, cross out the incorrect pronoun.

These sentences are adapted from *Moon Over Manifest*, by Clare Vanderpool.

The movement of the train rocked (I/me) like a lullaby.

(I/Me) closed my eyes to the dusty countryside and imagined the sign (I/me) knew only from stories.

(He/Him) does his best talking in stories, but in recent weeks, those had become few and far between.

When (I/me) was younger, (we/us) spent many a walking hour singing, making up rhymes, playing kick the can.

Uncle Henry won't mind giving (they/them) away to someone who actually wants to read (they/them).

The chain of that broken compass was long enough to stretch all the way back into his pocket, with (he/him) at one end and (I/me) at the other.

You can count on (I/me) to be truthful and certifiable in giving the honest-to-goodness scoop each and every week.

"We just figured (I/you) might like to meet some of the kids before (they/them) scatter to the four winds for the summer."

"(We/Us)'ll just head into town, then, as I need to pick up a letter for (we/us)."

Now, Gideon and (I/me) had been to many church services.

A proper-looking lady sat quietly in a rocking chair on the porch, not having the life in (she/her) to rock.

Maybe that was how I found comfort just then, even with (he/him) so far away.

I didn't know anything about Hattie Mae Harper, except what (she/her) wrote in her article.

I wondered how many of (they/them) I was up against.

But mostly (I/me) could taste the sadness in his voice when (he/him) told (I/me) (I/me) couldn't stay with him for the summer.

Exercise 52B: Possessive and Indefinite Pronouns

In these sentences, taken from *Further Chronicles of Avonlea*, by L. M. Montgomery, cross out the incorrect word in each set of parentheses.

"You should know that perfectly well, Mr. Patterson, better than anyone (does / do)."

Some (pities / pity) him.

The sound makes Christopher look up. Something in her face (irritates / irritate) him.

The little gray house, so close to the purring waves that in storms (its / their) spray splashed over (its / their) very doorstep, seemed deserted.

I hoped that spring might work (its / their) miracle upon her.

Although that scheme is not much good in Avonlea, where everybody (knows / know) your age.

None of the men in Glenby (was / were) good enough for her.

Naomi relaxed (her / their) grip on the girl's arm and sank back exhausted on the pillow.

"You (is / are) so good at understanding. Very few (is / are)."

All (was / were) enjoying themselves hugely.

We went down the road between the growths of young fir that bordered it. I smelled (its / their) balsam as we passed.

Each of the men (was / were) mutely imploring (his / their) neighbor to speak.

Everything (has / have) gone wrong.

Few of the Lincolns or Carewes (marries / marry) young, many not at all.

What was it? Was I, too, going mad, or WAS there something out there—(its / their) cries and moans, (its / their) longing for human love, yet ever retreating from human footsteps?

Many testimonies followed, each infused with the personality of the giver. Most of them (was / were) brief and stereotyped.

"If I cannot invite my father to see me married, no one (is / are) invited."

He said nothing—then or at any other time. From that day no reference to his wife or (her / their) concerns ever crossed his lips.

Several of her little playmates (has / have) gone to the harbor.

Exercise 52C: Writing Sentences from Diagrams

Use the diagrams below to reconstruct these sentences from *The Story of the World, Volume 1: Ancient Times*, by Susan Wise Bauer.

Write the original sentence on the blank below each diagram. Pay careful attention to each part of speech! Punctuate each sentence properly.

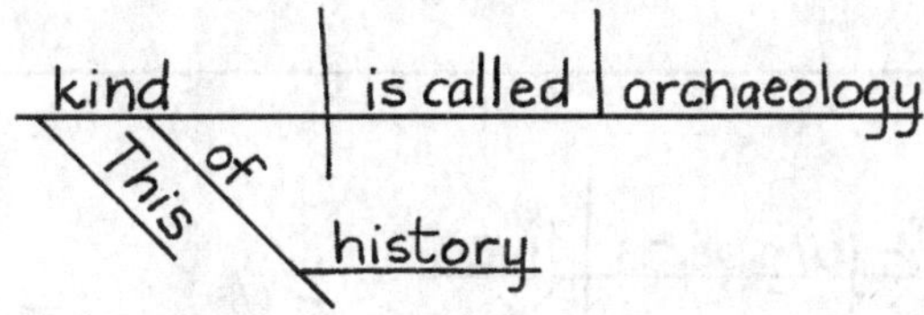

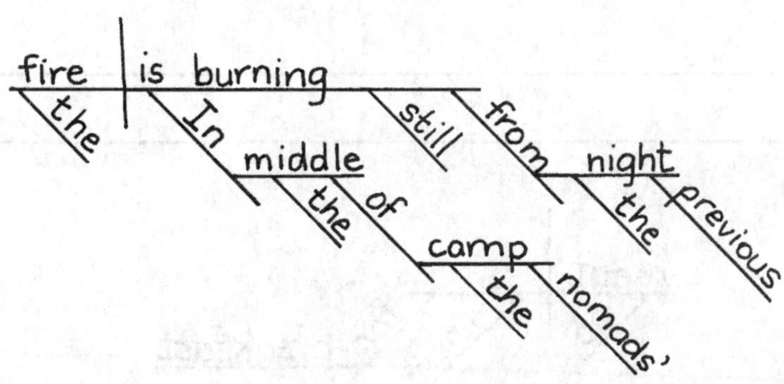

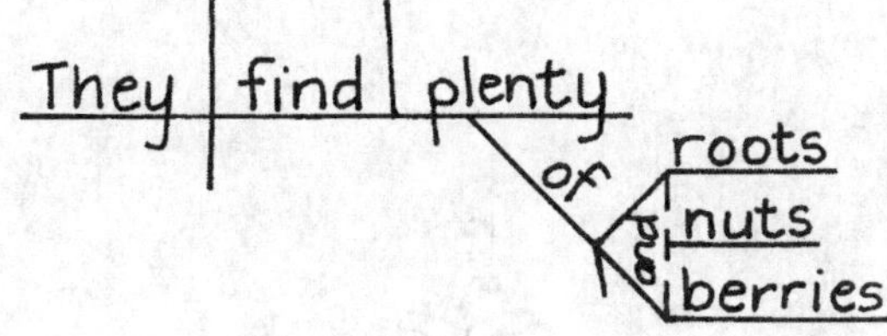

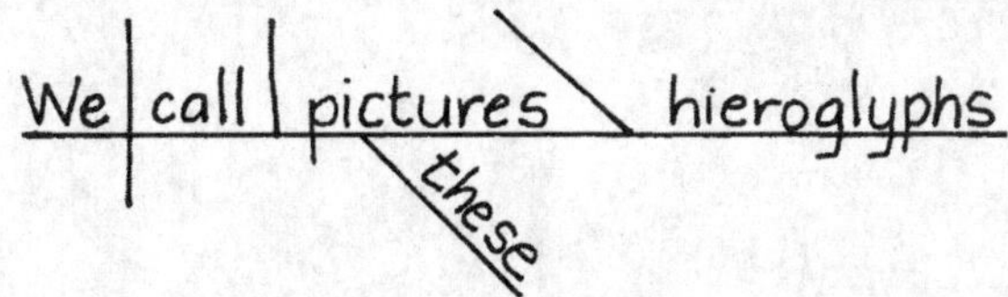

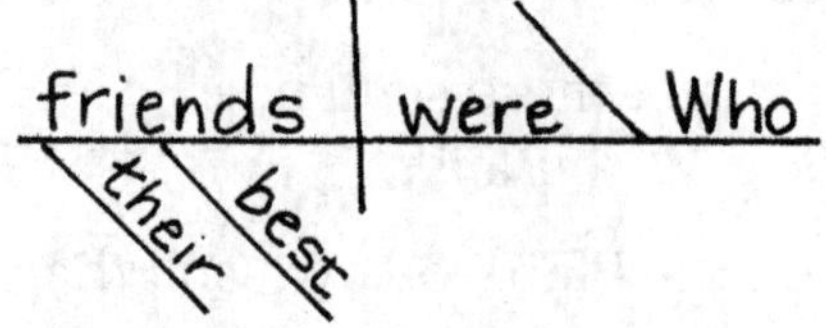
friends
were
Who
their
best

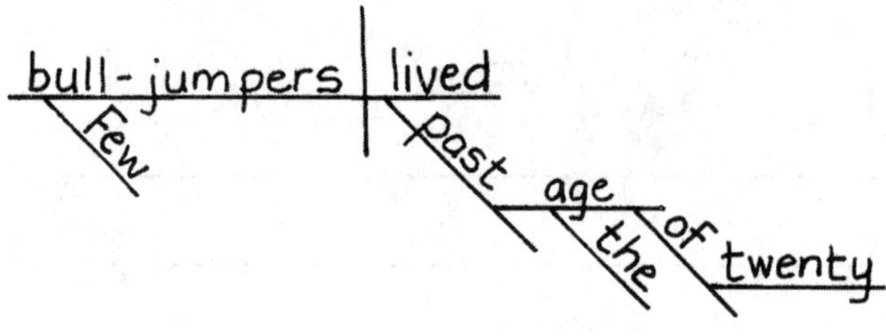
bull-jumpers
lived
Few
past
age
the
of
twenty

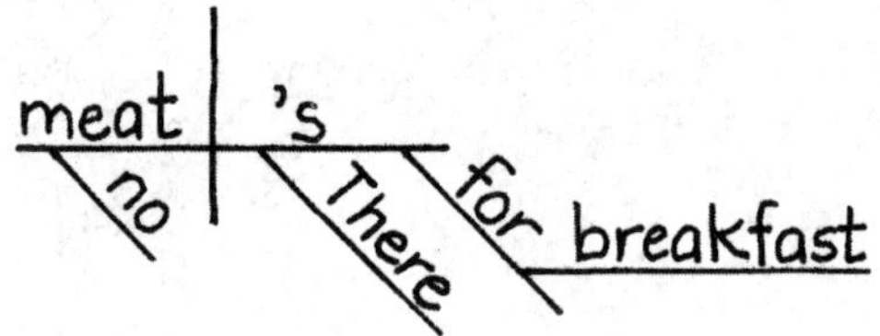
meat
's
no
There
for
breakfast

WEEK 14

Active and Passive Voice

— LESSON 53 —

Principal Parts
Troublesome Verbs

She set the set of sorted stuff
Beside the seat where she had sat.

English verbs have three principal parts.
The first principal part is the simple present.
The second principal part is the simple past.
The third principal part of a verb is found by dropping the helping verb from the perfect past.

Exercise 53A: Principal Parts of Verbs

Fill in the chart with the missing forms.

	First Principal Part Present	Second Principal Part Past	Third Principal Part Past Participle
I	decide		
I		sipped	
I		sold	
I			emptied
I	beat		
I			grown
I	become		
I		fought	

Troublesome Irregular Verbs

Verb	Principal Parts	Definition
sit	(sit, sat, sat)	to rest or be seated
set	(set, set, set)	to put or place something
lie	(lie, lay, lain)	to rest or recline
lay	(lay, laid, laid)	to put or place something
rise	(rise, rose, risen)	to get up or go up
raise	(raise, raised, raised)	to cause something to go up or grow up
let	(let, let, let)	to allow
leave	(leave, left, left)	to go away from or allow to remain

Exercise 53B: Using Correct Verbs

Choose the correct verb in parentheses. Cross out the incorrect verb.

The first thing we needed to do on our camping trip was to (set/sit) the tent up at our campsite.

Meg (let/leaved) me start the process. She had (lay/laid) out the equipment for fishing.

I (rose/raised) the tent poles and Meg helped me (set/sit) the sleeping bags inside.

We decided to (let/leave) the site and explore the lake.

I enjoyed (setting/sitting) by the water and waiting for the fish to bite.

Once we caught enough for our dinner, we headed back to camp and (set/sit) the wood in place for the campfire.

After we ate, we enjoyed (lying/laying) on the grass and naming the constellations we saw twinkling above us.

In the morning, I (set/sat) by the fire and (set/sat) the coffeepot over the flames.

Meg (rose/raised) from her sleeping bag and joined me for breakfast. We would (let/leave) the sun rise a bit more and then begin our hike.

Exercise 53C: Correct Forms of Troublesome Verbs

Fill in the blanks with the correct form of the indicated verb. The sentences are adapted from Mark Twain's *Autobiography of Mark Twain*.

He said that easier times would come by and by, and that the money could then be ________________ no doubt, and that he would enter into it cheerfully and with zeal and carry it through to the very best of his ability. (raise, simple past)

Mr. Rogers had _____________ Mrs. Clemens and me have our way. (let, past participle)

The best place of all to see the procession was, of course, from this rostrum, so I sauntered upon that rostrum, while as yet it was empty, and _____________ there. (sit, simple past)

In the summer they ___________ the table in the middle of that shady and breezy floor, and the sumptuous meals—well, it makes me cry to think of them. (set, simple past)

But I had checked myself there; for that way had ___________ madness. (lay, past participle)

That lady still ________________ in her bed at the principal hotel in Washington, disabled by the shock. (lie, simple present)

At last we all ________________ by one blessed impulse and went down to the street door without explanations—in a pile, and no precedence; and so parted. (rise, simple past)

Exercise 53D: Proofreading for Correct Verb Usage

The following excerpts are from *Little House in the Big Woods,* by Laura Ingalls Wilder. Find and correct fifteen errors in verb usage by crossing out the incorrect verbs and writing the correct forms above them. Be careful—some sentences might have more than one!

Then she mixed the pot-liquor with it and sat it away in a pan to cool. When it was cold it would be cutted in slices.

At night when Laura lie awake in the trundle bed, she listened and could not heard anything at all but the sound of the trees whispering together.

A wagon track runned before the house, but the little girl did not know where it gone.

Then they leaved the fire go out, and Pa took all the strips and pieces of meat out of the hollow tree. After that, they leaved it hanging to cool.

One night her father picked her up and carried her to the window so that she might saw the wolves. Two of them sitted in front of the house.

But she was safe inside the solid log walls. Good old Jack, the brindle bulldog, lied on guard in front of the door.

Then he lied away the traps, and he taked his fiddle out of its box and beginned to play.

The garden behind the house had been growing all summer. At night Jack keeped the deer away.

— LESSON 54 —

Verb Tense

Active and Passive Voice

past	simple
present	progressive
future	perfect

A simple verb simply tells whether an action takes place in the past, present, or future.
A progressive verb describes an ongoing or continuous action.
A perfect verb describes an action which has been completed before another action takes place.

Exercise 54A: Reviewing Tenses

Write the tense of each underlined verb above it. This excerpt is adapted from *The Story of a Great Schoolmaster*, by H. G. Wells. The first is done for you.

simple past

I knew him personally only during the last eight years of his life; I met him for the first time in 1914, when I was proposing to send my sons to his school. But our thoughts and interests drew us very close to one another, I have never missed an opportunity of meeting and talking to him, and I was the last person he spoke to before his sudden death. He was sixty-six years of age when he died. Those last eight years were certainly the richest and most productive of his whole career; he grew most in those years; he travelled farthest. I think I saw all the best of him. It is, I think, no disadvantage that I have known him only in his boldest and most characteristic phase. It saves me from confusion between his maturer and his earlier phases. He was a much stratified man. He had grown steadfastly all his life, he had shaken off many habitual inhibitions and freed himself from once necessary restraints and limitations. He was, I recall, a rock-climber; he was a mental rock-climber also, and though he was very wary of recalcitrance, there were times when his pace became so urgent that even his staff and his own family were tugging, breathless and perplexed, at the rope.

The door had been fastened upon the inner side, and the windows were blocked by old-fashioned shutters with broad iron bars.

He fastened the door upon the inner side.

In a sentence with an active verb, the subject performs the action.
In a sentence with a passive verb, the subject receives the action.

I punched you.
You were punched by me.

The Egyptians constructed pyramids.
Pyramids were constructed.
Pyramids were constructed by the Egyptians.

Active Verb	Passive Verb
Present Freddy tricks the alligator.	**is/are + past participle** The alligator is tricked by Freddy.
Past Freddy tricked the alligator.	**was/were + past participle** The alligator was tricked by Freddy.
Future Freddy will trick the alligator.	**will be + past participle** The alligator will be tricked by Freddy.
Progressive Present Freddy is tricking the alligator.	**is/are being + past participle** The alligator is being tricked by Freddy.
Progressive Past Freddy was tricking the alligator.	**was/were being + past participle** The alligator was being tricked by Freddy.
***Progressive Future** Freddy will be tricking the alligator.	***will be being + past participle** The alligator will be being tricked by Freddy.
Perfect Present Freddy has tricked the alligator.	**has/have been + past participle** The alligator has been tricked by Freddy.
Perfect Past Freddy had tricked the alligator.	**had been + past participle** The alligator had been tricked by Freddy.
Perfect Future Freddy will have tricked the alligator.	**will have been + past participle** The alligator will have been tricked by Freddy.

*The passive form of progressive future verbs is awkward and not often used.

State-of-being verbs do not have voice.

Exercise 54B: Distinguishing Between Active and Passive Voice

Identify the following sentences as *A* for active or *P* for passive. If you're not sure, ask yourself: Is the subject *doing* the verb, or is the verb *happening* to the subject?

The Great Wall of China was built during the time of the Ming Dynasty. ________

The idea for the wall was imagined by Emperor Qin Shi. ________

The people of China wanted to deter invaders. ________

The Great Wall runs over 5,000 miles of China's mountainous land. ________

The wall was created from stones and dirt. ________

The wall is made of several smaller walls linked together. ________

Much of the wall has been destroyed by the elements over the centuries. ________

During the wall's history, many dynasties repaired the crumbling structure. ________

Guard towers were erected at various points along the way. ________

Many times, merchants used the wall for travel. ________

Soldiers were deployed to protect the travelers. ________

The Three Inner Passes and Three Outer Passes were set along the wall. ________

These passes were heavily fortified. ________

Each year, over 10 million people visit the Great Wall. ________

The wall varies in height from 20 to 23 feet. ________

A car can be driven over the widest portions. ________

Runners can experience this historical site in the annual Great Wall Marathon. ________

Exercise 54C: Forming the Active and Passive Voice

Fill in the chart below, rewriting each sentence so that it appears in both the active and the passive voice. Be sure to keep the tense the same. The first is done for you.

ACTIVE	PASSIVE
A ballet dancer will often progress to pointe shoes after several years of hard work.	Pointe shoes are often progressed to after several years of hard work by a ballet dancer.
	The shoes' tips are formed by strong glue, cardboard, and fabric.

ACTIVE	PASSIVE
Prima ballerinas may go through a pair of pointe shoes in one performance.	
A dancer must strengthen her feet and ankles for pointe shoes.	
	Pointe shoes were first used in the 1800s.
	Some portions of the shoes are sewn on by the ballerinas themselves.

— LESSON 55 —

Parts of the Sentence
Active and Passive Voice

These sentences are adapted from *Treasury of American Indian Tales,* by Theodore Whitson Ressler.

Many traditional stories were related to him by his friends.

Little Rabbit lived a very happy and carefree life.

His mother and father were standing over him.

Someone or something was moving nearby.

Suddenly, Little Thunderbird felt very much alone.

— LESSON 56 —

Active and Passive Voice
Transitive and Intransitive Verbs

Active Voice	Passive Voice
Present	**am/is/are + past participle**
The farmer grows wheat.	Wheat is grown by the farmer.

Past	**was/were + past participle**
I made a cake.	The cake was made by me.
Future	**will be + past participle**
The princess will keep the key.	The key will be kept by the princess.
Progressive Present	**is/are being + past participle**
The farmer is growing wheat.	Wheat is being grown by the farmer.
Progressive Past	**was/were being + past participle**
I was making a cake.	The cake was being made by me.
Progressive Future	**will be being + past participle**
The princess will be keeping the key.	The key will be being kept by the princess.
Perfect Present	**has/have been + past participle**
The farmer has grown wheat.	Wheat has been grown by the farmer.
Perfect Past	**had been + past participle**
I had made a cake.	The cake had been made by me.
Perfect Future	**will have been + past participle**
The princess will have kept the key.	The key will have been kept by the princess.

I laugh out loud.
The baby slept soundly.
The queen will sit in the front row.
He died.

transire (Latin for "to pass over")

Transitive verbs express action that is received by some person or thing.
Intransitive verbs express action that is not received by any person or thing.

Common Intransitive Verbs

cough	go	arrive
sit	lie	rise
shine	sneeze	am, is, are, was, were

Common Transitive Verbs

love	eat	help
set	lay	raise
cut	hug	save

I am sitting on the front porch.
I lay down on the grass.
I will have risen early in the morning.

I am setting the heavy box down.
I laid my weary head on my arms.
I will have raised my hand at least once by the end of class.

Verbs That Can Be Used as Transitive or Intransitive

turn	break	speak
fly	run	spread

taste eat sing

The cook turns the meat on the spit.

I will spread gochujang mayonnaise on the burger bun.

He is singing a difficult aria.

The captain turned towards the sunset.

The mist spread across the river's surface.

He's singing in the shower.

The cook turns the meat on the spit.

____

I will spread gochujang mayonnaise on the burger bun.

____

He is singing a difficult aria.

____

Exercise 56A: Transitive and Intransitive Verbs

Underline each verb serving as a predicate in the following sentences. Write *T* above each transitive verb and *IT* above each intransitive verb. Circle the direct object of each transitive verb. If the transitive verb is passive, draw an arrow from the verb back to the subject to show that the subject receives the action of the verb.

These sentences are adapted from *Biology and Its Makers*, by William A. Locy.

Aristotle founded his Natural History only on observation of the structure, physiology, and development of animals.

Soon after the period of Aristotle the center of scientific investigation transferred to Alexandria.

Here mathematics and geography flourished, but natural history was little cultivated.

Ptolemy had erected a great museum and founded a large public library in Alexandria.

Aristotle founded his system of classification on a plan of organization.

Pliny replaced it by a highly artificial one, with a foundation of the incidental circumstance of the abodes of animals— in air, water, or on the earth.

The establishment of Harvey's view replaced Galen's view on the movement of the blood.

In 1597, Harvey graduated with an arts degree.

The ancients spoke of spirits and humors in the body.

His discovery created modern physiology.

For the first time ever in print, his book demonstrated the movement of blood in the body in a circuit.

The heartbeat supplied the propelling force.

The notochord occurred in all vertebrate animals.

Pasteur might have remained in this field of investigation.

Pasteur won his first scientific recognition at the age of twenty-five, in chemistry and molecular physics.

He applied his discoveries to the cure and prevention of diseases.

More than thirty "Pasteur institutes," with aims similar to the parent institution, have been established in different parts of the civilized world.

Exercise 56B: Active and Passive Verbs

In the blanks below, rewrite each sentence with an active verb so that the verb is passive. Rewrite each sentence with a passive verb so that the verb is active. You may need to add or rearrange words or phrases to make the sentences grammatical!

These sentences are slightly adapted from *Hanukkah for Kids*, by Leanne Annett.

Jewish families often eat sufganiyah, a jelly donut, during Hanukkah.

____

____

Many sufganiyot are coated in soft, powdered icing sugar.

____

____

Children may be given money and presents from their friends and relatives.

____

____

Often small chocolate coins are given as presents to the children as well.

____

____

The Hanukkah Menorah symbolizes the ancient temple and its Menorah.

____

____

One candle on the Menorah is lit each day.

____

____

Many people call Hanukkah "the Festival of Lights."

____

____

Exercise 56C: Diagramming

On your own paper, diagram every word in the following sentences. They are slightly adapted from *Chile: A Primary Source Cultural Guide*, by Jason Porterfield and Corona Brezina.

The Andes Mountains form a wall on the eastern side of Chile.

Chile's short rivers are unnavigable and full of rapids and cascades.

Much of Chile's folk tradition originated in Mapuche spiritual beliefs.

People placed dark stone and earth on hillsides and created geoglyphs.

WEEK 15

Specialized Pronouns

— LESSON 57 —

Parts of Speech
Parts of the Sentence
Intensive and Reflexive Pronouns

Anita made herself a huge brownie sundae!

Reflexive pronouns refer back to the subject.
Usually, reflexive pronouns act like objects.

Part of speech is a term that explains what a word does.
Part of the sentence is a term that explains how a word functions in a sentence.

He adapted himself to their knowledge.
He gave himself a task.
He praises in himself what he blames in others.

myself, himself, herself, itself, yourself, yourselves, ourselves, themselves

Intensive pronouns emphasize a noun or another pronoun.

The Queen of England herself gave the speech.
The Queen of England gave the speech herself.

DO
The Queen of England gave herself.

IO
The Queen of England gave herself the speech.

OP
The Queen of England gave the speech to herself.

Aristotle himself observed these variations.

He jumped into the sea and drowned himself.

Aristotle (himself) | observed | variations
these

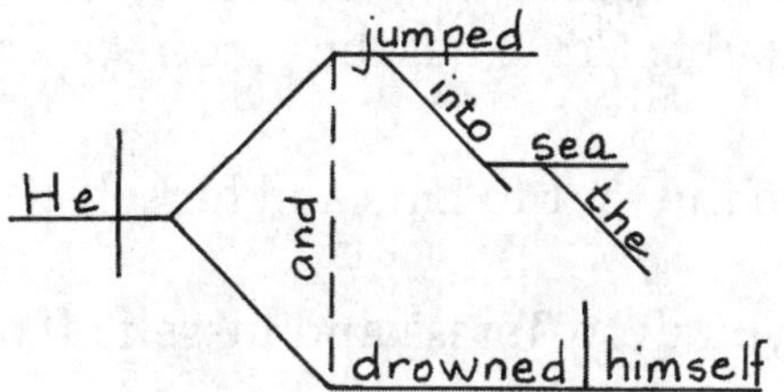

Do NOT use theirselves, hisself, or ourself.

Diana and myself cooked a casserole.
Diana and I cooked a casserole.
I myself cooked a casserole.
Take care of yourself.

Exercise 57A: Identifying Intensive and Reflexive Pronouns

Underline the intensive and reflexive pronouns in the following sentences. Above each pronoun, write *I* for intensive or *R* for reflexive. If the pronoun is reflexive, also mark it as *DO* (direct object), *IO* (indirect object), or *OP* (object of the preposition). The first is done for you.

R IO
She gave herself the gift of a trip for her birthday.

The class presented their project to the author himself.

Did you write that song yourself?

Isaias wants to ride in the backseat by himself.

The lab's roof collapsed on itself.

Mom bought herself a new car.

The actors themselves had no idea that the microphones were out.

We reserved the beach chairs for ourselves.

I myself have not finished the homework.

Please take out the trash yourself.

The elephants protected themselves from predators by circling around each other.

Exercise 57B: Using Intensive and Reflexive Pronouns Correctly

Each of the following sentences contains errors in the usage of intensive and reflexive pronouns. Cross out the incorrect word and write the correction above it.

I gave the tour to Luis and herself.

Did you drop Teresa and hisself off at the airport?

I ate the whole bag of chips myselves!

Ashleigh and Tina moved the couch theirselves.

The penguin hisself guarded the egg.

Irena asked Antonio and herself where they had found the book.

Exercise 57C: Diagramming Intensive and Reflexive Pronouns

On your own paper, diagram every word in the following sentences.

The valedictorian walked herself to the podium with great confidence.
I found the clue itself on an old piece of paper.
After their slideshow, I approved the plan myself.
The queen drove herself to her country estate.

— LESSON 58 —

Demonstrative Pronouns
Demonstrative Adjectives

Questions	Punch lines
What did the teacher say to make the student eat his quiz?	That opens up a whole new can of worms.
What did the customer in the butcher shop hear that scared him?	This will be a piece of cake!
What did the fisherman say when he dropped his bucket of bait?	These cost an arm and a leg.

Demonstrative pronouns demonstrate or point out something. They can take the place of a single word or a group of words.

this, that, these, those

"Your cousin wrote this," said Aunt Alexandra. "He was a beautiful character."

"Didn't know it was this dark. Didn't look like it'd be this dark earlier in the evening."

Demonstrative adjectives modify nouns and answer the question *which one*.

That was the only time I ever heard Atticus say it was a sin to do something . . .

"I destroyed his last shred of credibility at that trial, if he had any to begin with."

It was times like these when I thought my father, who hated guns and had never been to any wars, was the bravest man who ever lived.

I was beginning to notice a subtle change in my father these days, that came out when he talked with Aunt Alexandra.

"Dill, those were his own witnesses."

Mrs. Merriweather was one of those childless adults who find it necessary to assume a different tone of voice when speaking to children.

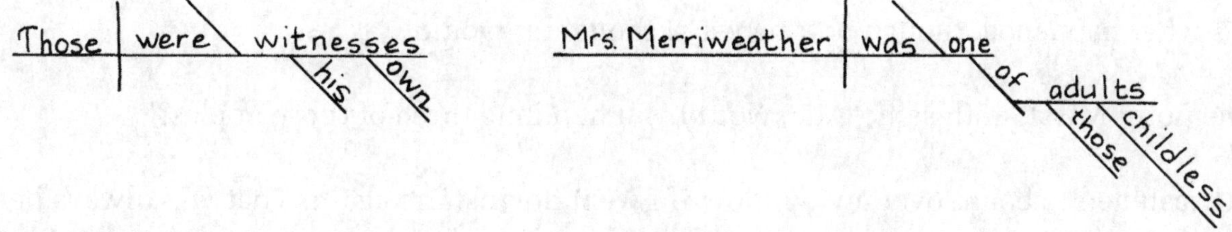

(The above sentences are from *To Kill a Mockingbird*, by Harper Lee.)

Did you see the coaster? That is one scary ride.

Raindrops on roses and whiskers on kittens, bright copper kettles and warm woolen mittens, brown paper packages tied up with strings–these are a few of my favorite things.

Exercise 58A: Demonstrative Pronouns and Demonstrative Adjectives

In the sentences below, label every occurrence of *this, that, these,* and *those* as either *DP* (demonstrative pronoun) or *DA* (demonstrative adjective). Draw an arrow from each demonstrative adjective to the noun it modifies. Label each demonstrative pronoun as *S* (subject), *DO* (direct object), *IO* (indirect object), or *OP* (object of the preposition).

These sentences are taken from *The War That Saved My Life*, by Kimberly Brubaker Bradley.

This story I'm telling starts out four years ago, at the beginning of the summer of 1939.

In the morning, though, those first words stuck in my head until I couldn't stand it anymore.

But I wouldn't lie about this.

It was just the two of us that morning, Mam gone I don't know where.

"Pretty soon you'll be going to school anyhow," I said, astonished I hadn't fully realized this before.

It seemed impossible, but all these men had come from one ship.

"These are the ornaments Becky and I put on our trees together."

I'd become a fighter, that summer.

That's what happened, though not the way I thought it would.

At one point Miss Smith said, "Ada, would you hand me three of those apples?"

She threatened to board over my window if I went downstairs again. That was always her threat to me.

The instant I said that, everything changed.

Her eyes narrowed. "I don't know what you're up to, girl. I don't know where you got all these words."

We were riding again, but this time we took a path Maggie chose, through the woods, down to the beach.

Exercise 58B: Demonstrative Pronouns

In the blank beneath each sentence, write a possible description of the thing or person that the underlined demonstrative pronoun stands for. Make sure to choose the correct number. (And use your imagination.)

This smells horrible!

Mom was delighted by those!

That seems like it would be scary.

These are ripe.

Exercise 58C: Diagramming

On your own paper, diagram every word in the following three sentences.

Before the storm, the mayor herself will describe this new evacuation plan for the city.

Where should I put these books and those supplies?

Some of that is on her mind.

— LESSON 59 —

Demonstrative Pronouns
Demonstrative Adjectives
Interrogative Pronouns
Interrogative Adjectives

Interrogative pronouns take the place of nouns in questions.

who, whom, whose, which, what

"Who started this?" said Uncle Jack.
"Talk like what in front of whom?" he asked.
Whose is that blanket?
Which is correct?

Whose blanket is missing?
What madness is this?
Which shoes are yours?

Interrogative adjectives modify nouns.

REMEMBER #1: Don't confuse *whose* and *who's.*

Whose orange flip-flops are those?	*Interrogative pronoun*
Who's cooking dinner?	*Contraction of* who is

I don't know whose/who's coming to dinner.

Whose/who's plate is still empty?

REMEMBER #2: Use *whom* as an object and *who* as a subject or predicate nominative.

CORRECT

Who started this?	*She started this. They started this. I started this. Jack started this.*
Talk like what in front of whom?	*In front of him? In front of her? In front of them? In front of Jack?*

Whom/Who is calling?

To whom/who did you speak?

REMEMBER #3: Diagram interrogative adjectives like any other adjective, and diagram interrogative pronouns like any other pronoun.

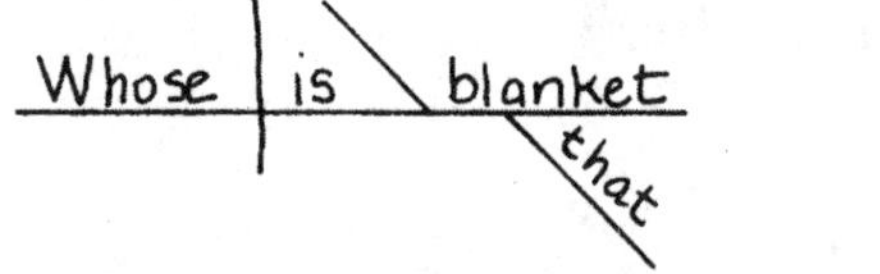

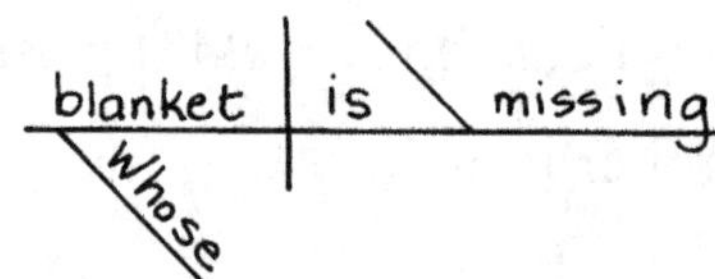

Exercise 59A: Identifying Demonstrative and Interrogative Pronouns

Underline all of the demonstrative and interrogative pronouns in the sentences. There may be more than one in each sentence.

These sentences are taken from *Alice's Adventures in Wonderland,* by Lewis Carroll.

"The March Hare will be much the most interesting, and perhaps as this is May it won't be raving mad—at least not so mad as it was in March." As she said this, she looked up, and there was the Cat again, sitting on a branch of a tree.

"I'm sure those are not the right words," said poor Alice, and her eyes filled with tears again as she went on.

"Beautiful Soup! Who cares for fish, game, or any other dish? Who would not give all else for two pennyworth only of beautiful Soup?"

"Why, what are *your* shoes done with?" said the Gryphon. "I mean, what makes them so shiny?"

"And now which is which?" she said to herself, and nibbled a little of the right-hand bit to try the effect.

First came ten soldiers carrying clubs; these were all shaped like the three gardeners, oblong and flat, with their hands and feet at the corners: next the ten courtiers; these were ornamented all over with diamonds, and walked two and two, as the soldiers did.

"I haven't the least idea what you're talking about," said Alice.

"Who is to give the prizes?" quite a chorus of voices asked.

Exercise 59B: Using Interrogative and Demonstrative Pronouns Correctly

Choose the correct word in parentheses. Cross out the incorrect word.

(Whose / Who's) coming to the beach with us today?

(Whose / Who's) towel is missing?

(Who / Whom) did you ask to meet us there?

With (who / whom) are you sharing a raft?

(This / These) are your fins, and (this / these) is your snorkel.

(That / Those) are mine.

(Whose / Who's) going in the water first?

(Who / Whom) wants to build a sandcastle?

(This / These) are strong waves!

(Who / What) should we eat first?

(Who / Whom) did you ask to swim?

(This / These) was a wonderful day together!

Exercise 59C: Diagramming Interrogative and Demonstrative Pronouns

On your own paper, diagram the following sentences.

Which is the right book for Algebra?

I must sweep that porch and those steps.

Whose is that beautiful garden?

Who made this?

She said that?

What is your name?

We laughed about this and that.

— LESSON 60 —

Pronoun Review

Sentences Beginning with Adverbs

A pronoun takes the place of a noun.
An antecedent is the noun that is replaced by the pronoun.

Personal Pronouns
I, me, my, mine
you, your, yours
he, she, him, her, it
his, hers, its
we, us, our, ours
they, them, their, theirs

Indefinite pronouns are pronouns without antecedents.

Singular

anybody	anyone	anything
everybody	everyone	everything
nobody	no one	nothing
somebody	someone	something
another	other	one
either	neither	each

Plural

both	few	many	several

Singular or Plural

all	any	most	none	some

Reflexive pronouns refer back to the subject.
myself, himself, herself, itself, yourself, yourselves, ourselves, themselves

She tripped and hurt herself.
She herself tripped.

Intensive pronouns emphasize a noun or another pronoun.

Demonstrative pronouns demonstrate or point out something. They can take the place of a single word or a group of words.
this, that, these, those

Interrogative pronouns take the place of nouns in questions.
who, whom, whose, which, what

Interrogative adjectives modify nouns.

What are you doing? Don't you know what direction to go?

That is she.
What is that?
Which is yours?
Where are you?
There you are.
So it is.

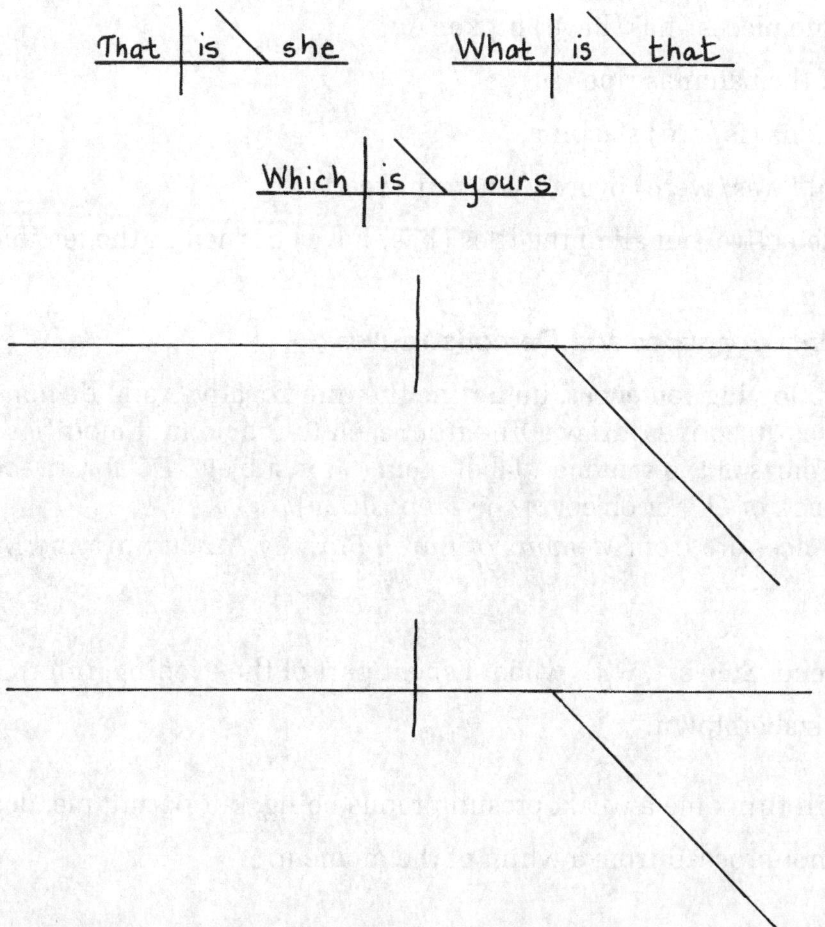

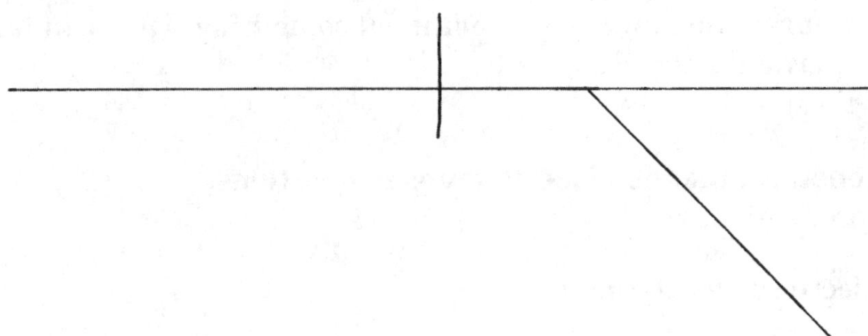

Exercise 60A: Singular/Plural Indefinite Pronouns

Cross out the incorrect verb in each sentence.

All of the competitors (was / were) at the field.

Most of the storm (has / have) passed.

None of the casserole (is / are) eaten.

Some of her game pieces (has / have) broken.

(Is / Are) any of the bananas ripe?

Some of the kittens (is / are) sleeping.

Most of the yard (was / were) overgrown with weeds.

I spoke to the detective, but all of the files (has / have) burned in the terrible fire.

Exercise 60B: Interrogatives and Demonstratives

In each of the following sentences, underline the interrogatives and demonstratives. If they are acting as adjectives, draw a line from each to the noun it modifies. If they are acting as other parts of the sentence, label them (*S* for subject, *DO* for direct object, *IO* for indirect object, or *OP* for object of the preposition).

These sentences are from *Memoirs of Aaron Burr*, by Aaron Burr and Matthew L. Davis.

Our mutual friend, Stewart, with whom I spent part of the evening, informed me you were still in Elizabethtown.

Perhaps you will think me a weak, presumptuous being; but permit me, dear sir, to assure you, this does not proceed from a whim of the moment.

Many of these letters, thus written, are now in existence.

I felt myself interested in the welfare of the province whose constitution you are now framing.

The armies were separated by a range of hills, at that time covered with wood, called the Heights of Gowannus.

What expeditions are on hand?

I have withdrawn abruptly. I would conceal that which I had not confidence to communicate.

What then will be your substitute?

Exercise 60C: Diagramming Practice

On your own paper, diagram every word of the following sentences, also taken from *Memoirs of Aaron Burr.*

What storms and tempests should I have avoided?

There is no better man.

Tryon ran and in his haste left all of his cattle and plunder behind him.

He spent much of his leisure time in the State Department.

— REVIEW 5 —

Weeks 13-15

Topics
Pronouns and Antecedents
Possessive Pronouns
Subject and Object Pronouns
Indefinite Pronouns (and Subject-Verb Agreement)
Troublesome Verbs
Active and Passive Voice
Conjugating Passive Voice
Intensive and Reflexive Pronouns
Demonstrative and Interrogative Pronouns

Review 5A: Types of Pronouns

Put each pronoun in the word bank in the correct category of pronoun.

myself its who what
our I us
them these themselves him
some she most
they this their himself
that all which

Personal Subject _______________ _______________ _______________

Personal Object _______________ _______________ _______________

Personal Possessive _______________ _______________ _______________

Indefinite _______________ _______________ _______________

Demonstrative _______________ _______________ _______________

Interrogative _______________ _______________ _______________

Intensive/Reflexive _______________ _______________ _______________

Review 5B: Using Correct Pronouns

Cross out the incorrect pronoun in parentheses.

The person riding the horse was (she/her).

Kiley, Abigail, Noah, and (I/me) carried the boxes into the warehouse.

The campers brought (their / they're) art projects to Vivaan and (I / me).

(Whose / Who's) signing up to bring snacks?

(Who / Whom) locked (hisself / himself) out?

Did those students raise the money all by (theirselves / themselves)?

(Who / Whom) are you riding with?

Treena and (I / myself) will pick up coffee for the group.

The last passengers on the plane were Jake and (he / him).

(There / their) is a new movie theater by (there / their) house, so (their / they're) going to see (their / they're) newest release tomorrow.

Review 5C: Pronouns and Antecedents

Circle the twenty-eight personal pronouns (subject, object, and possessive) in the following excerpts from *The Tale of Despereaux*, by Kate DiCamillo. Draw arrows to each pronoun's antecedent.

"Where are my babies?" said the exhausted mother when the ordeal was through. "Show to me my babies."

The father mouse held the one small mouse up high. "There is only this one," he said.

"Mon Dieu, just the one mouse baby?" asked the mother.

"Just the one. Will you name him?"

"All of that work for nothing," said the mother. She sighed. "Such a disappointment." She was a French mouse who had arrived at the castle long ago in the luggage of a visiting French diplomat. "Disappointment" was one of her favorite words. She used it often.

The mouse mother held a handkerchief to her nose and then waved it in front of her face. She sniffed. "I will name him. Yes. I will name this mouse Despereaux, for all the sadness, for the many despairs in this place. Now, where is my mirror?"

Her husband handed her a small shard of mirror. The mouse mother looked at her reflection and gasped aloud. "Toulèse," she said to one of her sons, "get for me my makeup bag. My eyes are a fright."

Review 5D: Agreement with Indefinite Pronouns

Choose the correct word in parentheses to agree with the indefinite pronouns. Cross out the incorrect word.

We wanted to stop for coffee, but nothing (seems / seem) to be open.

Did you see that some of the towels (is / are) still wet?

Pauline said that all of the pot pie (tastes / taste) burnt.

All of the branches (was / were) covered with ice.

A few of the students (sits / sit) outside for lunch.

It was so dark that each of the stars (was / were) very bright.

Any of those tools (works / work) for this project.

Everyone (laughs / laugh) at the comedian's new special.

Several pages (is / are) ripped.

(Does / Do) all of the chairs have cushions?

(Does / Do) all of the deck need painting?

Review 5E: Distinguishing Between Active and Passive Voice

Identify each underlined verb as *A* for active voice or *P* for passive voice. These sentences were taken from *Dirt*, by Bill Buford.

Ten pages were dedicated to making a sauce from an egg. ________

The peppers are roasted; then the tomatoes, but, according to the particularly French insistence of needing to remove the skin first. ________

Our host, the farmer, never used pesticides, not for any ideological reason necessarily, but because pesticides were expensive. ________

I had come to Lyon to learn how to cook French food. ________

George joined him, approaching on tiptoes. The boys then talked to the sheep. ________

Around a white platter, floppy circles of "tube food" were being arranged. ________

The practice is said to produce a more animated jumble of flavors than if everything had been plopped in at the same time. ________

We were lucky when we got a loaf hot from the oven, carried it home, and ate it with salty butter. ________

It was the bread, Bob's bread, that was talked about. ________

Review 5F: Troublesome Verbs

Choose the correct verb form in parentheses. Cross out the incorrect forms.

Dulce lives outside the small town of Antigua, Guatemala, where her family (raises / rises) coffee plants at their *finca*.

Every year, her parents (let / leave) her attend the festivities known as Semana Santa during the week that leads up to the Easter holiday.

Local artists plan out elaborate constructions called *alfombras*, which are intricate carpets of colored sawdust and fresh flowers (lying / laying) along each city block.

Often, artists will (lie / lay) local items such as coffee beans, fruits, or leaves from tropical plants on their *alfombras*.

On Good Friday, Dulce (sits / sets) on the bus riding into Parque Central, located in the heart of Antigua, where she will meet up with other girls from her church.

Together, they will walk to the street where they will (sit / set) up their *alfombra*. They will have only a few hours to create their masterpiece.

By the time the artisans have (risen / raised) from their posts on Good Friday evening, every street in Antigua will wear a brilliantly-colored carpet.

Nearly one million people have (let / left) their homes to line the sidewalks of the tiny town and watch as giant statues of saints are carried through the streets.

Local parishioners, dressed in long, dark robes, (rise / raise) the heavy statues to their shoulders and walk slowly down the avenues.

Dulce and her friends will (rise / raise) to their feet as the last statue passes and then begin the long walk to the bus stop.

As they (let / leave) the city behind, the sun will be (rising / raising) already.

Dulce waves goodbye to her friends, and she quietly opens the creaking gate that leads into her courtyard. Her mother is (lying / laying) fresh tortillas on a plate and pouring hot coffee for Dulce.

WEEK 16

Imposters

— LESSON 61 —

Progressive Tenses
Principal Parts
Past Participles as Adjectives
Present Participles as Adjectives

One Sunday afternoon in 1917, cousins named Frances Griffiths and Elsie Wright, aged nine and fifteen, saw some fairies and took clear snapshots of them with their box camera . . . In 1983, sixty-six years later, Elsie Wright and Frances Griffiths decided that it was time to confess what people had suspected all along. The fairies were paper dolls . . . propped up on the grass with pins.

—Kathryn Ann Lindskoog, *Fakes, Frauds, & Other Malarkey*

	First Principal Part Present	**Second Principal Part Past**	**Third Principal Part Past Participle**
	plan	planned	planned
	burst	burst	burst
	catch	caught	caught
	fall	fell	fallen

The planned vacation did not go well.

The burst balloon fit inside the honey jar.

The caught fish wriggled on the hook.

I climbed over the fallen tree.

The past participle of a verb can act as a descriptive adjective.

The freshly picked peaches were full of flavor.

As the clock struck twelve, he heard a rustling noise in the air.

By the side of the road, he saw a fox sitting.

Her mother stirred the pot of boiling water.

The snoring guards lay at the doorstep, fast asleep.

A simple verb simply tells whether an action takes place in the past, present, or future.

I thought, I think, I will think.

A perfect verb describes an action which has been completed before another action takes place.

I had thought, I have thought, I will have thought.

A progressive verb describes an ongoing or continuous action.

I was thinking, I am thinking, I will be thinking.

First Principal Part Present	Second Principal Part Past	Third Principal Part Past Participle	Present Participle
rustle	rustled	rustled	rustling
sit	sat	sat	sitting
snore	snored	snored	snoring
am	was	been	being

The present participle of a verb can act as a descriptive adjective.

The burst balloon fit inside the honey jar.

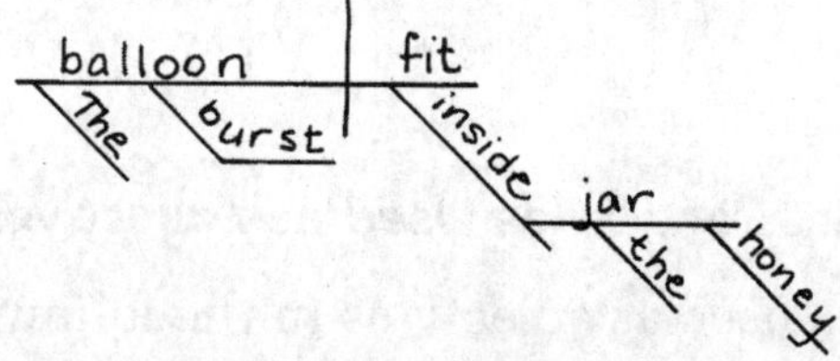

The snoring guards lay at the doorstep, fast asleep.

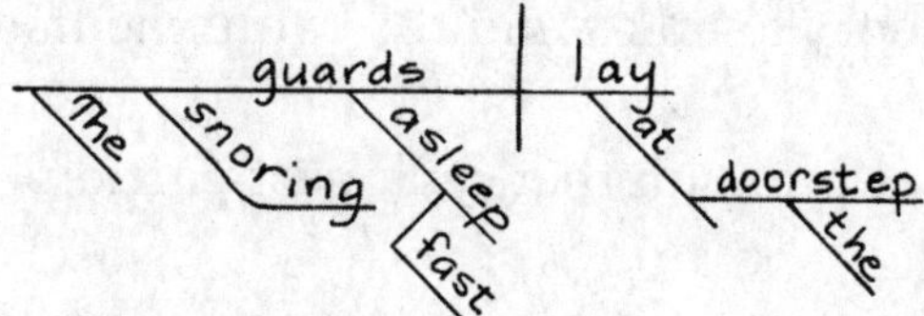

Sparkling stars shone.

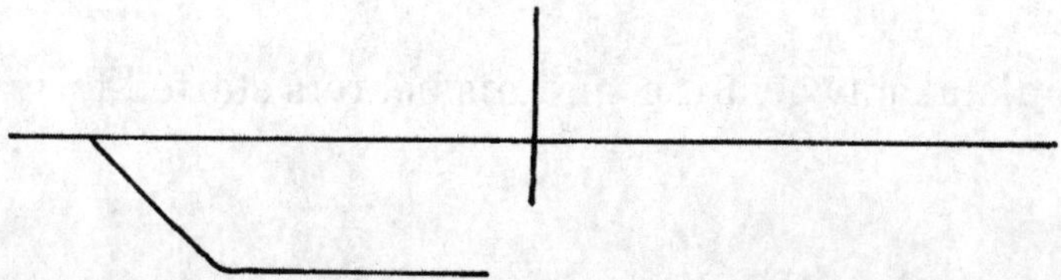

The forgotten cheese molded.

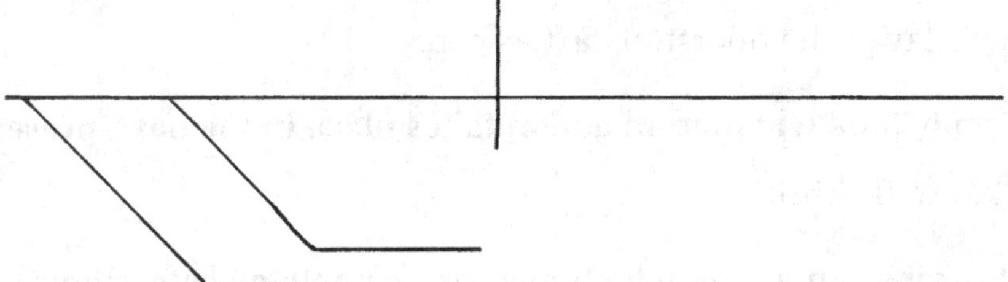

OPTIONAL:
The rustling leaves told us that the wind was rising.
The leaves, being rustled, signified the coming of fall.
Having rustled the leaves, the wind died down.
The leaves having been rustled, the wind died down.
The rustled leaves finally stilled.

Present (Active) Participle	Present (Passive) Participle	Perfect Present (Active) Participle	Perfect Present (Passive) Participle	Past Participle
add *-ing*	**being + past participle**	**having + past participle**	**having + been + past participle**	**add *-ed* (second principal part)**
rustling	being rustled	having rustled	having been rustled	rustled
eating				eaten
reading				read

Exercise 61A: Identifying Past Participles Used as Adjectives

Underline the past participles used as adjectives in the following sentences, taken from the classic short story "Tobermory," by the British short story writer Saki (given name: Hector Hugh Munro). In the story, which takes place at a house party, the guest Cornelius Appin teaches the cat Tobermory to talk—and the cat immediately begins to tell all of the secrets of the other guests!

Draw a line to the noun or pronoun that each past participle modifies.

In a minute Sir Wilfrid was back in the room, his face white beneath its tan and his eyes dilated with excitement.

His agitation was unmistakably genuine, and his hearers started forward in a thrill of awakened interest.

A Babel-like chorus of startled exclamation arose, amid which the scientist sat mutely enjoying the first fruit of his stupendous discovery.

In the midst of the clamour Tobermory entered the room and made his way with velvet tread and studied unconcern across to the group seated round the tea-table.

A shiver of suppressed excitement went through the listeners, and Lady Blemley might be excused for pouring out the saucerful of milk rather unsteadily.

With the disappearance of his too brilliant pupil Cornelius Appin found himself beset by a hurricane of bitter upbraiding, anxious inquiry, and frightened entreaty.

Exercise 61B: Identifying Present Participles Used as Adjectives

Underline the present participles used as adjectives in the following sentences, taken from *Time Cat: The Remarkable Journeys of Jason and Gareth*, by Lloyd Alexander. Jason has just discovered that his black cat, Gareth, can travel in time—and they're back in ancient Egypt, about to get into some serious trouble.

Draw a line to each word modified.

I was wondering if you thought there might be a special occasion coming up soon?

In the distance, Jason heard the sound of flutes and drums approaching.

Some carried sacred rattles; others held staves topped by glittering golden statues of cats.

Chanting voices filled the air with the "Hymn to the Great Cat."

There were several scribes, Jason saw, all carrying bundles of papyrus scrolls or clay tablets.

"Naturally," said the Chief Scribe, smiling blandly.

Before Jason could turn and race from the hall, the Chief Scribe scooped the bristling, spitting Gareth from his arms.

Exercise 61C: Diagramming Present and Past Participles Used as Adjectives

On your own paper, diagram the following sentences (adapted from *The Wild Cat Book*, by Fiona and Mel Sunquist).

A running cheetah covers 23 feet with each stride.
Cheetahs have enlarged lungs.
Hunting cheetahs prefer night hours.
A sleeping cheetah has retracted claws.

— LESSON 62 —

Parts of Speech and Parts of Sentences
Present Participles as Nouns (Gerunds)

The cuckoo is one of the great con artists of the animal world. It can trick other birds into raising its children by laying their eggs in the stranger's nest. When the cuckoo chicks hatch, the youngsters continue their parents' strategy by killing any other birds in the nest before they reveal their identity. Scientists have found the imposter cuckoo even fools the foster parent into thinking its chicks are still alive by flapping yellow patches on its wings. This also creates the illusion there are more mouths to feed and tricks the foster parents into delivering more food.

—Augustus Brown, *Why Pandas Do Handstands: And Other Curious Truths About Animals*

The running rabbit was darting towards the briar patch.

Part of speech is a term that explains what a word does.

A noun names a person, place, thing, or idea.

Part of a sentence is a term that explains how a word functions in a sentence.

subject direct object indirect object object of a preposition

A gerund is a present participle acting as a noun.

Careful sailing was the duty of the captain's mate.

This day was lost from pure whim, for the pleasure of going ashore.

Providence gives the deserving their due.

With the other hand, he repressed the beatings of his heart.

Running is my favorite exercise.

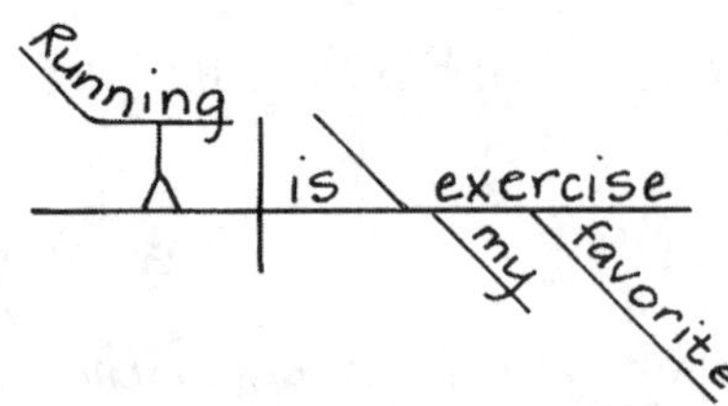

He feared falling.

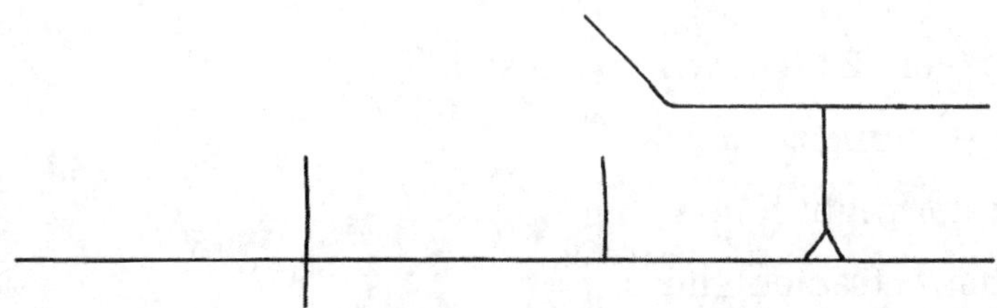

Exercise 62A: Identifying Gerunds

In the following sentences, loosely adapted from *The First Emperor: China's Terracotta Army*, by Jane Portal, underline each subject once and each predicate twice. Write *DO* above any direct objects of the predicate, *IO* above any indirect objects of the predicate, *OP* above any objects of prepositions, and *PN* above any predicate nominatives. Then, circle each gerund.

Building walls and digging ditches were required of Shang Yang's subjects.

The emperor went even further in asserting his central position in the cosmos.

His first task was constructing a tomb for his eternal dwelling.

Producing thousands of life-sized clay figures was an extraordinary task.

Techniques included coiling and rolling of clay, and the use of molds.

After drying at room temperature, the figures were put into a kiln for firing.

The craftsmen practiced painting the clothes of the figures.

Exercise 62B: Diagramming Verb Forms

On your own paper, diagram every word in the following sentences.

Digging peasants unearthed clay fragments.

Archaeologists have been locating 600 pits of terracotta figurines.

Choice specimens of clay warriors have been unearthed.

The unearthed warriors were facsimiles of the surrounding court.

720,000 workers were laboring on this project.

Shang Yang began conquering.

By conquering, Shang Yang became a hero to his adoring people.

— LESSON 63 —

Gerunds
Present and Past Participles as Adjectives
Infinitives
Infinitives as Nouns

The comings and goings of her acquaintances provided Mrs. Jennings great entertainment.

This circumstance was a growing attachment between her eldest girl and the brother of Mrs. John Dashwood.

The presence of the two Miss Steeles, lately arrived, gave Elinor pain.

An infinitive is formed by combining *to* and the first-person singular present form of a verb.

	Present Tense		Infinitive
	Singular	**Plural**	
First person	I give	we give	
Second person	you give	you give	____________
Third person	he, she, it gives	they give	
First person	I think	we think	
Second person	you think	you think	____________
Third person	he, she, it thinks	they think	
First person	I have	we have	
Second person	you have	you have	____________
Third person	he, she, it has	they have	

To err is human.
To forgive is divine.
—Alexander Pope

To wish was to hope.

To hope was to expect.
—Jane Austen

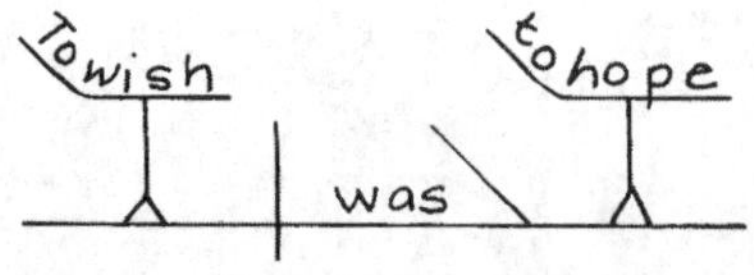

Exercise 63A: Identifying Gerunds and Infinitives

Underline the gerunds and infinitives in the following quotes about the nature of life. Identify the imposters as *G* for gerund or *I* for infinitive. Then, identify each gerund or infinitive as a subject (*S*), predicate nominative (*PN*), direct object (*DO*), or object of a preposition (*OP*).

When I went to school, they asked me what I wanted to be when I grew up.
—John Lennon

If life were predictable it would cease to be life, and be without flavor.
—Eleanor Roosevelt

The secret of success is to do the common thing uncommonly well.
—John D. Rockefeller Jr.

Try not to become a man of success. Rather become a man of value.
—Albert Einstein

If you want to achieve excellence, you can get there today. As of this second, quit doing less-than-excellent work.
—Thomas J. Watson

The greatest glory in living lies not in never falling, but in rising every time we fall.
—Nelson Mandela

If you genuinely want something, don't wait for it—teach yourself to be impatient.
—Gurbaksh Chahal

The only way out of the labyrinth of suffering is to forgive.
—John Green

I want to live and feel all the shades, tones and variations of mental and physical experience possible in my life.
—Sylvia Plath

The most important thing is to enjoy your life—to be happy—it's all that matters.
—Audrey Hepburn

I love to see a young girl go out and grab the world by the lapels.
—Maya Angelou

He wants to be nothing except what he is.
—Herman Hesse

To say goodbye is to die a little.
—Raymond Chandler

Exercise 63B: Diagramming Gerunds and Infinitives

On your own paper, diagram the following sentences.

I want to live and feel.

The secret of success is to do.

The greatest glory in living lies in rising.

Teach yourself to be.

The only way out of the labyrinth of suffering is to forgive.

— LESSON 64 —

Gerunds
Present and Past Participles
Infinitives
Gerund, Participle, and Infinitive Phrases

I love eating.

I love eating

A phrase is a group of words serving a single grammatical function.
I love eating pancakes with maple syrup, yellow cake with chocolate frosting, and grilled ribeye steaks.

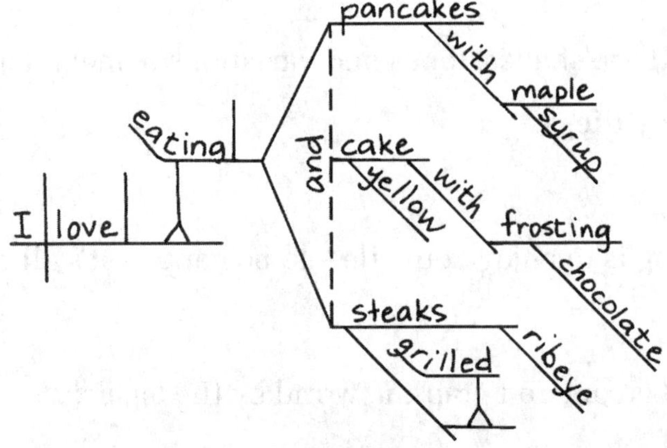

To give without expecting a reward is to receive an even greater gift.

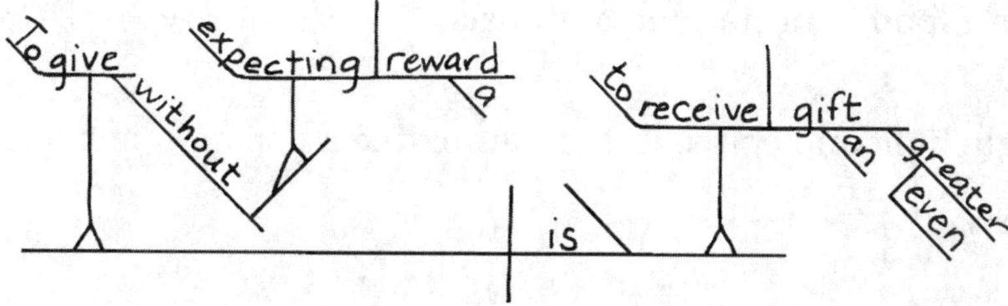

He saw the priceless antique vase shattered across the floor and scattered on the rug.

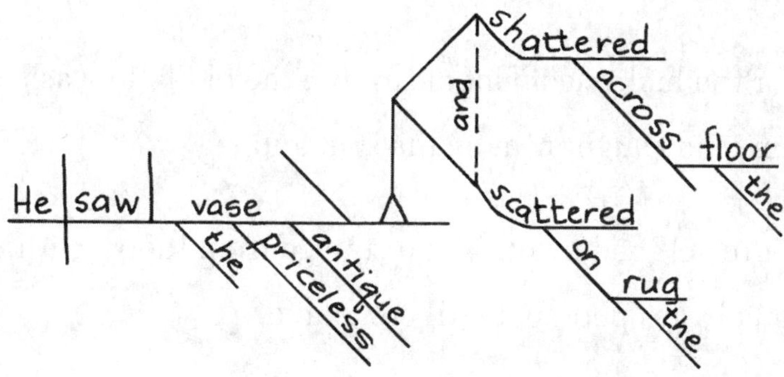

Exercise 64A: Identifying Phrases that Serve as Parts of the Sentence

In the following sentences, begin by underlining each prepositional phrase. Then, circle each group of words that contains a gerund, infinitive, or past participle. Each one serves as a part of the sentence. (Those circled phrases might include some of your prepositional phrases!) Label each circled phrase. Your options are: *ADJ* (adjective), *ADV* (adverb), *S* (subject), *IO* (indirect object), *DO* (direct object), *OC* (object complement), *OP* (object of the preposition), *PN* (predicate nominative), or *PA* (predicate adjective).

These sentences are taken from *A Wonder Book for Girls and Boys*, a retelling of classic Greek myths by the nineteenth-century American novelist Nathaniel Hawthorne.

The stick seemed to be alive in his hand, and to lend some of its life to Perseus.

Pandora tried to recollect the shape and appearance of the knot.

The young women had been having a fine time, weaving the flowers into wreaths, and crowning one another's heads.

Hastening forward, without ever pausing or looking behind, he heard the sea roaring at a distance.

An honest, hearty welcome to a guest works miracles with the fare, and is capable of turning the coarsest food to nectar and ambrosia.

He was exceedingly light and active in his figure, like a person much accustomed to gymnastic exercise.

To end the dispute was old Dame Scarecrow's aim, so she took the eye out of her forehead, and held it forth in her hand.

Thanking his stars for the lucky accident of finding the old fellow asleep, Hercules stole on tiptoe towards him, and caught him by the arm and leg.

His wife Baucis and himself had dwelt in the cottage from their youth, earning their bread by honest labor, always poor, but still contented.

Exercise 64B: Diagramming

On your own paper, diagram all of the sentences from Exercise 64A.

For the seventh sentence, only diagram:

"To end the dispute was old Dame Scarecrow's aim."

WEEK 17

Comparatives and Superlatives, Subordinating Conjunctions

— LESSON 65 —

Adjectives

Comparative and Superlative Adjectives

An adjective modifies a noun or pronoun.
Adjectives tell what kind, which one, how many, and whose.

The positive degree of an adjective describes only one thing.
The comparative degree of an adjective compares two things.
The superlative degree of an adjective compares three or more things.

Most regular adjectives form the comparative by adding *-r* or *-er*.
Most regular adjectives form the superlative by adding *-st* or *-est*.

Positive	**Comparative**	**Superlative**
large	larger	largest
big	bigger	biggest
silly	sillier	silliest

Spelling Rules

If the adjective ends in *-e* already, add only *-r* or *-st*.

noble	nobler	noblest
pure	purer	purest
cute	________	________

If the adjective ends in a short vowel sound and a consonant, double the consonant and add *-er* or *-est*.

red	redder	reddest
thin	thinner	thinnest
flat	________	________

If the adjective ends in *-y*, change the *y* to *i* and add *-er* or *-est*.

hazy	hazier	haziest
lovely	lovelier	loveliest
lucky	________	________

Many adjectives form their comparative and superlative forms by adding the word *more* or *most* before the adjective instead of using *-er* or *-est*.

unusual	more unusual	most unusual
fascinating	more fascinating	most fascinating
fun	more fun	most fun

She is more lovely than the dawn.
She is lovelier than the dawn.

She is the most lovely of all women.
She is the loveliest of all women.

The taller boy glanced around uneasily.

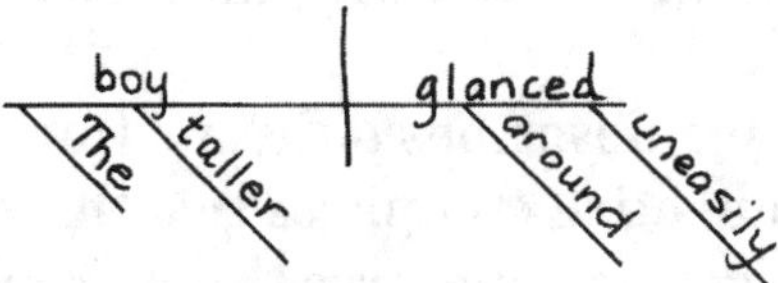

His more confident friend rang the doorbell.

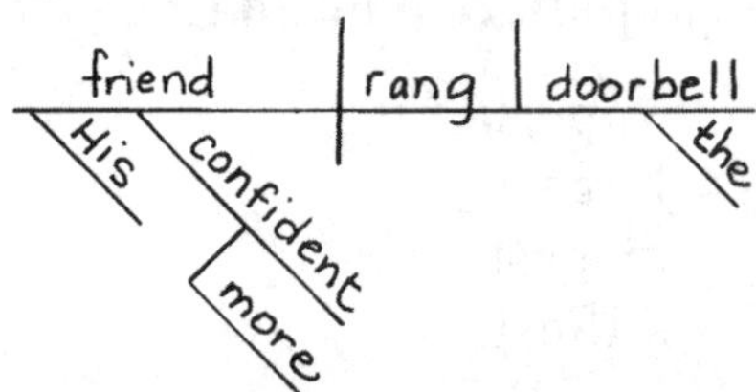

In comparative and superlative adjective forms, the words *more* and *most* are used as adverbs.

Exercise 65A: Identifying Positive, Comparative, and Superlative Adjectives

Identify the underlined adjective forms as *P* for positive, *C* for comparative, or *S* for superlative.

These speeches are all taken from the Elizabethan (1592) play *The Tragical History of Doctor Faustus*, by the English playwright Christopher Marlowe. Marlowe was born the same year as William Shakespeare, and many critics think that his use of language is as good as (or better than) Shakespeare's—but while Shakespeare lived to be 52 and wrote over 35 plays, Christopher Marlowe wrote only six plays before he was murdered at the age of 29, after an argument with three other men.

My <u>most excellent</u> lord, I am ready to accomplish your request in all things.

Nothing so <u>sweet</u> as magic is to him,

Which he prefers before his <u>chiefest</u> bliss.

Yea, <u>stranger</u> engines for the brunt of war,

Than was the <u>fiery</u> keel at Antwerp's bridge,
I'll make my servile spirits to invent.

When all is done, divinity is <u>best</u>.

But, leaving off this, let me have a wife,

The <u>fairest</u> maid in Germany.

Then up to Naples, <u>rich</u> Campania,

Whose buildings <u>fair</u> and <u>gorgeous</u> to the eye,

The streets straight forth, and paved with <u>finest</u> brick

'Twas made for man, therefore is man <u>more excellent</u>.

When Faustus had with pleasure taken the view

Of <u>rarest</u> things, and royal courts of kings,
He stayed his course, and so returned home,

Then read no more; thou hast attained that end:

A <u>greater</u> subject fitteth Faustus' wit.

<u>Brighter</u> art thou than flaming Jupiter
When he appeared to hapless Semele;

<u>More lovely</u> than the monarch of the sky

Break heart, drop blood, and mingle it with tears,

Tears falling from <u>repentant</u> heaviness

Of thy <u>most vile</u> and <u>loathsome</u> filthiness.

Exercise 65B: Forming Comparative and Superlative Adjectives

Fill in the blank with the correct form of the adjective in parentheses. These sentences are from another dramatic version of the Dr. Faustus legend: *Faust*, by the German poet Johann Wolfgang von Goethe, translated into English by Bayard Taylor.

Go, find yourself a ______________________ slave! (comparative of *obedient*)

Behind me, field and meadow sleeping,
I leave in deep, prophetic night,
Within whose dread and holy keeping
The ____________________ soul awakes to light. (comparative of *good*)

Why, just such talk as this, for me,
Is that which has the ____________________ features! (superlative of *attractive*)

But still the time may reach us, good my friend.
When peace we crave and ____________________ diet. (comparative of *luxurious*)

A ____________________ person you appear. (superlative of *fastidious*)

See, the entrancing
Whirl of their dancing!
All in the air are
____________________ and ____________________. (comparatives of *free* and *fair*)

Full well you know what here is wanting;
The crowd for ____________________ drink is panting. (superlative of *strong*)

The ____________________ stars from Heaven he requireth, (superlative of *fair*)
From Earth the __________ raptures and the ___________. (superlatives of *high* and *good*)

Bid the new career
Commence,
With ____________________ sense, (comparative of *clear*)
And the new songs of cheer
Be sung thereto!

No fount of ____________________ strength is in my brain: (comparative of *new*)

I am no hair's-breadth more in height,
Nor ________________, to the Infinite. (comparative of *near*)

Mephisto, seest thou there,
Alone and far, a girl ____________ and ____________? (superlatives of *pale* and *fair*)

And rival storms abroad are surging
A chain of ________________ action forging (superlative of *deep*)
From sea to land, from land to sea.
Round all, in wrathful energy.

I would I had a ________________ strain! (comparative of *cheerful*)

Exercise 65C: Diagramming Comparative and Superlative Adjectives

On your own paper, diagram the following sentences, from two modern versions of the Faust legend.

From Stephen Vincent Benét, "The Devil and Daniel Webster," a short story first published in 1936:

Lesser men will be made President and you will be passed over.

After supper he sent the family off to bed, for he had most particular business with Mr. Webster.

From Dorothy Sayers, "The Devil to Pay," a play first produced in 1939:

That is a most unjust accusation.

Tomorrow, we shall be richer and more powerful.

Try to look a little more respectable.

— LESSON 66 —

Adverbs
Comparative and Superlative Adverbs
Coordinating Conjunctions
Subordinating Conjunctions

An adverb describes a verb, an adjective, or another adverb.
Adverbs tell how, when, where, how often, and to what extent.

The positive degree of an adverb describes only one verb, adjective, or adverb.
The comparative degree of an adverb compares two verbs, adjectives, or adverbs.
The superlative degree of an adverb compares three or more verbs, adjectives, or adverbs.

Most adverbs that end in *–ly* form their comparative and superlative forms by adding the word *more* or *most* before the adverb instead of using *-er* or *-est*.

thoughtfully	more thoughtfully	most thoughtfully
sadly	more sadly	most sadly
angrily	more angrily	most angrily

A few adverbs ending in *-y* change the *-y* to *i* and add *-er* or *-est*.

early	earlier	earliest

He worked more efficiently.

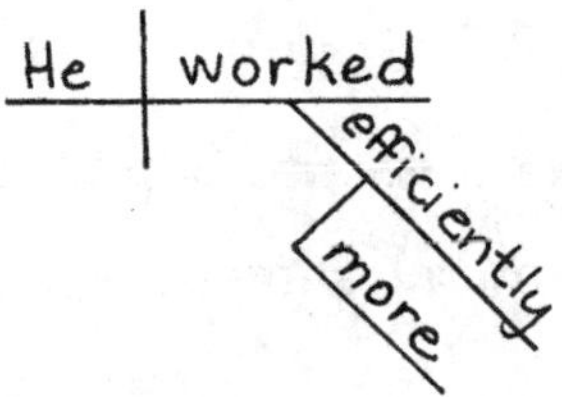

He worked more efficiently than his brother.

A conjunction joins two words or groups of words together.
and, or, nor, for, so, but, yet

A coordinating conjunction joins equal words or groups of words together.

The sun and the moon give us light.
The moon shines fitfully yet brightly.

A subordinating conjunction joins unequal words or groups of words together.

to subordinate: to place in a lower order or rank; to make secondary
  sub: from Latin preposition *sub,* beneath, under
  ordinate: from Latin verb *ordo,* to rank

He worked more efficiently than his brother.
He worked more efficiently than his brother [worked].

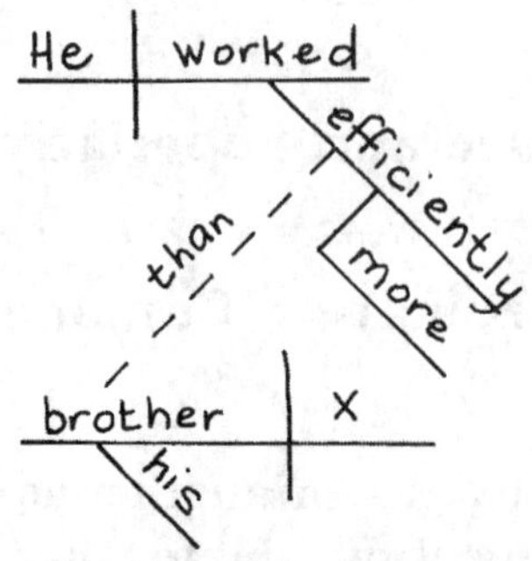

He is older than his brother.
He is older than his brother [is].

He | is \ older
than
brother | x
his

Exercise 66A: Diagramming Comparatives

Diagram the first two sentences on the frames provided. Diagram the remaining sentences on your own paper.

These are all adapted from a series of novels by the twentieth-century author Walter Farley. He first wrote the story of a fiery horse called the Black Stallion who was shipwrecked with a young boy named Alec Ramsay on a deserted island, and then afterwards wrote many more books about the Black Stallion, Alec, and all of the Black Stallion's descendants.

The Black Stallion
One sailor was more courageous than the rest.

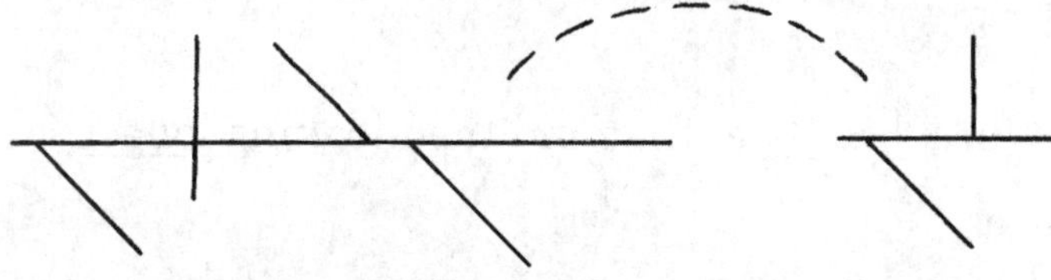

The Black Stallion Revolts
It was larger than the *Drake*.

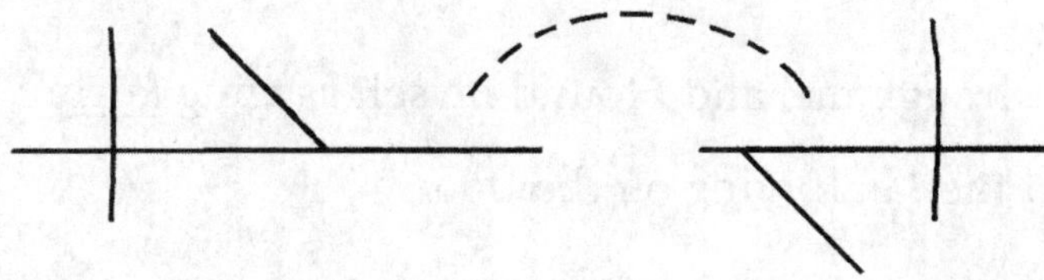

The Island Stallion
It was a long narrow room with a ceiling no higher than the tunnel.

The Black Stallion Revolts
It was more barren than any other part of the island.

The Black Stallion's Filly
The early afternoon was more balmy than hot.

Exercise 66B: Identifying Positive, Comparative, and Superlative Adverbs

Identify the underlined adverb forms as *P* for positive, *C* for comparative, or *S* for superlative.

These sentences are taken from the novel *Twice Shy*, by Dick Francis. Francis wrote dozens of novels about horse racing in England, and is considered one of the great suspense novelists of the twentieth century.

It appeared that what I'd told them so far did indeed interest them intensely.

The office was more accurately a sitting room with armchairs, television, bookshelves and pinewood paneling.

It took me a good hour to look everything up, and I thought that if I ever did begin to do it all seriously I would make myself a whole host of more easily accessible tables than those available in the record books.

Before we had finished eating, the telephone rang and most unexpectedly it was Ted Pitts calling from Switzerland.

The police had more moderately pointed out that if it was Angelo who woke first he might complete the job of murdering me: and Angelo was now in his unwaking sleep along the hallway, guarded by a constable night and day.

He looked from me to Jonathan, glancing at him briefly at first and then looking longer, more carefully, seeing what he didn't believe.

I thrust him again aside and opened the door, and found myself in a short passage which led into a large bedroom which was equipped most noticeably with another vast window looking out to the golf course.

An enveloping wave of weakness washed through me, and I found myself sagging fairly comprehensively against the cupboard and then half lying on the floor.

Cassie slept more peacefully than before, the cast becoming less of a problem as she grew used to it.

I was beginning to feel most dreadfully ill, with clamminess creeping over my skin and breaking into a sweat on my forehead.

He shoved the four planks into place between the cellar door and the refrigerator, casually remarking that during the night he'd sawn the wood to fit.

The psychopathic young man had at length erupted as a full-blown coarsened thug, no longer as Jonathan had described him, occasionally high on the drug of recklessness, but more plainly, comprehensively, violent.

Exercise 66C: Forming Comparative and Superlative Adverbs

Fill in the blank with the correct form of the adverb in parentheses.

These sentences are taken from the novel *To the Hilt*, by Dick Francis.

There was a full net of hay in the stall also, and a head collar for tying up a horse ______________________________ than with a bridle. [comfortably]

Then, as daylight ______________________________ arrived, I saddled and bridled him in the shelter. [positively]

"He usually paints nice-looking golf scenes, all sunshine with people enjoying themselves. Sells them to America ______________________________ than he can paint them, don't you, Al?" [fast]

"Well," I said, "when you gave me the Hilt to hide all those years ago, the first thing I thought about was metal detectors, because those things find gold almost ______________________________ than any other metal." [easily]

"Make him tell you. Hit him ______________________________." [hard]

The bothy faced west, which often gave me long mornings of near-perfect painting light, followed by warm afternoon glows that I'd at first subconsciously translated into mellowing glazes and then, when I found out those pictures sold ______________________________, into a commercial technique. [quickly]

Ivan gave it back to me again ______________________________, and I have brought it here today. [late]

— LESSON 67 —

Irregular Comparative and Superlative Adjectives and Adverbs

Exercise 67A: Best and Worst Games

Put the following games in the columns according to your opinion. (There are no correct answers—it all depends on you.)

Monopoly	The Game of Life	Scrabble
Sorry	Candy Land	Battleship

good: ________________ **bad:** ________________

better: ________________ **worse:** ________________

best: ________________ **worst:** ________________

Irregular Comparative and Superlative Adjectives

Adjective	Comparative Form	Superlative Form
good	better	best
bad	worse	worst
little	less	least
much	more	most
many	more	most

I have more legs than a snake.
The octopus has the most legs of the three.

Irregular Comparative and Superlative Adverbs

Adverb	Comparative Form	Superlative Form
well	better	best
badly	worse	worst
little	less	least
much	more	most
far	farther	farthest

Do not use *more* with an adjective or adverb that is already in the comparative form. Do not use *most* with an adjective or adverb that is already in the superlative form.

Use an adjective form when an adjective is needed and an adverb form when an adverb is needed.

INCORRECT	CORRECT	S LV ADV PA
The team played good.	The team played well.	I am (not) well.
The tomato smells badly.	The tomato smells bad.	

Common Linking Verbs
am, is, are, was, were, be, being, been
taste, feel, smell, sound, look, prove, grow, remain, appear, stay, become, seem

The music sounds beautiful/beautifully.

Exercise 67B: Using Comparatives and Superlatives Correctly

Choose the correct form in parentheses. Cross out the incorrect form.

These sentences are from the classic nineteenth-century horse novel *Black Beauty*, by Anna Sewell.

They often hurt themselves, often spoil (well / good) horses, and tear up the fields, and all for a hare or a fox, or a stag, that they could get (more easily / easier) some other way.

I always get on (well / good) with horses, and if I could help some of them to a fair start I should feel as if I was doing some (well / good).

When he brushed my head he went as (careful / carefully) over my eyes as if they were his own, and never stirred up any ill-temper.

Though he has not had much experience in driving, he has a (light / lightly) firm hand and a (quick / quickly) eye, and he is very (careful / carefully).

But this man went on laughing and talking, while at every step the stone became (more firmly / firmer) wedged between my shoe and the frog of my foot.

He stroked my face (kind / kindly).

Joe is the (best / most good) of grooms.

This often disordered my health, and made me sometimes (heavily / heavy) and (dully / dull), but (more often / oftener) restless and feverish.

I was sorry for Ginger, but of course I knew very little then, and I thought (most likely / likeliest) she made the worst of it.

The man, (fierce / fiercely) pulling at the head of the fore horse, swore and lashed (most brutally / brutallest).

He had kept his promise so (good / well) that York thought he might be (safer / safely) trusted to fill his place while he was away, and he was so clever and honest that no one else seemed so (good / well) fitted for it.

If you would take it off I am sure he would do (better / more good)—do try it.

The place is (more / most) than ten miles away from here, out in the country.

No one (more thoroughly / most thoroughly) understood his business than he did, and when he was all right there could not be a (faithfuller / more faithful) or (valuabler / more valuable) man.

We call them dumb animals, and so they are, for they cannot tell us how they feel, but they do not suffer (less / more little) because they have no words.

I love horses, and it riles me to see them (bad / badly) used; it is a (bad / badly) plan to aggravate an animal till he uses his heels; the (first / firstly) time is not always the (last / lastly).

There were also open spaces of fine short grass, with ant-hills and mole-turns everywhere; the (baddest / worst) place I ever knew for a headlong gallop.

I never was cleaned so (light / lightly) and (quick / quickly) as by that little old man.

A woman was standing at her garden gate, shading her eyes with her hand, and looking (eager / eagerly) up the road.

I needed no whip, no spur, for I was as (eager / eagerly) as my rider.

As we neared the corner I heard a horse and two wheels coming (rapid / rapidly) down the hill toward us.

Then he took a piece of iron the shape of my foot, and clapped it on, and drove some nails through the shoe quite into my hoof, so that the shoe was (firmly / firm) on. My feet felt very (stiffly / stiff) and (heavily / heavy), but in time I got used to it.

I know a (great / greatly) deal, and I can tell you there is not a (best / better) place for a horse all round the country than this. John is the (best / better) groom that ever was.

Exercise 67C: Using Correct Adverbs and Adjectives

Choose the correct word in parentheses. Cross out the incorrect word.

The two-year-old racehorse is growing (good / well). He's getting more muscular by the day.

The two-year-old racehorse is growing (good / well). He doesn't bite his groom any more!

The racehorse ran so (good / well)! He was much faster than the other horses in the race.

The broodmare remains (bad / badly); she tries to kick anyone who goes into her stall.

The broodmare remains (bad / badly); she hates her stall and wants to run around the pasture!

In the race, the steeplechasers did not run (slow / slowly); they were (good / well) at getting over fences!

The newborn foal doesn't feel (good / well) today. He had his shots this morning!

The vet looks (bad / badly) to the foal; he's carrying a syringe!

The vet looks (bad / badly). He's not wearing his glasses, and he can't see the markings on the syringe!

— LESSON 68 —

Coordinating and Subordinating Conjunctions
Correlative Conjunctions

When my mother makes *tacos al pastor*, she uses ancho chilies and pasilla chilies and cumin seed and garlic and pork roast and fresh cilantro.

A coordinating conjunction joins equal words or groups of words together.
and, but, for, nor, or, so, and yet

For dessert, I will have *tres leches* cake with fresh raspberries or caramel sandwich cookies with ice cream.
In my opinion, pork without pineapple is much better than pork with pineapple.

A subordinating conjunction joins unequal words or groups of words together.

We are cooking either pork roasts or goat chops tonight.
The patient was neither worse nor better.

Correlative conjunctions work in pairs to join words or groups of words.
Coordinating correlative conjunctions join equal words or groups of words.
both . . . and
not only . . . but/but also
either . . . or
neither . . . nor
although/though . . . yet/still
if . . . then

In the beginning, both the Sun and the Moon were dark.

Not only the town itself, but also the ranches in the neighborhood are built on hilltops.

Although he did not remember the way, still he pressed on.

If we run faster, then we will escape.

Though weary, still he presses on.

If unseated, then he will be unable to continue jousting.

Subordinating correlative conjunctions join unequal words or groups of words.
although/though . . . yet/still
if . . . then

In the beginning, the Sun and the Moon were dark.

In the beginning, both the Sun and the Moon were dark.

Although he did not remember, still he pressed on.

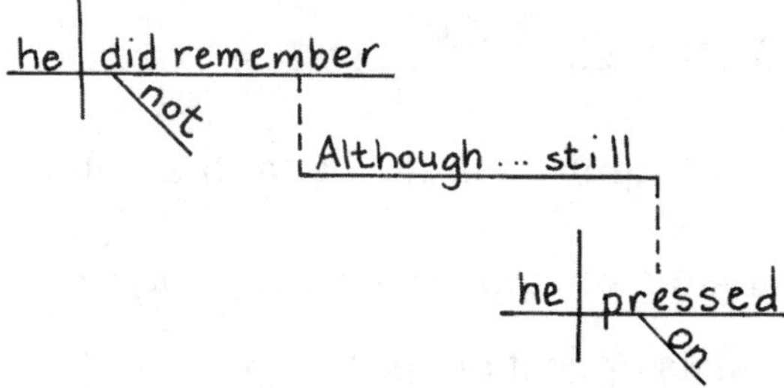

Both the grey foxes and the lion are watching for rabbits.

Not only the grey foxes but also the lion is watching for rabbits.
Either the mountain lion or the bears are growling.
Neither the butterflies nor the hummingbird was in the garden.

When compound subjects are connected by *not only . . . but/but also*, *either . . . or*, or *neither . . . nor*, the verb agrees with the subject that is closest to the verb.

Exercise 68A: Coordinating and Subordinating Correlative Conjunctions

In each of the following sentences, circle the correlative conjunctions. Underline the words or groups of words that the conjunctions connect. In the blank, write *C* for coordinating or *S* for subordinating.

These sentences have been slightly adapted from the 1909 collection *Persian Literature, Comprising THE SHÁH NÁMEH, THE RUBÁIYÁT, THE DIVAN, and THE GULISTAN, Volume 1.*

Though my life may be short, yet I may prove my love. ________

The country they inhabited was overrun with herds of wild boars, which destroyed not only the produce of their fields, but also the fruit and flowers in their orchards and gardens. ________

Not only has he despised my orders, but he has cruelly occasioned the untimely death of both. ________

His apprenticeship was spent in Arabic Bagdad, sitting at the feet of noted scholars, and taking in knowledge not only of his own Persian Sufism, but also of the science and learning of the Abbasid Caliphs. ________

If the truth must be told, then your life approaches its end. ________

His treasury was captured, and the soldiers of his army either killed or made prisoners of war. ________

My weapon must now be either dagger or I must draw my sword. ________

O king, thou art the willow-tree, all barren,
With neither fruit, nor flower. ________

He could neither sleep nor could he take food. ________

The register, including both old and young, was accordingly prepared. ________

Although your consideration for my happiness has passed away, I still wish to please you. ________

And though destruction spoke in every word,
Enough to terrify the stoutest heart,
Still he adhered to what he first resolved. ________

Though often wonderfully ornate, still his style is more sober than that of Háfiz. ________

Exercise 68B: Subject-Verb Agreement

Cross out the incorrect verb in each set of parentheses.

The first king of both the Medes and the Persians (was / were) a warrior chief named Madius.

Neither the Persian troops nor the Median commander (was / were) afraid of fighting the Scythians.

Legend says that both Nebuchadnezzar's palace and his great garden (was / were) built in honor of his Persian wife.

Both Cyrus and the Persian army (is / are) remembered for conquering the Medes.

Either camels or an elephant (was / were) used to fight against the Lydians.

Not only cavalry but also a siege engine (was / were) part of the conquest of Lydia.

Not only terror but also reward (was / were) Cyrus's strategies for retaining the loyalty of his people.

Either the Persians or Carthage (were / was) poised to become Rome's greatest enemy.

Exercise 68C: Diagramming

On your own paper, diagram every word of the following sentences, adapted from *The History of the Ancient World*, by Susan Wise Bauer.

The villain in the story is probably neither Cambyses nor Darius.

Themistocles died either from illness or from a dose of poison.

In 424, both Darius II's father and his half-brother died.

The patricians were gaining not only land but also money.

Neither Alexander's fury nor his charm could persuade his men.

WEEK 18

Clauses

— LESSON 69 —

Phrases
Sentences
Introduction to Clauses

A phrase is a group of words serving a single grammatical function.

A verb phrase is the main verb plus any helping verbs.

Four musketeers were waiting their turn.

A prepositional phrase begins with a preposition and ends with a noun or pronoun.

The center of the most animated group was a musketeer of great height.

A prepositional phrase that describes a noun or pronoun is called an adjective phrase.

He wore a long cloak of crimson velvet.

A prepositional phrase that describes a verb, adjective, or adverb is called an adverb phrase.

The young man advanced into the tumult and disorder.

(Sentences adapted from *The Three Musketeers,* by Alexandre Dumas.)

A clause is a group of words that contains a subject and a predicate.

Along with the tomato and garlic
Vinegar adds a little acid
While potatoes are roasting
Make the two sauces
Are salting and peppering generously
The sauce should not be
Two warm and delicious sauces

An independent clause can stand by itself as a sentence.

A sentence is a group of words that usually contains a subject and a predicate. A sentence begins with a capital letter and ends with a punctuation mark. A sentence contains a complete thought.

> *Can we measure intelligence without understanding it?* Possibly so. *Physicists measured gravity and magnetism long before they understood them theoretically. Maybe psychologists can do the same with intelligence.*
>
> Or maybe not.
>
> —James W. Kalat, *Introduction to Psychology*

A dependent clause is a fragment that cannot stand by itself as a sentence.

Although tapas bars are popular in Spain ____________

Patatas bravas are crispy potatoes eaten with a sauce ____________

Whether or not you choose to fry the potatoes on the stove ____________

Since this is a traditional Spanish dish ____________

Sprinkle lightly with salt ____________

Because my grandmother came to visit.
I cleaned up my room.

Because my grandmother came to visit, I cleaned up my room.

Dependent clauses begin with subordinating words.
Dependent clauses are also known as subordinate clauses.

Exercise 69A: Distinguishing Between Phrases and Clauses

Identify the following groups of words as *phrases* or *clauses*. The clauses may be independent or dependent, but you only need to identify them as *clauses*. In each clause, underline the subject once and the verb twice.

Small, lightly breaded, and fried fritters ____________

If you have eggs, potatoes, and onions ____________

Creamy, smooth, and very delicious ____________

Roll the dough into logs ____________

If fried until golden brown ____________

Cleaned squid are best for this recipe ____________

Plenty of garlic, pepper, and paprika ____________

Certainly they will ask for the recipe ____________

Tomato-based sauces with a little bit of spice ____________

Grilled octopus is served with olive oil ______________

Chopped and mixed with the rest of the stuffing ______________

Coat them in egg and breadcrumbs ______________

Unless you are not very hungry ______________

Exercise 69B: Distinguishing Between Independent and Dependent Clauses

Identify the following clauses as independent (*IND*) or dependent (*DEP*).

These clauses are adapted from José Andrés, *Tapas: A Taste of Spain in America*.

I arrived on these shores twelve years ago ___________

Who thought he knew it all ___________

Peoples that shaped Spanish cooking ___________

People will like your cooking ___________

Since I arrived in the United States ___________

Spanish food is more available than ever ___________

Although the conquistadors mistook them for truffles ___________

Tapas are a way of living and eating ___________

While they are chatting with their friends ___________

Press each olive ___________

Until the pit pops out ___________

Exercise 69C: Turning Dependent Clauses into Complete Sentences

Choose three of the dependent clauses below and attach independent clauses to them to form complete thoughts. Write your three new sentences on your own paper. (The dependent clause can go before or after the independent clause.)

since the Phoenicians first planted olive trees on the Iberian peninsula

when the tomato has broken down and deepened in color

and even though we don't use firewood in today's kitchens

after the cheeses have dried on wood shelves for twenty days and aged in the caves for four months

until the potatoes are slightly browned

because the clams add their own saltiness to the rice

— LESSON 70 —

Adjective Clauses
Relative Pronouns

Intro 70: Introduction to Adjective Clauses

The following sentences are taken from *Star Trek, The Official Guide to Our Universe: The True Science Behind the Starship Voyages*, written by Andrew Fazekas and published by National Geographic.

Complete each sentence by filling in the blank with the appropriate letter from the clauses below. (This is for fun, so just do your best—you might need to know something about the Star Trek universe to get them all right!)

The game makes the crew vulnerable to a plot by Ktarian Etana Jol, ______.

The *U. S. S. Enterprise* arrives at Deep Space Station K-7 after being called to protect a shipment bound for Sherman's Planet, ______.

Most of the action takes place within the Milky Way galaxy's Alpha Quadrant—except for *Voyager*, ______.

Amid tension, a trader arrives bearing tribbles: a fuzzy creature ______.

Vulcans are an ancient humanoid species ______.

A. which ended up in the Delta Quadrant
B. whom humans respected for their early development of warp drive technology
C. who planted the game on Will Riker in hopes of using mind control to take over the *Enterprise*-D
D. whose control the Federation and the Klingons are disputing
E. that Uhura delightedly adopts as a pet

Dependent clauses can act as adjectives, adverbs, or nouns.

An adjective clause is a dependent clause that acts as an adjective in a sentence, modifying a noun or pronoun in the independent clause.

They banded together in small groups that whispered and discussed and disputed.

A man who passed by spoke to them.

Relative pronouns introduce adjective clauses and refer back to an antecedent in the independent clause.
who, whom, whose, which, that

The men **who had been champions before Finn came** rallied the others against him.

Among the young princes was a boy **whom the High King preferred**.

The Chain of Silence was shaken by the servant **whose duty and honor it was.**

The thing **which was presented to us** is not true.

The people believed in gods **that the king did not accept**.

Use *who, whom,* and *whose* to refer to persons.
Use *which* to refer to animals, places, and things.
Use *that* and *whose* to refer to persons, animals, places, or things.

She saw him, and he saw her.

Use *P* for prepositions, *OP* for objects of prepositions, *ADJ* for adjectives, *ADV* for adverbs, *IO* for indirect objects, *DO* for direct objects, and *OC* for object complements.

I who speak to you have seen many evils.

At the door is a gentleman for whom no seat has been found.

He was the boy whom they called Little Fawn.

They are men whose happiness lies in ambition.

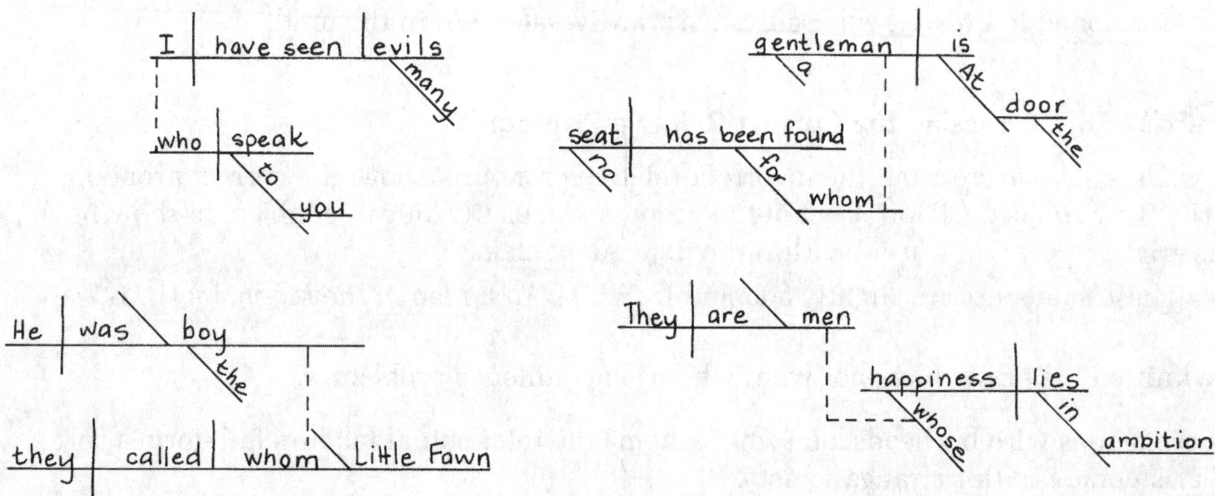

Exercise 70A: Identifying Adjective Clauses and Relative Pronouns

Underline the adjective clauses in the following sentences, and circle the relative pronouns. Draw an arrow from each relative pronoun to its antecedent.

These sentences are taken (and occasionally, very slightly condensed) from *The Hitchhiker's Guide to the Galaxy*, by Douglas Adams.

In moments of great stress, every life form that exists gives out a tiny subliminal signal.

Near them on the floor lay several rather ugly men who had been hit about the head with some heavy design awards.

The speech patterns you actually hear decode the brainwave matrix which has been fed into your mind by your Babel fish.

The Dentrassis are an unruly tribe of gourmands, a wild but pleasant bunch whom the Vogons had recently taken to employing as catering staff on their long-haul fleets.

As the others started after him he was brought up short by a Kill-O-Zap energy bolt that cracked through the wall in front of him and fried a small section of adjacent wall.

He didn't notice anything but the caterpillar bulldozers crawling over the rubble that had been his home.

Orbiting this at a distance of roughly ninety-eight million miles is an utterly insignificant little blue-green planet whose life forms are amazingly primitive.

The only place they registered at all was on a small black device called a Sub-Etha Sens-O-Matic which winked away quietly to itself.

Ford beckoned to Prosser, who sadly, awkwardly, sat down in the mud.

Exercise 70B: Choosing the Correct Relative Pronoun

In each sentence, cross out the incorrect relative pronoun. Above the correct pronoun, write S for subject, *OP* for object of the preposition, or *DO* for direct object to show how the relative pronoun is used within the dependent clause.

These sentences are slightly adapted from *The First Men in the Moon*, by H. G. Wells.

He knitted his brows like one (who / whom) encounters a problem.

These beings with big heads, on (who / whom) the intellectual labours fall, form a sort of aristocracy in this strange society.

I was a little sorry for the baker, (who / whom) was a very decent man indeed.

He told me of a work-shed he had, and of three assistants (who / whom) he had trained.

Gibbs, (who / whom) had previously seen to this responsibility, had suddenly attempted to shift it to the man who had been a gardener.

A man (who / whom) leaves the world when days of this sort are about is a fool!

They are a strange race with (who / whom) we must inevitably struggle for mastery.

Those (who / whom) have only seen the starry sky from the earth cannot imagine its appearance when the vague half-luminous veil of our air has been withdrawn.

Exercise 70C: Diagramming Adjective Clauses

On your own paper, diagram every word of the following sentences, slightly adapted from *The Essential Novels: Star Wars Legends 10-Book Bundle,* published by Random House in 2012.

She had interrogated a droid who had crawled out of the destruction.

The admiral was one for whom decisiveness had always been a career hallmark.

Cronal finally understood the terrible flaw that would bring the Order of the Sith to its ultimate destruction.

It would roll over Shadowspawn's base like a line of thunderheads whose clouds were toxic smoke, whose rain was fire.

— LESSON 71 —

Adjective Clauses
Relative Adverbs
Adjective Clauses with Understood Relatives

A phrase is a group of words serving a single grammatical function.
A clause is a group of words that contains a subject and a predicate.

An independent clause can stand by itself as a sentence.
A dependent clause is a fragment that cannot stand by itself as a sentence.

Dependent clauses begin with subordinating words.
Dependent clauses are also known as subordinate clauses.

Adjective clauses are also known as relative clauses because they relate to another word in the independent clause.

Relative pronouns introduce adjective clauses and refer back to an antecedent in the independent clause.
who, whom, whose, which, that

This was the very spot **where** a proud tyrant raised an undying monument to his own vanity.

He was going back to serve his country at a time **when** death was the usual reward for such devotion.

The reasons **why** he vented his ill humor on the soldiers were many.
—Adapted from *The Scarlet Pimpernel*, by Baroness Emmuska Orczy

Relative adverbs introduce adjective clauses and refer back to a place, time, or reason in the independent clause.
where, when, why

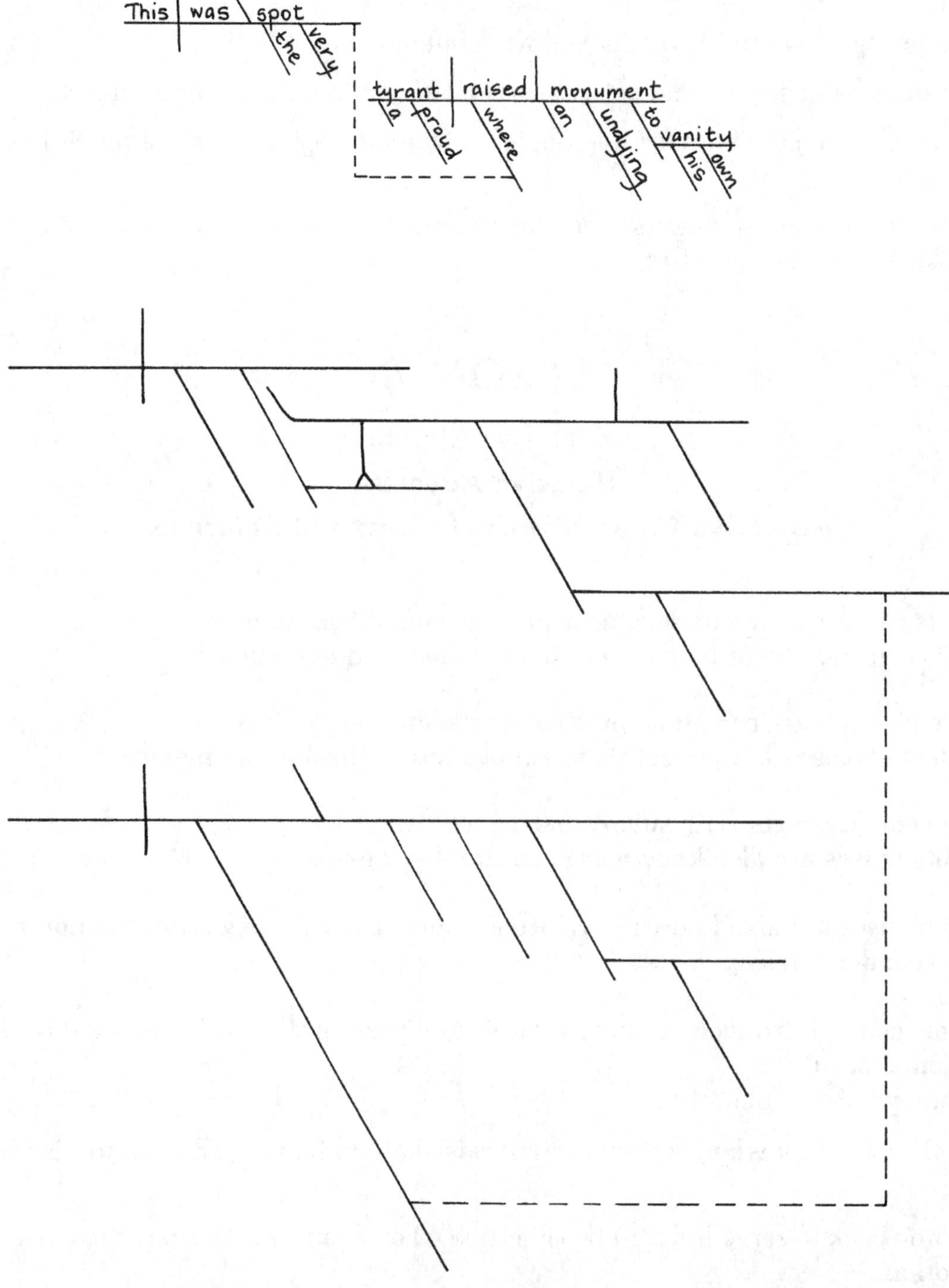

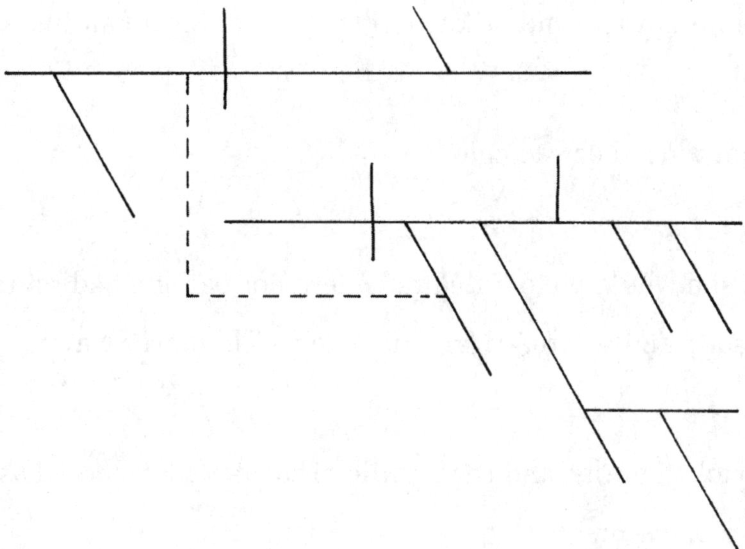

The evil men do lives after them.

I read the book you sent me.

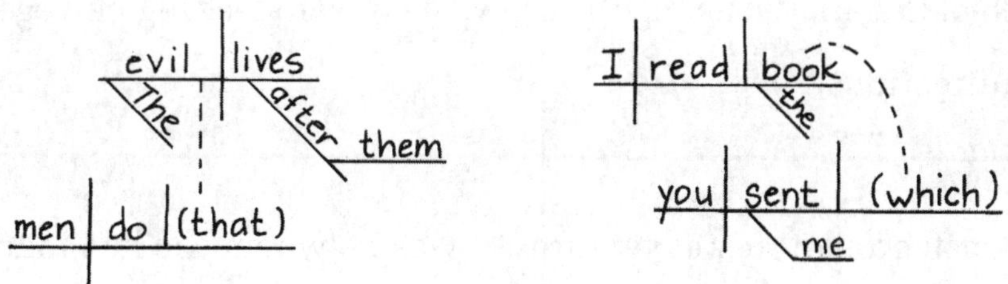

Exercise 71A: Relative Adverbs and Pronouns

In the following sentences, underline each adjective clause. Circle each relative word and label it as *RP* for relative pronoun or *RA* for relative adverb. Draw an arrow from each relative word back to its antecedent in the independent clause.

These sentences are taken from four works of fiction by the British-born writer Jhumpa Lahiri.

They walked past the mathematics building, where Mr. Sen taught his classes.

(*Interpreter of Maladies*)

It was centuries ago, when the Bay of Bengal's current was stronger.

(*The Lowland*)

Here was an explanation why her mother had gone.

(*The Lowland*)

My parents often hosted friends who came from New Jersey or New Hampshire for the weekend, to eat elaborate dinners and talk late into the evening about Indian politics.
(*Unaccustomed Earth*)

There were times when it had been so cold.
(*The Namesake*)

Just before Christmas she would go to Calcutta, where her parents had returned after a lifetime in Massachusetts and where, in January, she would marry Navin.
(*Unaccustomed Earth*)

That meant that her bucket, quilts, and the bundle of reeds which served as her broom all had to be braced under one arm.
(*Interpreter of Maladies*)

She shook the quilts once again underneath the letter boxes where she lived, then once again at the mouth of the alley, causing the crows who were feeding on vegetable peels to scatter in several directions.
(*Interpreter of Maladies*)

And yet they had met; after all her adventures, it was he whom she had married.
(*The Namesake*)

For the greater number of her twenty-nine years, Bibi Halldar suffered from an ailment that baffled family, friends, priests, palmists, spinsters, gem therapists, prophets, and fools.
(*Interpreter of Maladies*)

The following weekend, when he visited her again, the phone rang as they were having dinner.
(*The Lowland*)

You didn't have to tell me why you did it.
(*Interpreter of Maladies*)

Exercise 71B: Missing Relative Words

Draw a caret in front of each adjective clause and insert the missing relative pronoun. (For the purposes of this exercise, *which* and *that* and *whom* may be used interchangeably.)

The original sentences are slightly condensed from the comical spooky story "The Canterville Ghost," by Oscar Wilde.

The only thing that consoled him was the fact he had not brought his head with him.

He had been christened Washington by his parents, in a moment of patriotism he never ceased to regret.

This was the housekeeper Mrs. Otis, at Lady Canterville's earnest request, had consented to keep in her former position.

It was his most remarkable impersonation, one the Cantervilles had every reason to remember.

I have come from a modern country, where we have everything money can buy.

He had been very wicked, but he was really sorry for all he had done.

Washington was following with a lighted candle he had caught up from the table.

He thought of the Dowager Duchess he had frightened into a fit as she stood before the glass in her lace and diamonds.

Exercise 71C: Diagramming

On your own paper, diagram the following sentences from your first two exercises.

There were times when it had been so cold.

You didn't have to tell me!

It was centuries ago, when the Bay of Bengal's current was stronger.

He had been very wicked, but he was really sorry for all he had done.

— LESSON 72 —

Adverb Clauses

A clause is a group of words that contains a subject and a predicate.

A dependent clause is a fragment that cannot stand by itself as a sentence.
Dependent clauses begin with subordinating words.
Dependent clauses are also known as subordinate clauses.

Dependent clauses can act as adjective clauses, adverb clauses, or noun clauses.

Adverb clauses modify verbs, adjectives, and other adverbs in the independent clause. They answer the questions where, when, how, how often, and to what extent.

When the supper was finished, the king expressed a wish.

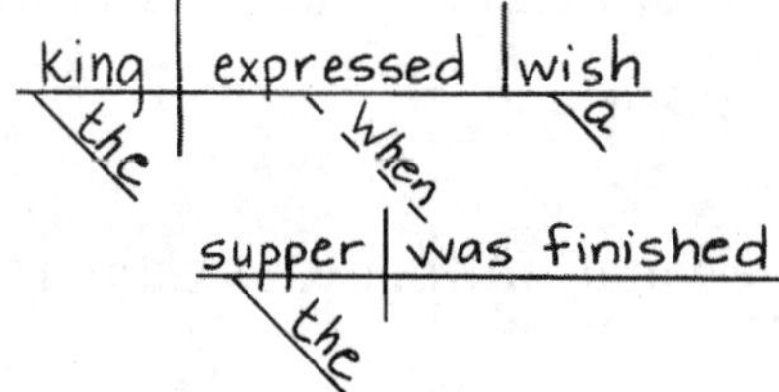

Adverb clauses can be introduced by adverbs.

Common Adverbs that Introduce Clauses
as (and its compounds: as if, as soon as, as though)
as if
how (and its compound: however)
when (and its compound: whenever)
whence
where (and its compounds: whereat, whereby, wherein, wherefore, whereon)
while
whither

A subordinating conjunction joins unequal words or groups of words together.

An honest enemy is better than an agreeable coward.

An honest enemy is better than an agreeable coward [is].

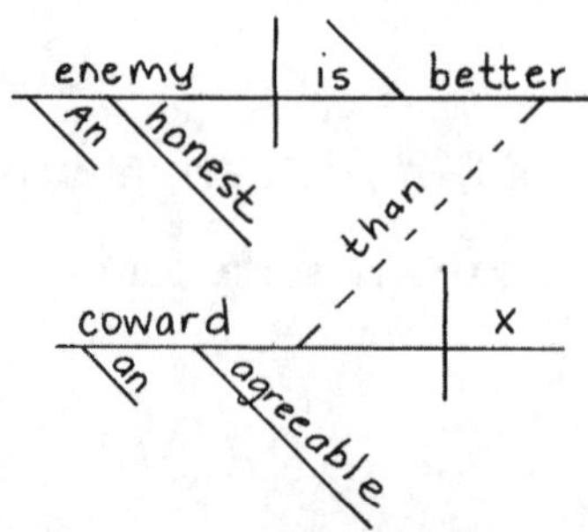

Subordinating conjunctions and subordinating correlative conjunctions often join an adverb clause to an independent clause.

Common Subordinating Conjunctions
after
although
as (as soon as)
because
before
if
in order that
lest
since
though
till
unless
until
although/though . . . yet/still
if . . . then

Because she loves Korean food, my aunt taught me to cook kimchi.

I will put six plates on the table unless our neighbors are also coming for dinner.

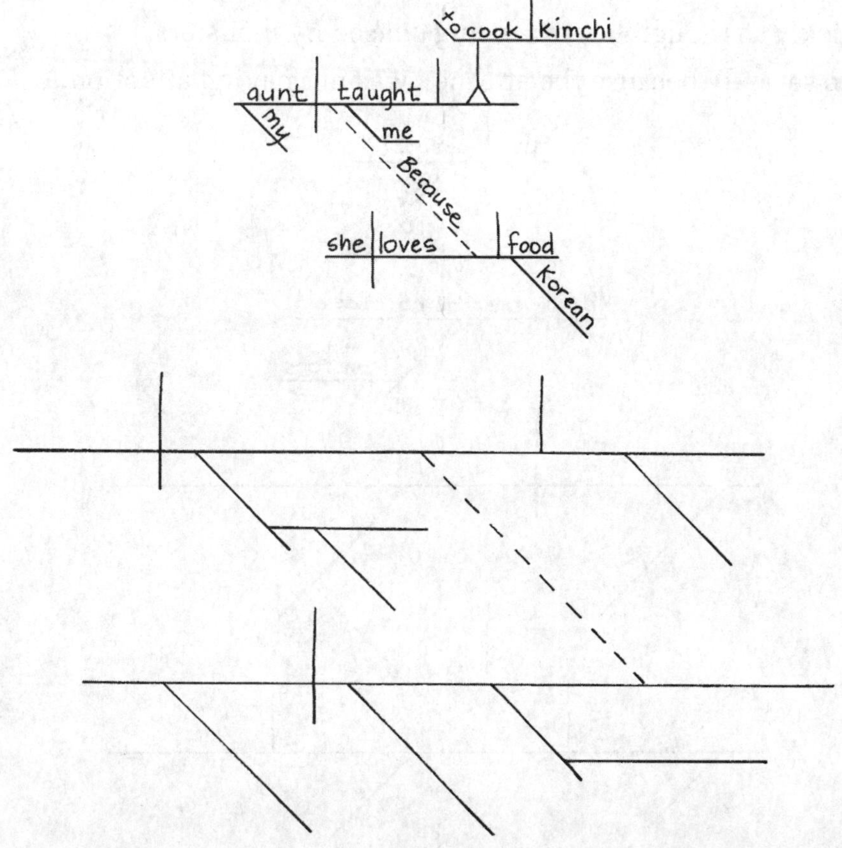

The task is difficult if you do not take care.
She was confident that she could reach the top of the mountain.

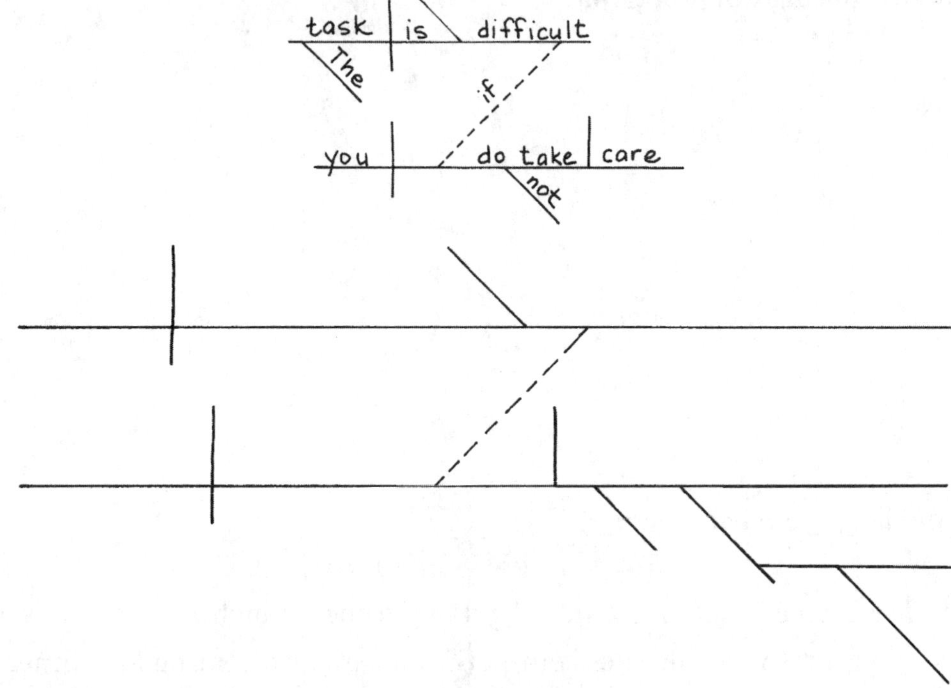

He sprinted quickly as though he were being chased by monsters.
The judge spoke severely because the attorney was not paying attention.

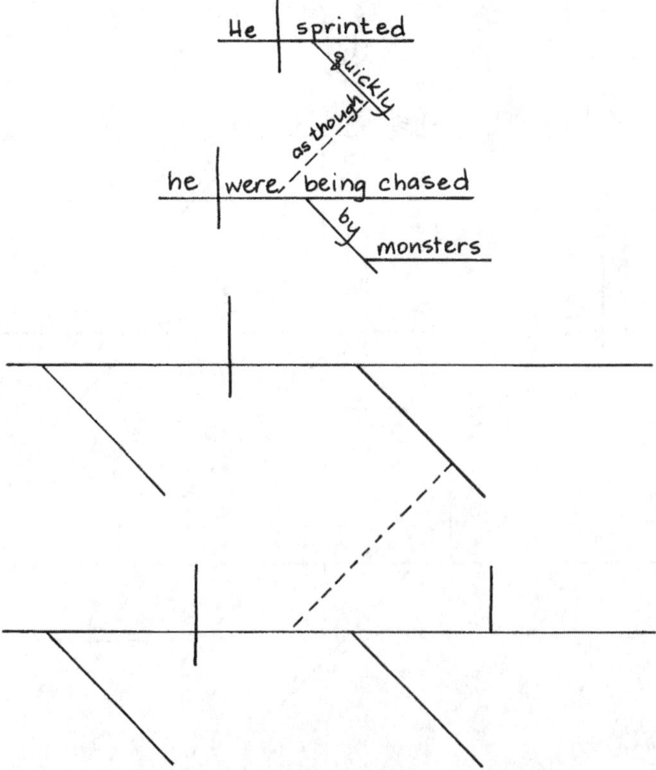

I will wait where I am.

I waited at the place where I had marked the ground.

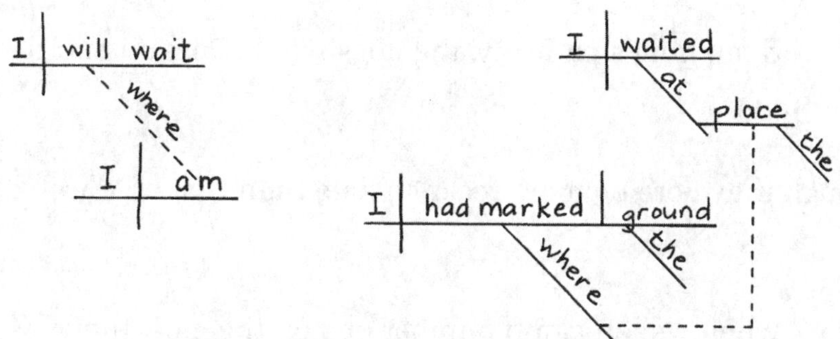

Exercise 72A: Adverb Clauses

In the following sentences, underline each adverb clause. Circle the subordinating word at the beginning of each clause and label it *ADV* for adverb or *SC* for subordinating conjunction. Draw an arrow from the subordinating word back to the verb, adverb, or adjective that the clause modifies.

These sentences are taken from a memoir written by Matthew Henson, who accompanied the explorer Robert Peary on seven different voyages to the Arctic in order to reach the North Pole. Henson was one of the only African-American Arctic explorers in the early years of the twentieth century. He's credited with the co-discovery of the North Pole, along with Robert Peary, in 1909.

My mother died when I was seven years old.

February 19, 1909: It was six a.m. when I routed out the boys for breakfast.

I am writing while the tea is brewing.

We were able to make better time because we had his trail to follow.

When the expedition returned, there were two who went back who had not come north with us.

He had scarcely set foot on the opposite floe when the floe on which he had been previously isolated swung off, and rapidly disappeared.

I knew little fear, though I did think of the ghosts of other parties, flitting in spectral form over the ice-clad wastes.

Neither Borup nor Marvin had caught up, but we felt that unless something had happened to them, they would surely catch up in a few more days.

While we were at work making a pathway, the dogs would curl up and lie down with their noses in their tails.

Our letters, although they bore no more recent a date than that of March 23, 1909, were eagerly read.

It was cold and dark when we left camp number one on the morning of March 2, at half past six o'clock.

Exercise 72B: Descriptive Clauses

In the following sentences, underline each dependent clause. Above each, write *ADVC* for adverb clause or *ADJC* for adjective clause. Circle each subordinating word and label it as *ADV* for adverb, *RP* for relative pronoun, or *SC* for subordinating conjunction. Draw an arrow from the subordinating word back (or forward) to the word in the independent clause that the dependent clause modifies.

These sentences are taken from the memoir *Touching My Father's Soul: A Sherpa's Journey to the Top of Everest*, by Jamling T. Norgay. Norgay's father, Tenzing Norgay, made the first ascent of Everest with the New Zealand climber Edmund Hillary. After standing on top of Everest, the two men always refused to say which one of them first set foot on the summit.

Jamling Norgay climbed Everest in 1996, following in his father's footsteps.

When I became an adult, and after my father's death, my desire to climb Everest only intensified.

I returned to Darjeeling with troubled thoughts, which began to invade my dreams.

We presented Rimpoche with kata blessing scarves, in which I enclosed some rupee notes.

Rimpoche may have been aware of the deaths on the mountain—the more than 150 who have died attempting to climb it, or about one for every five who have reached the summit.

Before 1951, when Nepal opened to the outside world for the first time, Everest expeditions were staged out of Darjeeling, a town that was created in the mid-1800s by the British raj as a hill station.

First ascents are generally recognized as successful only when the climbers return alive.

She bowed her head slightly in gratitude and said that although the entire afternoon had been quite windy, it was fortunate that the wind had stopped.

Jangbu helped Chen back to camp, where most climbers were still asleep, and returned him to his tent.

The Tibetans topped up the lamps with their own melted butter, which they had brought in vacuum flasks.

When they departed the South Col for the South Summit on May 26, carrying summit flags, my father was resigned to the possibility that they could reach the top.

Then, just as I was becoming used to the disappointment, the summit nearly surprised me.

Exercise 72C: Diagramming

On your own paper, diagram every word of the following sentences from the first two exercises.

We were able to make better time because we had his trail to follow.

When the expedition returned, there were two who went back who had not come to the north with us.

We presented Rimpoche with kata blessing scarves, in which I enclosed some rupee notes.

When they departed the South Col for the South Summit on May 26, carrying summit flags, my father was resigned to the possibility that they could reach the top.

— REVIEW 6 —

Weeks 16-18

Topics
Personal Pronouns: Subject, Object, Possessive, Reflexive
Verb Voice (Active and Passive)
Verb Tense
Adjectives
Gerunds and Participles
Phrases
Clauses (Independent and Dependent)

Review 6A: Pronouns

In the following sentences, taken from *Good Germs, Bad Germs: Health and Survival in a Bacterial World,* by Jessica Snyder Sachs, circle each pronoun. Label each as *S* (subject form of the personal pronoun), *O* (object form of the personal pronoun), *P* (possessive form of the personal pronoun), *R* (reflexive), *INT* (intensive), *I* (indefinite), *INTER* (interrogative), *D* (demonstrative), or *RP* (relative pronoun).

The Eubacteria make themselves known by their production of the more odiferous hydrogen sulfide—familiar the world over for its rotten-egg smell.

"In severe sepsis, while you don't see the major organ damage associated with septic shock, you have cells leaking fluids, bile mixing with blood, oxygen and water mixed together in the lungs," he explains. "It may be that when these barriers begin to fail at the cellular level, it's not long before the organs themselves give out."

Drug-resistant microbes made up 50 percent or more of the intestinal bacteria in more than one-third of his healthy volunteers—none of whom had taken antibiotics in more than six months.

Something was destroying Ricky's organs, but exactly what or where it lurked in his body remained maddeningly unclear.

For oral antibiotics, which get absorbed through the intestinal tract, the challenge is the opposite: to keep the drugs inactive until after they get absorbed.

Even after decades of being lectured about antibiotic abuse, too many doctors still think of antibiotics as benign and use them with a "what can it hurt?" attitude.

Vancomycin-resistant enterococcus made its U.S. hospital debut in 1988. Within five years it was showing up in nearly one in ten hospital patients, and the majority of those who spent several days or more on vancomycin. Fortunately, VRE caused no harm in and of itself so long as it stayed put in a patient's intestines.

The first of these is *Streptococcus sanguis*, a bacterium unsurpassed in its ability to cling to the smooth enamel face of small incisors.

All that was required was a little human trickery.

Review 6B: Using Comparative and Superlative Adjectives Correctly

Choose the correct form in parentheses. Cross out the incorrect form.

These sentences are taken from *The Story of Germ Life*, by H. W. Conn.

Bacteria are decidedly the (most small / smallest) living organisms which our microscopes have revealed.

Their numbers are (most great / greatest) near the surface of the ground, and decrease in the (more up / upper) strata of air.

This explanation will enable us (more clearly / clearer) to understand the relation of different bacteria to disease.

The (most interesting / interestingest) facts connected with the subject of bacteriology concern the powers and influence in Nature possessed by the bacteria.

A (importanter / more important) factor of soil fertility is its nitrogen content, without which it is completely barren.

The (more large / larger) doses of the past, intended to drive out the disease, have been everywhere replaced by (more small / smaller) doses designed to stimulate the lagging body powers.

From the very (most early / earliest) period, ever since man began to keep domestic cattle, he has been familiar with dairying.

Creameries which make the (most high / highest) priced and the (most uniform / uniformest) quality of butter are those in which the (most great / greatest) care is taken in the barns and dairies to insure cleanliness and in the handling of the milk and cream.

The butter maker has learned by long experience that ripened cream churns (more rapidly / rapider) than sweet cream, and that he obtains a (more large / larger) yield of butter therefrom.

After the (most thorough / thoroughest) washing which the milk pail receives from the kitchen, there will always be left many bacteria clinging in the cracks of the tin or in the wood, ready to begin to grow as soon as the milk once more fills the pail.

The cheese maker finds in the ripening of his cheese the (most difficult / difficultest) part of his manufacture.

The art of preparing flax is a process of getting rid of the worthless wood fibres and preserving the valuable, (more long / longer), (more tough / tougher), and (more valuable / valuablest) fibres, which are then made into linen.

Review 6C: Verbs

Underline the main verb (along with any helping verbs) in every clause below (both independent and dependent).

In the space above each verb, write the tense (*SIMP PAST, PRES, FUT; PROG PAST, PRES, FUT; PERF PAST, PRES, FUT*) and voice (*ACT* for active or *PASS* for passive). For state-of-being verbs, write *SB* instead of labeling voice.

If the verb is an action verb, also note whether it is transitive (*TR*) or intransitive (*INTR*).

The first is done for you.

These sentences are taken from the Victorian novel *The Tenant of Wildfell Hall*, by Anne Brontë.

SIMP FUT ACT INTR SIMP FUT SB
Perhaps he will stay among his friends till Christmas; and then, next spring, he will be off again.

Oh, it is cruel to leave me so long alone!

I have been accustomed to make him swallow a little wine or weak spirits-and-water, by way of medicine, when he was sick.

I know you will have a fellow-feeling for the old lady, and will wish to know the last of her history.

The servant had just brought in the tea-tray; and Rose was producing the sugar-basin and tea-caddy from the cupboard in the black oak side-board.

I glanced round the church.

Mrs. Markham, I beg you will not say such things.

We shall be constrained to regard ourselves as unwelcome intruders.

Well, I shall be neither careless nor weak.

I have had several letters from Arthur already.

Of him to whom less is given, less will be required, but our utmost exertions are required of us all.

All who were not attending to their prayer-books were attending to the strange lady.

I was annoyed at the continual injustice she had done me from the very dawn of our acquaintance.

Review 6D: Identifying Dependent Clauses

Underline each dependent clause in the following sentences. Circle the subordinating word. Label each clause as either adjective (*ADJ*) or adverb clause (*ADV*), and draw a line from each subordinating word to the word it modifies.

These sentences are taken from *The Annotated African American Folktales*, edited by Henry Louis Gates Jr. and Maria Tatar (Liveright, 2017).

From the Xhosa tale "The Story of Demane and Demazana"

Once upon a time there lived a brother and sister, who were twins and orphans. They decided to run away from their relatives because they had been treated so badly.

Not much later, Demane, who had found nothing that day but a swarm of bees, returned.

Zim went out to get some water, and while he was gone Demane took his sister out of the sack and put the bees in it.

Demane and Demazana took all of Zim's possessions, which were great in number, and soon they became wealthy people.

From the Congolese tale "The Story of the Four Fools"

One day a wizard met a boy who was sitting by the roadside, upset and weeping bitter tears.

The captain of the vessel summoned a storm and sent rain down on the glass boat, which shattered. But the carpenter mended it, and the hunter fired away at the rain until it stopped.

The carpenter then staked his claim, for he had twice mended the ship in which they were sailing.

From "The Maiden, the Frog, and the Chief's Son," a story with uncertain origins

One day the wife he disliked fell ill, and it was not long before she died.

She would take those scrapings and throw them into a pit where there were frogs.

Things went on like that, day after day, until it was time for the Festival.

When she reached the pit, she threw bits of food into it.

Review 6E: Present and Past Participles

Underline each present participle and past participle in the following sentences. Some are serving as nouns; others, as adjectives. Label adjective forms as *ADJ* and draw a line to the word modified. Label noun forms as *N* and write the part of the sentence that the noun is serving as.

These sentences are taken from *Origin Story: A Big History of Everything*, by David Christian.

We arrive in this universe through no choice of our own, at a time and place not of our choosing.

In 1992, the remains of an ancestor (referred to as Mungo 1) discovered by archaeologists in 1968 were finally returned to the local Aboriginal community.

Like many people, I struggled to link the isolated fields I studied.

We can see the links connecting the various scholarly landscapes, so we can think more deeply about broad themes such as the nature of complexity, the nature of life, even the nature of our own species!

I like to imagine a group of people sitting around a fire as the sun was setting forty thousand years ago.

In my imagined twilight conversations around the fire, there are girls and boys, older men and women, and parents and grandparents, some wrapped in animal furs and cradling babies. Children are chasing one another at the edge of the lake while adults are finishing a meal of mussels, freshly caught fish and yabbies, and wallaby steak.

Told over many nights and days, their stories describe the big paradigm ideas of the Lake Mungo people.

The problem is that in a globally connected world, there are so many local origin stories competing for people's trust and attention that they get in one another's way.

Sharing also allows us to test the details of our maps against millions of other maps.

Review 6F: Diagramming

On your own paper, diagram every word of the following sentences from *Miracle in Lake Placid: The Greatest Hockey Story Ever Told*, by John Gilbert.

The U.S. players hit the ice, absorbing the crowd's added enthusiasm, and immediately went to work.

The clock was ticking down when David Christian choreographed the goal that stunned the Russians and changed the course of the game.

The pass was headed for David Christian at the right point, but as it slid, Eruzione picked it off as he skated left to right to the slot; then he shot, low and to the left.

Setting up and scoring goals is the flashy part of hockey, but in the last 10 minutes of the biggest hockey game in U.S. history, the ability to think under intense defensive pressure was more important than any highlight-video scoring play.

WEEK 19

More Clauses

— LESSON 73 —

Adjective and Adverb Clauses
Introduction to Noun Clauses

A clause is a group of words that contains a subject and a predicate.

I know that a noun is the name of a person, place, thing, or idea.

I know an old lady who swallowed a fly while she was sitting on the front porch.

Dependent clauses can act as adjective clauses, adverb clauses, or noun clauses.

An adjective clause is a dependent clause that acts as an adjective in a sentence, modifying a noun or pronoun in the independent clause.
Relative pronouns introduce adjective clauses and refer back to an antecedent in the independent clause.

Adverb clauses modify verbs, adjectives, and other adverbs in the independent clause.
They answer the questions where, when, how, how often, and to what extent.
Adverb clauses can be introduced by adverbs.
Subordinating conjunctions and subordinating correlative conjunctions often join an adverb clause to an independent clause.

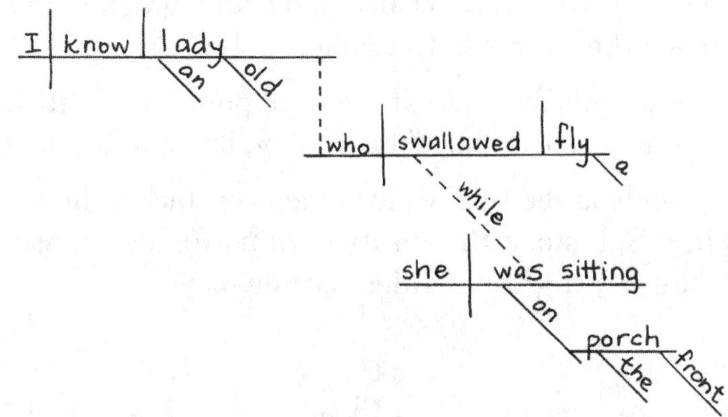

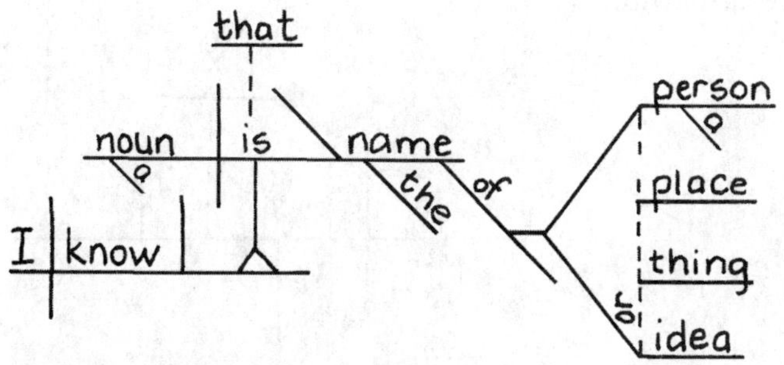

A noun clause takes the place of a noun.
Noun clauses can be introduced by relative pronouns, relative adverbs, subordinating conjunctions, or understood subordinating words.

I know where your lost keys are.

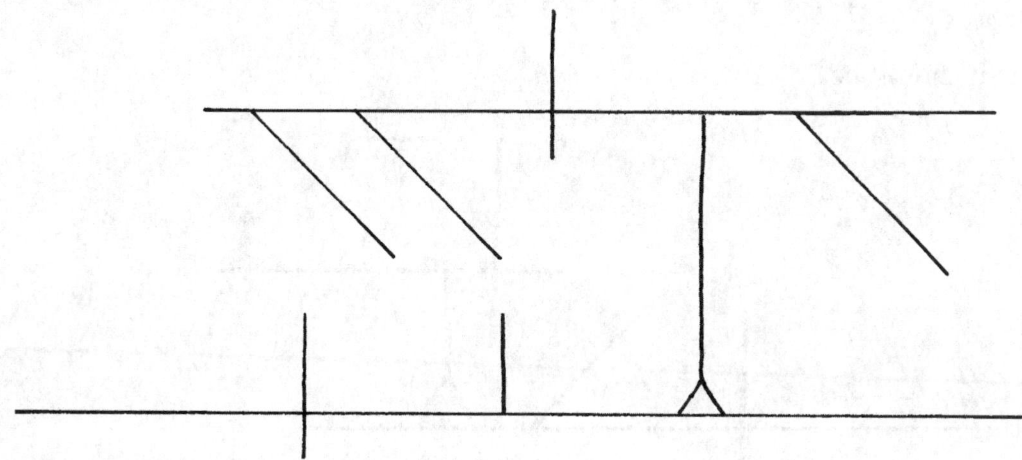

Whoever runs fastest will win the race.

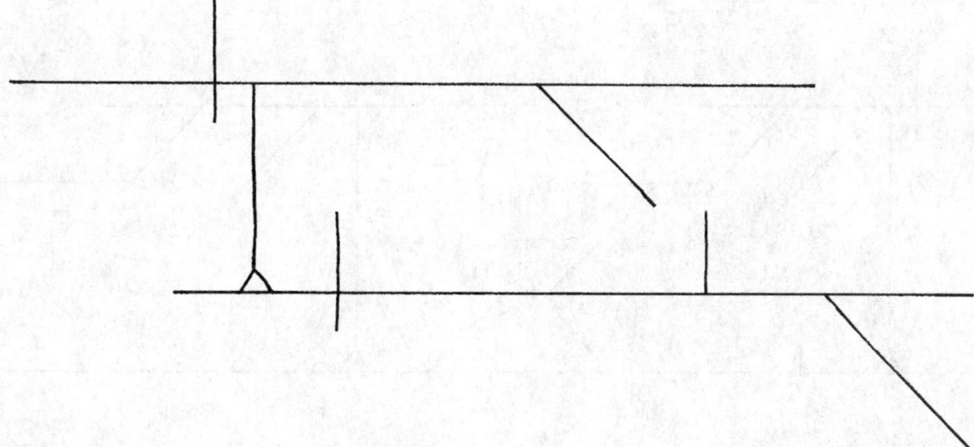

I really wish I had more chocolate.

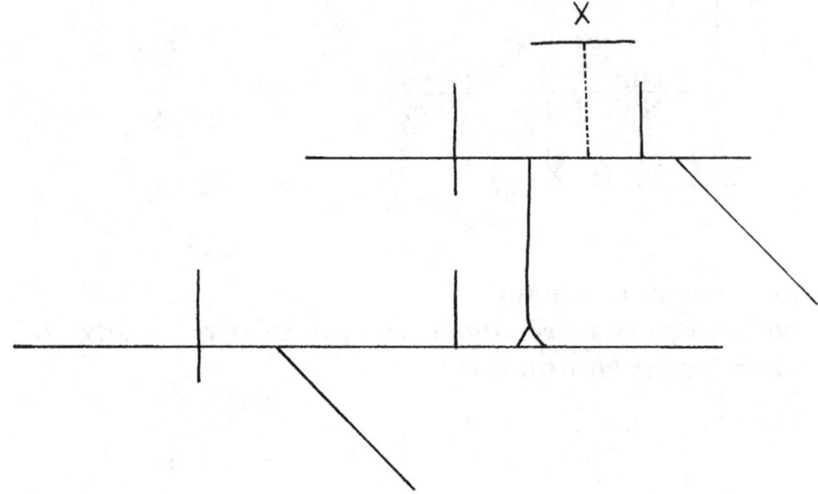

Nothing was as it should be.

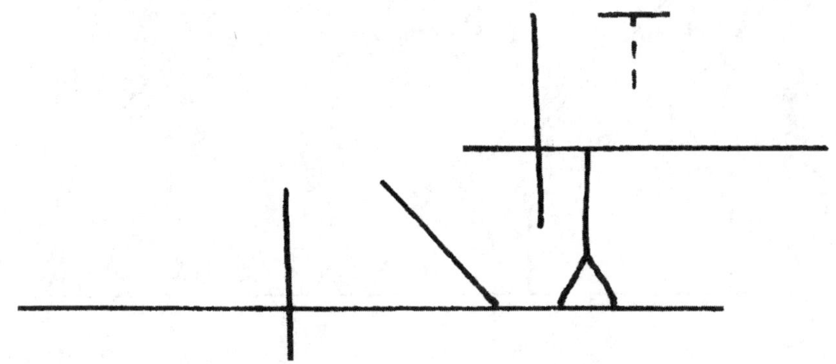

What matters most in this situation is how you feel about it.

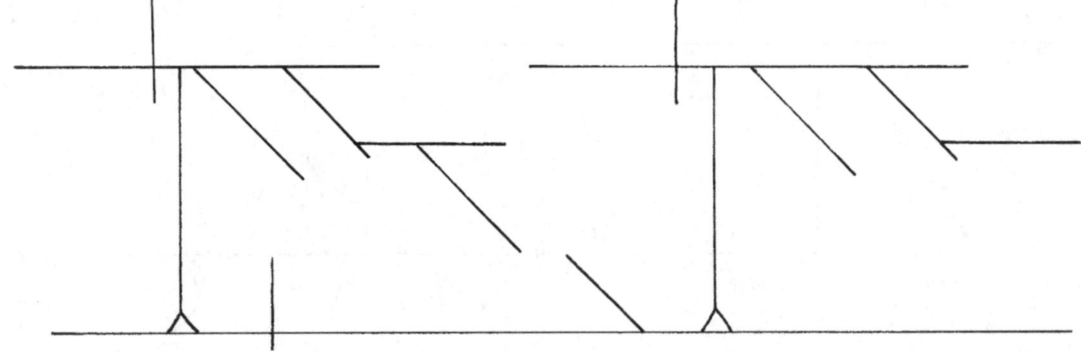

Exercise 73A: Identifying Clauses

In the following sentences, circle each dependent clause. Label each as *N* for noun, *ADJ* for adjective, or *ADV* for adverb. Also indicate the part of speech that each noun clause plays: subject (*S*), direct object (*DO*), predicate nominative (*PN*), or object of the preposition (*OP*). Draw a line from each adjective and adverb clause to the word it modifies.

Some of these clauses may have another clause within them! Do your best to find both, and ask your instructor for help if needed.

These sentences are slightly adapted from Nathaniel Hawthorne's *Tanglewood Tales.* The first is done for you.

N (DO)

Mother, I do believe it has started!

Jason knew that it would be impossible to withstand this blood-thirsty battalion with his single arm.

While they were crossing the pasture ground, the brazen bulls came towards Jason, lowing, nodding their heads, and thrusting forth their snouts, which, as other cattle do, they loved to have rubbed and caressed by a friendly hand.

But poor King Aegeus, day after day, infirm as he was, had clambered to the summit of a cliff that overhung the sea, and there sat watching for Prince Theseus, homeward bound.

He concluded that his dear son, whom he loved so much, and felt so proud of, had been eaten by the Minotaur.

That he trembles and cannot speak shows his guilt.

In the center of it there should be a noble palace, in which Cadmus might dwell, and be their king, with a throne, a crown, a sceptre, a purple robe, and everything else that a king ought to have.

All at once, Cadmus fancied he saw something glisten very brightly, first at one spot, then at another, and then at a hundred and a thousand spots together.

They brought along with them a great many beautiful shells; and sitting down on the moist sand, where the surf wave broke over them, they busied themselves in making a necklace, which they hung round Proserpina's neck.

The good Chiron taught his pupils how to play upon the harp, and how to cure diseases, and how to use the sword and shield.

The truth was that the Giant touched Mother Earth every five minutes.

Exercise 73B: Creating Noun Clauses

On your own paper, create five sentences by adding a noun clause into each of the blanks below.

If you have trouble coming up with a dependent clause, try starting out with one of the following subordinating words: *that, how, why, what/whatever, who/whoever* (these are always subjects within the dependent clause), *whom/whomever* (these are always objects within the dependent clause), *where, whether.* (This is not an exhaustive list of the possibilities—just a jumping-off place for you.)

I never knew ____.

________________________________ was the weirdest thing I ever saw.

Just don't forget ____.

A ridiculously exciting part of the movie was __________________________

________________________________.

Exercise 73C: Diagramming

On your own paper, diagram every word of the following sentences (slightly adapted from *Twice-Told Tales*, by Nathaniel Hawthorne).

One would have thought that the dark old man was chief ruler there.

Whatever secret hope had agitated him was quickly dispelled by Dorothy's next speech.

The secret of this phenomenon was that hatred had become the enjoyment of the wretch's soul.

He hardly knew whether he lived or only dreamed of living.

— LESSON 74 —

Clauses Beginning With Prepositions

The sun itself, which makes time, is elder by a year now.

Any man's death diminishes me, because I am involved in mankind.

What we call fortune here has another name above.

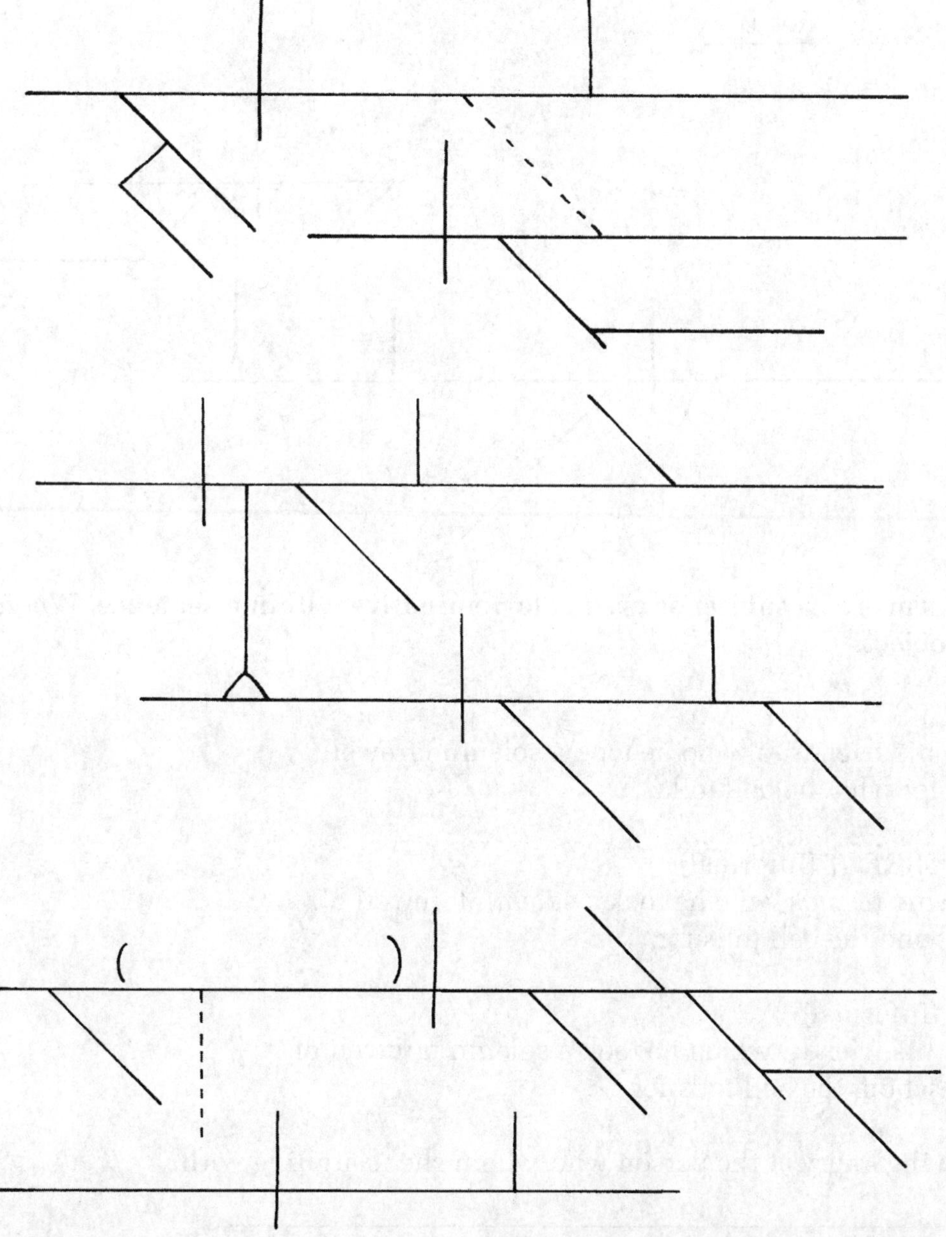

That carrack is the ship in which they are to sail.

He sent for his friends, of whom he took a solemn farewell.

Do not ask for whom the bell tolls.

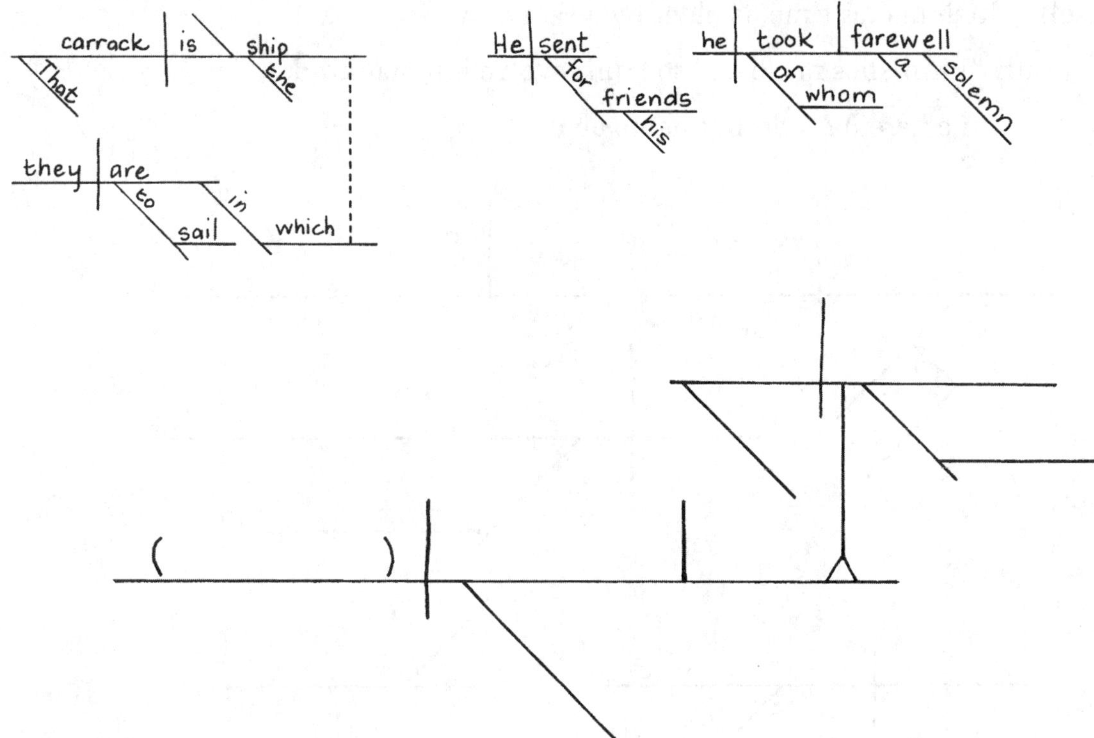

***Who* always acts as a subject or predicate nominative within a sentence. *Whom* always acts as an object.**

INCORRECT
He sent for his friends, of who he took a solemn farewell.
Do not ask for who the bell tolls.

ALSO INCORRECT (Informal)
He sent for his friends, who he took a solemn farewell of.
Do not ask who the bell tolls for.

CORRECT (Informal)
He sent for his friends, whom he took a solemn farewell of.
Do not ask whom the bell tolls for.

She is growing angry at the person who/whom she is arguing with.

____

Rude behavior is something I won't put up with!
Rude behavior is something up with which I will not put!

Exercise 74A: Adjective Clauses Beginning with Prepositions

In the following sentences, circle each adjective clause. Draw a line from the subordinating word back to the word the clause modifies. If the clause begins with a preposition, underline that preposition and label its object with *OP*.

These sentences are taken from the classic young adult novel *Dream of Fair Horses*, by Patricia Leitch.

The woman, whom we now knew as Mrs. Ramsay, was holding the pony while the girl saddled up.

The wooden fencing that surrounded the park was damaged.

Perdita was packed in next to a Shetland to whom she took an instant hatred, so that all the splendour and emotion of the ceremony rolled over me unnoticed.

Birds that had been stones shuffled and sang; two roe deer, bat-eared and alert, walked warily into the open; Perdita tugged at her reins wanting to graze.

I would bring her feed, which Mr. Ramsay had mixed for her the night before, and she would wait at her trough, glistening-eyed and anxious until I tipped the bucket of oats, bran and chop out into her trough.

Since there was hardly any space in which we could exercise I concentrated on walking and trotting, only asking her for an accuracy that was well within her scope.

At the celebration, one of Fran's songs was about the autumn people who were afraid to start on the winter journey.

As we swung past the judges Perdita was moving with a grace and assurance that no amount of grooming or schooling could have created.

I woke with a shock, starting abruptly into full awareness, trying to escape from something from which there was no escaping.

On Saturday mornings we hacked the hunters to the meets where the Ramsays would be waiting for us, and on Saturday evenings we sweated over weary, muddied horses and filthy tack.

I knew the way he could take a simple ordinary situation and turn and twist it until he made you see that the one thing you wanted was the one thing you couldn't possibly have.

Una has found a teacher whom she loves, who never even shouts at her, who accepts Una's spelling and arithmetic and appreciates Una's talent for keeping cupboards tidy and feeding school dinners to the infants.

Exercise 74B: Correct Use of *Who* and *Whom*

Choose the correct pronoun within the parentheses; cross out the incorrect pronoun.

These sentences are slightly condensed from *Original Sin*, a murder mystery set in a publishing office, by P. D. James.

To the left was a curved desk and a switchboard manned by a grey-haired, gentle-faced man (who/whom) greeted her with a smile before checking her name on a list.

It was she, Mandy, (who/whom) should have been nervous.

They were fond of each other; he was, he knew, the one person at Innocent House in (who/whom) she felt she could occasionally confide; but neither was demonstrative.

"Fortunately the printer (who/whom) received them was intelligent and thought some of the changes odd, so he telephoned to check."

But at least he would have someone with (who/whom) he could share the distresses of the day, a day which now seemed inordinate in length.

"No one was interested in (who/whom) he married."

Not for nothing were there those five shelves of crime paperbacks in her bedroom, Agatha Christie, Dorothy L. Sayers, Margery Allingham, Ngaio Marsh, Josephine Tey and the few modern writers (who/whom) Joan considered fit to join those Golden Age practitioners in fictional murder.

(Who / Whom) knew that better than (he / him)?

But the worst, Maggie confided, were the conceited, usually those whose books sold the least well, but (who / whom) demanded first-class fares, five-star hotels, a limousine and a senior member of staff to escort them, and (who / whom) wrote furious letters of complaint if their signings didn't attract a queue round the block.

"They're particular (who / whom) they get, I suppose."

"And (who / whom) is actually in charge now?"

Exercise 74C: Formal and Informal Diction

On your own paper, rewrite the bolded clauses (which are all written informally) in formal English, placing the preposition before its object. Then read each sentence out loud, substituting the formal clause for the informal clause.

The original sentences are all written formally! They are taken from the novel *The Marrow of Tradition*, by Charles W. Chesnutt.

Through the side door leading from the hall into the office, he saw the bell-boy **whom he had spoken to**, seated on the bench provided for the servants.

The fine old house **which they lived in** was hers.

The major had also invited Lee Ellis, his young city editor, **whom he had a great liking for apart from his business value,** and who was a frequent visitor at the house. These, with the family itself, which consisted of the major, his wife, and his half-sister, Clara Pemberton, a young woman of about eighteen, made up the eight persons **whom covers were laid for**.

An anxious half hour passed, **which the child lay quiet during**, except for its labored breathing.

He really thought him too much of a gentleman for the town, in view of the restrictions **which he must inevitably be hampered with**.

He had a habit of borrowing, right and left, small sums which might be conveniently forgotten by the borrower, **and which the lender would dislike to ask for**.

Exercise 74D: Diagramming

On your own paper, diagram every word of the following two sentences from *The Strivers' Row Spy*, by Jason Overstreet.

His disregard for what he was saying, when he was saying it, and whom he was saying it to was alarming.

The only possible end of the race problem in the United States to which we can now look without despair is one which embraces the fullest cooperation between white and black in all the phases of national activity.

— LESSON 75 —

Clauses and Phrases
Misplaced Adjective Phrases
Misplaced Adjective Clauses

In many East Asian countries, the day a baby is born is considered its first birthday.

The first birthday after a baby is born is considered its second birthday.

A phrase is a group of words serving a single grammatical function.

A clause is a group of words that contains a subject and a predicate.

Western birthdays are often celebrated with a cake made especially for the occasion.

The first reference to a "birthday cake" dates from 1785, when the Oxford Dictionary listed the phrase for the first time.

The young woman went to the awards ceremony with her father in a gorgeous ball gown.

She gave the cookie to the little girl made of gingerbread.

Paige gave a birthday cake to her cousin which she had baked herself.

Adjective clauses and phrases should usually go immediately before or after the noun or pronoun they modify.

Exercise 75A: Correcting Misplaced Modifiers

Circle the misplaced adjective clauses and phrases in the following sentences. Draw an arrow to the place where each modifier should be.

My brother blamed the weather for the game cancellation which was cold and rainy.

The bean stew was for our dinner simmering away on the stove.

The hen was pecking busily at the weeds in the back yard with the three fluffy yellow chicks.

The rocks passing by could easily fall down onto hikers balanced along the path.

The northern part of Africa was the home of the greatest Egyptian pharaoh, which borders the Mediterranean Sea.

The old deer skeleton had been there for months and months lying beside the hiking trail.

The grocery store clerk called her supervisor who had run out of change.

The hiker decided to go back to her group, afraid to lose the way.

The little girl ran happily home after talking to the librarian carrying her books in a backpack.

After the tourist paid for the map, he tucked the yellow-edged paper into his pocket with the pictures on it.

They said that the whole group had gotten lost together from their hotel.

All around the outside of the house which keeps the sun away from the large outer windows runs a screened porch.

Exercise 75B: Diagramming

Each of the following sentences contains a misplaced clause or phrase. On your own paper, diagram each sentence correctly, and then read the corrected sentence out loud to your instructor. These sentences are taken from *Grimm's Fairy Tales*!

The tailor with a black patch on her back had three strong sons and one goat.

When Rapunzel, which lay in a forest and had neither stairs nor door, was twelve years old, the Witch shut her into a tower.

Sleeping beside the fire, he called the other dwarves, and all of them were astonished to see Snow White who ran up.

— LESSON 76 —

Noun, Adjective, and Adverb Clauses
Restrictive and Non-Restrictive Modifying Clauses

Type of clause	Function in the sentence	Introduced by . . .	Diagram by . . .	Also known as
Adjective clause	Modifies a noun or pronoun in the main clause. Answers the questions *Which one? What kind? How many? Whose?*	. . . a relative pronoun, relative adjective, or relative adverb that refers back to a noun or pronoun in the main clause. The most common are *who, whom, whose, that, which, where, when, why.*	. . . placing every word of the dependent clause on a separate diagram below the diagram of the main clause. Connect the relative pronoun, adjective, or adverb to the word it refers to in the main clause with a dotted line.	Relative clause, dependent clause, subordinate clause
Adverb clause	Modifies a verb, adjective, or adverb in the main clause. Answers the questions *Where? When? How? How often? To what extent?*	. . . subordinating conjunctions, such as *when, until, before, after, as, while, where, although, unless, because, since, though, so that, even though.* (NOTE: There are many other subordinating conjunctions.)	. . . placing every word of the dependent clause EXCEPT for the subordinating word on a separate diagram below the diagram of the main clause. Draw a dotted line connecting the predicate of the dependent clause to the word modified in the independent clause, and write the subordinating word on the dotted line.	Subordinate clause, dependent clause

Type of clause	Function in the sentence	Introduced by . . .	Diagram by . . .	Also known as
Noun clause	Stands in as any part of the sentence that a noun can fill: subject, direct object, indirect object, predicate nominative, object of the preposition, appositive (see Lesson 94), object complement.	. . . most commonly, *that*. Can also be introduced by *who, whom, which, what, whether, why, when, where, how,* or other subordinating words.	. . . drawing a tree in the appropriate "noun" space on the diagram and placing each word in the noun clause on a diagram that sits on top of the tree. If the subordinating word only connects the dependent clause to the rest of the sentence and doesn't have a grammatical function *within* the dependent clause, diagram it on a line that floats above the predicate of the clause and is attached to the predicate by a dotted line.	Nominal clause, subordinate clause, dependent clause

Exercise 76A: Clause Review

The following sentence is the beginning of *Pride (A Pride and Prejudice Remix),* by Ibi Zoboi. Complete these steps:

1) Find and circle the dependent clauses. Label each one as adjective, adverb, or noun.
2) Identify and underline the subordinating word. If the subordinating word is understood, insert it and then underline it.
3) For the adverb and adjective clauses, draw a line from the subordinating word back to the word modified. For the noun clauses, identify the part of the sentence that each clause is serving as.
4) Diagram the sentence on your own paper.

It's a truth universally acknowledged that when rich people move into the hood, where it's a little bit broken and a little bit forgotten, the first thing they want to do is clean it up.

A restrictive modifying clause defines the word that it modifies. Removing the clause changes the essential meaning of the sentence.

A non-restrictive modifying clause describes the word that it modifies. Removing the clause doesn't change the essential meaning of the sentence.

In much of Asia, the day that a baby is born is considered to be its first birthday.

Wei's second birthday, which would have been considered his first in North America, was celebrated with a feast of long noodles and red-dyed eggs.

The movie, which lasted far too long, was quite boring.
I get very angry at people who talk during a movie.
My sister, who enjoys ballet and *muay thai* fighting, has gone to climb Denali.
She ran faster because there was a mountain lion behind her.

Only non-restrictive clauses should be set off by commas.

CORRECT
Hammurabi, who spent much of his life at war, created one of the first law codes.
INCORRECT
Hammurabi who spent much of his life at war created one of the first law codes.

CORRECT
The bricks that formed their city walls were made of mud.
INCORRECT
The bricks, that formed their city walls, were made of mud.

The king had no firm foundation on which to build. ____________________

The king had no firm foundation, on which to build. ____________________

Exercise 76B: Non-Restrictive Clauses and Missing Commas

In the following sentences (some slightly condensed from the original), underline each dependent clause. Place commas around each non-restrictive clause. Use the proofreader's mark: ^,. Leave sentences with restrictive clauses as they are.

From *Pride: A Pride and Prejudice Remix*, by Ibi Zoboi

In no time, Marisol who's two years younger is standing right beside me.

It's Darius who has a firm grip on my arm.

He plops down in his usual spot on the recliner chair and grabs an old Howard Zinn book that he's read a hundred times.

Now it looks like something that belongs in the suburbs, with its wide double doors, sparkling windows, and tiny manicured lawn.

From *Pride and Prejudice*, by Jane Austen

And with a low bow he left her to attack Mr. Darcy whose reception of his advances she eagerly watched.

Mr. Bennet was among the earliest of those who waited on Mr. Bingley.

But there is one of her sisters sitting down just behind you who is very pretty, and I dare say, very agreeable.

Mr. Collins invited them to take a stroll in the garden which was large and well laid out.

But, my dear sister, can I be happy, even supposing the best, in accepting a man whose sisters and friends are all wishing him to marry elsewhere?

Between Elizabeth and Charlotte there was a restraint which kept them mutually silent on the subject.

Exercise 76C: Restrictive Clauses and Unnecessary Commas

In the following sentences, underline each dependent clause. Some dependent clauses may have other dependent clauses within them—double underline clauses within clauses!

Delete the incorrect commas that have been placed around restrictive adjective clauses. Use proofreader's marks: ℓ. Leave sentences with non-restrictive clauses as they are.

From *Kingdom of Souls*, by Rena Barron

The few girls, who speak Tamaran, ask me what it's like living so far away in the Almighty Kingdom.

It's the name, my mother calls the street peddlers in the market, the ones, who sell worthless good luck charms.

I speak for he, who has no beginning and no end.

Grandmother nods, takes the bowl, and passes it to Sukar, who swallows hard.

"Don't worry, daughter," he says, folding the sleeves of my orange-and-blue kaftan, which matches his own.

A part of me is anxious to return home, where I'm not so much of an utter failure.

From *Louisa the Poisoner*, by Tanith Lee

March Mire lay at the heart of the great moors, a swamp so dangerous, that none but fools would venture into it, and seldom did they come out. There were however local legends of persons, who lived within the mire itself, creatures, that knew the two or three safe paths across the mud.

The other portion of the leather strap had remained with the police whistle, which the lone policeman had blown.

He sat down at the long table facing Louisa, and the wardress, whom Louisa had charmed the most, stood well back at the door.

The lady, to whom you refer, is here in the court?

Louisa had appeared devoted to Lord Maskullance, in whom possibly she had alone confided.

WEEK 20

Constructing Sentences

— LESSON 77 —

Constructing Sentences

Exercise 77A: Making Sentences out of Clauses and Phrases

The independent clauses below are listed in order and make up a story—but they're missing all their supporting pieces.

On your own paper, rewrite the story by attaching the dependent clauses and phrases in Lists 2 and 3 to the independent clauses in List 1 to make complete sentences. You may insert dependent clauses that act as adjectives or adverbs into the beginning, middle, or end of independent clauses (usually by putting them right before or after the word they modify), and you may change any capitalization or punctuation necessary. But do not add or delete words.

The first sentence has been constructed for you.

Crossing out each clause or phrase as you use it will help you not to repeat yourself!

List 1. Independent Clauses

~~Daedalus of Athens was the most skilful man.~~
His statues were so lifelike.
His buildings were the envy.

Minos chose Daedalus.
Daedalus travelled to Crete and built the Labyrinth.
Daedalus himself barely found the way out.

King Minos refused.
Daedalus built a pair of wings and a smaller pair.
The wings were made.
Together, father and son rose and began to fly.

But Icarus became too confident and flew.
The waxed cords began to melt.
His wings fell, and he plunged.

List 2. Dependent Clauses

because he could not leave by either land or sea
that they almost walked and spoke
that was full of winding passages
who saw them
when the Labyrinth was finished
as he drew closer to the sun
which was a monster with the head and shoulders of a bull and the body of a man

List 3. Phrases

of his time
for himself
for his son Icarus
~~an architect, sculptor, and stoneworker~~
higher and higher
of all
because of his fame
the king of Crete
a complicated maze
to allow Daedalus
to his death
of bird feathers
into the air
towards home
ignoring his father's calls
from his shoulders
into the ocean
to make a prison
held together with waxed linen cords
for the Minotaur
to return to Athens
across the ocean

FIRST SENTENCE

Daedalus of Athens was the most skillful man of his time—an architect, sculptor, and stoneworker.

— LESSON 78 —

Simple Sentences
Complex Sentences

A sentence is a group of words that usually contains a subject and a predicate.
A sentence begins with a capital letter and ends with a punctuation mark.
A sentence contains a complete thought.

(The following sentences are from *The Cricket in Times Square*, by George Selden.)

A mouse was looking at Mario.

Gradually the dirt that had collected on the insect fell away.

A complex sentence contains at least one subordinate clause.
A simple sentence contains one independent clause and no subordinate clauses.

But in all his days, and on all his journeys through the greatest city in the world, Tucker had never heard a sound quite like this one.

No matter what else is in a simple sentence, it will only have *one* subject-predicate set in it.

Then he folded a sheet of Kleenex, tucked it in the box, and put the cricket in it.

The thrumming of the rubber tires of automobiles, and the hooting of their horns, and the howling of their brakes made a great din.

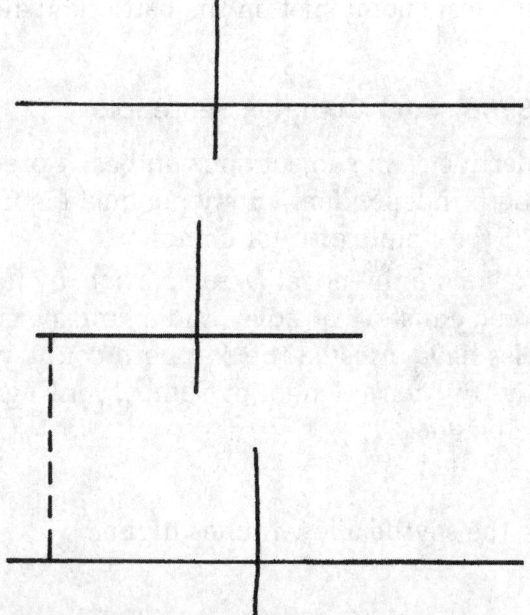

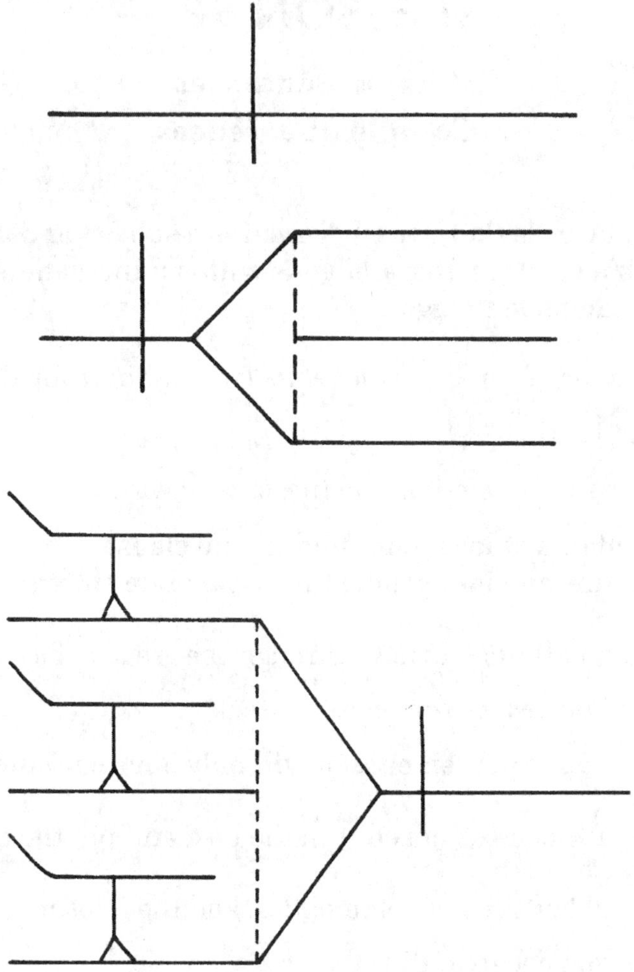

My closest friend and my greatest enemy met on the battlefield and fought bitterly.

Exercise 78A: Identifying Simple and Complex Sentences

In the sentences below, underline each subject once and each predicate twice. (Find the subjects and predicates in both independent and dependent clauses.) In the blank at the end of each sentence, write *S* for simple or *C* for complex.

These sentences are taken from the novel *Dread Nation*, by Justina Ireland. This novel, a creative cross between a historical novel and a fantasy, is set in the days just after the Civil War—when zombies have infested the southern countryside. The heroine, Jane McKeene, is a student at Miss Preston's School of Combat for Negro Girls, where she is learning to fight the zombie plague.

I swallow a groan and raise the scythe a few inches higher. ________

Miss Duncan waits until I'm about to scream from the holding before she gives me a small nod and turns back to the class. ________

I shake my arms out, one after another, willing the burn to go away. __________

So while I do believe Miss Duncan is a fine instructor, I do not believe that she is human. __________

I lift my weapon, focusing on Miss Duncan and trying to decide if she is indeed a revenant instead of thinking about the deep burning in my poor scrawny arms. __________

I slash the scythe across the empty air until my arms feel like overcooked green beans, limp and wobbly. __________

She is a crack shot with a rifle, invaluable in a long-range capacity. __________

Miss Anderson says the papers say he's going to cure the undead plague! __________

The crown jewel of my collection is the well-oiled Remington single-action, the close-range gun of choice for Miss Preston's girls. __________

Ruthie shakes her head and latches her tiny hand on my skirt, pulling me in the direction of Miss Preston's office. __________

During the Great Discord, right after the dead began to walk and before the Army finally got the shambler plague under control, the building was empty. __________

Ruthie pulls me through the main foyer and down into the left wing of the building, to the big office at the end. __________

Rumor is that Miss Preston's people had gone west to the Minnesota Territory before the war but came back when the undead got the better of them. __________

Exercise 78B: Forming Complex Sentences

On your own paper, rewrite each pair of simple sentences as a single complex sentence. The first is done for you. You will need to add a subordinating word to one of the sentences in each pair to turn it into a dependent clause.

In the last two sets of sentences, try to combine all three simple sentences into one complex sentence!

There may be more than one way to rewrite each sentence. Just make sure that your sentence is grammatical and reads well.

The original sentences are from *The Zombie Survival Guide: Complete Protection from the Living Dead*, by Max Brooks.

Zombies have caught fire.

Zombies will neither notice nor react to the engulfing flames in any way.

Zombies who have caught fire will neither notice nor react to the engulfing flames in any way.

There are hundreds of thousands of lethal compounds in this world.

It is impossible to discuss them all.

Never forget.

The body of the undead is, for all practical purposes, human.

A human body dies.

Its flesh is immediately set upon by billions of microscopic organisms.

A human body has been dead longer than twelve to eighteen hours.

A human body will be rejected as food.

It has been suggested.

Zombies possess night vision.

This fact explains their skill at nocturnal hunting.

A zombie's body is severely damaged.

It will continue to attack.

Nothing remains.

Exercise 78C: Diagramming

On your own paper, diagram the following four sentences. The sentences come from traditional Irish songs, which are reproduced here in italics so that you have context.

Beside each diagram, write the number of vertical lines dividing subjects from predicates, along with the label *S* for simple or *C* for complex.

The sentences are not difficult, but there may be a couple of interesting challenges here for you!

The Kilkenny Cats

There once were two cats of Kilkenny,
Each thought there was one cat too many.
So they fought and they fit,
And they scratched and they bit,
Till, excepting their nails
And the tips of their tails,
Instead of two cats, there weren't any.

Each thought there was one cat too many.

They scratched and bit until, instead of two cats, there weren't any.

Michael Finnigan

There was a boy called Michael Finnigan,
He grew whiskers on his chin-igan.
The wind came out and blew them in again.
Poor old Michael Finnigan, begin again.

There was an old man named Michael Finnigan,
Who went off fishing with a pinnigan.
He caught a fish, but it fell in again.
Poor old Michael Finnigan, begin again.

There was an old man named Michael Finnigan,
Who caught a cold and couldn't get well again.
Then he died, and had to begin again.
Poor old Michael Finnigan, begin again!

The wind came out and blew them in again.

There was an old man named Michael Finnigan who caught a cold and couldn't get well again.

— LESSON 79 —

Compound Sentences
Run-on Sentences
Comma Splice

(The sentences in this lesson are taken from *Pride and Prejudice*, by Jane Austen.)

Bingley had never met with more pleasant people or prettier girls in his life; everybody had been most kind and attentive to him; there had been no formality, no stiffness; he had soon felt acquainted with all the room.

A compound sentence is a sentence with two or more independent clauses.

Everybody was surprised.
Darcy, after looking at her for a moment, turned silently away.

Everybody was surprised, and Darcy, after looking at her for a moment, turned silently away.

A coordinating conjunction joins similar or equal words or groups of words together.
and, or, nor, for, so, but, yet

Run-on sentence

INCORRECT (run-on sentences)
I ran quickly down the road, it was a very long way to the end.
The rabbit leaped out of the bushes, the children watched with eager interest.

CORRECT
I ran quickly down the road**, but** it was a very long way to the end.
The rabbit leaped out of the bushes, **and** the children watched with eager interest.

Comma Splice

Mr. Bennet, you are wanted immediately.

We are all in an uproar.

Mr. Bennet, you are wanted immediately; we are all in an uproar.

colon :

semicolon ;

The envelope contained a sheet of elegant, little, hot-pressed paper, well covered with a lady's fair, flowing hand.

Elizabeth saw her sister's countenance change as she read it.

The envelope contained a sheet of elegant, little, hot-pressed paper, well covered with a lady's fair, flowing hand; and Elizabeth saw her sister's countenance change as she read it.

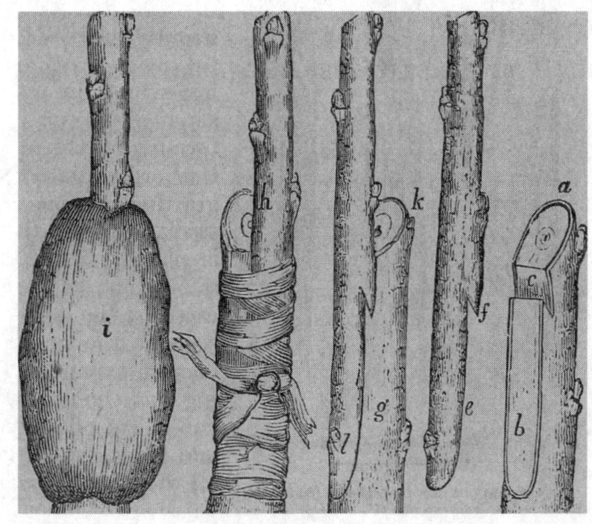

An illustration of splicing from A. J. Downing's 1889 manual *The Fruits and Fruit Trees of America*

The independent clauses of a compound sentence must be joined by a comma and a coordinating conjunction, a semicolon, or a semicolon and a coordinating conjunction. They cannot be joined by a comma alone.

Mr. Collins was not agreeable; his society was irksome, and his attachment to her must be imaginary.

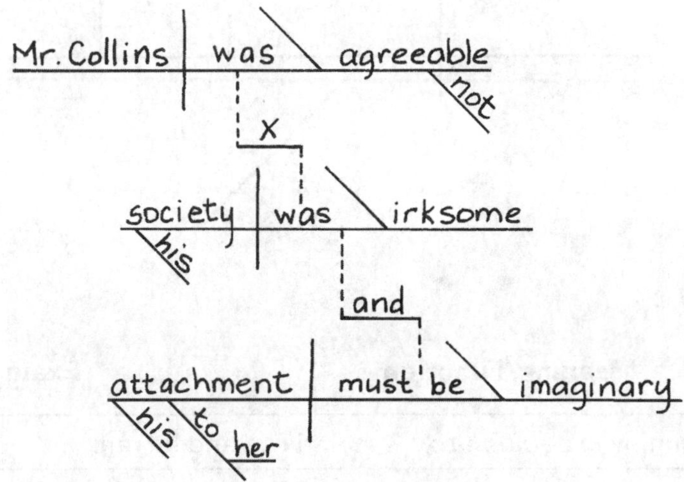

Mr. Collins is a conceited, pompous, narrow-minded, silly man; you know it, and you shall not defend Charlotte Lucas.

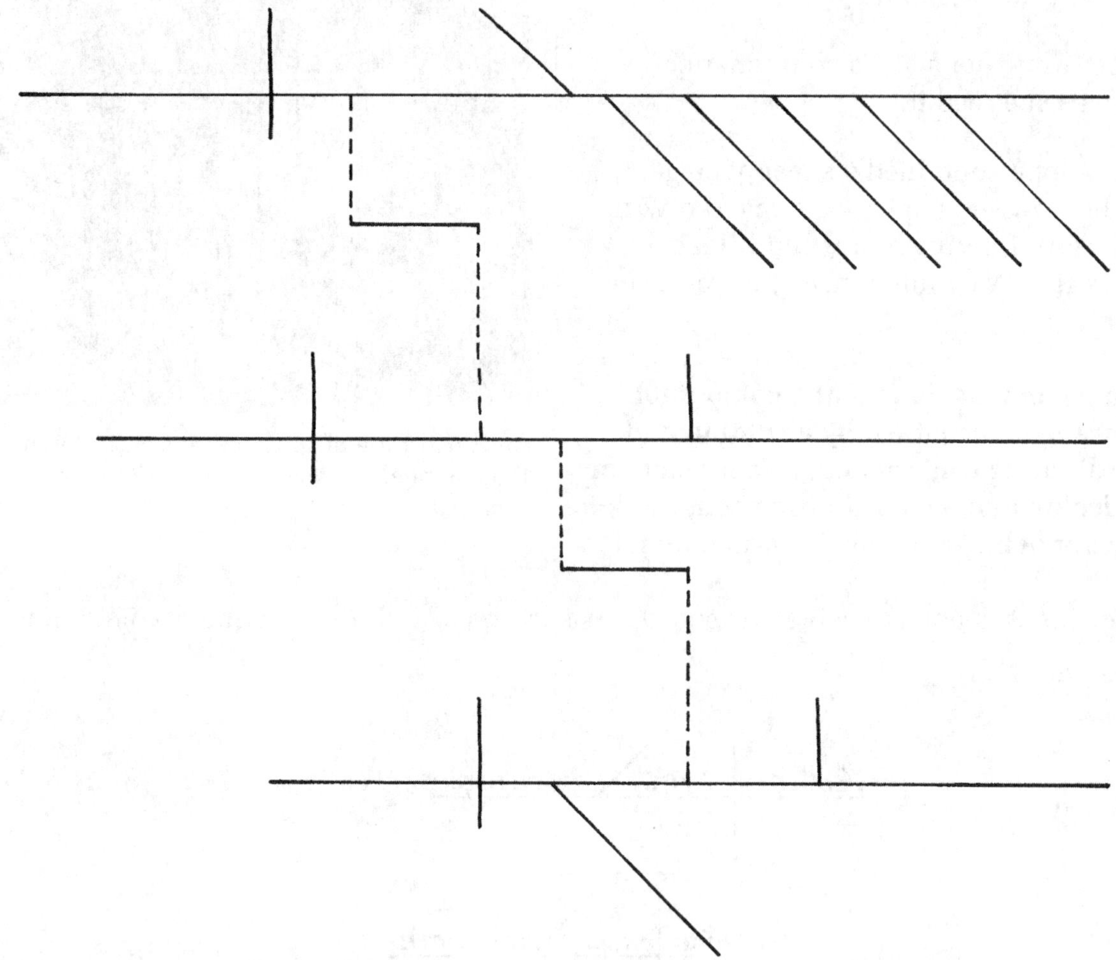

Coordinating Conjunction	Meaning/Function	Example
and	simply *in addition to*	I ran and he ran.
or	presents alternatives	He can teach or his assistant can teach.
nor	presents negative alternatives	He did not work, nor did he sleep.
for	*because*	I sang loudly, for I was happy.
so	showing results	He ate too much, so his stomach hurt.
but	*despite that*	I ran ten miles, but I wasn't tired.
yet	*nevertheless*	I had little money, yet I was content.

Exercise 79A: Forming Compound Sentences

Choose at least one independent clause from Column 1 and at least one independent clause from Column 2. Using correct punctuation and adding coordinating conjunctions as needed, combine the clauses into a compound sentence. (You may use more than two clauses, as long as your sentence makes sense!) Write your new compound sentences on your own paper. Use every clause at least once.

These clauses are taken from compound sentences written by Ernest Hemingway in his classic story *The Old Man and the Sea.*

Column 1	**Column 2**
I am a boy.	His head and back were dark purple.
The old man had taught the boy to fish.	He had no way of judging the time.
They sat on the Terrace.	In the sun the stripes on his sides showed wide and a light lavender.
Can you really remember that?	The boy loved him.
The newspaper lay across his knees.	The weight of his arm held it there in the evening breeze.
The old man went out the door.	Many of the fishermen made fun of the old man.
He was bright in the sun.	I must obey him.
The moon did not rise now until late.	Did I just tell it to you?
He was not angry.	The boy came after him.

Exercise 79B: Correcting Run-on Sentences (Comma Splices)

Using proofreader's marks (∧ to insert a coordinating conjunction, ∧, to insert a comma, ∧; to insert a semicolon), correct each of the run-on sentences below.

These are also taken from Ernest Hemingway's classic story *The Old Man and the Sea.*

The line was going out fast but steadily the fish was not panicked.

I'll keep yours and mine together on ice, we can share them in the morning.

He waited with the line between his thumb and his finger, watching it and the other lines at the same time, the fish might have swum up or down.

He was still sleeping on his face the boy was sitting by him watching him.

The old man leaned the mast with its wrapped sail against the wall the boy put the box and the other gear beside it.

But I have hurt them both badly neither one can feel very good.

The old man carried the mast on his shoulder, the boy carried the wooden box with the coiled, hard-braided brown lines, the gaff and the harpoon with its shaft.

The position actually was only somewhat less intolerable he thought of it as almost comfortable.

Exercise 79C: Diagramming

On your own paper, diagram every word of the following sentences from Ernest Hemingway's *The Old Man and the Sea.*

There was no pot of yellow rice and fish and the boy knew this too.

The line rose slowly and steadily and then the surface of the ocean bulged ahead of the boat and the fish came out.

They had eaten with no light on the table and the old man took off his trousers and went to bed in the dark.

The sail was patched with flour sacks and, furled, it looked like the flag of permanent defeat.

— LESSON 80 —

Compound Sentences

Compound-Complex Sentences

Clauses with Understood Elements

The rabbit jumped, and the lion roared, and the giraffe ambled.

The boy **who had the tickets** boarded the train, but his brother decided to hail a taxi instead; their mother knew **that they would both arrive home by bedtime.**

A compound-complex sentence is made up of two or more independent clauses, at least one of which is a complex sentence.

He was the proudest, most disagreeable man in the world, and everybody hoped that he would never come there again.

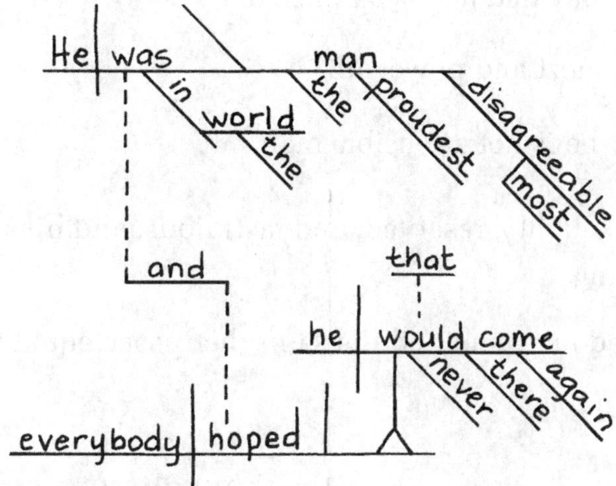

She could not recover from the surprise of what had happened; it was impossible to think of anything else; and, totally indisposed for employment, she resolved, soon after breakfast, to indulge herself in air and exercise.

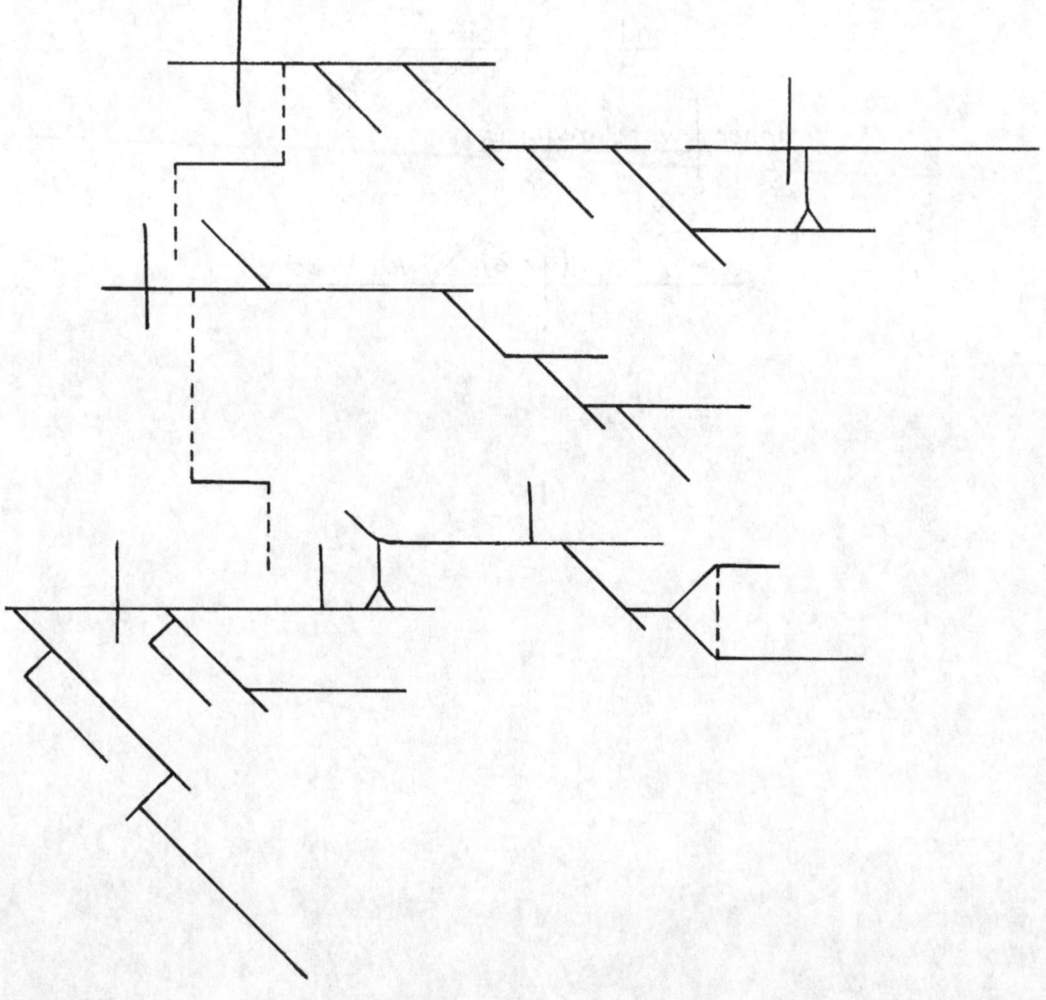

That was the weirdest thing I have ever seen.

The apples I bought yesterday had just been picked.

The speech he made was short and powerful.

He is vain, and you know he is not a sensible man.

He was at the same time haughty, reserved, and fastidious, and his manners, although well-bred, were not inviting.

The situation that troubled her remained the same, her peace equally disturbed by the circumstances.

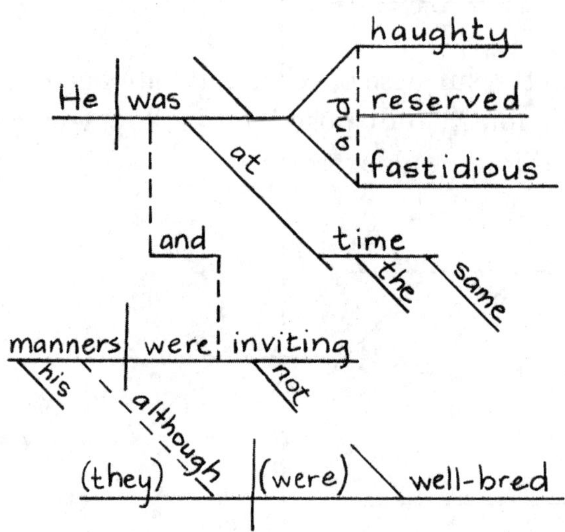

Exercise 80A: Analyzing Complex-Compound Sentences

The sentences below are all complex-compound sentences. For each sentence, carry out the following steps:

a) Cross out each prepositional phrase.
b) Circle any dependent clauses. Label them as *ADJ*, *ADV*, or *NOUN*. Draw a line from adjective and adverb clauses to the word modified. Label noun clauses with the part of the sentence that they function as.
c) Underline the subject of each independent clause once and the predicate twice.
d) Draw a vertical line between each simple and/or complex sentence.
e) Insert missing words (if any).

The first sentence has been done for you. Be careful—some dependent clauses may be within other dependent clauses!

These sentences are taken from a very famous nineteenth-century memoir called *Two Years Before the Mast*. The author, Richard Henry Dana Jr., left his college studies in 1834 and enlisted as a sailor on a merchant ship that was travelling from Boston, all the way around South America, back up to California. "Before the mast" was an expression that meant "where the common sailors sleep."

ADV

Early ~~in the morning~~ she was overhauling us a little, | but after the rain came on and the wind grew lighter, we began to leave her astern.

It was now the middle of April, the southeaster season was nearly over, and the light, regular winds, which blow down the coast, began to set steadily in, during the latter part of each day.

Among other bad practices, he frequently slept on his watch, and, having been discovered asleep by the captain, he was told that he would be turned off duty if he did it again.

Whatever your feelings may be, you must make a joke of everything at sea; and if you were to fall from aloft and be caught in the belly of a sail, and thus saved from instant death, it would not do to look at all disturbed, or to treat it seriously.

Some of the watch were asleep, and the others were quiet, so that there was nothing to break the illusion, and I stood leaning over the bulwarks, listening to the slow breathings of the mighty creatures,— now one breaking the water just alongside, whose black body I could see through the fog; and again another, which I could just hear in the distance, — until the low and regular swell seemed like the heaving of the ocean's mighty bosom to the sound of its own heavy and long-drawn respirations.

He told me that I could go home in the ship when she sailed (which I knew before); and, finding that I wished to be on board while she was on the coast, he said he had no objection, if I could find one of my own age to exchange with me for the time.

Exercise 80B: Constructing Complex-Compound Sentences

From each set of independent clauses, construct a single complex-compound sentence. You may turn any of the clauses into dependent clauses by adding subordinating words, insert any other words necessary, omit unnecessary words, and make any other needed changes, but try to keep the original meaning of each clause. You must use every clause in the set!

You may turn a clause into a prepositional phrase or another form, as long as your resulting sentence has at least two independent clauses and one dependent clause and contains all of the information in the listed clauses.

These sets of clauses are based on sentences from the opening chapter of the sea adventure novel *Master and Commander*, by Patrick O'Brian. The main character, Jack Aubrey, is a lieutenant in the British navy during the Napoleonic Wars (1803-1815). He is also an amateur musician. In this first chapter, he is waiting to find out if he will be given a ship to captain, and he also attends a chamber music concert.

Write your new sentences on your own paper. The first has been done for you.

He found something.
His hand was high in the air, beating time.
He lowered it, clenched his mouth shut and looked down at his feet.
The music was over.

He found that his hand was high in the air, beating time; he lowered it, clenched his mouth shut and looked down at his feet until the music was over.

It was a witty, agreeable minuet, no more.

It was succeeded by a curiously difficult, almost harsh last movement.

That piece seemed to be on the edge of saying something of the very greatest importance.

Jack Aubrey's face instantly changed from friendly ingenuous communicative pleasure to an expression of somewhat baffled hostility.

He could not but acknowledge something.

He had been beating the time.

He had certainly done so with perfect accuracy.

In itself the thing was wrong.

It was difficult to tell his age.

He had that kind of face.

That kind of face does not give anything away.

He was wearing a wig, a grizzled wig, apparently made of wire, and quite devoid of powder.

He might have been anything between twenty and sixty.

The volume of sound died away to the single whispering of a fiddle.

The steady hum of low conversation had never stopped at the back of the room.

The steady hum of low conversation threatened to drown it.

A soldier exploded in a stifled guffaw.

Jack looked angrily around.

His anger could not for the moment find any outward expression.

His anger took on the form of melancholy.

He thought of his shipless state.

He thought of half and whole promises made to him and broken.

He thought of the many schemes.

He had built up many schemes on visionary foundations.

Exercise 80C: Diagramming

On your own paper, diagram the following sentences from Ernest Hemingway's *The Old Man and the Sea.* Next to your diagram, label each sentence as compound (*C*), complex (*CX*), or compound-complex (*CCX*).

For an hour the old man had been seeing black spots before his eyes and the sweat salted his eyes and salted the cut over his eye and on his forehead.

But when the strain showed the fish had turned to come toward the boat, the old man rose to his feet and started the pivoting and the weaving pulling that brought in the line he gained.

He settled comfortably against the wood and took his suffering as it came and the fish swam steadily and the boat moved slowly through the dark water.

WEEK 21

Conditions

— LESSON 81 —

Helping Verbs
Tense and Voice
Modal Verbs

Helping Verbs
am, is, are, was, were
be, being, been
have, has, had
do, does, did
shall, will, should, would, may, might, must
can, could

In a sentence with an active verb, the subject performs the action.
In a sentence with a passive verb, the subject receives the action.

The progressive past tense uses the helping verbs *was* and *were*.
The progressive past passive voice uses the helping verbs *was/were being.*
The progressive present tense uses the helping verbs *am, is,* and *are*.
The progressive present passive voice uses the helping verbs *is/are being.*
The progressive future tense uses the helping verbs *will* and *be*.
The progressive future passive voice uses the helping verbs *will be being.*

Perfect past verbs describe an action that was finished in the past before another action began.
The active voice uses the helping verb *had.*
The passive voice uses the helping verbs *had been.*
Perfect present verbs describe an action that was completed before the present moment.
The active voice uses the helping verb *have.*
The passive voice uses the helping verbs *has/have been.*
Perfect future verbs describe an action that will be finished in the future before another action begins.
The active voice uses the helping verb *will have.*
The passive voice uses the helping verbs *will have been.*

NOTE: Shall and will are different forms of the same verb.

I do not believe in aliens.

He does not believe in aliens.

We did not believe in aliens (until they landed).

Do you believe in aliens?
Does he believe in aliens?
Did we believe in aliens (after they landed)?

I do too believe in aliens!
He does believe in aliens!
We did believe in aliens (once they had landed)!

Use the helping verbs *do, does,* and *did* to form negatives, ask questions, and provide emphasis.

	SIMPLE PRESENT		SIMPLE PRESENT EMPHATIC	
First person	I believe	we believe	I do believe	we do believe
Second person	you believe	you believe	you do believe	you do believe
Third person	he, she, it believes	they believe	he, she, it does believe	they do believe

	SIMPLE PAST		SIMPLE PAST EMPHATIC	
First person	I believed	we believed	I did believe	we did believe
Second person	you believed	you believed	you did believe	you did believe
Third person	he, she, it believed	they believed	he, she, it did believe	they did believe

We should be prepared for the arrival of alien spacecraft.
On earth, a Martian would weigh three times more than on Mars.
Strange creatures may visit Earth in our lifetime.
Alien invaders might want to conquer us.
The arrival of aliens must change our world.
We can scarcely imagine what that change will be.
We could find out that the aliens are friendly.

Modal verbs express situations that have not actually happened.
would, can, could, may, might: **possibility**
must, should: **obligation**
may: **permission**
can: **ability**

I would love to go eat a huge cheeseburger.
I can either sleep or eat.

I could probably finish my work by supper.
I may go down to the hamburger stand on the boardwalk.
I might get a burger with onions and Swiss cheese.

I must stop eating this cheeseburger!
I really should eat more vegetables.

Yes, you may eat that burger!

I can exercise self-control!

SIMPLE PRESENT MODAL		
First person	I could eat	We could eat
Second person	You could eat	You could eat
Third person	He could eat	They could eat

PERFECT PRESENT MODAL		
First person	I should have eaten	We should have eaten
Second person	You should have eaten	You should have eaten
Third person	She should have eaten	They should have eaten

I should've finished my work early; I could've finished it, if I'd had peace and quiet; I would've finished it, if everyone hadn't kept interrupting me.

Exercise 81A: Using *Do, Does*, and *Did*

In the blanks provided, rewrite the bolded verbs in the form described in brackets. Use the appropriate form of the helping verb along with any interrogatives or negatives necessary.

Don't forget that you may have to change the form of the verb! The first one is done for you.

These sentences are slightly adapted from Daniel Defoe's *Journal of the Plague Year*, an account of the 1665 bubonic plague that decimated the city of London.

When I speak of rows of houses being shut up, I **mean** shut up by the magistrates. [Turn into a negative statement]

When I speak of rows of houses being shut up, I do not mean shut up by the magistrates.

The making of so many fires, as above, **consumed** an unusual quantity of coals. [Provide emphasis]

The making of so many fires, as above, ______________ an unusual quantity of coals.

This hardship **exposed** me to any disaster. [Turn into a negative statement]

This hardship ________________ me to any disaster.

Any body **goes** by water these times. [Change into a question]

__________________ any body __________________ by water these times?

I **remember** how many died in the house itself. [Turn into a negative statement]

I __________________ how many died in the house itself.

You **stop** us on the king's highway, and pretend to deny us. [Change into a question]

__________________ you __________________ us on the king's highway, and pretend to deny us ____

But the next town behind me will, by the same rule, deny me leave to go back, and so they **starve** me between them. [Provide emphasis]

But the next town behind me will, by the same rule, deny me leave to go back, and so they __________________ me between them.

Our horsemen cannot pass with our baggage that way; it **leads** into the road that we want to go. [Turn into a negative statement]

Our horsemen cannot pass with our baggage that way; __________________ into the road that we want to go.

"Well, but," says I to him, "you **left** her the four shillings too." [Change into a question]

"Well, but," says I to him, "__________________ you __________________ her the four shillings too?"

The young woman, her mother, and the maid had been abroad on some occasion, though I **remember** what. [Turn into a negative statement]

The young woman, her mother, and the maid had been abroad on some occasion, though I __________________ what.

The magistrates **moderated and eased** families upon many occasions in this case. [Provide emphasis]

The magistrates __________________ families upon many occasions in this case.

But still my friend's observation was just, and it **appeared** that the people **recovered** faster and more in number. [Provide emphasis]

But still my friend's observation was just, and it __________________ that the people __________________ faster and more in number.

For though it is true that all the people **went** out of the city of London, yet I may venture to say that in a manner all the horses did. [Turn into a negative statement]

For though it is true that all the people __________________ out of the city of London, yet I may venture to say that in a manner all the horses did.

This is one of the reasons why I believed then, and **believe** still, that the shutting up houses thus by force was of little or no service in the whole. [Provide emphasis]

This is one of the reasons why I believed then, and ________________ still, that the shutting up houses thus by force was of little or no service in the whole.

The mourners **went** about the streets indeed, for nobody put on black or made a formal dress of mourning for their nearest friends. [Turn into a negative statement]

The mourners ________________ about the streets indeed, for nobody put on black or made a formal dress of mourning for their nearest friends.

First, it is so ordered, that every householder **cause** the street before his door to be clean swept all the week long. [Provide emphasis]

First, it is so ordered, that every householder ________________ the street before his door to be clean swept all the week long.

Exercise 81B: Modal Verbs

Fill in the blanks below with an appropriate helping verb (*should, would, may, might, must, can, could*) to form a modal verb. There may be more than one correct answer for each sentence. Use each helping verb at least once.

These sentences are taken from the anonymously written *A General History of the Pyrates, From Their First Rise and Settlement in the Island of Providence, to the Present Time.* Back in the author's day (the late seventeenth and early eighteenth centuries), writers capitalized any words that they thought were important—so we've kept the original capitalization in these excerpts. (Also, Defoe spelled *pirate* as *pyrate*, which is pronounced in exactly the same way!)

After you finish the exercise, be sure to read the original sentences in the *Answer Key.*

Caesar commanded that the Prisoners ________________ be brought and executed, according to the Laws in Cases of Pyracy.

You ________________ understand that these Men continually found Favours and Incouragers at Jamaica, and perhaps they are not all dead yet.

The Lords humbly besought her Majesty to use such Methods as she ________________ think proper for taking the said Island into her Hands.

Their Vessels were so small that they ________________ not attack a Ship of any Force.

He often proceeded to bully the Governor, not that I ________________ discover the least Cause of Quarrel betwixt them.

If such a one has but Courage, he ________________ certainly be a great Man.

How many you ________________ have killed of those that resisted you in the committing of your former Pyracies, I know now.

However, the Governor dissembled, received the Pyrates Invitation civilly, and promised that he and the rest ________________ go.

In the beginning he was very averse to this sort of Life, and ________________ certainly have escaped from it, had a fair Opportunity presented itself.

There are many Harbours to which Pyrates ________________ securely resort without Fear of Discovery from the Inhabitants.

Why ________________ Men, honestly disposed, give their Votes for such a Captain?

It came into his Head that the Tankard ________________ prove of some Use to him.

As to the Lives of our two female Pyrates, we ________________ confess they may appear a little Extravagant.

I understand how to navigate a Ship, and I ________________ soon teach you to steer.

He ________________ say little in Defence of himself.

It cannot be supposed that such a Man of War as this ________________ undertake any considerable Voyage, or attempt any extraordinary Enterprize.

Exercise 81C: Verb Tense and Voice

For each sentence below, underline each verb phrase (in both dependent and independent clauses) and identify the tense and voice of the verb. For state-of-being verbs that are neither active nor passive in voice, identify the tense and write *state-of-being*. Mark modal verbs as *perfect present modal, active* (or *passive*) or *simple present modal, active* (or *passive*). The first sentence is done for you.

These sentences are taken from *Treasure Island*, by Robert Louis Stevenson.

simple past, active — simple present modal, active — perfect past, active

Every day when he came back from his stroll he would ask if any seafaring men had gone by along the road.

That was Flint's treasure that we had come so far to seek.

I have seen him wringing his hands after such a rebuff, and I am sure the annoyance and the terror he lived in must have greatly hastened his early and unhappy death.

You may imagine how I felt when I heard this abominable old rogue addressing another in the very same words of flattery as he had used to myself.

Probably I should have told the whole story to the doctor, for I was in mortal fear lest the captain should repent of his confessions.

The captain had been struck dead by thundering apoplexy.

My heart was beating finely when we two set forth in the cold night upon this dangerous venture.

The ship is bought.

The thing was extremely small, even for me, and I can hardly imagine that it could have floated with a full-sized man.

Now, to tell you the truth, from the very first mention of Long John in Squire Trelawney's letter I had taken a fear in my mind that he might prove to be the very one-legged sailor whom I had watched for so long at the old Benbow.

— LESSON 82 —

Conditional Sentences
The Condition Clause
The Consequence Clause

(The following sentences are from *The Phantom Tollbooth*, by Norton Juster.)

If you have any more questions, please ask the giant.

If one is right, then ten are ten times as right.

If you are not perfectly satisfied, your wasted time will be refunded.

A condition is a circumstance that restricts, limits, or modifies.

Snow only falls when three conditions are met: the temperature up high is freezing, the temperature at ground level is freezing, and there are water droplets in the air.

A condition clause describes a circumstance that has not yet happened.
A consequence clause describes the results that will take place if the condition clause happens.

Unless it gets warmer, I will stay inside.

I will not go for a walk if it remains this cold.

When the temperature reaches 70 degrees, I will go outside.

Should it rain, I will not come.

Had he been fired, he could have left immediately.

Refuse my conditions, and I will become your enemy!

A conditional sentence expresses the conditions under which an action may take place. It contains a condition clause and a consequence clause.

CONDITION CONSEQUENCE
If you have any more questions, please ask the giant. ____________________

CONDITION CONSEQUENCE
If one is right, then ten are ten times as right. ____________________

CONDITION CONSEQUENCE
If you are not perfectly satisfied, your wasted time will be refunded. ____________________

First conditional sentences express circumstances that might actually happen.

The predicate of the condition clause is in a ____________________________ tense.

The predicate of the consequence clause is an ____________________________ or is in a

____________________________ or ____________________________ tense.

If only Rhyme and Reason were here, things would improve.

If you walked as fast as possible and looked at nothing but your shoes, you would arrive at your destination more quickly.

Second conditional sentences express circumstances that are contrary to reality.

The predicate of the condition clause is in a ______________________ tense.

The predicate of the consequence clause is in the ______________________ tense.

Modal verbs express situations that have not actually happened.

Simple Present

I would improve	We would improve
You would improve	You would improve
He would improve	They would improve

Perfect Past

I could have arrived	We could have arrived
You could have arrived	You could have arrived
She could have arrived	They could have arrived

If we had told you then, you might not have gone.

If the kingdom had been divided equally, both sons would now rule as kings.

Third conditional sentences express past circumstances that never happened.

The predicate of the condition clause is in the ______________________ tense.

The predicate of the consequence clause is in the ______________________ or

______________________ tense.

Exercise 82A: Identifying Conditional Sentences

Some of the sentences in this exercise are conditional sentences—and others are not! Identify each conditional sentence by writing a *C* in the margin. For each conditional sentence, label the clauses as *condition* or *consequence*.

These sentences are taken from the collection *The Oxford Book of Japanese Short Stories*, edited by Theodore William Goossen.

I would be so happy if you could come with me to the mountain.

Though twenty years had passed, Konko could still see Nichiyo's expression clearly.

If you're not here, I suppose they'll make me do the work of two.

Unless one managed to get into one of the cars—at the risk of life and limb—one would have to wait additional long hours.

I was attracted to things that had something of an impoverished beauty about them.

If the four had been making a pilgrimage to some nearby temple, their appearance would not have been extraordinary.

As soon as she saw him come in, she gave the command she had prepared for him.

On the ground, still locked, lay the steel shackle that had been fastened to the elephant's hind leg, as though the elephant had slipped out of it.

Let's go and see if your father's had any luck.

If only I could sew you a nice kimono, it would be a happy day.

Exercise 82B: Tense in Conditional Sentences

Fill in each blank below with the correct tense and form of the verb in brackets. Some sentences may have more than one possible correct answer.

These sentences are drawn from the anthologies *The Oxford Book of American Short Stories*, edited by Joyce Carol Oates, and *The World's Greatest Short Stories*, edited by James Daley.

Don't forget that the consequence clause might come before the condition clause!

First conditional sentences

If the speeches _______________ [state of being] successful, MacPherson _______________ [take] all the credit.

If we _______________ [meet] again, why, we _______________ [smile].

If I _______________ [speak] the truth it _______________ [state of being] my wife and my children who will pay in hardships for my outspokenness.

Snakes _______________ [negative form of hurt] you unless you _______________ [hurt] them.

We' _________ [go] before six o'clock if you _______________ [want] to sleep.

If you _______________ [shatter] this hour of peace, _______________ [think] of the mark on the wall.

Second conditional sentences

If Gabriel ever __________________ [break] the silence of the North, they ___________ [stand] together, hand in hand, before the great White Throne.

If, after reaching home, he __________________ [find] himself at any time in want of aid, a letter from him __________________ [state of being] sure of a reply.

If I __________________ [do] that, I __________________ [catch] myself out, and stretch my hand at once for a book in self-protection.

Third conditional sentences

If he and she __________________ [progressive form of *live*] in those days he ________ [see] ever so clearly the Cause for that fighting.

They __________________ perhaps __________________ [remained] with him longer, if those pushing up behind them __________________ [negative form of *make*] a longer peaceful observation impossible.

They __________________ [negative form of *have*] a more perfect day for a garden-party if they __________________ [order] it.

If someone __________________ [die] there normally, we __________________ still __________________ [progressive form of *have*] our party.

Exercise 82C: Diagramming

On your own paper, diagram these sentences, taken from J. R. R. Tolkien's *The Two Towers.* A conditional clause should be diagrammed like any other dependent clause.

Unless our enemies rest also, they will leave us far behind, if we stay to sleep.

None could pass the Teeth of Mordor and not feel their bite, unless they were summoned by Sauron, or knew the secret passwords that would open the Morannon, the black gate of his land.

— LESSON 83 —

Conditional Sentences

The Subjunctive

First conditional sentences express circumstances that might actually happen.
The predicate of the condition clause is in a present tense.
The predicate of the consequence clause is in an imperative, present, or future tense.

If we surrender and I return with you, will you promise not to hurt this man?

So bow down to her if you want, bow to her.

If she is otherwise when I find her, I shall be very put out.

Unless I am wrong (and I am never wrong), they are headed dead into the fire swamp.

Second conditional sentences express circumstances that are contrary to reality.
The predicate of the condition clause is in a past tense.
The predicate of the consequence clause is in the simple present modal tense.

I would not say such things if I were you!

If I had a month to plan, maybe I could come up with something.

If we only had a wheelbarrow, that would be something.

Third conditional sentences express past circumstances that never happened.
The predicate of the condition clause is in the perfect past tense.
The predicate of the consequence clause is in the perfect present modal or simple present modal tense.

But they would have killed Westley, if I hadn't done it.

CONTRARY TO FACT	FACT
If we surrender	We surrender.
If you want	We want.
If she is	She is.
If I were	I was.
If we had	We had.

Subjunctive verbs express situations that are unreal, wished for, or uncertain.
Indicative verbs affirm or declare what actually is.

I eat gingerbread men.

If I eat too many gingerbread men, I will not want any dinner.

The three little pigs build houses.

If the three little pigs build straw houses, the wolf will blow them all down.

INDICATIVE SIMPLE PAST		
First person	I was	we were
Second person	you were	you were
Third person	he, she, it was	they were

SUBJUNCTIVE SIMPLE PAST		
First person	I were	we were
Second person	you were	you were
Third person	he, she, it were	they were

CORRECT	I would not say such things if I were you!
INCORRECT	I would not say such things if I was you!

CORRECT	I was cold.
CORRECT	If I were cold, I would put on a hat.
INCORRECT	If I was cold, I would put on a hat.

He was smart.

If he __________ smart, he would go immediately.

I insist <u>that she leave the door open.</u>

I recommend <u>that he arrive early.</u>

The professor asked <u>that the student read out loud.</u>

	INDICATIVE SIMPLE PRESENT		**SUBJUNCTIVE SIMPLE PRESENT**	
First person	I leave	we leave	I leave	we leave
Second person	you leave	you leave	you leave	you leave
Third person	he, she, it leaves	they leave	he, she, it leave	they leave

It is vital that a life guard ____________ the children swim. [subjunctive present of *watch*]

The life guard ____________________ the children swim. [indicative present of *watch*]

The woman demanded that the mechanic __________ her car. [subjunctive present of *fix*]

The mechanic ________________ her car. [indicative present of *fix*]

My mother suggested that my sister ____________ to bed early. [subjunctive present of *go*]

My sister ______________ to bed early. [indicative present of *go*]

Exercise 83A: Subjunctive Forms in Folk Tales

Fill in each blank with the correct state-of-being verb. These sentences are taken from the tales collected by the Brothers Grimm.

If I __________ to fall from one of these great clods, I should undoubtedly break my neck.

I ______________ going to split the tre to get a little wood for cooking.

"Ah me!" cried the wife, "'if I ______________ but a thousand feet beneath the earth!"

But she set to work so nimbly, and pulled the lace so tight, that Snowdrop's breath was stopped, and she fell down as if she ______________ dead.

He ______________ undecided, and knew not if he ______________ worthy of this.

But as the king and queen had only twelve golden dishes for them to eat out of, they ______________ forced to leave one of the fairies out.

And they ______________ married that very day, and the soldier ______________ chosen to be the king's heir.

He has taken the chickens which I ______________ just going to serve up, off the dish, and has run away with them!

I wish you ___________ a raven and would fly away; then I should have a little peace!

The countryman then began to tell his tale, and said he ____________ going to take the goose to a christening.

I think if I ___________ to take another draught it would do me no harm.

When she ___________ emptying the beans into the pan, one dropped without her observing it, and lay on the ground beside a straw.

When he came to the sea, it looked blue and gloomy, though it ____________ very calm.

As they came near the brook they saw something like a large grasshopper jumping towards the water, as if it ______________ going to leap in.

Exercise 83B: Correct Verb Forms in Complex Sentences

In each pair of verb forms, cross out the incorrect form. These sentences are taken from Kate DiCamillo's modern fairy tale *The Tale of Despereaux: Being the Story of a Mouse, a Princess, Some Soup, and a Spool of Thread.*

The darkness had a physical presence as if it (was / were) a being all its own.

And so the prisoner took the cloth and draped it around his shoulders as if it (was / were) a cloak.

She (was / were) a natural-born cynic who lived in defiance of contracts!

I hope that the hair on the back of your neck stood up as you thought of Mig's fate and how it would be if it (was / were) your own.

And so he (was / were) reading the story as if it (was / were) a spell and the words of it, spoken aloud, could make magic happen.

When Despereaux stepped from the last stair onto the dungeon floor, Botticelli called out to him as if he (was / were) a long-lost friend.

"There is a rat in my soup" (was / were) the last words she uttered.

The king stamped his foot harder, and then harder still, so it seemed as if the whole castle, the very world, (was / were) shaking.

Terrible howls issued from the dark place, as if the castle itself (was / were) weeping.

But as soon as the princess said this, her mother (was / were) gone.

So the mouse raised his head and squared his shoulders and pushed the spool of thread forward again, into the kitchen, where he saw, too late, that there (was / were) a light burning.

Reader, if you (was / were) standing in the dungeon, you would certainly hear all of these disturbing and ominous sounds.

If I (was / were) standing in the dungeon, I would hear these sounds.

His paws (was / were) shaking and his muscles (was / were) jumping and the place where his tail should be (was / were) throbbing.

— LESSON 84 —

Conditional Sentences
The Subjunctive
Moods of Verbs
Subjunctive Forms Using *Be*

Tense
A simple verb simply tells whether an action takes place in the past, present, or future.
A progressive verb describes an ongoing or continuous action.
A perfect verb describes an action which has been completed before another action takes place.

The air was bracing, yet with a cold edge which made the travelers grateful for the cloaks

Medwyn had given them.

Voice
In a sentence with an active verb, the subject performs the action.
In a sentence with a passive verb, the subject receives the action.

It is not given to men to know the ends of their journeys.

Mood
Indicative verbs express real actions.
Subjunctive verbs express unreal actions.
Imperative verbs express intended actions.
Modal verbs express possible actions.

"Drink," the stranger said again, while Taran took the flask dubiously. "You look as

though I were trying to poison you."

There can be no victory over the Cauldron-Born, but with luck, we can hold.

First conditional sentences express circumstances that might actually happen.
The predicate of the condition clause is in a present tense.
The predicate of the consequence clause is an imperative, present or future tense.

Unless I am wrong (and I am never wrong), they are headed dead into the fire swamp.

Second conditional sentences express circumstances that are contrary to reality.
The predicate of the condition clause is in a past tense.
The predicate of the consequence clause is in the simple present modal tense.

If we only had a wheelbarrow, that would be something.

Third conditional sentences express past circumstances that never happened.
The predicate of the condition clause is in the perfect past tense.
The predicate of the consequence clause is in the perfect present modal or simple present modal tense.

But they would have killed Westley, if I hadn't done it.

SIMPLE PAST INDICATIVE
He left me behind.

SIMPLE PAST SUBJUNCTIVE SIMPLE PRESENT MODAL
If he left me behind, I would feel quite upset.

	INDICATIVE PRESENT (SIMPLE)		SUBJUNCTIVE PRESENT (SIMPLE)	
First person	I leave	we leave	I leave	we leave
Second person	you leave	you leave	you leave	you leave
Third person	he, she, it leaves	they leave	he, she, it **leave**	they leave

INDICATIVE He leaves at noon.
SUBJUNCTIVE It's important that he leave at noon.

	INDICATIVE PAST (SIMPLE)		SUBJUNCTIVE PAST (SIMPLE)	
First person	I was	we were	I were	we were
Second person	you were	you were	you were	you were
Third person	he, she, it was	they were	he, she, it were	they were

SIMPLE PRESENT MODAL PAST SUBJUNCTIVE
I <u>would</u> not <u>say</u> such things if I <u>were</u> you!

SIMPLE PRESENT INDICATIVE SIMPLE PAST SUBJUNCTIVE
CORRECT You look as though I were trying to poison you.

SIMPLE PRESENT INDICATIVE SIMPLE PAST INDICATIVE
INCORRECT You look as though I was trying to poison you.

I wish he were here.

A trace of a smile appeared on his face, as though he were savoring something pleasant.

	INDICATIVE PRESENT (SIMPLE)		SUBJUNCTIVE PRESENT (SIMPLE)	
First person	I am	we are	I be	we be
Second person	you are	you are	you be	you be
Third person	he, she, it is	they are	he, she, it be	they be

INDICATIVE I am well-organized.
SUBJUNCTIVE My job requires that I be well-organized.

INDICATIVE You are on time.
SUBJUNCTIVE I strongly suggest that you be on time.
SUBJUNCTIVE/MODAL Tomorrow, you should be on time.

He suggested that she be given a new task.

The captain ordered that the anchor be lifted.

It is vital that we all be properly prepared.

The present passive subjunctive is formed by pairing *be* with the *past participle* of a verb.

enjoy ____________________
juggle ____________________
plan ____________________
roast ____________________

Exercise 84A: Parsing Verbs

In the following sentences from the classic short story "The Yellow Wallpaper," by Charlotte Perkins Gilman, underline each predicate, in both main clauses and dependent clauses. Above each, write the tense, voice, and mood of the verb.

Tenses: Simple past, present, future; progressive past, present, future; perfect past, present, future
Voice: Active, passive (or state-of-being)
Mood: Indicative, subjunctive, imperative, modal, subjunctive/modal

Something to look out for: sometimes one helping verb will actually help out two different verbs! The first example of this has been done for you. Note that both verbs are modal (we have inserted the understood helping verb in brackets).

It is very seldom that mere ordinary people like John and myself secure ancestral halls for the summer.

simple present, active, modal — simple present, active, modal

A colonial mansion, a hereditary estate, I would say a haunted house, and [would] reach the height of romantic felicity—but that would be asking too much of fate!

Still I will proudly declare that there is something queer about it.

Else, why should it be let so cheaply?

I don't like our room a bit. I wanted one downstairs that opened on the piazza and had roses all over the window, and such pretty old-fashioned chintz hangings! but John would not hear of it.

I think sometimes that if I were only well enough to write a little it would relieve the press of ideas and rest me.

I wish I could get well faster.

But I must not think about that.

Even when I go to ride, if I turn my head suddenly and surprise it—there is that smell!

Such a peculiar odor, too! I have spent hours in trying to analyze it, to find what it smelled like.

Then he took me in his arms and called me a blessed little goose, and said he would go down cellar if I wished, and have it whitewashed into the bargain.

Exercise 84B: Forming Subjunctives and Modals

Fill in the blanks in the following sentences, from the classic novella *The Haunting of Hill House*, by Shirley Jackson, with the correct verb form indicated in brackets.

I think that I ________________ [simple present active modal of *like*] this better if I ________________ [simple past active subjunctive of *have*] the blankets over my head.

If I ________________ [perfect past active subjunctive of *see*, negative form] Hill House, __________ I __________ [simple present state-of-being modal] so unfair to these people?

You ________________ [perfect present active modal of *see*] the ham they had.

If it _______________ [perfect past active subjunctive of *happen*, negative form] you _______________ never _______________ [perfect present active modal of *come*] to Hill House.

What a farmer's wife you _______________ [perfect present active modal of *make*].

Eleanor, wondering if she _______________ [simple past state-of-being subjunctive] really here at all, and not dreaming of Hill House from some safe spot impossibly remote, looked slowly and carefully around the room.

Hill House was left jointly to the two sisters, who _______________ [perfect present state-of-being modal] quite young ladies by then.

He looked as though he _______________ [simple past state-of-being subjunctive] doggedly counting to a hundred.

Perhaps if I _______________ [simple present active subjunctive of *mention*, negative form] Hill House I will not be doing wrong.

She brought her hand up to the heavy iron knocker that had a child's face, determined to make more noise and yet more, so that Hill House _______________ [simple present state-of-being subjunctive] very sure she was there.

If we _______________ [simple present active subjunctive of *let*] you go off wandering by yourself we'd very likely never find you again.

For a few minutes she _______________ [perfect present passive modal of *persuade*] to believe that nothing had happened.

Exercise 84C: Diagramming

On your own paper, diagram the following sentences, from *Wide Sargasso Sea,* by Jean Rhys.

If some of the flowers were battered, the others smelt sweeter, the air was bluer and sparkling fresh.

Reality might disconcert her, bewilder her, hurt her, but it would not be reality.

It must have rained heavily during the night for the red clay was very muddy.

— REVIEW 7 —

Weeks 19-21

Topics
Phrases and Clauses
Adjective, Adverb, and Noun Clauses
Pronouns
Mood: Modal, Subjective, Imperative, Indicative
Conditional Sentences

Review 7A: Improving Sentences with Phrases

In the blanks below, supply phrases that meet the descriptions in brackets. You may supply more than one phrase in any blank, as long as at least one phrase fulfills the requirements (often, additional prepositional phrases may be needed). The first is done for you.

The original sentences are taken from Edith Nesbit's classic collection of tales, *The Book of Dragons*.

This is a challenging assignment—prepare to spend some time on it!

When you are finished, compare your sentences with the originals in the *Answer Key*.

adverbial prepositional phrase answering the question *where*

The Queen and the Princess were feeding the goldfish __in the courtyard fountains__

adverbial prepositional phrase answering the question *how*

__with crumbs of the Princess's eighteenth birthday cake__, when the King came into the

adjectival participle phrase describing the raven

courtyard, looking as black as thunder, with his black raven __hopping after him__.

adverbial prepositional phrase describing to what extent Nurse let go

The minute Nurse let go ____________________ Lionel bolted off

adverbial prepositional phrase describing how Lionel bolted off

____________________, and in the drawing room there were two very

adjectival prepositional phrase describing the gold coronets

grave-looking gentlemen in red robes with fur, and gold coronets __________.

adjectival past participle phrase describing the hedge

There was a great hedge at the end of this field, ____________________;

but the children found a place where there was a hole, and as no bears or wolves seemed to be just in that part of the hedge, they crept through and scrambled out of the frozen ditch on the other side.

adjectival present participle phrase describing the road

For in front of them, ________________, lay a great wide road of

adjectival present participle phrase describing the trees

pure dark ice, and on each side were tall trees ________________,

adjectival past participle phrase describing the strings of stars

and from the boughs of the trees hung strings of stars ________________,

prepositional phrase acting as a predicate adjective describing *like*

and shining so brightly that it was ________________.

adverbial prepositional phrase answering the question *where*

And as the dragon came ________________, following Johnnie

adverbial prepositional phrase answering the question *where*

and Tina ________________, he blinked his eyes as a cat does in

the sunshine, and he shook himself, and the last of his plates dropped off, and his wings

prepositional phrase acting as the predicate adjective describing *he*

with them, and he was ________________.

adjectival present participle phrase describing the dragon

For there, plain to be seen, was the dragon, as big as a barge, ________________,

adjectival present participle phrase describing the dragon / adjectival present participle phrase describing the dragon

and ________________ and ________________.

Review 7B: Improving Sentences with Clauses

Rewrite each sentence on your own paper, adding a dependent clause that meets the description in brackets. The first is done for you, with explanation provided.

The original sentences are taken from *My Father's Dragon*, by Ruth Stiles Gannett. When you are finished, compare your sentences with the originals in the *Answer Key*.

adjective clause describing *mane*

A lion was prancing about clawing at his mane, which was all snarled and full of blackberry twigs.

adverb clause describing *went* and answering the question *when*

________________ my father and the cat went down to the docks to the ship.

adverb clause describing *laughed* and answering the question *why*

My father and the dragon laughed themselves weak ________________.

adjective clause describing *clearing* and introduced by a relative adverb

It was the boar coming back from the big clearing ________________.

A pale moon came out from behind the clouds and my father could see _______________ (noun clause acting as a direct object)

_______________________________________.

It grew louder and louder _______________________________________. (adverb clause describing *grew* and answering the question *when*)

Why, this is just exactly _______________________________________! (noun clause acting as a predicate nominative)

The cat had told him _______________________________________, (noun clause acting as a direct object)

_______________________________________. (adjective clause modifying a noun within the noun clause)

Review 7C: Conditional Clauses

Label the following sentences as first, second, or third conditional by writing *1*, *2*, or *3* in the blank next to each one. Underline each conditional clause. Circle each consequence clause.

These sentences are taken from *Searching for Dragons*, by Patricia C. Wrede.

If she could guess his name, she could keep the baby. _______

If he hadn't been such a do-gooder, I wouldn't be in this mess. _______

And if I can't find her there, I'll swing through the Enchanted Forest on the way back. _______

If you're fool enough to travel through the Mountains of Morning without a companion, that's not my concern. _______

Mendanbar didn't like to think of what might happen if Kazul stayed missing for long. _______

He would have to apologize to the gargoyle sooner or later, unless he could figure out a way to muffle the noise while he worked. _______

If you'd really thought Kazul was here, you wouldn't have come at all. _______

Vanquish that, Cimorene—if you can! _______

It would cause a lot of trouble if I melted the King of the Enchanted Forest in the middle of Kazul's living room. _______

If it came to a fight, the Enchanted Forest and the Mountains of Morning would be very evenly matched. _______

But if I figure it out, I'll let you know. _______

So he kept the sword in the armory unless he could think of an excuse to use it. _______

Review 7D: Pronoun Review

The following sentences are taken from Patricia Wrede's *Dealing with Dragons.* Circle every pronoun. Label each as personal (*PER*), possessive (*POSS*), reflexive (*REF*), intensive (*INT*), demonstrative (*DEM*), interrogative (*INTER*), relative (*REL*), or indefinite (*IND*). Beside this label, add the abbreviation for the part of the sentence (or clause) that the pronoun serves as: adjective (*ADJ*), subject (*SUBJ*), predicate adjective (*PA*), direct object (*DO*), indirect object (*IO*), or object of the preposition (*OP*). (Intensive pronouns will not have one of these parts of speech—they act as appositives, which you'll cover in Lesson 94 if this is your first time through this course.)

The first has been done for you.

PER
SUBJ

Cimorene was quite sure that (they) were only taking her because her fairy godmother had told them that something had better be done about her, and soon. She kept this opinion to herself.

She was beginning to feel much less frightened, for the gray-green dragon reminded her of her great uncle, who was old and rather hard of hearing and of whom she was rather fond.

There weren't very many of them printed, and a lot of those were lost in a flood a few years later.

"How is that fireproofing spell of yours coming?" Morwen asked.

Fortunately the fireproofing spell was still in effect, and neither of them even felt warm, though Alianora lost the ends of her sleeves and Cimorene's hemline rose six scorched inches.

She felt a little warm, and her clothes had been reduced to a few charred rags, but that was nothing compared to what might have happened.

If you're that low on dried feverfew, take some of mine.

This wasn't getting anywhere.

A few, like the wolfsbane and feverfew, she could gather herself from the herbs that grew on the slopes of the mountains.

She was certain that the man was a wizard, though she had never met one before, and she did not want to agree to anything until she was sure of what she was agreeing to.

"If it wasn't a wizard, who was it?" the dragon at the far end of the table asked.

Review 7E: Parsing

In the sentences below, underline every verb or verb phrase that acts as the predicate of a clause (dependent or independent). Label each verb with the correct tense, voice, and mood.

Tenses: Simple past, present, future; progressive past, present, future; perfect past, present, future

Voice: Active, passive (or state-of-being)

Mood: Indicative, subjunctive, imperative, modal, subjunctive/modal

The first is done for you.

These sentences are taken from *The Yellow Fairy Book*, by Andrew Lang.

progressive present, active, indicative

You are looking for the Mother Dragon's mare who is galloping about among the clouds.

He was so vexed with his own folly that he did not attempt to explain his conduct, and things would have gone badly with him if his friends the fairies had not softened the hearts of his captors.

All the neighbouring kings had offered rich rewards to anyone who should be able to destroy the monster, either by force or enchantment, and many had tried their luck, but all had miserably failed. Once a great forest in which the Dragon lay had been set on fire; the forest was burnt down, but the monster had been unhurt.

Your prayers and your repentance come too late, and if I were to spare you everyone would think me a fool.

Very long ago, as old people have told me, there lived a terrible monster, who came out of thc North, and laid waste whole tracts of country, devouring both men and beasts; and this monster was so destructive that it was feared that no living creature would be left on the face of the earth.

He told them how the Dragon had been outwitted by his grandmother, and how he had heard from his own lips the answer to the riddle.

The King announced publicly that he would give his daughter in marriage, as well as a large part of his kingdom, to whosoever should free the country from the monster.

The Herd-boy did as he was told, and before he could have believed it possible he found himself in a big hall, where even the walls were made of pure gold.

The Emperor came himself with his most distinguished knights, and each impostor held up his arm just as if he were holding something.

Review 7F: Diagramming

On your own paper, diagram every word of the following two sentences from *The Yellow Fairy Book.*

Although the stranger's name and rank were unknown to Rosalie's father, he was really the son of the king of the Golden Isle, which had for capital a city that extended from one sea to another.

The Fairy entered with them, and warned the Queen that the Wizard King would shortly arrive, infuriated by his loss, and that nothing could preserve the Prince and Princess from his rage and magic unless they were actually married.

WEEK 22

Parenthetical Elements

— LESSON 85 —

Verb Review

INDICATIVE TENSES

SIMPLE		**Active**	**Passive**
	Past	he followed he was	he was followed
	Present	he follows he is	he is followed
	Future	he will follow he will be	he will be followed
PROGRESSIVE			
	Past	he was following he was being	he was being followed
	Present	he is following he is being	he is being followed
	Future	he will be following he will be being	he will be being followed
PERFECT			
	Past	he had followed he had been	he had been followed
	Present	he has followed he has been	he has been followed
	Future	he will have followed he will have been	he will have been followed

MODAL TENSES
(would OR should, may, might, must, can, could)

SIMPLE		Active	Passive
	Present	he would follow he would be	
PERFECT			
	Past	he would have followed he would have been	

SUBJUNCTIVE TENSES

SIMPLE		Active	Passive
	Past	he followed he were	
	Present	he follow he be	

Complete the following chart with the third-person-singular form of the verb indicated in the left-hand column. If you need help, ask your instructor.

INDICATIVE TENSES

		Active	Passive
SIMPLE			
abandon	Past	[he, she, it]	[he, she, it]
paint	Present	[he, she, it]	[he, she, it]
pay	Future	[he, she, it]	[he, she, it]
PROGRESSIVE			
soak	Past	[he, she, it]	[he, she, it]
shut	Present	[he, she, it]	[he, she, it]
spread	Future	[he, she, it]	[he, she, it]
PERFECT			
hug	Past	[he, she, it]	[he, she, it]
wring	Present	[he, she, it]	[he, she, it]
fly	Future	[he, she, it]	[he, she, it]

MODAL TENSES
(would OR should, may, might, must, can, could)

		Active	Passive
SIMPLE			
spring	Present	[he, she, it]	
PERFECT			
sleep	Past	[he, she, it]	

SUBJUNCTIVE TENSES

		Active	Passive
SIMPLE			
dive	Past	[he, she, it]	
sneer	Present	[he, she, it]	

On your own paper, write sentences that use each of the forms above as the predicate of an independent or dependent clause. If you need help (or ideas), ask your instructor.

— LESSON 86 —

Restrictive and Non-Restrictive Modifying Clauses
Parenthetical Expressions

In after-years Piglet liked to think that he had been in Very Great Danger during the Terrible Flood, but the only danger he had really been in was in the last half-hour of his imprisonment, when Owl, who had just flown up, sat on a branch of his tree to comfort him, and told him a very long story about an aunt who had once laid a seagull's egg by mistake, and the story went on and on, rather like this sentence, until Piglet, who was listening out of his window without much hope, went to sleep quietly and naturally, slipping slowly out of the window towards the water until he was only hanging on by his toes, at which moment luckily a sudden loud squawk from Owl, which was really part of the story, woke Piglet up and just gave him time to jerk himself back into safety and say, "How interesting, and did she?" when—well, you can imagine his joy when at last he saw the good ship *The Brain of Pooh* (Captain, C. Robin; 1st Mate, P. Bear) coming over the sea to rescue him.

—From *Winnie-the-Pooh*, by A. A. Milne

A restrictive modifying clause defines the word that it modifies. Removing the clause changes the essential meaning of the sentence.

A non-restrictive modifying clause describes the word that it modifies. Removing the clause doesn't change the essential meaning of the sentence.

Only non-restrictive clauses should be set off by commas.

Parentheses ( ) can enclose words that are not essential to the sentence.

singular: parenthesis
plural: parentheses

when Owl who had just flown up sat on a branch of his tree to comfort him

until Piglet who was listening out of his window without much hope went to sleep quietly

a sudden loud squawk from Owl which was really part of the story woke Piglet up

Parenthetical expressions often interrupt or are irrelevant to the rest of the sentence.

Punctuation goes inside the parentheses if it applies to the parenthetical material; all other punctuation goes outside the parentheses.

Parenthetical material only begins with a capital letter if it is a complete sentence with ending punctuation.

As soon as he saw his companion fall, the other soldier, with a loud cry, jumped out of the boat on the far side, and he also floundered through the water (which was apparently just in his depth) and disappeared into the woods of the mainland.

If you can swim (as Jill could) a giant bath is a lovely thing.

He had only once been in a ship (and then only as far as the Isle of Wight) and had been horribly seasick.

The cabin was very tiny but bright with painted panels (all birds and beasts and crimson dragons and vines) and spotlessly clean.

From the waist upward he was like a man, but his legs were shaped like a goat's (the hair on them was glossy black) and instead of feet he had goat's hoofs.

Get me a score of men-at-arms, all well mounted, and a score of Talking Dogs, and ten Dwarfs (let them all be fell archers), and a Leopard or so, and Stonefoot the Giant.

Edmund had had no gift, because he was not with them at the time. (This was his own fault, and you can read about it in the other book.)

Because it was such an important occasion they took a candle each (Polly had a good store of these in her cave).

I read the *Chronicles of Narnia* (all seven of them!) in three days.
Did you know that C. S. Lewis wrote the *Chronicles of Narnia* (all seven of them)?
C. S. Lewis and J. R. R. Tolkien were good friends (amazing, isn't it?).

Exercise 86A: Restrictive and Non-Restrictive Modifying Clauses

In the following sentences, mark each bolded clause as either *ADV* for adverb or *ADJ* for adjective, and draw an arrow from the clause back to the word modified. Some sentences contain more than one modifying clause—try to identify each one.

Then, identify each adjective clause as either restrictive (*R*) or non-restrictive (*NR*).

Finally, set off all of the non-restrictive adjective clauses with commas. Use the proofreader's mark (^,) for comma insertion. When you are finished, compare your punctuation with that of the original.

These sentences are very slightly condensed from *The Downstairs Girl*, by Stacey Lee, the story of Jo Kuan, a Chinese-American girl living in Atlanta in the late nineteenth century. The original commas around the non-restrictive clauses have been removed.

It was Robby's mother **who nursed me when I was a baby.**

And it was she **who told Old Gin about the secret basement under the print shop.**

Whitehall Street, the "spine" of Atlanta, rises well above the treetops with her stately brick and imposing stone buildings—along with the occasional Victorian house **that refuses to give up her seat at the table.**

She barely traipses in at nine **when the shop opens** and it's not even a quarter past eight.

Of course, I'd have to split the fee with Robby **whose six-foot height also draws attention, even as he keeps his eyes on the sidewalk.**

Fluffing up the sleeves of my russet dress **which have lost their puff and hang like a pair of deflated lungs** I carry myself a block farther to English's Millinery.

I set the boxes on our worktable **which is already weighed down with reams of felt.**

Servants are routinely blacklisted **when their services come to an end.**

I have been admiring the knot embellishment on my friend's hat, and she said it was made by the Chinese girl **who works here.**

Salt points to the top shelf **where we display the finest offerings** and with a wooden pole, Lizzie retrieves a straw hat in mauve with a cloud of tulle.

The Western and Atlantic Railroad was the first of several cuts in the pie **that divided Atlanta into six wards.**

I hurry to make it through **before it closes.**

It was Old Gin **who stayed when the others moved on.**

Exercise 86B: Identifying Parenthetical Expressions

Identify each parenthetical expression as phrase, dependent clause, or complete sentence. These sentences are taken from Charles Darwin's classic account of his five-year round-the-world journey of exploration and discovery, *The Voyage of the Beagle.*

CHALLENGE EXERCISE

Provide a fuller description of each expression. What kind of phrase, clause, or sentence is it? What does it do or modify?

When you are finished, ask your instructor for the fuller explanations. Compare your descriptions to these explanations.

All the fireflies, which I caught here, belonged to the Lampyridae (in which family the English glowworm is included), and the greater number of specimens were of Lampyris occidentalis.

It excited the liveliest admiration that I, a perfect stranger, should know the road (for direction and road are synonymous in this open country) to places where I had never been.

We everywhere saw great numbers of partridges (Nothura major).

In the evening the Saurophagus takes its stand on a bush, often by the roadside, and continually repeats without a change a shrill and rather agreeable cry, which somewhat resembles articulate words: the Spaniards say it is like the words "Bien te veo" (I see you well), and accordingly have given it this name.

To begin with, the Polyborus Brasiliensis: this is a common bird, and has a wide geographical range; it is most numerous on the grassy savannahs of La Plata (where it goes by the name of Carrancha), and is far from unfrequent throughout the sterile plains of Patagonia.

We here had the four necessaries of life "en el campo,"—pasture for the horses, water (only a muddy puddle), meat and firewood.

It is remarkable that in all the different kinds of glowworms, shining elaters, and various marine animals (such as the crustacea, medusae, nereidae, a coralline of the genus Clytia, and Pyrosma), which I have observed, the light has been of a well-marked green colour.

As long as the ground remains moist in the salitrales (as the Spaniards improperly call them, mistaking this substance for saltpeter), nothing is to be seen but an extensive plain composed of a black, muddy soil, supporting scattered tufts of succulent plants.

They described it as being less than the common ostrich (which is there abundant), but with a very close general resemblance.

Here (at Bahia Blanca) the walls round the houses are built of hardened mud, and I noticed that one, which enclosed a courtyard where I lodged, was bored through by round holes in a score of places.

Exercise 86C: Punctuating Sentences with Parenthetical Expressions

All of the following sentences, taken from Leo Tolstoy's classic novel *Anna Karenina* (translated by Constance Garnett), have misplaced punctuation marks! Draw an arrow from each incorrect mark back to the place where the mark *should be.*

Wasn't it you (and didn't we all appreciate it in you)? who forgave everything, and moved simply by Christian feeling was ready to make any sacrifice?

Though it's a pity to take him from his work (but he has plenty of time!,) I must look at his face; will he feel I'm looking at him?

Levin deliberately took out a ten rouble note, and, careful to speak slowly, though losing no time over the business, he handed him the note, and explained that Pyotr Dmitrievitch (what a great and important personage he seemed to Levin now, this Pyotr Dmitrievitch, who had been of so little consequence in his eyes before)! had promised to come at any time.

Dressing without hurry (he never hurried himself, and never lost his self-possession,) Vronsky drove to the sheds.

On the day of the wedding, according to the Russian custom (the princess and Darya Alexandrovna insisted on strictly keeping all the customs,) Levin did not see his betrothed, and dined at his hotel with three bachelor friends, casually brought together at his rooms.

He doesn't believe even in my love for my child, or he despises it (just as he always used to ridicule it.)

She stopped suddenly, and glanced inquiringly at her husband (he did not look at her.)

No one else in Stepan Arkadyevitch's place, having to do with such despair, would have ventured to smile (the smile would have seemed brutal;) but in his smile there was so much of sweetness and almost feminine tenderness that his smile did not wound, but softened and soothed.

And it vaguely came into Levin's mind that she herself was not to blame (she could not be to blame for anything,) but what was to blame was her education, too superficial and frivolous. ("That fool Tcharsky: she wanted, I know, to stop him, but didn't know how to.)"

As he approached her, his beautiful eyes shone with a specially tender light, and with a faint, happy, and modestly triumphant smile (so it seemed to Levin,) bowing carefully and respectfully over her, he held out his small broad hand to her.

— LESSON 87 —

Parenthetical Expressions

Dashes

(The sentences in this lesson are from Lewis Carroll's novel *Through the Looking-glass.)*

A little provoked, she drew back, and after looking everywhere for the queen (whom she spied out at last, a long way off), she thought she would try the plan, this time, of walking in the opposite direction.

There was a Beetle sitting next to the Goat (it was a very queer carriage-full of passengers altogether).

Or—let me see—suppose each punishment was to be going without a dinner; then, when the miserable day came, I should have to go without fifty dinners at once!

I can see all of it when I get upon a chair—all but the bit behind the fireplace.
I can see all of it when I get upon a chair, all but the bit behind the fireplace.

But the beard seemed to melt away as she touched it, and she found herself sitting quietly under a tree—while the Gnat (for that was the insect she had been talking to) was balancing itself on a twig just over her head, and fanning her with its wings.

Parentheses ( ) can enclose words that are not essential to the sentence.
Parenthetical expressions often interrupt or are irrelevant to the rest of the sentence.
Punctuation goes inside the parentheses if it applies to the parenthetical material; all other punctuation goes outside the parentheses.
Parenthetical material only begins with a capital letter if it is a complete sentence with ending punctuation.

Dashes — — can enclose words that are not essential to the sentence.
Dashes can also be used singly to separate parts of a sentence.

I read Lewis Carroll's poem "Jabberwocky" which, I thought, was very weird.
I read Lewis Carroll's poem "Jabberwocky" which—I thought—was very weird.
I read Lewis Carroll's poem "Jabberwocky" which (I thought) was very weird.

Commas make a parenthetical element a part of the sentence.
Dashes emphasize a parenthetical element.
Parentheses minimize a parenthetical element.

1. You can set off parenthetical elements in three different ways.
2. You can turn a dependent clause into a parenthetical element just by putting it inside dashes or parentheses.
3. You can use a dash in place of a comma to emphasize the part of the sentence that follows.

The independent clauses of a compound sentence must be joined by a comma and a coordinating conjunction, a semicolon, or a semicolon and a coordinating conjunction. They cannot be joined by a comma alone.

CORRECT
Alice ventured to taste it, and finding it very nice (it had, in fact, a sort of mixed flavour of cherry tart, custard, pineapple, roast turkey, toffee, and hot buttered toast) she very soon finished it off.

INCORRECT
Alice ventured to taste it, and finding it very nice, it had, in fact, a sort of mixed flavour of cherry tart, custard, pineapple, roast turkey, toffee, and hot buttered toast, she very soon finished it off.

Exercise 87A: Types of Parenthetical Expressions

Identify each parenthetical expression as phrase, dependent clause, or sentence.

These sentences are taken from *A Walk in the Woods*, Bill Bryson's account of his attempt to hike along the Appalachian Trail.

CHALLENGE EXERCISE

Provide a fuller description of each expression. What kind of phrase, clause, or sentence is it? What does it do or modify?

When you are finished, ask your instructor for the fuller explanations. Compare your descriptions to these explanations.

From Georgia to Maine, it wanders across fourteen states, through plump, comely hills whose very names—Blue Ridge, Smokies, Cumberlands, Catskills, Green Mountains, White Mountains—seem an invitation to amble.

It would be useful (I wasn't quite sure in what way, but I was sure nonetheless) to learn to fend for myself in the wilderness.

The Appalachians are the home of one of the world's great hardwood forests—the expansive relic of the richest, most diversified sweep of woodland ever to grace the temperate world—and that forest is in trouble.

I heard four separate stories (always related with a chuckle) of campers and bears sharing tents for a few confused and lively moments; stories of people abruptly vaporized ("tweren't nothing left of him but a scorch mark") by body-sized bolts of lightning when caught in sudden storms on high ridgelines; of tents crushed beneath falling trees, or eased off precipices on ballbearings of beaded rain and sent paragliding onto distant valley floors, or swept away by the watery wall of a flash flood; of hikers beyond counting whose last experience was of trembling earth and the befuddled thought "Now what the—?"

At least nine hikers (the actual number depends on which source you consult and how you define a hiker) have been murdered along the trail since 1974.

Our only apparent option was to pitch our tents—if we could in this wind—crawl in, and hope for the best.

I hadn't expected to buy so much—I already owned hiking boots, a Swiss army knife, and a plastic map pouch that you wear around your neck on a piece of string, so I had felt I was pretty well there—but the more I talked to Dave the more I realized that I was shopping for an expedition.

The mound of provisions that a minute ago had looked so pleasingly abundant and exciting—all new! all mine!—suddenly seemed burdensome and extravagant.

I lay saucer-eyed in bed reading clinically precise accounts of people gnawed pulpy in their sleeping bags, plucked whimpering from trees, even noiselessly stalked (I didn't know this happened!) as they sauntered unawares down leafy paths or cooled their feet in mountain streams.

Exercise 87B: Punctuating Parenthetical Expressions

On either side of each bolded parenthetical expression, place parentheses, dashes, or commas. There are not necessarily correct answers for these, but compare them to the originals when you have finished.

These sentences are taken from *The Mother Tongue: English and How It Got That Way*, by Bill Bryson.

Indeed Robert Burchfield, editor of the *Oxford English Dictionary*, created a stir in linguistic circles on both sides of the Atlantic when he announced his belief that American English and English English are drifting apart so rapidly that within 200 years the two nations won't be able to understand each other at all.

For the airlines of 157 nations **out of 168 in the world**, it is the agreed international language of discourse.

When companies from four European countries **France, Italy, Germany, and Switzerland** formed a joint truck-making venture called Iveco in 1977, they chose English as their working language because, as one of the founders wryly observed, "It puts us all at an equal disadvantage."

English is **in short** one of the world's great growth industries.

Altogether about 200,000 English words are in common use, more than in German **184,000** and far more than in French **a mere 100,000**.

The Italians even have a word for the mark left on a table by a moist glass ***culacino*** while the Gaelic speakers of Scotland, not to be outdone, have a word for the itchiness that overcomes the upper lip just before taking a sip of whiskey. **Wouldn't they just?** It's *sgriob*. And we have nothing in English to match the Danish *hygge* **meaning "instantly satisfying and cozy"**, the French *sang-froid*, the Russian *glasnost*, or the Spanish *macho*, so we must borrow the term from them or do without the sentiment.

Few English-speaking natives **however well educated** can confidently elucidate the difference between **say** a complement and a predicate or distinguish a full infinitive from a bare one.

A third **and more contentious** supposed advantage of English is the relative simplicity of its spelling and pronunciation.

We possess countless examples of pithy phrases **"life is short," "between heaven and earth," "to go to work"** which in other languages require articles.

And why **come to that** can we be overwhelmed or underwhelmed, but not semi-whelmed or **if our feelings are less pronounced** just whelmed?

Moreover all children everywhere learn languages in much the same way: starting with simple labels **"Me"**, advancing to subject-verb structures **"Me want"**, before progressing to subject-verb-emphatics **"Me want now"**, and so on.

Most adults tend **even when they are not aware of it** to speak to infants in a simplified, gitchy-goo kind of way.

Exercise 87C: Using Dashes for Emphasis

On your own paper, rewrite the next four sentences, substituting dashes for the underlined punctuation marks and making any other capitalization or punctuation changes needed.

These sentences are taken from Bill Bryson's 2019 book *The Body: A Guide for Occupants.*

Six of these (carbon, oxygen, hydrogen, nitrogen, calcium, and phosphorus) account for 99.1 percent of what makes us, but much of the rest is a bit unexpected.

The cell is full of busy things, ribosomes and proteins, DNA, RNA, mitochrondria, and much other cellular arcana. But none of those are themselves alive. The cell itself is just a compartment, a kind of little room: a cell, to contain them, and of itself is as nonliving as any other room.

DNA exists for just one purpose, to create more DNA.

— LESSON 88 —

Parenthetical Expressions
Dashes
Diagramming Parenthetical Expressions

We met the new neighbors today, who, we think, are very pleasant people.
It was a glorious morning—a cool, sunny, sweet-scented morning.
The chef decided to put liver, which was one of his favorites, on the dinner menu.
The liver (which most diners didn't order) was cooked with onions and red wine.

Recognizing Parenthetical Elements

Dashes and parentheses always turn a clause or phrase into a parenthetical element—even if there's actually a grammatical relationship between the clause or phrase and the rest of the sentence.

If a clause or phrase is set off by commas, but doesn't have a clear grammatical relationship to the rest of the sentence, it is parenthetical.

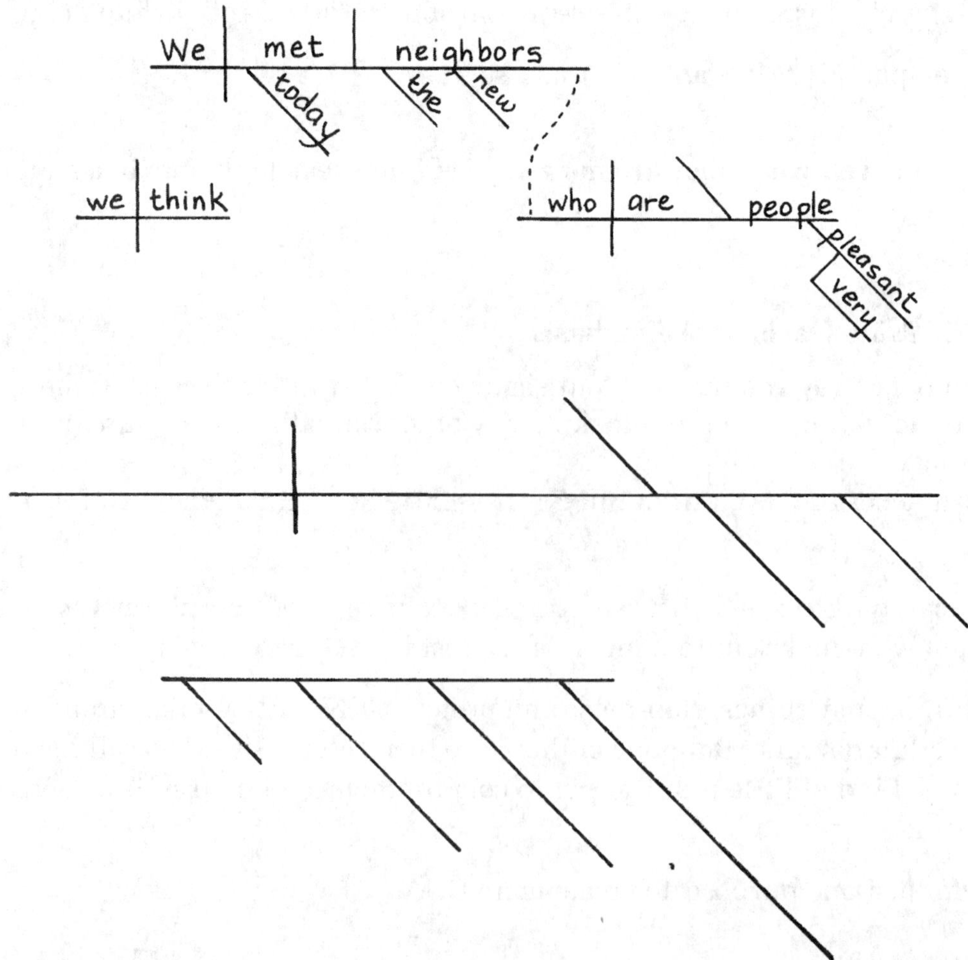

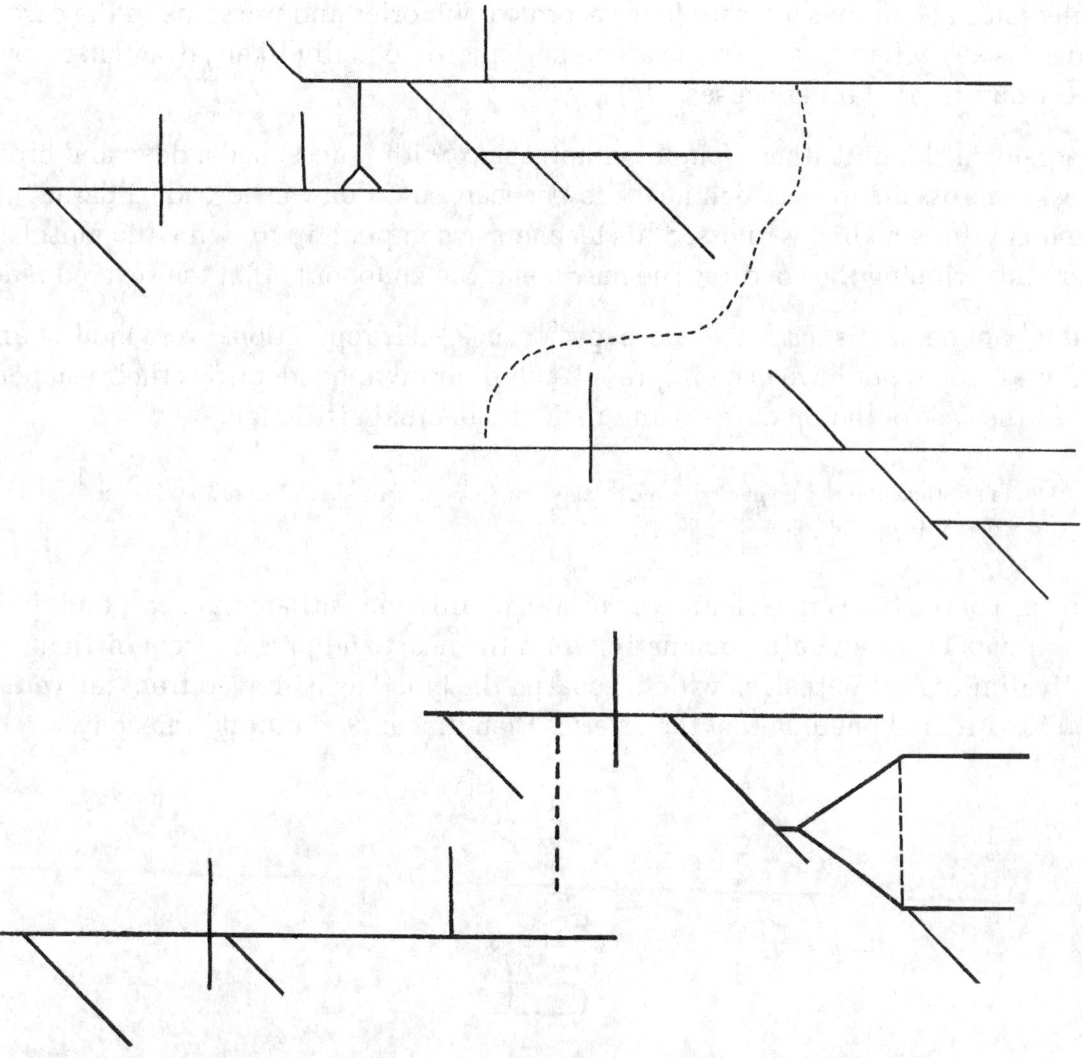

The train—can you believe it?—was on time (a rare and happy occurrence!).

Exercise 88A: Diagramming Parenthetical Expressions

On your own paper, diagram each of the following sentences.

These sentences are taken from *The Prince of Medicine*, a biography of the Roman physician Galen written by Susan P. Mattern. (Some have been slightly condensed.) They are meant to be challenging! Do your best, and ask your instructor for help if you get frustrated. When you are finished, compare your answers to the *Answer Key*. (There may be more than one way to diagram these elements.)

Death and mortal illness, in Rome, was not especially associated with old age (and very few of Galen's recorded patients are old), nor even necessarily with childhood.

Galen and his patients visited the public baths daily or even twice daily (although the wealthiest had private baths in their houses).

Some gladiatorial epitaphs attest to long records of victories and missions in the career of the deceased—killed finally in the arena perhaps, or, equally likely, dead later from infected wounds, or of other causes.

One gladiator, a "knight" (these fought on horseback with lances) had a deep and broadly gaping gash across his lower thigh near the kneecap, so Galen was forced ("I dared") to exceed anything he had witnessed his teachers accomplish in drawing the muscles together and stripping the covering (he may mean the epitenon) off of the severed tendons.

Galen does not name his teachers—perhaps because their reputations were modest and these names would not have been impressive on their own; he identifies their teachers (except in the case of the Epicurean) and their intellectual affiliation.

Note to Student: If this is your first time through the *Grammar for the Well-Trained Mind* course, you may skip the following sentence.

The purpose of the lungs in Galen's system was mainly to ventilate the heart and thus regulate innate heat—an entity emanating from the heart and present from birth (it gradually diminished with age), which, cooking the blood as it arrived from the veins, injected it with vital pneuma that the arteries then distributed around the body.

WEEK 23

Dialogue and Quotations

— LESSON 89 —

Dialogue

"I'm sorry, Ender," Valentine whispered. She was looking at the band-aid on his neck.

Ender touched the wall and the door closed behind him. "I don't care. I'm glad it's gone."

"What's gone?" Peter walked into the parlor, chewing on a mouthful of bread and peanut butter.

Ender did not see Peter as the beautiful ten-year-old boy that grown-ups saw, with dark, thick, tousled hair and a face that could have belonged to Alexander the Great. Ender looked at Peter only to detect anger or boredom, the dangerous moods that almost always led to pain. Now as Peter's eyes discovered the band-aid on his neck, the telltale flicker of anger appeared.

Valentine saw it too. "Now he's like us," she said, trying to soothe him before he had time to strike.

—From *Ender's Game*, by Orson Scott Card

Dialogue: the actual words characters speak
Narrative: the rest of the story

Dialogue is set off by quotation marks.

A dialogue tag identifies the person making the speech.
When a dialogue tag comes after a speech, place a comma, exclamation point, or question mark inside the closing quotation marks.

"I ate the cookie," my brother said.
"I ate seventeen cookies!" my brother exclaimed.
"Do you think I'll be sick?" my brother asked.

INCORRECT:
"I ate the cookie." My brother said.

When a dialogue tag comes before a speech, place a comma after the tag. Put the dialogue's final punctuation mark inside the closing quotation marks.

My brother said, "I ate the cookie."

My brother exclaimed, "I ate seventeen cookies!"

My brother asked, "Do you think I'll be sick?"

Speeches do not need to be attached to a dialogue tag as long as the text clearly indicates the speaker.

"I've watched through his eyes, I've listened through his ears, and I tell you he's the one. Or at least as close as we're going to get."

"That's what you said about the brother."

"The brother tested out impossible. For other reasons. Nothing to do with his ability."

"Same with the sister. And there are doubts about him. He's too malleable. Too willing to submerge himself in someone else's will."

"Not if the other person is his enemy."

"So what do we do? Surround him with enemies all the time?"

"If we have to."

—From *Ender's Game,* by Orson Scott Card

Usually, a new paragraph begins with each new speaker.

CORRECT:
"I'm not afraid to say what I think," George retorted. "I wish you could be honest too."
"I'm not afraid to say what I think," George retorted, "whether or not you like it."

INCORRECT: (Run-on sentence):
"I'm not afraid to say what I think," George retorted, "I wish you could be honest too."

INCORRECT: (Ends with a sentence fragment):
"I'm not afraid to say what I think," George retorted. "Whether or not you like it."

When a dialogue tag comes in the middle of a speech, follow it with a comma if the following dialogue is an incomplete sentence. Follow it with a period if the following dialogue is a complete sentence.

Exercise 89A: Punctuating Dialogue

The excerpt below is from Robert Louis Stevenson's classic novel *The Strange Case of Dr. Jekyll and Mr. Hyde.* Most of the dialogue is missing quotation marks, and some of it is missing ending punctuation as well. Do your best to supply the missing punctuation marks. (Don't use proofreader's marks—just write the punctuation directly into the sentences.)

The passage describes the first encounter of the lawyer Mr. Utterson with the mysterious Mr. Hyde, a man Mr. Utterson has long suspected of committing crimes.

When you are finished, compare your version with the original.

The steps drew swiftly nearer, and swelled out suddenly louder as they turned the end of the street. The lawyer, looking forth from the entry, could soon see what manner of man he had to deal with. He was small and very plainly dressed and the look of him, even at that distance, went somehow strongly against the watcher's inclination. But he made straight for the door, crossing the roadway to save time; and as he came, he drew a key from his pocket like one approaching home.

Mr. Utterson stepped out and touched him on the shoulder as he passed. Mr. Hyde, I think?

Mr. Hyde shrank back with a hissing intake of the breath. But his fear was only momentary; and though he did not look the lawyer in the face, he answered coolly enough: That is my name. What do you want

I see you are going in returned the lawyer. I am an old friend of Dr. Jekyll's—Mr. Utterson of Gaunt Street—you must have heard of my name; and meeting you so conveniently, I thought you might admit me.

You will not find Dr. Jekyll; he is from home replied Mr. Hyde, inserting the key. And then suddenly, but still without looking up, How did you know me he asked.

On your side said Mr. Utterson will you do me a favour?

With pleasure replied the other. What shall it be?

Will you let me see your face asked the lawyer.

Mr. Hyde appeared to hesitate, and then, as if upon some sudden reflection, fronted about with an air of defiance; and the pair stared at each other pretty fixedly for a few seconds. Now I shall know you again said Mr. Utterson. It may be useful

Yes returned Mr. Hyde, it is as well we have met; and à propos, you should have my address And he gave a number of a street in Soho.

"Good God!" thought Mr. Utterson, "can he, too, have been thinking of the will?" But he kept his feelings to himself and only grunted in acknowledgment of the address.

And now, said the other, how did you know me?

By description was the reply.

Whose description?

We have common friends said Mr. Utterson.

Common friends, echoed Mr. Hyde, a little hoarsely Who are they?

Jekyll, for instance, said the lawyer.

He never told you cried Mr. Hyde, with a flush of anger. I did not think you would have lied

Come said Mr. Utterson that is not fitting language.

The other snarled aloud into a savage laugh; and the next moment, with extraordinary quickness, he had unlocked the door and disappeared into the house.

Exercise 89B: Writing Dialogue Correctly

On your own paper, rewrite the following sentences as dialogue, using the past tense for the dialogue tags. Use the notations in parentheses to help you.

You may choose to place dialogue tags before, in the middle, or after dialogue, or to leave the tags out completely. But you must have at least one sentence with a dialogue tag that comes before, at least one sentence with a dialogue tag that comes after, at least one speech with the dialogue tag in the middle, and at least one speech with no dialogue tag at all.

The text in italics is part of the scene and should be included in your final version, but it isn't dialogue.

When you are finished, compare your answers with the original.

This passage was slightly condensed from *The Railway Children*, by Edith Nesbit. The three "railway children" are Robert (Bobbie), Peter, and their youngest sister Phyllis. In this part of the story, they are having the kind of argument that siblings often have—a silly argument that blows up because they're all on edge for another reason!

(Bobbie says) "I was using the rake."

(Peter says) "Well, I'm using it now."

(Bobbie says) "But I had it first."

(Peter says) "Then it's my turn now."

And that was how the quarrel began.

(There is some heated argument and then Peter says) "You're always being disagreeable about nothing."

(Bobbie is holding onto the rake's handle and says) "I had the rake first."

(Peter says) "Don't—I tell you I said this morning I meant to have it. Didn't I, Phil?"

Phyllis said she didn't want to be mixed up in their rows. And instantly, of course, she was.

(Peter says) "If you remember, you ought to say."

(Bobbie says) "Of course she doesn't remember—but she might say so."

(Peter says) "I wish I'd had a brother instead of two whiny little kiddy sisters."

This was always recognised as indicating the high-water mark of Peter's rage.

(Bobbie wants to say) "Don't let's quarrel. Mother hates it so."

But though she tried hard, she couldn't. Peter was looking too disagreeable and insulting.

(Bobbie snaps) "Take the horrid rake, then."

And she suddenly let go her hold on the handle. Peter had been holding on to it too firmly, and he staggered and fell over backward, the teeth of the rake between his feet.

(Before she can stop herself, Bobbie says) "Serve you right."

Mother put her head out of the window, and it wasn't half a minute after that she was in the garden kneeling by the side of Peter.

(Mother says) "Now, are you hurt?"

Exercise 89C: Proofreading

Using the following proofreader's marks, correct these incorrect sentences. The originals are from *Catching Fire*, by Suzanne Collins.

Insert quotation marks: ❛❜
insert comma: ^,
insert period: ⊙
insert question mark: ^?
insert exclamation point: ↑!
delete: ℓ
move punctuation mark: ↷

"You're hideous, you know that, right"? I ask him. Buttercup nudges my hand for more petting, but we have to go "Come on, you".

"Aren't you supposed to be on a train" he asks me.

"They're collecting me at noon" I answer.

"Shouldn't you look better" he asks in a loud whisper? I can't help smiling at his teasing, in spite of my mood. "Maybe a ribbon in your hair or something"? He flicks my braid with his hand and I brush him away.

"Don't worry By the time they get through with me I'll be unrecognizable" I say.

I nudge his shoulder "Get up" I say loudly, because I've learned there's no subtle way to wake him.

"Is everything all right, Katniss" she asks?

"It's fine. We never see it on television, but the president always visits the victors before the tour to wish them luck", I say brightly.

My mother's face floods with relief "Oh. I thought there was some kind of trouble".

— LESSON 90 —

Dialogue

Direct Quotations

The stranger said, "I have come far seeking Mali and have found great wealth here. But I must tell your king that great wealth that the world has not seen is worth less to your children's children than a rumor of water to a people dying of thirst."

The elders wondered silently about this stranger who presumed to lecture the king of Mali, but they were much too polite to say anything that might make a guest feel less than welcome.

"You will have to go to Niani, the capital city, to speak with the *mansa*—that is, the king—of Mali," said Musa Weree, with a smile that seemed to mask a secret.

But the stranger showed no interest in Niani. "The king has heard me!" he said.

—From *Mansa Musa: The Lion of Mali*, by Khephra Burns

During the two months he remained in Mali, Ibn Battuta paid grudging respect to the safety and justice of the kingdom: "A traveler may proceed alone among them, without the least fear of a thief or robber," he noted.

In Sulayman's twenty-four years on the throne, Mali remained firmly under his authority. Sulayman surrounded himself with the trappings of an emperor:

gold arms and armor; ranks of courtiers and Turkish mamluks, warrior slaves bought from Egypt, surrounding him. They were required to keep solemn and attentive in his presence: "Whoever sneezes while the king is holding court," al-'Umari explains, "is severely beaten."

—From *The History of the Renaissance World,* by Susan Wise Bauer

Dialogue: the exact words of a speaker
Direct quotation: the exact words of a writer

Dialogue tags attach dialogue to a speaker.
Attribution tags attach direct quotations to a writer.

When an attribution tag comes after a direct quote, place a comma, exclamation point, or question mark inside the closing quotation marks.

"Many ships sank that day," the chronicler wrote.
"Seventeen ships sank that day!" the chronicler lamented.
"Who can say how many lives were lost?" the chronicler mourned.

INCORRECT:
"Many ships sank that day." The chronicler wrote.

When an attribution tag comes before a direct quote, place a comma after the tag. Put the dialogue's final punctuation mark inside the closing quotation marks.

According to the chronicler, "Many ships sank that day."
The chronicler tells us, "Seventeen ships sank that day!"
One witness asked, "Who can say how many lives were lost?"

When an attribution tag comes in the middle of a direct quotation, follow it with a comma if the remaining quote is an incomplete sentence. Follow it with a period if the remaining quote is a complete sentence.

"Many ships," the chronicler tells us, "sank that day."
"Seventeen ships sank that day," the chronicler tells us. "Who can say how many lives were lost?"

Speeches do not need to be attached to a dialogue tag as long as the text clearly indicates the speaker.

Every direct quote must have an attribution tag.

CORRECT:

The soldiers chased Yazdegerd north into the province of Kirman, but the Arab army was caught in a blizzard and froze. "The snow reached the height of a lance," al-Tabari says. Only the commander, one soldier, and a slave girl survived, the latter because her owner slit open the stomach of a camel and packed her inside it to keep her warm.

—*The History of the Medieval World,* by Susan Wise Bauer

INCORRECT:

The soldiers chased Yazdegerd north into the province of Kirman, but the Arab army was caught in a blizzard and froze. “The snow reached the height of a lance.” Only the commander, one soldier, and a slave girl survived, the latter because her owner slit open the stomach of a camel and packed her inside it to keep her warm.

Exercise 90A: Punctuating Dialogue

The passage of dialogue below, from L. Frank Baum’s *Glinda of Oz*, is missing punctuation. Write in all of the missing punctuation marks (insert them directly rather than using proofreader’s marks). When you are finished, compare your answers to the original.

Is that all the Book says asked Ozma.

Every word said Dorothy, and Ozma and Glinda both looked at the Record and seemed surprised and perplexed.

Tell me, Glinda said Ozma, who are the Flatheads

I cannot, your Majesty confessed the Sorceress Until now I never have heard of them, nor have I ever heard the Skeezers mentioned. In the faraway corners of Oz are hidden many curious tribes of people, and those who never leave their own countries and never are visited by those from our favored part of Oz, naturally are unknown to me. However, if you so desire, I can learn through my arts of sorcery something of the Skeezers and the Flatheads.

I wish you would answered Ozma seriously. You see, Glinda, if these are Oz people they are my subjects and I cannot allow any wars or troubles in the Land I rule, if I can possibly help it.

Very well, your Majesty said the Sorceress, I will try to get some information to guide you. Please excuse me for a time, while I retire to my Room of Magic and Sorcery

May I go with you asked Dorothy, eagerly.

No, Princess. was the reply. It would spoil the charm to have anyone present.

So Glinda locked herself in her own Room of Magic and Dorothy and Ozma waited patiently for her to come out again.

Exercise 90B: Punctuating Direct Quotations

In the sentences below, the authors quote various experts talking and writing about Mars. Write in all of the missing punctuation marks (insert them directly rather than using proofreader's marks). When you are finished, compare your answers to the original sentences.

The camera had fog in it and some of the scan lines failed, causing streaks across the frame. The resolution was awful recalls JPL engineer John Casani. You really couldn't see much. But the images would presumably get better as *Mariner 4* came closer and closer to the planet, imaging it as the sun struck the landscape more obliquely, picking up more contrast.

Upon seeing the pictures, Lyndon Johnson sighed It may be—it may just be—that life as we know it... is more unique than many have thought.

The reality of the cold, hard, desolate world was beyond anything that scientists had imagined, beyond even the imaginations of the great science-fiction writers. Craters? Why didn't we think of craters Isaac Asimov, upon seeing the Mariner 4 images, reportedly asked a friend.

Inside the book, Lowell scrawled Hurry!

—Sarah Stewart Johnson, *The Sirens of Mars: Searching for Life on Another World*

The key ingredient is water. People often say how amazingly robust life is McKay says. My reaction is the opposite. It always needs water. If we had the trick of learning to live without water, life would be hardier.

They happened upon the Antarctic coastline after "a magical journey of towering mountains and shining glaciers in the memorable phrase of one chronicler of their travels.

But then, Buzz Aldrin has always dreamed of an encore: walking on Mars. I think we can all say with confidence that we are closer to Mars today than we have ever been Aldrin had said earlier that same year.

When Scott and his team happened upon them, they were astounded. The hillsides were covered with a coarse granitic sand strewn with numerous boulders he recorded in his diaries.

—Elizabeth Howell and Nicholas Booth, *The Search for Life on Mars: The Greatest Scientific Detective Story of All Time*

Exercise 90C: Attribution Tags

In the following excerpts, taken from Stephen O'Meara and William Sheehan's *Mars: The Lure of the Red Planet*, find and underline the direct quotes that are missing their attribution tags. When you are finished, ask your instructor to check your work.

Then, compare the excerpts with the originals found in the *Answer Key.* Circle each attribution tag in the *Answer Key.*

On paper, *Pathfinder's* purpose was to get something—anything—to land on Mars. "After [that]," project scientist Matthew Golombek said, "whatever we did was pretty much considered gravy."

The most common size was from a few centimeters to about 20 centimeters (8 inches). "We wanted rocks and we got rocks." Ares Vallis was supposed to be a geological wonderland and it was.

The consensus swelled unanimously: "The area shows the effect of catastrophic flooding." Torrents of water, perhaps having a volume equal to that of all the Great Lakes combined, had washed down the valley from the southeast, carved the trough, and deposited the boulders. "In a typical flood like this on Earth," Golombek explained, "we would expect to see big rocks deposited during the first rush of water. Then, as the water volume and speed lessen, we see dust and smaller particles deposited around the rocks."

To make identifying the rocks easier, the scientists quickly began naming them. "Within hours scientists were jostling for position in front of wall-sized prints of the lander's pictures and demanding to name the rocks."

The Assyrians were, moreover, preoccupied with astrological affairs; even more than the Babylonians had been, they were enchanted by the strangely compelling and still potent idea that the motions, positions, and brightnesses of the heavenly bodies in some unfathomable way controlled human destiny. "Astrology connected the life of man so closely with the heavens that the stars and their wanderings began to occupy an important place in his thoughts and activities."

Alas, Aristarchus's idea, like Heracleides', attracted scant attention at the time. "Why did the Greeks develop a heliocentric hypothesis and then let it fall by the wayside?"

The date of the eclipse had been predicted long before by astronomers, and Tycho, as his early biographer Pierre Gassendi wrote, "thought of it as divine that men could know the motions of the stars so accurately that they could long before foretell their places and relative positions."

— LESSON 91 —

Direct Quotations
Ellipses
Partial Quotations

> A few clouds of dust moving to and fro signify that the army is encamping. Humble words and increased preparations are signs that the enemy is about to advance. Violent language and driving forward as if to the attack are signs that he will retreat. When the light chariots come out first and take up a position on the wings, it is a sign that the enemy is forming for battle. Peace proposals unaccompanied by a sworn covenant indicate a plot. When there is much running about and the soldiers fall into rank, it means that the critical moment has come. When some are seen advancing and some retreating, it is a lure.
>
> —Sun Tzu, *The Art of War,* trans. Lionel Giles

> The good general not only deceives the enemy himself, but assumes that his enemy is always deceiving him: "Humble words and increased preparations are signs that the enemy is about to advance," Sun Tzu explains. "Violent language and driving forward as if to the attack are signs that he will retreat . . . Peace proposals unaccompanied by a sworn covenant indicate a plot." Both Confucius and Sun-Tzu, roughly contemporary as they are, offer a philosophy of order, a way of dealing with a disunified country; stability through the proper performance of social duties, or stability through intimidation.
>
> —Susan Wise Bauer, *The History of the Ancient World*

Ellipses show where something has been cut out of a sentence.

élleipsis Greek for "omission"
ellipsis (singular), ellipses (plural)

The Roman historian Varro mentions an early division of Rome's people into three "tribes" of some kind.

The attackers were thoroughly thrashed, since the army of debtors that came

charging out to meet them was, as Livy puts it, "spoiling for a fight."

The present participle of a verb can act as a descriptive adjective.

The city needed laws "which every individual citizen could feel that he had . . .

consented to accept."

Every direct quote must have an attribution tag.
A second or third quote from the same source does not need another attribution tag, as long as context makes the source of the quote clear.

A clause is a group of words that contains a subject and a predicate.
A dependent clause is a fragment that cannot stand by itself as a sentence.
Dependent clauses begin with subordinating words.
Dependent clauses are also known as subordinate clauses.

Adjective clauses are also known as relative clauses because they relate to another word in the independent clause.
Relative pronouns introduce adjective clauses and refer back to an antecedent in the independent clause.
A noun clause takes the place of a noun.

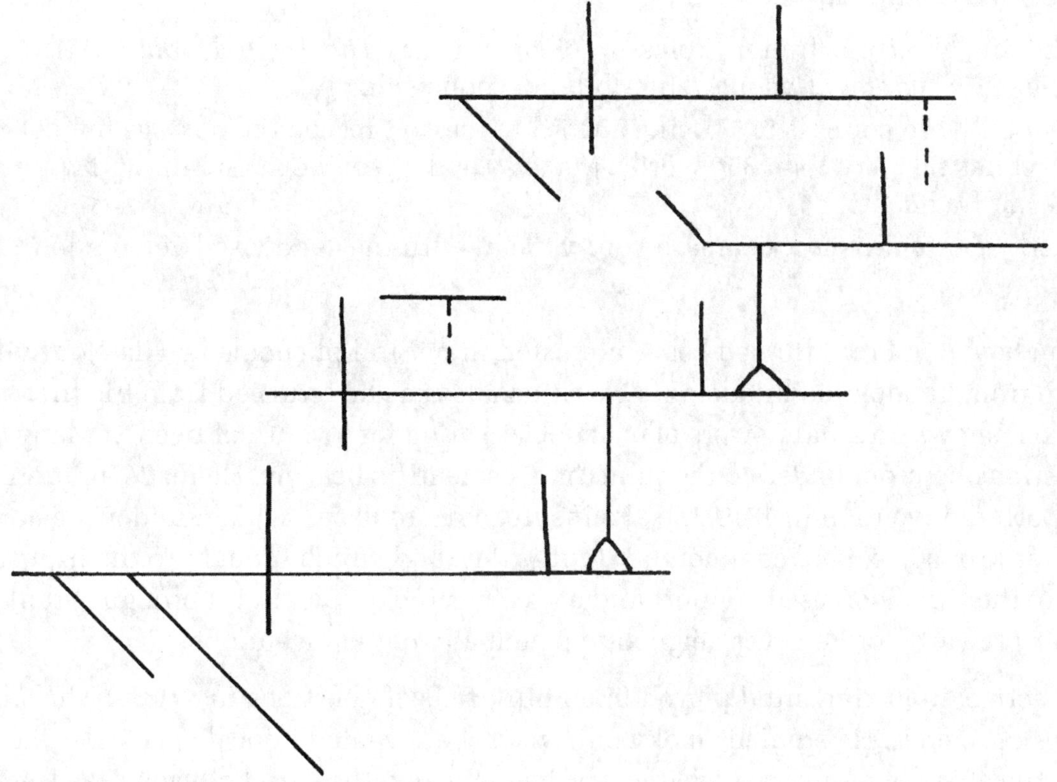

The city of Veii, Livy writes, had "inflicted worse losses than she suffered," which means that the siege had significantly weakened the Roman army.

Such was the fall of Veii, the wealthiest city of Etruria. Even her final destruction witnessed to her greatness, for after a siege of ten summers and ten winters, during which she inflicted worse losses than she suffered, even when her destined hour had come she fell by a stratagem and not by direct assault.
—Livy, *The Early History of Rome*

He had heard, "in the silence of the night," an inhuman voice saying, "Tell the magistrates that the Gauls are coming."

Direct quotes can be words, phrases, clauses, or sentences, as long as they are set off by quotation marks and form part of a grammatically correct original sentence.

Exercise 91A: Using Ellipses

The following excerpt is from the classic science history *The Age of Invention: A Chronicle of Mechanical Conquest*, by Holland Thompson.

The total word count is 576. Using a word processor, retype the passage but condense it so that it has no more than 350 words. Make sure that you don't end up with run-on sentences or fragments!

When you are finished, compare your version with the condensed version found in the *Answer Key*.

From boyhood Franklin had been interested in natural phenomena. His "Journal of a Voyage from London to Philadelphia", written at sea as he returned from his first stay in London, shows unusual powers of exact observation for a youth of twenty. Many of the questions he propounded to the Junto had a scientific bearing. He made an original and important invention in 1749, the "Pennsylvania fireplace," which, under the name of the Franklin stove, is in common use to this day, and which brought to the ill-made houses of the time increased comfort and a great saving of fuel. But it brought Franklin no pecuniary reward, for he never deigned to patent any of his inventions.

His active, inquiring mind played upon hundreds of questions in a dozen different branches of science. He studied smoky chimneys; he invented bifocal spectacles; he studied the effect of oil upon ruffled water; he identified the "dry bellyache" as lead poisoning; he preached ventilation in the days when windows were closed tight at night, and upon the sick at all times; he investigated fertilizers in agriculture. Many of his suggestions have since borne fruit, and his observations show that he foresaw some of the great developments of the nineteenth century.

His fame in science rests chiefly upon his discoveries in electricity. On a visit to Boston in 1746 he saw some electrical experiments and at once became deeply interested. Peter Collinson of London, a Fellow of the Royal Society, who had made several gifts to the Philadelphia Library, sent over some of the crude electrical apparatus of the day, which Franklin used, as well as some contrivances he had purchased in Boston. He says in a letter to Collinson: "For my own part, I never was before engaged in any study that so engrossed my attention and my time as this has lately done."

Franklin's letters to Collinson tell of his first experiments and speculations as to the nature of electricity. Experiments made by a little group of friends showed the effect of pointed bodies in drawing off electricity. He decided that electricity was not the result of friction, but that the mysterious force was diffused through most substances, and that nature is always alert to restore its equilibrium. He developed the theory of positive and negative electricity, or plus and minus electrification. The same letter tells of some of the tricks which the little group of experimenters were accustomed to play upon their wondering neighbors. They set alcohol on fire, relighted candles just blown out, produced mimic flashes of lightning, gave shocks on touching or kissing, and caused an artificial spider to move mysteriously.

Franklin carried on experiments with the Leyden jar, made an electrical battery, killed a fowl and roasted it upon a spit turned by electricity, sent a current through water and found it still able to ignite alcohol, ignited gunpowder, and charged glasses of wine so that the drinkers received shocks. More important, perhaps, he began to develop the theory of the identity of lightning and electricity, and the possibility of protecting buildings by iron rods. By means of an iron rod he brought down electricity into his house, where he studied its effect upon bells and concluded that clouds were generally negatively electrified. In June, 1752, he performed the famous experiment with the kite, drawing down electricity from the clouds and charging a Leyden jar from the key at the end of the string.

Exercise 91B: Partial Quotations

On your own paper, rewrite each of the statements below two times. Each rewritten statement must contain a partial quotation. Draw the partial quotation from the bolded sentences that follow each statement. The authors of the bolded sentences are provided for you—be sure to include an attribution tag for each direct quote!

You may change and adapt the statements freely.

At least one of your sentences should contain a very short one- to three-word quote; one should contain a preposition phrase, gerund phrase, participle phrase, or infinitive phrase; and one should quote a dependent clause.

If you need help, ask your instructor to show you sample answers.

The invention of the wheel allowed farmers to haul loads across land easily for the first time.

Before wheeled vehicles were invented, really heavy things could be moved efficiently only on water, using barges or rafts, or by organizing a larger hauling group on land. Some of the heavier items that prehistoric, temperate European farmers had to haul across land all the time included harvested grain crops, hay crops, manure for fertilizer, firewood, building lumber, clay for pottery making, hides and leather, and people.

—David W. Anthony, *The Horse, the Wheel, and Language*

The physicist Percy Spencer invented the microwave oven while working for the defense contractor Raytheon.

The ever-inventive Percy Spencer opened another important door for Raytheon when he decided to experiment with the well-known warming capacity of the microwaves emitted by magnetrons. Spencer, intrigued by a candy bar that melted in his pocket when he was near an operating magnetron, decided to see what the waves would do to popcorn kernels and was delighted to find that they quickly popped. The next day he exploded an egg by the same means.

—Alan Earls and Robert Edwards, *Raytheon Company*

The Internet, a network that connects other networks together, began as ARPANET, a military project linking computers together.

Bob Taylor had been the young director of the office within the Defense Department's Advanced Research Projects Agency overseeing computer research, and he was the one who had started the ARPANET. The project had embodied the most peaceful intentions—to link computers at scientific laboratories across the country so that researchers might share computer resources.

—Matthew Lyon and Katie Hafner, *Where Wizards Stay Up Late*

Exercise 91C: Diagramming

On your own paper, diagram every word of the following sentences. These are taken from *Beyond: Our Future in Space*, by Chris Impey. In the chapter where these sentences occur, Impey is discussing the role of Germany's rocket scientists during World War II in developing the technology that would eventually be used in space flight.

Ask your instructor for help if you get stuck! Do your best, and then compare your answers with the *Answer Key*.

The V-2 was far more advanced than any of Goddard's rockets, but he was convinced the Germans had "stolen" his ideas.

The architect of the V-2 was the most controversial figure in the history of rocketry: Wernher von Braun.

After seeing film footage of the successful launch of a V-2 prototype, Hitler personally made von Braun a professor—an exceptional honor for a thirty-one-year-old engineer.

Scientists use counterfactual thinking as a high-level skill for developing theories, by asking, "What might be but isn't, and why?"

— LESSON 92 —

Partial Quotations
Ellipses
Block Quotes
Colons
Brackets

If a direct quotation is longer than three lines, indent the entire quote one inch from the margin in a separate block of text and omit quotation marks.

If you change or make additions to a direct quotation, use brackets.

And I doubt not but posterity will find many things, that are now but Rumors, verified into practical Realities. It may be some ages hence, a voyage to the Southern unknown Tracts, yea possibly the Moon, will not be more strange than one to America. To them, that come after us, it may be as ordinary to buy a pair of wings to fly into remotest Regions; as now a pair of Boots to ride a Journey. And to confer at the distance of the Indies by Sympathetick conveyances, may be as usual to future times, as to us in a litterary correspondence. The restauration of gray hairs to Juvenility, and renewing the exhausted marrow, may at length be effected without a miracle: And the turning of the now comparative desert world into a Paradise, may not improbably be expected from late Agriculture.

Now those, that judge by the narrowness of former Principles, will smile at these Paradoxical expectations: But questionless those great Inventions, that have in these later Ages altered the face of all things; in their naked proposals, and meer suppositions, were to former times as *ridiculous.* To have talk'd of a *new Earth* to have been discovered, had been a Romance to Antiquity. And to sayl without sight of Stars or shoars by the guidance of a Mineral, a story more absurd, than the flight of Daedalus.

—Joseph Glanvill, *Scepsis Scientifica: Or, Confest Ignorance, The Way to Science; In an Essay of the Vanity of Dogmatizing and Confident Opinion*

In 1661, the English philosopher Joseph Glanvill predicted the invention of "many things, that are now but Rumors." Among them were space travel, airplanes, and conversation over long distances. In his essay *Scepsis Scientifica,* Glanvill admits that these inventions seem farfetched, but he argues that the discovery of a new continent must have seemed just as unlikely:

> It may be some ages hence, a voyage to the Southern unknown Tracts, yea possibly the Moon, will not be more strange than one to America. To them, that come after us, it may be as ordinary to buy a pair of wings to fly into remotest Regions; as now a pair of Boots to ride a Journey. And to confer at the distance of the Indies by Sympathetick conveyances, may be as usual to future times, as to us in a litterary correspondence . . . [T]hose great Inventions, that have in these later Ages altered the face of all things . . . were to former times as *ridiculous.* To have talk'd of a *new Earth* [the North and South American continents] to have been discovered, had been a Romance [Glanvill means a "fairy tale"] to Antiquity.

Glanvill goes on to point out that navigating a ship by compass ("the guidance of a Mineral," as he puts it) instead of by the stars must have seemed just as impossible to ancient sailors as moon travel does to people of his own day.

When using a word processing program, leave an additional line space before and after a block quote.

Block quotes should be introduced by a colon (if preceded by a complete sentence) or a comma (if preceded by a partial sentence).

As the English philosopher Joseph Glanvill predicted in 1661,

> It may be some ages hence, a voyage to the Southern unknown Tracts, yea possibly the Moon, will not be more strange than one to America. To them, that come after us, it may be as ordinary to buy a pair of wings to fly into remotest Regions; as now a pair of Boots to ride a Journey.

If you change or make additions to a direct quotation, use brackets.

Exercise 92A: Writing Dialogue Correctly

The following speeches, from the classic 1951 novel *All-of-a-Kind Family,* are listed in the correct order but are missing their dialogue tags. On your own paper, rewrite the speeches as dialogue, making use of the dialogue tags below. You must place at least one dialogue tag before a speech, one in the middle of a speech, and one following a speech.

A list of the rules governing dialogue follows, for your reference.

When you are finished, compare your dialogue to the original passage in the *Answer Key.*

All-of-a-Kind Family tells the story of five Jewish girls growing up in New York City in 1912. In this scene, the sisters are plotting a way to save enough money to buy their father a birthday present, something they've never been able to do before.

List 1. Dialogue (in Correct Order)

If we all saved our pennies for the next week, we'd have enough money

I'll save my pennies

But that won't leave us any money to spend for a whole week We won't be able to buy any candy or anything for a whole week?

Well, can't you give up your candy for a week?

What about the library lady? We promised to give her a penny every Friday

Oh, dear, I forgot all about that

Aren't we finished paying for that old book yet?

The library lady said we'd be all paid up in about three weeks

That's just fine! Only Papa's birthday is next week

Maybe she'll let us skip a week

List 2. Dialogue Tags (Not in Correct Order)

Gertie chimed in
Ella said
Ella demanded
said Ella
Sarah reminded them
Sarah said
Henny asked
wailed Henny
Henny retorted
suggested Charlotte

List 3. For Reference: Rules for Writing Dialogue

A dialogue tag identifies the person making the speech.

When a dialogue tag comes after a speech, place a comma, exclamation point, or question mark inside the closing quotation marks.

When a dialogue tag comes before a speech, place a comma after the tag. Put the dialogue's final punctuation mark inside the closing quotation marks.

Speeches do not need to be attached to a dialogue tag as long as the text clearly indicates the speaker.

Usually, a new paragraph begins with each new speaker.

When a dialogue tag comes in the middle of a speech, follow it with a comma if the following dialogue is an incomplete sentence. Follow it with a period if the following dialogue is a complete sentence.

Exercise 92B: Using Direct Quotations Correctly

On your own paper, rewrite the following three paragraphs, inserting at least one quote from each of the following three sources into the paragraph. Use the following guidelines:

a) At least one quote must be a block quote.
b) At least one quote must be a complete sentence.
c) At least one quote must be a partial sentence incorporated into your own sentence.
d) Each quote must have an attribution tag.
e) At least one quote must be condensed, using ellipses.
f) You must make at least one change or addition that needs to be put in brackets.

A list of the rules governing direct quotations follows, for your reference.

You may make whatever changes are needed to the paragraphs. When you are finished, compare your paragraphs to the sample answer in the *Answer Key.*

List 1. Paragraphs

Epilepsy: the Greeks called it the "sacred disease," but they were not the first. In Sumer, around 2,000 BCE, a scribe describes an epileptic convulsion.

For nearly a millennium and half, epileptic seizures were thought to be a sign that a god or demon was present. The Babylonians, who followed the Sumerians in the lands between the Tigris and the Euphrates, blamed demons who infested sufferers because of uncleanness. In the Greece of the pre-Socratics, epilepsy was a punishment sent by Poseidon (if the sufferer made hoarse sounds) or the earth-goddess Cybele (if the seizure was stronger on the right side of the body and involved the gnashing of teeth).

Hippocrates, the fifth-century BCE doctor from the Greek island of Kos, off the coast of Asia Minor, disagreed. He argued that disease is caused by purely physical factors that can be discovered by physicians—with epilepsy as Exhibit A.

Unlike priests and sorcerers, Hippocrates bases his explanation of epilepsy on his observations: Men who suffer head injuries are far more likely to suffer unexpected convulsions, so the cause of this syndrome is clearly located in the head. The Greeks were unclear about what exactly went on, up there inside the skull, but the jelly inside the head obviously controlled the body. Convulsions of the muscles and joints obviously began with a problem inside the skull.

List 2. Sources

If his seizure always seizes him in the evening, his eyes are clouded, his ears ring. If a sick man's neck turns to the right, time and again, while his hands and feet are paralysed, his eyes are now closed, now rolling, saliva flows from his mouth, he makes sounds, then it is caused by the hand of the moon-god Shin. He opens his eyes time and time again, he bites his tongue; he does not know himself when it seizes him.

—A Sumerian scribe, describing an epileptic convulsion around 2,000 BCE

It is thus with regard to the disease called Sacred: it appears to me to be nowise more divine nor more sacred than other diseases, but has a natural cause from which it originates like other affections. Men regard its nature and cause as divine from ignorance and wonder, because it is not at all like to other diseases. And this notion of its divinity is kept up by their inability to comprehend it.

—Hippocrates, *On the Sacred Disease*

In these ways I am of the opinion that the brain exercises the greatest power in the man. This is the interpreter to us of those things which emanate from the air, when it happens to be in a sound state.

—Hippocrates, *On the Sacred Disease*

List 3. For Reference: Rules for Using Direct Quotations

When an attribution tag comes after a direct quote, place a comma, exclamation point, or question mark inside the closing quotation marks.

When an attribution tag comes before a direct quote, place a comma after the tag. Put the dialogue's final punctuation mark inside the closing quotation marks.

When an attribution tag comes in the middle of a direct quotation, follow it with a comma if the remaining quote is an incomplete sentence. Follow it with a period if the remaining quote is a complete sentence.

Direct quotes can be words, phrases, clauses, or sentences, as long as they are set off by quotation marks and form part of a grammatically correct original sentence.

An ellipsis shows where something has been cut out of a sentence.

Every direct quote must have an attribution tag.

If a direct quotation is longer than three lines, indent the entire quote one inch from the margin in a separate block of text and omit quotation marks.

If you change or make additions to a direct quotation, use brackets.

WEEK 24

Floating Elements

— LESSON 93 —

Interjections
Nouns of Direct Address
Parenthetical Expressions

Oh dear, I've dropped my keys.
Oops! The keys fell through the grate into the sewer.
Alas, I will not be able to unlock my door.
Whew! That was a close one.
Whoa, let's just slow down here for a minute.
Hush, I'm on the phone.

inter between
jacere to throw

Interjections express sudden feeling or emotion. They are set off with commas or stand alone with a closing punctuation mark.

Friends, Romans, countrymen, lend me your ears!
Stars, hide your fire!
I am afraid, my dear, that you are too late.
Run, baby, run.
Get down, dog!

Nouns of direct address name a person or thing who is being spoken to. They are set off with commas. They are capitalized only if they are proper names or titles.

Parentheses ( ) can enclose words that are not essential to the sentence.
Parenthetical expressions often interrupt or are irrelevant to the rest of the sentence.
Punctuation goes inside the parentheses if it applies to the parenthetical material; all other punctuation goes outside the parentheses.
Parenthetical material only begins with a capital letter if it is a complete sentence with ending punctuation.
Parenthetical expressions can also be set off by commas.

The doctor was so late, in fact, that the baby was born before he arrived.

To be sure, she will tell a very plausible story.

When Marco Polo travelled to China he crossed, as it were, the horizon of European knowledge.

Fear was, no doubt, the greatest enemy the army had.

In a word, he supported the other candidate.

These things are always difficult, you know.

Short parenthetical expressions such as the following are usually set off by commas: *in short, in fact, in reality, as it were, as it happens, no doubt, in a word, to be sure, to be brief, after all, you know, of course.*

Whew! That was a close one.

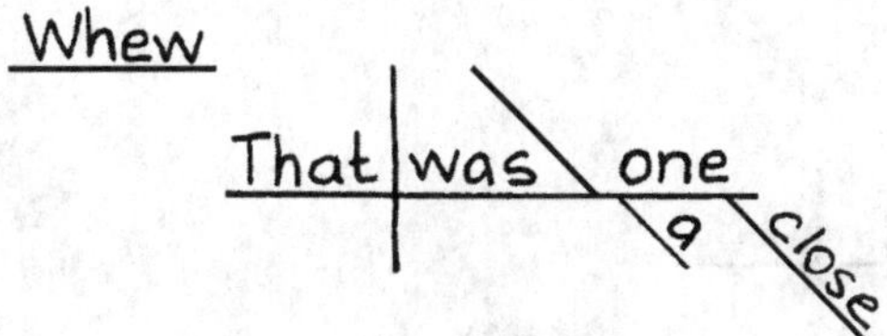

Friends, Romans, countrymen, lend me your ears!

In a word, he supported the other candidate.

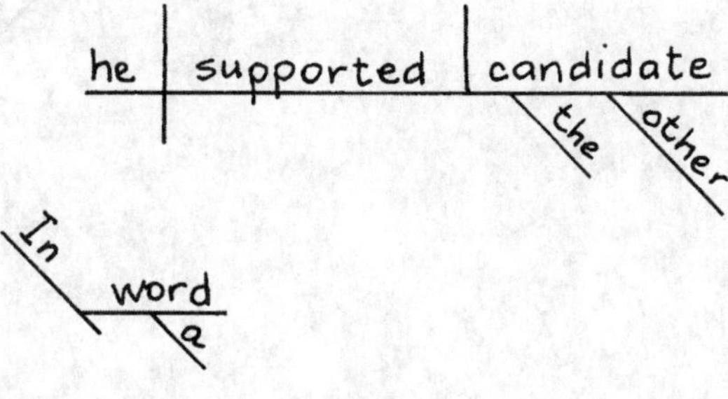

The following sentences are taken from *The Scarlet Pimpernel*, by Baroness Emmuska Orczy.

Your heroism, your devotion, which I, alas, so little deserved, have atoned for that unfortunate episode of the ball.

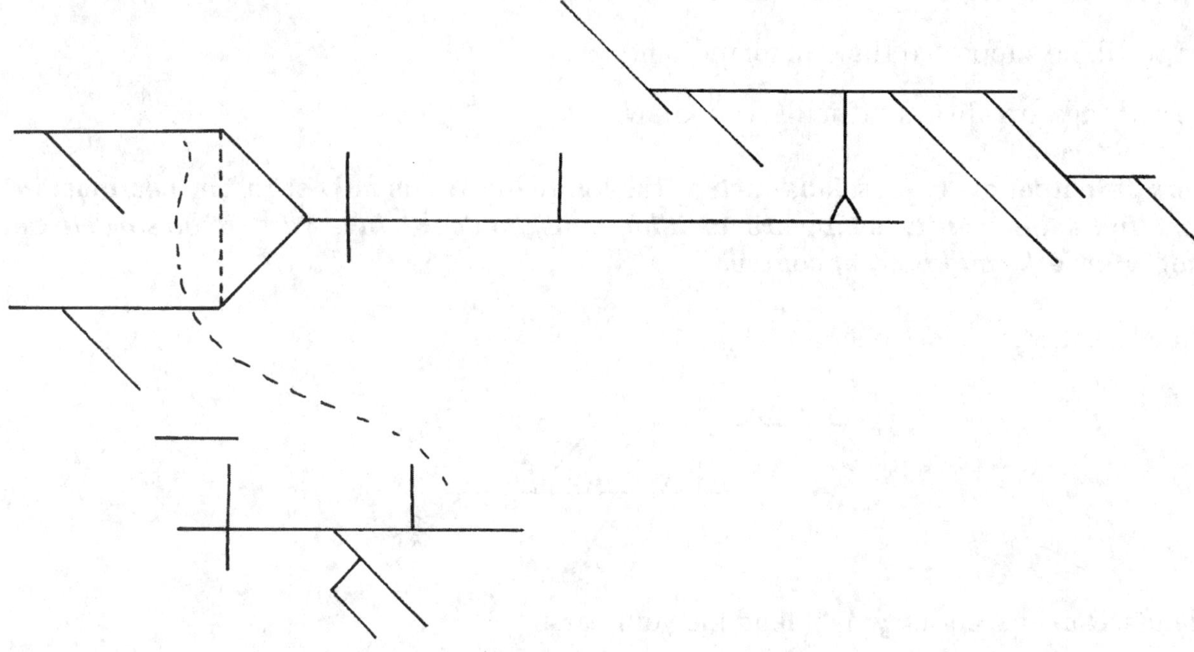

Do you impugn my bravery, Madame?

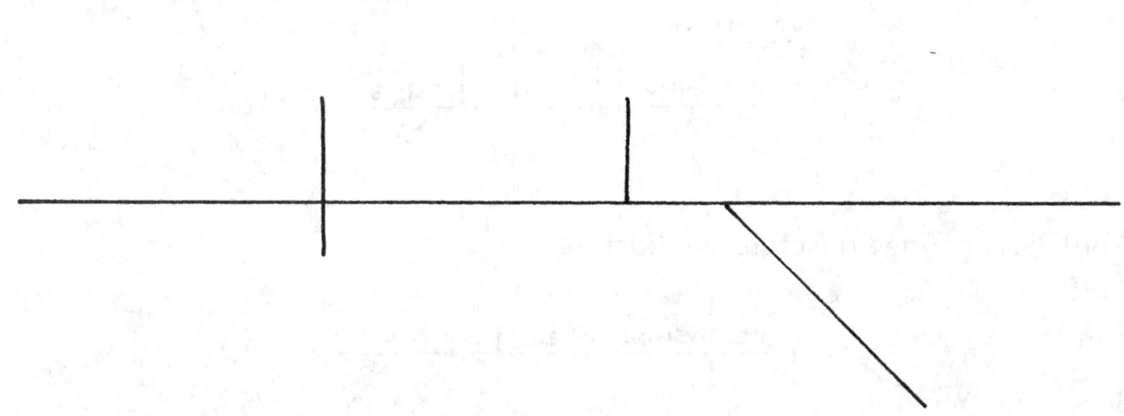

This restriction, of course, did not apply to her, and Frank would, of course, not dare to oppose her.

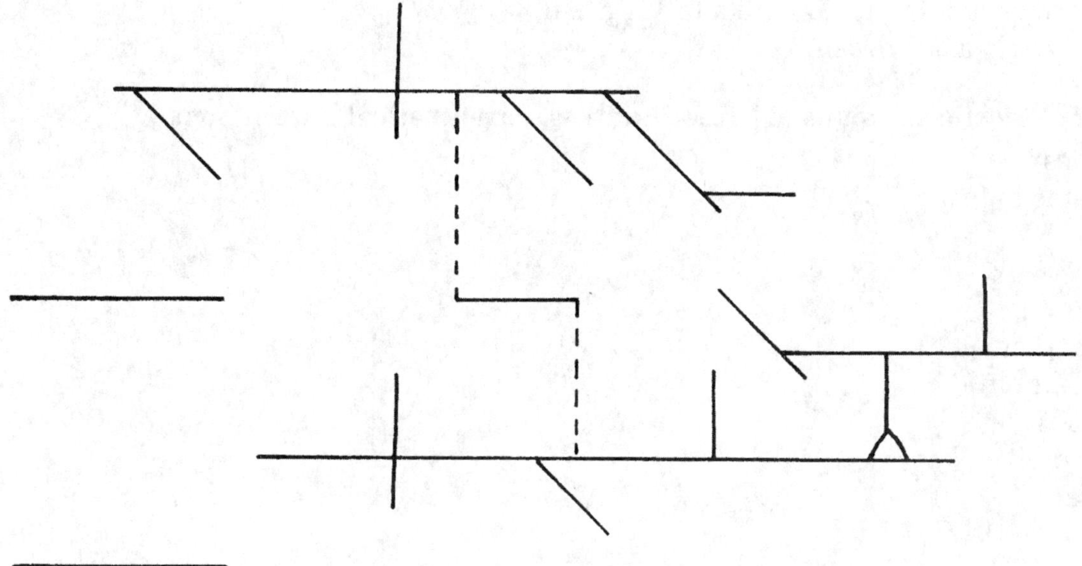

The storm will, no doubt, snarl the traffic.

There is no doubt that the storm is coming.

We aren't ready yet, you know.

You know that we aren't ready yet.

The snow caused school to be cancelled, of course.

In case of snow, school is cancelled as a matter of course.

Exercise 93A: Using Floating Elements Correctly

On your own paper, rewrite the following sentences in List 1, inserting interjections, nouns of direct address, and parenthetical expressions from List 2. You must use every item in List 2 at least once. Every sentence in List 1 must have at least one insertion.

Interjections may either come before or after sentences on their own, or may be incorporated directly into the sentence.

List 1. Sentences

Now the foxes and chickens will have fun together!
You'll feel much better now.
Why are you weeping?
This journey is the most exciting one we've ever set out on.
The giant has nothing better to do.
That is the loudest screaming I have ever heard!
What can you see out of the window?

I didn't get enough magic soup to eat at dinner.
What will become of Hansel and Gretel?
I will have nothing to do with a talking fish!
This is only a bad dream.

List 2. Interjections, Nouns of Direct Address, Parenthetical Expressions

besides
it seems to me
alas
well
oh ho
there, there
my dear child
my darling
after all
hurrah
bravo
Ji-woo

Exercise 93B: Parenthetical Expressions

In the following pairs of sentences, underline each subject once and each predicate twice (in both independent and dependent clauses). In each pair, cross out the parenthetical expression that is not essential to the sentences. If the expression is used as an essential part of the sentence, circle it and label it with the correct part of the sentence (e.g., *prep phrase acting as adj, subject and predicate*, etc.). If it acts as a modifier, draw an arrow to the word it modifies.

The play, I hesitate to say, is the worst one I've ever seen.

I hesitate to say that he flat-out lied, but he certainly misled me.

A hippo, not a crocodile, is the most dangerous animal in the river.

An alligator is not a crocodile, although many people mix them up.

The rocket launch, in my opinion, is doomed to fail.

That politician has drastically fallen in my opinion!

If you please the king, he may grant your request!

If you please, do not leave muddy tracks all over the marble floor.

Darn it, I jammed my finger again!

Stop saying "darn it"!

Exercise 93C: Diagramming

On your own paper, diagram every word of the following sentences. Several of them can be diagrammed in more than one way—when you're finished, compare your answers with the Key and look at the instructor's notes to understand the difference!

These are taken from three novels and a short story by the pioneering speculative fiction writer Octavia Butler.

From *Kindred*

The years hadn't changed her much, and, of course, they hadn't changed me at all.

No, Dana, I just didn't pay any attention.

From *Parable of the Sower*

Today is our birthday—my fifteenth and my father's fifty-fifth.

From *Parable of the Talents*

These were stupid affairs—wastes of life and treasure.

From "Bloodchild"

He looked young—my brother's age perhaps.

— LESSON 94 —

Appositives

Rome, the Eternal City, is built on seven hills that lie on both sides of the Tiber River.

Dubrovnik, the Pearl of the Adriatic, is a walled seaside fortress in Croatia.

Helsinki, the White City of the North, gets no sunshine at all for about fifty days every winter.

In Mumbai, the City of Dreams, almost seven million people ride the trains every day.

Chinese tin miners founded the Malaysian city Kuala Lumpur, the Golden Triangle, in 1857.

The people of Sydney, the Harbour City, celebrate Harbour Day, a commemoration of the first convict ships landing in Sydney Cove, on January 26.

An appositive is a noun, pronoun, or noun phrase that usually follows another noun and renames or explains it.

Rome's first ruler, Romulus, killed his brother and seized power.
In the Middle Ages, many Spanish Jews, *Conversos*, migrated to Dubrovnik.
A 1981 movie about the USSR, *Reds,* was actually filmed in Helsinki.

Rome is built on seven hills that lie on both sides of the Tiber River.
Dubrovnik is a walled seaside fortress in Croatia.
Helsinki gets no sunshine at all for about fifty days every winter.

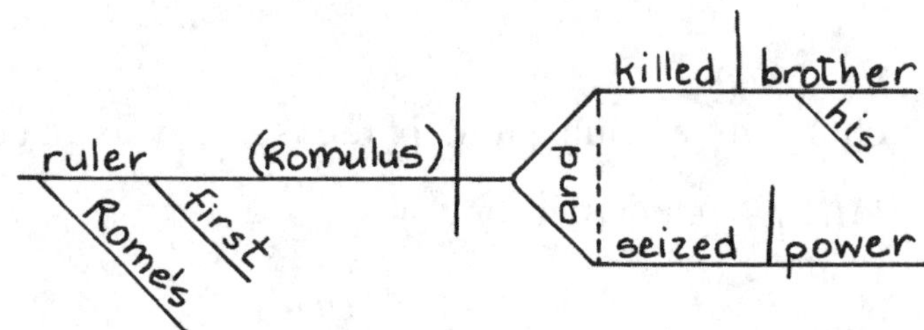

In Mumbai, the City of Dreams, almost seven million people ride the trains every day.

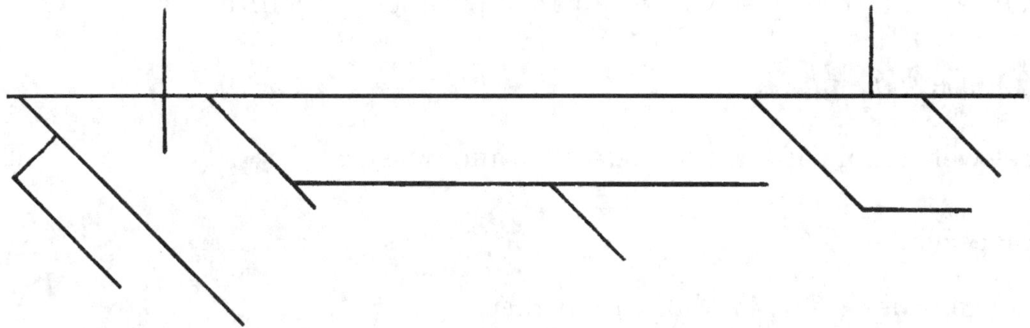

Chinese tin miners founded the Malaysian city Kuala Lumpur, the Golden Triangle, in 1857.

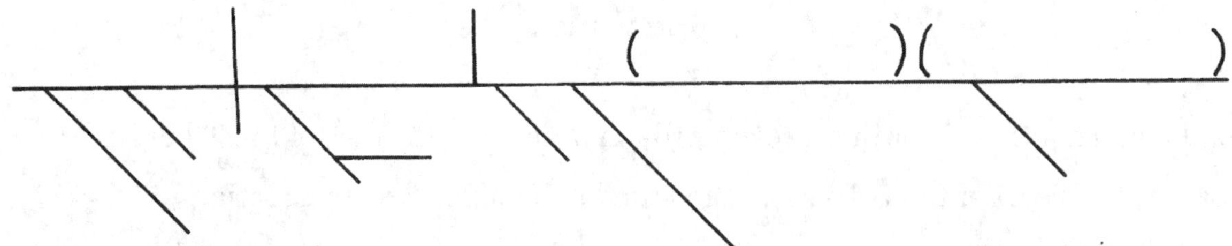

An appositive is a noun, pronoun, or noun phrase that usually follows another noun and renames or explains it.

The wisest philosopher of the ancients, Socrates wrote nothing.

A better-known destination, Marseilles is less picturesque than the surrounding villages.

An ancient breed, the Kuvasz protects helpless livestock.

Appositives are set off by commas.

The wisest philosopher of the ancients, Socrates, wrote nothing.

A better-known destination, Marseilles, is less picturesque than the surrounding villages.

An ancient breed, the Kuvasz, protects helpless livestock.

An appositive that occurs within a sentence has commas both before and after it. An appositive at the beginning of a sentence has one comma that follows it. An appositive at the end of a sentence has one comma that precedes it.

My grandfather, Aquilino Ramos, makes the best pork adobo I've ever eaten.

The best supper ever, pineapple chicken adobo waited for us on the table.

My grandfather prepared a fantastic meal, squid adobo with tomatoes.

An appositive is a noun, pronoun, or noun phrase that usually follows another noun and renames or explains it. Appositives are set off by commas.

Exercise 94A: Using Appositives

On your own paper, rewrite each group of sentences below as a single sentence using one or more appositives. You may make any necessary changes to the original sentences.

The harp is the oldest musical instrument played by humans.
Harps have strings that are plucked with fingers.

Alfred the Great was king of the Saxons in the ninth century.
Alfred the Great established the first professorship of music in Britain.

Troubadors travelled through medieval Europe.
Troubadors were singers of love songs, serenades, rounds, and shepherd's chants.

Palestrina was a sixteenth-century composer.
Palestrina was Italian.
Palestrina came to Rome to study music.
Rome was the greatest city in Italy.

Counterpoint is the addition of a second melodic line to an already existing melody.
Both melodic lines move constantly.
The melodic lines are related to each other.

Half of Johann Sebastian Bach's compositions are fugues.
Fugues are musical pieces that repeat a theme, using counterpoint.

Exercise 94B: Identifying Appositives

In each of the following sentences, underline the subject(s) once and the predicate(s) twice (in both independent and dependent clauses). Circle each appositive or appositive phrase.

These sentences are taken from the novel *Bel Canto*, by Ann Patchett.

They waited, father and son, without speaking, until finally the darkness fell and the first breath of music stirred from someplace far below them.

Tiny people, insects, really, slipped out from behind the curtains, opened their mouths, and with their voices gilded the walls with their yearning, their grief, their boundless, reckless love that would lead each one to separate ruin.

It was his oldest daughter, Kiyomi, who bought him his first recording of Roxane Coss for his birthday.

It was soaring, that voice, warm and complicated, utterly fearless.

It was Mr. Hosokawa's selection, the aria from *Rusalka*, which she had just completed when the lights went out.

He did not seek something achingly obscure, an aria from *Partenope* perhaps, so as to prove himself an aficionado.

The only music would be after dinner, Roxane Coss and her accompanist, a man in his thirties from Sweden or Norway with fine yellow hair and beautiful, tapering fingers.

Two hours before the beginning of Mr. Hosokawa's birthday party, President Masuda, a native of this country born of Japanese parents, had sent a note of regret saying that important matters beyond his control would prevent him from attending the evening's event.

Into the presidential void, the Vice President, Ruben Iglesias, stepped forward to host the party.

Exercise 94C: Diagramming

On your own paper, diagram every word of the following five sentences from Exercise 94B.

It was his oldest daughter, Kiyomi, who bought him his first recording of Roxane Coss for his birthday.

It was soaring, that voice, warm and complicated, utterly fearless.

It was Mr. Hosokawa's selection, the aria from *Rusalka,* which she had just completed when the lights went out.

Into the presidential void, the Vice President, Ruben Iglesias, stepped forward to host the party.

— LESSON 95 —

Appositives
Intensive and Reflexive Pronouns
Noun Clauses in Apposition
Object Complements

myself, himself, herself, itself, yourself, yourselves, ourselves, themselves

Reflexive pronouns refer back to the subject.
Intensive pronouns emphasize a noun or another pronoun.

I may have expressed myself badly.

I myself was never top in anything!

An appositive is a noun, pronoun, or noun phrase that usually follows another noun and renames or explains it. Appositives are set off by commas.

I may have expressed myself badly.

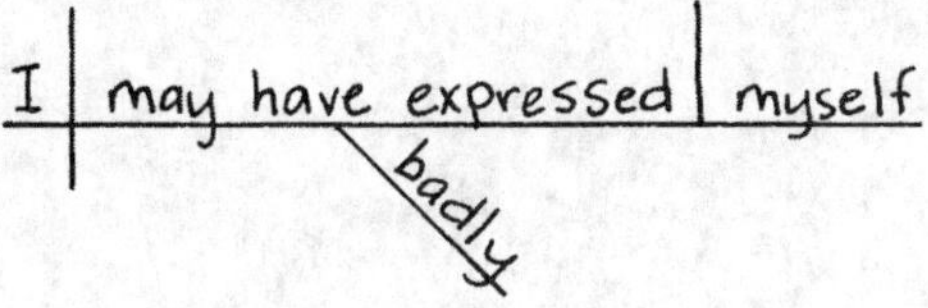

I myself was never top in anything!

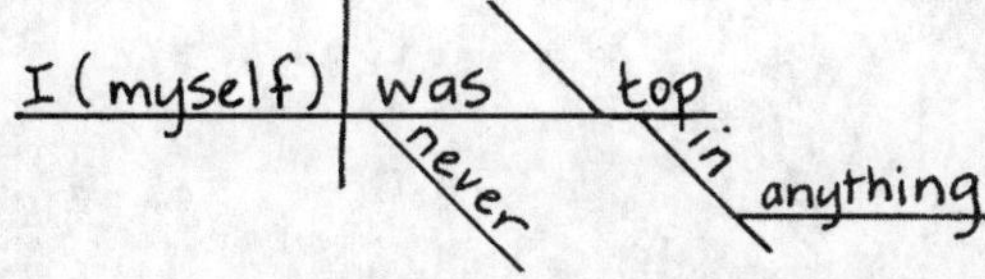

The author, Fyodor Dostoyevsky, was born in Moscow in 1821.

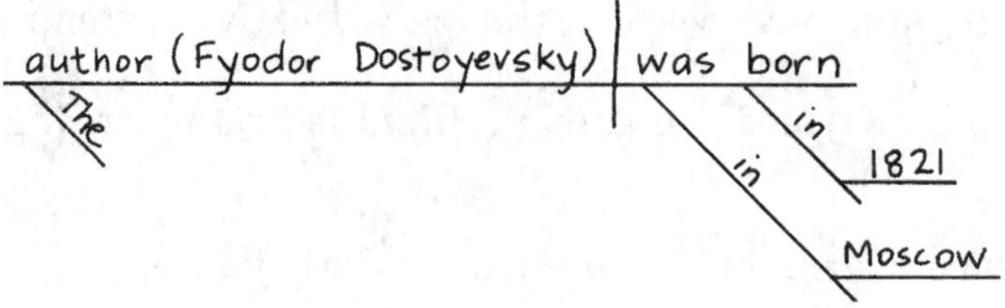

Exercise 95A: Reflexive and Intensive Pronoun Review

In the following sentences, taken from poems written by Robert Frost, underline each reflexive or intensive pronoun. Put parentheses around each intensive pronoun. Label each reflexive pronoun with one of the following labels: *DO* (direct object of a verb form), *IO* (indirect object of a verb form), *PN* (predicate nominative), or *OP* (object of a preposition).

For *DO* pronouns *ONLY,* draw an arrow from the label back to the verb or verb form that is affecting it.

He was hard on himself. I couldn't find

That he kept any hours—not for himself.

—"The Code"

He gave his own poor iliac a wrench

And plunged himself head foremost in the trench.

—"Haec Fabula Docet"

He lingered for some word she wouldn't say,

Said it at last himself, "Good-night."

—"Snow"

I armed myself against such bones as might be

With the pitch-blackened stub of an ax-handle.

—"The Census-Taker"

I am overtired

Of the great harvest I myself desired.

—"After Apple-Picking"

We could have some arrangement

By which I'd bind myself to keep hands off.

—"Home Burial"

Nothing to say to all those marriages!

She had made three herself to three of his.

—"Place for a Third"

Then she climbed slowly to her feet,

And walked off, talking to herself or Paul.

—"Paul's Wife"

Turn the farm in upon itself

Until it can contain itself no more.

—"Build Soil"

The earth itself is liable to the fate

Of meaninglessly being broken off.

—"The Lesson for Today"

Make yourself up a cheering song of how

Someone's road home from work this once was.

—"Directive"

Isn't it pretty much the same idea?

You said yourself you weren't avoiding work.

—"From Plane to Plane"

We'd kept all these years between ourselves

So as to have it ready for outsiders.

—"The Witch of Coos"

Something we were withholding made us weak

Until we found out that it was ourselves.

—"The Gift Outright"

Men fumble at the possibilities

When left to guess forever for themselves.

—"A Masque of Reason"

A dependent clause can act as an appositive if it renames the noun that it follows.

The article's argument, that studying grammar is good for your brain, didn't convince me.

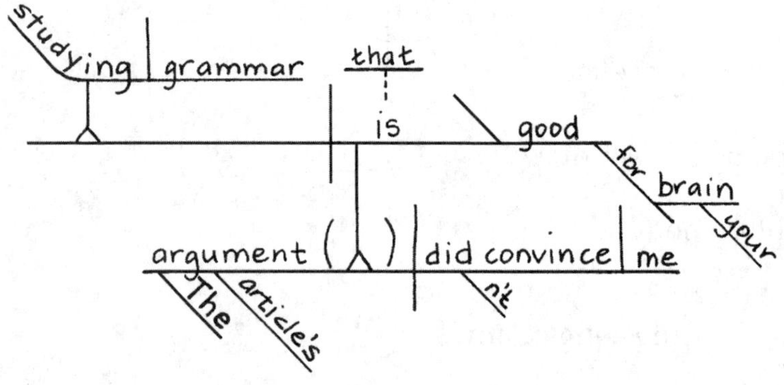

Don't forget our story, that we left early and didn't stop on the way.

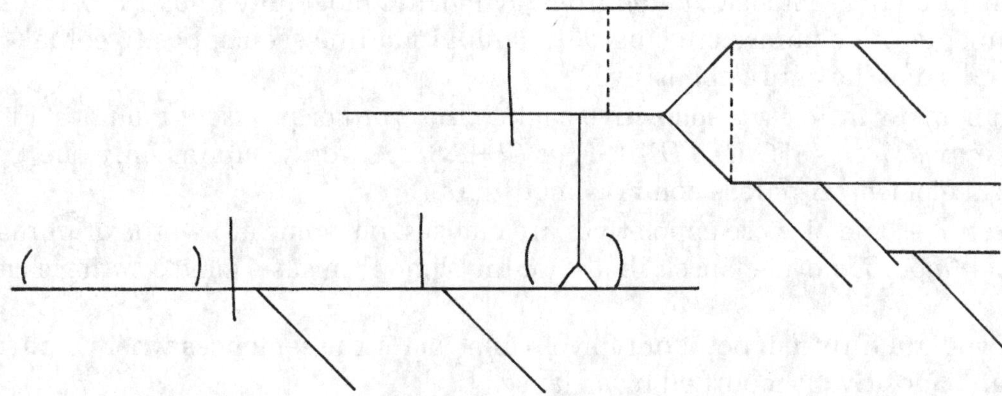

Dependent clauses can act as adjective clauses, adverb clauses, or noun clauses.

An adjective clause is a dependent clause that acts as an adjective in a sentence, modifying a noun or pronoun in the independent clause. Relative pronouns introduce adjective clauses and refer back to an antecedent in the independent clause.

A noun clause takes the place of a noun. Noun clauses can be introduced by relative pronouns, relative adverbs, or subordinating conjunctions.

Reread the story that made you happy.

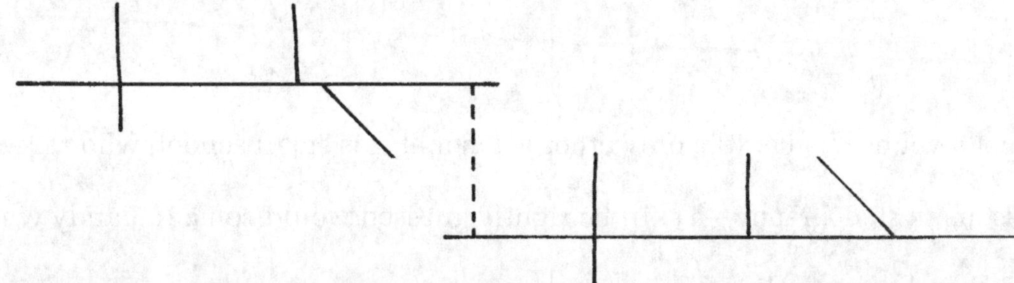

An object complement follows the direct object and renames or describes it.

The story, a long boring tale that seemed to go on forever, took up most of the evening.

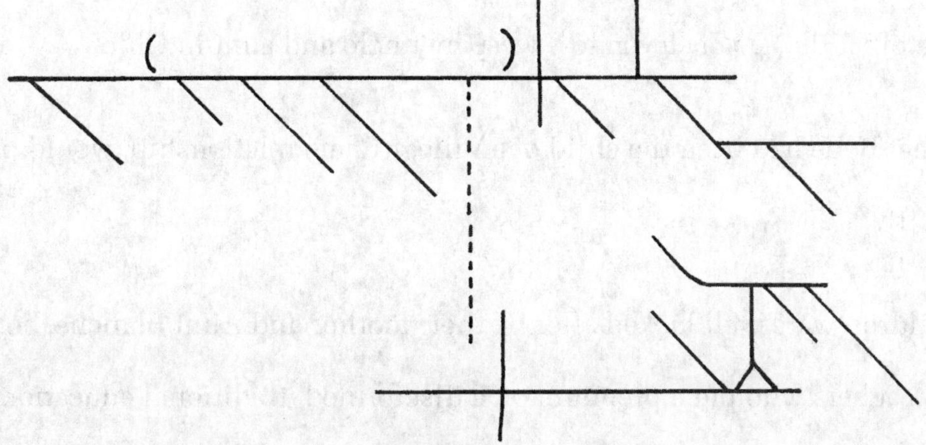

Exercise 95B: Identifying Appositives

Each of the following sentences, taken from Jay Parini's biography *Robert Frost: A Life*, contains an appositive phrase or clause. Find and underline each appositive. Make sure that you underline the entire appositive!

Draw an arrow from each appositive back to the word or phrase it renames. Finally, label each appositive as *WORD*, *PHRASE*, or *CLAUSE*. A word contains only one grammatical element. A phrase contains modifiers.

Be careful—some of these appositives are clauses, but some are words or phrases that are then *modified* by a clause! That's not the same thing as a clause *acting* as an appositive.

When you are finished, point out to your instructor the sentences where a phrase acting as an appositive is modified by a clause.

He was a poet who took nothing for granted, who could cast his thoughts upon the objects around him, as Emerson—a central figure in Frost's imagination—urged poets to do.

According to family legend, the poet's brash, talented father, William Prescott Frost, Jr., warned the doctor who delivered his son that he would shoot him if anything went wrong.

Will Frost met a young teacher (the only other teacher at this small school) who agreed to give him lessons in stenography—a skill he rightly guessed would come in handy when he turned his hand to journalism.

Her father, Thomas Moodie, was drowned at sea when she was eight; her mother, Mary, shipped Belle off at the age of eleven to a wealthy uncle and aunt in Ohio.

The rumor, that Belle had been the child of an illegitimate relationship, would persist in the Frost family.

The Frost children were well looked after by their mother and Aunt Blanche, both experienced teachers who put a premium on a disciplined, traditional education.

When Robbie was five, arrangements were made for him to attend a private kindergarten in the home of a Russian woman, Madame Zitska, even though he had to go halfway across the city of San Francisco by horse-drawn omnibus to get there.

On warm Sundays in spring, they often went to the botanical displays at Woodward's Gardens in the old mission district—the setting for "At Woodward's Gardens," which Frost published in 1936.

Another book of Scottish interest that she introduced to her children was *The Scottish Chiefs* (1810), a work of popular history by Jane Porter.

Robbie liked to set off alone on foot, often hiking to Nob Hill, where the new millionaires—men such as Charles Crocker, Leland Stanford, Mark Hopkins and D. D. Colton—were building huge Victorian houses as monuments to their own egos, crafting them from the best imported materials.

Will Frost actually managed to work at the newspaper on May 5, the day before he died at age thirty-four.

In particular, Grandfather Frost, with his flowing white beard and small, wire-rimmed glasses—an important man in this working-class community, and a dominant figure in this small mill town—seemed austere.

Grandmother Frost, an intense, nervous woman, was scarcely any warmer.

The undeniable truth, that her son had a gift for learning, was clear to Belle Frost by now.

During the summer of 1889, Frost devoted himself in the evenings and on weekends to reading books not found in the classical course at Lawrence: Cooper's *The Deerslayer* and *The Last of the Mohicans*, Mary Hartwell Catherwood's *The Romance of Dollard*, and Prescott's *History of the Conquest of Mexico.*

Elinor was a year and half older than Frost, and had missed a good deal of school owing to a mysterious disease called "slow fever"—a sickness that entailed fevers and periods of acute exhaustion.

Frost sat the Harvard entrance exams in October 1891, as expected, finishing seventh in English literature, a subject he had never studied formally in school.

Frost determined to go his own way, or to seem to go his own way, as in "The Road Not Taken," his most famous poem, which he ends with a wry self-critical note that he will be telling people "with a sigh" that he "took the road less traveled by."

Frost's new knowledge, that teaching children was not for him, compelled him to search for other ways to earn a living.

Exercise 95C: Diagramming

On your own paper, diagram every word of these sentences from Exercise 95B.

He was a poet who took nothing for granted, who could cast his thoughts upon the objects around him, as Emerson—a central figure in Frost's imagination—urged poets to do.

Will Frost met a young teacher (the only other teacher at this small school) who agreed to give him lessons in stenography—a skill he rightly guessed would come in handy when he turned his hand to journalism.

The rumor, that Belle had been the child of an illegitimate relationship, would persist in the Frost family.

Robbie liked to set off alone on foot, often hiking to Nobb Hill, where the new millionaires—men such as Charles Crocker, Leland Stanford, Mark Hopkins and D. D. Colton—were building huge Victorian houses as monuments to their own egos, crafting them from the best imported materials.

> **Note to Student:** In the above sentence, *such as* functions as a single preposition (a synonym for *like*).

— LESSON 96 —

Appositives
Noun Clauses in Apposition
Absolute Constructions

I am absolutely serious, my friend.

The whole story is absolutely untrue.

There is absolutely no question as to the alibi!

He appeared to be in an absolute frenzy.

Her face and voice were absolutely cold and expressionless.

Having no near relations or friends, I was trying to make up my mind what to do, when I ran across John Cavendish. (Adjective)

Our efforts having been in vain, we had abandoned the matter. **(Absolute construction)**

Semantic: having to do with meaning

(Greek *sēmantikós*, "having meaning")

An absolute construction has a strong semantic relationship but no grammatical connection to the rest of the sentence.

To tell the truth, an idea, wild and extravagant in itself, had once or twice that morning flashed through my brain.

Dr. Bauerstein remained in the background, his grave bearded face unchanged.

He has lived by his wits, as the saying goes.

To tell the truth, an idea, wild and extravagant in itself, had once or twice that morning flashed through my brain.

To tell truth
the

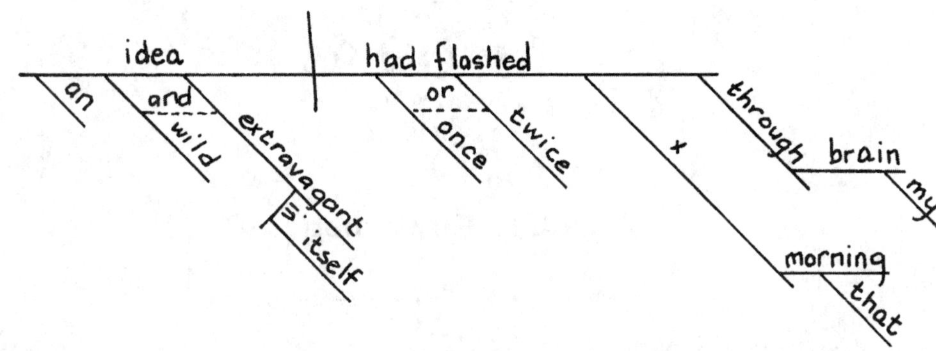

Dr. Bauerstein remained in the background, his grave bearded face unchanged.

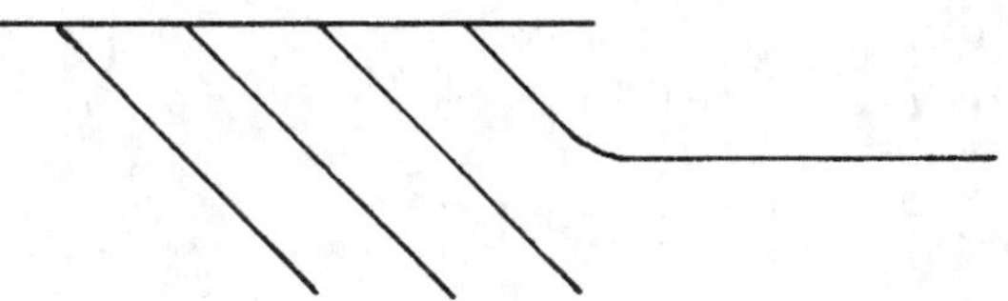

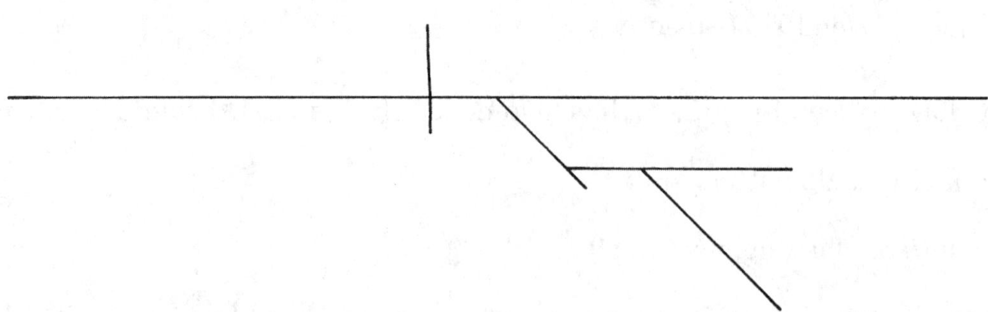

He has lived by his wits, as the saying goes.

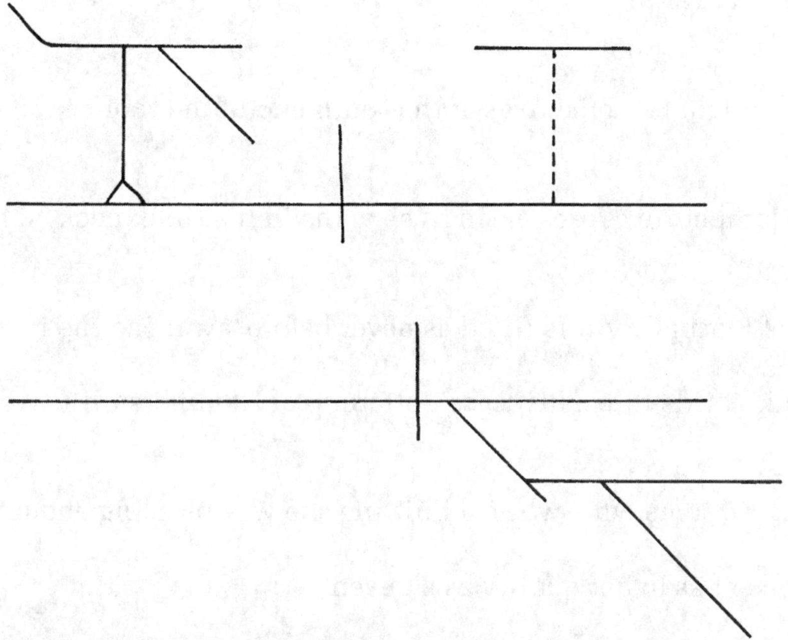

Exercise 96A: Identifying Absolute Constructions

In the following sentences, taken from *The Princess Bride*, by William Goldman, circle the absolute constructions. Label each absolute construction as *CL* for clause or *PHR* for phrase. For clauses, underline the subject of each clause once and the predicate twice.

He spoke from inside, his dark face darkened by shadow.

Now granted, things had improved since the farm boy had come to slave for him—no question, the farm boy had certain skills, and the complaints were quite nonexistent now—but that didn't make his the finest cows in Florin.

The farm boy did have good teeth, give credit where credit was due.

There was much to be done now, with Westley gone, and more than that, ever since the Count had visited, everyone in the area had increased his milk order.

But travel consumed time, ships and horses being what they were, and the time away from Florin was worrying.

This double door, it might be noted, was at the south end of the room.

At 8:23:55 Prince Humperdink rose roaring, the veins in his thick neck etched like hemp.

The Great Square of Florin City was filled as never before, awaiting the introduction of Prince Humperdink's bride-to-be, Princess Buttercup of Hammersmith.

There were, to be sure, some who, while admitting she was pleasing enough, were withholding judgement as to her quality as a queen.

Buttercup did not know how long she was out, but they were still in the boat when she blinked, the blanket shielding her.

Exercise 96B: Appositives, Modifiers, and Absolute Constructions

The sentences below, taken from *Strong Poison*, by the British mystery novelist Dorothy Sayers, each contain phrases or clauses set off by dashes. Some are appositives, some are modifiers, and some are absolute constructions. Identify them by writing *APP*, *MOD*, or *AC* above each one. For appositives and modifiers, draw an arrow back to the word being renamed or modified.

Since that time—and she is now twenty-nine years old—she has worked industriously to keep herself.

At this point the elderly spinster on the jury was seen to be making a note—a vigorous note, to judge from the action of her pencil on the paper.

The dates of these occasions cannot be ascertained with any certainty—they were informal parties—but there is some evidence that there was a meeting towards the end of March.

After the third attack—the one in May—the doctor advises Boyes to go away for a change, and he selects the northwest corner of Wales.

A very cold letter, you may think—almost hostile in tone.

I shall not have to keep your attention very much longer, but I do ask for it at this point, specially—though you have been attending most patiently and industriously all the time—because now we come to the actual day of the death itself.

The omelette—the only dish which did not go out to the kitchen—was prepared by Philip Boyes himself and shared by his cousin.

At 9:15 Boyes leaves Mr. Urquhart's house in Woburn Square, and is driven in a taxi to the house where Miss Vane has her flat, No. 100 Doughty Street—a distance of about half a mile.

Now you have been told—and the medical witnesses all agree in this—that if a person takes arsenic, a certain proportion of it will be deposited in the skin, nails and hair.

The prisoner had the means—the arsenic—she had the expert knowledge, and she had the opportunity to administer it.

And the girl—who has got rather fed up with him—thinks of a grand scoop that will make both of them best-sellers.

She took everything—money, jewels, horses, carriages, all the rest of it—and turned it into good consolidated funds.

Well, the long and short of it was that the eldest sister, Jane—the one who married the schoolmaster—would have nothing to do with the family black sheep.

Poisoning is a passion that grows upon you—like drink or drugs.

Exercise 96C: Diagramming

On your own paper, diagram every word of the following sentences, taken from the mystery novel *Murder Must Advertise*, by Dorothy Sayers.

Miss Rossiter and Miss Parton are our guardian angels—type our copy, correct our grammar, provide us with pencils and paper and feed us on coffee and cake.

Like a cat, which, in his soft-footed inquisitiveness, he rather resembled, he made himself acquainted with his new home.

What disgusting stuff cauliflower could be—a curdle of cabbage!

This pencil—a natty scarlet, as you observe, with gold lettering—didn't come from any of Darling's branches.

— REVIEW 8 —

Weeks 22-24

Topics
Parenthetical Expressions
Dashes, Colons, and Brackets
Dialogue and Dialogue Tags
Direct Quotations and Attribution Tags
Ellipses and Partial Quotations
Block Quotes
Interjections
Nouns of Direct Address
Appositives
Noun Clauses in Apposition
Absolute Constructions

Review 8A: Definition Fill-in-the-Blank

You learned many definitions in the past three weeks! Fill in the blanks in the definitions below with one of the terms from the list. Many of the terms will be used more than once.

commas	comma	parentheses
line space	dashes	coordinating conjunction
semicolon	colon	paragraph
appositive	appositives	absolute construction
period	attribution tag	exclamation point
parenthetical expression	interjections	dialogue tag
question mark	brackets	ellipses
restrictive modifying clause	nouns of direct address	quotation marks
nonrestrictive modifying clause	closing quotation marks	short parenthetical expressions

________________________ can enclose words that are not essential to the sentence.

________________________ can also be used singly to separate parts of a sentence.

____________________________ make a parenthetical element a part of the sentence.

____________________________ emphasize a parenthetical element.

______________________ minimize a parenthetical element.

The independent clauses of a compound sentence must be joined by a ____________ and a ______________________, a ______________________, or a ______________________ and a ______________________. They cannot be joined by a ______________________ alone.

A ______________________ defines the word that it modifies. Removing the clause changes the essential meaning of the sentence.

A ______________________ describes the word that it modifies. Removing the clause doesn't change the essential meaning of the sentence.

______________________ can enclose words that are not essential to the sentence.

A ______________________ often interrupts or is irrelevant to the rest of the sentence. Punctuation goes inside the ______________________ if it applies to the ______________________; all other punctuation goes outside the ______________________.

A ______________________ only begins with a capital letter if it is a complete sentence with ending punctuation.

A ______________________ can also be set off by commas.

______________________ such as the following are usually set off by commas: *in short, in fact, in reality, as it were, as it happens, no doubt, in a word, to be sure, to be brief, after all, you know, of course.*

Only a ______________________ should be set off by commas.

An ______________________ is a noun, pronoun, or noun phrase that usually follows another noun and renames or explains it. ____________ are set off by ______________________.

A dependent clause can act as an ______________________ if it renames the noun that it follows.

When a ______________________ comes before a speech, place a ______________________ after the tag. Put the dialogue's final punctuation mark inside the ______________________.

______________________ show where something has been cut out of a sentence.

A second or third quote from the same source does not need another _______________, as long as context makes the source of the quote clear.

Direct quotes can be words, phrases, clauses, or sentences, as long as they are set off by _______________ and form part of a grammatically correct original sentence.

If a direct quotation is longer than three lines, indent the entire quote one inch from the margin in a separate block of text and omit _______________.

If you change or make additions to a direct quotation, use _______________.

When using word processing software, leave an additional _______________ before and after a block quote.

Block quotes should be introduced by a _______________ (if preceded by a complete sentence) or a _______________ (if preceded by a partial sentence).

_______________ express sudden feeling or emotion. They are set off with _______________ or stand alone with a closing punctuation mark.

_______________ name a person or thing who is being spoken to. They are set off with _______________. They are capitalized only if they are proper names or titles.

An _______________ has a strong semantic relationship but no grammatical connection to the rest of the sentence.

Speeches do not need to be attached to a _______________ as long as the text clearly indicates the speaker.

Usually, a new _______________ begins with each new speaker.

When a _______________ comes in the middle of a speech, follow it with a _______________ if the following dialogue is an incomplete sentence. Follow it with a _______________ if the following dialogue is a complete sentence.

When an _______________ comes after a direct quote, place a _______________, _______________, or _______________ inside the closing quotation marks.

When an ____________________ comes before a direct quote, place a ____________________ after the tag. Put the dialogue's final punctuation mark inside the ____________________ .

When an ____________________ comes in the middle of a direct quotation, follow it with a ____________________ if the remaining quote is an incomplete sentence. Follow it with a ____________________ if the remaining quote is a complete sentence.

Every direct quote must have an ____________________.

Review 8B: Punctuating Restrictive and Non-Restrictive Clauses, Compound Sentences, Interjections, Parenthetical Expressions, Items in Series, and Nouns of Direct Address

The sentences below contain restrictive clauses, nonrestrictive clauses, interjections, parenthetical expressions, items in series, and nouns of direct address. Some are compound sentences. But all of them have lost their punctuation! Insert all necessary punctuation directly into the sentences (use the actual punctuation marks rather than proofreader's marks).

These sentences are taken from the story "Hansel and Gretel," found in *Grimms' Fairy Tales*, collected by the nineteenth-century German folklorists Jacob Grimm and Wilhelm Grimm, translated into English by Edgar Taylor and Marian Edwardes.

O you fool then we must all four die of hunger!

The moon shone brightly and the white pebbles which lay in front of the house glittered like real silver pennies.

Now children lay yourselves down by the fire and rest we will go into the forest and cut some wood.

Hansel took his little sister by the hand and followed only the pebbles which shone like newly coined silver pieces.

On the way into the forest Hansel crumbled the bread which had been given him and he often threw a morsel on the ground.

When the moon came they set out but they found no crumbs the many thousands of birds which fly about in the woods and fields had picked them all up.

Hansel who liked the taste of the roof tore down a great piece of it and Gretel pushed out the whole of one round window-pane sat down and enjoyed herself with it.

Oh you dear children who has brought you here?

The old woman had only pretended to be so kind she was in reality a wicked witch who lay in wait for children and had only built the little house of bread in order to entice them there.

Get up lazy thing fetch some water and cook something good for your brother he is in the stable outside and is to be made fat.

Gretel began to weep bitterly but it was all in vain for she was forced to do what the wicked witch commanded.

Hansel however stretched out a little bone to her and the old woman who had dim eyes could not see it.

She pushed poor Gretel out to the oven which was already shooting up flames of fire.

Then Gretel gave her a push that drove her far into the oven and shut the iron door and fastened the bolt which was on it.

Gretel, however, ran like lightning to Hansel she opened his little shed and let him out.

Their father had not known one happy hour since he had left the children in the forest the cruel stepmother as it happened was dead.

Then all anxiety was at an end and they lived together in perfect happiness.

Review 8C: Dialogue

In the following passage from "How the Camel Got His Hump" (from the *Just So Stories*, by Rudyard Kipling), all of the punctuation around, before, and after the lines of dialogue is missing. Insert all necessary punctuation directly into the sentences (use the actual punctuation marks rather than proofreader's marks).

There is a special challenge in the excerpt! If you can't find it, your instructor will point it out to you.

In the beginning of years, when the world was so new and all, and the Animals were just beginning to work for Man, there was a Camel, and he lived in the middle of a Howling Desert because he did not want to work; and besides, he was a Howler himself.

So he ate sticks and thorns and tamarisks and milkweed and prickles, most 'scruciating idle; and when anybody spoke to him he said Humph

Presently the Horse came to him on Monday morning, with a saddle on his back and a bit in his mouth, and said Camel, O Camel, come out and trot like the rest of us.

Humph said the Camel; and the Horse went away and told the Man.

Presently the Dog came to him, with a stick in his mouth, and said Camel, O Camel, come and fetch and carry like the rest of us.

Humph said the Camel; and the Dog went away and told the Man.

Presently the Ox came to him, with the yoke on his neck and said Camel, O Camel, come and plough like the rest of us.

Humph said the Camel; and the Ox went away and told the Man.

At the end of the day the Man called the Horse and the Dog and the Ox together, and said Three, O Three, I'm very sorry for you (with the world so new-and-all); but that Humph-thing in the Desert can't work, or he would have been here by now, so I am going to leave him alone, and you must work double-time to make up for it.

That made the Three very angry (with the world so new-and-all), and they held a palaver, and an *indaba*, and a *punchayet*, and a pow-wow on the edge of the Desert; and the Camel came chewing on milkweed *most* 'scruciating idle, and laughed at them. Then he said Humph and went away again.

Presently there came along the Djinn in charge of All Deserts, rolling in a cloud of dust (Djinns always travel that way because it is Magic), and he stopped to palaver and pow-pow with the Three.

Djinn of All Deserts said the Horse is it right for any one to be idle, with the world so new-and-all?

Certainly not said the Djinn.

Well said the Horse there's a thing in the middle of your Howling Desert (and he's a Howler himself) with a long neck and long legs, and he hasn't done a stroke of work since Monday morning. He won't trot.

Whew said the Djinn, whistling that's my Camel, for all the gold in Arabia! What does he say about it?

He says Humph said the Dog and he won't fetch and carry.

Does he say anything else?

Only Humph and he won't plough said the Ox.

Very good said the Djinn I'll humph him, if you will kindly wait a minute.

The Djinn rolled himself up in his dust-cloak, and took a bearing across the desert, and found the Camel most 'scruciatingly idle, looking at his own reflection in a pool of water.

My long and bubbling friend said the Djinn what's this I hear of your doing no work, with the world so new-and-all?

Humph said the Camel.

The Djinn sat down, with his chin in his hand, and began to think a Great Magic, while the Camel looked at his own reflection in the pool of water.

You've given the Three extra work ever since Monday morning, all on account of your 'scruciating idleness said the Djinn; and he went on thinking Magics, with his chin in his hand.

Humph said the Camel.

I shouldn't say that again if I were you said the Djinn You might say it once too often.

Review 8D: Parenthetical Expressions, Appositives, Absolute Constructions

Each one of the sentences below contains an element not closely connected to the rest of the sentence: parenthetical, appositive, or absolute.

In each sentence, find and circle the unconnected element (word, phrase, or clause). Above it, write *PAR* for parenthetical, *APP* for appositive, or *AB* for absolute.

In the blank at the end of the sentence, note whether the element is set apart with commas (*C*), parentheses (*P*), dashes (*D*), or some other mark (*O*).

These are taken from "A Boyhood in Scotland," a personal essay by the great nineteenth-century nature writer John Muir.

One fine day, as the story goes, when the bell was ringing gently, the pirate put out to the rock. _______

This happened, I think, before I was sent to school. _______

I couldn't imagine what the doctor, a tall, severe-looking man in black, was doing to my brother. _______

When I was a little boy at Mungo Siddons's school, a flower-show was held in Dunbar, and I saw a number of the exhibitors carrying large handfuls of dahlias, the first I had ever seen. _______

Our bedroom was adjacent to the ghost room, which had in it a lot of chemical apparatus—glass tubing, glass and brass retorts, test-tubes, flasks, etc.—and we thought that those strange articles were still used by the old dead doctor. _______

David (not to be outdone) crawled up to the top of the window-roof and got bravely astride of it; but in trying to return he lost courage and began to cry. _______

After attaining the manly, belligerent age of five or six years, very few of my schooldays passed without a fist fight. _______

We even carried on war, class against class, in those wild, precious minutes. _______

Every boy owned some sort of craft whittled from a block of wood and trimmed with infinite pains—sloops, schooners, brigs, and full-rigged ships, with their sails and string ropes properly adjusted and named for us by some old sailor. _______

Our most exciting sport, however, was playing with gunpowder. _______

Like squirrels that begin to eat nuts before they are ripe, we began to eat apples about as soon as they were formed, causing (of course) desperate gastric disturbances to be cured by castor oil. _______

Our portions were consumed in about a couple of minutes; then off to school. _______

We had hens in our back yard, and on the next Saturday we managed to swallow a couple of raw eggs apiece, a disgusting job. _______

These were my first excursions—the beginnings of lifelong wanderings. _______

Review 8E: Direct Quotations

In the following two excerpts from two different books about hoaxes and conspiracies, the bolded quotations have not been properly punctuated. Rewrite the paragraphs on your own paper or with your own word processor. (You do not need to include the author and title information!) Punctuate and space the quotations properly.

When you are finished, circle any places where words have been left out of the direct quotations. Underline any places where words or punctuation has been added to the direct quotations. Then compare your answers with the original.

Donna Henes, a self-proclaimed **artist and ritual-maker,** gathered about a hundred people in New York City to publicly stand eggs up at the exact moment of the vernal equinox on March 20, 1983. This event was covered by the *New Yorker* magazine, and a story about it appeared in its April 4, 1983 issue, describing how Ms. Henes handed out eggs to the onlookers, making them promise not to stand any up before the appointed time. Around 11:39 PM she upended an egg and announced **Spring is here**

Everyone in the crowd, us included, got busy balancing eggs the *New Yorker* effused. **Honest to God, it works** The unnamed reporter was not so convinced, however, as to swallow this line whole.

—Philip C. Plait, *Bad Astronomy: Misconceptions and Misuses Revealed, from Astrology to the Moon Landing "Hoax"*

It's also tempting to simply label conspiracy theories as either "mainstream" or "fringe." Journalist Paul Musgrave referenced this dichotomy when he wrote in the *Washington Post* **Less than two months into the administration, the danger is no longer that Trump will make conspiracy thinking mainstream. That has already come to pass... [S]uch untruths may now be driving government policy in realms as disparate as immigration policy and civil rights.** What Musgrave is talking about is a fairly small shift in a dividing line on the conspiracy spectrum.

—Slightly adapted from Mick West, *Escaping the Rabbit Hole: How to Debunk Conspiracy Theories Using Facts, Logic, and Respect*

Review 8F: Diagramming

On your own paper, diagram every word of the following sentences from the first chapter of the novel *When We Were Orphans*, by the British novelist Kazuo Ishiguro (the 2017 winner of the Nobel Prize in literature).

Each sentence contains words set off by a dash, but each of these function as a different part of the sentence. Be ready to explain to your instructor briefly how the different words set off by dashes function!

Ask for help if necessary.

Eventually he flopped down into the sofa, and we were able to exchange news—our own and that of old schoolfriends.

After a while, I grew angry—at myself, at Osbourne, at the whole proceedings.

I did not notice until later—one needs a second magnifying glass to read the engraving—that it was manufactured in Zurich in 1887.

I believe it was at this point I finally assented to his suggestion for the evening—an evening which, as I shall explain, was to prove far more significant—and showed him out.

WEEK 25

Complex Verb Tenses

— LESSON 97 —

Verb Tense, Voice, and Mood
Tense Review (Indicative)
Progressive Perfect Tenses (Indicative)

Moods
- Indicative
- Subjunctive
- Imperative
- Modal

(The following sentences are from Beverly Cleary's novel *Fifteen*.)

He spoke rapidly, as if he <u>were</u> anxious to get the words out of the way.

Mood: ______________________

And <u>be</u> home by ten thirty.

Mood: ______________________

To hide her discomfort she <u>took</u> small bites of ice cream.

Mood: ______________________

<u>Should</u> they <u>talk</u> awhile, or <u>should</u> she <u>suggest</u> that they leave, or <u>should</u> she <u>wait</u> for him to suggest it?

Mood: ______________________

Indicative verbs express real actions.
Subjunctive verbs express unreal actions.
Imperative verbs express intended actions.
Modal verbs express possible actions.

Here everything looked brand-new, as if the furniture had been delivered only the day before.

Mood: ______________________

Voice: ______________________

Now the fat pug dog rose and shook himself, scattering his hair over the carpet.

Mood: ______________________

Voice: ______________________

Voice
In a sentence with an active verb, the subject performs the action.
In a sentence with a passive verb, the subject receives the action.

Tense
A simple verb simply tells whether an action takes place in the past, present, or future.
A progressive verb describes an ongoing or continuous action.
A perfect verb describes an action which has been completed before another action takes place.

Exercise 97A: Review of Indicative Tenses

The following partially completed chart shows the active and passive tenses of the regular verb *help* (in the third-person singular), the irregular verb *leave* (in the third-person plural), and the irregular verb *send* (in the first-person singular). Review your indicative tenses by completing the chart now.

		Active	Passive
SIMPLE TENSES			
help *leave* *send*	Past	he helped they I	he they were I
help *leave* *send*	Present	he they I send	he is they I
help *leave* *send*	Future	he they will leave I	he will be they I

		Active	Passive
PROGRESSIVE TENSES			
help *leave* *send*	Past	he they I was	he was being helped they I
help *leave* *send*	Present	he they I am sending	he is they I
help *leave* *send*	Future	he they will be I	he they I will be being sent
PERFECT TENSES			
help *leave* *send*	Past	he they had left I	he had been they I
help *leave* *send*	Present	he has they I	he they I have been sent
help *leave* *send*	Future	he they I will have	he will have been helped they I

A progressive perfect verb describes an ongoing or continuous action that has a definite end.

progressive perfect past

I had been running for half an hour before I decided to stop.

progressive perfect present

I have been running all morning.

progressive perfect future

I will have been running for an hour by the time you arrive.

PAST

Simple	I rejoiced over my grammar!
Progressive	I was rejoicing over my grammar.
Perfect	I had rejoiced over my grammar.
Progressive Perfect	I had been rejoicing over my grammar, until I realized I had done the wrong exercises.

PRESENT

Simple	I enjoy this schoolwork!
Progressive	I am enjoying this schoolwork.
Perfect	I have enjoyed this schoolwork.
Progressive Perfect	I have been enjoying this schoolwork, but unfortunately I have to stop now and go play Minecraft.

FUTURE

Simple	I will expect to receive a prize!
Progressive	All afternoon, I will be expecting to receive a prize.
Perfect	By dinner time, I will have expected to receive my prize.
Progressive Perfect	By dinner time, I will have been expecting to receive a prize for at least four hours.

PROGRESSIVE PERFECT PAST

Active The house had been showing signs of wear.

Passive The house had been being shown to prospective buyers for months.

PROGRESSIVE PERFECT PRESENT

Active I have been sending letters out every day.

Passive I have been being sent to the post office by my mother every day.

PROGRESSIVE PERFECT FUTURE

Active Come June, the professors will have been teaching Latin for two years.

Passive Come June, the students will have been being taught Latin for two years.

PROGRESSIVE PERFECT TENSES

Past	**Active**	**Passive**
Active: helping verb had + *helping verb* been + *present participle* *Passive: helping verb* had + *helping verb phrase* been being + *past participle*	I had been amusing you had been amusing he, she, it had been amusing we had been amusing you had been amusing they had been amusing	I had been being amused you had been being amused he, she, it had been being amused we had been being amused you had been being amused they had been being amused
Present	**Active**	**Passive**
Active: helping verb have *or* has + *helping verb* been + *present participle* *Passive: helping verb* have *or* has + *helping verb phrase* been being + *past participle*	I have been amusing you have been amusing he, she, it has been amusing we have been amusing you have been amusing they have been amusing	I have been being amused you have been being amused he, she, it has been being amused we have been being amused you have been being amused they have been being amused

PROGRESSIVE PERFECT TENSES

Future	Active	Passive
Active: helping verb phrase will have been *+ present participle*	I will have been amusing you will have been amusing he, she, it will have been amusing	I will have been being amused you will have been being amused he, she, it will have been being amused
Passive: helping verb phrase will have been being *+ past participle*	we will have been amusing you will have been amusing they will have been amusing	we will have been being amused you will have been being amused they will have been being amused

Perfect Future Passive	The students will have been taught Latin very thoroughly.
Progressive Perfect Future Passive	Come June, the students will have been being taught Latin for two years.
Progressive Perfect Future Passive (Understood)	Come June, the students will have been taught Latin for two years.

Exercise 97B: Parsing Verbs

Identify the tense, voice, and mood of each underlined verb. You may abbreviate (*PROG, PERF, SIMP, PAST, PRES, FUT* for tense; *ACT, PASS, ST-OF-BE* for voice; *IND, SUBJ, MOD* for mood).

The first is done for you.

These sentences have been slightly adapted from *The Old Curiosity Shop*, by Charles Dickens.

SIMP PAST, ACT, IND

She added that there was no harm in what she had been doing, but it was a great secret—a secret which she did not even know herself.

If no such suspicion had been awakened by his speech, his wiry hair, dull eyes, and sallow face would still have been strong witnesses against him.

There were suits of mail standing like ghosts in armour here and there, fantastic carvings, tapestry and strange furniture that might have been designed in dreams.

I have been rendered uneasy by what you said the other night, and can only plead that I have done all for the best.

"I'm sorry I have an appointment in the city," said Quilp, looking at his watch, "or I should have been very glad to have spent half an hour with you."

"Wait until dusk," returned Mr Groves. "You will have eaten your suppers by then."

Yet it was strange that she had been imagining this figure so very distinctly.

Unless my aunt sends me a remittance, I shall have gone without a room for the night.

"She is sleeping soundly," he said, "but no wonder. Angel hands have strewn the ground deep with snow."

She wished they could be told how much she thought about them, and how she had watched them as they walked together, by the river side at night.

You shall not be permitted to fly in the face of your superiors in this exceedingly gross manner!

Exercise 97C: Completing Sentences

Complete the following sentences by providing an appropriate verb in the tense and voice indicated beneath each blank. (All verbs are in the indicative mood.)

The little lake on the edge of the farm ______________________ for the last few
progressive perfect present, active
years, as the weather has gotten hotter and dryer.

The rebel leader ______________________ in four different attempts to take
perfect present, passive
over the government of her country.

For the last twelve hours, the ultra-marathoner ________________ through the desert.
progressive perfect present, active

By tomorrow, the enormous birthday cake ____________________________ and
perfect future, passive (compound!)

________________.
perfect future, passive

By tomorrow night, the entire cake ________________________ by hungry guests.
perfect future, passive

By the time I go to college, I __________________________ grammar for ten years!
progressive perfect future, active

The flower __________________________ better than ever, since it ____________
progressive present, active ... progressive perfect present, active

in the full sunlight.

Unless the borrower has completed the application, his debt ________ not ____________
perfect future, passive

in time for him to take out another loan.

For years before the pandemic began, poor tenants __________________________
progressive perfect past, passive

at every possible opportunity.

The gigantic towers __________________________ for years, and they still aren't
progressive perfect present, passive

ready for tenants to move in!

— LESSON 98 —

Simple Present and Perfect Present Modal Verbs

Progressive Present and Progressive Perfect Present Modal Verbs

Modal verbs express situations that have not actually happened.

Should, would, may, might, must, can, could

Would, may, might, can, could: **possibility**

He was afraid that, in a little while, death ____________ meet him.

I fear that we ____________ never see him in this life again.

Oh, that I ____________ strike a blow for him before I die!

Only a knight of true valor ____________ hope to win.

Madam, how then ____________ I help you?

Must, should: **obligation**

I _______________ find a man whom I can truly love.

You _______________ do homage to King Arthur for your kingdom.

May: **permission**

_______________ I go to Camelot, to see the jousting?

Can: **ability**

Nothing _______________ heal his wound on this side of the water.

	Simple Present Modal (Active)	
First person	I could help	we could help
Second person	you could help	you could help
Third person	he, she, it could help	they could help

	Perfect Present Modal (Active)	
First person	I should have helped	we should have helped
Second person	you should have helped	you should have helped
Third person	he, she, it should have helped	they should have helped

MODAL TENSES

	Simple Present	**Simple Past**	**Simple Future**
Active	I should help	none	none
Passive	I should be helped	none	none
	Progressive Present	**Progressive Past**	**Progressive Future**
Active	I could be helping	none	none
Passive	I could be being helped	none	none
	Perfect Present	**Perfect Past**	**Perfect Future**
Active	I would have helped	none	none
Passive	I would have been helped	none	none
	Progressive Perfect Present	**Prog Perfect Past**	**Prog Perfect Future**
Active	I might have been helping	none	none
Passive	I might have been being helped	none	none

Use the simple present or progressive present when the situation isn't happening in the present.

Since I slept badly last night, I might go take a nap.

mood	indicative	modal
tense		
voice		

People are being left in the hospital when they could be being nursed at home.

mood	indicative	
tense		
voice		

Use the perfect present or the progressive perfect present when the situation didn't happen in the past.

I was eating cheese and crackers when I could have been sitting down to a big juicy steak.

mood	indicative	
tense	progressive past	
voice	active	

While the floors were being scrubbed, I could have vacuumed the rugs.

mood	indicative	
tense	progressive past	
voice	passive	

Modal Present: Simple or Progressive
Modal Past: Perfect or Progressive Perfect

MODAL TENSE FORMATION

Simple Present

Active	I can help	modal helping verb + first-person singular
Passive	I should be helped	modal helping verb + *be* + past participle

Progressive Present

Active	I might be helping	modal helping verb + *be* + present participle
Passive	I could be being helped	modal helping verb + *be* + being + past participle

Perfect Present

Active	I would have helped	modal helping verb + *have* + past participle
Passive	I may have been helped	modal helping verb + *have* + been + past participle

Progressive Perfect Present

Active	I must have been helping	modal helping verb + *have* + *been* + present participle
Passive	I could have been being	modal helping verb + *have* + *been* + *being* + past participle

Exercise 98A: Parsing Verbs

In the following sentences from *Moby-Dick*, by Herman Melville, find and underline each modal verb. Write the tense and voice of each modal verb above it. (For state-of-being verbs, the voice is simply *state-of-being*.) The first is done for you.

simple present, passive

Ahab gave orders that not an oar should be used, and no man must speak but in whispers.

But in the foamy confusion of their mixed and struggling hosts, the marksmen could not always hit their mark; and this brought about new revelations of the incredible ferocity of the foe.

Beelzebub himself might climb up the side and step down into the cabin to chat with the captain, and it would not create any unsubduable excitement in the forecastle.

Meanwhile, the whale he had struck must also have been on its travels.

For who could tell but what the next morning, as soon as I popped out of the room, the harpooneer might be standing in the entry, all ready to knock me down!

One packed rush was made to the side, and every eye counted every ripple, as moment followed moment, and no sign of either the sinker or the diver could be seen.

A nose to the whale would have been impertinent.

What just before might have seemed to him a thing most momentous, now seems but a part of the general joke.

For one of them may have received a transfer of letters from some third, and now far remote vessel; and some of those letters may be for the people of the ship she now meets.

Some at least of the imaginative impressions about to be presented may have been shared by most men.

To accomplish his object Ahab must use tools.

The lines, of which, hardly an instant before, not one hand's breadth could have been gained, were now in long quick coils flung back all dripping into the boats.

That for six thousand years—and no one knows how many millions of ages before—the great whales should have been spouting all over the sea—this is surely a noteworthy thing.

The headsman should stay in the bows from first to last; he should both dart the harpoon and the lance, and no rowing whatever should be expected of him, except under circumstances obvious to any fisherman.

Exercise 98B: Forming Modal Verbs

Fill in the blanks with the missing modal verbs. Using the helping verbs indicated, put each action verb provided into the correct modal tense.

Around the reef, we ____________________________ fish of every luminous color that ______________________________________.

helping verb: could
simple present active of *see*

helping verb: could
simple present passive of *imagine*

Sharks ______________________________ their bodies out of the water, but only partly, and only with great effort.

helping verb: can
simple present active of *raise*

Our guide ______________________________, because the entire party decided to scuba dive down into the cold depths of the ocean.

helping verb: must
progressive perfect present active of *convince*

Huge bull sharks, we later learned, ______________________________ as close as fifty yards off our private beach.

helping verb: may
perfect present passive of *see*

I ______________________________ the catastrophe that followed!

helping verb: might
perfect present active of *expect*

Before our vacation was finished, we ______________________________ the loss of nearly all of our colleagues!

helping verb: would
progressive present active of *mourn*

To be so aggressive, the sharks ______________________________ for food for many weeks before we arrived on the scene.

helping verb: must
progressive perfect present passive of *starve*

The epic battle between swimmers and sharks ___________________________ again and again over the coming years.

helping verb: would
simple present passive of *retell*

Magazine subscribers the world over ______________________________ about our struggle against the bull sharks for years to come, and the story _________________ the popularity of Shark Bay for all time.

helping verb: would
progressive present active of *read*

helping verb: may
perfect present active of *destroy*

— LESSON 99 —

Modal Verb Tenses
The Imperative Mood
The Subjunctive Mood
More Subjunctive Tenses

Indicative verbs express real actions.
Subjunctive verbs express unreal actions.
Imperative verbs express intended actions.
Modal verbs express possible actions.

Turn to the end of your book.
Eat more vegetables!
Go away.

Be checked by a doctor before you come back to work.

The present passive imperative is formed by adding the helping verb *be* to the past participle of the verb.

Subjunctive verbs express situations that are unreal, wished for, or uncertain.

If we kept our ponies up in the winter time, we gave them fodder to eat.

We kept our ponies up in the winter time, and we gave them fodder to eat.

	Simple Present Subjunctive State-of-Being Verb		**Simple Past Subjunctive State-of-Being Verb**	
First person	I be	we be	I were	we were
Second person	you be	you be	you were	you were
Third person	he, she, it be	they be	he, she, it were	they were

Should you be in town, come by and see me.

If I were a bird, I would fly across the water.

	Simple Present Subjunctive Action Verb: Active		**Simple Present Subjunctive Action Verb: Passive**	
First person	I leave	we leave	I be left	we be left
Second person	you leave	you leave	you be left	you be left
Third person	he, she, it leave	they leave	he, she, it be left	they be left

He leaves early to avoid traffic.
I suggest that he leave early to avoid traffic.

The present passive subjunctive is formed by pairing *be* with the past participle of a verb.

The tent was left behind.
The guide recommended that the tent be left behind.

	Simple Past Subjunctive Action Verb: Active		Simple Present Subjunctive Action Verb: Passive	
First person	I left	we left	I were left	we were left
Second person	you left	you left	you were left	you were left
Third person	he, she, it left	they left	he, she, it were left	they were left

If I left early, I might be able to pick up the milk.
I left early to pick up the milk.

If I were left behind, I would be upset.
I was left behind, which made me very upset.

Simple Future Subjunctive Action Verb: Active	Simple Future Subjunctive Action Verb: Passive
None	None

Use the simple past subjunctive state-of-being verb, plus an infinitive, to express a future unreal action.

If I were to die tomorrow, I would have no regrets.

PROGRESSIVE TENSES

	Progressive Present Subjunctive Action Verb: Active	
First person	I am leaving	we are leaving
Second person	you are leaving	you are leaving
Third person	he, she, it is leaving	they are leaving

	Progressive Present Subjunctive Action Verb: Passive	
First person	I am being left	we are being left
Second person	you are being left	you are being left
Third person	he, she, it is being left	they are being left

If I be running late, I must throw myself upon your kind mercies.

If I am running late, I will call you.

It is unlikely that I am being penalized.

	Progressive Past Subjunctive **Action Verb: Active**	
First person	I **were** leaving	we were leaving
Second person	you were leaving	you were leaving
Third person	he, she, it **were** leaving	they were leaving

	Progressive Past Subjunctive **Action Verb: Passive**	
First person	I **were** being left	we were being left
Second person	you were being left	you were being left
Third person	he, she, it **were** being left	they were being left

If I were running in the race, I would certainly win.

I was running in the race.

If I were being left behind, I would make a huge fuss.

I was being left behind.

Progressive Future Subjunctive
Action Verb: Active

None

Progressive Future Subjunctive
Action Verb: Passive

None

PERFECT TENSES

	Perfect Present Subjunctive **Action Verb: Active**	
First person	I have left	we have left
Second person	you have left	you have left
Third person	he, she, it has left	they have left

	Perfect Present Subjunctive **Action Verb: Passive**	
First person	I have been left	we have been left
Second person	you have been left	you have been left
Third person	he, she, it has been left	they have been left

	Perfect Past Subjunctive Action Verb: Active	
First person	I had left	we had left
Second person	you had left	you had left
Third person	he, she, it had left	they had left

	Perfect Past Subjunctive Action Verb: Passive	
First person	I had been left	we had been left
Second person	you had been left	you had been left
Third person	he, she, it had been left	they had been left

Perfect Future Subjunctive
Action Verb: Active

None

Perfect Future Subjunctive
Action Verb: Passive

None

PROGRESSIVE PERFECT TENSES

	Progressive Perfect Present Subjunctive Action Verb: Active	
First person	I have been leaving	we have been leaving
Second person	you have been leaving	you have been leaving
Third person	he, she, it has been leaving	they have been leaving

	Progressive Perfect Present Subjunctive Action Verb: Passive	
First person	I have been being left	we have been being left
Second person	you have been being left	you have been being left
Third person	he, she, it has been being left	they have been being left

	Progressive Perfect Past Subjunctive **Action Verb: Active**	
First person	I had been leaving	we had been leaving
Second person	you had been leaving	you had been leaving
Third person	he, she, it had been leaving	they had been leaving

	Progressive Perfect Past Subjunctive **Action Verb: Passive**	
First person	I had been being left	we had been being left
Second person	you had been being left	you had been being left
Third person	he, she, it had been being left	they had been being left

Progressive Perfect Future Subjunctive
Action Verb: Active

None

Progressive Perfect Future Subjunctive
Action Verb: Passive

None

Exercise 99A: Complete the Chart

Fill in the missing forms on the following chart. Use the verbs indicated above each chart, in order. The first form on each chart is done for you.

INDICATIVE

(aggravate, build, dazzle, forget, bless, hurry, interrupt, keep, leave, lighten, murder, twist)

Indicative Tense	Active Formation	Examples	Passive Formation	Examples
Simple present	Add *-s* in third- person singular	I aggravate he, she, it ______	*am*/*is*/*are* + past participle	I am aggravated you ______ he, she, it ______

Indicative Tense	Active Formation	Examples	Passive Formation	Examples
Simple past	Add *-d* or *-ed*, or change form	I ______	was/*were* + past participle	I ______ you ______
Simple future	+ *will* OR *shall*	they ______	*will be* + past participle	it ______
Progressive present	*am/is/are* + present participle	I ______ you ______ he, she, it ______	*am/is/are being* + past participle	I ______ you ______ he, she, it ______
Progressive past	*was/were* + present participle	I ______ you ______ he, she, it ______	*was/were being* + past participle	I ______ you ______ he, she, it ______
Progressive future	*will be* + present participle	I______	*will be being* + past participle	it ______
Perfect present	*has/have* + past participle	I ______ you ______ he, she, it ______	*has/have been* + past participle	I ______ you ______ he, she, it ______
Perfect past	*had* + past participle	they ______	*had been* + past participle	you ______
Perfect future	*will have* + past participle	we ______	*will have been* + past participle	they ______

Indicative Tense	Active Formation	Examples	Passive Formation	Examples
Progressive perfect present	*have/has been* + present participle	I ______ he, she, it ______	*have/has been being* + past participle	I ______ he, she, it ______
Progressive perfect past	*had been* + present participle	you ______	*had been being* + past participle	you ______
Progressive perfect future	*will have been* + present participle	you ______	*will have been being* + past participle	they ______

MODAL

(avoid, freeze, poison, try)

Modal Tense	Active Formation	Examples	Passive Formation	Examples
Simple present	modal helping verb + simple present main verb	I could avoid you ______ he, she, it ______	modal helping verb + *be* + past participle	I ______ they ______
Progressive present	modal helping verb + *be* + present participle	I ______	modal helping verb + *be* + *being* + past participle	it ______
Perfect present	modal helping verb + *have* + past participle	you ______	modal helping verb + *have* + *been* + past participle	it ______

Modal Tense	Active Formation	Examples	Passive Formation	Examples
Progressive perfect present	modal helping verb + *have been* + present participle	I __________	modal helping verb + *have been being* + past participle	we __________

IMPERATIVE
(chase, mock)

Imperative Tense	Active Formation	Examples	Passive Formation	Examples
Present	simple present form without subject	Chase ! __________!	*be* + past participle	__________! __________!

SUBJUNCTIVE
(capture, deceive, destroy, gather, honor, scold, tweak, underestimate)

Subjunctive Tense	Active Formation	Examples	Passive Formation	Examples
Simple present	no change in any person	I capture you __________ he, she, it __________ we __________ you __________ they __________	*be* + past participle	I __________ they __________

Subjunctive Tense	Active Formation	Examples	Passive Formation	Examples
Simple past	**same as indicative:** add *-d* or *-ed*, or change form	I ______ you ______ he, she, it ______	*were* + past participle	it ______
Progressive present	**same as indicative:** *am/is/are* + present participle	I ______ you ______ he, she, it ______	**same as indicative:** *am/is/are being* + past participle	I ______ you ______ he, she, it ______
Progressive past	*were* + present participle	I ______ you ______ he, she, it ______	*were being* + past participle	I ______ you ______ he, she, it ______
Perfect present	**same as indicative:** *has/have* + past participle	I ______ he, she, it ______ they ______	**same as indicative:** *has/have been* + past participle	I ______ he, she, it ______ they ______
Perfect past	**same as indicative:** *had* + past participle	we ______	**same as indicative:** *had been* + past participle	we ______

Subjunctive Tense	Active Formation	Examples	Passive Formation	Examples
Progressive perfect present	**same as indicative:** *have/has been* + present participle	I ______ you ______ he, she, it ______	**same as indicative:** *have/has been being* + past participle	I ______ you ______ he, she, it ______
Progressive perfect past	**same as indicative:** *had been* + present participle	you ______	**same as indicative:** *had been being* + past participle	you ______

Exercise 99B: Parsing

Write the mood, tense, and voice of each underlined verb above it. The first is done for you. These sentences are taken from *The Great Brain*, by John D. Fitzgerald.

subjunctive
past
state-of-being

If there were one man in all of Adenville who would order the first water closet ever seen in town, that man had to be Papa.

You would think a man smart enough to be an editor and publisher would be smart enough not to let himself be swindled.

We were beating with sticks on Mamma's washtubs, pretending to be drummers in a band.

Aunt Bertha, who had lived with us since the death of her husband, was greasing a bread pan with bacon rinds.

I was positive that Papa had been swindled again on another crazy invention.

Papa came home for lunch with Sweyn, who had been helping at the newspaper office.

I thought ahead to the time when I would be graduating from the sixth grade in Adenville, like Sweyn would in June of that year.

"You go round up ten more kids. Tell them they not only get to see the digging of the first cesspool for a water closet for a penny, but also that they will be served refreshments."

With his great brain I knew he could have influenced me, but he didn't even try.

You can bet Mr. Thompson would have made it his business to find out why.

I knew from the color of the sign that Howard must have the mumps.

They knew Jimmie Peterson must have been in on it, but I didn't say so.

He said that the current is so swift it could have carried them all to their deaths.

"It is all right, Mamma," Tom said, as if he led ten kids into our kitchen every day.

I would have gone with them if Uncle Mark had asked me.

—LESSON 100—

Review of Moods and Tenses
Conditional Sentences

First conditional sentences express circumstances that might actually happen.
The predicate of the condition clause is in a present tense.
The predicate of the consequence clause is an imperative or is in a present or future tense.

> If we surrender and I return with you, will you promise not to hurt this man?
> So bow down to her if you want, bow to her.
> If she is otherwise when I find her, I shall be very put out.
> Unless I am wrong (and I am never wrong), they are headed dead into the fire swamp.

Second conditional sentences express circumstances that are contrary to reality.
The predicate of the condition clause is in a past tense.
The predicate of the consequence clause is in the simple present modal tense.

I would not say such things if I were you!
If I had a month to plan, maybe I could come up with something.
If we only had a wheelbarrow, that would be something.

Third conditional sentences express past circumstances that never happened.
The predicate of the condition clause is in the perfect past tense.
The predicate of the consequence clause is in the perfect present modal or simple present modal tense.

But they would have killed Westley, if I hadn't done it.

If I were you, I would go home.

If I were you, I would be dancing with joy.

If I had been wrong, I would say so now.

If I had been wrong, I would be apologizing with sincerity.

If I had been wrong, I would have said so.

If I had been wrong, I would have been running for my life.

(The examples below are adapted from Mary Shelley's *Frankenstein*.)

First conditional sentences express circumstances that might actually happen.
The predicate of the condition clause is in a present tense.
The predicate of the consequence clause is an imperative or is in a present or future tense.

If I fail, you will see me again soon, or never.

If you believe that she is innocent, rely on the justice of our laws.

If I could bestow animation upon lifeless matter, I might renew life.

Second conditional sentences express circumstances that are contrary to reality.
The predicate of the condition clause is in a past tense.
The predicate of the consequence clause is in the simple or progressive present modal tense.

Unless such symptoms had been shown early, a sister or brother could never suspect the other of fraud.

If you cherished a desire of revenge against me, you would be rejoicing in my destruction.

Third conditional sentences express past circumstances that never happened.
The predicate of the condition clause is in the perfect past tense.
The predicate of the consequence clause is in any modal tense.

If she had earnestly desired it, I should have willingly given it to her,

If you had known me as I once was, you would not recognize me in this state of degradation.

If the voice of conscience had been heeded, Frankenstein would yet have lived.

Exercise 100A: Conditional Sentences

Identify the following sentences (taken from the popular South Korean novel *Kim Jiyoung, Born 1982*, written by Cho Nam-Joo, translated into English by Jamie Chang) as first, second, or third conditional by writing a *1*, *2*, or *3* in the blank next to each.

If Grandma had been alive, she would have ripped into Eunyoung. _______

If you like someone, you're friendlier and nicer to them. _______

And if I work, don't you spend my pay, too? _______

If she ever came across another part-time job that offered the hours and pay she wanted, she would take it, regardless of what it was. _______

It'll ruin this company's reputation if word gets around in the field. _______

I can apologize if I came on too strong. _______

If the woman hadn't said that to her, Jiyoung would have lived in fear for even longer. _______

If you catch a falling snowflake and make a wish, it comes true. _______

Even if they do manage to find new work, it is quite common for them to end up with jobs that are more menial than their previous employment. _______

Exercise 100B: Parsing

Write the correct mood, tense, and voice above each underlined verb. These sentences are taken from *A Book of Myths*, by Jean Lang.

It was a sunless world in which land, air, and sea were mixed up together.

The East Wind rushed across the Ægean Sea, seizing the sails with cruel grasp and casting them in tatters before it, snapping the mast as though it were but a dry reed by the river.

Before its furious charge, even the heart of a hero might have been stricken.

If I boasted, by my boast I must stand.

Prometheus knew that at any moment he could have brought his torment to an end.

The children said farewell to Lîr, who must have wondered at the tears that stood in Finola's eyes.

So sure were they of that love from the very first moment that it seemed as though they must have been born loving one another.

The day before their hurried flight from Erin, Ainle and Ardan had been playing chess with Conor, the king.

An embassy was sent by the king to the oracle of Apollo.

All your strength will be wanted to hold the horses in.

He told her all that had been, all that might have been.

You will have a little grave apart to yourself.

If by a miracle I should return, look you to yourself, Roland!

Exercise 100C: Diagramming

On your own paper, diagram every word of the following sentences from *The Complete Idiot's Guide to Game Theory*, by Edward Rosenthal. (You may not be interested in game theory, but you should still be able to understand the grammar of these sentences!)

If you need help, ask your instructor.

Often in this book we have relied on games having a certain set of rules that the players must follow.

On the other hand, if you simply divided up the $120 equally, neither you, Jennifer, nor Dan should have any worries about getting a raw deal.

If one of the players gets greedy and plays one defection too many, the other player will employ a so-called trigger strategy: to defect forever after.

WEEK 26

More Modifiers

—LESSON 101—

Adjective Review

Adjectives in the Appositive Position

Correct Comma Usage

It was a dark and stormy night; the rain fell in torrents, except at occasional intervals, when it was checked by a violent gust of wind which swept up the streets (for it is in London that our scene lies), rattling along the house-tops, and fiercely agitating the scanty flame of the lamps that struggled against the darkness.

—From *Paul Clifford*, by Edward Bulwer-Lytton

An adjective modifies a noun or pronoun.
Adjectives tell what kind, which one, how many, and whose.
Descriptive adjectives tell what kind.
A descriptive adjective becomes an abstract noun when you add *-ness* to it.
Possessive adjectives tell whose.

Hastings kissed the duke's hand in silence.

Nouns become adjectives when they are made possessive.
Form the possessive of a singular noun by adding an apostrophe and the letter *s*.

duchess ________________

Form the possessive of a plural noun ending in *-s* by adding an apostrophe only.

emperors ________________

Form the possessive of a plural noun that does not end in *-s* as if it were a singular noun.

noblemen ________________

Since choice was mine, I chose the man love could not choose, and took this sad comfort to my heart.

—From *The Last of the Barons*, by Edward Bulwer-Lytton

An adjective that comes right before the noun it modifies is in the attributive position. An adjective that follows the noun it modifies is in the predicative position.

On the floor is the image of a dog in mosaic, with the well-known motto "Cave canem" upon it.

My name is well known, methinks, in Pompeii.
—From *The Last Days of Pompeii*, by Edward Bulwer-Lytton

Possessive Pronouns (Adjectives)

Attributive	**Predicative**
my	mine
your	yours
his, her, its	his, hers, its
our	ours
your	yours
their	theirs

The eyes were soft, dark, and brilliant, but dreamlike and vague; the features in youth must have been regular and beautiful, but their contour was now sharpened by the hollowness of the cheeks and temples.

His face was far less handsome than Marmaduke Nevile's, but infinitely more expressive, both of intelligence and command,—the features straight and sharp, the complexion clear and pale, and under the bright grey eyes a dark shade spoke either of dissipation or of thought.
— From *The Last of the Barons*, by Edward Bulwer-Lytton

Appositive adjectives directly follow the word they modify.

The sea, blue and tranquil, bounded the view.

To add to the attractions of his house, his wife, simple and good-tempered, could talk with anybody, take off the bores, and leave people to be comfortable in their own way.

It was a spot remote, sequestered, cloistered from the business and pleasures of the world.

The latter was a fine dark-eyed girl, tall, self-possessed, and dressed plainly indeed, but after the approved fashion.
—From *Alice: or, The Mysteries*, by Edward Bulwer-Lytton

When three or more nouns, adjectives, verbs, or adverbs appear in a series, they should be separated by commas.

"Wrinkles" in the comma rule:

1. **When three or more items are in a list, a coordinating conjunction before the last term is usual but not necessary.**

   The horse spun, bucked, kicked with abandon.
   The horse spun, bucked, and kicked with abandon.

   Chickens, roosters, ducks filled the yard.
   Chickens, roosters, and ducks filled the yard.

   I ran quickly, efficiently, easily.
   I ran quickly, efficiently, and easily.

   It was a spot remote, sequestered, cloistered.
   It was a spot remote, sequestered, and cloistered.

   It was a dark, stormy, frightening night.
   It was a dark, stormy, and frightening night.

2. **When three or more items are in a list and a coordinating conjunction is used, a comma should still follow the next-to-last item in the list.**

   The fourteen-year-old loved her sisters, Taylor Swift, and Jennifer Lawrence.
   The fourteen-year-old loved her sisters, Taylor Swift and Jennifer Lawrence.

   Oranges, apples, and plums filled the fruit bowl.
   Oranges, apples and plums filled the fruit bowl.

3. **When two or more adjectives are in the attributive position, they are only separated by commas if they are equally important in meaning.**

   Monday was a tiring, difficult day.
   Monday was a tiring and difficult day.
   Monday was a difficult, tiring day.

   The old man was wearing a grey wool overcoat.
   The old man was wearing a grey and wool overcoat.
   The old man was wearing a wool grey overcoat.

   INCORRECT: Monday was a tiring difficult day.
   INCORRECT: The old man was wearing a grey, wool overcoat.

Exercise 101A: Identifying Adjectives

Underline every adjective (including verb forms used as adjectives) in the following sentences, from *The Custom of the Country*, by Edith Wharton.

Draw an arrow from each adjective to the word it modifies.

Above each adjective, write *DESC* for descriptive or *POSS* for possessive. Then, label each as in the attributive (*ATT*) or appositive (*APP*) position.

Do not underline articles! There are just too many of them.

Mrs. Heeny, a stout professional-looking person in a waterproof, her rusty veil thrown back, and a shabby alligator bag at her feet, followed the mother's glance with good-humoured approval.

Her pale soft-cheeked face, with puffy eyelids and drooping mouth, suggested a partially-melted wax figure which had run to double-chin.

Mr. Spragg, having finished the last course of his heterogeneous meal, was adjusting his gold eyeglasses for a glance at the paper when Undine trailed down the sumptuous stuffy room, where coffee-fumes hung perpetually under the emblazoned ceiling and the spongy carpet might have absorbed a year's crumbs without a sweeping.

About them sat pallid families, richly dressed, and silently eating their way through a bill-of-fare which seemed to have ransacked the globe for gastronomic incompatibilities; and in the middle of the room a knot of equally pallid waiters, engaged in languid conversation, turned their backs by common consent on the persons they were supposed to serve.

Presently her attention was drawn to a lady in black who was examining the pictures through a tortoise-shell eyeglass adorned with diamonds and hanging from a long pearl chain.

The realities lay about him now: the books jamming his old college bookcases and overflowing on chairs and tables; sketches too—he could do charming things, if only he had known how to finish them!—and, on the writing-table at his elbow, scattered sheets of prose and verse; charming things also, but, like the sketches, unfinished.

His imagination, peopled with such varied images and associations, fed by so many currents from the long stream of human experience, could hardly picture the bareness of the small half-lit place in which his wife's spirit fluttered.

Exercise 101B: Punctuation Practice

The sentences below are missing all of their punctuation marks! Using everything you have learned about punctuation, insert correct punctuation. You may simply write the punctuation marks in, rather than using proofreader's marks.

These sentences are taken from the modern gothic novel *The Haunting of Hill House*, by Shirley Jackson, first published in 1959.

Each of these people then received a letter from Dr. Montague extending an invitation to spend all or part of a summer at a comfortable country house old but perfectly equipped with plumbing electricity central heating and clean mattresses.

His aunt who was the owner of Hill House was fond of pointing out that her nephew had the best education the best clothes the best taste and the worst companions of anyone she had ever known she would have leaped at any chance to put him safely away for a few weeks.

It was made of gray stone grotesquely solid jammed hard against the wooden side of the house with the insistent veranda holding it there.

On either side of them the trees silent relinquished the dark color they had held paled grew transparent and stood white and ghastly against the black sky.

They could hear the laughter of the children and the affectionate amused voices of the mother and father the grass was richly thickly green the flowers were colored red and orange and yellow the sky was blue and gold and one child wore a scarlet jumper and raised its voice again in laughter tumbling after a puppy over the grass.

Within walls continued upright bricks met neatly floors were firm and doors were sensibly shut silence lay steadily against the wood and stone of Hill House and whatever walked there walked alone.

Exercise 101C: Diagramming

On your own paper, diagram the following sentences from the modern gothic stories *Revenge: Eleven Dark Tales*, by Yoko Ogawa, translated by Stephen Snyder.

Each sentence has a different variation of items in a series, separated by commas. When you're finished diagramming, try to tell your instructor what they are.

Each sentence also has a different kind of element set off by a dash! Also try to tell your instructor what grammatical function each of these elements serves.

The light in the glass display case was pleasant and soft, the pastries looked beautiful, and the stool was quite comfortable—I liked the place, in spite of the service.

She rearranged her scarf, tapped the toe of her shoe, and anxiously fidgeted with the clasps on a black leather wallet—apparently used to collect her accounts.

First, I turned off our refrigerator and emptied it: last night's potato salad, ham, eggs, cabbage, cucumbers, wilted spinach, yogurt, some cans of beer, pork—I pulled everything out and threw it aside.

—LESSON 102—

Adjective Review
Pronoun Review
Limiting Adjectives

(All sentences in this lesson are taken from *The Two Towers*, by J. R. R. Tolkien.)

They had come to the desolation that lay before Mordor: the lasting monument to the dark labour of its slaves that should endure when all their purposes were made void; a land defiled, diseased beyond all healing—unless the Great Sea should enter in and wash it with oblivion.

brown curling hair	old tired horse
long black hair	white horse
snowy hair	running horse
his hair	king's horse

Descriptive adjectives *describe* by giving additional details.
Limiting adjectives *define* by setting limits.

Descriptive Adjectives	**Limiting Adjectives**
Regular	Possessives
Present participles	Articles
Past participles	Demonstratives
	Indefinites
	Interrogatives
	Numbers

The articles are *a, an*, and *the*.

Demonstrative pronouns demonstrate or point out something. They take the place of a single word or a group of words.

this, that, these, those

Demonstrative adjectives modify nouns and answer the question *which one*.

If those unhappy hobbits are astray in the woods, it might draw them hither.

The prisoners are NOT to be searched or plundered; those are my orders.

Indefinite pronouns are pronouns without antecedents.

Singular

anybody	anyone	anything
everybody	everyone	everything
nobody	no one	nothing
somebody	someone	something
another	other	one
either	neither	each

Plural
both few many several

Singular or Plural
all any most none some

I do not understand all that goes on myself, so I cannot explain it to you. Some of us are still true Ents, and lively enough in our fashion, but many are growing sleepy, going tree-ish, as you might say.

Indefinite adjectives modify nouns and answer the questions *which one* and *how many*.

We will ride for a few hours, gently, until we come to the end of the valley.

The cord hurts us, yes it does, it hurts us, and we've done nothing.

Some are quite wide awake, and a few are, well, ah, well, getting Entish.

Each Palantir replied to each, but all those in Gondor were ever open to the view of Osgiliath.

Interrogative pronouns take the place of nouns in questions.
who, whom, whose, what, which

Interrogative adjectives modify nouns.

Then if not yours, whose is the wizardry?

At whose command do you hunt Orcs in our land?

Which way do we go from here?

How far back his treachery goes, who can guess?

Cardinal numbers represent quantities (one, two, three, four . . .).
Ordinal numbers represent order (first, second, third, fourth . . .).

Treebeard was at their head, and some fifty followers were behind him.

Fifteen of my men I lost, and twelve horses, alas!

"Not Elves," said the fourth, the tallest, and as it appeared, the chief among them.

Gollum was the first to get up.

It was his turn to sleep first, and he was soon deep in a dream.

Exercise 102A: Identifying Adjectives

The following excerpt are taken from the novel *Madam, Will You Talk?* by the modern gothic writer Mary Stewart.

Underline every word that acts as an adjective.

Do not include phrases or clauses acting as adjectives. Also, do not include articles. (There are just too many!)

Label each one using the following abbreviations:

Descriptive Adjectives		**Limiting Adjectives**	
Regular	*DA-R*	Possessives	*LA-P*
Present participles	*DA-PresP*	~~Articles~~	~~*LA-A*~~
Past participles	*DA-PastP*	Demonstratives	*LA-D*
		Indefinites	*LA-IND*
		Interrogatives	*LA-INT*
		Numbers	*LA-N*

A white-painted trellis wall separated the court on one side from the street, and beyond it people, mules, cars, buses, moved about their business up and down the narrow thoroughfare. But inside the vine-covered trellis it was very still and peaceful. The gravel between the little chairs was carefully raked and watered; shade lay gently across the tables.

His face, which had, even in the slight courtesies of small-talk, betrayed humour and a quick intelligence at work, seemed suddenly to mask itself, to become older. Some impalpable burden almost visibly dropped on to his shoulders. One was conscious, in spite of the sensitive youth of his mouth, and those childish thin wrists and hands, of something that could meet and challenge a quite adult destiny on its own ground, strength for strength.

The couple under the palm tree might have sat anywhere for the portrait of Suburban England Abroad. Dressed as only the British can dress for a sub-tropical climate—that is, just as they would for a fortnight on the North-East coast of England—they sat sipping their drinks with wary enjoyment, and eyeing their seventeen-year-old daughter with the sort of expression that barnyard fowls might have if they suddenly hatched a flamingo.

For she was startling to say the least of it. She would have been pretty in a fair English fashion, but she had seen fit to disguise herself by combing her hair in a flat thick mat down over one side of her face. From behind the curtain appeared one eye, blue-shadowed to an amazing appearance of dissipation.

Exercise 102B: Analysis

The passage above shows you how a good writer uses adjectives: a mix of colorful descriptive adjectives and sparer, simpler limiting adjectives.

The total word count of the excerpt is 270 words. Now count each type of adjective and fill out the following chart:

Descriptive Adjectives		**Limiting Adjectives**	
Regular	________	Possessives	________
Present participles	________	~~Articles~~	________
Past participles	________	Demonstratives	________
		Indefinites	________
		Interrogatives	________
		Numbers	________

Total Descriptive Adjectives ________ Total Limiting Adjectives ________

Total Adjectives Used ________

Good prose can't be reduced to *just* formulas—but formulas can give you some extra help in writing well. The total word count of the excerpt is 270 words. You can figure out what fraction of the total word count is taken up by adjectives by dividing the total word count by the total number of adjectives used. Work that sum now, and ask your instructor for help if necessary.

$\overline{)270}$

The calculation above tells you that 1 out of every ____________ [insert answer to division problem!] words in this passage is an adjective. In other words, adjectives do not make up more than about 1/______ of this descriptive writing.

Now let's look at the relationship between limiting and descriptive adjectives. Complete the following division problem:

[number of limiting adjectives] ________ $\overline{)\qquad\qquad}$ [number of descriptive adjectives]

The calculation above tells you that 1 out of every ____________ [insert answer to second division problem!] adjectives used is a limiting adjective.

Ask your instructor to share the last part of this exercise with you.

Exercise 102C: Using Adjectives

On your own paper, rewrite the passage below. It is taken from Mary Stewart's modern Gothic novel *Thunder on the Right*—but most of the adjectives (except for articles) have been removed. The blanks show where adjectives should go. Some of the blanks represent two adjectives!

Follow these guidelines:

- Use at least one compound, hyphenated adjective.
- Use at least one indefinite adjective.
- Use at least two present participles acting as adjectives.
- Use at least two past participles acting as adjectives.
- Use at least two adjectives in one of the blanks.
- Use at least one possessive adjective.

It was a _______________ afternoon. The road lifted _______________ length before them along the hillside, the valley _______________ itself in curve after curve. The road was, to begin with, narrowly _______________, with _______________ meadows _______________ sharply to the stream bed on the right, to rise again beyond the water in _______________ pastures where cattle grazed with slowly _______________ bells. The valley twisted toward the south, and before them the _______________ barrier of _______________ peaks which barred it had, miraculously, parted, and now valley and road were cupped between _______________ slopes _______________, _______________ in sunlight, toward still more _______________ crests of blue that brushed the sky. And these, _______________ with distance, _______________ in with snow and shadow against the _______________ fingers of cloud that clung to them were, unbelievably, but the _______________ ridges of the _______________ barriers beyond... She turned off the road into the track—it was little more—that climbed the _______________ valley. She walked steadily, and soon, as she rounded a curve of the track, she saw, _______________ distance ahead of her, set back against the mountainside to the left, the _______________ walls of the convent. A _______________ tower jutted up to catch the sunlight, vividly _______________ against a rampart of pines beyond, and, even as Jennifer glimpsed it and guessed _______________ nature, she heard, _______________ out of the _______________ wind, the _______________ sound of a bell. She tilted her head to listen, _______________ , her _______________ being pierced, _______________ through, ______________ with a ______________ delight. But presently the ______________ beauty of that ______________ note, insisting beat by beat upon the strangeness of the place, took her with a ______________ sensation, part pleasure and part fear, and wholly ______________. To her, suddenly, in that ______________ haunt of bells and ______________ waters, the mission on which she was bound seemed to lose reality.

—LESSON 103—

Misplaced Modifiers
Squinting Modifiers
Dangling Modifiers

The party organizer passed around stuffed mushrooms to the guests on tiny bamboo mats.

Churning inexorably towards the coast, we breathlessly watched the weather reports about the hurricane.

Miranda spotted a blue heron on the way home.

The movie star rode through the crowds of fans in a limousine.

The inconsiderate child was kicking the back of the airplane seat.
The child was kicking the inconsiderate back of the airplane seat.

Mari upset almost every colleague she worked with.
Mari almost upset every colleague she worked with.

I slept for barely an hour.
I barely slept for an hour.

A misplaced modifier is an adjective, adjective phrase, adverb, or adverb phrase in the wrong place.

The chocolate fudge cake that I baked recently fell off the table onto the dirty floor.

Doing fifty chin-ups quickly strengthens your biceps.

My friend said on Monday we would go camping.

A squinting modifier can belong either to the sentence element preceding or the element following.

After reading more on the subject, the article turned out to be incorrect.

The experiment failed, not having procured the correct ingredients.
Exhausted by long days at work, the secretary's joy was unbounded when the office closed because of snow.

A dangling modifier has no noun or verb to modify.

How to Fix a Dangling Modifier

1. Provide the missing word in the main clause.

   After reading more on the subject, I discovered that the article was incorrect.

2. Turn the dangling phrase into a clause by putting the missing word(s) into the phrase itself.

   After I read more on the subject, the article turned out to be incorrect.

INCORRECT: Having been delayed by traffic, the bride's frustration was easily understood.

1. Provide the missing noun or verb in the main clause.

   ____

   ____

2. Turn the dangling phrase into a clause by putting the missing noun or verb into the phrase itself.

   ____

   ____

Exercise 103A: Correcting Misplaced Modifiers

Circle each misplaced modifier, and draw an arrow to the place in the sentence that it should occupy.

We watched our daughter drive away through the window.

The shopowner chased after the thief filled with indignation.

The singer was standing in the lobby with an armful of flowers.

We all decided to meet up for a Labor Day picnic in May.

Weeping and afraid, the vast dark kitchen was cold and frightening to the lost child.

I had just gotten up when I caught sight of a wolf wearing a bathrobe.

The horses were finally corralled by the animal handlers galloping wildly across the field.

Burnt to a crisp, the campers did not enjoy the s'mores as much as they had hoped.

Piled full of mushrooms with thyme sauce, I passed the platter to my dinner guests.

The exhausted man threw himself into the hammock gasping for air.

Exercise 103B: Clarifying Squinting Modifiers

Circle each squinting modifier. On your own paper, rewrite each sentence twice, eliminating the ambiguity by moving the squinting modifier to produce sentences with two different meanings. Insert commas and change capitalization/punctuation as needed. (And be aware—you might be able to eliminate the ambiguity by simply changing punctuation!)

Sprinting up hills quickly builds up your cardiovascular endurance.

Screaming at the top of your lungs often upsets other people.

She told us that she went for a long jog after she finished the chocolate cake.

Let's be sure that we celebrate the play's ending with a big party.

Our director said that we seemed too nervous during the rehearsal.

Actors who get nervous rarely turn out be superstars.

If you jog slowly you will get faster and faster.

I explained to my son when the lightning struck he would need to be careful.

Exercise 103C: Rewriting Dangling Modifiers

On your own paper, rewrite each of these sentences twice, using each of the strategies described in the lesson. You should feel free to change and add verbs and other words, as long as the meaning of the sentence remains the same.

The first is done for you! Notice that the first answer supplies the missing subject that the modifier describes, while the second turns the dangling modifier into a dependent clause.

These have been adapted from *The Disappearing Spoon and Other True Tales of Madness, Love, and the History of the World from the Periodic Table of the Elements*, by Sam Kean.

When you've finished rewriting your sentences, your instructor will show you the originals.

Lying there with the glass stick under my tongue, the thermometer would slip from my mouth when I would answer an imagined question out loud, and shatter on the hardwood floor.

Lying there with the glass stick under my tongue, I would answer an imagined question out loud, and the thermometer would slip from my mouth and shatter on the hardwood floor.

As I was lying there with the glass stick under my tongue, I would answer an imagined question out loud, and the thermometer would slip from my mouth and shatter on the hardwood floor.

ORIGINAL SENTENCE

Lying there with the glass stick under my tongue, I would answer an imagined question out loud, and the thermometer would slip from my mouth and shatter on the hardwood floor, the liquid mercury in the bulb scattering like ball bearings.

Lusting for gold, mercury was considered the most potent and poetic substance in the universe by medieval alchemists.

First presented with the jumble of the periodic table, mercury was found nowhere.

Force-feeding people a mercury chloride sludge, their teeth and hair fell out from this pet treatment.

Dredging around in the steamy vats, their hair and wits were gradually lost (like the mad hatter in *Alice in Wonderland*), because hat manufacturers once used a bright orange mercury wash to separate fur from pelts.

—LESSON 104—

Degrees of Adjectives

Comparisons Using *More, Fewer,* and *Less*

Good, better, best,
Never let it rest,
Till your good is better,
And your better, best.
—Julia Richman, *School Work 3,* No. 2 (June 1904)

And summer days were sad and long,
And sad the uncompanioned eyes,
And sadder sunset-tinted leaves.
Of all sad words of tongue or pen,
The saddest are these: "It might have been!"
—John Greenleaf Whittier

The positive degree of an adjective describes only one thing.
The comparative degree of an adjective compares two things.
The superlative degree of an adjective compares three or more things.

Most regular adjectives form the comparative by adding *-r* or *-er.*
Most regular adjectives form the superlative by adding *-st* or *-est.*

positive	comparative	superlative
______________	______________	______________

Irregular adjectives may change form completely.

positive	comparative	superlative
______________	______________	______________

For a moment the general did not reply; he was smiling his curious red-lipped smile. Then he said slowly, "No. You are wrong, sir. The Cape buffalo is not the most dangerous game." He sipped his wine. "Here in my preserve on this island," he said in the same slow tone, "I hunt more dangerous game."
—Richard Connell, "The Most Dangerous Game" (1924)

Many adjectives form their comparative and superlative forms by adding the word *more* or *most* before the adjective instead of using *-er* or *-est.* In comparative and superlative adjective forms, the words *more* and *most* are used as adverbs.

positive	comparative	superlative
______________	______________	______________

So long as people will drink, drink will be made; and so long as drink is made, there will be those to sell it. Well, the more the restrictions, the fewer to sell; the fewer to sell, the less sold; the less sold, the less made; the less made, the less drunk; the less drunk, the fewer the inebriates—and that's what the temperance people are after.

—*The Grip,* Vol. 20, 1882

The more thoroughly we searched, the fewer treasures we found.
The more love I offered, the less enthusiasm he showed.

Use *fewer* for concrete items and *less* for abstractions.

He would do very well if he had fewer cakes and sweetmeats sent him from home.
I wanted to tease you a little to make you less sad.

—Charlotte Bronte, *Jane Eyre*

In comparisons using *more . . . fewer* and *more . . . less, more* and *less* can act as either adverbs or adjectives, and *the* can act as an adverb.

We searched (the) more thoroughly. We found (the) fewer treasures.
I offered (the) more love. He showed (the) less enthusiasm.

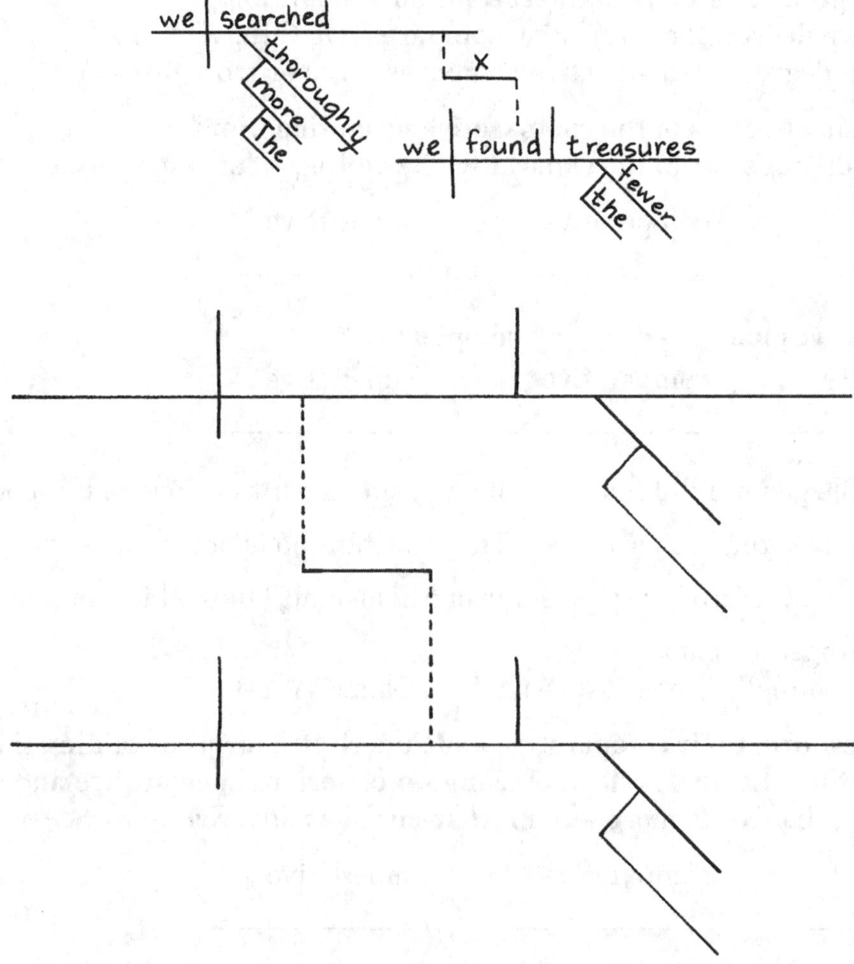

The more the building shook, the less he wanted to be there.

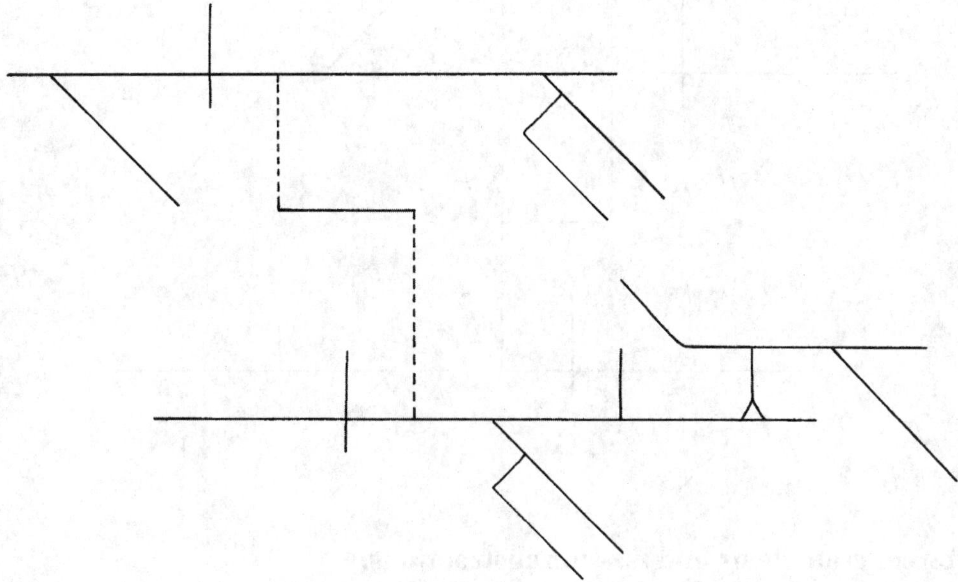

The more the building shook, the more we held on.
The less we saw, the less we knew.

The more the wave rose, the faster we ran.
The less we worried, the better we felt.
The happier we were, the more we rejoiced.
The louder the wind, the fewer words we were able to exchange.

The better we felt, the longer we stayed.
The longer the tail grew, the better the horse could swat flies.

The better we felt, the longer we stayed.

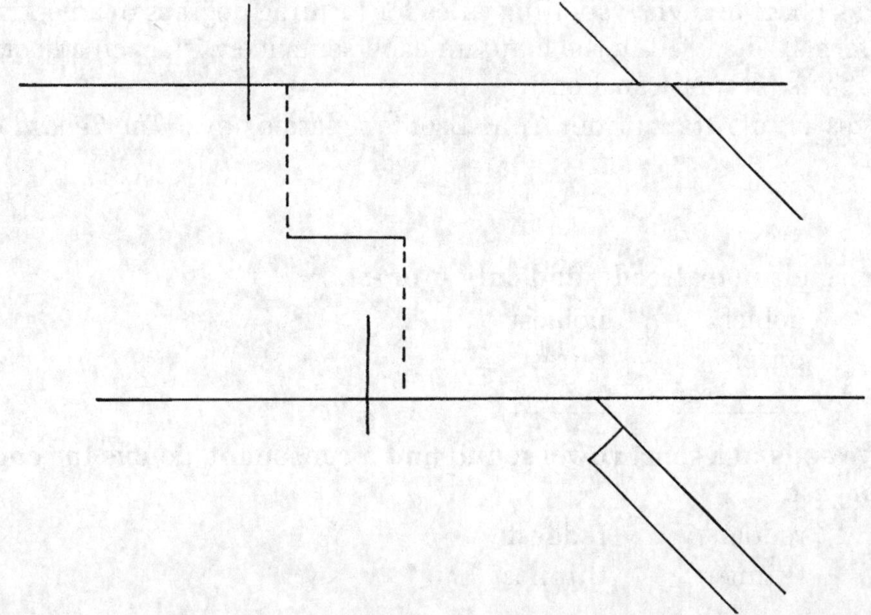

The longer the tail grew, the better the horse could swat flies.

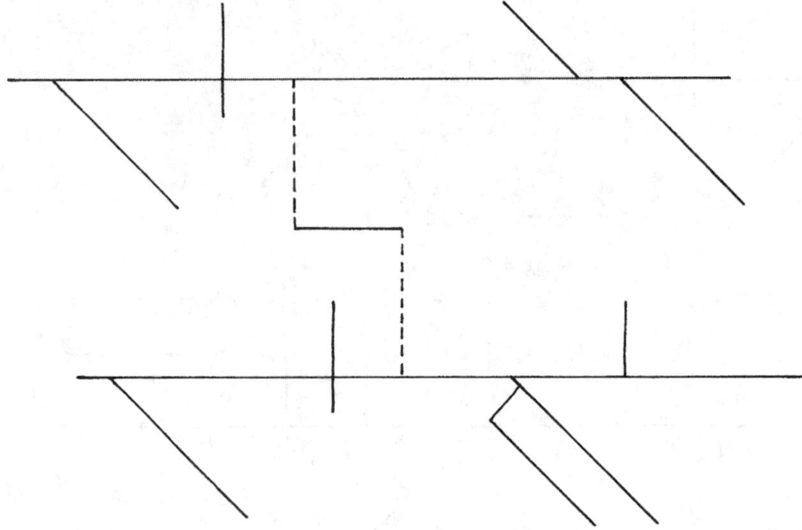

Use *fewer* for concrete items and *less* for abstractions.

Comparisons can be formed using a combination of *more* and *fewer* or *less;* a combination of *more* and *more* or *fewer/less* and *fewer/less*; a combination of *more* or *fewer/less* with a comparative form; or simply two comparative forms.

In comparisons using *more, fewer,* and *less, more* and *less* can act as either adverbs or adjectives, and *the* can act as an adverb.

In comparisons using two comparative forms, the forms may act as either adverbs or adjectives, and *the* can act as an adverb.

Exercise 104A: Positive, Comparative, and Superlative Adjectives

Use the following chart to review spelling rules for forming degrees of adjectives. Fill in the missing forms. Then, fill in the blank in each sentence with each adjective indicated in brackets (properly spelled!).

The sentences are all drawn from Anne Bronte's classic novel *The Tenant of Wildfell Hall.*

Spelling Rules:

If the adjective ends in e already, add only *-r* or *-st.*

noble	nobler	noblest
pure	purer	purest
fine	_______	_______

If the adjective ends in a short vowel sound and a consonant, double the consonant and add *-er* or *-est.*

red	redder	reddest
thin	thinner	thinnest
flat	_______	_______

If the adjective ends in *-y*, change the *y* to *i* and add *-er* or *-est*.

hazy hazier haziest
muddy _______ _______

Her sister, Mary, was several years _______________, several inches _______________, and of a _______________, _______________ build—a plain, quiet, sensible girl, who had patiently nursed their mother, through her last long, tedious illness, and been the housekeeper, and family drudge, from thence to the present time. [in order, the comparatives of *old*, *tall*, *large*, and *coarse*]

If you persist, I must regard you as my _______________ foe. [the superlative of *deadly*]

None of our gentlemen had the _______________ pretensions to a literary taste, except Mr. Hargrave; and he, at present, was quite contented with the newspapers and periodicals of the day. [the superlative of *small*]

Arthur was clad in his _______________ clothes, and wrapped in a coarse woolen shawl. [the superlative of *plain*]

We must defer the enjoyment of your hospitality till the return of _______________ days and _______________ nights. [in order, the comparatives of *long* and *warm*]

But I shall say no more against her: I see that she was actuated by the best and _______________ motives in what she has done; and if the act is not a wise one, may heaven protect her from its consequences! [the superlative of *noble*]

It was a _______________, _______________, _______________ beauty—lovely indeed, but with far less dignity and depth of soul—without that indefinable grace, that keenly spiritual yet gentle charm, that ineffable power to attract and subjugate the heart—my heart at least. [in order, the comparatives of *young*, *slight*, and *rosy*]

Yesterday morning, one of October's _______________, _______________ days, Milicent and I were in the garden enjoying a brief half-hour together with our children, while Annabella was lying on the drawing-room sofa, deep in the last new novel. [in order, the superlatives of *bright* and *lovely*]

She was, and I believe still is, one of the ______________ and ______________ wives in England. [in order, the superlatives of *happy* and *fond*]

When she was returned to the silence and solitude of her own home, it would be my _____ opportunity. [the superlative of *fit*]

If a cold ensued, the ______________ the better—it would help to account for the sullen moods and moping melancholy likely to cloud my brow for long enough. [comparative of *severe*]

But for you, I might sink into the ______________ condition of self-indulgence and carelessness about the wants of others. [the superlative of *gross*]

Exercise 104B: Forming Comparisons

Rewrite each set of independent clauses so that they form a comparative sentence making use of *more*, *less*, *fewer*, and/or comparative forms. The first is done for you.

When you are finished, ask your instructor to show you the original sentences, which are taken from the nonfiction book *No Filter: The Inside Story of Instagram*, by Sarah Frier.

The first is done for you.

A user went out more times.
They got more virtual prizes.

The more times a user went out, the more virtual prizes they got.

Facebook got bigger.
Facebook had more power to shape global politics.

____

____

Instagram grew bigger.
Users strived for followers, likes, and comments.

____

____

Instagram's network got stronger.
Instagram's network became an alternative to Facebook for restaurant menus.

____

____

He made the deal faster.
Systrom was less likely to call someone who would give advice unfavorable to Facebook.

___

___

A network became bigger.
The unintended consequences of its decisions grew bigger.

___

___

More people joined the product.
They produced more content.
There were more slots in the news feed for brands to place ads.

___

___

Exercise 104C: Using *Fewer* and *Less*

Complete the sentences by filling in each blank with either *fewer* or *less.*

The original sentences are taken from David Kirkpatrick's nonfiction book *The Facebook Effect: The Inside Story of the Company That Is Connecting the World.*

But he couldn't understand why Zuckerberg thought Facebook, which had far ___ users at that point, was worth several times what he'd paid for MySpace.

If Accel invested it would be very intimately involved, which might mean ___ freedom.

It and its business partners learn a lot about us, but in general we know far ___ about it and exactly how the company is using our data.

That was tough enough to deal with in the quaint days of the News Feed controversy, when Facebook had ___ than 10 million users.

Though it had ___ features than Thefacebook, it was experiencing a similar stratospheric uptake—by the end of the month about two-thirds of undergraduates had registered.

Its strategy was to go after ___ snooty schools that the elite Thefacebook hadn't yet targeted.

They typically had ___ users at each new campus so they could add more schools without putting as much demand on their systems as Thefacebook's hordes did.

At other moments the phrase made even ____________ sense.

Some consumer-oriented companies now put ____________ emphasis on their website and more on their Facebook page.

Exercise 104D: Diagramming

On your own paper, diagram every word of the following sentences from *The Green Fairy Book*, by Andrew Lang.

The second, third, and fourth sentences all contain challenges (although not related to the comparison elements!). Do your best, and ask your instructor for help if you need it.

The more he howled the more the others laughed.

The more he walked towards the light the further away it seemed.

Her stepmother's heart wasn't in the least touched, and the more the poor girl did, the more she asked her to do.

While I do my household tasks you had better stay in bed, since the more one sleeps the less one need eat.

WEEK 27

Double Identities

—LESSON 105—

Clauses with Understood Elements
Than as Conjunction, Preposition, and Adverb
Quasi-Coordinators

I like chocolate better than vanilla.
Other than pistachio, I'll eat any flavor of ice cream.
I am more than satisfied with chocolate, but less than happy with pistachio.
I will starve rather than eat pistachio.

A coordinating conjunction joins equal words or groups of words together.
A subordinating conjunction joins unequal words or groups of words together.

He worked more efficiently than his brother.
He worked more efficiently than his brother [worked].

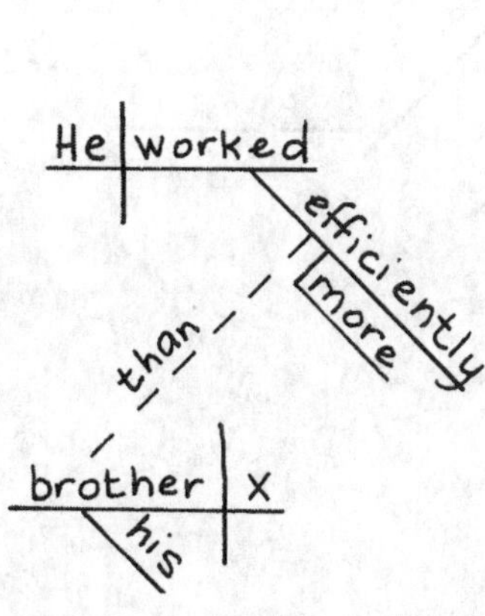

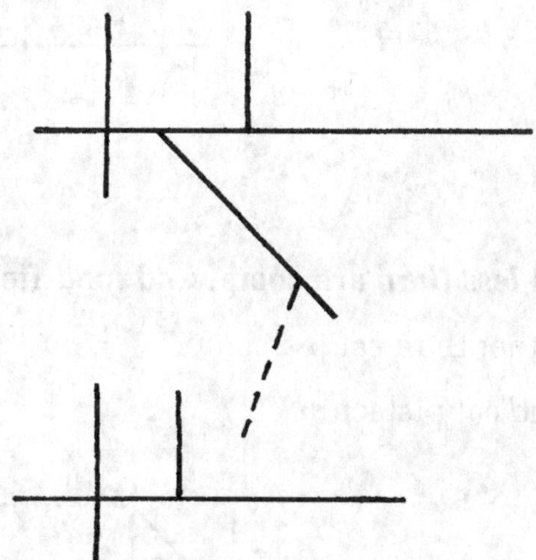

Tomorrow should be sunnier than today.
A new broom sweeps better than an old one.
The cook added more salt than he should have.

I love him more than you.

He is stronger than I.

INCORRECT: He is stronger than me.

He is stronger than I am.

not He is stronger than me.

When *than* is used in a comparison and introduces a clause with understood elements, it is acting as a subordinating conjunction.

Other than pistachio, I'll eat any flavor of ice cream.

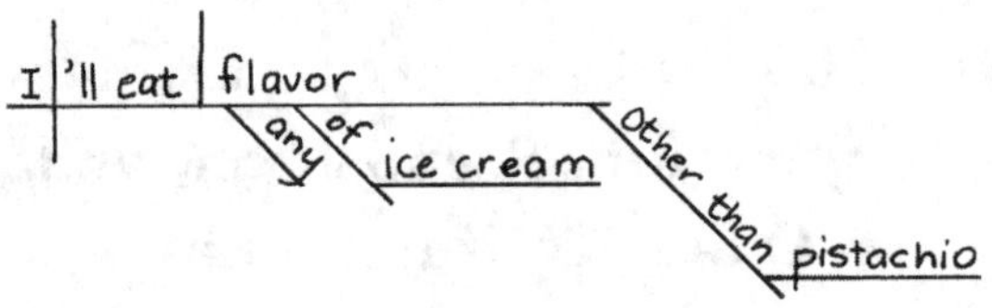

***Other than* is a compound preposition that means "besides" or "except."**

I am more than satisfied with chocolate, but less than happy with pistachio.

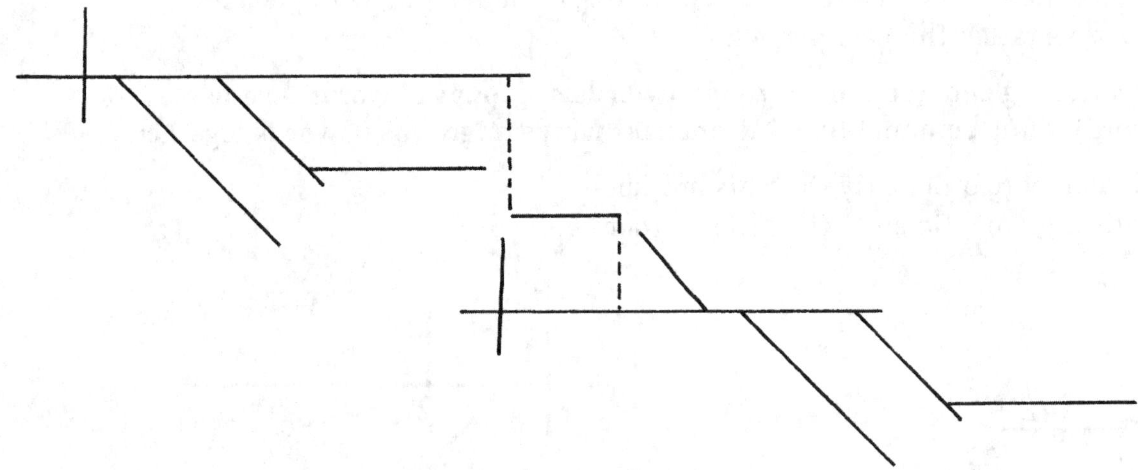

***More than* and *less than* are compound modifiers.**

I will starve rather than eat pistachio.

I will starve *and* eat pistachio.

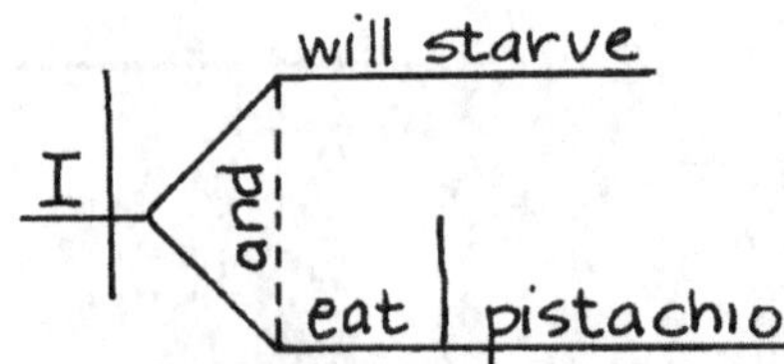

Quasi-coordinators link compound parts of a sentence that are unequal. Quasi-coordinators include *rather than, sooner than, let alone,* and *not to mention.*

I will starve rather than eat pistachio.

I
will starve
rather than
eat pistachio

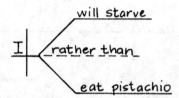

Rather than going home, she drove back up to the lake.

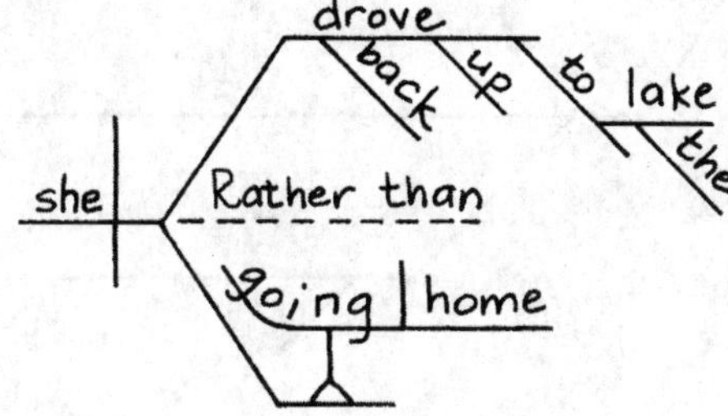

He could not keep up with Patel, let alone Krishna.

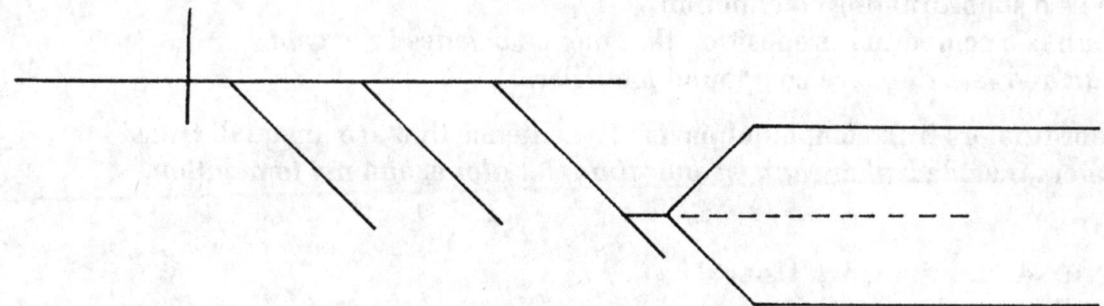

The expense, not to mention the risk, was simply too great.

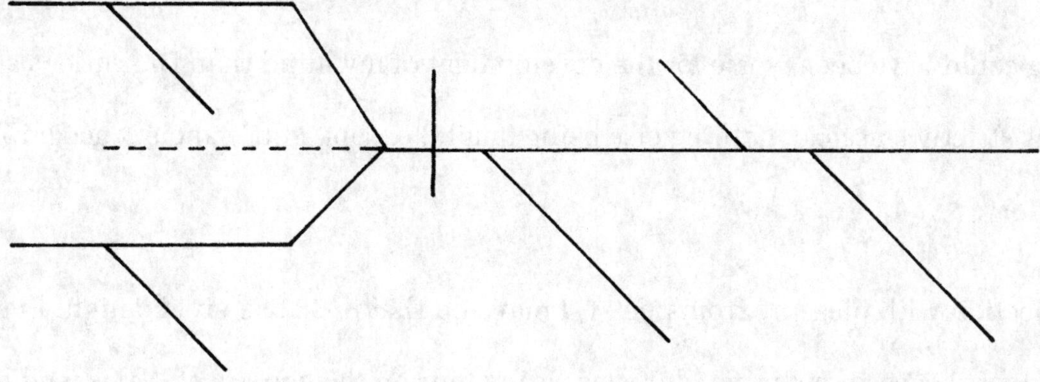

He would walk in a hailstorm sooner than pay ten dollars for a cab.

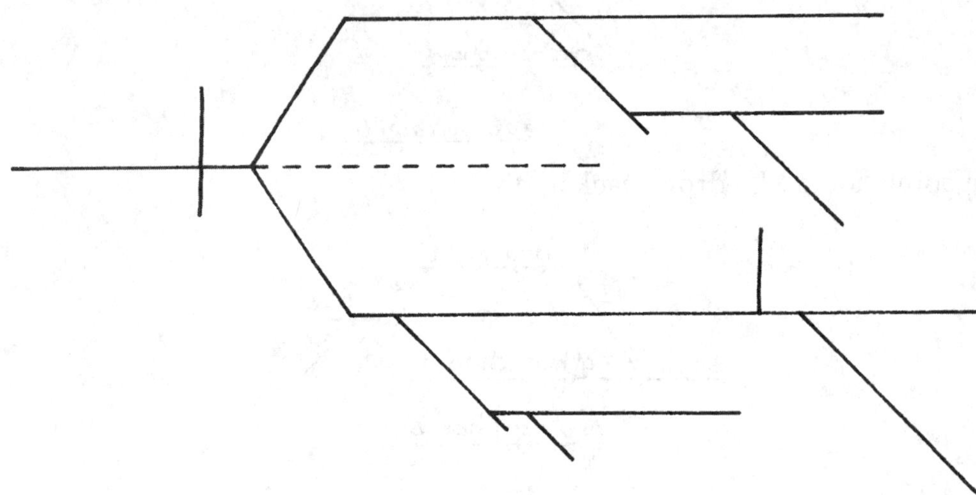

When *than* is used in a comparison and introduces a clause with understood elements, it is acting as a subordinating conjunction.
***Other than* is a compound preposition that means *besides* or *except*.**
***More than* and *less than* are compound modifiers.**

Quasi-coordinators link compound parts of a sentence that are unequal. Quasi-coordinators include *rather than, sooner than, let alone,* and *not to mention*.

Exercise 105A: Comparisons Using *Than*

Each of the following sentences, taken from *The Autobiography of Charles Darwin*, by (who else?) Charles Darwin, contains a comparison clause introduced by *than* and missing some of its words. Using carets, do your best to insert the missing words.

Nothing could have been worse for the development of my mind than Dr. Butler's school, as it was strictly classical, nothing else being taught, except a little ancient geography and history.

In connection with pleasure from poetry, I may add that in 1822 a vivid delight in scenery was first awakened in my mind, during a riding tour on the borders of Wales, and this has lasted longer than any other aesthetic pleasure.

Nothing has left a more vivid picture on my mind than these evenings at Maer.

On first examining a new district nothing can appear more hopeless than the chaos of rocks; but by recording the stratification and nature of the rocks and fossils at many points, always reasoning and predicting what will be found elsewhere, light soon begins to dawn on the district, and the structure of the whole becomes more or less intelligible.

I discovered, though unconsciously and insensibly, that the pleasure of observing and reasoning was a much higher one than that of skill and sport.

I saw more of Lyell than of any other man, both before and after my marriage.

A man with a mind more highly organised or better constituted than mine, would not, I suppose, have thus suffered; and if I had to live my life again, I would have made a rule to read some poetry and listen to some music at least once every week; for perhaps the parts of my brain now atrophied would thus have been kept active through use.

Exercise 105B: Identifying Parts of the Sentence

In the following sentences, from *How Star Wars Conquered the Universe: The Past, Present, and Future of a Multibillion Dollar Franchise,* by Chris Taylor, identify each bolded word or phrase as *SC* for subordinating conjunction, *QC* for quasi-coordinator, *PREP* for preposition, *ADJ* for adjective, or *ADV* for adverb.

She is more intelligent and adept **than** Buck.

No sooner had he sat on the stone **than** he was up with a yell, and running down the trail.

There are multiple Vaders in every garrison, and naturally no event should have **more than** one Vader.

There was, Sean discovered, **more than** enough iron in the Earth's core to construct two million Death Stars.

$16 million was a better outcome **than** anyone around Lucas could imagine, save for Spielberg.

In 1978, the company sold **more than** forty-two million Star Wars items; the majority, twenty-six million, were action figures.

The Internet had barely become a gathering place for Star Wars fans, **let alone** Stormtrooper costume owners.

Foster had also written the novelization of *Dark Star*—**not to mention** a whopping ten Star Trek novelizations based on that franchise's animated series.

Leigh Brackett died **less than** a month later.

On the other hand, the new film was a darker beast **than** its predecessor, a fairy tale of the grimmer, Grimm variety.

Something often forgotten today is that many members of the audience were **less than** okay with such openended endings.

Once again, the comedic target was something **other than** Star Wars.

Other than that, the Force is largely a mystery.

This time it was a freak avalanche **rather than** a freak desert storm.

Lucas added a wisecracking, two-headed announcer to the pod race, **rather than** have Jabba the Hutt himself introduce the racers.

Exercise 105C: Diagramming

On your own paper, diagram every word of the following sentences, taken from the original *Star Wars Trilogy* novels by George Lucas.

But there was nothing to see other than the darkening expanses of snow and ice.

Once forward, he fell rather than sat in the pilot's seat and immediately began checking readouts and gauges.

It's the ship that made the Kessel run in less than twelve standard timeparts!

The sleekly elongated ship was larger and even more ominous than the five wedge-shaped Imperial Star Destroyers guarding it.

—LESSON 106—

The Word *As*

Quasi-Coordinators

Middle English *alswa* "similarly" *as*

> The twenty-fourth object would be as big as a sugar cube, the twenty-seventh would be about the size of a large mammal, the fifty-fourth would be the size of the planet Jupiter and the fifty-seventh would be about as big as the Sun, where even atoms are destroyed by gravity, leaving a mixture of nuclei and free electrons called a plasma.
>
> — John R. Gribbin, *The Scientists: A History of Science Told Through the Lives of Its Greatest Inventors*

The twenty-fourth object would be as big as a sugar cube ^. (is big)

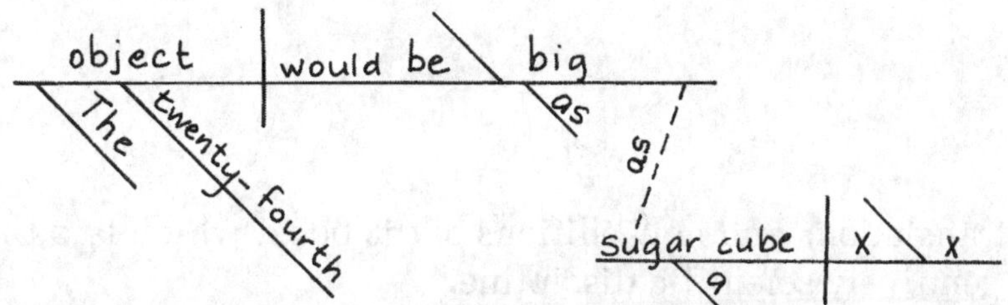

(The following sentences are all from Gribbin's *The Scientists* as well.)

. . . [A]n equally important factor, as many people have argued, was the depopulation of Europe by the Black Death . . .

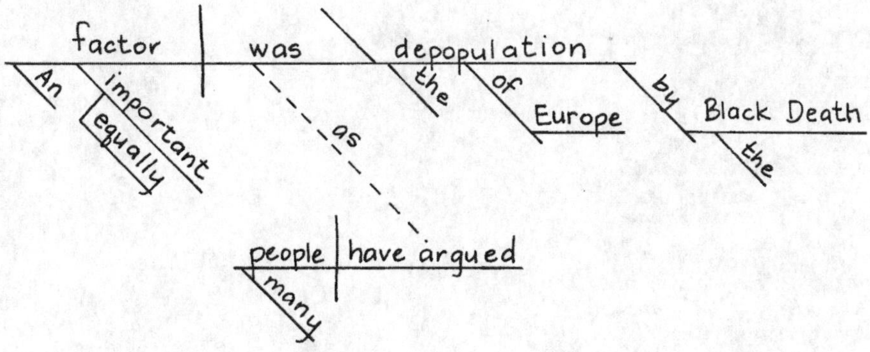

As long as Frederick remained on the throne, Tycho was able to enjoy an unprecedented amount of freedom to run his observatory just as he liked.

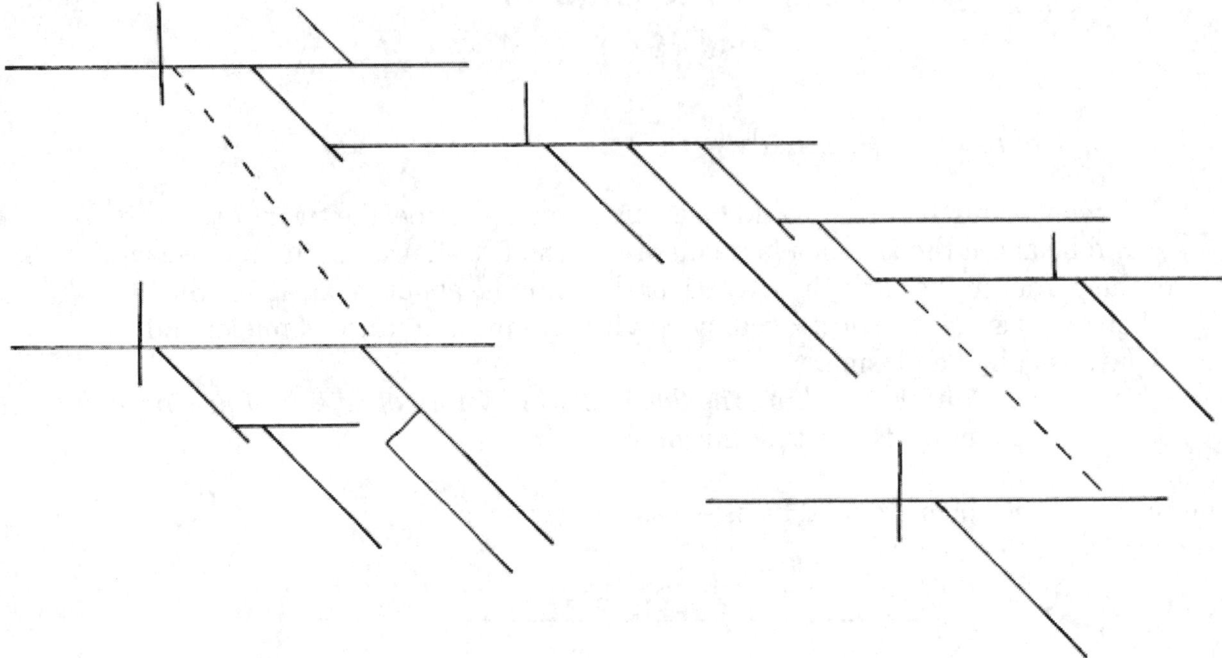

There were many translations and new editions of the book, which laid the foundations for chemistry as a genuinely scientific discipline.

Lavoisier . . . played a full part in the activities of the Academy, and during his time as a member worked on very many reports covering topics as diverse as . . . meteorites, cultivation of cabbages, the minerology of the Pyrenees and the nature of the gas arising from cesspools.

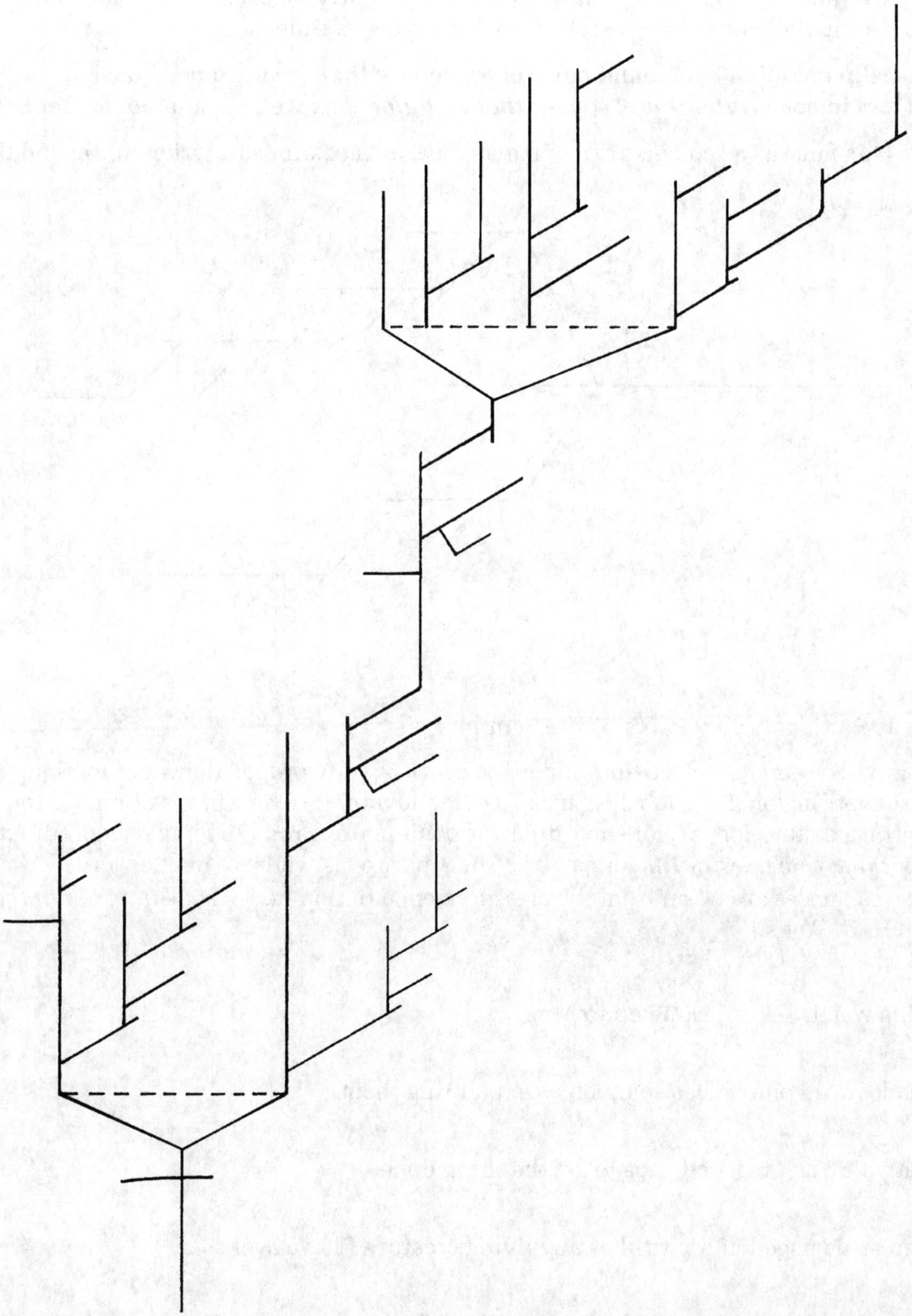

At the time of his marriage, as well as considerable property, Charles Cavendish had a disposable annual income of at least £2000, which grew as time passed.

Quasi-coordinators link compound parts of a sentence that are unequal. Quasi-coordinators include *rather than, sooner than, let alone, as well as,* and *not to mention.*

As well as his fame as a geologist, Darwin also received acclaim as a writer, in the mould of Lyell.

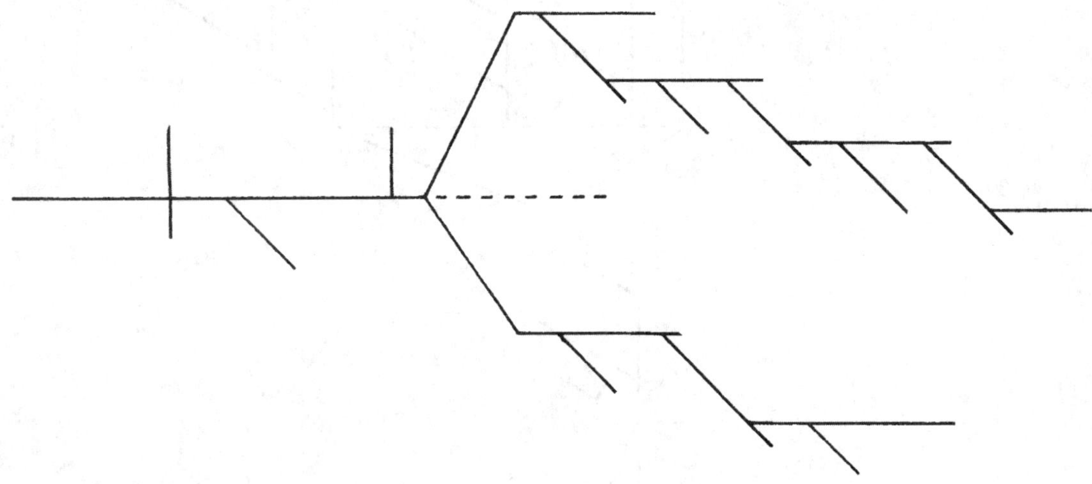

Exercise 106A: Identifying Parts of the Sentence

In the following sentences, find and underline every adverb, preposition, conjunction, and quasi-coordinator. Then label each as *ADV* for adverb, *PREP* for preposition, *CC* for coordinating conjunction, *SC* for subordinating conjunction, and *QC* for quasi-coordinator. Remember that a quasi-coordinator can be a short phrase as well as a single word.

These sentences are taken from the classic science fiction novel *The First Men in the Moon*, by H. G. Wells.

He had his watch out as I came up to him.

Nothing clears up one's ideas so much as explaining them.

The great point, as I insisted, was to get the thing done.

He looked as damaged and pitiful as any living creature I have ever seen.

The sky outside was as black as the darkness within the sphere, but the shape of the open window was marked by an infinite number of stars.

I was half-inclined to go back into the moon without him, rather than seek him until it was too late.

For a time, whether it was long or short I do not know, there was nothing but blank darkness.

Men have watched this planet systematically with telescopes for over two hundred years.

Instantly my coat tails were over my head, and I was progressing in great leaps and bounds, and against my will, towards him.

Then I hauled the blanket from beneath my feet and got it about me and over my head and eyes.

He turned me about and pointed to the brow of the eastward cliff, looming above the haze about us, scarce lighter than the darkness of the sky.

I twisted my head round as well as my bonds would permit.

Exercise 106B: Diagramming

On your own paper, diagram every word of the following sentences, very slightly adapted from *A History of Chemistry*, written by Bernadette Bensaude-Vincent and Isabelle Stengers, translated by Deborah van Dam.

Ask for help if you need it!

As early as the beginning of the eighteenth century, Olivier de Serres had pointed out the presence of sugar in beets.

In Alexandria, crossroads of culture and commerce, "chemistry" as a body of knowledge and experience devoted to retrieving a legacy, to deciphering, reconstructing, and transmitting a lost science, was born.

An apparently more modest path was to use the method of the "table makers," as they were called, not as a condensed and convenient way to present chemical knowledge, but as an end in itself.

—LESSON 107—

Words That Can Be Multiple Parts of Speech

(The sentences from this lesson have been slightly adapted and condensed from *Bleak House*, by Charles Dickens.)

But ______________________ ______________________

I had an illness, but it was not a long one.

He has never hurt anybody but himself.

For ______________________ ______________________

I can answer for him as little as for you.

I should have been ashamed to come here to-day, for I know what a figure I must seem to you two.

About ______________________ ______________________

You could hear the horses being rubbed down outside the stable and being told to "Hold up!" and "Get over," as they slipped about very much on the uneven stones.

What with making notes on a slate about jams, and pickles, and preserves, and bottles, and glass, and china, and a great many other things; and what with being generally a methodical, old-maidish sort of foolish little person, I was so busy that I could not believe it was breakfast-time when I heard the bell ring.

Yet ______________________ ______________________

Is he here yet?
At this time, Jo has not yet died.
It is good, yet it could be improved.

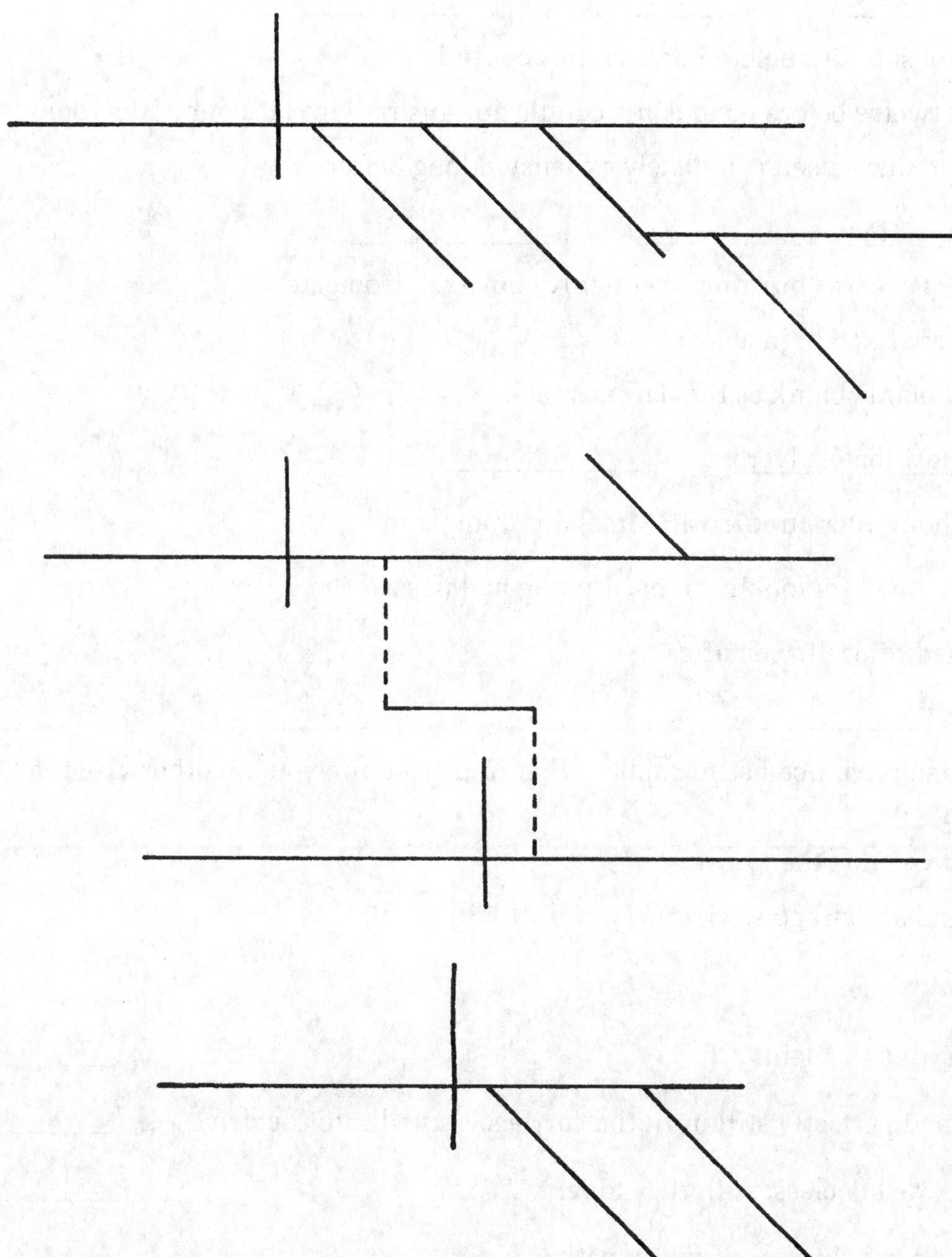

Any pronoun adjective adverb

I could not reproach myself any less.

It would be an insult to the discernment of any man with half an eye to tell him so.

I wonder whether any of the gentlemen remembered him.

I then asked Richard whether he had thought of any more congenial pursuit.

I thought it was impossible that you could have loved me any better.

Before ______________ ______________ ______________

Weariness of soul lies before her, as it lies behind.

It was past twelve before he took his candle and his radiant face out of the room.

He seemed to have been completely exhausted long before.

Above preposition ______________ ______________

The flame of gas was burning so sullenly above the iron gate.

His eyes were fixed high above.

But it is all blank, blank as the darkness above.

After preposition adverb ______________

In half an hour after our arrival, Mrs. Jellyby appeared.

I once more saw him looking at me after he had passed the door.

He presented himself soon after.

Otherwise ______________ ______________ ______________

We are not so prejudiced as to suppose that in private life you are otherwise than a very estimable man.

How could you do otherwise?

Love her and all will go well; otherwise, all will go ill.

Still

It is quite still and silent. ______________

She remained perfectly still until the carriage turned into the drive. ______________

The cause was hopeless; still, they fought. ______________

Still yourself, my dear, and wait in patience. ______________

In the still, the woods seemed massively hushed in sleep. ______________

Exercise 107A: Identifying Parts of Speech

Identify the part of speech of each underlined word by writing the correct abbreviation above it: *N* (noun), *PRO* (pronoun), *V* (verb), *ADJ* (adjective), *ADV* (adverb), *PREP* (preposition), *CC* (coordinating conjunction), or *SC* (subordinating conjunction).

These sentences are taken from the novel *Hard Times*, by Charles Dickens.

He had virtually retired from the wholesale hardware trade before he built Stone Lodge, and was now looking about for a suitable opportunity of making an arithmetical figure in Parliament.

Not that a ditch was new to me, for I was born in a ditch.

As she straightened her own figure, and held up her head in adapting her action to her words, the idea crossed Stephen that he had seen this old woman before, and had not quite liked her.

When Tom appeared before dinner, though his mind seemed heavy enough, his body was on the alert; and he appeared before Mr. Bounderby came in.

I have been uneasy for the consequences of his being so involved, but I have kept these secrets until now, when I trust them to your honour.

Now that I have asked you so much, tell me the end.

O Tom, Tom, do we end so, after all my love!

I beg your pardon, sir, for being troublesome—but—have you had any letter yet about me?

As soon as I was big enough to run away, of course I ran away.

She sat at the window, when the sun began to sink behind the smoke; she sat there, when the smoke was burning red, when the colour faded from it, when darkness seemed to rise slowly out of the ground, and creep upward, upward, up to the house-tops, up the church steeple, up to the summits of the factory chimneys, up to the sky.

She was so constrained, and yet so careless; so reserved, and yet so watchful; so cold and proud, and yet so sensitively ashamed of her husband's braggart humility.

As Stephen had but a little while ago instinctively addressed himself to her, so she now instinctively addressed herself to Rachael.

All her wildness and passion had subsided; but, though softened, she was not in tears.

He went his way, but she stood on the same spot, rubbing the cheek he had kissed with her handkerchief, until it was burning red.

The more I spoke to him, the more he hid his face; and at first he shook all over.

He darted on until he was very near this figure.

Exercise 107B: Diagramming

On your own paper, diagram every word of the following sentences from *Hard Times*. If you need help, ask your instructor!

He wanted nothing but his whip.

They all assumed to be mighty rakish and knowing, they were not very tidy in their private dresses, they were not at all orderly in their domestic arrangements, and the combined literature of the whole company would have produced but a poor letter on any subject.

> **Note to Student:** The first independent clause of the above sentence contains two understood elements. If you cannot find them, ask your instructor for help! (This is a difficult clause.)

I have explained to Miss Louisa—this is Miss Louisa—the miserable but natural end of your late career; and you are to expressly understand that the whole of that subject is past, and is not to be referred to any more.

That could hardly be, she knew, until an hour past midnight; but in the country silence, which did anything but calm the trouble of her thoughts, time lagged wearily.

—LESSON 108—

Nouns Acting as Other Parts of Speech
Adverbial Noun Phrases

Exercise 108A: Nouns

These sentences are taken from the memoir *Bird by Bird: Some Instructions on Writing and Life*, by Anne Lamott. Identify the part of the sentence that each noun plays by labelling it as *S* for subject, *PN* for predicate nominative, *APP* for appositive, *DO* for direct object, or *OP* for object of the preposition.

It doesn't come from outside or above.

Books were revered in our house, and great writers admired above everyone else.

Keep moving; let them spend some time together, let them jam for a while.

I always show my work to one or two people before sending a copy to my editor or agent.

It is work and play together.

We found my parents rejoicing over the arrival of my dad's new novel, the first copy off the press.

Every so often at a writing conference, people get taken aside by wonderful writers who love their story and who help them in some pivotal way.

A moral position is not a slogan, or wishful thinking. Cornucopia.

Exercise 108B: Nouns as Other Parts of Speech

Each of the following sets of sentences is missing one of the nouns from the exercise above—but the noun is also functioning as a part of speech!

Your task: figure out which noun can fill every blank.

When you are done, label the part of speech of each word in the blanks (*N* for noun, *ADJ* for adjective, *ADV* for adverb, *PREP* for preposition, *V* for verb, *SC* for subordinating conjunction). The first is partially done for you.

The sentences are taken from Anne Lamott's memoir *Traveling Mercies: Some Thoughts on Faith.*

COPY
____

____________ it down and tape it to the refrigerator.

N One day not long after, she sidled up to me at school and asked me if I had an extra copy of the book I wrote about being a mother.

____

After breakfast, he went off to swim with a friend, and I went ______________ to look at the mountain peak in daylight.

I just remembered that sometimes you start with the ______________ and you get it right.

______________ the windows were trees and roses, the eastern shores of San Francisco Bay, blue waters, blue sky: birds, life, motion, stillness.

____

He pointed to where a hawk hung just ______________ the wall of cliffs which runs the length of the beach.

From up ______________ it looked fertile and abandoned, surrounded by nondescript suburban houses and anonymous buildings.

Mt. Tamalpais loomed ______________, and we hiked her windy trails many weekends.

____

I sat in the movie theater and cried for a ______________.

It became clear that Sam would need me to hold onto him ______________ we were in the water.

I suddenly remembered the cave where the prophet Elijah hung out ______________ waiting to be either killed by Ahab or saved by God.

____

My father believes in hard ______________

We lurched and crashed along until finally we nosed right into the greasy ______________ deck of the tire shop.

I lay on my bed pretending to read but watching him ______________: he is a very slow writer, looking like a thoughtful old person with arthritis and bad vision.

____

It made me feel helpless in the best possible ______________________.

The laughter rose from ______________________ below, from below my feet.

Let me put it this ______________________, Annie.

Mary and her lamb went into the school.

Mary and her lamb went home.

He followed her to school on Monday.

He followed her to school one day.

An adverbial noun tells the time or place of an action, or explains how long, how far, how deep, how thick, or how much. It can modify a verb, adjective, or adverb. An adverbial noun plus its modifiers is an adverbial noun phrase.

Before the lamb had travelled a mile, Mary turned around.

The road to school was two miles long.

The mud puddle in the road was three inches deep.

The lamb splashed in the puddle until he was covered with inch-thick mud.

The lamb splashed in the puddle until he was covered with mud an inch thick.

The storm continued all night.

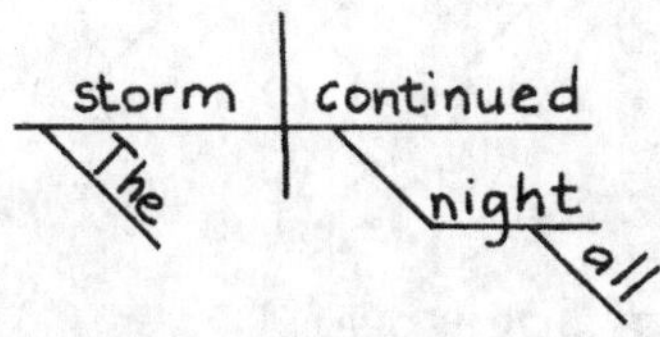

The earth's mantle is roughly 1,800 miles thick.

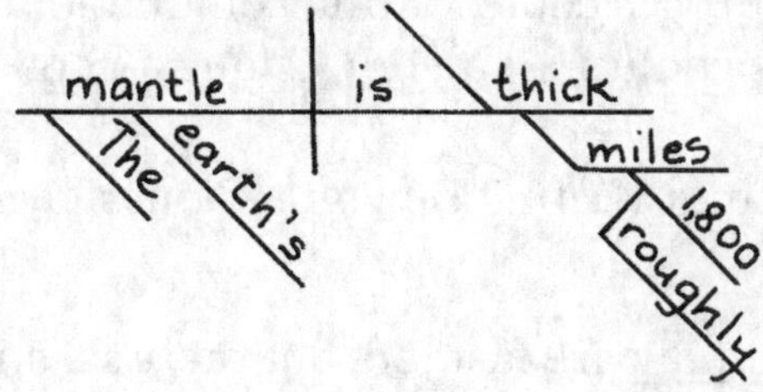

He slept eight hours and then woke up early the next morning.

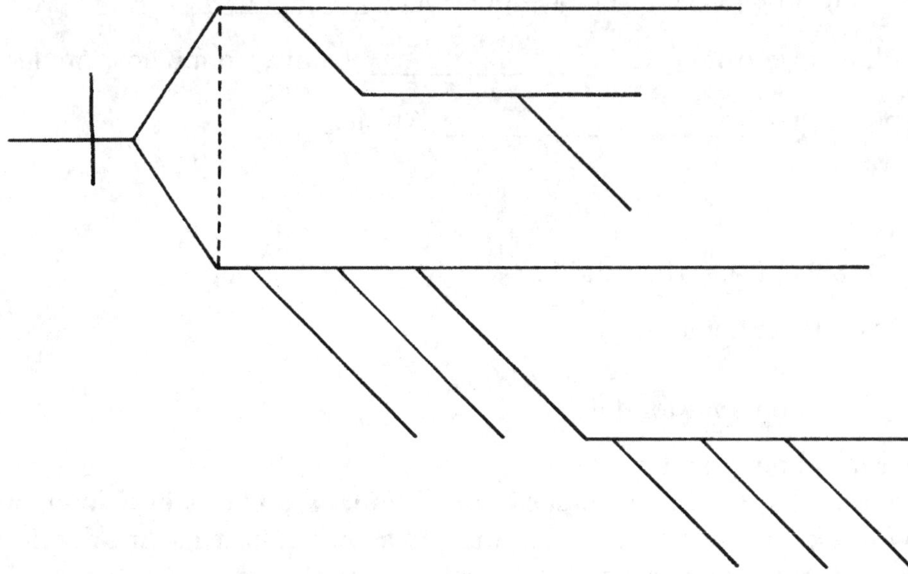

After our delicious picnic lunch, we walked the two miles to the battlefield.

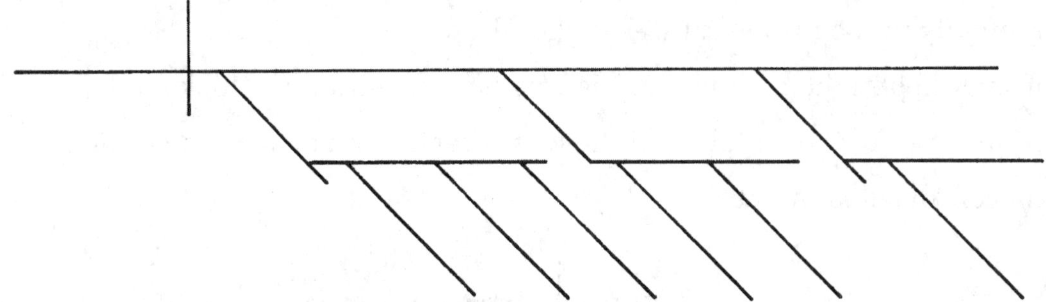

Exercise 108C: Identifying Parts of Speech

Identify the part of speech of each underlined word by writing the correct abbreviation above it: *N* (noun), *ADV-N* (adverbial noun), *PRO* (pronoun), *V* (verb), *ADJ* (adjective), *ADV* (adverb), *PREP* (preposition), *CC* (coordinating conjunction), *CorrC* (correlative conjunction), *SC* (subordinating conjunction), or *QC* (quasi-coordinator). Not all labels may be used!

These sentences are taken from *Writing Down the Bones*, by Natalie Goldberg.

The new roller pens that are out now are fast too, but there's a slight loss of control.

Sometimes, instead of writing in a notebook, you might want to directly type out your thoughts.

Out of this fertile soil bloom our poems and stories.

Don't hold too tight; allow it to come out how it needs to rather than trying to control it.

I've bought hundreds over the years.

They know what well the water they drink comes from, that their cat who ran away two years ago will not return.

Read a lot, listen well and deeply, and write a lot.

I try to fill a notebook a month.

Within a month one of the stories was accepted by a very fine magazine.

That day in the studio my conscious mind was frustrated and had no idea that I had written anything good, but below my discursive, critical thoughts that buzz around like a swarm of mosquitoes, my hand was busy recording first thoughts and writing a very present piece.

If you begin too exactly, you will stay precise but never hit the exact mark that makes the words vibrate with the truth that goes through the present, past, and future.

You can sit down and time yourself and add to the original work that second, third, or fourth time you wrote on something.

People will react however they want; and if you write poetry, get used to no reaction at all.

If you find yourself checking the clock too much as you write, say to yourself you are going to keep writing until three (or four or five) pages, both sides, are filled or until the cake is baked.

All that heat goes into the making of that cake.

A writer must say yes to life, to all of life: the water glasses, the Kemp's half-and-half, the ketchup on the counter.

If the class is too large and it will take up too much time, we alternate the people who will read after each round, so you might read every other time instead of every time.

The piece I read I later typed up and entitled "Slow Seeing the World Go Round," about my grandmother drinking water, raising children, and leaving the world without socks, salamis, or salt.

Exercise 108D: Adverbial Noun Phrases

Fourteen of the following sentences, from Stephen King's *On Writing*, contain adverbial nouns or adverbial noun phrases (possibly more than one!). The rest do not.

Circle each adverbial noun or noun phrase, and draw an arrow from the circle to the word modified. The first is done for you..

She gave birth to Joe less than three hours later.

Most of the nine months I should have spent in the first grade I spent in bed.

The money the sisters sent her each month covered the groceries but little else.

That year my brother David jumped ahead to the fourth grade and I was pulled out of school entirely.

I would be paid sixty-four hundred dollars a year, which seemed an unthinkable sum after earning a dollar-sixty an hour at the laundry.

We talked for another half an hour, but I don't remember a single word of what we said.

There was no sense of exhilaration, no buzz—not that day—but there was a sense of accomplishment that was almost as good.

It occurs to me, in a muddled sort of way, that an hour before I was taking a walk and planning to pick some berries in a field that overlooks Lake Kezar.

At one moment I had none of this; at the next I had all of it.

I drove home, had a brief nap, and then set out on my usual walk.

If I don't write every day, the characters begin to stale off in my mind—they begin to seem like characters instead of real people.

I was only passing the time on a late spring afternoon, but two months later *Cavalier* magazine bought the story for two hundred dollars.

According to the story, a friend came to visit him one day and found the great man sprawled across his writing desk in a posture of utter despair.

I'd usually find that treasured tee-shirt or my favorite Nikes deep under the bed months later, looking sad and abandoned among the dust kitties.

I should have stayed home, I think; going for a walk today was a really bad idea.

Ten years or so later, after I'd sold a couple of novels, I discovered "The Night of the Tiger" in a box of old manuscripts and thought it was still a perfectly respectable tale, albeit one obviously written by a guy who had only begun to learn his chops.

My wife has put up with a lot from me over the years, but her sense of humor stretches only so far.

He looks at himself a moment longer in the mirror, lips pink and eyes bleak, then slowly returns to the table.

Exercise 108E: Diagramming

On your own paper, diagram every word of the following sentences, slightly adapted from Exercise 108D.

The money the sisters sent her each month covered the groceries but little else.

There was no sense of exhilaration, no buzz—not that day—but there was a sense of accomplishment that was almost as good.

I should have stayed home, I think; going for a walk today was a really bad idea.

Ten years later, after I'd sold a couple of novels, I discovered "The Night of the Tiger" in a box of old manuscripts and thought it was still a perfectly respectable tale, albeit one obviously written by a guy who had only begun to learn his chops.

> **Note to Student:** The word *albeit* is a conjunction (but not a commonly used one!).

WEEK 28

— REVIEW 9 —

Weeks 25-27

Topics
Progressive Perfect Indicative Tenses
Progressive Present and Progressive Perfect Present Modal Verbs
Conditional Sentences
Adjectives in the Appositive Position
Correct Comma Usage
Limiting Adjectives
Misplaced, Squinting, and Dangling Modifier Comparisons
Using *More*, *Fewer*, and *Less* Quasi-Coordinators
Words That Can Be Multiple Parts of Speech
Nouns Acting as Other Parts of Speech
Adverbial Nouns

Review 9A: Definition Fill-in-the-Blank

In the last three weeks, you learned (and reviewed) even *more* definitions than in Weeks 22, 23, and 24! Fill in the blanks in the definitions below with one of the terms from the list. Many of the terms will be used more than once.

abstract noun
adjectives
adverbs
attributive
comma
compound modifiers
dangling modifier
descriptive adjective
future
indefinite pronouns
interrogative pronouns
modal
passive
perfect
plural
predicative
progressive perfect
second conditional
singular
subjunctive
third conditional
active
adverb
apostrophe
cardinal numbers
commas
compound preposition
demonstrative adjectives
fewer
imperative
indicative
less
noun
past
perfect past
positive
present
progressive present
simple
squinting modifier
subordinating conjunction
adjective
adverbial noun
appositive
clause
comparative
coordinating conjunction
demonstrative pronouns
first conditional
indefinite adjectives
interrogative adjectives
misplaced modifier
ordinal numbers
past participle
perfect present
possessive adjective
progressive
quasi-coordinators
simple present
state-of-being
superlative

_________________________ represent quantities (one, two, three, four . . .).

_________________________ represent order (first, second, third, fourth . . .).

_________________________ demonstrate or point out something. They take the place of a single word or a group of words.

_________________________ modify nouns and answer the question *Which one*?

_________________________ are pronouns without antecedents.

_________________________ modify nouns and answer the questions *Which one*? and *How many*?

A _________________________ tells what kind.

A _________________________ becomes an _________________________ when you add *-ness* to it.

A _________________________ tells whose.

A _________________________ becomes an _________________________ when it is made possessive.

Form the possessive of a _________________________ noun by adding an _______________ and the letter *s*.

Form the possessive of a _________________________ noun ending in *-s* by adding an _________________________ only.

Form the possessive of a _________________________ noun that does not end in *-s* as if it were a _________________________ noun.

_________________________ verbs express real actions.

_________________________ verbs express situations that are unreal, wished for, or uncertain.

_________________________ verbs express intended actions.

_________________________ verbs express possible actions and situations that have not actually happened.

The present passive imperative is formed by adding the helping verb *be* to the _________________________ of the verb.

The present passive subjunctive is formed by pairing *be* with the _________________________ of a verb.

Use the simple past subjunctive ____________________ verb, plus an infinitive, to express a future unreal action.

____________________ sentences express circumstances that might actually happen. The predicate of the condition clause is in a ____________________ tense. The predicate of the consequence clause is an ____________________ or is in a ____________________ or ____________________ tense.

____________________ sentences express circumstances that are contrary to reality. The predicate of the condition clause is in a ____________________ tense. The predicate of the consequence clause is in the ____________________ or ____________________ modal tense.

____________________ sentences express past circumstances that never happened. The predicate of the condition clause is in the ____________________ tense. The predicate of the consequence clause is in the ____________________ modal or ____________________ modal tense.

An ____________________ that comes right before the noun it modifies is in the ____________________ position.

An ____________________ that follows the noun it modifies is in the ____________ position.

____________________ adjectives directly follow the word they modify.

When three or more nouns, adjectives, verbs, or adverbs appear in a series, they should be separated by ____________________.

More than and *less than* are ____________________.

An ____________________ tells the time or place of an action, or explains *how long, how far, how deep, how thick,* or *how much.* It can modify a verb, ____________________ or ____________________.

An ____________________ plus its modifiers is an ____________________ phrase.

A ____________________ is an adjective, adjective phrase, adverb, or adverb phrase in the wrong place.

A ____________________ can belong either to the sentence element preceding or the element following.

A ____________________ has no noun or verb to modify.

A ______________________ joins equal words or groups of words together.

A ______________________ joins unequal words or groups of words together.

__________________ link compound parts of a sentence that are unequal. ___________ include *rather than, sooner than, let alone, as well as*, and *not to mention*.

When three or more items are in a list, a ______________________ before the last term is usual but not necessary.

When three or more items are in a list and a ______________________ is used, a ______________________ should still follow the next-to-last item in the list.

When two or more adjectives are in the ______________________ position, they are only separated by ______________________ if they are equally important in meaning.

______________________ take the place of nouns in questions.

______________________ modify nouns.

The ______________________ degree of an adjective describes only one thing.

The ______________________ degree of an adjective compares two things.

The ______________________ degree of an adjective compares three or more things.

Most regular adjectives form the ______________________ by adding *-r* or *-er.*

Most regular adjectives form the ______________________ by adding *-st* or *-est.*

Many adjectives form their ______________________ and ______________________ forms by adding the word *more* or *most* before the adjective instead of using *–er* or *–est.* In ______________________ and ______________________ adjective forms, the words *more* and *most* are used as ______________________.

Use ______________________ for concrete items and ______________________ for abstractions.

In comparisons using *more . . . fewer* and *more . . . less, more* and *less* can act as either ______________________ or ______________________ and *the* can act as an ______________________.

In comparisons using two comparative forms, the forms may act as either ___________ or ______________________, and *the* can act as an ______________________.

When *than* is used in a comparison and introduces a ______________________ with understood elements, it is acting as a ______________________.

Other than is a ______________________ that means "besides" or "except."

In a sentence with an ______________________ verb, the subject performs the action.

In a sentence with a ______________________ verb, the subject receives the action.

A ______________________ verb simply tells whether an action takes place in the past, present, or future.

A ______________________ verb describes an ongoing or continuous action.

A ______________________ verb describes an action which has been completed before another action takes place.

A ______________________ verb describes an ongoing or continuous action that has a definite end.

Review 9B: Parsing

Above each underlined verb, write the complete tense, the voice (or note *state-of-being*), and the mood. The first verb is done for you.

These sentences are from *Salamandastron: A Tale of Redwall*, by Brian Jacques.

perfect past, active, indicative

Many and many a long season had come and gone since that fateful midwinter day in the Southwest Lands.

Above the tideline stood the great citadel of Salamandastron, the mountainous shell that had once been a volcano when the world was young.

Through countless ages it had been ruled by the mysterious badger Lords and their friends, the hares of the Long Patrol.

I know for a fact that the center of that mountain is packed with gold, silver, jewels, armor, swords, encrusted shields and all manner of wonderful weapons. Just think, if you owned a fifth part of all that, every creature in the land would be bowing their heads and fighting to kiss your footpaws.

Now I think that between five warriors like ourselves we could manage to slip a dagger in his ribs while we're congratulating him on a job well done.

It should have been worn by your brother Urthstripe.

The previous night had been spent swapping life stories with their new friends.

You must have chirruped like a cricket too early.

Samkim covered his eyes, realizing what had happened.

If I had known that Ferahgo was in the area of my son's home I would never have gone out into the woodland that day to gather snowdrops.

Lately I have been saying strange poems and singing songs that I have never even heard before—most of you have heard me.

That way the only place it will have left to run will be straight into this pool.

Salamandastron had been breached—the horde of Ferahgo was within the mountain.

Since dawn King Glagweb had been peering over the edge of the pit, watching Mara intently.

I want this poisoner myself, but if we are to capture him we must act with all speed.

If the spirit of Redwall is trying to tell us something, then the least we can do is listen!

Hey, Migroo, they might've gone this way.

Review 9C: Provide the Verb

Complete each song line or stanza by providing an appropriate verb in the tense indicated. You may want to use the chart in Lesson 99 for reference.

If there are two blanks for a single verb, the helping verb (or verbs) is divided from the main verb by another part of the sentence.

If you can't think of a verb, ask your instructor for help.

When you are finished, compare your answers to the original lines.

Note to Student: The following lines are all taken from popular musicals.

present progressive, active, indicative

I ____________________ not ____________________ away my shot!

—*Hamilton*

present perfect, active, indicative

____________________ I actually ____________________?

—*Wicked*

simple past, passive, indicative

They ____________________ by rows and rows of the finest virtuosos, the cream of ev'ry famous band.

—*The Music Man*

simple present, active, indicative / simple present, active, modal

I ____________________ you ____________________ me why.

—*Frozen*

perfect present, active, indicative

We ____________________ never ____________________ you in in the first place!

—*Les Miserables*

present, active, imperative / present, active, imperative

____________________ every mountain, ____________________ high and low.

—*The Sound of Music*

simple future, active, indicative

Who ____________________ this wonderful morning?

—*Oliver*

perfect present, active, indicative

A new day ____________________.

—*Cats*

perfect past, active, indicative

But the moon ____________________, and so had Christopher MacGill.

—Brigadoon

progressive past, active, indicative

Well, I ____________________ along by the banks of the river, when seven fat cows came up out of the Nile.

—Joseph and the Amazing Technicolor Dreamcoat

Note to Student: The following lyrics are all from nineteenth century operettas (short, usually comic operas that also include spoken dialogue) by playwright W. S. Gilbert and composer Arthur Sullivan.

May that which now is the far-off horizon

simple future, active, indicative

(But which ____________________ then ____________________ the middle distance),
In fruitful promise be exceeded only

perfect future, active, indicative

By that which ____________________, in the meantime,

Into a new and glorious horizon!

—The Sorcerer

perfect past, passive, indicative

Unspeak the oaths that never ____________________,

simple present, passive, modal

And break the vows that never ____________________!

—Utopia Limited

perfect present, passive, indicative

Well, he ____________________,

perfect present, active, indicative

and my father ____________________ me here to claim his hand.

—The Gondoliers

simple present, passive, modal

I ____________________ much ____________________ if I thought it was.

—The Gondoliers

simple present, passive, subjunctive

If from my sister I ____________________,

It could be borne—

I should, no doubt, be horrified,

simple present, active, modal

But I ____________________ it.

—The Gondoliers

perfect present, passive, modal

Our views ____________________ hastily ____________________ on insufficient grounds.

—*The Gondoliers*

With a pleasure that's emphatic,
We retire to our attic

perfect present, passive, indicative

With the gratifying feeling that our duty ____________________!

—*The Gondoliers*

simple past, passive, indicative

When you were a prattling babe of six months old you ____________________ by proxy to no less a personage than the infant son and heir of His Majesty the immeasurably wealthy King of Barataria!

—*The Gondoliers*

Review 9D: Identifying Adjectives and Punctuating Items in a Series

In the following poem, "The Cremation of Sam McGee," by Robert Service, carry out the following three steps:

a) Underline once and label all adjectives (except for articles), using the following abbreviations:

Descriptive Adjectives		Limiting Adjectives	
Regular	DA-R	Possessives	LA-P
Present participles	DA-PresP	~~Articles~~	~~LA-A~~
Past participles	DA-PastP	Demonstratives	LA-D
Infinitives	DA-Inf	Indefinites	LA-IND
		Interrogatives	LA-INT
		Numbers	LA-N

b) Circle all adjectives that are in the predicate or in the predicative position and draw an arrow from each back to the noun it modifies.

c) Identify proper adjectives as *DA-R Prop.*

There are strange things done in the midnight sun

By the men who moil for gold;

The Arctic trails have their secret tales

That would make your blood run cold;

The Northern Lights have seen queer sights,
But the queerest they ever did see
Was that night on the marge of Lake Lebarge
I cremated Sam McGee.

Now Sam McGee was from Tennessee, where the cotton blooms and blows.
Why he left his home in the South to roam round the Pole God only knows.
He was always cold, but the land of gold seemed to hold him like a spell;
Though he'd often say in his homely way that he'd "sooner live in hell."

On a Christmas Day we were mushing our way over the Dawson trail.
Talk of your cold! through the parka's fold it stabbed like a driven nail.
If our eyes we'd close, then the lashes froze, till sometimes we couldn't see;
It wasn't much fun, but the only one to whimper was Sam McGee.

And that very night as we lay packed tight in our robes beneath the snow,
And the dogs were fed, and the stars o'erhead were dancing heel and toe,
He turned to me, and, "Cap," says he, "I'll cash in this trip, I guess;
And if I do, I'm asking that you won't refuse my last request."

Well, he seemed so low that I couldn't say no: then he says with a sort of moan:
"It's the cursèd cold, and it's got right hold till I'm chilled clean through to the bone.
Yet 'taint being dead, it's my awful dread of the icy grave that pains:
So I want you to swear that, foul or fair, you'll cremate my last remains."

A pal's last need is a thing to heed, so I swore I would not fail;
And we started on at the streak of dawn, but God! he looked ghastly pale.
He crouched on the sleigh, and he raved all day of his home in Tennessee;
And before nightfall a corpse was all that was left of Sam McGee.

There wasn't a breath in that land of death, and I hurried, horror driven,
With a corpse half-hid that I couldn't get rid because of a promise given;
It was lashed to the sleigh, and it seemed to say: "You may tax your brawn and brains,
But you promised true, and it's up to you to cremate those last remains."

Now a promise made is a debt unpaid, and the trail has its own stern code.
In the days to come, though my lips were dumb, in my heart how I cursed that load.
In the long, long night, by the lone firelight, while the huskies, round in a ring,
Howled out their woes to the homeless snows—O God! how I loathed the thing!

And every day that quiet clay seemed to heavy and heavier grow;
And on I went, though the dogs were spent and the grub was getting low;
The trail was bad, and I felt half mad, but I swore I would not give in;
And I'd often sing to the hateful thing, and it hearkened with a grin.

Till I came to the marge of Lake Lebarge, and a derelict there lay;
It was jammed in the ice, but I saw in a trice it was called the "Alice May."
And I looked at it, and I thought a bit, and I looked at my frozen chum:
Then, "Here," said I, with a sudden cry, "is my cre-ma-tor-eum."

Some planks I tore from the cabin floor, and I lit the boiler fire;
Some coal I found that was lying around, and I heaped the fuel higher;
The flames just soared, and the furnace roared—such a blaze you seldom see;
And I burrowed a hole in the glowing coal, and I stuffed in Sam McGee.

Then I made a hike, for I didn't like to hear him sizzle so;
And the heavens scowled, and the huskies howled, and the wind began to blow.
It was icy cold, but the hot sweat rolled down my cheeks, and I don't know why;
And the greasy smoke in an inky cloak went streaking down the sky.

I do not know how long in the snow I wrestled with grisly fear;
But the stars came out and they danced about ere again I ventured near;
I was sick with dread, but I bravely said: "I'll just take a peep inside.
I guess he's cooked, and it's time I looked," ... then the door I opened wide.

And there sat Sam, looking cool and calm, in the heart of the furnace roar;
And he wore a smile you could see a mile, and he said: "Please close that door.
It's fine in here, but I greatly fear you'll let in the cold and storm—
Since I left Plumtree, down in Tennessee, it's the first time I've been warm."

Review 9E: Correcting Modifiers

The following sentences all have modifier problems!

Rewrite each sentence correctly on your own paper, and be ready to explain the solution out loud to your instructor. You may need to add or delete words or phrases—as long as the sentence makes sense, that's fine. There may be more than one way to fix each sentence.

Bleating noisily, the farm was filled with the sounds of sheep.

Between cows and sheep, sheep are definitely the most loud animal.

However, ducks win the prize for the annoyingest animal.

After being fed, the farm is much quieter.

That big white duck in the nest that is busy laying an egg is the oldest duck in the pen.

The biggest sheep in the paddock who butts the other sheep is a bully.

That ram knocked down the fence because he is the powerfullest animal in the pasture.

Wandering through the farm, the smell of all the manure was overpowering me!

The chickens seemed to require less scoops of grain than the ducks.

That horse is the beautifullest of all the horses with the white mane and tail.

The mare with the chestnut foal in the front paddock asked for treats when I walked by.

To run a successful farm, fields have to be planted on time and properly fertilized.

The pigs are pastured the most far away from the farmhouse.

The spotted pig with the huge jowls I was afraid of seemed like it might jump out of the pen and attack me.

After walking around the farm, afternoon tea with cream scones satisfied my hunger.

Review 9F: Identifying Adverbs

In the following sentences, taken from *The Shepherd's Life*, by James Rebanks, carry out the following steps:

a) Underline each word, phrase, or clause that is acting as an adverb.
b) Draw a line from the word/phrase/clause to the verb form, adjective, or adverb modified.
c) Above the word or phrase, note whether it is a regular adverb (*ADV*), an adverbial noun or noun phrase (*AN*), a prepositional phrase (*PrepP*), an infinitive phrase (*INF*), a present participle phrase (*PresP*), a past participle phrase (*PastP*), an adverbial clause (*C*), or a relative adverb introducing an adjective clause (*RA*).

Remember: Within a phrase or clause acting as an adverb, there might also be an adverb modifying an adjective or verb form. Underline these adverbs a second time. There might even be a third adverb or adverbial phrase in some phrases and clauses—underline those three times! And keep your eyes open for the one sentence that might need four underlinings—or possibly five.

The earth spins through the vastness of space. The grass comes and goes with the warmth of the sun.

We farm in a valley called Matterdale, between the first two rounded fells that emerge on your left as you travel west on the main road from Penrith.

There is a stolen moment each early summer when I climb that fell and sit with my sheepdogs and have half an hour to take the world in.

The swallows explode outwards from the barn door. They fledged a couple of days ago, and whole families head out to the fields, where they hawk all day over the grass and thistles. Fingers of pink and orange light are now creeping over the fell sides.

I drive through the village past cars being pushed into drives by folk who've just returned from trying to get to work in the local town, beaten by the snow.

Two or three of us are sent up the left-hand side of the fell, after Joe, to sweep out the sheep across the fell to the right, with one of us peeling off to hold them that way every half mile or so.

One of the other shepherd's dogs nips my hand as I push the sheep through.

When the last ones are sorted, the shepherds walk their sheep home for clipping.

Sometimes I am left alone somewhere on the mountain, waiting for the others.

Review 9G: Comma Use

The following sentences have lost all of their commas. Insert commas directly into the text (no need to use proofreader's marks) wherever needed.

These sentences were taken from *The Secret Life of Cows*, by Rosamund Young.

Cows are individuals as are sheep pigs and hens and I dare say all the creatures on the planet however unnoticed unstudied or unsung.

If when a young calf tries to eat some hay it is repeatedly pushed away by bigger stronger cattle and it then works out that by squeezing in under its mother's chin it will be able to eat in peace that seems to me an example of useful practical intelligence.

At our farm Kite's Nest the calves stay with their mothers for as long as they choose.

Cows can be highly intelligent or slow to understand: friendly considerate aggressive docile inventive dull proud or shy.

Where cattle have adequate living space freedom from competition for food licence to roam freely and above all where they can live in family groups in which there is a preponderance of mature animals immunity to lung and stomach worms can be established.

Calves play games together copying and learning constantly.

In *The Shepherd's Calendar* John Clare wrote "The ass... will eager stoop/to pick the sprouting thistle up."

Farmed birds should be allowed to follow their behavioural instincts grow at their natural rate eat safe food and live dignified lives.

When hens are healthy and happy their feathers shine their eyes are bright and alert and they spend all day being as busy as bees: pecking grazing chopping pulling running investigating digging playing and singing contentedly.

It is widely accepted that animals such as cats dogs and horses usually kept in small numbers and given individual attention are capable of exhibiting symptoms of boredom and unhappiness that they can pine and grieve and show signs of feeling unwell.

When we have had occasion to treat a farm animal as a pet because of illness accident or bereavement it has exhibited great intelligence a huge capacity for affection and an ability to fit in with an unusual routine.

Review 9H: Conjunctions

In the following sentences, from the short story collection *Tales of Men and Ghosts*, by Edith Wharton, find and circle every conjunction. Label each as coordinating (*C*), compound coordinating (*COMC*), subordinating (*SUB*), compound subordinating (*CSUB*), coordinating correlative (*CC*), subordinating correlative (*SC*), or quasi-coordinator (*QC*).

His attempts at self-destruction were as futile as his snatches at fame!

He stood a little way off, looking down at her with a gaze that was both hesitating and constrained.

He had spoken painfully at first, as if there were a knot in his throat; but each time he repeated the words he found they were easier to say.

But as he walked away, his fears dispelled, the sense of listlessness returned on him.

As he did so he noticed that the reporter was accompanied by a tall man with grave compassionate eyes.

I had always wanted to do her some service, to justify myself in my own eyes rather than hers; and here was a beautiful embodiment of my chance.

He was as inexpressive as he is to-day, and yet oddly obtrusive: one of those uncomfortable presences whose silence is an interruption.

It was his face, really, rather than his words, that told her, as she furtively studied it, the tale of failure and slow discouragement which had so blurred its handsome lines.

For a time he was content to let himself go on the tranquil current of this existence; but although his auditors gave him for the most part an encouraging attention, which, in some, went the length of really brilliant and helpful suggestion, he gradually felt a recurrence of his old doubts.

At length he discovered that on certain days visitors from the outer world were admitted to his retreat; and he wrote out long and logically constructed relations of his crime, and furtively slipped them into the hands of these messengers of hope.

Neave *wanted* what he appreciated—wanted it with his touch and his sight as well as with his imagination.

I thought this shrewd of Archie, as well as generous; and I saw the wisdom of Dredge's course.

Of course she laid stress on the fact that his ideas were the object of her contemplation; but he was pleasantly aware, from the lady's tone, that she guessed him to be neither old nor ridiculous.

Review 91: Identifying Independent Elements

The following sentences, taken from the novel *Austenland*, by Shannon Hale, all contain independent elements: absolutes (*ABS*), parenthetical expressions (*PE*), interjections (*INT*), nouns of direct address (*NDA*), appositives (*APP*), and/or noun clauses in apposition (*NCA*).

Locate, underline, and label each one. If an independent element occurs within another independent element, underline it twice.

Jane's mother, Shirley, came to visit and brought along Great-Aunt Carolyn.

"Really, Jane, I don't know how you survive here," said Shirley, picking the brittle leaves from among the sallow green ones.

I'm sure your poor aunt wants to relax, but it's like a sauna in here and not a moment of silence—traffic, car alarms, sirens nonstop.

She took a scolding stance, hand on hip.

Carolyn smiled, her uncountable cheek wrinkles gathered into a few deeper ones.

Hours later, when the nameless driver stopped the car and opened her door, Jane found herself in the quaint, green, rolling countryside she recognized from travel brochures, the sky as cloudy as all English October skies ought to be, and the ground, of course, unpleasantly damp.

Let me assure you that we will still do all in our power to make your visit, such as it is, enjoyable.

Mrs. Wattlesbrook settled down to quiz her on the items of study—how to play the card games whist and speculation, general etiquette, current events of the Regency period, and so on.

Mrs. Wattlesbrook was reminding Jane of Miss April, the spiteful, tight-bunned, glossy-lipped, stick-cracking ballet teacher of her elementary school years.

Review 9J: Words with Multiple Identities

In the following sentences, taken from the Jane Austen novel *Persuasion*, identify each bolded word as a noun (*N*), verb (*V*). adverb (*ADV*), adjective (*ADJ*), pronoun (*PRO*), preposition (*PREP*), subordinating conjunction (*SC*), or coordinating conjunction (*CC*).

He was **at that time** a very young man, **just** engaged in the study of the law; and Elizabeth found him extremely agreeable, and every **plan** in his **favour** was confirmed.

I am not particularly disposed to **favour** a tenant.

Depend **upon** me **for** taking **care that** no tenant has **more** than his **just** rights.

For you **alone**, I think and **plan**.

It would be going **only** to multiply trouble to the others, and **increase** his own distress; and a much better scheme followed and was acted **upon**.

She ventured to **hope** he did not always read **only** poetry.

All equality of alliance must **rest** with Elizabeth, **for** Mary had merely connected herself with an **old country** family of respectability and large fortune, and had therefore given **all** the honour and received none.

The **country** round Lyme is very fine.

He could plainly see **how old all** the **rest** of his family and acquaintance were growing.

He would go, **though** I told him **how ill** I was.

Like many other great moralists and preachers, she had been eloquent on a point in **which** her own conduct would **ill** bear examination.

Anne felt **that** she had gained nothing **but** an **increase** of curiosity.

I am sure neither Henrietta nor I should **care at all** for the play, **if** Miss Anne could not be with us.

Mrs. Musgrove was giving Mrs. Croft the history of her eldest daughter's engagement, and **just** in **that** inconvenient tone of voice **which** was perfectly audible while it pretended to be a whisper.

If I could explain to you **all this**, and **all that** a man can bear and do, and glories to do, for the sake of **these** treasures of his existence!

In the **quieter** professions, there is a toil and a labour of the mind, **if** not of the body, **which seldom** leaves a man's looks to the natural effect of time.

Review 9K: Phrases, Clauses, and Absolutes

The following paragraph, from Charles Dickens' novel *Barnaby Rudge*, is made up of one single sentence! This exercise should give you a sense of just how an accomplished writer can string together MANY different sentence elements to create a vivid scene.

First, read the sentence as it was written, in paragraph form. (You might want to read it out loud.)

> There he sat, watching his wife as she decorated the room with flowers for the greater honour of Dolly and Joseph Willet, who had gone out walking, and for whom the tea-kettle had been singing gaily on the hob full twenty minutes, chirping as never kettle chirped before; for whom the best service of real undoubted china, patterned with divers round-faced mandarins holding up broad umbrellas, was now displayed in all its glory; to tempt whose appetites a clear, transparent, juicy ham, garnished with cool green lettuce-leaves and fragrant cucumber, reposed upon a shady table, covered with a snow-white cloth; for whose delight, preserves and jams, crisp cakes and other pastry, short to eat, with cunning twists, and cottage loaves, and rolls of bread both white and brown, were all set forth in rich profusion; in whose youth Mrs V. herself had grown quite young, and stood there in a gown of red and white: symmetrical in figure, buxom in bodice, ruddy in cheek and lip, faultless in ankle, laughing in face and mood, in all respects delicious to behold—there sat the locksmith among all and every these delights, the sun that shone upon them all: the centre of the system: the source of light, heat, life, and frank enjoyment in the bright household world.

Then, look at the version of the sentence that follows. Each part of the sentence has been placed on a separate line. For each part, point out the following:

- Identity: Is it a phrase, clause, independent element (*IND*)—or other?
- Type: If it's a phrase, is it prepositional (*PrepP*), present participle (*PresP*), past participle (*PastP*), or infinitive (*INF*)? If it's a clause, is it independent (*IND*) or subordinate (*SUB*)? And if it's *other*, how would you describe it?
- Part of speech: Then, identify whether the part serves as an adjective (*ADJ*), adverb (*ADV*), appositive (*APP*), noun—or something else.
- Finally, in the last blank, if the part modifies, renames, or otherwise relates to another word in the sentence, list that word.

We have completed a few of the blanks below, to show you how it's done.

There are two things to keep in mind! First, a sentence part might contain other elements (for example, a past participle phrase might contain a prepositional phrase), but only identify the main sentence part on each line; don't worry about any other phrases contained within it. See the first completed example below—the clause *There he sat* contains the adverbial present participle phrase *watching his wife*, but there is no need to identify this separately.

Second, a couple of the parts are divided by yet another part! Where that happens, we have placed ellipses to connect the parts together.

Take some time over this. Ask your instructor for help if necessary. And, if you get frustrated, just remember—we could have asked you to diagram this sentence!

	Identity	Type	Part of Speech	Related to (if any) (modifies or renames)
There he sat, watching his wife	clause	ind	main	none
as she decorated the room				
with flowers				
for the greater honour of Dolly and Joseph Willet,	phrase	prep	adv	decorated
who had gone out walking,				
and for whom the tea-kettle had been singing gaily on the hob				
full twenty minutes,				
chirping as never kettle chirped before;				

	Identity	Type	Part of Speech	Related to (if any) (modifies or renames)
for whom the best service of real undoubted china... was now displayed				
patterned with divers round-faced mandarins				
holding up broad umbrellas,				
in all its glory;				
to tempt whose appetites				
a clear, transparent, juicy ham... reposed				
garnished with cool green lettuce-leaves and fragrant cucumber				
upon a shady table,				
covered with a snow-white cloth;				
for whose delight,				
preserves and jams, crisp cakes and other pastry, short to eat... and cottage loaves, and rolls of bread both white and brown, were all set forth				
with cunning twists				
in rich profusion;				
in whose youth Mrs V. herself had grown quite young, and stood there				
in a gown of red and white:				
symmetrical in figure,				
buxom in bodice,				
ruddy in cheek and lip,				

	Identity	Type	Part of Speech	Related to (if any) (modifies or renames)
faultless in ankle,				
laughing in face and mood,				
in all respects delicious to behold—				
there sat the locksmith				
among all and every these delights,				
the sun				
that shone upon them all:				
the centre of the system:				
the source of light, heat, life, and frank enjoyment				
in the bright household world.				

WEEK 29

Still More Verbs

—LESSON 109—

Hortative Verbs

Subjunctive Verbs

A hortative verb encourages or recommends an action.

Latin *hortari*: to encourage or urge

English derivatives:
to exhort (verb): to urge, or to give urgent recommendations
I exhorted him to keep running despite his weariness.
hortative (adjective): encouraging or urging on
Patience, Charity, and Praise-God are all hortative names.

Let's be more careful next time.

Let's run faster.

Let's be finished now.

In first-person plural hortative verbs, the helping verb *let* is used.
The state-of-being verb takes the form *be*.
The active verb is the same form as the present active indicative.
The passive verb combines *be* with the past participle.

May you be happy.

May you walk in joy.

May you be saved from your own foolishness.

In second-person hortative verbs, the helping verb *may* is used.
The state-of-being verb takes the form *be*.
The active verb is the same form as the present active indicative.
The passive verb combines *be* with the past participle.

Let the trumpets be sounded.

May no creature on earth be silent.

Let the Lord of the Black Lands come forth.

Third-person hortative verbs use the helping verbs *let* or *may*.
The state-of-being verb takes the form *be*.
The active verb is the same form as the present active subjunctive.
The passive verb combines *be* with the past participle.

Active indicative, first person	We **sing** with happiness.
second person	You **sing** with happiness.
Active hortative, first person	Let us **sing** with happiness.
second person	May you **sing** with happiness.
Active indicative, third person	He **sings** with happiness.
Active subjunctive, third person	Should he **sing**, he will be happy.
Active hortative, third person	Let him **sing** with happiness.

May you travel safely.
Let us travel safely.

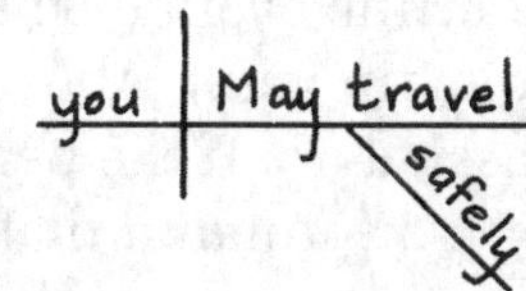

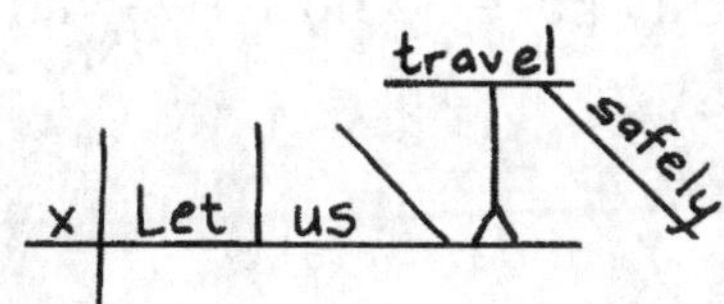

An object complement follows the direct object and renames or describes it.

DO OC
We elected Marissa leader.

May the evildoers come forth.
Let the Lord of the Black Lands come forth.

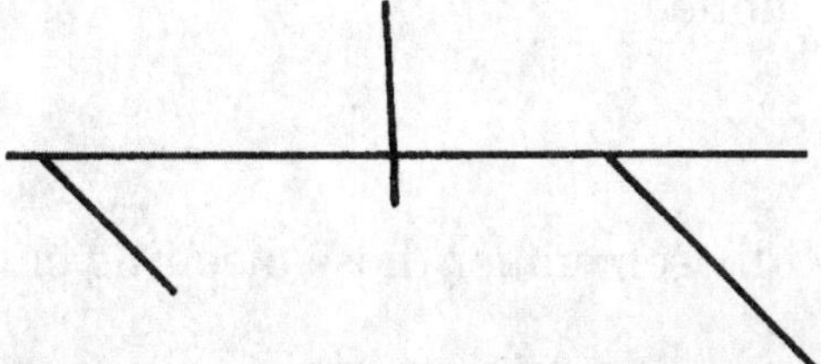

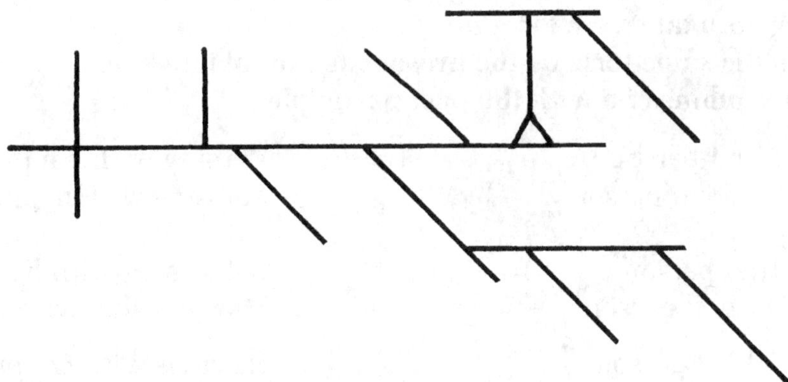

Exercise 109A: Identifying Hortative Verbs

Speechmakers are often exhorting their readers—so they tend to use many hortative verbs! In the following sentences, underline every element of each hortative verb (*let* or *may*, any other helping verbs, and the main verb). Above the underlined verb, identify it as state-of-being (*SB*), active (*A*), or passive (*P*). If the person or thing being exhorted is present in the sentence, circle the noun or pronoun that identifies him/her/it, and identify it as *S* for subject or *O* for object.

Be careful—some sentences may have no hortative verbs at all!

The first is done for you.

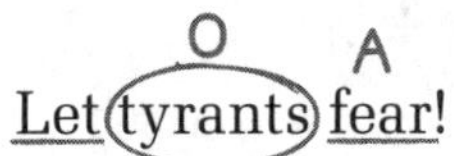

—"Speech to the Troops at Tilbury," Elizabeth I

And let me warn you that it is dangerous to copy the example of a nation whose crimes, towering up to heaven, were thrown down by the breath of the Almighty, burying that nation in irrevocable ruin!

In the fervent aspirations of William Lloyd Garrison, I say, and let every heart join in saying it:

God speed the year of jubilee
The wide world o'er!

If I do forget, if I do not faithfully remember those bleeding children of sorrow this day, "may my right hand forget her cunning, and may my tongue cleave to the roof of my mouth!"

You may rejoice, I must mourn.

—"What to the Slave Is the Fourth of July?," Frederick Douglass

Let him remember also that the worth of the ideal must be largely determined by the success with which it can in practice be realized.

Let us try to level up, but let us beware of the evil of leveling down.

Long may you carry yourselves proudly as citizens of a nation which bears a leading part in the teaching and uplifting of mankind.

Let those who have, keep, let those who have not, strive to attain, a high standard of cultivation and scholarship. Yet let us remember that these stand second to certain other things.

—"Citizenship in a Republic," Theodore Roosevelt

Before you discuss the resolution, let me place before you one or two things.

May it be that the reins will be placed in the hands of the Parsis, for instance—as I would love to see happen—or they may be handed to some others whose names are not heard in the Congress today.

Let me, however, hasten to assure that I am the same Gandhi as I was in 1920.

—"Quit India," Mahatma Gandhi

But let the men of Hartford imagine that they were not in the position of being voters at all, that they were governed without their consent being obtained, that the legislature turned an absolutely deaf ear to their demands, what would the men of Hartford do then?

—"Freedom or Death," Emmeline Pankhurst

You are hemmed in on all sides; all your plans are clearer than the day to us; let me remind you of them.

With malice toward none, with charity for all, with firmness in the right as God gives us to see the right, let us strive on to finish the work we are in, to bind up the nation's wounds, to care for him who shall have borne the battle and for his widow and his orphan, to do all which may achieve and cherish a just and lasting peace among ourselves and with all nations.

Both parties deprecated war, but one of them would make war rather than let the nation survive, and the other would accept war rather than let it perish, and the war came.

— "Second Inaugural Address," Abraham Lincoln

Wherefore, O conscript fathers, let the worthless be gone,—let them separate themselves from the good,—let them collect in one place,—let them, as I have often said before, be separated from us by a wall; let them cease to plot against the consul in his own house,—to surround the tribunal of the city pretor,—to besiege the senate-house with swords,—to prepare brands and torches to burn the city; let it, in short, be written on the brow of every citizen, what his sentiments are about the republic.

— "The First Oration Against Catiline," Cicero

Exercise 109B: Rewriting Indicative Verbs as Hortative Verbs

Hortative verbs also appear frequently in song lyrics! In the lines below, the statements and commands in bold type originally contained hortative verbs. On your own paper, rewrite each bolded clause so that the main verbs are hortative. Then, compare your answers with the original.

If you need help, ask your instructor.

It will happen that the shadow's call will fly away.

They will talk, if they want to!

The river will run,
The dreamers will wake the nation.

The rough times ahead will become triumphs in time.

She will defend our laws, and ever give us cause
To sing with heart and voice, God save the Queen!

He can sink or **he can swim,**
He doesn't care for me, and I don't care for him.

Exercise 109C: Diagramming

On your own paper, diagram every word of each sentence. These come from speeches made by three nineteenth-century women who fought for women's *suffrage*—the right for women to vote. This right was not granted to American women until 1920, just one hundred years ago.

May these statements lead you to reflect upon this subject, that you may know what woman's condition is in society—what her restrictions are, and seek to remove them.
—Lucretia Mott, "Discourse on Woman" (1849)

And let not woman hesitate to enter upon the work before her from any fear of transcending the bounds of her sphere.
—Amelia Bloomer, "Most Terribly Bereft" (1855)

Let it be remembered, finally, that it has ever been the pride and boast of America that the rights for which she contended were the rights of human nature.
—Susan B. Anthony, quoting James Madison in "Is It a Crime to Vote?" (1872)

—LESSON 110—

Transitive Verbs
Intransitive Verbs
Sit/Set, Lie/Lay, Rise/Raise
Ambitransitive Verbs

The reindeer broke the first house apart.

The ice between the two floes broke apart.

Transitive verbs express action that is received by some person or thing.
Intransitive verbs express action that is not received by any person or thing.

ambi- from the Latin: prefix meaning "both"

ambidextrous ______________________________

ambiguous ______________________________

ambitransitive both transitive and intransitive

When I hear my voice on a record I absolutely loathe my voice. I cannot stand my voice.
—Roger Daltrey

Music in the soul can be heard by the universe.
—Laozi

Transitive verbs can be active or passive.
Intransitive verbs can only be active.

I hate thunderstorms.
The goat bleated.

***Sit*, *lie*, and *rise* are intransitive.**
***Set*, *lay*, and *raise* are transitive.**

(simple present)	Strong women _____________ above adverse circumstances.
(simple present)	The waiter _____________ the coffee carefully on the table.
(progressive past)	The hen _____________ four or five eggs every week.
(simple present)	She _____________ primly on the elaborate throne.
(simple past)	The farmer _____________ corn, wheat, and rye.
(progressive present)	The horse _____________ peacefully on its side in the pasture.

The cook tied on his apron and set to work.
The travelers set off first thing in the morning.
As we reached the ocean, the sun was setting.

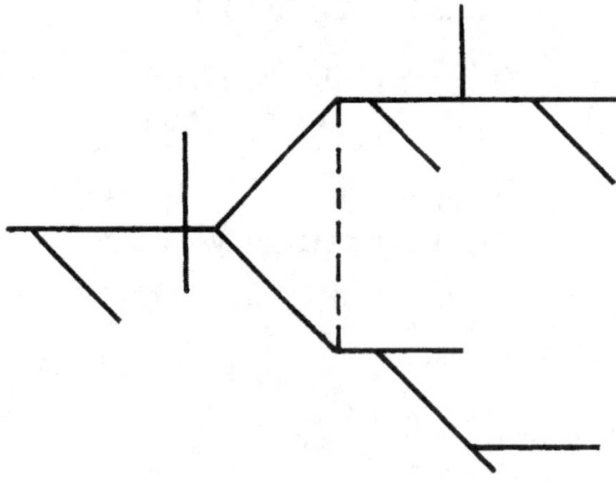

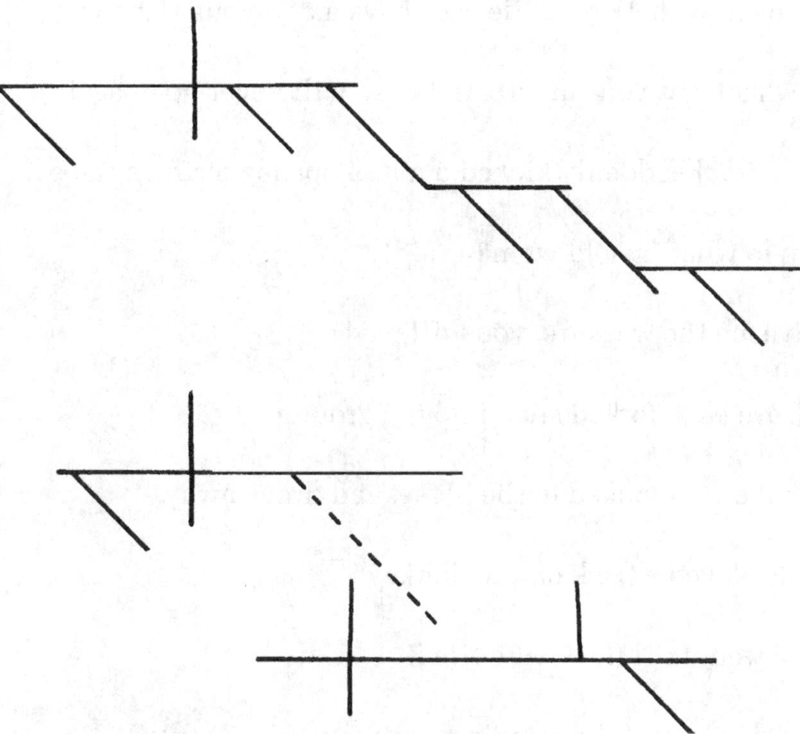

Transitive verbs can be active or passive.
Intransitive verbs can only be active.
Ambitransitive verbs can be either transitive or intransitive.
Transitive verbs express action that is received by some person or thing.
Intransitive verbs express action that is not received by any person or thing.

Exercise 110A: Ambitransitive Verbs

Each one of the sentences below (adapted from the book *African Folk Tales*, edited by Hugh Vernon-Jackson) contains at least one ambitransitive verb. For each sentence, carry out the following steps:

a) Underline the action verbs that are acting as predicates (in both independent and subordinate clauses), and label each one as *TR* for transitive or *INTR* for intransitive.
b) Circle the direct object of each active transitive verb. Remember that clauses and phrases can act as objects and subjects, as well as single words.
c) Choose two sentences with transitive verbs. On your own paper, rewrite them so that the verb becomes passive. You may need to supply additional subjects or other parts of speech!
d) Choose two sentences with intransitive verbs. Rewrite them so that the verbs become transitive. You may need to supply additional objects or other parts of speech!

But as he washed it, it broke.

You have broken the calabash, and I am glad.

Now, the tortoise knew that crocodile eggs have a delicious flavour.

Unless you do what I say, your mouth and nose will never open again!

The frightened animal suddenly kicked out and opened a rift in the earth beneath him.

Pay no attention to what the old woman said!

If you do not give me the treasure, you will pay!

The leopards drove each forked stick into the ground.

He picked up the reins, clucked to the horse, and drove away.

The three rascals played a trick on the donkey.

The tiger cubs played until they were tired.

Ali gave the traveller one of the remaining camels.

You ate my cake without asking my permission!

The she-goat and her children were hungry, and so they sat down and ate.

Please help us with our camels!

The traveller shouted, but no one helped.

He shouted his pain to the sky.

Exercise 110B: The Prefix *Ambi-*

Using a dictionary or thesaurus, find two more words using the prefix *ambi-* where the prefix carries the meaning of "both." On your own paper, write the words and their definitions, and then use each correctly in a sentence. If the word is too technical for you to write an original sentence, you may locate a sentence using an internet search and write it down.

Exercise 110C: Diagramming

On your own paper, diagram every word of the following quotations.

When you are finished, label each action verb occupying a predicate space with *T* for transitive or *INT* for intransitive.

Live in the sunshine, swim the sea, drink the wild air.
—Ralph Waldo Emerson

If you set your goals ridiculously high and it's a failure, you will fail above everyone else's success.
—James Cameron

I have learned over the years that when one's mind is made up, this diminishes fear.
—Rosa Parks

The best and most beautiful things in the world cannot be seen or even touched—they must be felt with the heart.
—Helen Keller

In three words I can sum up everything I've learned about life: it goes on.
—Robert Frost

— LESSON 111 —

Ambitransitive Verbs
Gerunds and Infinitives
Infinitive Phrases as Direct Objects
Infinitive Phrases with Understood *To*

I may not succeed, but I will try.

Try the chocolate cake.

The concert-goers tried arriving early.

Every night, he tries to go to bed by ten.

A gerund is a present participle acting as a noun.
An infinitive is formed by combining *to* and the first-person singular present form of a verb.

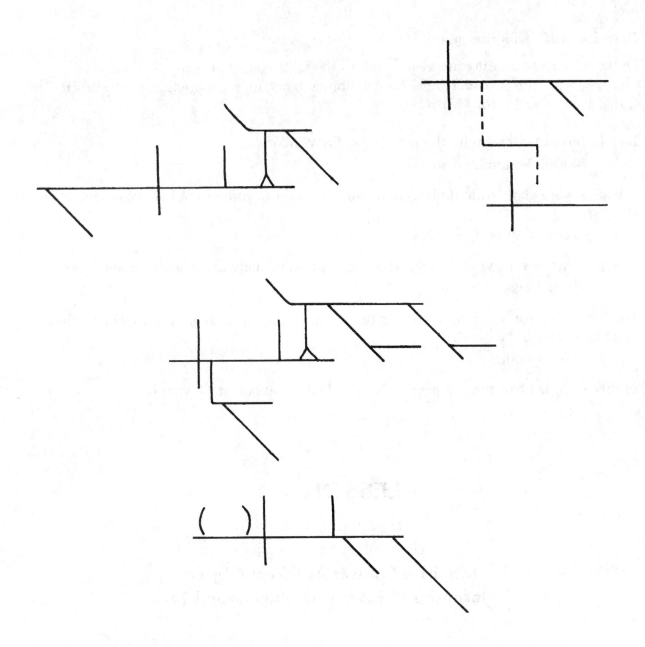

Mother told me to clean my room.

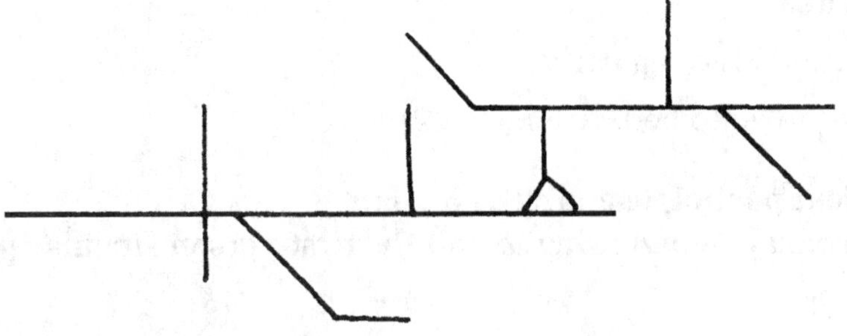

The duchess ordered the maid to arrange the flowers.

His mistake made me lose money.

You must come and make Lizzy marry Mr. Collins, for she vows she will not have him.
—*Pride and Prejudice*

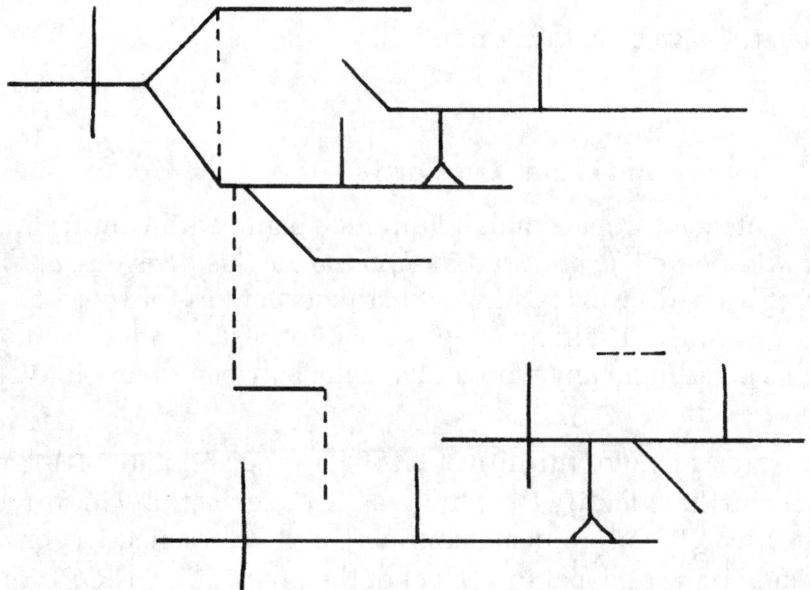

I was made to love you.

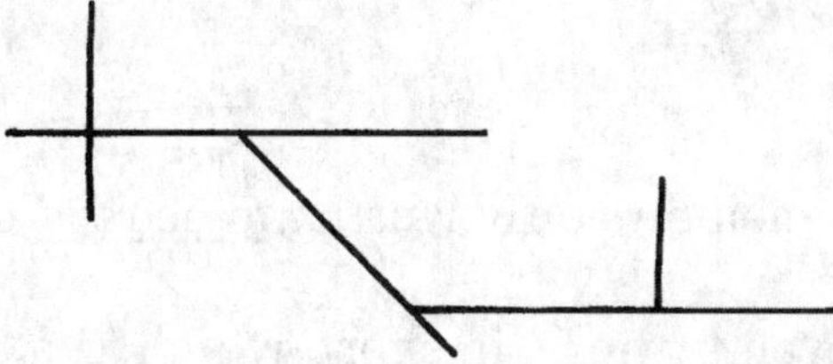

He was good enough to sing.

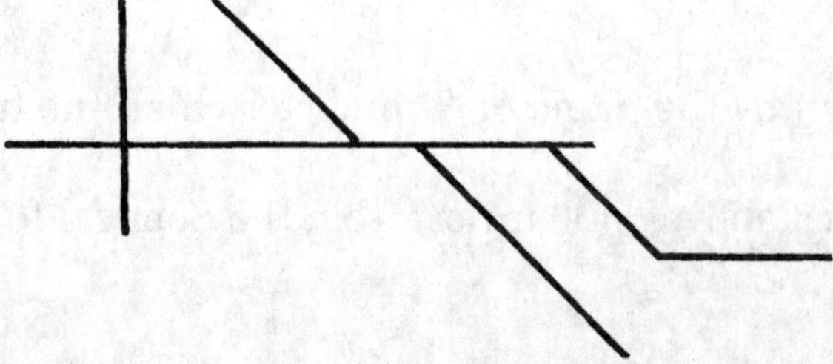

You ought to go home.

You | need | to go home

You | should go | home

You | ought to go | home

The politician ought to have been thrown in jail.

The politician should have been thrown in jail.

Exercise 111A: Infinitives and Other Uses of *To*

In the following sentences, from Olaudah Equiano's eighteenth-century memoir *The Interesting Narrative of the Life of Olaudah Equiano, or Gustavas Vassa, the African, Written By Himself,* underline every phrase that incorporates the word *to.* For infinitives, underline just the infinitive itself; for prepositional phrases, underline just the preposition and its object (and any words that come between them); for verb phrases, underline the entire verb.

- Label each phrase as *INF* for infinitive, *PREP* for prepositional, or *V* for verb.
- For infinitives, further identify the phrase as *S* for subject, *DO* for direct object, *PA* for predicate adjective, *PN* for predicate nominative, *ADJ* for adjective, or *ADV* for adverb.
- For prepositional phrases, label the object of the preposition as *OP.*
- For verb phrases, parse the verb, giving tense, voice, and mood.
- For infinitive adjective and adverb phrases, draw an arrow back to the word modified.

The first is done for you.

INF ADV INF ADV

People generally think those memoirs only worthy to be read or remembered which abound in great or striking events, those, in short, which in a high degree excite either admiration or pity: all others they consign to contempt and oblivion.

That part of Africa, known by the name of Guinea, to which the trade for slaves is carried on, extends along the coast above 3400 miles, from the Senegal to Angola, and includes a variety of kingdoms.

All are taught the use of these weapons; even our women are warriors, and march boldly out to fight along with the men.

This speech seemed to confound him; he began to recoil: and my heart that instant sunk within me.

Indeed such were the horrors of my views and fears at the moment, that, if ten thousand worlds had been my own, I would have freely parted with them all to have exchanged my condition with that of the meanest slave in my own country.

I inquired of these what was to be done with us; they gave me to understand we were to be carried to these white people's country to work for them.

I at that time began to understand him a little, and refused to be called so, and told him as well as I could that I would be called Jacob; but he said I should not, and still called me Gustavus; and when I refused to answer to my new name, which at first I did, it gained me many a cuff; so at length I submitted, and was obliged to bear the present name, by which I have been known ever since.

I am sensible I ought to entreat your pardon for addressing to you a work so wholly devoid of literary merit!

I now thought my condition much mended; I had sails to lie on, and plenty of good victuals to eat; and every body on board used me very kindly, quite contrary to what I had seen of any white people before; I therefore began to think that they were not all of the same disposition.

When I came to Spithead, I found we were destined for the Mediterranean, with a large fleet, which was now ready to put to sea.

I now knew what it was to work hard; I was made to help to unload and load the ship.

To my no small surprise, and very great joy, the captain confirmed every syllable that I had said: and even more; for he said he had tried different times to see if I would make any attempt of this kind, both at St. Eustatia and in America, and he never found that I made the smallest.

Exercise 111B: Diagramming

On your own paper, diagram every word of the following sentences from *Common Sense*, by Thomas Paine. Ask for help if you need it!

To God, and not to man, are all men accountable on the score of religion.

To unite the sinews of commerce and defense is sound policy; for when our strength and our riches play into each other's hand, we need fear no external enemy.

For as in absolute governments the King is law, so in free countries the law ought to be King; and there ought to be no other.

When we are planning for posterity, we ought to remember, that virtue is not hereditary.

> **Note to Student:** This last sentence has several challenging elements in it! Do your best and ask for help as needed.

We are endeavoring, and will steadily continue to endeavor, to separate and dissolve a connexion which hath already filled our land with blood; and which, while the name of it remains, will be the fatal cause of future mischiefs to both countries.

— LESSON 112 —

Principal Parts

Yet More Troublesome Verbs

Exercise 112A: Verb Definitions

For each definition, choose the best term from the word bank. Write it into the blank next to the definition.

imperative	present participle	second principal part
third principal part	transitive verb	modal
subjunctive	gerund	hortative
first principal part	ambitransitive verb	progressive verb
infinitive	perfect verb	simple verb
intransitive verb	indicative	

Describes an ongoing or continuous action	
Expresses intended actions	
Expresses action that is received by some person or thing	
Affirms or declares what actually is	
Present participle acting as a noun	
Expresses situations that are unreal, wished for, or uncertain	
A verb form ending in *-ing*	
Encourages or recommends an action	
Can be either transitive or intransitive	
The simple present (first-person singular)	
Expresses possible actions	
Describes an action which has been completed before another action takes place	
The same as the simple past verb form	

Formed by combining *to* and the first-person singular present form of a verb	
Expresses action that is not received by any person or thing	
Simply tells whether an action takes place in the past, present, or future	
The perfect past verb form, minus helping verbs	

English verbs have three principal parts.

First principal part: The Simple Present (Present)

(I) pontificate	(I) sing	(I) cut	(I) become

Second principal part: The Simple Past (Past)

(I) pontificated	(I) sang	(I) cut	(I) became

Third principal part: The Perfect Past, Minus Helping Verbs (Past Participle)

(I have) pontificated	(I have) sung	(I have) cut	(I have) become

pontificate, pontificated, pontificated
sing, sang, sung
cut, cut, cut
become, became, become

***Sit*, *lie*, and *rise* are intransitive.**
***Set*, *lay*, and *raise* are transitive.**

lie		**lay**		**lay**	
Simple Past		**Simple Present**		**Simple Past**	
I lay	we lay	I lay	we lay	I laid	we laid
you lay	you lay	you lay	you lay	you laid	you laid
he, she, it lay	they lay	he, she, it lays	they lay	he, she, it laid	they laid

(simple past) The child ____________ out her clothes for the birthday party the night before.

(simple past) She got sunburned because she ______________ out in the sun too long.

(simple present) ______________ down and go to sleep now.

(simple present) ______________ your head down and close your eyes.

	First Principal Part Present	Second Principal Part Past	Third Principal Part Past Participle
I	lie	lay	lain
	lay	laid	laid
	sit	sat	sat
	set	set	set
	rise	rose	risen
	raise	raised	raised

Exercise 112B: Using Troublesome Verbs Correctly

In the following sentences from the anonymous collection *English Fairy Tales*, fill in the blanks.

The first blank (above the sentence) should be filled in with the first principal part of the correct verb: *lie* or *lay* in the first set of sentences, *sit* or *set* in the second set, and *rise* or *raise* in the third set.

You will be able to tell from the context of the sentence whether you should use the transitive verbs *lay, set,* and *raise* (if the verb is passive, or has a direct object), or the intransitive verbs *lie, sit,* and *rise* (if the action of the verb is not passed on to any other word in the sentence).

The second blank (in the sentence itself) should be filled in with the correct form of that verb.

simple present active indicative of ___________

Here _______________ Tom Thumb, King Arthur's knight,
Who died by a spider's cruel bite.

simple past active indicative of ___________

He _______________ down on the ground, and shading his eyes with one hand, looked up into the sky, and pointed heavenwards with the other hand.

simple past active indicative of ___________

On went Johnny-cake, and by-and-by he came to a fox that _______________ quietly in a corner of the fence.

simple present active indicative of ___________

Wife, bring me the hen that _______________ the golden eggs.

Mr. Vinegar, you foolish man, you blockhead, you simpleton; you went to the fair, and

simple past active indicative of __________

______________ out all your money in buying a cow.

The Laidly Worm crawled and crept, and crept and crawled till it reached the Heugh or

simple present active indicative of __________

rock of the Spindlestone, round which it coiled itself, and ______________ there basking with its terrible snout in the air.

simple past active indicative of __________

So at last she lifted the frog up on to her lap, and it ______________ there for a time.

Wash me, and comb me,

simple present active imperative of __________

And ______________ me down softly.

simple present active imperative of __________

And in ______________ me on a bank to dry,

That I may look pretty,

When somebody passes by.

simple past active indicative of __________

And then she ______________ down upon the bed of the Little, Small, Wee Bear; and that was neither too high at the head, nor at the foot, but just right.

simple present active imperative of __________

Get off your horse and ______________ down.

One came up roaring with open mouth to devour him, when he struck it with his wand,

simple past active indicative of __________

and ______________ it in an instant dead at his feet.

His mother, who was very sorry to see her darling in such a woeful state, put him into a

simple past active indicative of __________

teacup, and soon washed off the batter; after which she kissed him, and ______________ him in bed.

simple past active indicative of __________

The Brownie at Hilton Hall would play at mischief, but if the servants ______________ out for it a bowl of cream, or a knuckle cake spread with honey, it would clear away things for them, and make everything tidy in the kitchen.

**

active infinitive of ___________

And they had each a chair ______________ in; a little chair for the Little, Small, Wee Bear; and a middle-sized chair for the Middle Bear; and a great chair for the Great, Huge Bear.

Well, who should be there but her master's son, and what should he do but fall in love

simple past active indicative of ___________

with her the minute he ______________ eyes on her.

simple present active imperative of ___________

But ______________ ye down; but woe, O, woe,
That ever ye were born,
For come the King of Elfland in,
Your fortune is forlorn.

The king was so charmed with his address that he ordered a little chair to be made, in

simple present active modal of ___________

order that Tom might ______________ upon his table, and also a palace of gold, a span high, with a door an inch wide, to live in.

Jack was so lazy that he would do nothing but bask in the sun in the hot weather, and

simple present active indicative of ___________

______________ by the corner of the hearth in the winter-time.

simple past active indicative of ______________

So she took them in, and ______________ them down before the fire, and gave them milk

active infinitive of ___________

and bread; now Katie was a very brave girl, so she offered ______________ up with him.

perfect past active indicative of ___________

However, the last day of the last month he takes her to a room she'______________ never ______________ eyes on before.

simple past active indicative of ___________

She came to the stile, ______________ down the candles, and proceeded to climb over.

simple past active indicative of ___________

And after they were married all the company ______________ down to the dinner.

passive infinitive of ______________

Mr. Fitzwarren ordered a chair ______________ for him, and so he began to think they were making game of him.

simple past active indicative of ______________

She ______________ down on a stool in the kitchen, and law! how she did cry!

simple past active indicative of ______________

And all the day the girl ______________ trying to think of names to say to it when it came at night.

simple past active indicative of ______________

He travelled till he came to a big stone, and there he ______________ down to rest.

**

simple present active indicative of ______________

As twelve o clock rings, however, the sick prince ______________, dresses himself, and slips downstairs.

simple past active indicative of ______________

Mr. Fox cursed and swore, and drew his sword, ______________ it, and brought it down upon the hand of the poor lady.

simple past active indicative of ______________

So Kate gave him a third bite, and he ______________ quite well, dressed himself, and sat down by the fire.

active infinitive of ______________

Childe Rowland was just going ______________ it to his lips, when he looked at his sister and remembered why he had come all that way.

active infinitive of ______________

Dick now tried ______________, but was obliged to lie down again, being too weak to stand, for he had not eaten any food for three days.

simple present active modal of ______________

Then the fairies would fan him till he could ______________ again and go on dancing.

simple past active indicative of ______________

It ______________ to the boy's knees and still more water was poured.

King Arthur and his whole court were so sorry at the loss of their little favourite that they

simple past active indicative of ______________

went into mourning and ______________ a fine white marble monument over his grave.

	First Principal Part **Present**	Second Principal Part **Past**	Third Principal Part **Past Participle**
I	give	gave	given
	come	came	come
	write	wrote	written
	go	went	gone
	eat	ate	eaten

She had gave her outgrown shoes to her sister.

Has she came home from the movies yet?

The policeman had wrote her a speeding ticket.

When Mom got home, I had already went to bed.

He has ate his dinner too fast.

Exercise 112C: More Principal Parts

Fill in the chart below with the missing principal parts of each verb. (You may use a dictionary if necessary.) Some are regular, and some are irregular.

Then, in the sentences below from Ben Bova's science fiction novel *Neptune*, fill in the blanks with the correct verb, in the tense, mood, and voice indicated in brackets at the end of each sentence. Each verb is used one time.

	First Principal Part **Present**	Second Principal Part **Past**	Third Principal Part **Past Participle**
I	am		
	read		
	withstand		
	eat		

	First Principal Part **Present**	Second Principal Part **Past**	Third Principal Part **Past Participle**
	live		
	notify		
	inform		
	change		
	test		
	choose		
	find		
	see		
	take		
	breathe		
	pull		
	detain		

We ____________________ some of the fishes and other organisms down there for analysis. [perfect present, active, modal]

The mission ________________________ nearly a century to get there. [simple future, active, indicative]

We __________________________ them to see if they have elevated levels of potassium or sulfur. [perfect present, active, modal]

It __________________________ devastating. [perfect present, state-of-being, modal]

As calmly as if she __________________________ from a textbook, Francine went on. [past progressive, active, subjunctive]

Even the built-in desk opposite the small sofa was clear of papers or any other sign that someone __________________________ in this suite for weeks. [perfect past progressive, active, indicative]

They _______ all _________ already ______________ of this meeting. [perfect past, passive, indicative]

He wanted to breathe the same air she _______________________. [progressive present, active, modal]

We have considered the possibility, and we _______________________ that this idea of an alien invasion is pure conjecture! [perfect present, active, indicative]

I believe he ____________ well _______________________ cryonic preservation once he realized his submersible was beyond recovery. [perfect present, active, modal]

Darby _________________________ to it that you won't be here to plead your case. [perfect present, active, indicative]

Once the planet Uranus was found by William Herschel in 1781, studies of its motion indicated that it _________________________ slightly out of its predicted orbit by the gravitational tug of an unseen, more distant planet. [progressive past, passive, indicative]

Its walls _______________________ invading armies and rebelling Hungarians for many centuries. [perfect past, active, indicative]

The creatures of Neptune's deep ocean _________________________ almost everything. [perfect past, active, indicative]

I _______________________ aboard this station against my will! [progressive present, passive, indicative]

I ______________ not _______________________ of any emergency. [perfect present, passive, indicative]

But he _______________________ course. [perfect present, active, modal]

WEEK 30

Still More About Clauses

— LESSON 113 —

Clauses and Phrases

The sentences in this lesson are taken from *Redwall,* by Brian Jacques.

> All eyes were on the Father Abbot. He took a dainty fork loaded precariously with steaming fish. Carefully he transferred it from plate to mouth. Chewing delicately, he turned his eyes upwards then closed them, whiskers atwitch, jaws working steadily, munching away, his tail curled up holding a napkin which neatly wiped his mouth.
>
> —Brian Jacques, *Redwall*

A clause is a group of words that contains a subject and a predicate.

An independent clause can stand by itself as a sentence.

A sentence is a group of words that usually contains a subject and a predicate. A sentence begins with a capital letter and ends with a punctuation mark. A sentence contains a complete thought.

A phrase is a group of words serving a single grammatical function.

A dependent clause is a fragment that cannot stand by itself as a sentence.

Dependent clauses can act as adjective clauses, adverb clauses, or noun clauses.

An adjective clause is a dependent clause that acts as an adjective in a sentence, modifying a noun or pronoun in the independent clause.

Relative pronouns (*who, whom, whose, which, that*) introduce adjective clauses and refer back to an antecedent in the independent clause.

Relative adverbs (*where, when, why*) introduce adjective clauses when they refer back to a place, time, or reason in the independent clause.

Matthias started to slide down the rope on the Mossflower side of the wall, where the woods came close up to the Abbey.

The Father Abbot halted in front of the wall on which hung a long tapestry.

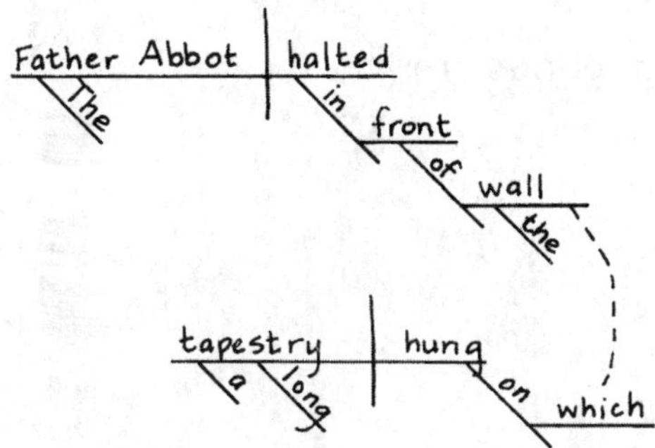

He arrived here in the deep winter when the Founders were under attack from many foxes, vermin, and a great wildcat.

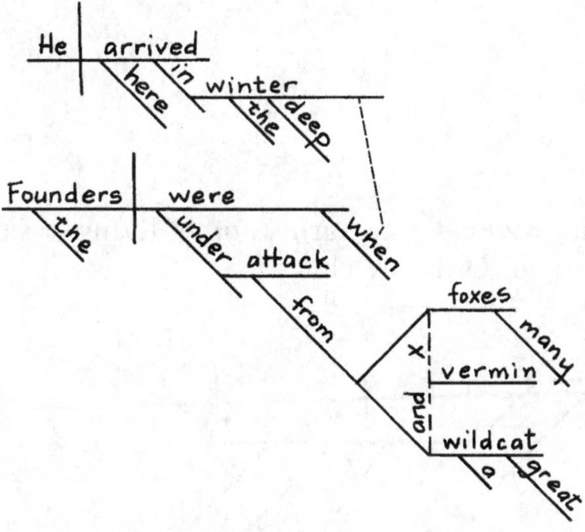

Adverb clauses can be introduced by adverbs.

Common adverbs that introduce adverbial clauses are as follows:

as and its compounds (as if, as soon as, as though)
how and its compound (however)
when and its compound (whenever)
whence
where and its compounds (whereat, whereby, wherein, wherefore, whereon)
while
whither

Her blunt claws churned the roadside soil as she propelled the cart through a gap in the hawthorn hedge, down to the slope of the ditch where she dug her paws in, holding the cart still and secure while John Churchmouse and Cornflower's father jumped out and wedged the wheels firmly with stones.

A subordinating conjunction joins unequal words or groups of words together.

Subordinating conjunctions and subordinating correlative conjunctions often join an adverb clause to an independent clause.

Common subordinating conjunctions are:

after
although
as (as soon as)
because
before
if
in order that
lest
since
though
till
unless
until
although/though . . . yet/still
if . . . then

All the mice took a solemn vow never to harm another living creature, unless it was an enemy that sought to harm our Order by violence.

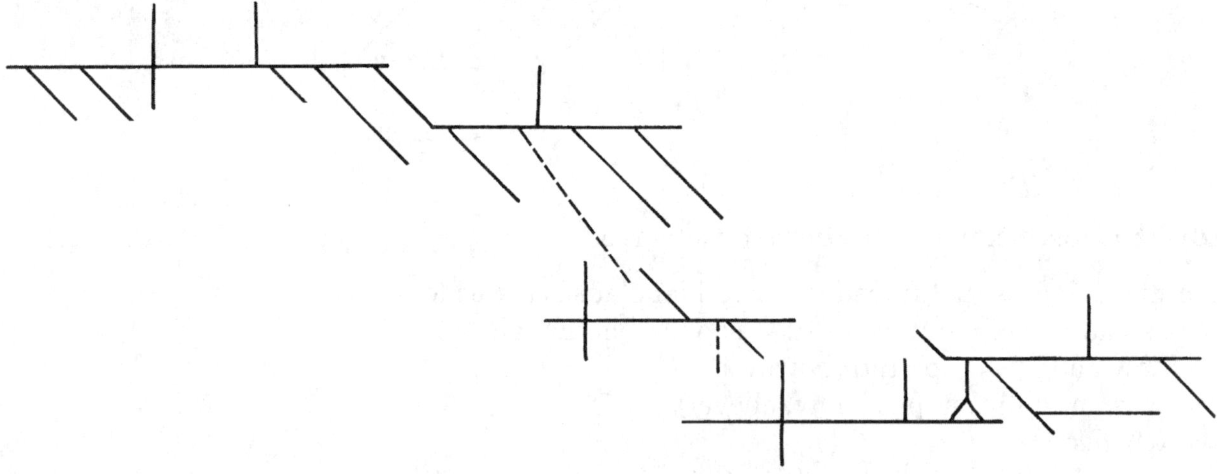

A noun clause takes the place of a noun. Noun clauses can be introduced by relative pronouns, relative adverbs, or subordinating conjunctions.

Somewhere there had to be a clue, a single lead that might tell him where the resting place of Martin the Warrior could be found, or where he could regain possession of the ancient sword for his Abbey.

The defenders stood and cheered in the depression above what had once been Killconey's tunnel.

It is because you are kind and good.

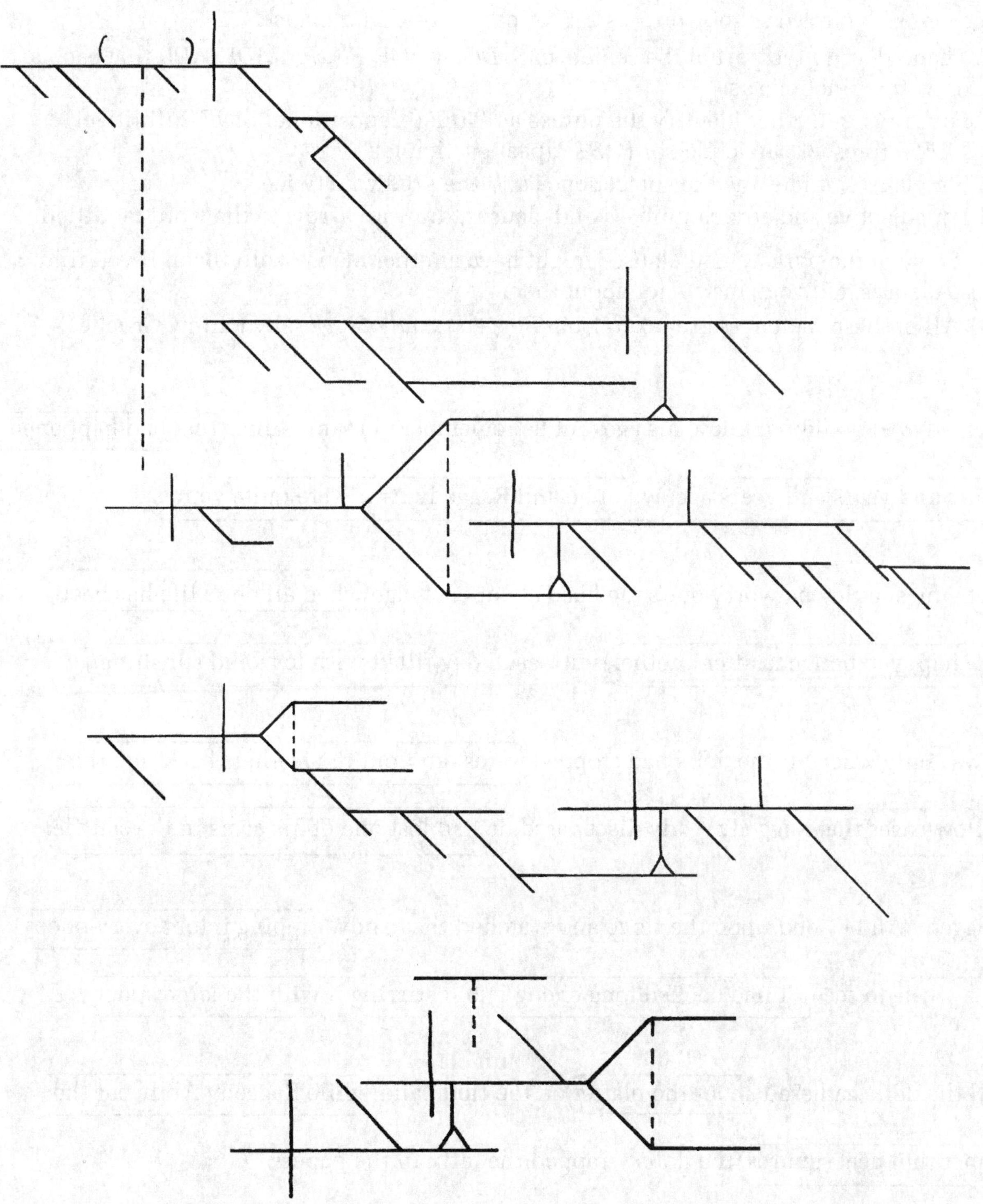

Exercise 113A: Phrases and Clauses

Identify each circled set of words as *PH* for phrase or *CL* for clause.

- Then, identify the part of the sentence (*S, DO, IO, OP, PN, PA, ADV, ADJ*) that each set of words functions as.
- For phrases, further identify the phrase as *PREP* (prepositional), *INF* (infinitive), *PRESP* (present participle), or *PASTP* (past participle).
- For clauses, underline the subject once and the predicate twice.
- For adjective and adverb phrases and clauses, draw an arrow to the word modified.

Some of the phrases and clauses might have another clause with them! If you find these clauses, tell your instructor about them.

All of these sentences are taken from *Raggedy Andy Stories*, by Johnny Gruelle.

Raggedy Andy did not know his age, but he remembered many things that had happened years and years and years ago when he and Raggedy Ann were quite young.

But why should one worry one's rag head about one's age when all one's life has been one happy experience after another, with each day filled with love and sunshine?

It was only when all the dolls had stopped to rest and put the feathers back into the pillow cases that Raggedy Andy discovered he had lost one of his arms in the scuffle.

Raggedy Andy stood upon the stove and watched the candy, dipping into it every once in a while to see if it had cooked long enough, and stirring it with the large spoon.

All the dolls gathered about the platter on the floor, and while Raggedy Andy cut the paper into neat squares, the dolls wrapped the taffy in the papers.

Then the taffy was put into a large bag, and with much pulling and tugging it was finally dragged up into the nursery, where a window faced out toward the street.

A wooden horse, covered with canton flannel and touched lightly with a paint brush dipped in black paint to give him a dappled gray appearance, was one of the presents.

Then, as all the dolls' merry laughter rang out, Raggedy Andy stopped rubbing his hands, and catching Raggedy Ann about the waist, he went skipping across the nursery floor with her, whirling so fast neither saw they had gone out through the door until it was too late.

All the dolls took turns putting their ears to the mouth of the beautiful shell.

The coloring consisted of dainty pinks, creamy whites and pale blues, all running together just as the coloring in an opal runs from one shade into another.

Exercise 113B: Diagramming

On your own paper, diagram every word of the following sentences, taken from *Sweets: A History of Candy*, by Tim Richardson.

In 1866 Fry launched a dark chocolate bar filled with a mint fondant: Fry's Chocolate Cream.

These bars are not modern versions of Fry's original plain bars, but of the second important innovation in chocolate-bar history: the bar that is not all chocolate.

In 1913, the Swiss chocolatier Jules Sechaud created the technology for making moulded chocolate shells into which fondant could be poured (as opposed to simply dipping hard centres in chocolate) and the chocolate assortment was transformed.

The citizens of every country believe that their own chocolate is "real" chocolate, and that anything else is an inferior version.

The breakfast tradition of chocolate with churros (long fried pastries) can be found in a cafe or two in many Spanish towns today, and the visitor used to pre-sweetened eating chocolate might be surprised to find that one adds sugar to this drink, as one might with coffee.

— LESSON 114 —

Restrictive and Non-Restrictive Modifying Clauses
Punctuating Modifying Clauses
Which and *That*

Why does the mechanism of the p-value, which seems so reasonable, work so very badly in this setting?

If the first throw is tails and the second is heads, an event which happens 1/4 of the time, Paul gets two ducats.

—From *How Not to Be Wrong: The Power of Mathematical Thinking*, by Jordan Ellenberg

A non-restrictive modifying clause describes the word that it modifies. Removing the clause doesn't change the essential meaning of the sentence. Only non-restrictive clauses should be set off by commas.

A restrictive modifying clause defines the word that it modifies. Removing the clause changes the essential meaning of the sentence.

I especially like the "Methods" section, which starts "One mature Atlantic Salmon (*Salmo salar*) participated in the fMRI study."

I especially like the "Methods" section which starts "One mature Atlantic Salmon (*Salmo salar*) participated in the fMRI study."

A noun clause takes the place of a noun. Noun clauses can be introduced by relative pronouns, relative adverbs, or subordinating conjunctions.

In principle, if you carry out a powerful enough study, you can find out, which it is.

The reason the 0.999 . . . problem is difficult is, that it brings our intuitions into conflict.

An appositive is a noun, noun phrase, or noun clause that usually follows another noun and renames or explains it. Appositives are set off by commas.

The Goldbach conjecture, that every even number greater than 2 is the sum of two primes, is another one that would have to be true if primes behaved like random numbers.

The chocolate brownies that
The chocolate brownies which

The chocolate brownies that were on the counter are gone now.

The chocolate brownies, which were made with olive oil instead of butter, have been sitting on the counter since lunch time.

When the relative pronoun introducing a modifying clause refers to a thing rather than a person, *which* introduces non-restrictive clauses and *that* introduces restrictive clauses.

"These are but shadows of the things that have been," said the Ghost.

It was shrouded in a deep black garment, which concealed its head, its face, its form, and left nothing of it visible save one outstretched hand.

He lived in chambers which had once belonged to his deceased partner.

At last she said, and in a steady, cheerful voice, that only faltered once, "I have known him walk with—I have known him walk with Tiny Tim upon his shoulder, very fast indeed."

—From *A Christmas Carol,* by Charles Dickens

That's certainly an impressive figure, but one which clearly indicates that the percentage doesn't mean quite what you're used to it meaning.

—From *How Not to Be Wrong,* by Jordan Ellenberg

He lived in chambers that had once belonged to his deceased partner.
At last she said, and in a steady, cheerful voice, which only faltered once, "I have known him walk with—I have known him walk with Tiny Tim upon his shoulder, very fast indeed."
That's certainly an impressive figure, but one that clearly indicates that the percentage doesn't mean quite what you're used to it meaning.

Exercise 114A: Restrictive and Non-Restrictive Adjective Clauses

Find every adjective clause in the following sentences, taken from *T. Rex and the Crater of Doom,* by Walter Alvarez, and then follow these steps:

a) Underline each adjective clause.
b) Circle the relative pronoun that introduces each clause.
c) Draw an arrow from the pronoun back to the word modified.
d) Label each clause as *R* for restrictive or *NR* for nonrestrictive.
e) Draw an asterisk or star next to each sentence that does not follow the which/that rule.

We come into this world in ignorance of everything that happened before we were born.

The normal circulation of the ocean, which delivered oxygen to its depths, slowed down as a result of the warming.

Looking back across the abyss of time which separates us from the Cretaceous, we can somehow feel nostalgia for a long-lost world, one which had its own rhythm and harmony.

The Solar System abounds in comets and asteroids, some even bigger than the one which was nearing Earth on that day 65 million years ago.

Even if the impact site had been on oceanic crust that had been subducted, tsunami erosion of the surrounding continental margins might reveal where the crater had been.

A few of these asteroids and comets are diverted into orbits which cross that of the Earth.

The 108-megaton impact of the comet which ended the Cretaceous was therefore equivalent to the explosion of 10,000 times the entire nuclear arsenal of the world (although the impact explosion was not nuclear).

Throughout the decade of the 1980s, more and more evidence was discovered that supported the impact theory for the KT extinction, but the impact site remained frustratingly elusive.

But land above sea level is the main site of erosion, which levels hills and mountains and removes sediment previously deposited.

Before long, unmanned probes to other planets and moons sent back images which made it clear that impact craters are the rule in the solar system, not the exception.

Exceptions like the scablands of eastern Washington, which seemed to require catastrophic causes, were explained away or ignored.

The energy escapes in the form of photons which ricochet around inside the star, sustaining the pressure that keeps the gravity of the star from shrinking it to a much smaller size.

It was a suggestion that sounded reasonable to astronomers, who have photographed supernovas, and to physicists, who understand the nuclear processes that make stars explode.

Exercise 114B: Dependent Clauses Within Dependent Clauses

The following sentences all contain dependent clauses that have other dependent clauses within them.

Underline the whole of each one of these dependent clauses (including additional dependent clauses that act as nouns or modifiers within it). Draw a box around the subject of the main dependent clause, and underline its predicate twice. In the right-hand margin, write the abbreviation for the part of the sentence that the main dependent clause is fulfilling: *N-SUB* for a noun clause acting as subject, *N-PN* for predicate nominative, *N-DO* for direct object, *N-OP* for object of the preposition, *N-APP* for appositive, and then *ADJ* for adjective and *ADV* for adverb. For adjective and adverb clauses, draw a line from the label back to the word in the main independent clause that is modified.

Then, circle any additional clauses that fall within the main dependent clause. Label each clause, above the circle, in the same way: *N-SUB* for a noun clause acting as subject, *N-PN* for predicate nominative, *N-DO* for direct object, *N-OP* for object of the preposition, *N-APP* for appositive, and then *ADJ* for adjective and *ADV* for adverb. For adjective and adverb clauses, draw a line from the label back to the word in the main dependent clause modified.

The first is done for you.

These are all taken from *Fire in the Sky: Cosmic Collisions, Killer Asteroids, and the Race to Defend Earth*, by Gordon L. Dillow.

ADV

Because meteorites are usually named for the town closest to where they are found, the meteorites collected by Volz and others came to be known as Canyon Diablo meteorites— ADV
and soon "Canyon Diablos" were featured in every important meteorite collection.

Barringer eventually learned that the meteorites found around the crater also contained small percentages of platinum and iridium, which are rare in the Earth's crust but relatively abundant in asteroids.

Strangely enough, while deciding that Meteor Crater was not the result of a cosmic impact, Gilbert got the notion that the craters on the Moon were the result of cosmic impacts, not volcanos as everyone thought.

I'll admit that given the breadth and scope of the universe, it seems likely that there is life somewhere beyond our own little planet.

It's been said that time transforms the improbable into the certain, that anything that can happen will happen, given enough time.

The problem is that because asteroids don't reflect much sunlight, they're hard to spot even with powerful telescopes, especially the smaller ones—which may be a good thing for our peace of mind.

It was at that moment that he came up with an idea, an almost breathtakingly audacious idea, one that he would pursue for the next quarter century.

For example, when a Great Comet appeared in 1910 a French scientist warned that when Earth passed through the comet's tail it would be enveloped in deadly cyanogen gas, which could "possibly snuff out all life on the planet."

Exercise 114C: Diagramming

On your own paper, diagram every word of the following three sentences. If you need help, ask your instructor.

These are from *The Asteroid Threat: Defending Our Planet from Deadly Near-Earth Objects*, by William E. Burrows. They describe the massive meteor that struck near the Russian city of Chelyabinsk on February 15, 2013.

The asteroid—which had become a meteor when it plunged into the atmosphere and then meteorites when the wall of air broke it into large fragments—was about fifty-six feet in diameter, weighed more than seven thousand tons, and was made of rock that was probably laced with nickel and iron.

The Comprehensive Nuclear-Test-Ban Treaty Organization reported that the sound wave registered on sensors from Greenland to Antarctica, making it the largest ever detected by its network.

The force of the explosion was deeply frightening to those who saw and felt it because it showed them, in the most dramatic way, how vulnerable living creatures and their habitats are to the indomitable violence of nature.

—LESSON 115—

Conditional Sentences

Conditional Sentences as Dependent Clauses
Conditional Sentences with Missing Words
Formal *If* Clauses

The sentences in this lesson are from *Pride & Prejudice & Zombies*, by Jane Austen and Seth Grahame-Smith.

simple past, active, subjunctive

I have nothing to say against him; he has felled many a zombie; and if he had the fortune he

simple present, active, modal,

ought to have, I should think you could not do better. SECOND

Active verbs are active or passive in voice.
State-of-being verbs do not have voice.
Subjunctive verbs express situations that are unreal, wished for, or uncertain.

If my children are silly, I must hope to be always sensible of it. ____________

If I had known as much this morning I certainly would not have called him. __________

If I were not afraid of judging harshly, I should be almost tempted to demand satisfaction.

____

First conditional sentences express circumstances that might actually happen.
The predicate of the condition clause is in a present tense.
The predicate of the consequence clause is an imperative or is in a present or future tense.

Second conditional sentences express circumstances that are contrary to reality.
The predicate of the condition clause is in a past tense.

The predicate of the consequence clause is in the simple or progressive present modal tense.

Third conditional sentences express past circumstances that never happened.
The predicate of the condition clause is in the perfect past tense.
The predicate of the consequence clause is in any modal tense.

In her postscript it was added that if Mr. Bingley and his sister pressed them to stay

longer, she could spare them.

However, I recollected afterwards that if he had been prevented going, the wedding need

not be put off.

If he fears me, why come hither?

If he no longer cares for me, why silent?

Should you wish to, meet me in the drawing room.

Formal conditional sentences drop *if* from the condition clause and reverse the order of the subject and helping verb.

Were you not otherwise agreeable, I should be forced to remove your tongue with my saber.

If he fears me, why come hither?

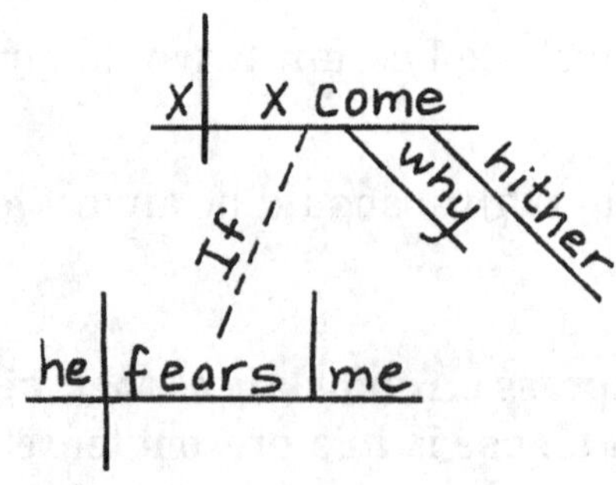

If he no longer cares for me, why silent?

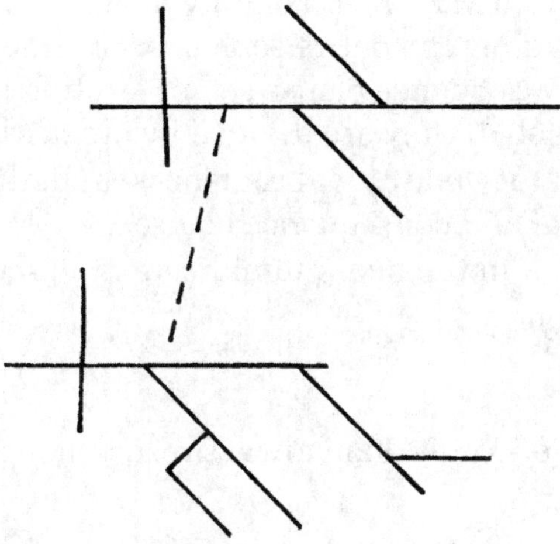

Should you wish, meet me in the drawing room.

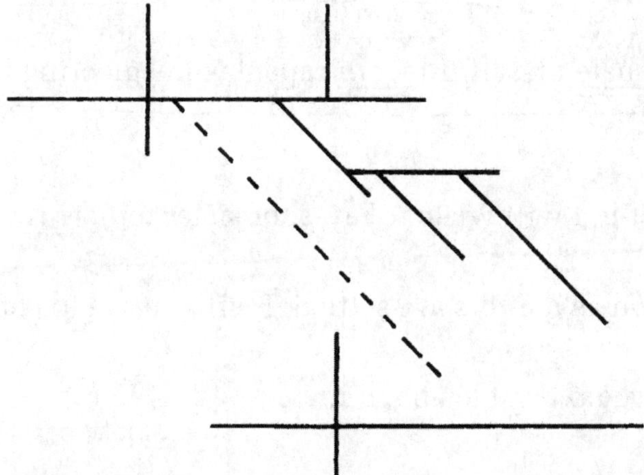

Were you not otherwise agreeable, I should be forced to remove your tongue with my saber.

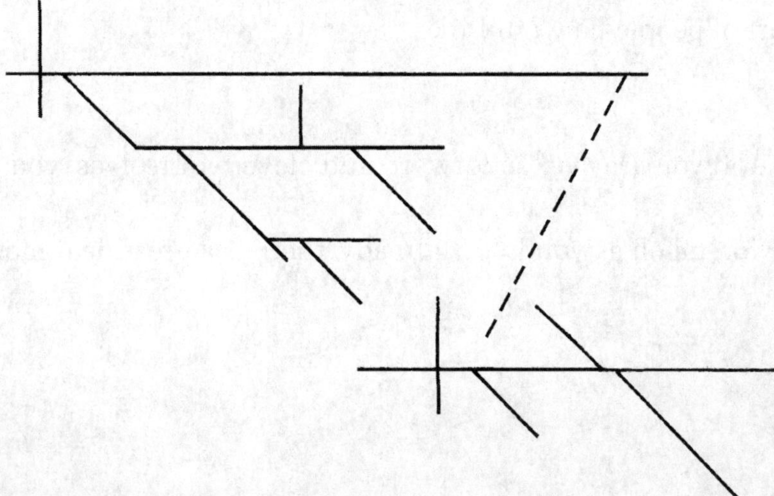

Exercise 115A: Conditional Clauses

In the following sentences from *Mansfield Park*, by Jane Austen, circle every conditional sentence. This may mean circling the entire sentence, circling only the part of it that makes up the conditional-consequence clause set, or circling the conditional and consequence clauses separately if they are divided by other words.

After you have circled the conditional sentences, underline twice and then parse the predicate in each conditional and consequence clause.

Finally, write a *1*, *2*, or *3* in the blank to indicate *first*, *second*, or *third conditional*. The first is done for you.

Whatever I can do, as you well know, I am always ready enough to do for the good of those I love; and, though I could never feel for this little girl the hundredth part of the regard I bear your own dear children, nor consider her, in any respect, so much my own, I should hate myself if I were capable of neglecting her. (simple present, active, modal — should hate; simple present, state-of-being, subjunctive — were) 1

So, if you are not against it, I will write to my poor sister tomorrow, and make the proposal; and, as soon as matters are settled, I will engage to get the child to Mansfield; you shall have no trouble about it. ______

If he knew them better, he would value their society as it deserves; for they are in fact exactly the sort of people he would like. ______

And remember that, if you are ever so forward and clever yourselves, you should always be modest; for, much as you know already, there is a great deal more for you to learn. ______

If I could suppose my aunt really to care for me, it would be delightful to feel myself of consequence to anybody. ______

Dear sister, if you consider my unhappy state, how can she be any comfort to me? ______

If I could wish it for my own sake, I would not do so unjust a thing by the poor girl. ______

There will be little rubs and disappointments everywhere, and we are all apt to expect too much; but then, if one scheme of happiness fails, human nature turns to another; if the first calculation is wrong, we make a second better. ______

If I were you, I should not think of the expense. ______

Now, at Sotherton we have a good seven hundred, without reckoning the water meadows; so that I think, if so much could be done at Compton, we need not despair. ______

If she had been riding before, I should not have asked it of her. ______

Should her disposition be really bad, we must not, for our own children's sake, continue her in the family; but there is no reason to expect so great an evil. ______

My dear Edmund, if you were but in orders now, you might perform the ceremony directly. ______

Don't act yourself, if you do not like it, but don't expect to govern everybody else. ______

And though Dr. Grant is most kind and obliging to me, and though he is really a gentleman, and, I dare say, a good scholar and clever, and often preaches good sermons, and is very respectable, *I* see him to be an indolent, selfish *bon vivant*, who must have his palate consulted in everything; who will not stir a finger for the convenience of any one; and who, moreover, if the cook makes a blunder, is out of humour with his excellent wife. ______

Exercise 115B: Diagramming

On your own paper, diagram every word of the following sentences from *Mansfield Park*. Do your best, and ask your instructor for help if you need it. (You might want to use some scratch paper as well.)

If he is to die, there will be two poor young men less in the world; and with a fearless face and bold voice would I say to any one, that wealth and consequence could fall into no hands more deserving of them.

Were you even less pleasing—supposing her not to love you already (of which, however, I can have little doubt)—you would be safe.

A most scandalous, ill-natured rumour has just reached me, and I write, dear Fanny, to warn you against giving the least credit to it, should it spread into the country.

> **Note to Student:** This sentence has an unusual connection between condition and consequence! Do your best to find it, and then ask your instructor for an explanation.

—LESSON 116—

Words That Can Be Multiple Parts of Speech
Interrogatives
Demonstratives
Relative Adverbs and Subordinating Conjunctions

Exercise 116A: Words Acting as Multiple Parts of Speech

Use these sentences, taken from *The Middle Moffat*, by Eleanor Estes, to identify the parts of speech that the bolded words can serve as. The first blank is filled in for you. Fill in the blanks with the correct labels from the following list:

conjunction	interjection	preposition	adverb
adjective	noun	pronoun	verb

The **middle** Moffat was going to be the **middle** bear. adjective

The **middle** of the earth was a mysterious place like the **middle** of the night, and the **middle** of the ocean, too, where there very likely were waterspouts, whirlpools, and mermaids. ______

Mama was making all the costumes, **even** the bear heads. ______

Maybe she had grown up some, too, and she hadn't **even** known it. ______

Of course, Mama would have to sit out front there with the regular people, **even** though she had made the costumes. ______

To **even** things up, Janey could join the basketball team. ______

She was pointing **right** straight at that little parlor organ. ______

She hoped she was doing some good for the **right** side. ______

Sylvie could play the organ with **both** hands and the hands played different parts. ______

They always went to school together and they came home together, too, **both** at noon time and in the afternoon. ______

For weeks the teacher had talked of little **else** in school. ______

But where **else** could she keep the photographs of all her nephews? ______

She would try it on somebody **else**. ______

And **all** winter Joey had shamefully neglected the oldest inhabitant's furnace. ______

Soon there it was, **all** whole again. ____________

"Boy, oh, boy" was **all** he could say. ____________

Jane sat in the big armchair, her legs flung over **one** of the arms. ____________

One night there were lamb chops for dinner. ____________

All the same she did feel scared **inside**. ____________

Jane's laugh was more of an **inside** job. ____________

She looked **around** to see if anybody else had heard what he said. ____________

Usually when Wallie Bangs marched **around** the house he wouldn't even notice them. ____________

She watched Jane all the way **up** the street, even forgetting her lollipop. ____________

But the ball shot **up** and **up** and clean through the basket again, as beautifully as the first time. ____________

Besides, she really owed him a visit **since** he had come to her organ recital. ____________

But Nancy got mad at her and had not spoken **since**. ____________

She ran down the stairs and out the **back** door, slamming it. ____________

Big boys at the **back** of the hall put their fingers in their mouths and whistled. ____________

Jane wished they'd come **back**. ____________

---

who, whom, whose, what, which

Interrogative pronouns take the place of nouns in questions.
Interrogative adjectives modify nouns.

Interrogative Pronouns	**Interrogative Adjectives**
Who was Dragging Canoe?	Whose side was Dragging Canoe on?
With whom did Dragging Canoe fight?	What war did he fight?
What did Dragging Canoe do?	Which tribe did Dragging Canoe belong to?
Which of his countrymen followed him?	

In the American Revolution, Dragging Canoe fought against the colonists who were rebelling against the British.

Dragging Canoe and his brother chiefs, whom he had known for many years, joined together and allied with the British.

Dragging Canoe told his tribesmen to consider the case of the Delaware, whose land had been swallowed by the American colonies.

At first, the American colonists did not know what Dragging Canoe was planning.

Dragging Canoe led attacks on the settlements which were in southeast North America.

The interrogative words *who, whom, whose, what*, and *which* can also serve as relative pronouns in adjective clauses or introductory words in noun clauses.

What was the name of Dragging Canoe's father? ____________________

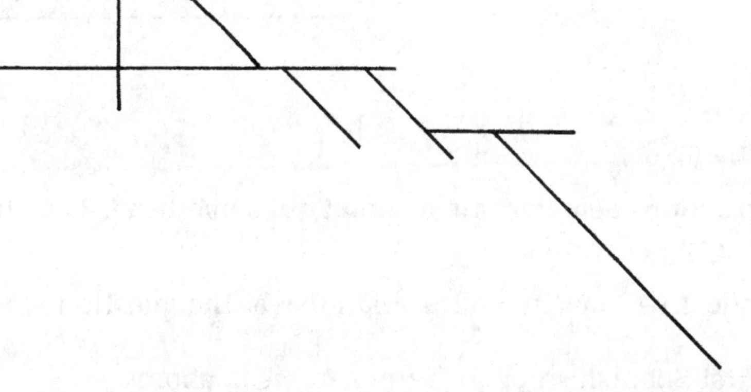

What five towns did Dragging Canoe build? ____________________

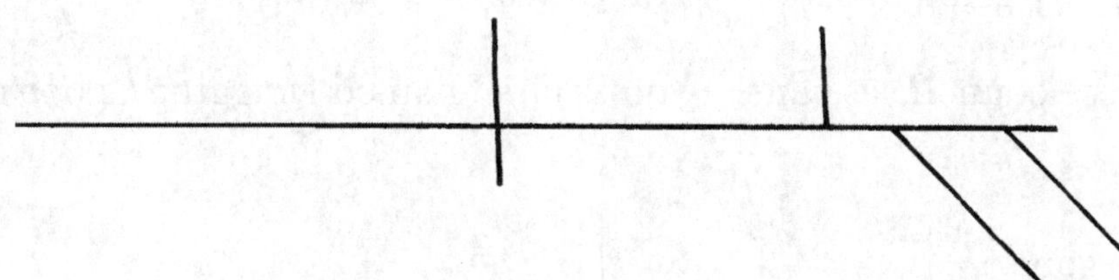

Dragging Canoe did not believe what the governor of North Carolina told him. ____________________

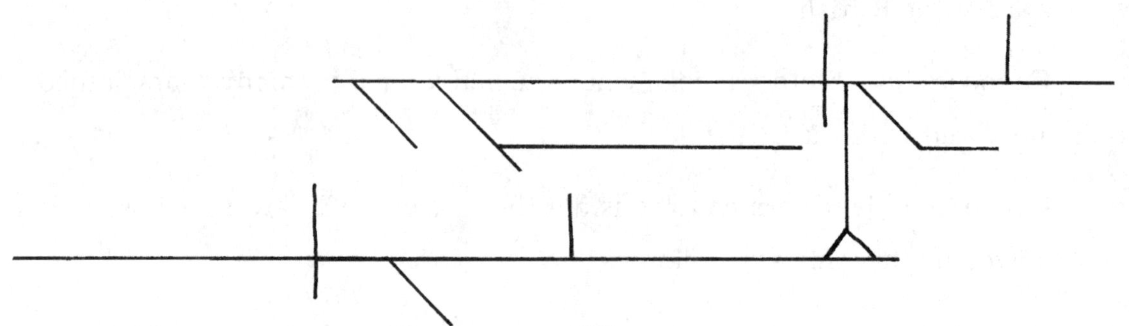

Dragging Canoe led the Cherokees who refused to stay neutral. ______________________

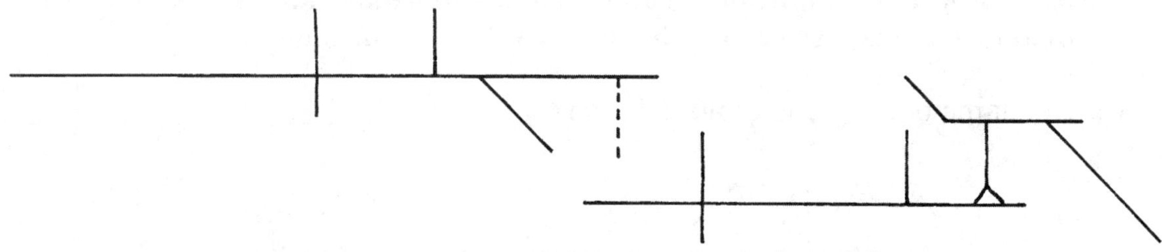

this, that, these, those

Demonstrative pronouns demonstrate or point out something. They take the place of a single word or a group of words.

Demonstrative adjectives modify nouns and answer the question *which one*.

Those were the first Spanish ships to touch American shores.

While a young boy, this future chief wanted to accompany his father, Attakullakulla, and a Cherokee war party going to battle the Shawnee.

During one of these council sessions, a young chief named Dragging Canoe exploded into prominence.

Now that hope is gone.

This was the first invasion of the Middle Towns by an enemy force on record.
—From Pat Alderman, *Nancy Ward: Cherokee Chieftainess, Dragging Canoe: Cherokee-Chickamauga War Chief*

He had come to the council because of his admiration for that great chief.

They set off at a rapid pace, little guessing that a silent scout followed them.

That would be a catastrophe for the Cherokee and their allies.

An adverb describes a verb, an adjective, or another adverb.
Adverbs tell how, when, where, how often, and to what extent.

Relative adverbs introduce adjective clauses and refer back to a place, time, or reason in the independent clause.

where, when, why

(The remaining sentences in the lesson are slightly adapted from *Trail of Tears: The Rise and Fall of the Cherokee Nation*, by John Ehle.)

It was the orderly village to which he was heir, and where his mother was the pivot of the world.

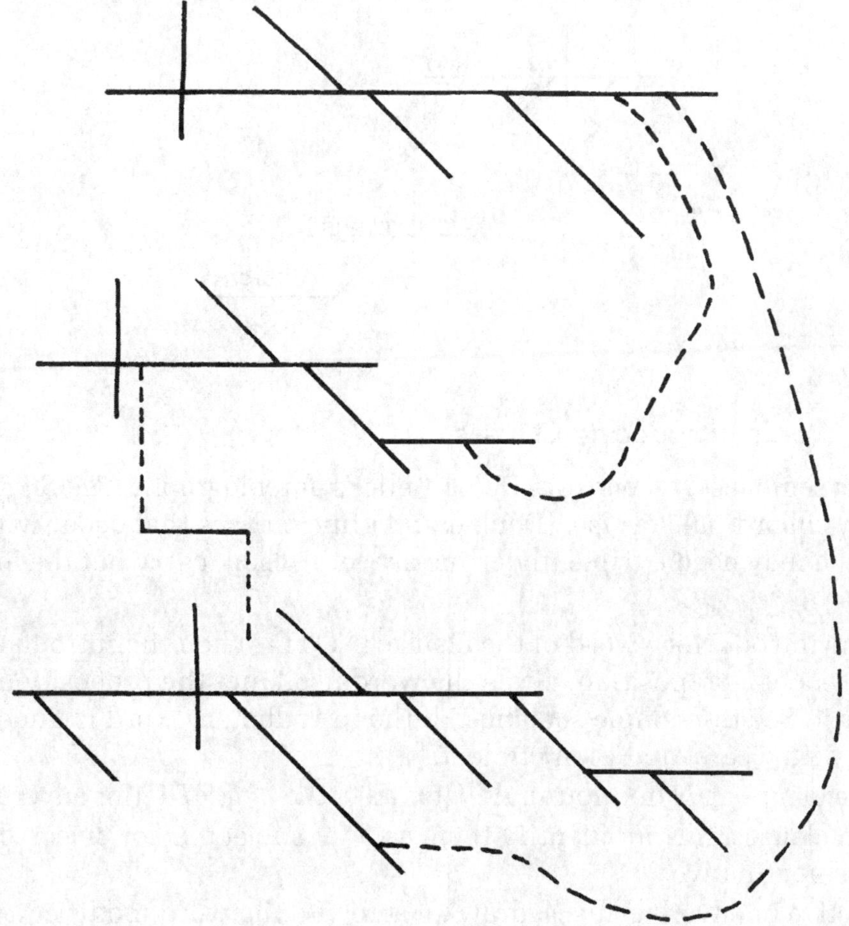

My heart rejoices when I look upon you.

Adverbs can act as subordinating conjunctions when they connect adverb clauses to a verb, adjective, or adverb in the main clause.

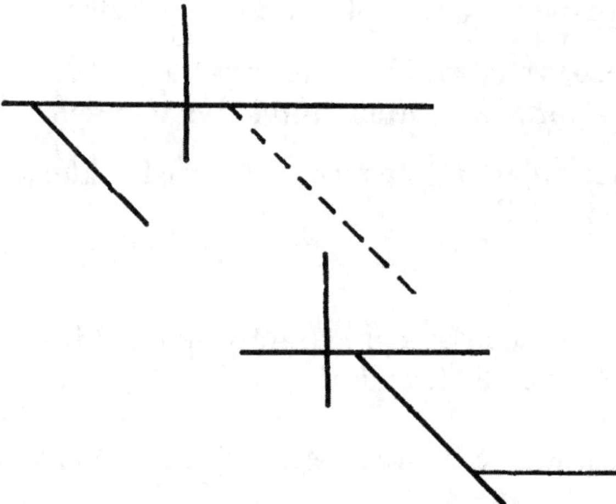

Their land was taken away because they fought for the British.

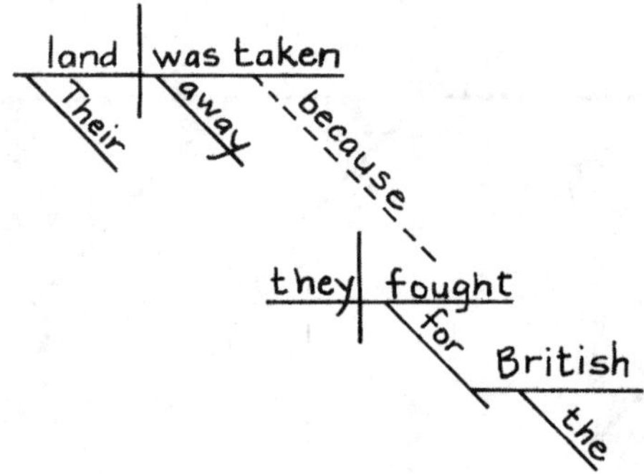

Exercise 116B: Words Introducing Clauses

In the following sentences, taken from Helen Keller's autobiography *The Story of My Life*, underline every subordinate clause. (Double underline clauses that occur within other clauses—and you may need a triple underline as well!) Then, carry out the following steps:

a) Circle the introductory word of the clause. (NOTE: When the introductory word is the object of a preposition, circle the word itself, not the preposition that precedes it. See the sample sentence.) If the introductory word is understood, insert it with a caret and then circle it.
b) Label the clause as *N* (for noun), *ADJ* (for adjective), or *ADV* (for adverb).
c) For noun clauses, further identify them as *S* for subject, *O* for object, or *PN* for predicate nominative.
d) For adjective or adverb clauses, draw an arrow to the word modified.
e) Finally, label the introductory word as one of the following: *RP* for relative pronoun, *RAdj* for relative adjective (a relative pronoun functioning as an adjective and introducing an adjective clause), *RAdv* for relative adverb, *SC* for subordinating conjunction, or *A-SC* for adverb functioning as a subordinating conjunction.

The first sentence is done for you, but notice that several selections contain more than one sentence—be sure to carry out these steps for each one!

SC ADJ

My mother solved the problem by giving it as her wish that I should be called after her

RAdj ADJ

mother, whose maiden name was Helen Everett. But in the excitement of carrying me to church my father lost the name on the way, very naturally, since it was one in which he had declined to have a part.

Then, in the dreary month of February, came the illness which closed my eyes and ears and plunged me into the unconsciousness of a new-born baby.

I especially remember the tenderness with which my mother tried to soothe me in my wailing hours of fret and pain, and the agony and bewilderment with which I awoke after a tossing half sleep, and turned my eyes, so dry and hot, to the wall away from the once-loved light, which came to me dim and yet more dim each day.

At five I learned to fold and put away the clean clothes when they were brought in from the laundry, and I distinguished my own from the rest. I knew by the way my mother and aunt dressed when they were going out, and I invariably begged to go with them.

It seemed as if the spirit of spring had passed through the summer-house.

Her words puzzled me very much because I did not then understand anything unless I touched it.

It was because she seized the right moment to impart knowledge that made it so pleasant and acceptable to me.

How much of my delight in all beautiful things is innate, and how much is due to her influence, I can never tell.

That night, after I had hung my stocking, I lay awake a long time, pretending to be asleep and keeping alert to see what Santa Claus would do when he came.

I also remember the beach, where for the first time I played in the sand.

It seemed to me that there could be nothing more beautiful than the sun, whose warmth makes all things grow.

What joy it was to lose myself in that garden of flowers, to wander happily from spot to spot, until, coming suddenly upon a beautiful vine, I recognized it by its leaves and blossoms, and knew it was the vine which covered the tumble-down summer-house at the farther end of the garden!

Exercise 116C: Diagramming

(You didn't think you'd escape diagramming, did you?)

On your own paper, diagram every word of the following sentences from the memoir *Unbowed*, by Nobel Peace Prize winner Wangari Maathai.

If you need help, ask your instructor.

For rural people, traveling to town was a novelty and you didn't go unless you had something to do, since it was not a place to hang around.

Those who had not embraced Christianity, who still held on to and advocated for local customs, were called Kikuyus, while those who had converted were called *athomi*.

> **Note to Student:** You'll have to think outside the box to diagram this one! Do your best, and ask your instructor for help if needed.

Literally translated, this means "people who read."

When independence came and there was a program through which people could purchase land, Kikuyus like my father were in a position to buy some of the settlers' farms on which many had lived as squatters.

I had never anticipated that I would be discriminated against on the basis of my gender as often as I was, or that I could be belittled even while making a substantial contribution to society.

WEEK 31

Filling Up the Corners

After the feast (more or less) came the Speech. Most of the company were, however, now in a tolerant mood, at that delightful stage which they called "filling up the corners." They were sipping their favourite drinks, and nibbling at their favourite dainties, and their fears were forgotten. They were prepared to listen to anything, and to cheer at every full stop.

—J. R. R. Tolkien, *The Fellowship of the Ring*

— LESSON 117 —

Interrogative Adverbs
Noun Clauses
Forming Questions
Affirmations and Negations
Double Negatives

An adverb describes a verb, an adjective, or another adverb.
Adverbs tell how, when, where, how often, and to what extent.

Relative adverbs introduce adjective clauses and refer back to a place, time, or reason in the independent clause.

where, when, why

I found a shop where I could buy cheese and chocolate.

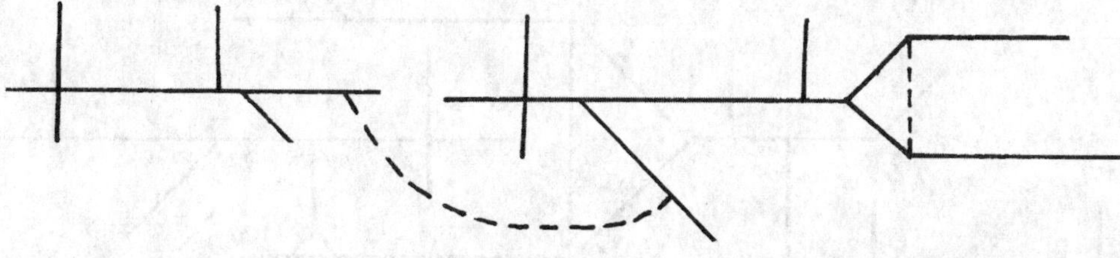

Where did you get the cheese and chocolate?

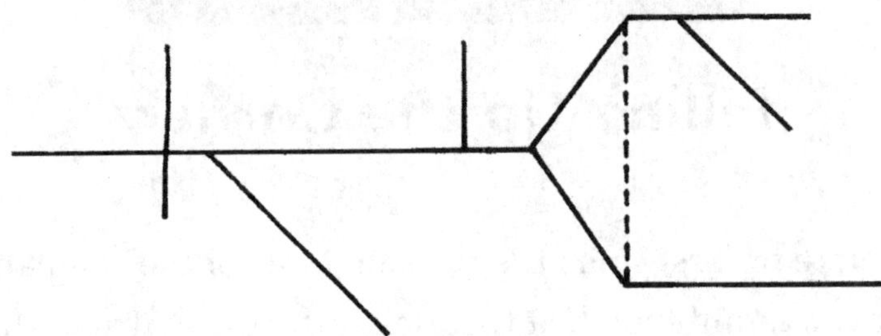

He asked me where I got the cheese and chocolate.

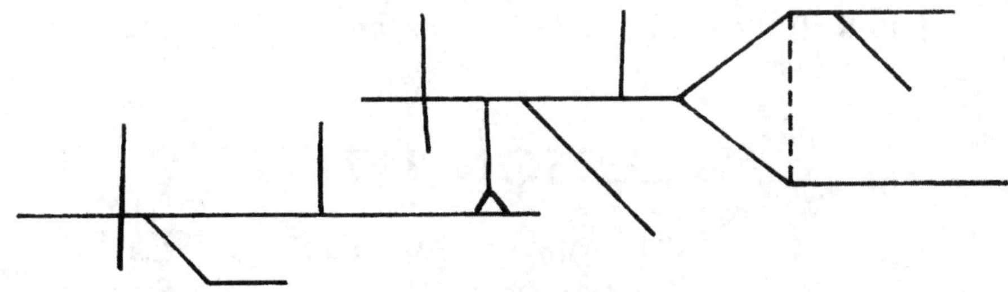

An interrogative adverb asks a question.

where, when, why, how

The interrogative adverbs can also introduce noun clauses.

I desired to know how this thing came to Gollum, and how long he had possessed it.

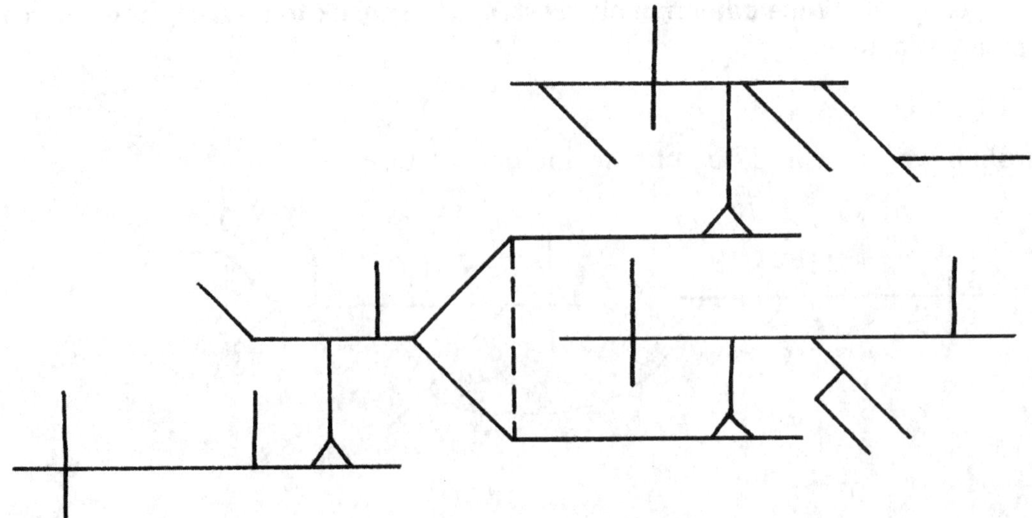

How do the Wise know that this ring is his?

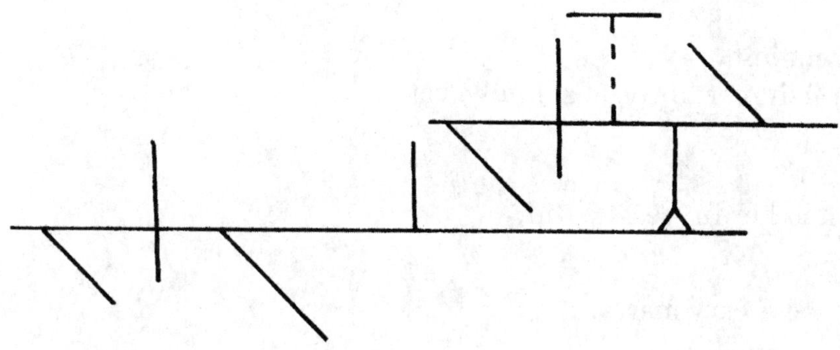

You are hungry.
Are you hungry?

You would like a big bowl of pozole.
Would you like a big bowl of pozole?

Use the helping verbs *do, does,* and *did* to form negatives, ask questions, and provide emphasis.

He fixed green pozole with sliced avocados.
Did he fix green pozole with sliced avocados?

Simple Present

I do	we do
you do	you do
he, she it, does	they do

Simple Past

I did	we did
you did	you did
he, she it did	they did

They love to nibble on chalupas.
Do they love to nibble on chalupas?

Who is bringing the bread pudding with flaming brandy?

What kind of frosting are you using for the cake?

When will the mangos be ripe enough to make mango cake?

Which limes did you use in the lime pudding?

Whom have you invited to the party?

How many loaves of challah did you bake?

Whose presents are those?

An affirmation states what is true or what exists.
A negation states what is not true or does not exist.

Adverbs of affirmation
yes, surely, definitely, certainly, absolutely, very

Did he invite her in?
And he invited her in; yes, he did.

Were they merry?
Surely they were very merry.

Was the roast chicken ready?
The roast chicken was definitely ready to eat.

Were the mushrooms good?
The mushrooms were absolutely delicious.

Adverbs of negation	**Adjective of negation**
no, not, never	no

Did anyone go hungry?
No man, woman, or child went hungry.

When did they stop feasting?
They did not stop feasting until well after sundown.

How much merriment was there?
Never was there so much merriment.

There is not no doubt.

I haven't heard no good of such folk.

I don't know nothing about jewels.

Do not use two adverbs or adjectives of negation together.

Exercise 117A: Identifying Adverbs, Interrogative and Demonstrative Pronouns and Adjectives, and Relatives

In the following sentences, from *The Adventures of Sherlock Holmes*, by Arthur Conan Doyle, follow these steps (note that some double underlining might be required):

a) Label each bolded word as one of the following:

ADV for adverb

Draw an arrow from the adverb to the word modified.
If the adverb also introduces a clause, underline the clause.

PRO for pronoun

If the pronoun has an antecedent, label the antecedent as *ANT*. If the pronoun introduces a clause, underline the clause.

Label each pronoun as *S* for subject, *PN* for predicate nominative, *DO* for direct object, *IO* for indirect object, *OP* for object of the preposition, or *ADJ* (see below).

ADJ for adjective

Draw an arrow from the adjective to the word modified. If the adjective introduces a clause, underline the clause.

SC for subordinating conjunction

Underline the dependent clause introduced by the conjunction.

b) Label each underlined clause as *ADV-C* for adverb clause, *ADJ-C* for adjective clause, or *N-C* for noun clause.

c) Draw an arrow from each *ADV-C* and *ADJ-C* clause back to the word modified. Label each *N-C* noun clause as *S* for subject, *DO* for direct object, *IO* for indirect object, or *OP* for object of the preposition.

d) Label each *N-C* noun clause as *S* for subject, *DO* for direct object, *IO* for indirect object, or *OP* for object of the preposition.

The first is done for you.

ADV-C
ADV
Stay **where** you are.

I was half-dragged up to the altar, and before I knew **where** I was I found myself mumbling responses **which** were whispered in my ear, and vouching for things of **which** I knew nothing, and generally assisting in the secure tying up of Irene Adler, spinster, to Godfrey Norton, bachelor.

Where could I find him?

What do you make of it all?

I was still balancing the matter in my mind **when** a hansom cab drove up to Briony Lodge, and a gentleman sprang out.

And **when** will you call?

But, after all, if he is satisfied, **why** should I put ideas in his head?

Mr. Merryweather is the chairman of directors, and he will explain to you **that** there are reasons **why** the more daring criminals of London should take a considerable interest in this cellar at present.

But then, **when** I found **how** I had betrayed myself, I began to think.

I do not know **how** the bank can thank you or repay you.

But **how** could you guess **what** the motive was?

It proved to be **that** of a young gentleman **whose** name, as it appears from an envelope **which** was found in his pocket, was John Openshaw, and **whose** residence is near Horsham.

Whose house is it?

It is clear **that** Mrs. Toller knows more about **this** matter than anyone else.

If there's police-court business over **this**, you'll remember **that** I was the one **that** stood your friend, and **that** I was Miss Alice's friend too.

I shall stand behind **this** crate, and do you conceal yourselves behind **those**.

The man **who** entered was a sturdy, middle-sized fellow, some thirty years of age, clean-shaven, and sallow-skinned, with a bland, insinuating manner, and a pair of wonderfully sharp and penetrating grey eyes.

But if he is innocent, **who** has done it?

And yet I question, sir, whether, in all your experience, you have ever listened to a more mysterious and inexplicable chain of events than **those which** have happened in my own family.

All emotions, and **that** one particularly, were abhorrent to his cold, precise but admirably balanced mind.

Exercise 117B: Forming Questions

On your own paper, rewrite the following statements as questions.

Use each of the three methods for forming questions (adding an interrogative pronoun, reversing the subject and helping verb, or adding the helping verb *do, does*, or *did* in front of the subject and adjusting the tense of the main verb) at least once. You may change tenses, add or subtract words, or alter the statements in any other necessary ways, as long as the meaning remains the same.

These statements are all adapted from the titles of classic pop and rock songs! When you have transformed your statements into questions, compare them with the originals.

I should stay or I should go.
Someone let the dogs out.
You can feel the love tonight.
You have ever seen the rain.
I will see you again, at some point.
The frequency is something, Kenneth.
You hear what I hear.
It would be nice.
You have done something for me lately.
You love me.
The flowers have gone somewhere.

Exercise 117C: Affirmations and Negations

On your own paper,

- Rewrite each of the following affirmative statements as a negation, using one adverb or adjective of negation. You may add or subtract words or change tenses as necessary.
- Rewrite each of the following negative statements as an affirmative, using at least one adverb of affirmation.
- Rewrite any double negation as an affirmative, also using at least one adverb of affirmation.

When you are finished, compare your answers with the original sentences, which were all taken from *The Return of Sherlock Holmes*, by Sir Arthur Conan Doyle.

She was engaged to me.

And as you value your life, go across the moor.

Your case has no features of great interest.

The recital of these events must not be painful to you.

If we cannot prove it this would turn Lestrade's argument against himself.

It was evident that we had not miscalculated his movements.

Outside, the street was not deserted.

I am certainly to blame, Mr. Holmes.

The fugitives definitely did use the road.

His Grace is very friendly to anyone.

— LESSON 118 —

Diagramming Affirmations and Negations
Yet More Words That Can Be Multiple Parts of Speech

Comparisons Using *Than*
Comparisons Using *As*

Are you ready for your lesson?
Absolutely.
Do you remember the definition of a noun?
Definitely.
How sure are you?
Very.
Have you forgotten it?
No.

Will you ever forget it?
Never.

Affirmative and negative adverbs can also act as interjections.

Never

Absolutely

I can be **very** deaf when I need.

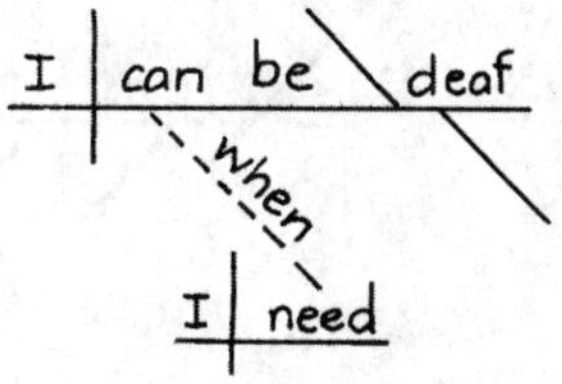

I | can be \ deaf
when
I | need

Yes, I will paint you, Juanico.

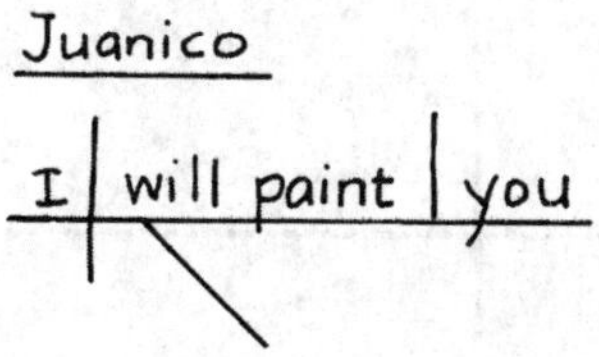

Juanico

I | will paint | you

You will **never** be beaten again.

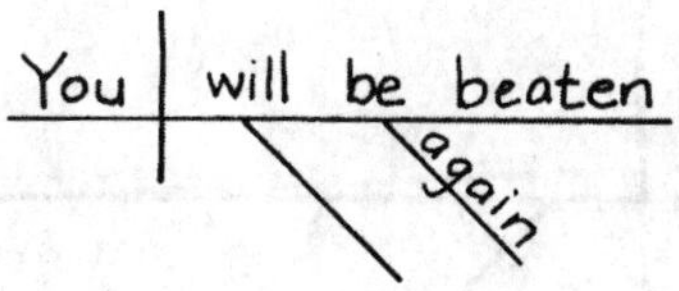

You | will be beaten
again

I am **no** longer a slave.

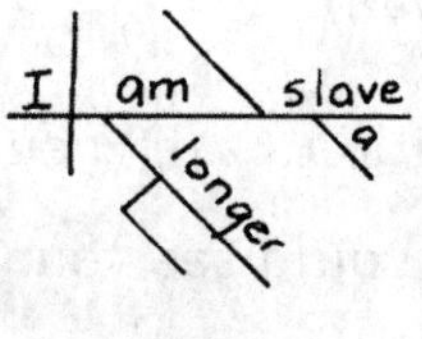

I | am \ slave
a
longer

(From *I, Juan de Pareja*, by Elizabeth Borton de Treviño)

Yes, I said.

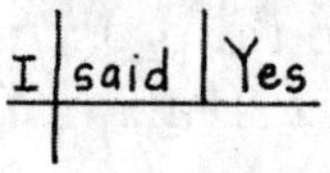

I | said | Yes

He's unbeatable and drops the dehuller with a fat Yes.

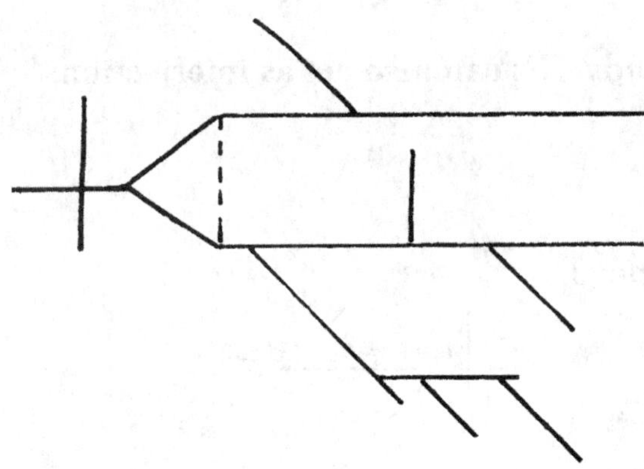

(From *Drown*, by Junot Diaz)

Father might say no.

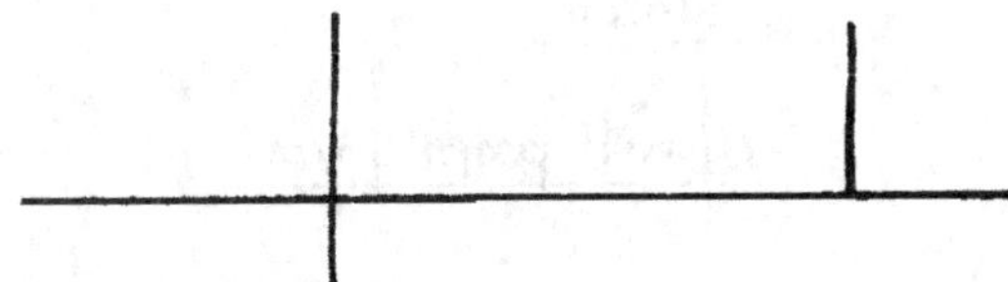

It has no shoestrings.

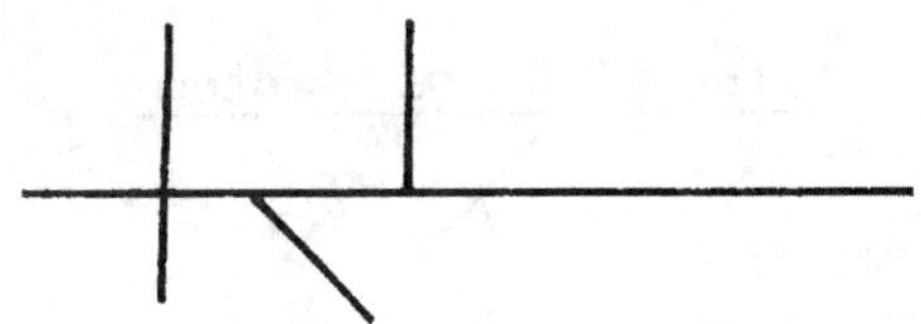

(From *The Dreamer*, by Pam Muñoz Ryan)

QC: quasi-coordinator PREP: preposition ADV: adverb SC: subordinating conjunction

The stone was black and shiny, so you could see your reflection as well as the blooming trees and the clouds in the sky.
—From *Return to Sender*, by Julia Alvarez

Mamadre nodded and smiled as she left the room.

As my partner, how do you think we should proceed?
—From *The Dreamer*, by Pam Muñoz Ryan

When we arrived, nothing was as promised.
—From *Esperanza Rising*, by Pam Muñoz Ryan

His affections became poems, as warm and supple as the wool of a well-loved sheep.
—From *The Dreamer*, by Pam Muñoz Ryan

When *than* is used in a comparison and introduces a clause with understood elements, it is acting as a subordinating conjunction.

That wool is warmer than my wool.

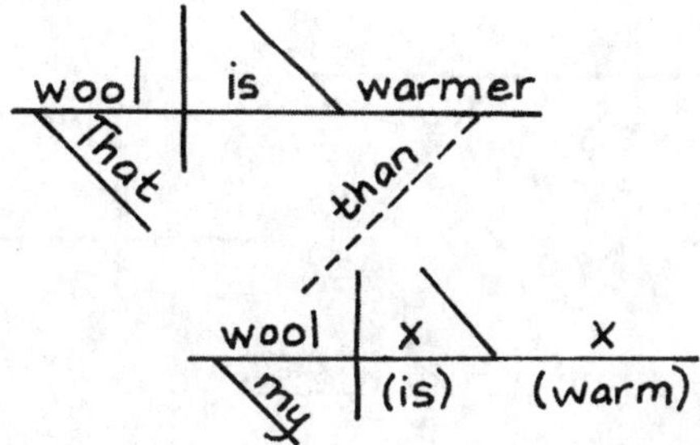

His affections became poems, as warm and supple as the wool of a well-loved sheep.
—From *The Dreamer,* by Pam Muñoz Ryan

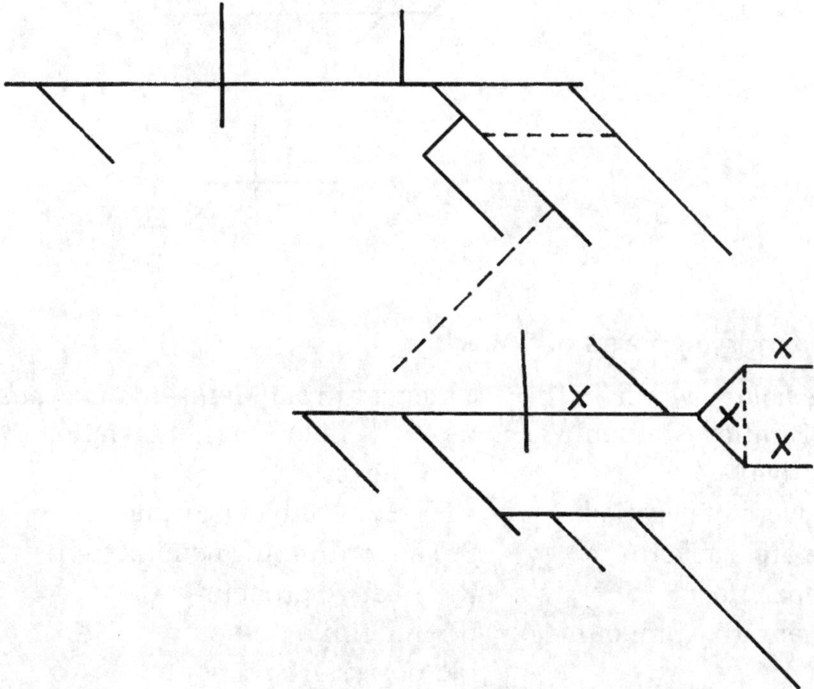

I did as he asked.

He had the same concerns as you have had.

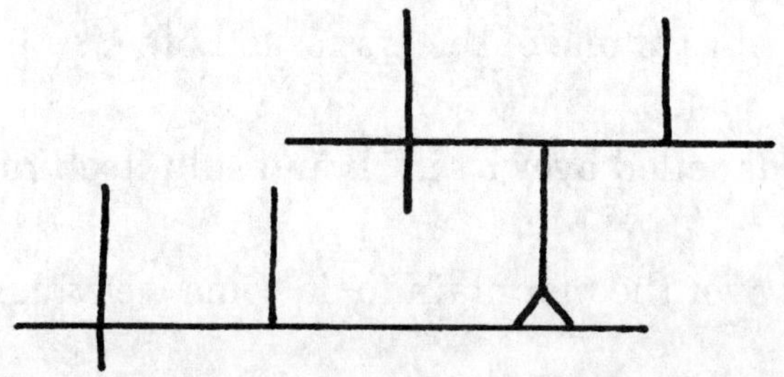

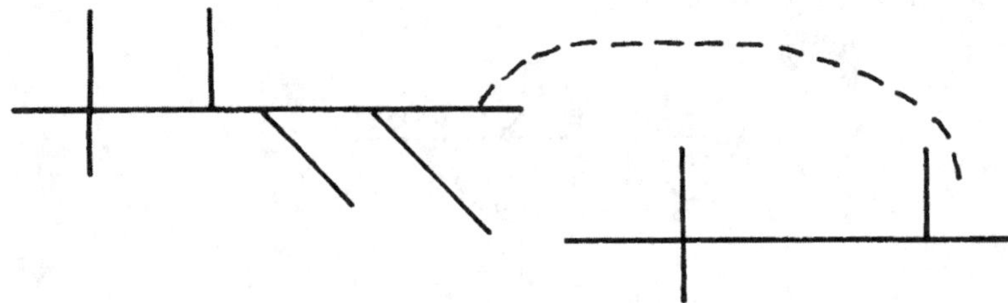

The farmer struggled with the same difficulties as you.

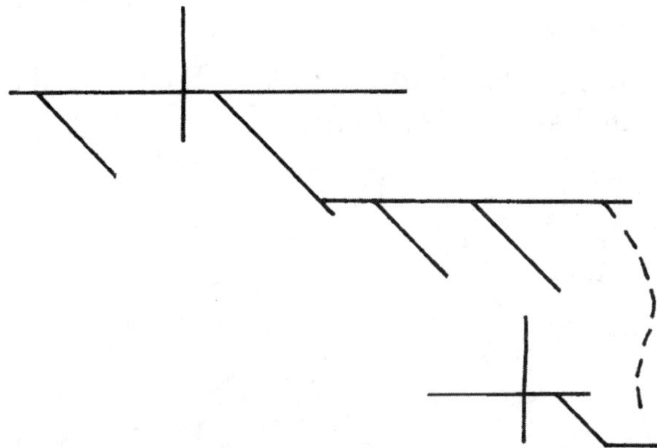

Exercise 118A: Identifying Parts of Speech

Label each of the bolded words in these sentences (from *Myths and Legends from Korea*, edited by James Huntley Grayson) with one of the following abbreviations.

ADJ: adjective
ADV: adverb
ADV-N: adverb of negation
ADV-A: adverb of affirmation
ADV-R: relative adverb
SC: subordinating conjunction
PREP: preposition
RP: relative pronoun
DP: demonstrative pronoun
IP: indefinite pronoun
N: noun
PP: possessive pronoun

Where a subordinating conjunction introduces a comparison clause with missing words, draw a caret and insert the missing words.

As he fell to the ground, his body transformed **into** the body of a great tiger.

The feather of **one** of the wings of **one** of the cranes fell **off**.

With that, one of the gourds rolled **over by** itself and split itself **into two**.

One day, the mother went **over** the mountain to do some weaving.

Then he was able to shoot the handle **off** a pitcher of water **without** breaking the pitcher.

Soon, Rabbit got **onto** the turtle's back and set **off on** the journey to the Dragon Palace.

The throat of the tiger was **as** dark **as** a tunnel.

He lived for **three** years **as** a refugee in the house of Morok.

The king put **on** the ragged clothes **which** the stranger had left **behind** and went **back** to his palace.

The old woman hid the boy **behind** the folding screen.

The front legs were short and the **back** legs were long.

Upon coming **back** from drawing water, she followed the tracks of the two brothers.

There was a tortoise on **whose back** a chant was inscribed.

In the **end**, there were **no** noises.

When he is born, you will **no longer** be **lonely**.

Before setting **forth**, however, he **quite** forgot to divest himself of his garments.

The two ravens formed **quite** a contrast!

That widow worked **so** hard raising her young children **that** her cold bones became coarse.

I asked the beggar why **this** should be **so**.

If an animal can have compassion, **so** should a human.

So saying, he fell **down** in worship in the **middle** of the road.

Wash your hands in the **middle** part of the river.

She floated **down** the river to the mountains in the east.

Exercise 118B: Diagramming

On your own paper, diagram every word of the following sentences from *Chinese Fairy Tales and Fantasies*, edited by Moss Roberts and Sengyi Zheng. Ask your instructor for help if you need it.

The giant took him to a cave containing mounds of such things as tiger sinew, deer tail, and elephant tusk.

The giant lowered his head as if he were thinking; then he nodded as if he understood.

He was as tall as a tree, with eyes like pots, mouth like a basin, and teeth a foot long.

Yes, how did you know?

And each time she answered, "Yes."

Having no choice, the scholar paid his respects to the tree and, after giving a full account of the situation, put the question to the tree, "So then, does the wolf have the right to eat me?"

— LESSON 119 —

Idioms

I'm confused because I don't know what you are **driving at**.

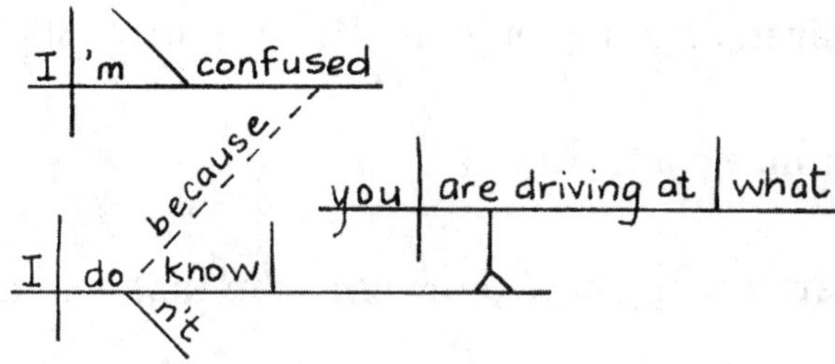

We did our best, but we failed, and now it is **back to the drawing board**.

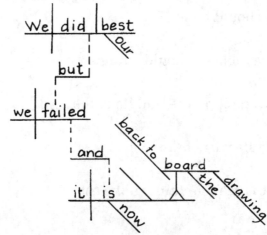

I know you think you've solved the problem, **but you're barking up the wrong tree.**

I know you think you've solved the problem, **but you have the wrong solution.**

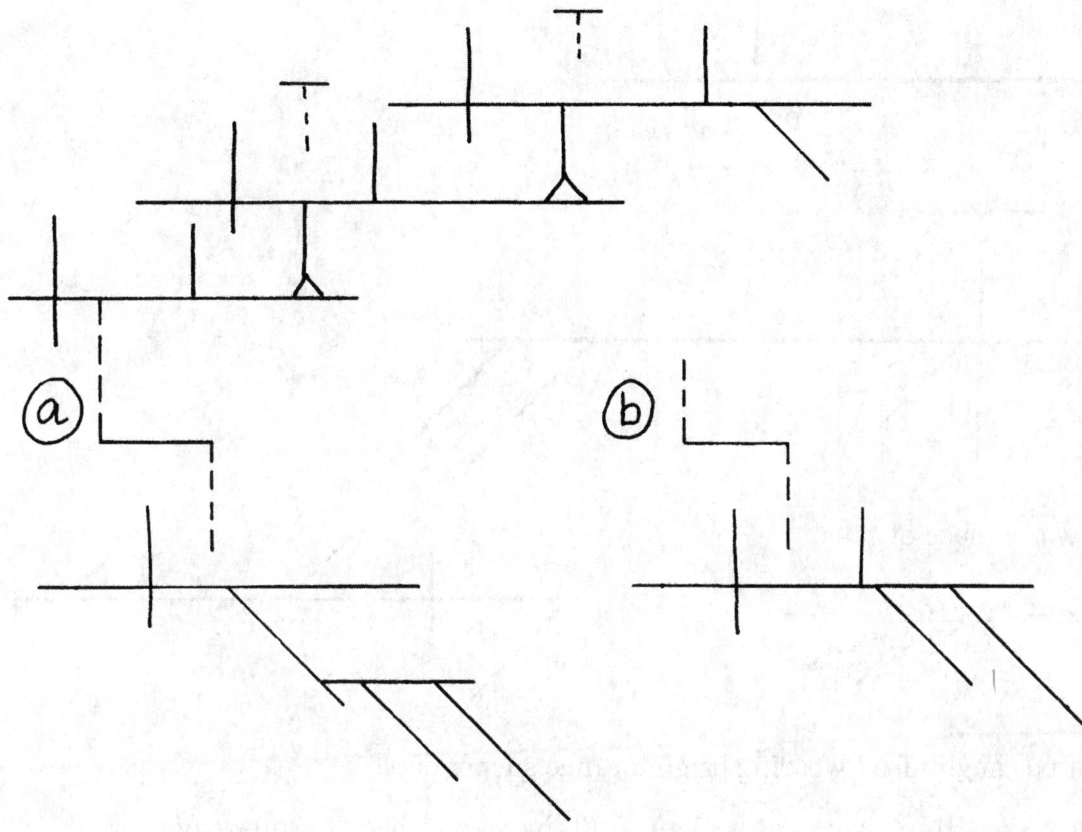

Yes, we lost the soccer game, but there's no point crying over spilt milk.

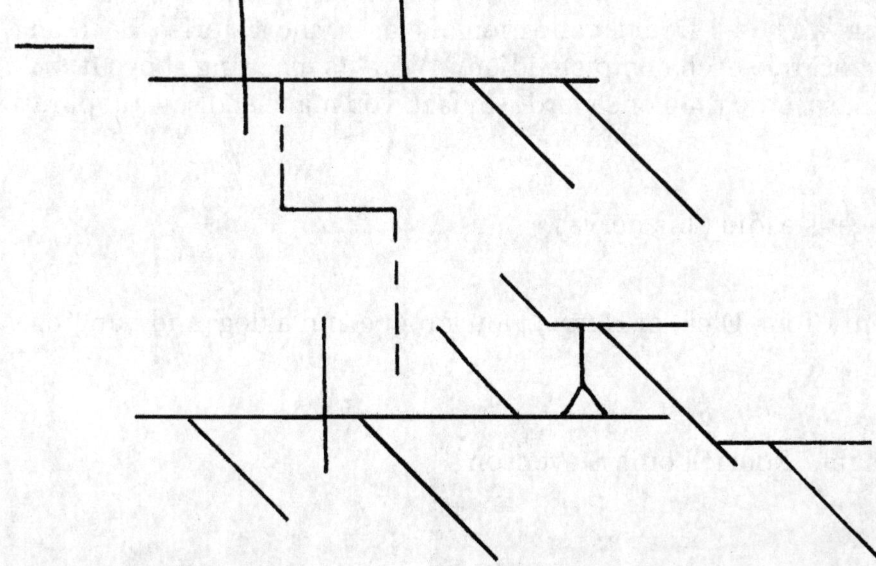

You might enjoy acting, but don't give up your day job!

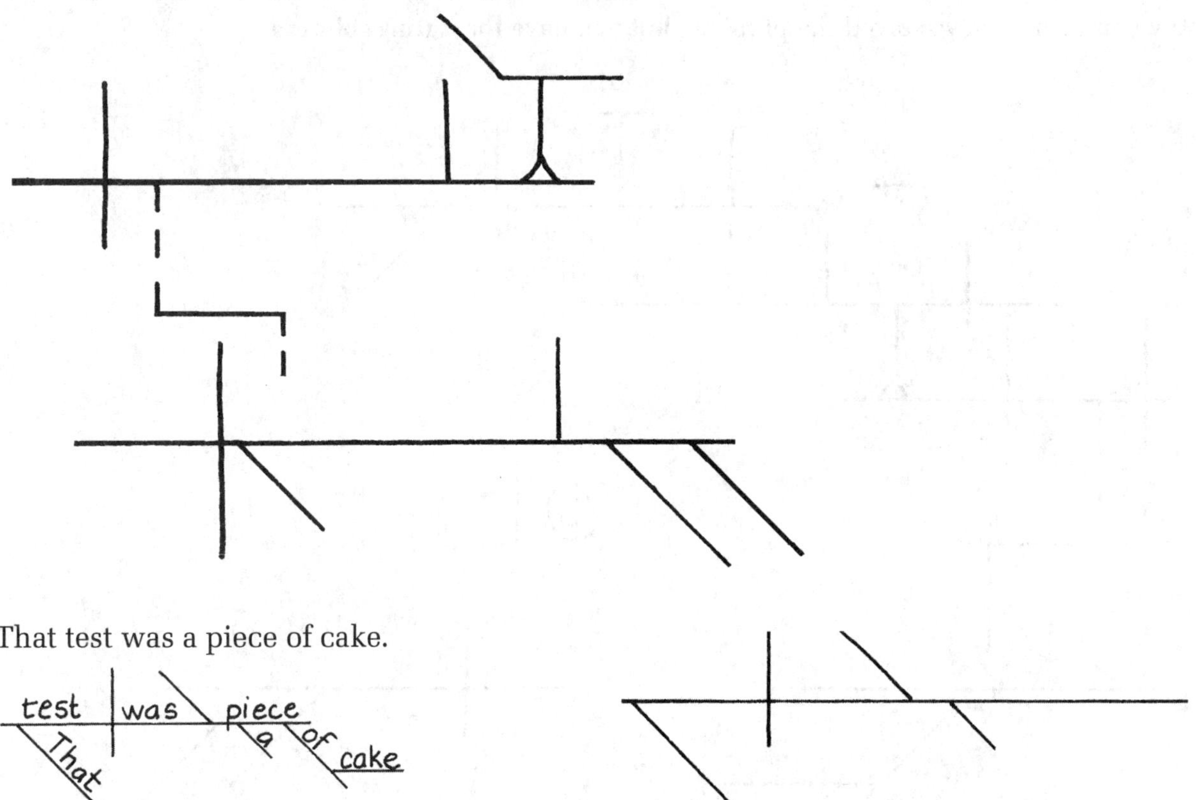

That test was a piece of cake.

I wouldn't be caught dead wearing bright orange suspenders!

My business idea didn't work out, so I guess I'll have to go back to square one.

Exercise 119A: Explaining Idioms

The following sentences are all taken from a collection of classic short stories. Each one contains at least one idiom! Circle each complete idiom. Write its meaning above it in your own words. (You can use more than one word—in fact, you may need several phrases.)

But the gravity of the danger steadied his nerves.

I have no trumpet; I am only Tom, Dick, or Harry; I am a rogue and a dog, and hanging's

too good for me.

—"A Lodging for the Night," Robert Louis Stevenson

Dancing was instantaneous, Mrs. Fennel privately enjoining the players on no account to let the dance exceed the length of a quarter of an hour.

They noticed to their surprise that he stood before them the picture of abject terror—his knees trembling, his hand shaking so violently that the door-latch by which he supported himself rattled audibly.

Shepherdess Fennel fell back upon the intermediate plan of mingling short dances with short periods of talk and singing.

—"The Three Strangers," Thomas Hardy

She sang bits of old songs and Psalms, stopping suddenly, mingling the Psalms of David and the diviner words of his Son and Lord with homely odds and ends of ballads.

—"Rab and His Friends," John Brown

Still, in spite of all this strenuous attention to forms, Tom had a lurking dread that the devil, after all, would have his due.

"You have made so much money out of me," said the speculator.

—"The Devil and Tom Walker," by Washington Irving

Above all, meanwhile, this high consciousness prevailed.

"Why, my dear man," Julia cried, "you take the wind straight out of my sails!"

—"Julia Bride," Henry James

Exercise 119B: Diagramming

On your own paper, diagram every word of the following sentences, taken from Agatha Christie's classic mystery novel *The Mysterious Affair at Styles*.

When you are finished, tell your instructor what each idiom means! Several sentences have more than one idiom. Ask for help if you need it.

Having no near relations or friends, I was trying to make up my mind what to do, when I ran across John Cavendish.

A wink's as good as a nod—from you.

One's gorge does rise at sitting down to eat with a possible murderer!

I felt glad that the decision had been taken out of his hands.

The only fly in the ointment of my peaceful days was Mrs. Cavendish's extraordinary, and, for my part, unaccountable preference for the society of Dr. Bauerstein.

Exercise 119C: Finding Idioms

On your own paper, rewrite the following four sentences, replacing the bolded words in each with an idiom that means the same thing.

Ask for help if you need it!

Don't talk to the track team about the big loss at State Finals—it's a real **event that is very hard to talk or think about!**

I've got to **recognize to your face just how hard you've worked**—you managed to get all the way to the semifinals even though you only started playing tennis two years ago!

I know that talking about the loss just **makes the loss even worse than it already was**, because you tried so hard right to the end.

When you're working out this often, you **eat so much that I can barely keep the refrigerator and the pantries filled with food!**

—LESSON 120—

Troublesome Sentences

Grammar is the art of speaking or writing a language correctly.
—William Greatheed Lewis, *A Grammar of the English Language* (1821)

Perfect grammar—persistent, continuous, sustained—is the fourth dimension, so to speak: many have sought it, but none has found it.
—Mark Twain, *Autobiography* (posthumous edition, 1925)

Grammar is to literary composition what a linch-pin is to a waggon. It is a poor pitiful thing in itself; it bears no part of the weight; communicates nothing to the force; adds not in the least to the celerity; but, still the waggon cannot very well and safely go on without it; she is constantly liable to reel and be compelled to stop, which, at the least, exposes the driver to be laughed at, and that, too, by those who are wholly unable to drive themselves.

—William Cobbett, *Grammar of the English Language* (1818)

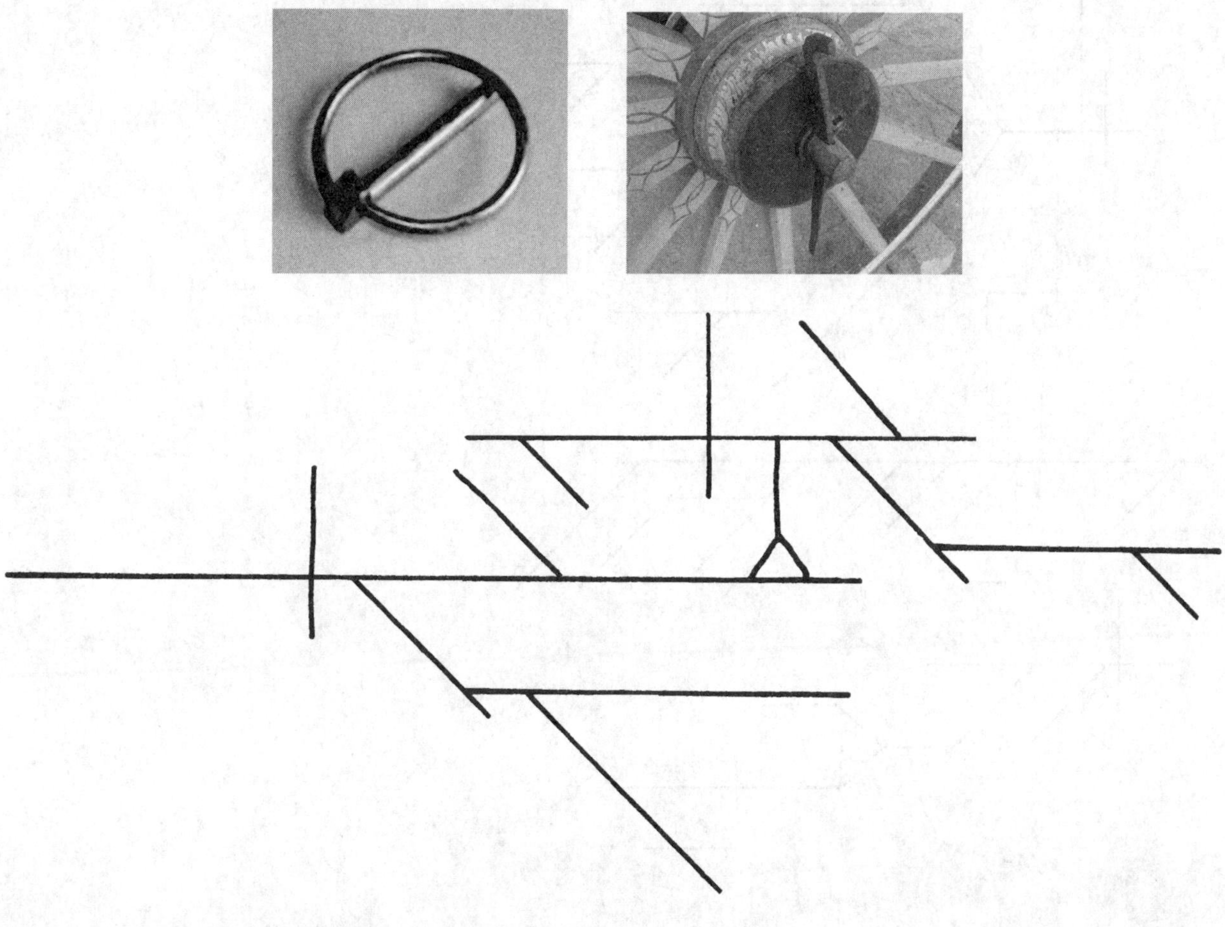

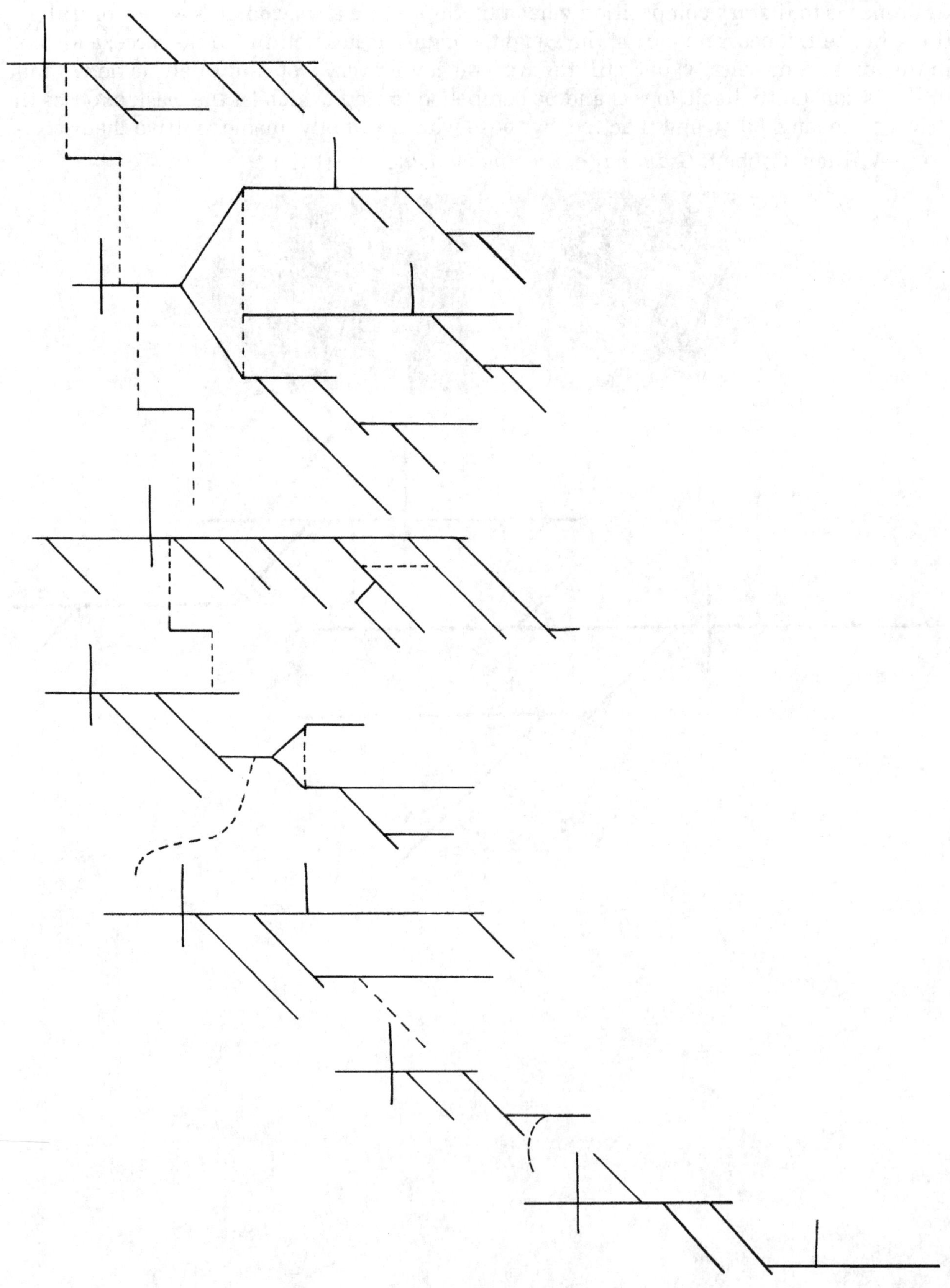

Exercise 120A: A Selection of Challenging Sentences

After your instructor discusses each sentence with you, diagram it on your own paper.

These sentences are taken from *Frankenstein: or, the Modern Prometheus*, by Mary Wollstonecraft Shelley.

When I returned home my first care was to procure the whole works of this author, and afterwards of Paracelsus and Albertus Magnus.

I have described myself as always having been imbued with a fervent longing to penetrate the secrets of nature.

Chance—or rather the evil influence, the Angel of Destruction, which asserted omnipotent sway over me from the moment I turned my reluctant steps from my father's door—led me first to M. Krempe, professor of natural philosophy.

Such were the professor's words—rather let me say such the words of the fate—enounced to destroy me.

He appeared about fifty years of age, but with an aspect expressive of the greatest benevolence; a few grey hairs covered his temples, but those at the back of his head were nearly black.

The raising of ghosts or devils was a promise liberally accorded by my favourite authors, the fulfilment of which I most eagerly sought; and if my incantations were always unsuccessful, I attributed the failure rather to my own inexperience and mistake than to a want of skill or fidelity in my instructors.

WEEK 32

—REVIEW 10—

Weeks 29-31

Topics
Hortative Verbs
Ambitransitive Verbs
Infinitive Phrases as Objects
Infinitive Phrases With Understood *To*
Principal Parts of Irregular Verbs
Noun Clauses as Appositives
Which/That in Restrictive and Non-Restrictive Clauses
Formal Conditionals
Words Acting as Multiple Parts of Speech
Affirmations and Negations
Idioms

Review 10A: The Missing Words Game

Fill in each blank below with the exact *form* described—but choose your own words!

Show your answers to your instructor, who will insert them into the matching blanks in the short essay in the *Answer Key*.

Your instructor will then show you the original essay—and your version.

passive past participle ______________________

indicative perfect future active verb (third-person singular) ______________________

demonstrative pronoun, singular ______________________

adverb of affirmation ______________________

adverb of time ______________________

adverb of time ______________________

modal simple present state-of-being verb (third-person singular) ______________________

noun, either concrete or abstract, singular or plural ______________________

adverb of time ______________________

number ______________________

modal simple present state-of-being verb (third-person singular) ____________________

abstract noun, singular ____________________

parenthetical expression ____________________

idiom expressing the extent of something ____________________

infinitive, present active ____________________

possessive adjective ____________________

abstract noun, singular ____________________

abstract noun, singular ____________________

possessive adjective ____________________

indicative simple future perfect passive verb (third-person singular) ____________________

demonstrative adjective ____________________

relative adverb ____________________

indicative present passive verb (third-person singular) ____________________

adverb of quantity ____________________

relative adverb ____________________

adjective that can also be a noun ____________________

adjective ____________________

concrete noun, singular ____________________

modal simple present passive verb (third-person singular) ____________________

indicative simple future active verb (third-person singular) ____________________

present participle acting as a singular noun ____________________

concrete noun, singular ____________________

concrete noun, singular ____________________

adverb of time ____________________

noun that can also be an adjective ____________________

modal simple present passive verb (third-person plural) ____________________

demonstrative pronoun, plural ____________________

modal simple present passive verb (third-person singular) ____________________

demonstrative pronoun, plural ______________________

relative pronoun ______________________

adverb of frequency ______________________

infinitive, present passive ______________________

adverb ______________________

present participle acting as a noun ______________________

possessive adjective ______________________

indefinite adjective ______________________

modal simple present active verb (third-person plural)______________________

abstract noun, singular ______________________

adverb of affirmation ______________________

modal simple present active verb (third-person singular) ______________________

correlative conjunctions (two) ______________________

adverb acting as subordinating word ______________________

infinitive, present active ______________________

compound adverb ______________________

present participle acting as an adverb ______________________

concrete noun, singular ______________________

adverb of affirmation ______________________

abstract noun, singular ______________________

abstract noun, singular ______________________

imperative simple present active verb, singular ______________________

present participle acting as an adverb ______________________

modal simple present active verb (second-person singular) ______________________

abstract noun, singular ______________________

imperative simple present active verb, singular ______________________

compound adverb ______________________

present participle acting as a noun ______________________

reflexive pronoun ____________________

adverb of negation ____________________

hyphenated compound adjective ____________________

hyphenated compound adjective ____________________

preposition ____________________

modal simple present passive verb (third-person singular) ____________________

subjunctive simple present active verb (third-person singular) ____________________

predicate adjective ____________________

concrete noun, plural ____________________

adjective of quantity ____________________

adjective ____________________

concrete noun, plural ____________________

demonstrative pronoun, singular ____________________

abstract noun, singular ____________________

present participle acting as a noun ____________________

present participle acting as a noun ____________________

adverb of affirmation ____________________

abstract noun, singular ____________________

abstract noun, singular ____________________

concrete noun, plural ____________________

predicate adjective, compound, hyphenated ____________________

predicate adjective ____________________

adverb of degree ____________________

adjective ____________________

modal simple present active verb (third-person plural) ____________________

concrete noun, plural ____________________

modal simple present passive verb (third-person plural) ____________________

predicate adjective that can also be a preposition or adverb ____________________

Review 10B: Identifying Infinitive Phrases, Noun Clauses, and Modifying Clauses

In the following sentences, follow these four steps:

a) Identify every set of underlined words as *INF* for infinitive phrase, *PREP* for prepositional phrase, or *CL* for clause.
b) Label each phrase or clause as *ADV* for adverb, *ADJ* for adjective, or *N* for noun.
c) For adjective and adverb phrases and clauses, draw an arrow from the label to the word modified.
d) For noun phrases and clauses, add the appropriate part of the sentence label: *S* for subject, *DO* for object, *IO* for indirect object, *OP* for object of a preposition, *PN* for predicate nominative, *APP* for appositive.

Note: Some sets of words are within other sets of words, so you'll see some double underlining! If you see double underlining, be sure to follow the instructions for both sets of underlined words.

The first sentence is done for you.

Like the sentences from the last exercise, these are taken from *The Book of Household Management,* by Mrs. Isabella Beeton, an English journalist who lived in London. The Book of Household Management was a tremendous best-seller, was a standard gift to new wives for a century, and is still in print today. At least half of it was recipes for what were considered standard meals for a household!

CL ADV PREP ADV

When all is well stirred, put the pudding into a buttered basin, tie it down with a cloth, plunge it into boiling water, and boil for 1-1/4 hour.

As not only health but life may be said to depend on the cleanliness of culinary utensils, great attention must be paid to their condition generally, but more especially to that of the saucepans, stewpans, and boilers. Inside they should be kept perfectly clean, and where an open fire is used, the outside as clean as possible.

Now place them in the oven for a few minutes, to acquire a nice brown colour, and serve them on a napkin, with custard sauce flavoured with vanilla, or a *compôte* of any fruit that may be preferred.

In English meadows sorrell is usually left to grow wild; but in France, where it is cultivated, its flavour is greatly improved.

To all these directions the cook should pay great attention, nor should they, by any means, be neglected by the mistress of the household, who ought to remember that cleanliness in the kitchen gives health and happiness to home, whilst economy will immeasurably assist in preserving them.

A well-ventilated larder, dry and shady, is better for meat and poultry, which require to be kept for some time.

Stew the rice very gently in the above proportion of new milk, and, when it is tender, pour it into a basin; stir in the butter, and let it stand to cool; then beat the eggs, add these to the rice with the sugar, salt, and any flavouring that may be approved, such as nutmeg, powdered cinnamon, grated lemon-peel, essence of bitter almonds, or vanilla.

When the soup is cold, the fat may be much more easily and completely removed; and when it is poured off, care must be taken not to disturb the settlings at the bottom of the vessel, which are so fine that they will escape through a sieve.

Cut the cold hare into neat slices, and put the head, bones, and trimmings into a stewpan, with 3/4 pint of water; add the mace, allspice, seasoning, onion, and herbs, and stew for nearly an hour, and strain the gravy; thicken it with butter and flour, add the wine and ketchup, and lay in the pieces of hare, with any stuffing that may be left.

When the whole is well blended together, mould it into balls, or whatever shape is intended, roll them in flour, and poach in boiling water, to which a little salt should have been added.

Review 10C: Parsing

Parse every bolded verb in the following sentences, taken from another best-selling book by Isabella Beeton: *Mrs. Beeton's Dictionary of Every-Day Cookery.*

Provide the following information:

Person: First, second, or third
Number: Sing. or pl.
Tense: Simple past, present, or future; perfect past, present, or future; progressive past, present, or future; or progressive perfect present
Voice: Active, passive, or state-of-being
Mood: Indicative, subjunctive, imperative, hortatory, or modal
If the verb is also emphatic, add this label to the mood.

The first bolded verb is done for you.

The principal art in composing good rich soup is so to proportion the several ingredients that the flavour of one **shall** not **predominate** over another, and that all the articles of which it **is composed shall form** an agreeable whole.

3rd sing., simple future, active, indicative

Boil gently for ¼ hour, or until the fruit is tender; but take care not to let it break, as the appearance of the dish **would be spoiled were** the fruit **reduced** to a pulp.

For a nursery pudding, the addition of the latter ingredients **will be found** quite superfluous, as also the paste round the edge of the dish.

Put in the fish, heat it gradually, but **do** not **let** it boil, or it **will be broken**.

The above is the proportion of milk which we think **would convert** the flour into a stiff paste; but **should** it **be found** too much, an extra spoonful or two of flour **must be put** in.

Mix with it by degrees all, or a portion, of the gravy that **will have run** from it, and a little clarified butter; **add** the seasoning, put it in small pots for use, and cover with a little butter just warmed and poured over.

Plunge the stems into boiling water, and, by the time the water is cold, the flowers **will have revived**.

We heard a gentleman who, when he **might have had** a wing, declare his partiality for a leg, saying that he **had been obliged** to eat legs for so long a time that he **had** at last **come** to like them better than the other more prized parts.

Mince the fowl not too finely, and **make** it hot in the Béchamel sauce, to which the nutmeg, pepper and salt, and cream, **have been added**.

Then put them into a stewpan, cover them with water, and **let** them boil until tender, and, if the onions **should be** very strong, change the water after they **have been boiling** for ¼ hour.

They **may be served** in their skins, and **eaten** with a piece of cold butter and a seasoning of pepper and salt; or they **may be peeled**, and a good brown gravy poured over them.

The jelly is then done, and **may be poured** into moulds which **have been** previously **soaking** in water, when it **will turn** out nicely for dessert or a side dish.

The gravy **should be boiling** before it **is poured** into the tureen.

After this pickle **has been made** from 4 to 5 months, the liquor **may be strained** and **bottled**, and **will be found** an excellent lemon ketchup.

Gravies and sauces **should be sent** to table very hot; and there is all the more necessity for the cook to see to this point, as, from their being usually served in small quantities, they **are** more liable to cool quickly than if they **were** in a larger body.

In speaking of confectionary, it **should be remarked** that many preparations come under that head; for the various fruits, flowers, herbs, roots, and juices, which, when boiled with sugar, **were** formerly **employed** in pharmacy as well as for sweetmeats, were called confections, from the Latin word conficere, 'to make up;' but the term confectionary embraces a very large class indeed of sweet food, many kinds of which **should** not **be attempted** in the ordinary cuisine.

Review 10D: *Which* and *That* Clauses

In the following sentences, from Isabella Beeton's *Book of Needlework*, underline each clause introduced by *which* or *that*. If *that* is understood, use a caret to insert it. If a *which* or *that* clause falls within another clause, underline the entire larger clause once, and the clause-within-a-clause a second time.

- Label each clause as *ADJ* for adjective, *ADV* for adverb, or *N* for noun.
- For adjective and adverb clauses, draw an arrow back to the word modified.
- For noun clauses, label the part of the sentence that the clause fulfills (*S*, *PN*, *DO*, *IO*, *APP*).
- Finally, label each adjective clause as *R* for restrictive or *NON-R* for nonrestrictive.

The first sentence is done for you.

The needlework called Tatting in England, *Frivolité* in French, and *Frivolitäten* in German, is a work which seems, from all accounts, to have been in favour several generations ago.

ADJ R

Take the end of the shuttle which comes out from the loop between the forefinger and thumb of the right hand, and strain the cotton very tightly towards the right.

We think it would be better to leave the repetitions to the judgment of the worker.

After this, withdraw the second left-hand finger, which is *above* the cotton, and pass it again under that cotton, so as to draw up the loop.

The Venetian Bar is so simple that it hardly needs description.

Then take some crochet cotton, which must be finer than the cotton used for tatting, and work a row of double stitches over the thread which joins the circles.

Draw up very tightly the cotton over which you work, so that the circles form a rosette, which is closed by sewing together the two corresponding purl of the first and last circle.

Lace is of two kinds—pillow lace, which is made upon a cushion or pillow, and point lace, which is made of stitches or *points* worked in patterns by hand, which are joined by various stitches forming a groundwork, also the result of the needle above.

Repeat from beginning, taking care that the next oval be close to the last.

This insertion consists of 2 rows of three-branched patterns which lie opposite each other, and are joined by slanting rows of knots.

Before beginning to work this pattern, thread the beads which take the place of purl stitches, and which are slipped in between two double stitches.

We shall merely say that the centre circle is always worked separately, and that the cotton is fastened on afresh to work the eight outer leaves.

Take thicker cotton than that with which you work; never commence with a knot, and do not take a thread longer than sixteen or eighteen inches.

Great care should be taken that the material on which you embroider is not puckered.

The two loops that remain at the end are cast off together after winding the cotton round the needle.

Run some cord in the top of the bag to match one of the colours used, and make the tassel for the bottom from the silk that is remaining after working the crochet.

One great advantage of netting is that each stitch is finished and independent of the next, so that if an accident happens to one stitch it does not, as in crochet or knitting, spoil the whole work.

Review 10E: Words Acting as Multiple Parts of Speech

In each set of sentences below, underline the repeated word. Label each occurrence as *N* for noun, *V* for verb, *PRO* for pronoun, *ADV* for adverb, *ADJ* for adjective, *PREP* for preposition, *CC* for coordinating conjunction, or *SC* for subordinating conjunction.

These sentences are all taken from *The American Woman's Home: or, Principles of Domestic Science*, by the nineteenth-century writer Harriet Beecher Stowe. You may be more familiar with Stowe's anti-slavery novel *Uncle Tom's Cabin*. But Stowe also wrote over two dozen other books, including the how-to text *The American Woman's Home*.

Under the sink are shelf-boxes placed on two shelves run into grooves, with other grooves above and below.

This is all a mistake; for, as a fact, in close sleeping-rooms the purest air is below and the most impure above.

This cast-iron pipe is surrounded by a brick flue, through which air passes from below to be warmed by the pipe.

A certain degree of warmth in the stomach is indispensable to digestion; so, when the gastric juice is cooled below this temperature, it ceases to act.

It is useful to be able to move the shelves, and increase or diminish the spaces between.

As a general rule, meals should be five hours apart, and eating between meals avoided.

Even so, in our long winters, multitudes of delicate people subsist on the daily waning strength which they acquired in the season when windows and doors were open.

I have often returned from church doubting whether I had not committed a sin in exposing myself so long to its poisonous air.

As long as the paper remains, the candle will burn.

Every woman should train her children in this important duty of home life on which health and comfort so much depend.

Having duly arranged for the physical necessities of a healthful and comfortable home, we next approach the important subject of beauty in reference to the decoration of houses.

The oven is the space under and around the back and front sides of the fire-box.

Another useful appendage is a common tin oven, in which roasting can be done in the front of the stove.

Probably you could make the cover more cheaply by getting the cloth and trimming its edge with a handsome border.

Cover this with a green English furniture print.

In like manner, each motion of the arm and fingers has one muscle to produce it and another to restore to the natural position.

The cushion to be cut square, with side pieces; stuffed with hair, and stitched through like a mattress.

The following, then, may be put down as the causes of a debilitated constitution from the misuse of food.

Down these two corner-flues passes the current of hot air and smoke, having first drawn across the corrugated oven-top.

What animals use is provided by vegetables, and what vegetables require is furnished by animals.

The use of ivy in decorating a room is beginning to be generally acknowledged.

This is prevented by enlarging the closets on each side, so that their walls meet the ceiling under the garret floor.

When watering, set a pail under, for it to drip into.

The under couch is like the upper couch, except for its different dimensions.

Review 10F: Idioms

Circle each idiom in the following sentences. Above each one, write its meaning within the sentence. The first is done for you.

These sentences are taken from *The Gospel of Germs*, by Nancy Tomes. The book examines how the housekeeping standards and principles taught by nineteenth-century housekeeping manuals affected the way that Americans thought about disease and germs.

explained their reasons as related to

Converts to the germ theory often (painted a chilling picture) of an environment saturated with these invisible enemies.

They produced countless lectures, exhibits, posters, films, and pamphlets that preached to millions of Americans from all walks of life the same hygenic message.

Exposed to the continual refrain that "little things were not trifles," they began to look at familiar habits with new eyes.

By seizing the hygienic high ground, they gained a useful advantage over their less affluent and sanitarily savvy fellow plumbers, who were more likely to run afoul of the regulations.

From the 1880s on, the new style toilet quickly came to embody the cutting edge of hygienic design.

The "whited sepulchre" image had a particularly keen edge for women of the genteel classes.

Under his watchful eye, Rockwell proceeded with the renovations that Waring had recommended in his preliminary report.

Last but not least, they urinated and defecated in chamber pots and outdoor privies with little regard for where the contents ended up in relation to the community water supply.

In the name of public health, hotels were gradually required to change the sheets between each patron's use of a room.

Review 10G: Ambitransitive Verbs

In the following sentences, underline each action verb that acts as a predicate. Mark each of these verbs as *T* for transitive or *IT* for intransitive. For transitive verbs, draw an arrow from the label *T* to the word that receives the action of the verb.

These sentences are taken from another nineteenth-century household manual: *Women, Plumbers, and Doctors, or, Household Sanitation*, by Harriette Merrick Plunkett. The book is all about how proper cleanliness in the home can prevent disease (a major preoccupation of nineteenth-century writers!).

A new sphere of usefulness and efficiency opens with the knowledge that an ounce of prevention is worth a ton of cure.

Ball-floats open the pipe when the water is lowered.

We will give the reply which Professor C. F. Chandler, of New York, gave.

She thought she had done her whole duty; but her vigilance gave out at the ground floor.

After all the little errands are done, bed-time is come!

The men of the house come and go.

The plow does not sprout and spring up into a stalk of maize, but it breaks and mellows the soil.

When oil is burned too high in a lamp, the lamp breaks.

Cheese kept in a cool larder will mellow over time.

We must continually eat and drink and be nourished!

For many parents, running errands eats two good hours out of the day.

There are whole families who all drink tea or coffee.

The energy of the spring growth runs its course by summer.

The waste water runs into different drains, according to the season.

We should all understand the details as well as the theory of sanitation.

The best gardeners understand perfectly.

Once the construction is completed, the workers should paint on the following day.

Gas and drain pipes must be painted a distinct color.

When you let the sunshine in, you drive the doctor out.

The market-wagons drive between the buildings without proper care.

Review 10H: Hunt and Find

In the following sentences, find, underline, and label each of the following:

- Progressive verb (provide exact tense, voice, and mood!)
- Action verb that can also be a linking verb
- Hortative verb
- Subjunctive verb (provide exact tense and voice)
- Demonstrative pronoun acting as a subject
- Intensive pronoun
- Compound adjective in the attributive position
- Possessive adjective
- Infinitive phrase acting as a subject
- Object complement
- Consequence clause
- Adjective clause introduced by a relative pronoun
- Noun clause acting as a direct object
- Noun clause acting as a predicate nominative
- Present participle acting as the object of a preposition
- Present participle acting as a subject
- Present participle phrase acting as an adverb
- Past participle acting as an adjective in the predicative position

These sentences are all taken from the 1907 book *The Chemistry of Cooking and Cleaning: A Manual for Housekeepers*, by Ellen H. Richards and S. Maria Elliott. It was one of the first domestic science handbooks to treat the scientific aspects of housework.

We live in an invisible atmosphere of dust, we are constantly adding to this atmosphere by the processes of our own growth and waste, and, finally, we shall go the way of all the earth, contributing our bodies to the making of more dust.

That which costs little or nothing is seldom appreciated; so this all-abundant, freely-given light is often shut out through man's greed or through mistaken economy.

As far as possible, let the exterior of the house be bathed in sunlight.

Nature's supply of pure air is sufficient for all, but to have it always in its pure state requires knowledge and constant, intelligent action.

If the finish be removed or broken by deep scratches, the wood itself absorbs the grease and dust, and the stain may have to be scraped out.

Whether to boil or not to boil the clothes depends largely upon the purity of the materials used and the degree of care exercised.

Many persons feel that the additional disinfection which boiling ensures is an element of cleanness not to be disregarded, while others insist that boiling yellows the clothes.

Another reason for kneading is that the bubbles of gas may be broken up into as small portions as possible.

The cook must remember that the butter absorbed from her cake tin or the olive oil on her salad is food, as well as the flour and eggs.

The secret of the cooking of vegetables is the judicious production of flavor.

Review 10I: Conditionals and Formal Conditionals

In each of the following conditional sentences, parse the underlined verbs, giving tense, voice (*active*, *passive*, or *state-of-being*), and mood. Then, classify the sentences as first, second, or third conditional by placing a *1*, *2*, or *3* in the blank at the beginning.

These sentences are taken from *The Secret History of Home Economics: How Trailblazing Women Harnessed the Power of Home and Changed the Way We Live*, by Danielle Dreilinger.

The first verb is parsed for you.

Remember that the condition can come before the consequence—or the other way around!

simple present, active, subjunctive

_____ If home economists miss this boat, they may never catch another one like it.

_____ Of course, if we seriously valued this work that makes our lives much easier, that in some cases makes it possible for people to work outside the home as (for instance) welders, we might improve the pay of the people who do it.

_____ Special diets had to start three days before takeoff, prepared to clinically antibacterial standards, for it would be awful if an astronaut got food poisoning in space.

_____ If there is justice in the nation, there will be peace in the world.

_____ If corporations didn't do something to regain trust, the government would intervene.

_____ If she had lived ten years longer, how much good she could have done!

_____ If we don't come out of it and change the narrative, it will disappear.

_____ If everyone did her part, peace and quiet might someday reign again.

_____ If I had been white, I think that would have been a huge difference.

_____ Richards laid down her dictum most concisely in one of the most passionate speeches of her life, an impromptu retort at an otherwise all-male educational conference whose attendees told her that schools wouldn't have to teach housekeeping if women stayed home.

_____ The country could not succeed, he said, if it continued to give Black citizens a separate and unequal education.

_____ The club members wouldn't like it, Melville said, if the great Tuskegee leader ate in the club dining room.

_____ If you want kids to learn home economics, and maybe even liberate future adult women from unequal housework, make the class mandatory.

_____ If she had known, she would not have told them to quit their jobs.

Review 10J: Affirmations and Negations

The following sentences all contain adverbs of affirmation and negation. Circle each one, and label them as *AFF* or *NEG.*

Then, choose three sentences and rewrite them on your own paper, turning affirmatives into negatives and vice versa. Show your sentences to your instructor.

All of these sentences are taken from the 1871 handbook *Miss Beecher's Domestic Receipt-Book: Designed as a Supplement to Her Treatise on Domestic Economy*, by Catharine Esther Beecher.

When a woman has good sense and good taste, these are some of the things she will not do.

She will not be particularly anxious to know what the fashion is, in dress and furniture.

Nor will she be disturbed if found deficient in these particulars.

Fresh air is absolutely necessary for good health.

It is very desirable that every family should have a constant supply of good bread.

Constantly stirring porridge surely preserves it from growing sour or musty.

Be careful to have clean dish towels, and never use them for other purposes.

The careful and benevolent housekeeper will certainly receive her reward.

Constantly finding fault is inconsistent with a truly amiable character.

Fat is indeed the offending ingredient in most dishes which disturb weak stomachs.

Green peas need no soaking, and must boil not more than an hour.

Review 10K: Diagramming

On your own paper, diagram every word of the following sentences, taken from the 1841 text *A Treatise on Domestic Economy*, by Catharine Esther Beecher.

Every person should be dressed so loosely, that, when sitting in the posture used in sewing, reading, or study, the lungs can be as full and as easily inflated as they are without clothing.

Of course, confinement to one position, for a great length of time, tends to weaken the muscles thus strained.

This shows the evil of confining young children to their seats, in the schoolroom, so much and so long as is often done.

If a parent perceives that a child is growing crooked, the proper remedy is to withdraw it from all pursuits which tax one particular set of muscles, and turn it out to exercise in sports, or in gardening, in the fresh air, when all the muscles will be used, and the whole system strengthened.

Review 10L: Explaining A Long Sentence

Tell your instructor the following pieces of grammatical information about the following very long sentence! It is taken from the 1823 textbook *A New System of Practical Domestic Economy.*

Follow these steps:

a) Underline each subordinate clause. Describe the identity and function of each clause and give any other useful information (introductory word, relationship to the rest of the sentence, etc.). Insert any understood words, using the ^.

b) Circle each phrase. Describe the identity and function of each phrase and give any other useful information.

c) Parse all verbs acting as predicates.

If you need help, ask your instructor.

That the winds on the north-eastern coast of the kingdom are as violent as, and much colder than, those in the south-western counties, cannot for a moment be doubted; yet it is an important fact, that in the former situation there are some very striking specimens of that beautiful tree, which seems not only to defy the weather, but even to flourish in their exposed situation, throwing out their spreading branches in all directions, both with and against the wind, and covered with a foliage, rich, full, and verdant, even to their very summit.

WEEK 33

Mechanics

—LESSON 121—

Capitalization Review
Additional Capitalization Rules
Formal and Informal Letter Format
Ending Punctuation

what an amazing place london was to me when i saw it in the distance and how i believed all the adventures of all my favourite heroes to be constantly enacting and re-enacting there and how i vaguely made it out in my own mind to be fuller of wonders and wickedness than all the cities of the earth i need not stop here to relate

What an amazing place London was to me when I saw it in the distance, and how I believed all the adventures of all my favourite heroes to be constantly enacting and re-enacting there, and how I vaguely made it out in my own mind to be fuller of wonders and wickedness than all the cities of the earth, I need not stop here to relate.

—Charles Dickens, *David Copperfield*

A proper noun is the special, particular name for a person, place, thing, or idea. Proper nouns always begin with capital letters.

1. Capitalize the proper names of persons, places, things, and animals.

boy	manuel
store	macy's
car	ford
horse	secretariat

2. Capitalize the names of holidays.

lent

ramadan

new year's day

3. Capitalize the names of deities.

zeus

buddha

holy spirit

god

4. Capitalize the days of the week and the months of the year, but not the seasons.

wednesday	february	spring
thursday	april	fall
saturday	september	winter

5. Capitalize the first, last, and other important words in titles of books, magazines, newspapers, stories, poems, and songs.

book	*green eggs and ham*
magazine	*the new yorker*
newspaper	*the philadelphia inquirer*
movie	*the hunger games: catching fire*
television show	*agents of s.h.i.e.l.d.*
story	"the lottery"
poem	"stopping by woods on a snowy evening"
song	"happy birthday to you"
chapter in a book	"an unexpected party"

6. Capitalize and italicize the names of ships, trains, and planes.

ship	*santa maria*
train	*hogwarts express*
plane	*air force one*

The titles *mister*, *madame*, and *miss* are capitalized and abbreviated *Mr.*, *Mrs.*, and *Miss* when placed in front of a proper name.

Miss Snevellicci made a graceful obeisance, and hoped Mrs. Curdle was well, as also Mr. Curdle, who at the same time appeared.
—Charles Dickens, *The Life and Adventures of Nicholas Nickleby*

A proper adjective is formed from a proper name. Proper adjectives are capitalized. Words that are not usually capitalized remain lowercase even when they are attached to a proper adjective.

	Proper Noun	**Proper Adjective**
Person	shakespeare	the shakespearean play
	kafka	a kafkaesque dilemma
Place	italy	an italian city
	korea	a non-korean tradition
Holiday	labor day	the labor day picnic
	christmas	an anti-christmas sentiment
Month	september	september storms
	december	the post-december blues

Capitalize the personal pronoun *I*.

Interjections express sudden feeling or emotion. They are set off with commas or stand alone with a closing punctuation mark.

I have prayed over them, oh, I have prayed so much.
Ahem! That is my name.
Ha, ha! The liars that these traders are!
—Charles Dickens, *David Copperfield*

Capitalize the interjection *O*. It is usually preceded by, but not followed by, a comma.

For a few weeks it was all well enough, but afterwards, O the weary length of the nights!

But, O dear, O dear, this is a hard world!
—Kenneth Grahame, *The Wind in the Willows*

After an interjection followed by an exclamation point, the next word may be lowercase.

Oh! let me see it once again before I die!
Alas! how often and how long may those patient angels hover above us!
—Charles Dickens, *The Life and Adventures of Nicholas Nickleby*

Capitalize the address, date, greeting, closing, and signature of a letter.

Your Street Address
Your City, State, and ZIP Code

June 14, 2018

Well-Trained Mind Press
18021 The Glebe Lane
Charles City, Virginia 23030

Dear Editors:

Thank you for *Grammar for the Well-Trained Mind.* It is the most exciting grammar book I have ever read. I only wish I could spend more time doing grammar.

Please publish more grammar books immediately.

Sincerely,

SIGNATURE

Your Greatest Fan

Your Street Address
Your City, State, and ZIP Code

June 14, 2018

Well-Trained Mind Press
18021 The Glebe Lane
Charles City, Virginia 23030

Dear Editors:

Thank you for *Grammar for the Well-Trained Mind.* It is the most exciting grammar book I have ever read. I only wish I could spend more time doing grammar.

Please publish more grammar books immediately.

Sincerely,

SIGNATURE

Your Greatest Fan

Abbreviations are typically capitalized when each letter stands for something.

The WHO has expressed concern about the Zika virus and its rapid spread.
Why did NASA cancel the lunar exploration program?
OPEC was founded in 1960 in Baghdad.

Capitalize the first word in every line of traditional poetry.

"The Elephant"
by Hilaire Belloc

When people call this beast to mind,
They marvel more and more
At such a little tail behind,
So large a trunk before.

A sentence is a group of words that contains a subject and a predicate. A sentence begins with a capital letter and ends with a punctuation mark.

A statement gives information. A statement always ends with a period.
An exclamation shows sudden or strong feeling. An exclamation always ends with an exclamation point.
A command gives an order or makes a request. A command ends with either a period or an exclamation point.
A question asks something. A question always ends with a question mark.

Look ahead, Rat

Hooray, this is splendid

I wonder which of us had better pack the luncheon-basket

Presently they all sat down to luncheon together

Exercise 121A: Proofreading

Use proofreader's marks to insert the missing capital letters and punctuation marks into the following sentences. These are taken from *The Worst Journey in the World,* by the English explorer Apsley Cherry-Garrard—an account of an attempt to reach the South Pole in 1911 during which several other explorers died.

capitalize letter: ≡ make letter lowercase: /
insert period: ⊙ insert exclamation point: ↑
insert comma: ^, insert question mark: ^?
insert quotation marks: ∨"

If a word or phrase should be italicized, indicate this by underlining.

the terra nova sailed from the west india dock london on june 1 1910 and from cardiff

on june 15

she made her way to new zealand refitted and restowed her cargo took on board ponies dogs motor sledges certain further provisions and equipment as well as such members of her executive officers and scientists as had not travelled out in her and left finally for the south on november 29 1910

mr evans mr day and myself could eat more as we are just beginning to feel the tightening of the belt

lo for there among the flowers and grasses

only the mightier movement sounds and passes

owing to press contracts and the necessity of preventing leakage of news the terra nova had to remain at sea for twenty four hours after a cable had been sent to england

as a rule great sheets spread over the seas which fringe the antarctic continent in the autumn grow thicker and thicker during the winter and spring and break up when the temperatures of sea and air rise in summer

the discovery left new zealand on christmas eve 1901 and entered the belt of pack ice which always has to be penetrated in order to reach the comparatively open sea beyond

it was a great disappointment to dr wilson that no emperor penguin embryos were obtained during the cruise of the discovery

oh what joy

when and under what conditions the cape crozier rookery was eventually visited and emperor eggs secured is graphically told in the winter journey

on the 8th the morning was still separated from the discovery by eight miles of fast ice campbell and his five companions were finally landed at cape adare and built their hut close to borchgrevinck's old winter quarters

to our amazement we found their snowed-up tent some 140 geographical miles from hut point only 11 geographical miles from one ton camp

inside the tent were the bodies of scott wilson and bowers

oh no said campbell we always sang it on inexpressible island

in addition to scotts last expedition and priestleys antarctic adventures griffith taylor has written an account of the two geological journeys of which he was the leader and of the domestic life of the expedition at hut point and at cape evans in a book called with scott: the silver lining

Exercise 121B: Correct Letter Mechanics

The following text is a letter written by the scientist Carl Sagan, on behalf of the Voyager Interstellar Record Committee, to the pioneering rock-and-roll musician Chuck Berry.

On your own paper (or with your own word-processing program), rewrite or retype the text so that it is properly formatted, punctuated, and capitalized. You may choose either letter format from this lesson.

The first three sentences in the letter are one paragraph, while the last sentence is its own separate paragraph.

The abbreviation *c/o* stands for "in care of" and is used when the person you're writing to has to be contacted through someone else (such as an agent or other representative).

When you are finished, compare your letter with the two versions in the *Answer Key*.

carl sagan cornell university ithaca new york october 15 1986 mr chuck berry

c/o mr nick miranda 12825 four winds farm drive st. louis mo 63131 dear chuck berry

when they tell you your music will live forever you can usually be sure theyre exaggerating. but johnny b goode is on the voyager interstellar records attached to nasas voyager spacecraft—now two billion miles from earth and bound for the stars. These records will last a billion years or more. go johnny go carl sagan

—LESSON 122—

Commas
Semicolons
Additional Semicolon Rules
Colons
Additional Colon Rules

1. A comma and coordinating conjunction join compound sentences.
2. Commas separate three or more items in a series.
3. Commas separate two or more adjectives that come before a noun (as long as the adjectives can exchange position).
4. A comma precedes the *and* before the last item last item in a series of three or more (the "Oxford comma").
5. Commas set off terms of direct address.
6. Commas set off non-restrictive adjective clauses.
7. Commas set off parenthetical expressions that are closely related to the sentence.
8. Commas set off most appositives (unless the appositive is only one word and very closely related to the word it renames).
9. Commas may surround or follow interjections.
10. Commas may surround or follow introductory adverbs of affirmation and negation.
11. Commas may set off introductory adverb and adjective phrases.
12. In dates, commas separate the day of the week from the day of the month and the day of the month from the year.
13. In addresses, commas separate the city from the state.
14. Commas follow the greeting and closing of a friendly letter, and the closing of a formal letter.
15. Commas divide large numbers into sets of thousands.
16. A comma follows a dialogue tag or attribution tag that precedes a speech or quote.
17. A comma comes after a speech or quote if a dialogue tag or attribution tag follows.
18. A comma may divide a partial sentence from the block quote it introduces.
19. Commas may be used at any time to prevent misunderstanding and simplify reading.

Exercise 122A: Comma Use

In the blank at the end of each sentence, write the number from the list above that describes the comma use. If more than one number seems to fit equally well, write all suitable numbers.

These sentences are from *South: The Story of Shackleton's Last Expedition 1914-1917*, written by the polar explorer Ernest Shackleton himself.

We sailed from London on Friday, August 1, 1914, and anchored off Southend all Saturday. ________

On the following Saturday, August 8, the *Endurance* sailed from Plymouth, obeying the direct order of the Admiralty. ________

They were big, sturdy animals, chosen for endurance and strength, and if they were as keen to pull our sledges as they were now to fight one another all would be well. ________

Worsley, Wild, and I, with three officers, kept three watches while we were working through the pack, so that we had two officers on deck all the time. ________

I do not know who had been responsible for some of the dogs' names, which seemed to represent a variety of tastes. ________

They were as follows Rugby, Upton Bristol, Millhill, Songster, Sandy, Mack, Mercury, Wolf, Amundsen, Hercules, Hackenschmidt, Samson, Sammy, Skipper, Caruso, Sub, Ulysses, Spotty, Bosun, Slobbers, Sadie, Sue, Sally, Jasper, Tim, Sweep, Martin, Splitlip, Luke, Saint, Satan, Chips, Stumps, Snapper, Painful, Bob, Snowball, Jerry, Judge, Sooty, Rufus, Sidelights, Simeon, Swanker, Chirgwin, Steamer, Peter, Fluffy, Steward, Slippery, Elliott, Roy, Noel, Shakespeare, Jamie, Bummer, Smuts, Lupoid, Spider, and Sailor. ________

No, I do not like the idea of drifting on a berg. ________

The first day of the New Year (January 1, 1915) was cloudy, with a gentle northerly breeze and occasional snow-squalls. ________

This takes us into open water, where we make S. 50° W. for 24 miles. ________

The sun, which had been above the horizon for two months, set at midnight on the 17th, and, although it would not disappear until April, its slanting rays warned us of the approach of winter. ________

On the 23rd, for example, we put down a 2 ft. dredge and 650 fathoms of wire. __________

Having, therefore, determined as nearly as possible that portion of the deck immediately above these cases, we proceeded to cut a hole with large ice-chisels through the 3-in. planking of which it was formed. __________

However, in spite of occasional setbacks due to unfavourable winds, our drift was in the main very satisfactory, and this went a long way towards keeping the men cheerful. __________

"All theories about the swell being non-existent in the pack are false," wrote the anxious master. __________

The independent clauses of a compound sentence must be joined by a comma and a coordinating conjunction, a semicolon, or a semicolon and a coordinating conjunction. They cannot be joined by a comma alone.

He knew—as the Athenians and Persians did not—exactly when the flooding of the Nile was about to occur, and he managed to hold the combined invasion force off until the waters began to rise rapidly around him.

Thousands of years ago, groups of hunters and gatherers roamed across Asia and Europe, following mammoth herds that fed on the wild grasses. Slowly the ice began to retreat; the patterns of the grass growth changed; the herds wandered north and diminished.

They eat and drink, and thank him for his generosity; but Atrahasis himself, knowing that the feast is a death meal, paces back and forth, ill with grief and guilt.

—Susan Wise Bauer, *The History of the Ancient World*

Block quotes should be introduced by a colon (if preceded by a complete sentence) or a comma (if preceded by a partial sentence).

Piankhe did not try to wipe out his enemies. Instead, he chose to see Egypt as a set of kingdoms, with himself as High King over them:

> Amun of Napata has appointed me governor of this land,

he wrote in another inscription,

> as I might say to someone: "Be king," and he is it, or: "You will not be king," and he is not.

—Susan Wise Bauer, *The History of the Ancient World*

Use a colon after the salutation of a business letter.

The White House
1600 Pennsylvania Ave NW
Washington, DC 20500

Dear Mr. President

Use a colon to separate the hour from minutes in a time.

I went to bed at 11 59 on December 31.

Use a colon to separate the chapter from verse in a Biblical reference.

According to Ecclesiastes 12 12, "much study wearies the body."

If items in a series contain commas within the items, semicolons may separate two or more items in a series.

If semicolons separate items in a series, a colon may set off the series.

Around the tomb complex, buildings recreated in stone the materials of traditional Egyptian houses: walls of stone, carved to look like reed matting; stone columns shaped into bundles of reeds; even a wooden fence with a partly open gate, chiseled from stone.

Like the Great Pyramid, the Sphinx has attracted its share of nutty theories: it dates from 10,000 B.C. and was built by a disappeared advanced civilization; it was built by Atlanteans (or aliens); it represents a zodiacal sign, or a center of global energy.

Between 4000 and 3000 B.C. is known as the Naqada Period, and was once divided into three phases: the Amratian, which runs from 4000 to 3500 B.C.; the Gerzean, from 3500 to 3200 B.C.; and the Final Predynastic, from 3200 to 3000 B.C.

—Susan Wise Bauer, *The History of the Ancient World*

A colon may introduce a list.

Stripped of personality, prehistoric peoples too often appear as blocks of shifting color on a map: moving north, moving west, generating a field of cultivated grain, or corralling a herd of newly domesticated animals.

Many thousands of years ago, the Sumerian king Alulim ruled over Eridu: a walled city, a safe space carved out of the unpredictable and harsh river valley that the Romans would later name Mesopotamia.

Plague, drought, and war: these were enough to upset the balance of a civilization that had been built in rocky dry places, close to the edge of survival.

—Susan Wise Bauer, *The History of the Ancient World*

For emphasis, a colon may introduce an item that follows a complete sentence, when that item is closely related to the sentence.

But the historian's task is different: to look for particular human lives that give flesh and spirit to abstract assertions about human behavior.

But the historian's task, to look for particular human lives that give flesh and spirit to abstract assertions about human behavior, is different.

Exercise 122B: Capitalization and Punctuation

Insert all missing punctuation and correct all capitalization in the text that follows. Use these proofreader's marks:

capitalize letter: ≡	make letter lowercase: /
insert period: ⊙	insert exclamation point: ^!
insert comma: ^,	insert question mark: ^?
insert colon: ^:	insert semicolon: ^;
insert dash: (—)	insert quotation marks: ∨"
insert hyphen: △	

If a word or phrase should be italicized, indicate this by underlining.

122B.1: Sentences

the search for the northwest passage languished for several years following baffins voyages

thomas jamess voyage was financed by merchants from the port of bristol luke foxe was sailing under the royal sponsorship of king charles i

james set sail from bristol on may 3 1631 and foxe left from london on may 5

following rumors of gold the spaniards moved north through modern day georgia and into present day south carolina

pizarro and orellana soon discovered that the legendary land of cinnamon did not exist all they encountered were endless jungles and scattered villages

an eyewitness to the carnage wrote the whole number of indians that died in this town were two thousand and five hundred little more than less

they paused for almost two months at a village called aparia where they built a second larger ship they called the victoria to complement the smaller and cramped san pedro

champlain and twenty seven men prepared to spend the winter in a tiny enclave they suffered from dysentery and scurvy and by the time more settlers arrived in the spring only champlain and eight others were still alive

but now reinforced champlain continued his explorations in the summer of 1609 he became the first recorded european to visit lake champlain on the border between modern day vermont and new york

one explorer named jean nicolet spent several years as a fur trader among the native inhabitants in modern day western ontario where he heard about other tribes that lived to the west and south along the shores of an unknown bay

the native people with whom he lived referred to them by the name people of the sea

—the age of exploration by andrew a kling

122B.2: Letter Format

The following letters were both written by J. R. R. Tolkien, author of *The Lord of the Rings*.

In the first letter, Tolkien is complaining to his editor that *The Fellowship of the Ring*, the first book in his new trilogy, isn't going anywhere because he's all out of ideas!

In the second, Tolkien is writing a Santa Claus letter to one of his sons. He used to write these letters every Christmas.

(In Britain, the day of the month comes before the month, not after as in the United States, but the same punctuation rules still apply!)

20 northmoor road
oxford england

17 february 1938

c a furth, allen & unwin
40 museum street
london england

dear mr furth,

the hobbit sequel is still where it is, and i have only the vaguest notions of how to proceed. not ever intending any sequel, i fear i squandered all my favorite 'motifs' and characters on the original Hobbit

yours sincerely
j r r tolkien

christmas house
north pole

22 december 1923

master john francis tolkien
11 st. mark's terrace
leeds england

my dear john
it is very cold today and my hand is very shaky—i am nineteen hundred and twenty seven years old on christmas day—lots older than your great-grandfather, so i can't stop the pen wobbling, but i hear that you are getting so good at reading that i expect you will be able to read my letter.

a cold kiss from,
father nicholas christmas

122B.3: Quotes

In a 2012 *esquire* article, essayist tom junod told the story of leonard sim and recounted how his invention had shaped the experience of visiting a georgia water park with his daughter. junod noted that with the rise of FastPass and its ilk, ordinary ticket holders find themselves waiting longer, and end up taking fewer rides than they did in the past, even as wealthier park goers cruise by. the experience of the line becomes an infernal humiliation he wrote and the experience of avoiding the line becomes the only way to enjoy the water park. He mourns the passing of the small-d democratic experience of waiting in a wet bathing suit with people of all sizes shapes and colors, and sees the stratification that has replaced it as signifying much more than merely jumping a line

it sounds like an innovative answer to the problem that everybody faces at an amusement park, and one perfectly in keeping with the approaches currently in place at airports and even on some crowded american highways perfectly in keeping with the two tiering of america you can pay for one level of access, or you can pay for another. If you have the means, you can even pay for freedom. theres only one problem Cutting the line is cheating, and everyone knows it. children know it most acutely know it in their bones and so when they've been waiting on a line for a half-hour and a family sporting yellow plastic flash passes on their wrists walks up and steps in front of them, they can't help asking why that family has been permitted the privilege of perpetrating what looks like an obvious injustice. And then you have to explain not just that they paid for it but that you haven't paid enough that the $100 or so that you've ponied up was just enough to teach your children that they are second- or third class citizens

the end result junod concluded is that "your experience—what you've paid full price for—has been devalued

— The velvet rope economy, by nelson d schwartz

—LESSON 123—

Colons
Dashes
Hyphens
Parentheses
Brackets

But the historian's task is different: to look for particular human lives that give flesh and spirit to abstract assertions about human behavior.

But the historian's task is different—to look for particular human lives that give flesh and spirit to abstract assertions about human behavior.
—Susan Wise Bauer, *The History of the Ancient World*

A colon may introduce an item that follows a complete sentence, when that item is closely related to the sentence.

Dashes — — can enclose words that are not essential to the sentence.
Dashes can also be used singly to separate parts of a sentence.

A dash is twice as long as a hyphen.
When you write a dash, make it a little longer than a hyphen.
When you type a dash, use two hyphens for each dash.

well-educated (hyphen)
Well—that was a mistake. (dash)

Hyphens connect some compound nouns.

self-confidence
wallpaper
air conditioning

Hyphens connect compound adjectives in the attributive position.

self-confident woman
the woman was self confident

Hyphens connect spelled-out numbers between twenty-one and ninety-nine.

seventy-one balloons
he turned seventy-one on Friday

Hyphens divide words between syllables at the end of lines in justified text.

. . . worth inhabiting by reason of its barrenness; and indeed, both for-
saking it because of the prodigious number of tigers, lions, leopards,
and others of the furious creatures which harbour there; so that the . . .

> . . . worth inhabiting by reason of its barrenness; and indeed, both forsaking it because of the prodigious number of tigers, lions, leopards, and others of the furious creatures which harbour there; so that the . . .

Parentheses ( ) can enclose words that are not essential to the sentence.
Parenthetical expressions often interrupt or are irrelevant to the rest of the sentence.
Punctuation goes inside the parentheses if it applies to the parenthetical material; all other punctuation goes outside the parentheses.
Parenthetical material only begins with a capital letter if it is a complete sentence with ending punctuation.

> I had no sooner said so, but I perceived the creature (whatever it was) within two oars' length.

Commas make a parenthetical element a part of the sentence.
Dashes emphasize a parenthetical element.
Parentheses minimize a parenthetical element.

> "Particularly," said I, aloud (though to myself), "what should I have done without a gun, without ammunition, without any tools to make anything, or to work with, without clothes, bedding, a tent, or any manner of covering?"
>
> Accordingly, having spent three days in this journey, I came home (so I must now call my tent and my cave); but before I got thither the grapes were spoiled; the richness of the fruit and the weight of the juice having broken them and bruised them, they were good for little or nothing; as to the limes, they were good, but I could bring but a few.
>
> Well, to take away this discouragement, I resolved to dig into the surface of the earth, and so make a declivity; this I began, and it cost me a prodigious deal of pains (but who grudge pains who have their deliverance in view?); but when this was worked through, and this difficulty managed, it was still much the same, for I could no more stir the canoe than I could the other boat.
>
> I first laid all the planks or boards upon it that I could get, and having considered well what I most wanted, I got three of the seamen's chests, which I had broken open, and emptied, and lowered them down upon my raft; the first of these I filled with provisions—bread, rice, three Dutch cheeses, five pieces of dried goat's flesh (which we lived much upon), and a little remainder of European corn, which had been laid by for some fowls which we brought to sea with us, but the fowls were killed.
>
> —Daniel Defoe, *Robinson Crusoe*

Exercise 123A: Hyphens

Many (but not all) of the following sentences contain words that should be hyphenated. Insert a hyphen into each word that needs one.

From their mid twenties in most social groups, from adolescence in elite circles, women experienced a cycle of childbirth and nursing and childbirth again.

Poor women gave birth every twenty four to thirty months.

Unproductive marriages in sixteenth century Venice threatened the survival of her ruling class and left citizen houses in fourteenth century Florence, according to Dante, "vuote di famiglia," childless.

Her contemporary, the Englishwoman Margaret Denton Verney, bore twelve children over a twenty eight year period, while the Florentine Alessandra Macinghi Strozzi, a descendent of the Alberti and Strozzi commercial dynasties of Florence, gave birth to eight children in the decade from 1426 to 1436.

From the fourteenth through the seventeenth century, the women of the noble Venetian Donato family may have achieved in each generation the average maximum biological fertility: twelve births.

In fifteenth century Venice, Magdalucia, the wife of the nobleman Francesco Marcello, gave birth to twenty six children: nearly one per year for all the years of her fertility.

Both pregnancy and birth overwhelmed the English mystic Margery Kempe, whose difficult labor precipitated a six month depression.

—*Women of the Renaissance*, by Margaret L. King

She commissioned paintings from Michelangelo and Titian, and was on a first name basis with the Holy Roman Emperor.

In the third century C.E., it was there that the emperor Caracalla chose to erect a magnificent temple to the Greco Egyptian god Serapis.

Vittoria is dressed in a rich blue and red gown, with locks of her long reddish brown hair flowing onto her shoulders.

In the sixteenth century, Italy was not a unified country—it became a nation state only in the 1860s—but was made up of small kingdoms and city states that were either self governed or under the control of foreign powers.

Six hundred thousand ducats were already owed to the imperial troops before the Battle of Pavia began.

Ferrante's near betrayal of Charles would have been in Vittoria's mind when she received the request to come to Milan.

In early December, 1525, she and her entourage stopped in Viterbo, roughly fifty miles north of Rome.

The d'Avalos family, as we have seen, arrived in Italy with the first Spanish kings in the mid fifteenth century.

—*Renaissance Woman: The Life of Vittoria Colonna*, by Ramie Targoff

Exercise 123B: Parenthetical Elements

The following sentences, slightly condensed from *The Life of Cesare Borgia*, by Rafael Sabatini, each contain at least one parenthetical element.

Set off each bolded set of words with commas, dashes, or parentheses. Choose the punctuation marks that seem to fit best.

Within those bolded sets of words, you may see an additional parenthetical element that is underlined. Be sure to punctuate this one as well!

Then, compare your answers with the original punctuation in the *Answer Key*.

King Alfonso had already fled the kingdom **January 25**, abdicating in favour of his brother Federigo.

This aim was later to be carried into actual **if ephemeral** fulfillment by Cesare Borgia.

He paid all salaries promptly a **striking departure <u>it would seem</u> from what had been usual under his predecessor** and the effect was soon seen.

There would be fresh difficulties, owing **of course** to Orsini's enmity to the existing Florentine government.

It may not be amiss **though <u>perhaps</u> no longer very necessary after what has been written** to say a word about his social position.

The letter written from Spoleto expresses his regret that **on the occasion of his passage through Florence <u>on his way from Pisa to Spoleto</u>** he should not have time to visit.

The circumstance of their father being a Pope not only was not accounted extraordinarily scandalous **if scandalous at all** but, on the contrary rendered them eligible for princely alliances.

Whether or not Lodovico had him poisoned **a charge which <u>after all</u> rests on no proof** his death most certainly lies at his ambitious uncle's door.

Such was the person of the young king **he was twenty-four years of age at the time** who poured his legions into Rome.

The House of Farnese was to give dukes to Parma and reach the throne of Spain **in the person of Isabella Farnese** before becoming extinct in 1758.

On April 23 we see him on horseback accompanying the Pope through Rome, and **as usual** he is attended by his hundred armed grooms in black.

He made haste **therefore** to agree to the surrender of Castel Bolobnese to the duke.

Roderigo de Lanzol y Broja alone remained **notably, the only prominent member of his house** to face the enmity of the Sacred College.

He left behind him most of his precious artillery, his tents and carriages, and the immense Neapolitan booty, which he had loaded **says Gregorovius** onto twenty thousand mules.

Her widowhood was short however for in the same year **on June 6** she took a second husband, possibly at the instance of Roderigo Borgia, who did not wish to leave her unprotected; that **at least** is the general inference, although there is very little evidence upon which to base it.

—LESSON 124—

Italics
Quotation Marks
Ellipses
Single Quotation Marks
Apostrophes

In *Around the World in Eighty Days,* Jules Verne describes the arrival of the steamer *Mongolia* at the port of Suez.

Capitalize and italicize the names of ships, trains, and planes.

Italicize the titles of lengthy or major works such as books, newspapers, magazines, major works of art, and long musical compositions.

Use quotation marks for minor or brief works of art and writing or portions of longer works such as short stories, newspaper articles, songs, chapters, and poems.

Watership Down	"The Chief Rabbit"
The Hobbit	"An Unexpected Party"
The New York Times	"In Julia Child's Provençal Kitchen"
National Geographic	
The *Mona Lisa* of Da Vinci	"Saint Jerome in Penitence," by Dürer
The *David* of Michelangelo	
1812 Overture, by Tchaikovsky	
The opera *Carmen*, by Bizet	"Toreador Song"
	"Scarborough Fair"
	"The Lottery"
The *Odyssey*	"Stopping by Woods on a Snowy Evening"
	"The Raven"

Italicize letters, numbers, and words if they are the subject of discussion. In plural versions, do not italicize the *s*.

The letter *A* begins the alphabet, and a *Z* concludes it.

Most Americans hate the word *moist.*

*A*s and *F*s are hard to write in calligraphy.

Italicize foreign words not adopted into English.

What we call "rapid-eye-movement sleep" the French call *sommeil paradoxal* (paradoxical sleep) because the body is still but the mind is extremely active.
—Pamela Druckerman, *Bringing Up Bébé*

Mark Twain was the nom de plume of Samuel Langhorne Clemens.

English doesn't borrow from other languages. English follows other languages down dark alleys, knocks them over and goes through their pockets for loose grammar.
—Sir Terry Pratchett

Use quotation marks for minor or brief works of art and writing or portions of longer works such as short stories, newspaper articles, songs, chapters, and poems.

Then there crawled from the bushes a dozen more great purple spiders, which saluted the first one and said, "The web is finished, O King, and the strangers are our prisoners."

Dorothy did not like the looks of these spiders at all. They had big heads, sharp claws, small eyes and fuzzy hair all over their purple bodies.

—L. Frank Baum, *Glinda of Oz*

Direct quotations are set off by quotation marks.

Fear of spiders might come in part from children's stories, which often portray spiders as hostile predators. In *Glinda of Oz,* L. Frank Baum writes about a Spider King and his army of "great purple spiders, which . . . said, 'The web is finished, O King, and the strangers are our prisoners.'"

A quote within a quote is surrounded by single quotation marks.

An apostrophe is a punctuation mark that shows possession. It turns a noun into an adjective that tells whose.

Form the possessive of a singular noun by adding an apostrophe and the letter *s*.

spider	wand
web	sorceress

Form the possessive of a plural noun ending in *-s* by adding an apostrophe only.

spiders	troubles
fields	lakes

Form the possessive of a plural noun that does not end in *-s* as if it were a singular noun.

sheep	hangmen
geese	teeth

A contraction is a combination of two words with some of the letters dropped out. An apostrophe shows where the letters have been omitted.

they are ____________________

was not ____________________

were not ____________________

I am ____________________

Exercise 124A: Proofreading Practice

The sentences below, taken from novels by Terry Pratchett, have lost most punctuation and capitalization. Insert all missing punctuation marks, and correct all capitalization errors. When you are finished, compare your sentences with the originals.

Use these proofreader's marks:

capitalize letter: ≡	make letter lowercase: /
insert period: ⊙	insert exclamation point: ↑
insert comma: ^,	insert question mark: ^?
insert colon: ^:	insert semicolon: ^;
insert apostrophe: ∨'	insert quotation marks: ∨"
insert dash: (—)	insert hyphen: ^-

If a word or phrase should be italicized, indicate this by underlining.

nine tenths of the universe in fact is the paperwork.

exciting eh said a hoarse voice by deaths ear.

it belonged to quoth the raven who had attached himself to the household as the death of rats' personal transport and crony

right on this point was the world turtle, elephants, the little orbiting sun, and all

it was a bitter winters night

well, now she said because shed learned a lot in the last twenty years or so that's as may be and ill always do the best i can ask anyone

the trouble was that he was the kind of person who, having decided to be an interesting person, would first of all try to find a book called how to be an interesting person and then see whether there were any courses available.

why, he could talk about all kinds of clocks mechanical clocks magical clocks water clocks first clocks floral clocks candle clocks sand clocks cuckoo clocks the rare hershebian beetle clocks

but enough of this perhaps said lady lejean stepping back you make clocks and we

it was three oclock

jeremy looked shocked the alloy i didnt think anyone outside the guild knew about that.

—thief of time

indeed sir and may I remind you that he will be leaving us very shortly

yes, but vimes began but his wife silenced him with a smile

she had a special smile for these occasions it was warm and friendly and carved out of rock the man thus addressed looked around for help support and guidance or escape but there was none the crowd was deathly silent

he very nearly gloated at the downfall of his enemy and slammed his copy of the ankh-morpork times open at the crossword page on to his desk

—snuff

you will set sail at dawn and rendezvous in the channel with the maid of liverpool just returned from san francisco.

no indeed captain you were born forty five years ago the second son of mr and mrs bertie samson and christened lionel after your grandfather said mr black calmly lowering his package to the deck

mau paddled over to a large hehe fish which he managed to drag aboard

—nation

Exercise 124B: Foreign Phrases That Are Now English Words

The following phrases and words are now part of English and are usually not italicized. Using a dictionary, look up each one. In the blank, write the original language that the word belongs to, the meaning in English, and the meaning in the original language. The first is done for you.

cul-de-sac French, a dead-end street, "bottom of the sack"

avatar ______________________________

patio ______________________________

vigilante ______________________________

angst ______________________________

a la carte ______________________________

de facto ______________________________

coup de grace ______________________________

nom de plume ______________________________

WEEK 34

Advanced Quotations & Dialogue

—LESSON 125—

Dialogue
Additional Rules for Writing Dialogue
Direct Quotations
Additional Rules for Using Direct Quotations

Use dialogue in fiction and to bring other voices into memoir, profiles, and reporting.

> A man was thought to be the painter of "Portrait of an Unknown Lady" when it went on sale in 2014 at an auction in the southern English city of Salisbury. It was bought by Bendor Grosvenor, an art dealer and historian who recognized the work as Carlile's.
>
> In an interview with *The Telegraph*, Mr. Grosvenor said that the artist's style "is quite recognizable if you know what it looks like."
>
> —Roslyn Sulcas, "A 17th-Century Portrait Will Be the Earliest Painting by a Woman at the Tate," *The New York Times,* Sept. 21, 2016

A dialogue tag identifies the person making the speech.

When a dialogue tag comes after a speech, place a comma, exclamation point, or question mark inside the closing quotation marks before the tag.

When a dialogue tag comes before a speech, place a comma after the tag. Put the dialogue's final punctuation mark inside the closing quotation marks.

> "There goes Tommaso the painter," the people would say, watching the big awkward figure passing through the streets on his way to work.

> Diamante said to Filippo, "You have learned well, and it is time now to turn your work to some account."

Speeches do not need to be attached to a dialogue tag as long as the text clearly indicates the speaker.

> The father gave a hopeless sigh and turned away. "So, you will be a painter."

Usually, a new paragraph begins with each new speaker.

Michelangelo said nothing, but he mounted the scaffolding and pretended to chip away at the nose with his chisel. Meanwhile he let drop some marble chips and dust upon the head of the critic beneath. Then he came down.

"Is that better?" he asked gravely.

"Admirable!" answered the artist. "You have given it life."

"I am growing too old to help you," Leonardo said, but Raphael shook his head. "I will go with you to the ends of the earth," he said.

When a dialogue tag comes in the middle of a speech, follow it with a comma if the following dialogue is an incomplete sentence. Follow it with a period if the following dialogue is a complete sentence.

"The boy!" said one brother, nudging the other, "has found his brains at last."

The painter's quick eyes examined the work with deep interest. "Send him to me at once," he said. "This is indeed marvellous talent."

—Amy Steedman, *Knights of Art: Stories of the Italian Painters*

RULES FOR USING DIRECT QUOTATIONS

Direct quotations are set off by quotation marks.

Every direct quote must have an attribution tag.

When an attribution tag comes after a direct quote, place a comma, exclamation point, or question mark inside the closing quotation marks.

"Frederick, is God dead?" asked Sojourner Truth.

When an attribution tag comes before a direct quote, place a comma after the tag. Put the quote's final punctuation mark inside the closing quotation marks.

The orator paused impressively, and then thundered in a voice that thrilled his audience with prophetic intimations, "No, God is not dead; and therefore it is that slavery must end in blood!"

When an attribution tag comes in the middle of a direct quotation, follow it with a comma if the remaining quote is an incomplete sentence. Follow it with a period if the remaining quote is a complete sentence.

"A new world had opened up to me," Douglass wrote. "I lived more in one day than in a year of my slave life."

"It was my good fortune," he writes, "to get out of slavery at the right time, to be speedily brought in contact with that circle of highly cultivated men and women, banded together for the overthrow of slavery, of which William Lloyd Garrison was the acknowledged leader."

Direct quotes can be words, phrases, clauses, or sentences, as long as they are set off by quotation marks and form part of a grammatically correct original sentence.

In his autobiography Douglass commends Mr. Johnson for his "noble-hearted hospitality and manly character."

Ellipses show where something has been cut out of a sentence.

If a direct quotation is longer than three lines, indent the entire quote one inch from the margin in a separate block of text and omit quotation marks.

In a footnote to the *Life and Times of Garrison* it is stated:

> This enterprise was not regarded with favor by the leading abolitionists, who knew only too well the precarious support which a fifth anti-slavery paper . . . must have . . . As anticipated, it nearly proved the ruin of its projector; but by extraordinary exertions it was kept alive.

If you change or make additions to a direct quotation, use brackets.

Parker Pillsbury reported that "though it was late in the evening when the young man closed his remarks, none seemed to know or care for the hour. . . . The crowded congregation had been wrought up almost to enchantment during the whole long evening, particularly by some of the utterances of the last speaker [Douglass], as he turned over the terrible apocalypse of his experience in slavery."

A quote within a quote is surrounded by single quotation marks.

ADDITIONAL RULES FOR DIRECT QUOTATIONS

Use direct quotations to provide examples, cite authorities, and emphasize your own points.

An attribution tag may be indirect.

In the wild songs of the slaves he read, beneath their senseless jargon or their fulsome praise of "old master," the often unconscious note of grief and despair.

A colon may introduce a direct quote.

Douglass spent a year under Covey's ministrations, and his life there may be summed up in his own words: "The overwork and the brutal chastisements of which I was the victim, combined with that ever-gnawing and soul-destroying thought, 'I am a slave—a slave for life,' rendered me a living embodiment of mental and physical wretchedness."

—Charles W. Chesnutt, *Frederick Douglass*

To quote three or fewer lines of poetry, indicate line breaks by using a slanted line and retain all original punctuation and capitalization.

Likewise, Paul Laurence Dunbar's 1895 poem "We Wear the Mask" anticipates the "two-ness" of African-American existence expressed most poignantly and poetically by Du Bois nearly a decade later. Dunbar most famously writes: "We wear the mask that grins and lies,/It hides our cheeks and shades our eyes,—/This debt we pay to human guile".

—Rebecka Rutledge Fisher, *Habitations of the Veil*

Four or more lines of poetry should be treated as a block quote.

> In his poem, "We Wear the Mask," Dunbar speaks of a double-consciousness that had been forced on African-Americans:
>
> > We wear the mask that grins and lies,
> > It hides our cheeks and shades our eyes,—
> > This debt we pay to human guile;
> > With torn and bleeding hearts we smile,
> > And mouth with myriad subtleties.
>
> Dunbar's biographer, Benjamin Brawley, wrote that Dunbar's poetry "soared above race and touched the heart universal."
>
> —Joseph Nazel, *Langston Hughes*

Any poetic citation longer than one line may be treated as a block quote.

Direct quotes should be properly documented.

—LESSON 126—

(Optional)
Documentation

In *101 Gourmet Cookies for Everyone*, author Wendy Paul claims that her Chocolate Chip Pudding Cookies are "by far the softest chocolate chip cookies" that can be found.[1]

[1] Wendy Paul, *101 Gourmet Cookies for Everyone* (Bonneville Books, 2010), p. 18.

A sentence containing a direct quote should be followed by a citation.

A superscript number may lead to a citation at the bottom of the page (a footnote) or the end of the paper (an endnote).

1. Footnotes and endnotes should follow this format:

   Author name, *Title of Book* (Publisher, year of publication), p. #.

   If there are two authors, list them like this:

   Author name and author name, *Title of Book* (Publisher, year of publication), p. #.

   If your quote comes from more than one page of the book you're quoting, use *pp.* to mean "pages" and put a hyphen between the page numbers.

   Author name, *Title of Book* (Publisher, year of publication), pp. #-#.

   If a book is a second (or third, or fourth, etc.) edition, put that information right after the title.

Author name, *Title of Book*, 2nd ed. (Publisher, year of publication), p. #.

If no author is listed, simply use the title of the book.

Title of Book (Publisher, year of publication), p. #.

All of this information can be found on the copyright page of the book.

2. Footnotes should be placed beneath a dividing line at the bottom of the page. If you are using a word processing program, the font size of the footnotes should be about 2 points smaller than the font size of the main text.

3. Endnotes should be placed at the end of the paper, under a centered heading, like this:

ENDNOTES

[1] Wendy Paul, *101 Gourmet Cookies for Everyone* (Bonneville Books, 2010), p. 18.

[2] Author, *Title of Book* (Publisher, year of publication), p. #.

For a short paper (three pages or less), the endnotes can be placed on the last page of the paper itself. A paper that is four or more pages in length should have an entirely separate page for endnotes.

4. The second time you cite a book, your footnote or endnote only needs to contain the following information:

[2] Author last name, p. #.

5. If a paragraph contains several quotes from the same source, a single citation at the end of the entire paragraph can cover all quotations.

Every work mentioned in a footnote or endnote must also appear on a final Works Cited page.

WORKS CITED

Paul, Wendy. *101 Gourmet Cookies for Everyone*. Springville, UT: Bonneville Books, 2010.

1. List sources alphabetically by the author's last name.
2. The format should be: Last name of author, first name. *Title of Book*. City of publication: Publisher, year of publication.
3. If the work has no author, list it by the first word of the title (but ignore the articles *a*, *an*, and *the*).
4. If the city of publication is not a major city (New York, Los Angeles, London, Beijing, New Delhi, Tokyo), include the state (for a U.S. publisher) or country (for an international publisher).
5. For a short paper (three pages or less), the Works Cited section may be at the bottom of the last page. For a paper of four or more pages, attach a separate Works Cited page.

Additional Rules for Citing Sources (Turabian)

1. Magazine articles

In a footnote or endnote, use the following style:

[1] Author name, "Name of article." *Name of Magazine*, Date of publication, page number.

[2] Jacqueline Harp, "A Breed for Every Yard: Black Welsh Mountain Sheep Break New Ground." *Sheep!*, September/October 2013, p. 27.

In Works Cited, use the following style:

Author last name, first name. "Name of article." *Name of Magazine* volume number: issue number (Date of publication), total number of pages article takes up in magazine.

Harp, Jacqueline. "A Breed for Every Yard: Black Welsh Mountain Sheep Break New Ground." *Sheep!* 34:5 (September/October 2013), pp. 26–28.

2. Websites

In a footnote or endnote, use the following style:

[3] Author/editor/sponsoring organization of website, "Name of article," URL (date accessed).

[4] Mallory Daughtery, "Baa Baa Black and White Sheep Treats," http://www.southernliving.com/home-garden/holidays-occasions/spring-table-settings-centerpieces-00400000041389/page8.html (accessed Sept. 12, 2013).

In Works Cited, use the following style:

Author/editor/sponsoring organization of website. "Name of article." URL (date accessed).

Daughtery, Mallory. "Baa Baa Black and White Sheep Treats." http://www.southernliving.com/home-garden/holidays-occasions/spring-table-settings-centerpieces-00400000041389/page8.html (accessed Sept. 12, 2013).

3. Ebooks with flowing text (no traditional page numbers)

In a footnote or endnote, use the following style:

[5] Author name, *Name of book* (Publisher, date), Name of ebook format: Chapter number, any other information given by ebook platform.

[6] Paul de Kruif, *Microbe Hunters* (Harvest, 1996), Kindle: Ch. 7, Loc. 2134.

In Works Cited, use the following style:

Author last name, author first name. *Title of book*. City of publication: Publisher, date. Name of ebook format.

de Kruif, Paul. *Microbe Hunters*. Fort Washington, PA: Harvest, 1996. Kindle.

In-text citations may be used in scientific or technical writing.

The chemical reactions that take place within Chocolate Chip Pudding Cookies make them "by far the softest chocolate chip cookies" (Paul 2010, 18) that can be found.

About Turabian

The style described in this lesson is the most common one for student papers. It is known as "Turabian," after Kate Turabian, the head secretary for the graduate department at the University of Chicago from 1930 until 1958.

Kate Turabian had to approve the format of every doctoral dissertation and master's thesis submitted to the University of Chicago. These papers were supposed to follow the format of the *University of Chicago Manual of Style*, but the *Manual of Style* is huge and complicated and many students couldn't figure out exactly how to use it. So Kate Turabian wrote a simplified version of the *Manual of Style*, intended just for the use of students writing papers. It was called *A Manual for Writers of Research Papers, Theses, and Dissertations*, and her book has sold over eight million copies.

Alternative Styles for Citation

A. **Turabian** (most common for students)

FOOTNOTE/ENDNOTE

[1] Susan Cooper, *Silver on the Tree* (Atheneum, 1977), p. 52.

IN-TEXT CITATION

(Cooper 1977, 52)

WORKS CITED

Cooper, Susan. *Silver on the Tree*. New York: Atheneum, 1977.

B. **Chicago Manual of Style**

FOOTNOTE/ENDNOTE

[1] Susan Cooper, *Silver on the Tree* (New York: Atheneum 1977), p. 52.

IN-TEXT CITATION

(Cooper 1977, 52)

WORKS CITED

Cooper, Susan. 1977. *Silver on the Tree*. New York: Atheneum, 1977.

C. **APA** (American Psychological Association, the standard for science writing)

FOOTNOTE/ENDNOTE

APA does not recommend the use of footnotes or endnotes.

IN-TEXT CITATION

(Cooper, 1977, p. 52)

WORKS CITED

Cooper, S. (1977). *Silver on the tree.* Atheneum.

D. **MLA** (Modern Language Association, more often used in the arts and humanities)

FOOTNOTE/ENDNOTE

MLA does not recommend the use of footnotes or endnotes for citations. They should only be used to direct the reader to additional books or resources that should be consulted.

IN-TEXT CITATION

(Cooper 52)

WORKS CITED

Cooper, Susan. *Silver on the Tree.* New York, NY, United States: Atheneum, 1977. Print.

—LESSON 127—

Practicing Direct Quotations and Correct Documentation

Your assignment: Write a short essay called "Four Wicked Rulers." The four wicked rulers are Ashurnasirpal II of Assyria, Nero of Rome, Krum of Bulgaria, and Henry VIII of England. In the sources below, you'll see some praise for each of these rulers—but your essay should focus on the wickedness of each one!

Your essay should be at least 250 words, although it will probably need to be longer.

You must quote directly from at least FIVE of the sources listed below, footnote each direct quote, and put all five on your Works Cited page. You MUST include both a quote from the journal article listed below AND from the website history.co.uk among your sources (and you can use more than five sources, if you prefer).

Your essay must include the following:

a) a brief quote that comes before its attribution tag
b) a brief quote that comes after its attribution tag
c) a brief quote divided by its attribution tag
d) a block quote
e) a quote that is incorporated into a complete sentence and serves a grammatical function within that sentence
f) a quote that has been altered with either brackets or ellipses (these must be your own alterations, not those that are already in the sources below!)
g) a second quote from the same source

One quote can fulfill more than one of these requirements. If you need help, ask your instructor.

Note to Student: There's a challenge below you haven't seen yet—two books by the same author, Susan Wise Bauer!

You've learned that your first reference to a book should be a full listing of author, title, publisher, date, and page number, but that the second time, you can simply list the author's last name and the page number.

If the author has written *two* books that you reference, you have to add a little more information! If Julia Smith wrote *A Guide to Giant Owls* and *Handbook of Pygmy Owls* and you quote both, you still give a full citation for the first time you quote each book, but then the second time you need to specify which book you're citing—so instead of

Smith, 42

you would write

Smith, *A Guide to Giant Owls*, 42

or

Smith, *Handbook of Pygmy Owls*, 42

Note that you don't have to provide any other information, because that all came in your first citation of each book.

Author: Stanley Sandler, ed.
Title of Book: *Ground Warfare: An International Encyclopedia*, Vol. I
City of Publication: Santa Barbara, CA
Publisher: ABC-CLIO, Inc.
Date: 2002

67

Ashurnasirpal II (r. 883-859 BCE) was the king who forged Assyria into one of the dominant powers of the Near East... [He] campaigned continuously during his reign, directing his efforts to the north against the Aramean states... All of these states, in one form or another, became vassals to Assyria. Moreover, Ashurnasirpal established a long line of fortresses to protect Assyrian trade routes... Ashurnasirpal restructured the Assyrian state and army (which had been weak for centuries), created a large bureaucracy, continued a policy of deporting conquered peoples, and claims in his annals to have used psychological warfare on his enemies by performing public displays of cruelty, mass executions, and the burning of disloyal vassal cities.

Author: Susan Wise Bauer
Title of Book: *The History of the Ancient World: From the Earliest Accounts to the Fall of Rome*
City of Publication: New York
Publisher: W. W. Norton
Date: 2007

338

In Ashurnasirpal there appeared, full-blown, the delight in cruelty which tagged at the heels of almost every Assyrian king who followed. "I put up a pillar at the city gate," Ashurnasirpal explains, recording his dealings with a city which had revolted and killed its Assyrian-appointed governor, "and I skinned the chiefs who revolted against me, and covered the pillar with their skins. I walled up others in the middle of the pillar itself, and some of them I impaled on stakes and arranged them around the pillar. Inside the city, I skinned many more and covered the walls with their skins. As for the royal officials, I cut off their members." He varied this, at other times, by making heaps of cut-off noses and ears, gouging out eyes, and tying heads to vines throughout the gardens of conquered cities like obscene and decaying fruit. "I made one pillar of the living," he remarks, a particularly nasty Assyrian invention where living prisoners were laid one on top of another and covered with plaster to make a column. "I cut off their ears and their fingers, of many I put out the eyes… their young men and maidens I burned in the fire."

Name of Article: "The Making of the Bulgarian Nation"
Author: V. N. Zlatarski
Magazine: *The Slavonic Review*
Date: December 1925
Volume and issue number: Volume 4, Number 11
Page range of article: 362-383

368

The plan for uniting the Balkan Slavs and strengthening the Slavonic element in the state was carried on and extended

369

under the warlike and energetic Khan Krum (802-814). After crushing the Avars and extending the northern frontier of Bulgaria to the rivers Tisza and Prut and to the Carpathians, Krum advanced south-westward in the steps of his predecessors and succeeded in adding the Sofia region and the lands along the upper Stuma and Mesta to his khanate… [This] brilliant victory exalted the Khan of Bulgaria in the eyes of the Imperial Slavs as the conqueror of the Romaic Basileus, and so paved the way for the expansion of the state towards the south-west. Krum… carried away by his great success and by the idea that the Byzantine Emperor could be defeated… launched a series of fierce attacks on Constantinople, which brought no profit to the state and served only to hasten his end…

371

At the time of his campaigns in Thrace and of his expeditions against Constantinople, he took large numbers of prisoners, whom he subsequently transplanted to various parts of his country.

Author: Susan Wise Bauer
Title of Book: *The History of the Medieval World: From the Conversion of Constantine to the First Crusade*
City of Publication: New York
Publisher: W. W. Norton
Date: 2010

400

The Bulgarian khan was named Krum, and under his rule—which began sometime between 796 and 803—Bulgaria swelled into a major power... Around 805, Krum invaded the territory of the once-great Avars and folded it into his own, which brought his empire directly to the eastern border of Charlemagne. Deciding not to wait until Krum became even more powerful, the emperor of Constantinople, Nikephoros, declared war on the Bulgarians and began to arm his troops.

It took him over a year to get the troops on the road, partly because he had to put down a palace rebellion in the middle of his preparations. But by 808, he was moving troops into the Strymon river valley, on the southern Bulgarian border. Krum's men descended on them before they were at full strength and drove them back, killing a number of soldiers and officers and (even more damaging) capturing all of the money Nikephoros had sent along with his generals to use for payroll—eleven hundred pounds of gold, according to Theophanes.

Hostilities now began in earnest. In 809, Krum led his army against the city of Serdica, a frontier city within Byzantine territory, and captured it, slaughtering six thousand Byzantine soldiers and hundreds of civilians... It took Nikephoros I (who was again distracted by yet another rebellion at home, this one brought about by his decision to raise everyone's taxes) more than a year to prepare his army for a return attack. He had decided that the only appropriate response was to wipe Krum out entirely, and to that end he imported soldiers from Thracia and Asia Minor to beef up the depleted

401

forces at Constantinople... Krum's defenders were defeated and pushed backwards as the Byzantine army advanced... But Krum was not finished. He had retreated, along with every man he could recruit, into the mountains through which the Byzantine army would have to march on their way home, and had built a wooden wall across the pass. On July 25, heading for Constantinople in triumph, Nikephoros and his men ran directly into the wooden wall. The Bulgarians attacked the trapped army as it piled up in front of the barrier. Nikephoros, fighting at the front, was killed almost at once. Soldiers who tried to climb the wall and escape fell into an enormous ditch that the Bulgarians had dug on the other side and filled with burning logs.

The Byzantine troops were slaughtered. Krum beheaded the emperor's corpse, stuck the head on a pole, and—once the flesh had rotted off—had the skull coated in silver so that he could use it as a drinking goblet.

Author: Samuel G. Goodrich
Title of Book: *Famous Men of Ancient Times*
City of Publication: Boston, MA
Publisher: Thompson, Brown & Co.
Date: 1864

69

[Nero] delivered himself from the sway of his mother, and at last ordered her to be assassinated. This unnatural act of barbarity shocked some of the Romans; but Nero had his devoted adherents; and when he declared that he had taken away his mother's life to save himself from ruin, the senate applauded his measures, and the people signified their approbation… Nero sacrificed to his fury or caprice all such as obstructed his pleasures, or stood in the way of his inclinations.

In the night he generally sallied out from his palace, to visit the meanest taverns and the scenes of debauchery in which Rome abounded. In his nocturnal riots he was fond of insulting the people in the streets, and on one occasion, an attempt to offer violence to the wife of a Roman senator nearly cost

70

him his life… His conduct, however, soon became more censurable; he was guilty of various acts which cannot be even named with decency. The cruelty of his nature was displayed in the sacrifice of his wives Octavia and Poppæa; and the celebrated writers, Seneca, Lucan, Petronius, &c., became the victims of his wantonness. The Christians did not escape his barbarity. He had heard of the burning of Troy, and as he wished to renew that dismal scene, he caused Rome to be set on fire in different places. The conflagration became soon universal, and during nine successive days the fire was unextinguished. All was desolation; nothing was heard but the lamentations of mothers whose children had perished in the flames, the groans of the dying, and the continual fall of palaces and buildings.

71

Nero was the only one who enjoyed the general consternation. He placed himself on a high tower and he sang on his lyre the destruction of Troy; a dreadful scene which his barbarity had realized before his eyes. He attempted to avert the public odium from his head, by a feigned commiseration of the sufferings of his subjects, and by charging the fire upon the Christians. He caused great numbers of them to be seized and put to death. Some were covered with the skins of wild beasts, and killed by dogs set upon them; others were crucified; others were smeared with pitch and burned, at night, in the imperial gardens, for the amusement of the people!

Author: C. Suetonius Tranquillus
Translator: Alexander Thomson
Title of Book: *The Lives of the Twelve Caesars, Vol. 6*
City of Publication: London
Publisher: G. Bell & Sons
Date: 1896

> **Note to Student:** Ancient texts sometimes use section numbers with Roman numerals rather than page numbers to indicate the place of the quote!

XXVI. Petulancy, lewdness, luxury, avarice, and cruelty, [Nero] practised at first with reserve and in private, as if prompted to them only by the folly of youth; but, even then, the world was of opinion that they were the faults of his nature, and not of his age. After it was dark, he used to enter the taverns disguised in a cap or a wig, and ramble about the streets in sport, which was not void of mischief. He used to beat those he met coming home from supper; and, if they made any resistance, would wound them, and throw them into the common sewer. He broke open and robbed shops; establishing an auction at home for selling his booty. In the scuffles which took place on those occasions, he often ran the hazard of losing his eyes, and even his life; being beaten almost to death by a senator, for handling his wife indecently. After this adventure, he never again ventured abroad at that time of night, without some tribunes following him at a little distance. In the day-time he would be carried to the theatre incognito in a litter, placing himself upon the upper part of the proscenium, where he not only witnessed the quarrels which arose on account of the performances, but also encouraged them. When they came to blows, and stones and pieces of broken benches began to fly about, he threw them plentifully amongst the people, and once even broke a praetor's head.

XXXIV. His mother being used to make strict inquiry into what he said or did, and to reprimand him with the freedom of a parent, he was so much offended, that he endeavoured to expose her to public resentment, by frequently pretending a resolution to quit the government, and retire to Rhodes. Soon afterwards, he deprived her of all honour and power, took from her the guard of Roman and German soldiers, banished her from the palace and from his society, and persecuted her in every way he could contrive; employing persons to harass her when at Rome with law-suits, and to disturb her in her retirement from town with the most scurrilous and abusive language, following her about by land and sea. But being terrified with her menaces and violent spirit, he resolved upon her destruction, and thrice attempted it by poison. Finding, however, that she had previously secured herself by antidotes, he contrived machinery, by which the floor over her bed-chamber might be made to fall upon her while she was asleep in the night. This design miscarrying likewise, through the little caution used by those who were in the secret, his next stratagem was to construct a ship which could be easily shivered, in hopes of destroying her either by drowning, or by the deck above her cabin crushing her in its fall. Accordingly, under colour of a pretended reconciliation, he wrote her an extremely affectionate letter, inviting her to Baiae, to celebrate with him the festival of Minerva. He had given private orders to the captains of the galleys which were to attend her, to shatter to pieces the ship in which she had come, by falling foul of it, but in such manner that it might appear to be done accidentally. He prolonged the entertainment, for the more convenient opportunity of executing the plot in the night; and at her return for Bauli, instead of the old ship which had conveyed her to Baiae, he offered that which he had contrived for her destruction. He attended her to the vessel in a very cheerful mood, and, at parting with her, kissed her breasts; after which he sat up very late in the night, waiting with great anxiety to learn the issue of his project. But receiving information that every thing had fallen out contrary to his wish, and that she had saved herself by swimming,—not knowing what course to take, upon her freedman, Lucius Agerinus bringing word, with great joy, that she was safe and well, he privately dropped a poniard by him. He then commanded the freedman to be seized and put in chains, under pretence of his having been employed by his mother to assassinate him; at the same time ordering her to be put to death, and giving out, that, to avoid punishment for her intended crime, she had laid violent hands upon herself.

Author/Editor/Sponsoring Organization: Sky History by the A&E Network
Name of Web Article: "The Killer King: How Many People Did Henry VIII Execute?"
URL: https://www.history.co.uk/article/the-killer-king-how-many-people-did-henry-viii-execute
Date of access: Use the date on which you are writing your essay

Henry VIII (1491 – 1547) is perhaps the most well known of all England's monarchs, notably for the fact that he had six wives and beheaded two of them. Besides presiding over sweeping changes that brought the nation into the Protestant Reformation and changed England's faith, the infamous monarch, ridiculed for his obesity, was also subject to raging mood swings and paranoia. It is estimated that during his 36 years of rule over England he executed up to 57,000 people, many of whom were either members of the clergy or ordinary citizens and nobles who had taken part in uprisings and protests up and down the country… Simply broadcasting or discussing an opinion against the paranoid king could put even the most influential of citizens, including nobility, in the Tower of London. Worse fates were to await those who he believed were against him; for if someone dared to be against Henry, they were also against God. Such an offence was dealt with by the relatively humane swift swing of the axe. But for those accused of heresy, witchcraft and treason a far worse fate was in store for condemned victims through the barbaric acts of being burned at the stake or hanged, drawn and quartered. It is interesting to note that members of aristocracy and gentry could not be legally tortured unlike commoners.

Author: Herbert Beerbohm Tree
Title of Book: *Henry VIII and His Court*, 6th ed.
City of Publication: London
Publisher: Cassell & Co.
Date: 1911

3

Masterful, cruel, crafty, merciless, courageous, sensual, through-seeing, humorous, mean, matter of fact, worldly-wise, and of indomitable will, Henry the Eighth is perhaps the most outstanding figure in English history. The reason is not far to seek. The genial adventurer with sporting tendencies and large-hearted proclivities is always popular with the mob, and "Bluff King Hal," as he was called, was of the eternal type adored by the people. He had a certain outward and inward affinity with Nero. Like Nero, he was corpulent; like Nero, he was red-haired; like Nero, he sang and poetised; like Nero, he was a lover of horsemanship, a master of the arts and the slave of his passions. If his private vices were great, his public virtues were no less considerable. He had the ineffable quality called

4

charm, and the appearance of good-nature which captivated all who came within the orbit of his radiant personality. He was the "beau garçon," endearing himself to all women by his compelling and conquering manhood. Henry was every inch a man, but he was no gentleman. He chucked even Justice under the chin, and Justice winked her blind eye...

119

The night Anne Boleyn was executed he supped with Jane Seymour; they were betrothed the next morning, and married ten days later. It is also recorded that on the day following Katharine's death, Henry went to a ball, clad all in yellow.

Author: G. J. Meyer
Title of Book: *The Tudors: The Complete Story of England's Most Notorious Dynasty*
City of Publication: New York
Publisher: Delacorte Press
Date: 2010

31

On top of all his other blessings, Henry had the inestimable advantage—one that fit beautifully with his increasingly grandiose conception

32

of his own place in the world—of happening to rule at a time when the curious idea of the divine right of kings was becoming fashionable across much of Europe. The emergence of this notion was understandable as a reaction to the bloody instability of recent generations, and as an expression of the widespread hunger for law and order and therefore for strong central government. But it gave crowned heads a justification for turning themselves into despots with no obligations to anyone. It fed Henry VIII's inclination to think of himself as a quasi-divine being whom heaven intended to be all powerful... Henry remained lord and master of everyone around him for so long, and became so accustomed not only to doing whatever he wished, but to making everyone else do as he wished and being applauded for doing so, that he lost contact with the commonplace realities of human experience. Power corrupts, as Acton famously said, and a generation into Henry's reign there was beginning to hang over him the stench of corruption, of something like spiritual death. He was slipping into the special realm of fantasy reserved for those deprived too long of the simple truth even—or especially—about themselves. In ancient Greece or Rome he might have declared himself a god. Living in Christian England on the threshold of the modern world, he had to settle for being treated like a god....

292

No ruler in the history of England had reaped a bounty of gold to compare with Henry's, and yet somehow it had all ended with the economy of the kingdom in a parlous state and its government virtually bankrupt. And there had been absolutely no reason why things had to end up this way; it had all been Henry's doing, and he had done it for no better reason than the satisfaction of his own appetites and the demands of his swollen ego.

WEEK 35

Introduction to Sentence Style

The definitions in this lesson use the categories laid out by Thomas Kane in *The New Oxford Guide to Writing.*

—LESSON 128—

Sentence Style: Equal and Subordinating
Sentences with Equal Elements: Segregating, Freight-Train, and Balanced

But, in a larger sense, we cannot dedicate—we cannot consecrate—we cannot hallow this ground.
—Abraham Lincoln, "The Gettysburg Address"

We shall defend our island, whatever the cost may be; we shall fight on the beaches, we shall fight on the landing grounds, we shall fight in the fields and in the streets, we shall fight in the hills; we shall never surrender.
—Winston Churchill, "We Shall Fight on the Beaches"

An equal sentence is made up of a series of independent grammatical elements.

Years and years ago, when I was a boy, when there were wolves in Wales, and birds the color of red-flannel petticoats whisked past the harp-shaped hills, when we sang and wallowed all night and day in caves that smelt like Sunday afternoons in damp front farmhouse parlors, and we chased, with the jawbones of deacons, the English and the bears, before the motor car, before the wheel, before the duchess-faced horse, when we rode the daft and happy hills bareback, it snowed and it snowed.
— Dylan Thomas, *A Child's Christmas in Wales*

Even when pressed by the demands of inner truth, men do not easily assume the task of opposing their government's policy, especially in time of war.
—Martin Luther King, "Beyond Vietnam—A Time to Break Silence"

A subordinating sentence is made up of both independent and dependent elements.

Equal sentences can be segregating, freight-train, or balanced.

Segregating sentences express a single idea each and occur in a series.

The barn was still dark. The sheep lay motionless. Even the goose was quiet.
—E. B. White, *Charlotte's Web*

He hadn't found any doweling that day. He hadn't checked the generator. He hadn't cleaned up the pieces of mirror. He hadn't eaten supper; he'd lost his appetite. That wasn't hard. He lost it most of the time.
—Richard Matheson, *I Am Legend*

They disappear among the poplars. The meadow is empty. The river, the meadow, the cliff and cloud. The princess calls, but there is no one, now, to hear her.
—John Fowles, *The Ebony Tower*

Freight-train sentences link independent clauses together to express a combined idea.

He was energetic and devout; he was polite and handsome; his fame grew in the diocese.
—Lytton Strachey, *Eminent Victorians*

There was much game hanging outside the shops, and the snow powdered in the fur of the foxes and the wind blew their tails.
—Ernest Hemingway, "In Another Country"

I'm very young, I have no real friend here in the barn, it's going to rain all morning and all afternoon, and Fern won't come in such bad weather.
—E. B. White, *Charlotte's Web*

Balanced sentences are made up of two equal parts, separated by a pause.

Darkness is cheap, and Scrooge liked it.
—Charles Dickens, *A Christmas Carol*

It is a far, far better thing that I do, than I have ever done; it is a far, far better rest that I go to than I have ever known.
—Charles Dickens, *A Tale of Two Cities*

But there is something that I must say to my people, who stand on the warm threshold which leads into the palace of justice: In the process of gaining our rightful place, we must not be guilty of wrongful deeds.
—Martin Luther King, "I Have a Dream"

Exercise 128A: Identifying Sentence Types

In the blank that follows each sentence or set of sentences, write *S* for segregating, *FT* for freight-train, or *B* for balanced.

He missed the surface all together, his legs flew up above his head, and he found himself lying on the top of the prostrate Rat. ________

O my how cold the water was, and O, how very wet it felt. ________

Now, look here. Let's be sensible. You are the very animals I wanted. You've got to help me. It's most important! ________

The dusk advanced on him steadily, rapidly, gathering behind and before; and the light seemed to be draining away like flood-water. ________

He ran up against things, he fell over things and into things, he darted things and dodged round things. ________

His paper of half-finished verses slipped from his knee, his head fell back, his mouth opened, and he wandered by the verdant banks of dream rivers. ________

—Kenneth Grahame, *The Wind in the Willows*

His folk are known for hewers of wood and drawers of water, but in truth his father has been a schoolmaster. ________

He lives in a room above a courtyard behind a tavern and he comes down at night like some fairybook beast to fight with the sailors. ________

There was a strange silence in the room. The men looked like mud effigies. Finally someone began to laugh. Then another. Soon they were all laughing together. Someone bought the judge a drink. ________

He swung with the bottle and the kid ducked and he swung again and the kid stepped back. ________

—Cormac McCarthy, *Blood Meridian*

And the child grew, and she brought him to Pharaoh's daughter, and he became her son. (Exodus 2:10) ________

But his delight is in the law of the Lord, and in His law he meditates day and night. (Psalm 1:2) ________

For we are God's fellow workers; you are God's field, you are God's building. (1 Cor. 3:9) ________

—New King James Version of the Bible

Mademoiselle caught the twinkle, and she laughed, and Gerald laughed too. ________

Against a little hill to the left was a round white building with pillars, and to the right a waterfall came tumbling down among mossy stones to splash into the lake. ________

This is an enchanted garden, and that's an enchanted castle, and I'm jolly well going to explore. ________

Beyond the rose garden was a yew hedge with an arch cut in it, and it was the beginning of a maze like the one in Hampton Court. ________

The princess went first, and Kathleen carried her shining train; then came Jimmy and Gerald came last. ________

The sun was blazing in at the window, the eight-sided room was very hot, and everyone was getting cross. ________

Do say you are. You've had your joke with me. Don't keep it up. I don't like it. ________

Invisible arms clasped her, a hot invisible cheek was laid against hers, and warm invisible tears lay wet between the two faces. ________

Everyone was very hungry, and more bread and butter had to be fetched. ________

—Edith Nesbit, *The Enchanted Castle*

—LESSON 129—

Subordinating Sentences: Loose, Periodic, Cumulative, Convoluted, and Centered

In a loose sentence, subordinate constructions follow the main clause.

People always think that happiness is a far away thing, something complicated and hard to get.

—Betty Smith, *A Tree Grows in Brooklyn*

He was pacing the room swiftly, eagerly, with his head sunk upon his chest and his hands clasped behind him.

—Arthur Conan Doyle, "A Scandal in Bohemia"

The spotlight has often been focused on me because I was a late bloomer who turned out to be a prodigy, and perhaps, more than that, because I am a black woman excelling in a white world.

—Misty Copeland, *Life in Motion: An Unlikely Ballerina*

In a periodic sentence, subordinate constructions precede the main clause.

To be, or not to be: that is the question.

—William Shakespeare, *Hamlet*

When Galileo and Newton looked at nature, they saw simplicity.

—Edward Dolnick, *The Clockwork Universe: Isaac Newton, the Royal Society, and the Birth of the Modern World*

Some years ago—never mind how long precisely—having little or no money in my purse, and nothing particular to interest me on shore, I thought I would sail about a little and see the watery part of the world.

—Herman Melville, *Moby-Dick*

A cumulative sentence puts multiple subordinate constructions before or after the main clause.

Beyond the obvious facts that he has at some time done manual labour, that he takes snuff, that he is a Freemason, that he has been in China, and that he has done a considerable amount of writing lately, I can deduce nothing else.
—Arthur Conan Doyle, "The Red-Headed League"

Lastly, she pictured to herself how this same little sister of hers would, in the after-time, be herself a grown woman; and how she would keep, through all her riper years, the simple and loving heart of her childhood; and how she would gather about her other little children, and make their eyes bright and eager with many a strange tale, perhaps even with the dream of Wonderland of long ago; and how she would feel with all their simple sorrows, and find a pleasure in all their simple joys, remembering her own child-life, and the happy summer days.
—Lewis Carroll, *Alice's Adventures in Wonderland*

In a convoluted sentence, subordinate constructions divide the main clause.

The dorm, with two narrow beds to a room, didn't just house dancers studying with ABT.
—Misty Copeland, *Life in Motion: An Unlikely Ballerina*

We, the people of the United States, in order to form a more perfect union, establish justice, insure domestic tranquility, provide for the common defense, promote the general welfare, and secure the blessings of liberty to ourselves and our posterity, do ordain and establish this Constitution for the United States of America.
—The Constitution of the United States

They knew, without my needing to spell it out, every setback or curve in the road: that I had fought for ten years to be recognized, to show that I had the talent and ability to dance in classical ballets.
—Misty Copeland, *Life in Motion: An Unlikely Ballerina*

In a centered sentence, subordinate constructions come on both sides of the main clause.

With an apology for my intrusion, I was about to withdraw when Holmes pulled me abruptly into the room and closed the door behind me.
—Arthur Conan Doyle, "The Red-Headed League"

And having got rid of this young man who did not know how to behave, she resumed her duties as hostess and continued to listen and watch, ready to help at any point where the conversation might happen to flag.
—Leo Tolstoy, *War and Peace*

Exercise 129A: Identifying Subordinating Sentences

In each sentence, underline the subject(s) of the main clause once and the predicate twice.

Label each sentence in the blank that follows it as *L* for loose, *P* for periodic, *CUMUL* for cumulative, *CONV* for convoluted, or *CENT* for centered. For the purpose of this exercise, any sentence with three or more phrases and dependent clauses before or after the main clause should be considered cumulative. If two or fewer phrases or dependent clauses come before or after the main clause, the sentence should be classified as loose or periodic. Don't worry too much about figuring out exactly how many phrases or clauses are in the sentence—just do your best.

If phrases or clauses come before *and* after the main clause, the sentence is centered, no matter how many other phrases or clauses there are.

If any phrases or clauses come between the subject, predicate, and any essential parts of the main clause (objects, predicate nominatives, or predicate adjectives), the sentence is convoluted, no matter how many other phrases and clauses there are.

Spring was moving in the air above and in the earth below and around him, penetrating even his dark and lowly little house with its spirit of divine discontent and longing. ________

Jumping off all his four legs at once, in the joy of living and the delight of spring without its cleaning, he pursued his way across the meadow till he reached the hedge on the further side. ________

He thought his happiness was complete when, as he meandered aimlessly along, suddenly he stood by the edge of a full-fed river. ________

As he sat on the grass and looked across the river, a dark hole in the bank opposite, just above the water's edge, caught his eye. ________

Absorbed in the new life he was entering upon, intoxicated with the sparkle, the ripple, the scents and the sounds and the sunlight, he trailed a paw in the water and dreamed long waking dreams. ________

So the dismal Mole, wet without and ashamed within, trotted about till he was fairly dry, while the Rat plunged into the water again, recovered the boat, righted her and made her fast, fetched his floating property to shore by degrees, and finally dived successfully for the luncheon-basket and struggled to land with it. ________

On reaching the town they deposited Toad in the second-class waiting-room, giving a porter twopence to keep a strict eye on him. ________

He could see the imprints of them in the mud, running along straight and purposeful, leading direct to the Wild Wood. ________

In the side of what had seemed to be a snow-bank stood a solid-looking little door, painted a dark green. ________

A couple of high-backed settles, facing each other on either side of the fire, gave further sitting accommodations for the sociably disposed. ________

In the embracing light and warmth, warm and dry at last, with weary legs propped up in front of them, and a suggestive clink of plates being arranged on the table behind, it seemed to the storm-driven animals, now in safe anchorage, that the cold and trackless Wild Wood just left outside was miles and miles away, and all that they had suffered in it a half-forgotten dream. ________

The hedgehogs, who were just beginning to feel hungry again after their porridge, and after working so hard at their frying, looked timidly up at Mr. Badger. ________

After luncheon, accordingly, when the other two had settled themselves into the chimney-corner and had started a heated argument on the subject of *eels*, the Badger lighted a lantern. ________

The Mole was staggered at the size, the extent, the ramifications of it all; at the length of the dim passages, the solid vaultings of the crammed store-chambers, the masonry everywhere, the pillars, the arches, the pavements. ________

He was running here and there, opening doors, inspecting rooms and cupboards, and lighting lamps and candles and sticking them up everywhere. ________

Then the brutal minions dragged the hapless Toad from the Court House, shrieking, praying, protesting; across the marketplace, where the playful populace, always as severe upon detected crime as they are sympathetic and helpful when one is merely "wanted," assailed him with jeers, carrots, and popular catch-words; past hooting school children, their innocent faces lit up with the pleasure they ever derive from the sight of a gentleman in difficulties; across the hollow-sounding drawbridge, below the spiky portcullis, under the frowning archway of the grim old castle, whose ancient towers soared high overhead; past guardrooms full of grinning soldiery off duty, past sentries who coughed in a horrid, sarcastic way, because that is as much as a sentry on his post dare do to show his contempt and abhorrence of crime; up time-worn winding stairs, past men-at-arms in casquet and corselet of steel, darting threatening looks through their vizards; across courtyards, where mastiffs strained at their leash and pawed the air to get at him; past ancient warders, their halberds leant against the wall, dozing over a pasty and a flagon of brown ale; on and on, past the rack-chamber and the thumbscrew-room, past the turning that led to the private scaffold, till they reached the door of the grimmest dungeon that lay in the heart of the innermost keep. ________

—Kenneth Grahame, *The Wind in the Willows*

He wanders west as far as Memphis, a solitary migrant upon that flat and pastoral landscape. _________

They disembark aboard a lighter, settlers with their chattels, all studying the low coastline, the thin bight of sand and scrub pine swimming in the haze. _________

The sun that rises is the color of steel. _________

The old man shuffled through the gloom, his head bent to clear the low ceiling of woven limbs and mud. _________

The wind moaned in the section of stovepipe that was run through the roof above them to quit the place of smoke. _________

Three men sat on the box, not unlike the dead themselves or spirit folk, so white they were with lime and nearly phosphorescent in the dusk. _________

Across the street sat a man on a bench dimly lit in the doorlight from the cafe. _________

—Cormac McCarthy, *Blood Meridian*

According to the grace of God which was given to me, as a wise master builder I have laid the foundation. (1 Cor. 3:10) _________

But on the contrary, when they saw that the gospel for the uncircumcised had been committed to me, as the gospel for the circumcised was to Peter (for He who worked effectively in Peter for the apostleship to the circumcised also worked effectively in me toward the Gentiles), and when James, Cephas, and John, who seemed to be pillars, perceived the grace that had been given to me, they gave me and Barnabas the right hand of fellowship. (Gal. 2:7-9) _________

We give thanks to the God and Father of our Lord Jesus Christ, praying always for you, since we heard of your faith in Christ Jesus and of your love for all the saints; because of the hope which is laid up for you in heaven, of which you heard before in the word of the truth of the gospel, which has come to you, as it has also in all the world, and is bringing forth fruit, as it is also among you since the day you heard and knew the grace of God in truth; as you also learned from Epaphras, our dear fellow servant, who is a faithful minister of Christ on your behalf, who also declared to us your love in the Spirit. (Col. 1:3-8) _________

If then you were raised with Christ, seek those things which are above, where Christ is, sitting at the right hand of God. (Col. 3:1) _________

I, John, both your brother and companion in the tribulation and kingdom and patience of Jesus Christ, was on the island that is called Patmos for the word of God and for the testimony of Jesus Christ. (Rev. 1:9) _________

—New King James Version of the Bible

The wide High Street, even at the busy morning hour almost as quiet as a dream-street, lay bathed in sunshine. ________

Then came a glimmer of daylight that grew and grew, and presently ended in another arch that looked out over a scene so like a picture out of a book about Italy that every one's breath was taken away, and they simply walked forward silent and staring. ________

The three children remained breathless, open-mouthed, staring at the sparkling splendours all about them, while the Princess stood, her arm stretched out in a gesture of command, and a proud smile on her lips. ________

He turned from fixing it by an ingenious adaptation of his belt to find the others already decked with diadems, necklaces, and rings. ________

And the minds of the three played with granted wishes—brilliant yet thoroughly reasonable—the kind of wish that never seems to occur to people in fairy tales when they suddenly get a chance to have their three wishes granted. ________

By wonderful luck—beginner's luck, a card-player would have told him—he had discovered a burglary on the very first night of his detective career. ________

The men were taking silver out of two great chests, wrapping it in rags, and packing it in baize sacks. ________

The three met Mabel opportunely at the corner of the square where every Friday the stalls and the awnings and the green umbrellas were pitched, and poultry, pork, pottery, vegetables, drapery, sweets, toys, tools, mirrors, and all sorts of other interesting merchandise were spread out on trestle tables, piled on carts whose horses were stabled and whose shafts were held in place by piled wooden cases, or laid out, as in the case of crockery and hardware, on the bare flagstones of the market-place. ________

For this hall in which the children found themselves was the most beautiful place in the world. ________

—Edith Nesbit, *The Enchanted Castle*

—LESSON 130—

Practicing Sentence Style

Choose one of the following assignments:

Exercise 130A: Rewriting

The following list of events, from the traditional story "Little Red Riding-hood" as collected by the French author Charles Perrault in 1696, needs to be rewritten as a story.

Think this is an easy task? Just remember that this story must have at least one of each of the following types of sentences:

Segregating (at least three sentences in a row)
Freight-Train
Balanced
Loose
Periodic
Cumulative (with four or more subordinate phrases/clauses; main clause can come either first or last)
Convoluted
Centered

AND the story must be at least 500 words long and make good sense.

So you can't simply write out the story you remember from your childhood picture books—you're going to have to put some brainpower into this assignment!

there was a little country girl in a village
her mother and her grandmother loved her
the grandmother made her a red riding-hood
the hood was very flattering
the little girl wore it all the time
everyone called her "Little Red Riding-hood"
her mother made custards
her grandmother was ill
her grandmother lived in another village
the village was through the forest and beyond the mill
her mother told her to take custards and butter to her grandmother
Little Red Riding-hood started off
she had to go through a forest
she met Gaffer Wolf
Gaffer Wolf wanted to eat her
Gaffer Wolf did not eat her
There were timber-cutters in the forest
Gaffer Wolf asked where she was going
it is dangerous to listen to a wolf talk
she did not know it was dangerous
she told Gaffer Wolf what she was doing

Gaffer Wolf asked where the grandmother lived
she told him
the Wolf offered to go as well
the Wolf would go one way
Little Red Riding-hood would go the other way
the Wolf ran the shortest way
Little Red Riding-hood went the long way
she gathered nuts
she chased butterflies
she made flower bouquets
the Wolf got to the grandmother's house
he knocked on the door
the grandmother asked who was there
the Wolf said that he was Little Red Riding-hood
the Wolf said that he had custard and butter
the grandmother was ill
she said to pull the bobbin (latch)
the Wolf pulled the bobbin
the Wolf opened the door
the Wolf had not eaten for three days
the Wolf ate the grandmother
the Wolf shut the door
the Wolf got into the grandmother's bed
the Wolf waited for Little Red Riding-hood
she got there later
she knocked on the door
the Wolf asked who was there
the Wolf had a big voice
Little Red Riding-hood heard the big voice
Little Red Riding-hood was afraid
she thought her grandmother had a cold
she said who she was
she said that she had custard and butter
the Wolf softened his voice
the Wolf said to pull the bobbin (latch)
she pulled the bobbin
she opened the door
the Wolf hid under the bedclothes

the Wolf told her to put the food on a stool
the Wolf told her to climb into bed
Little Red Riding-hood put on her nightgown
she got into bed
she was surprised at how her grandmother looked
she said that her grandmother had large arms
the Wolf said that it made it better to hug her
she said that her grandmother had huge ears
the Wolf said that it was easier to hear her
she said her grandmother had enormous eyes
the Wolf said that it was easier to see her
she said that her grandmother had sharp teeth
the Wolf said that it was to eat her
the Wolf ate her

Exercise 130B: Original Composition

Write an original composition of at least 400 words, with at least one of each of the following types of sentences:

Segregating (at least three sentences in a row)
Freight-Train
Balanced
Loose
Periodic
Cumulative (with four or more subordinate phrases/clauses; main clause can come either first or last)
Convoluted
Centered

This composition may be one of the following:

a) A plot summary of one of your favorite books or movies,
b) A narrative of some event, happening, trip, or great memory from your past,
c) A scene from a story that you create yourself, or
d) Any other topic you choose.